Fatal Sunday

CAMPAIGNS & COMMANDERS

GREGORY J. W. URWIN, SERIES EDITOR

CAMPAIGNS AND COMMANDERS

Fatal Sunday

George Washington, the Monmouth Campaign, and the Politics of Battle

Mark Edward Lender
and
Garry Wheeler Stone

University of Oklahoma Press | Norman

Library of Congress Cataloging-in-Publication Data

Names: Lender, Mark Edward, 1947– author. | Stone, Garry Wheeler, author.
Title: Fatal Sunday : George Washington, the Monmouth Campaign, and the politics of battle / Mark Edward Lender and Garry Wheeler Stone.
Description: Norman : University of Oklahoma Press, 2016. | Series: Campaigns and commanders ; volume 54 | Includes bibliographical references and index.
Identifiers: LCCN 2015041929 | ISBN 978-0-8061-5335-3 (hardcover) ISBN 978-0-8061-5748-1 (paper) Subjects: LCSH: Monmouth, Battle of, Freehold, N.J., 1778. | Washington, George, 173–1799—Military leadership.
Classification: LCC E241.M7 L54 2016 | DDC 973.4/1092—dc23
LC record available at http://lccn.loc.gov/201504192

Fatal Sunday: George Washington, the Monmouth Campaign, and the Politics of Battle is Volume 54 in the Campaigns and Commanders series.

The paper in this book meets the guidelines for permanence and durability of the Committee on Production Guidelines for Book Longevity of the Council on Library Resources, Inc. ∞

Interior layout and composition: Alcorn Publication Design

With love and gratitude for
Penny Booth Page and Sara Jane Withers

Contents

List of Illustrations ix
Preface xi

1. The Audit of War: The Military Situation, 1777–1778 3
2. A General under Fire: George Washington and His Critics 19
3. Antagonists: The British and American Armies 45
4. Toward a New Campaign 76
5. The Matter of Major General Charles Lee 105
6. The Roads to Monmouth I: Henry Clinton's March 123
7. The Roads to Monmouth II: The Continental Advance 159
8. General Lee's Orders: Expectations and Misunderstandings 184
9. Battlefield and Village 200
10. Morning at Monmouth I: The Opening Round 233
11. Morning at Monmouth II: General Lee's Battle 249
12. Commanders in Conflict: The Washington and Lee Affair 282
13. Buying Time: The Point of Woods and the Hedgerow 298
14. The Great Cannonade 318
15. Death in the Afternoon: The Battle of Detachments 331
16. Aftermath of Battle: The Living and the Dead 353
17. The British and the French: Departures and Arrivals 372
18. Constructing Victory, Settling Scores 382
19. A Campaign in Retrospect: Assessments and Legacies 404

Epilogue 427

Appendix A. Monmouth: A Campaign and Battle Chronology, 16 June–6 July 1778 441
Appendix B. Continental Army Order of Battle 451
Appendix C. British Army Order of Battle 463

Notes 471
Bibliography 549
Index of Military Units 577
General Index 581

Illustrations

Figures

Washington Rallying the Troops at Monmouth	218
George Washington	219
Sir Henry Clinton	220
Charles Lee	221
Charles Cornwallis	222
Philemon Dickinson	223
William Livingston	224
John Graves Simcoe	225
Daniel Morgan	226
Richard Butler	227
Henry Laurens	228
Eleazer Oswald	229
Tennent's Meeting House	230
Sir Charles Grey	231
Anthony Wayne	232

Maps

New Jersey and Eastern Pennsylvania, 1777–78	20
The British Routes to Monmouth, June 1778	125
The Continental Army Routes to Monmouth, June 1778	160
The Rival Army Encampments, 27 June 1778	185
The Village of Monmouth Court House (Freehold)	202
The Farms on the Western Battlefield	207

Steuben's Escape 242
Lee's Advance Stalls at the West Morass 252
Lee Marches to Contact 257
Counterattack 267
Washington Encounters the Retreating Vanguard 287
Melee at the Point of Woods 301
Bloody Action at the Hedgerow 307
The Grenadiers Cross the Bridge 311
The Great Cannonade 321
Washington Resumes the Offensive 334
Wayne Attacks the British Rear 343
The British Route to Sandy Hook 351

Preface

The Battle of Monmouth was fought on Sunday, 28 June 1778—the *Fatal Sunday* of this volume's title. The bulk of the action took place just outside the village of Monmouth Court House (modern Freehold), New Jersey, the seat of Monmouth County. It was one of the largest battles in the War for American Independence, was the longest single day of combat, and marked the effective end of British efforts to achieve a military victory in the northern colonies. The battle was part of a three-week campaign in mid-June and early July—the time it took the British to evacuate Philadelphia, march across central New Jersey, and reach safety in New York City. It pitted the rival commanders in chief, the American George Washington and the Briton Sir Henry Clinton, directly against one another; it was the only time they met in the open field. Monmouth saw some particularly dramatic and bitter fighting, and it was the root of subsequent military and political controversies that reverberated through the army, in the Continental Congress, and across the rebellious colonies. It was a battle that gripped the public imagination, with many Americans initially believing it heralded an early end to the conflict. But even after these hopes had faded, and long after the guns had fallen silent, aspects of the Battle of Monmouth remained matters of contention. Some stories would echo into American folklore.

For patriots, Monmouth had immediate significance. At daybreak on Monday, 29 June, exhausted rebel soldiers, who had slept on their arms expecting a resumption of the fighting, discovered that the battle was over. The British were gone, having moved out during the night; the astonished Continentals and their militia compatriots held the field. It was the first time in over a year that troops under General Washington could make such a claim. Elated, they made the most of the result. "It is Glorious for America," Colonel Israel Shreve, commanding the Second New Jersey Regiment, wrote his wife, Polly. "The Enemy was Drove off the Ground," he exulted, "and many British Grenadiers and Light Infantry lay weltering in their gore."[1] Shreve's excitement was typical, Colonel William Irvine was equally overjoyed. "The Americans never [held] the field" before, he wrote a friend, but they did this time and trounced "the pride of the British Tyrant" in the bargain.[2] Beyond such satisfaction, the rejoicing had an element of sweet revenge. One soldier wrote home that the enemy dead were the same men who had beaten the Continentals the year before at Brandywine and elsewhere, making the results now all the more glorious. Brigadier General Anthony Wayne, in the thick of the fighting at Monmouth, was especially satisfied. He relished a none-too-subtle jab at certain young women of Philadelphia—those who had courted the attentions of occupying redcoat officers. Wayne asked a friend in the city to "tell the Phila. Ladies" their former beaus had "humbled themselves on the Plains of Monmouth."[3] Among rebel officers, desperate to even the score with the British after long months of frustration, the story was the same: The Continentals had met the flower of the King's army in a fair fight and had brought it low.

Yet the British saw the Monmouth affair in strikingly different terms. Lieutenant General Clinton winked at American boasts. Washington could claim victory all he liked, but in reality, Clinton coolly observed, "Nothing, surely, can be more ridiculous." He had orders to get his army back to New York, which he had successfully executed. During the march from Philadelphia, he not only had brought his army through the heart of enemy territory but also had done so in the face of superior numbers without the loss of even a single wagon. He believed he had done well enough; his only real disappointment lay in the fact that Washington never gave him a chance for a general action.[4] Sharing their commander's assessment of events, some of Clinton's subordinates used hyperbole as expertly as the Americans ever did. Hessian captain Johann Ewald, whose jaegers were in almost constant action during the march, considered the campaign a marvel. "The retreat of Xenophon and his Ten Thousand Greeks," he wrote, "could not have had more hardships on their marches than we endured," and yet the army reached safety.[5] Officially at least, the British were well pleased with their performance.

In assessing the outcome at Monmouth, some able historians, early and modern, have split the difference between British and American accounts. In her 1805 history of the Revolution, Mercy Otis Warren, hardly likely to flatter the British, took exactly this perspective: "After the battle of Monmouth," she wrote, "both parties boasted their advantages, as is usual after an indecisive action."[6] There is a certain logic to this middle ground. On the American side, it is possible to discount inflated victory claims and still credit a gritty battlefield performance. The rebel army that fought on 28 June was a force to reckon with, and there is a great deal to be said for seeing the battle as the Continental Army's "coming of age."[7] On the other hand, Clinton would have evacuated New Jersey regardless of anything Washington had done; if the British commander had refused to reengage after Monmouth, he had done so fairly certain that Washington was not about to offer a showdown fight. Under the circumstances, Clinton acted professionally and got his army to New York for redeployment.

So there it is: a hard-fought battle with no clear decision in the field, one in which both sides took some satisfaction, and one that seemingly did not alter the fortunes of war. From a purely tactical perspective, it would be hard to argue with the conclusion of historian Willard Wallace: "if ever a battle was a drawn struggle, Monmouth was it."[8]

This tactical perspective, however, may be too limited, for it may have obscured an appreciation of the strategic intentions of the commanders, the significance of the engagement, and especially its aftermath. The Monmouth campaign occurred during a particularly interesting and fluid period during the Revolution. The context of the war was changing. In late 1777 the British had lost an entire army at Saratoga, and by early 1778 the French alliance and the rejuvenation of the Continental Army during the Valley Forge winter promised to alter the strategic balance. British military plans, including redeployments that had led directly to the evacuation of Philadelphia and the action at Monmouth, raised additional questions about future operations. Certainly patriot political and military prospects appeared to be brightening, but the future was anything but clear.

Thus, as the British planned their move across New Jersey and as General Washington and his subordinates pondered their response, they did so amid open questions about the future conduct of the war, including its new international dimensions. There also were questions about the capabilities of patriot arms and, perhaps most significantly, the abilities of Washington himself. Indeed, as the Monmouth campaign opened, the general was something of an unknown quantity. Despite his flashes of brilliance at Trenton and Princeton and the regard many patriots had for his character and dedication, his performance as commander in chief was questionable.

Some contemporaries could not forget the painful defeats around New York in 1776 or the bitter loss of Philadelphia in 1777. This was no record to support a reputation in arms, and as early as late 1776 there were doubts about Washington's fitness to command. Among others, Adjutant General Joseph Reed and, most notably, Major General Charles Lee, the army's second-ranking officer, groused indiscreetly (but reasonably) at Washington's performance.[9] Worse came the following year: The defeats around Philadelphia stood in bold relief against Major General Horatio Gates's victory at Saratoga, triggering unflattering (for Washington) comparisons between the two patriot commanders.

That Washington's generalship had drawn censure was no surprise. Historically, it was (and has been) no rare thing to sack losing generals: consider the generals Abraham Lincoln relieved before finding U. S. Grant, or the commanders tossed out of their jobs (and lucky to keep their heads) by the government of revolutionary France. After Major General Arthur St. Clair's 1777 retreat from Fort Ticonderoga, even John Adams mused about shooting underachieving commanders.[10] Viewed in this light, the Revolution presented something of an exception since the patriot commander in chief actually kept his job. But the criticisms of 1777 were serious, and at least some disaffected leaders in the army and civil circles, including Congress, toyed with trading Washington for Gates. Their plans, such as they may have been, had jelled loosely in the so-called Conway Cabal. Fortunately for Washington, his critics were better at talk than action, and they fell into embarrassed silence when their slights became known. He had weathered the storm, but he and many of his military and civilian allies believed there had been a serious plot to replace him.[11] Nevertheless, however inchoate or even foolish the general's critics may have been, the fact is that he had serious doubters in and out of the army, and there were legitimate questions about his record.

Beyond Washington's performance on the battlefield, however, lay broader questions about the capabilities and future of the army itself. Throughout the months at Valley Forge, and especially in early 1778, the general had worked feverishly at improving supply and training and on the myriad tasks inherent in reinforcing, reequipping, and reorganizing the depleted Continental regiments. Success in these areas would factor heavily in the army's future performance, and securing the necessary resources taxed Washington's administrative and political skills to the utmost. Often frustrated, he dealt tactfully with civilian authorities, most of whom understood the necessity of military reform but often quibbled over details.[12] Some even questioned why patriot forces delayed offensive action, their desire to avenge the loss of Philadelphia blinding them to the disabling realities still confronting the recovering patriot regulars. At Valley Forge, nothing came easily.

There was even a challenge to Washington's vision for the army's future. He was adamant in his belief that only a professionally trained, regular Continental Army could stand up to the British in the field; this, he insisted, was the key to ultimate victory. But not everyone agreed, including some members of Congress and others active in political circles. In particular, General Lee refused to believe American regulars could ever beat redcoats at their own game. Trained on a "European Plan," Lee warned, American troops would "make an Aukward Figure, be laugh'd at as a bad Army by their enemy, and defeated in every Renecontre which depends on Manoevres."[13] But most officers agreed with the commander in chief and loyally supported his efforts to reorganize and retrain the army, although there is little doubt criticisms of their chief, from whatever quarter and for whatever reason, left many of them smarting.

Thus on 18 June 1778, when the first Continental units broke camp at Valley Forge to shadow Clinton into New Jersey, Washington fully understood that a great deal rested on his performance and that of his army. But while the general was still in command, he was not above criticism. And though it was clear that the army that marched out of Valley Forge was better than the one that had straggled into that encampment following the disappointments of 1777, it was not clear how much better. Perhaps the only thing that was clear was that the pursuit of the British would test both the rebel general and his remodeled battalions. An additional major defeat, or even a lackluster campaign, could well have triggered another and more concerted challenge to his leadership; he and officers loyal to him must have understood this. There is no question the general wanted at least some modest success in 1778 to compensate for his poor showing the previous year. For Washington, the stakes of the new campaign would be as much political as military.

Washington got rather more than a modest success. The patriot commander in chief emerged from the Monmouth campaign with his critics cowed into silence; his potential rivals in the officer corps routed or, in the case of General Lee, actually disgraced; and his military reputation praised in terms fit for an Alexander or a Caesar. In fact, the aftermath of Monmouth saw Washington with his prestige so enhanced that, for the rest of the war, he was beyond any real censure, much less any challenge to his command. It is not too much to say that the campaign confirmed the patriot commander in his status as the proverbial "man on the white horse," or in James Flexner's parlance, the "indispensable man."[14] This was a dramatic reversal of fortune in any event, but it was all the more remarkable in that it derived from what some careful studies have insisted was a drawn battle.

Was this really possible? Victories usually make military reputations and keep generals in their jobs, not tactical standoffs. This observation alone is enough to raise questions about what actually happened near Freehold on 28 June. Have we profoundly misunderstood some critical aspects of the battle? Were the results of the fighting more far reaching than previous scholarship would have us believe? A reassessment of events immediately after Monmouth suggests this was indeed the case, and these same developments held the key to Washington's ability finally to consolidate his hold on the army. Indeed, this book will argue that the Monmouth campaign was the hinge upon which the fate of his command turned, the point at which the general was able to put to rest questions about his competence and silence his critics once and for all. Monmouth was the key to why Washington kept his job, and thus its significance looms considerably greater than a hard-fought draw.

How this turn of events came about involved more than the results of combat. Much depended on the steps Washington and his lieutenants took to burnish his reputation in the aftermath of the battle—in effect, to convince patriots that Monmouth had been a major triumph, no matter what the tactical realities may have been, and to use this perception to enhance Washington's stature. None of this is to imply that the general and his army had not fought well at Monmouth—far from it (as we will see). But it does assert the politics of battle—the skirmishes in Congress and the campaign for public opinion that both preceded and followed the engagement—were for General George Washington every bit as important as the battle itself.

The narrative of *Fatal Sunday* is that of a military campaign, but the main point of the book is political—the subtitle's "politics of battle." The politics and battle are interwoven, and thus an understanding of military operations, including the details of the fighting on 28 June, is central. Such an understanding, however, is more readily proposed than realized. Some fifty years ago, in an essay on Charles Lee, historian John Shy observed, "there is no satisfactory account of the Monmouth campaign."[15] His comment remains accurate. Any number of authors have tried to make sense of the fighting, and their efforts have suffered from no dearth of evidence.[16] In fact, the problem has been quite the reverse. The Monmouth campaign involved thousands of patriot and British troops, and it took place in a relatively populated region. Thus plenty of eyewitnesses had more than enough time to see or experience at least some aspect of events, and they produced a plethora of contemporary accounts. But as is the case with most history, these accounts were refracted through the proverbial fog of war, personal and political biases, honest mistakes, and the eyes of those who simply did not understand what they saw. Also in the mix and contributing to the confusion were elements of Continental and international political developments, bitterly clashing personalities, evolving British and American tactical considerations, changing conditions within the patriot and royal armies, geography, and as events transpired, even the weather. Of course, much the same can be said of most military operations, but at Monmouth the impact of all these factors seemed especially pronounced. No wonder historians generally have considered Monmouth to be one of the most difficult of all engagements of the Revolution to understand. "It remains to this day the hardest battle of the war to chronicle," wrote Robert Bray and Paul Bushnell, "let alone to analyze."[17]

If a better understanding of the battle and its consequences emerges in these pages, it stems from access to a remarkable trove of research materials—no doubt the largest available to any scholar of the subject and many unavailable to previous studies. These include American and British manuscripts and other original sources as well as a wide range of newer scholarship on specific aspects of the Monmouth campaign. We have drawn heavily on British and translated Hessian sources in an effort to clarify the royal army's movements and the thinking of its commanders and soldiers. The results of battlefield archaeology, a wealth of pension applications, and new cartography have assisted greatly in deciphering the course of the fighting and in correcting many misconceptions about how the rival forces maneuvered as they did. More-recent studies, including valuable unpublished research, provide often-graphic detail on individual units, while the use of pension records and private correspondence add an important dimension to our appreciation of the personal experience of combat in the eighteenth century. The publication of important documentary editions, notably *Letters of Delegates to Congress* and the *Papers of George Washington* (Revolutionary War Series), has offered rich insights into a range of patriot opinions on and reactions to the campaign and its implications.

What emerges is the clearest tactical and strategic view we have of what happened at Monmouth. Our account insists that while events there were complicated indeed, they nevertheless were explicable. Beyond the battlefield narrative, this study also explains how the Monmouth campaign became one of the pivotal events in George Washington's career as commander in chief. Inasmuch as Washington's fate was intertwined with that of the Revolution, we have argued that the Battle of Monmouth must be recognized as a pivotal moment in the success of the struggle for independence itself.

A note on terminology and organization is in order. We have used the word "patriots" or "patriot," with a small "p," as something of a pronoun. It denotes individuals who favored the cause of independence as well as the forces that fought against Great Britain. Depending upon its context, the term includes Continental, militia, or other rebel combatants. "Patriot" comes in handy when "rebel," "irregular," or "militia" appears repeatedly in a sentence or paragraph; it is a stylistic usage. We use "whig," a contemporary term for those opposed to Britain, in the same way. As such, "patriot" and "whig" carry no moral connotation. Indeed, in taking up arms for the King, plenty of loyalists fully believed they were patriots as well, and they believed as firmly in their cause as their rebellious neighbors did. In the same vein "tory," with a small "t," simply denotes an American standing with the King (who gets a capital "K").

The narrative cites the movements of dozens of individual units: regiments, battalions, divisions, wings, and others. To avoid confusion between patriot and British outfits, we have adopted another editorial usage. The names of American units are spelled out—for example, the Second New Jersey Regiment—while

British units have numerical designations—for example, the 42nd Regiment of Foot.

An abbreviation also deserves note. The transcript of the court-martial of Major General Charles Lee is the best single source of information on the Battle of Monmouth. Used carefully and coordinated with other contemporary sources, the court-martial record has allowed us to present a coherent account of the fighting on the morning of 28 June 1778. There are several versions of the transcript, however, each with some minor differences. We have used a privately printed version—*Proceedings of a Court-Martial . . . for the Trial of Major-General Lee*—from 1864, a reprint of the original that appears complete in all respects and is readily available to scholars.[18]

The Battle of Monmouth is the central event in this book. Matters of historical interpretation, especially regarding the command of George Washington and the consequences for the Revolutionary cause generally, hinge on the events of 28 June 1778. Yet the approach to the battlefield is gradual. The early chapters dwell on the context and stakes of the upcoming campaign: the military situation in early 1778 and British and patriot strategic concerns, the status of Washington as commander in chief, the state of the rival armies, and the personalities central to understanding events in the field. The narrative moves to active operations in chapter 6 as the British begin their march across New Jersey and patriot forces react. The battle itself and related events fill another nine chapters. These deal—not always chronologically—with the leadership and operations of patriot and royal forces and specifically address the controversies that have plagued efforts to interpret what actually happened at Monmouth Court House. The final chapters then consider the engagement in retrospect, looking at the influence of the fighting on public opinion (patriot and loyalist), assessing the performance of both armies, and examining the political implications of the battle and its aftermath. It is these latter chapters that argue that it was the Battle of Monmouth that allowed Washington to consolidate his preeminent position in the army—and thus in the Revolution.

This book has had a long gestation period. It began two decades ago as a lengthy public-history project for American History Workshop, Inc., on behalf of the Monmouth Battlefield State Park. Over time, other scholarly undertakings and employment changes placed *Fatal Sunday* on and off hold. Still, bits and pieces have appeared in print and in paper presentations, and with the long-delayed publication of this book, it is a pleasant task to thank a number of individuals for their help (and their patience). At the David Library of the American Revolution, David Fowler was a constant source of encouragement and research assistance. Garry Wheeler Stone has been a close collaborator, and in particular, his meticulous efforts to map the battle have been central to understanding the events of 28 June 1778. With every good reason, his name appears as coauthor. James T. Raleigh, Daniel M. Sivilich, and Michael S. Adelberg provided any number of research leads and generously shared the results of their own research; we have cited Dan's work frequently. John U. Rees has produced some remarkable manuscripts on individual units, routes of march, and casualties at Monmouth as well as technical aspects of military equipage. We have relied on his work as well, and he has our genuine thanks. So do Harry M. Ward, Lynn Simms, and William Welsch, all of whom carefully read chapters and provided valuable critiques. We also appreciated the useful insights of Kent McGaughy. At Kean University, Frank J. Esposito and Terry Golway took time to review the manuscript while laboring over projects of their own; old friends make good critics. Thanks as well to old friend Ron Herrsche. The University of Oklahoma Press supplied three anonymous reviewers for *Fatal Sunday* (although Gregory J. W. Urwin was not so anonymous); we appreciated these readers' enthusiasm for the manuscript, and we took their suggestions for improvements seriously. Many thanks indeed. At the New Jersey Historical Commission, which long ago supplied vital research support, Richard Waldron and Mary Murrin were always helpful and have our deepest gratitude. We owe a great deal to the Special Collections staff at the Alexander Library of Rutgers University, especially Ron Becker and Bonita Grant, who helped us mine the wonderful manuscripts in their care. The libraries at the New Jersey Historical Society, the Monmouth County Historical Society, Morristown National Historical Park, the Virginia Historical Association, the Historical Society of Pennsylvania, the Historical Society of Delaware Historical Society, Massachusetts Historical Society, the Library of Virginia, and the Maryland Historical Society all yielded valuable material. Joseph Lee Boyle, former historian at Valley Forge National Historical Park, shared with us everything he found on the battle.

Many archives provided valuable cartographic information, including the Camden County Historical Society, the Library of Congress, the New-York Historical Society, and Princeton University. At the New Jersey State Archives, Bette Epstein has been a constant friend for over twenty years. Likewise, at the Monmouth County Archives, Mary Ann Kiernan helped research the farms and roads west of Monmouth Court House. At the New Jersey Department of Environmental Protection Geographic Information Systems Office, Craig Coutros compiled the 1930 aerial photographs that gave us access to a preindustrial agrarian landscape. The current and former staff members of the Monmouth County GIS Office not only provided contemporary aerial photography of the larger battlefield but also patiently coached Garry Stone in digital mapping—particular thanks to Michael Thorne, Eric Anderson, and Michael Dunzello. West Jersey History Round Table members Edward Fox, Peter Hamilton, and Paul Schopp helped map the south Jersey roads. The National Park Service's American Battlefield Protection Program and BRAVO (the Battlefield Restoration and Archaeological Volunteer Organization) provided funding for computer equipment and cartographic programs.

We certainly want to thank everyone at the University of Oklahoma Press for their support in turning our manuscript into a book. Editor in Chief Chuck Rankin, Amy Hernandez, Stephanie Evans, and Rowan Steineker were always available, professional, and encouraging, while Kevin Brock, editor extraordinaire, provided superb editorial service and advice. It was a pleasure working with them. To all of these individuals, and many others too numerous to name who lent us their time, advice, and assistance, we offer our sincerest gratitude.

A final thanks goes to our wives, Penny Booth Page and Sara Jane Withers. They are good critics (how many drafts have they read?) and the best of company in walking the still-beautiful countryside where two armies fought so long ago.

Fatal Sunday

CHAPTER 1

THE AUDIT OF WAR

THE MILITARY SITUATION, 1777–1778

Early in the afternoon of 24 May 1778, thirteen days after formally relinquishing command of His Majesty's troops in the rebellious American colonies, General Sir William Howe boarded the Royal Navy frigate HMS *Andromeda* and sailed from British-occupied Philadelphia. He was returning to Great Britain, and as *Andromeda* dropped downriver toward Delaware Bay and the Atlantic, Sir William must have realized any glimpse he had of the city would be his last. It was also the last he would see of the army he had led since 1775, the army that triumphantly entered the de facto rebel capital in September 1777. From the deck of *Andromeda* it must have seemed long ago.

Up to the time of his departure, Howe was a popular commander in chief. An affable man and no martinet, he socialized easily and enjoyed the company of his brother officers (and his mistresses); he also appreciated the theater and a well-prepared table. Howe's pleasures, however, never kept him from his duty. He was a good officer, one of the British army's best. He had seen action in the Seven Years' War (1756–63), including combat in North America and Europe, and was an expert in the use of light infantry. When Britain finally realized it would have to fight a major war in America, Lord North's government wanted to win the contest as quickly as possible. For that purpose it carefully selected Howe for the top command over generals with considerably greater seniority. Lord George Germain, secretary of state for the American Department, told Parliament that Howe (along with Lieutenant Generals John Burgoyne and Henry Clinton, who traveled with him to America) was the man best suited to defeat the rebellion. George Washington agreed: in late 1775 the Continental commander in chief assessed the British general as "the most formidable enemy America has."[1]

Howe was indeed a formidable opponent. In the field he had been generally intelligent and personally brave. Yet he was seldom hard driving, and some of his men sensed that Sir William lacked an instinct for the enemy's jugular. In 1776 he had beaten Washington badly on Long Island, an action that won the British commander a knighthood. At Brooklyn Heights, however, he had failed to order a final assault that could have destroyed the opposing army. Howe then drove the battered patriots out of New York and across New Jersey, but he halted for the winter rather than chase them across the Delaware River. He paid heavily for this decision: The ensuing affairs at Trenton and Princeton stung his army and galvanized the rebels, perhaps blasting whatever chance the British had to break the rebellion through military force. The campaign of 1777 had been equally disappointing. Following heavy fighting, Howe managed to take Philadelphia and send Congress scurrying a hundred miles west to rustic York. Nevertheless, he had neither crushed the rebellion nor finished off the shaken Continental Army, and critics of his leadership—from which so much was expected—were asking why.

While Howe always vigorously defended his decisions in the American command, he winced at the criticisms of his leadership. As early as October 1777, discouraged by what he felt was a lack of support from the government of Lord Frederick North (and especially on the part of his civilian chief, Germain), he had asked to be relieved. Indecision on what to do about the American War delayed an answer, with Germain finally approving his request only in February 1778. Even then the ministry failed to dispatch an immediate replacement, and Sir William, however impatient to be away, had little choice but to remain at his post. It was only on 11 May that General Sir Henry Clinton formally relieved him as commanding general.[2]

While awaiting relief, Howe remained popular in the army. In a tribute to their departing chief, his officers organized a magnificent sendoff party. The "Meschianza" had involved a fabulous banquet, a round of gay parties, a regatta, fireworks, and a final display in which an allegory of fame assured the general, "Thy laurels shall never fade."[3] The mood upon Howe's actual leave taking, however, was decidedly somber. There were no change-of-command ceremonies, just emotional goodbyes from brother officers and on Howe's part, a number of heart-felt public and private expressions of gratitude to his subordinates. The general himself was subdued; he fully understood that he was returning to England under a cloud and would have to defend his performance in America. Among many of his contemporaries, even those who wished him well, the snarky observation of Horace Walpole, English *litterateur,* politico, and sometime wag, seemed on the mark. The general had returned, Walpole coolly noted, "much richer in money than in laurels."[4]

If Howe's departure closed a signal chapter in the War of Independence, it quickly opened a new one. Barely a month after Sir William left, his army, under a new commander, would fight the rebel army at the village of Monmouth Court House in the heart of New Jersey. Measured in miles, the road to Monmouth was relatively short: only some sixty miles from Philadelphia and about seventy-five from Valley Forge. But from the wider perspective of the war, the road—metaphorically—was considerably longer and more complicated. For the British, the backdrop to the battle involved the strategic and political ramifications of Howe's campaign of 1777 and the subsequent change of command that brought Clinton to the post of commander in chief. For the rebellious Americans, the background story was, if anything, more tumultuous. Before the Continental Army marched out of Valley Forge and into New Jersey, the patriots had witnessed a searching examination of Washington's military acumen and swirling controversies over the future conduct of the war. In addition, the French political and military alliance with the rebellious colonies brought an international dimension to the conflict, a development that would force both sides to reconsider their strategic and operational plans. The influence and interplay of these factors mapped the contours of the war to 28 June 1778, and any understanding of what led to the Battle of Monmouth must begin with them.

General Howe's War

Walpole's quip about Howe's dearth of laurels, while perhaps unkind to the general, applied equally to the entire British war effort; by early 1777 it too had produced few laurels. In fact, 1777 had been one of the most disappointing, if not catastrophic, years in the annals of British arms. Lieutenant General Burgoyne's drive out of Canada—an attempt to reach Albany, New York, and thereby cut New England off from the colonies to the south—had ended in spectacular failure. In October Burgoyne had surrendered his entire army to Continental major general Horatio Gates at Saratoga. A blow serious enough by itself, the Saratoga disaster was only one factor, albeit a significant one, in a larger British malaise.

Howe would have insisted that his performance was better than Burgoyne's, but in reality it was little more conclusive. Over the spring of 1777, he had done his best to draw George Washington into a general engagement in central New Jersey, but the patriot general never took the bait. June saw a series of skirmishes, some involving very stiff fighting, as Sir William maneuvered against his elusive adversary. Finally, on 8 July, convinced that the Continentals would not give him a showdown fight, Howe abandoned the state, thus foregoing an overland march on Philadelphia, his target for the upcoming campaign. Philadelphia was less than seventy miles from the forward British garrison at New Brunswick, New Jersey, but Howe feared that such a march would leave Washington loose in his rear, able to strike at his communications, hit while the British were crossing the Delaware, or even turn east and attack New York. An overland march was too risky.

Instead, in late July Sir William's army took ship for Pennsylvania. The voyage was bitterly frustrating. Plans calling for a quick trip from New York to Philadelphia, striking toward the rebel city up Delaware Bay, dissolved in the face of contrary winds and doubts about being able to land safely somewhere below Philadelphia. There were too many questions about the nature of whig (patriot) defenses along and in the Delaware River. Again the risks appeared too great. The alternative was another month at sea, most of it in blazing August heat, as the invasion fleet sailed south around the Virginia capes and up the length of Chesapeake Bay. Only on 25 August were the groggy and miserable troops and animals able to land below Head of Elk, Maryland.[5] The delays in New Jersey and on the voyage had cost the British three months of the campaign season. Once rested, on 3 September Howe's army skirmished with American light infantry at Cooch's Bridge, Delaware, then six days later battered the Continental Line at Brandywine; on the twenty-sixth the British marched unopposed into Philadelphia.

Yet the rebel army still showed plenty of fight. Washington counterattacked at Germantown on 4 October, but fog, an overly complicated attack plan, poor coordination, and plain bad luck prevented a patriot victory. Howe won, but the battle had been a near thing. Rebel garrisons held out stubbornly below Philadelphia at Forts Mercer and Mifflin, blocking the Delaware River to the Royal Navy and threatening to choke off supplies to the city. It took until mid-November, with plenty of bitter fighting, to force the defenders from the forts. Howe had won his victories, but none were decisive.

December saw the end of active campaigning. On the fourth Howe sallied to confront the rebels at White Marsh, some thirteen miles from the Philadelphia, but this led only to several days of inconclusive skirmishing. Washington refused to commit to a general engagement. On the eighth Sir William returned to Philadelphia and settled into the city for the season; Washington moved to take up winter quarters at Valley Forge. The British had wounded but had failed to destroy the patriot army, and Howe was unable to prevent rebel forces from harassing British foraging parties and patrols in the countryside. In return, the royal commander had suffered some 1,500 casualties during the campaign, a bit less than 10 percent of his army.[6] While not disabling, these losses were disturbing. Parliamentary reticence over the costs of the war, as well as the government's worries over political opposition to the conflict, worked against the dispatch of significant reinforcements. Over the rest of the winter and into the early spring of 1778, additional losses occurred due to sickness, desertion, and small-unit operations around Philadelphia and in New Jersey. The victories of the Brandywine campaign proved largely hollow.

The only real prize was Philadelphia itself, and there was no denying the fall of the City of Brotherly Love dealt a blow to rebel pride. Yet even this triumph was questionable. Philadelphia, as Howe soon discovered, was never the strategic center of the rebellion. Its capture lacked the military, psychological, or political importance of taking a European capital; Congress simply transplanted itself to York and carried on. Philadelphia itself proved a drain on British resources. Having occupied it, Howe needed to govern it, a task to which his army was barely equal. The city provided his men with warm and secure quarters over the winter, but the minutia of maintaining local services and security demanded constant attention. Such matters as fire and police protection, local commerce, the civil courts, and sanitation could not be ignored if Philadelphia was to remain habitable. These functions were also critical to encouraging loyalist support, which would evaporate if the occupation appeared inept or only temporary. Howe understood that he needed help.

In an effort to create a viable civilian administration, the general turned to Joseph Galloway, Pennsylvania's most prominent tory, naming him to the newly created post of superintendent general of Philadelphia. He wanted Galloway to help run the machinery of local government and to rally his fellow Pennsylvanians to the royal cause. For his part Galloway was optimistic, thinking his prior service to the province would carry weight with popular opinion. Born in Maryland in 1731, Galloway moved with his father to Pennsylvania in 1740. Well educated, he studied law and subsequently practiced in Philadelphia, where he rose to political and social eminence. From 1757 to 1775 he served in the Pennsylvania House of Representatives, as speaker from 1766 to 1774. He considered himself a patriot and stood with the colonials when they protested imperial measures to tighten control of American affairs after 1763. Indeed, in 1774 as a Pennsylvania delegate, Galloway played a significant role in the First Continental Congress, authoring a substantial proposal—the "Galloway Plan"—to settle the constitutional relationship between the colonies and Great Britain. But he balked at independence, and in 1776 he fled to New York and joined Howe. (At this, the rebel Pennsylvania Assembly convicted him of high treason in absentia and confiscated his considerable estates.)[7]

Galloway took his new role as superintendent seriously. He was able to organize a night watch and to keep the street lamps lit and did his best to revive local business activity. But it soon became evident that he was powerless without Howe's active intervention. The frustrated loyalist in fact enjoyed little authority or influence, and the general, for all practical purposes, had to govern the city by decree. As Howe believed that his army lacked the force to administer the city *and* to deal with General Washington simultaneously, he never seriously considered a move against Valley Forge, even as the patriot commander was struggling to hold his weakened forces together.[8]

Worse, the British had to fight to sustain themselves in the city. As desperate as things were at Valley Forge, Washington was still able to make life dangerous for redcoat detachments moving into the countryside. The rebel general, knowing only too well what it was like to command an army short on food, forage, and supplies, tried to turn the tables on Howe. Militia and Continental patrols actively harassed British foraging and reconnaissance operations, forcing Sir William to send strong escorts with units leaving the lines around Philadelphia and Germantown. Foraging and supply shipments arriving via the Royal Navy kept the occupying troops fed, but over the winter, casualties from small-unit actions became a fact of life.

When he had to, the royal commander in chief was willing to go far afield to secure supplies for his men and animals. Forays included raids into New Jersey, where stocks of food and forage were relatively plentiful. Howe dispatched one of the strongest such expeditions in late March 1778, sending a party under Colonel Charles Mawhood across the Delaware to forage in Salem and Cumberland Counties. Washington had defeated the colonel the year before at Princeton, but this time the British officer was more successful. On the twenty-first and twenty-third, Mawhood badly bloodied two separate patriot militia detachments at Hancock's Bridge and Quinton's Bridge. He also gathered a rich haul of forage, though thoroughly outraging local civilians. Rebels claimed that the British had massacred helpless militiamen, some of whom had surrendered. For his part, Mawhood threatened to arm local tories and to lay waste the homes and property of prominent patriots. Colonel Elijah Hand of the Cumberland County militia knew a propaganda coup when he saw one. He decried what he claimed was wanton British brutality and warned Mawhood that such conduct would "injure your cause more than ours: it will increase your enemies and our army."[9] The British paid for their forage with a public-relations debacle, and the incident put New Jerseyans on their guard against future enemy incursions—a fact that helped the British not at all when they marched across the state the following June.

The alternatives to foraging and other patrol duties were safer for the troops but not always productive. With Howe avoiding major operations, the rank and file spent long hours on routine garrison duty: watching approaches to the city, guarding and moving supplies, cleaning equipment, and all of the other daily chores essential to maintaining a military force. There were ample off-duty hours, though. Taverns did a roaring business, and incidents of drunkenness, vandalism, and brawling among soldiers and civilians kept the military-justice system occupied. In their free time officers enjoyed the civic pleasures of Philadelphia, including the society of prominent tories and local belles, and they pursued a range of amusements. Literature, gambling, mistresses, theater, entertaining on a lavish scale, cockfights, horseracing, cricket, and religious gatherings all had their devotees as officers sought to "kill dull hours" and drive off boredom.[10] Efforts in this regard were such that some historians have described an army that had grown soft.[11]

In fact, such perspectives are mistaken. Activities pursued in Philadelphia were typical of urban garrison life in the eighteenth century, and the army had little trouble shifting from the gaming tables and barracks to the field. Recall the example of Colonel Mawhood: no one in southern New Jersey could accuse him of going soft in garrison. An army in garrison, however, was not going to destroy an enemy. Absent a winter campaign, the conquest of the rebel capital had gained Howe little more than the privilege of spending the winter there. In retrospect, it is hard to argue with Benjamin Franklin, who upon being informed that Howe had captured Philadelphia supposedly responded, "it would be more proper to say that Philadelphia has taken Sir William Howe."[12]

There were other disappointments as well. In particular, the British commander's hopes that operations in Pennsylvania would rally tory support amounted to little more than that. As early as December 1776, during the planning for Howe's 1777 campaign, Galloway and other Pennsylvania loyalists encouraged the general to expect thousands of tories to rise at the appearance of the King's army. Some predicted that local recruits would be numerous enough to handle garrison and other routine duties, thus freeing more veterans for field operations. Indeed, the seeming potential of loyalist support was an important factor in Sir William's decision to go to Pennsylvania in the first place. Shortly after landing near Head of Elk in late August, Howe issued a proclamation assuring inhabitants of Pennsylvania, Delaware, and eastern Maryland of the peaceable intentions of the royal army. He also invited all those in rebellion to return to their allegiance.[13] This approach had worked in 1776 in New York and New Jersey, where thousands of residents formally renewed their allegiance to the King.[14]

There were some limited successes. Recruiters for a proposed battalion of "Pennsylvania Loyalists" appealed to "All Intrepid Able-Bodied Heroes" to enlist in "Defence of their Country, Laws and Constitution, against the arbitrary Usurpations of a tyrannical Congress." Besides winning "Laurels," the recruiting pitch ran, at the end of the war veterans would receive fifty acres of land "where every gallant Hero may retire, and enjoy his Bottle and his Lass."[15] Eventually, the offer tempted some two hundred volunteers, far short of expectations. In addition to the Pennsylvania Loyalists, between the autumn of 1777 and spring of 1778 the British raised eleven other provincial units of various kinds from Pennsylvania, Maryland, and New Jersey. Some became effective outfits and accompanied the army on the trek across New Jersey in June, but most were understrength and indifferently equipped and disciplined. They did not add appreciably to the army's capabilities.[16] In the end, relatively few residents declared for the King, and of those who did even fewer were willing to bear arms. Most were Philadelphians without military intentions and who, once they had shown their colors, needed British protection against the vengeance of patriot neighbors. All of this was a disappointment to Howe, who ultimately conceded that he had been taken in by falsely optimistic reports of loyalist strength.[17]

Had he thought about it, Sir William could have predicted the poor turnout. In late 1776 thousands of New Jersey residents declared for the King when the British army swept through that colony. After Trenton and Princeton, however, and the subsequent royal withdrawal from most of the province, New Jersey tories paid the price for their outspoken allegiance. Without the King's army to protect them, these loyalists found themselves virtually powerless in the face of vengeful patriots. Furious whigs hounded them, arrested their leaders (and executed some), and eventually confiscated many tory estates. Thousands fled to exile within British lines.[18] By the time Howe tried to rally loyalists in and around Philadelphia, the plight of their New Jersey counterparts was well known, and potential friends of the King understood that openly professing a political allegiance was a calculated risk, one relatively few choose to take. Thus if Howe was to defeat the rebels, he would have to do it largely with His Majesty's regulars.

After taking Philadelphia, however, the British general failed to make any real effort to strike at Washington's battered forces. Customarily, eighteenth-century European armies avoided winter campaigns, but these did occur when commanders saw opportunities or felt that they had no choice (Washington demonstrated as much at Trenton and Princeton). In early 1778 Howe had opportunity. He knew the Continental Army was suffering from the cold weather, poor commissary and quartermaster support, and a stream of desertions.[19] It was in no condition to fight a major action. Thus a British winter campaign seemed in order, and many junior officers and tories urged Howe to strike. Indeed, at Valley Forge rebel officers wondered why the winter passed without a British effort against them.[20] Major Henry "Light Horse Harry" Lee (father of Robert E. Lee) was astonished. Howe was well supplied, his opponent in desperate circumstances, yet "it is wonderful how he could omit venturing a winter campaign, to him promising every advantage, and to his antagonist, menacing every ill."[21] But the blow never fell.

There never has been a satisfactory explanation for Sir William's inaction. Howe insisted that the defenses at Valley Forge were too strong and that, anyway, he did not have enough forage to sustain a new campaign. He also may have overestimated Washington's strength. In April 1778 at least one report from a rebel prisoner told of 25,000 men at Valley Forge, more than double the actual total.[22] Yet all of this has the ring of excuses rather than explanations. Certainly Howe was better informed than to believe that Washington had so many men, in addition to which a march to Valley Forge was a matter of a day or two, possible even with short forage. Historian Ira Gruber has suggested a more likely reason for Howe's inertia: the general was too preoccupied with plans to go home, and to defend his conduct of the war, to consider any offensive operations.[23] This seems nearer the truth, for the British commander had wearied of the conflict and its frustrations.

Enter the French: The Game Changes

As Howe brooded on his disappointments and awaited relief, and while Washington struggled to hold his army together, events moved beyond both of them. For the British, Sir William's failure to produce definitive military or political results soon became a secondary issue. Indeed, the 1777 campaign had triggered a diplomatic disaster of the first magnitude, a development that dramatically changed the character of the war. On 6 February 1778 France and America signed a Treaty of Amity and Commerce; that same day France recognized the independence of the United States and formalized a military alliance. The British saw the French move for what it was—a step toward war—and prepared for the worst. Yet Lord North's government did not want a wider war; operations in America had been costly in money and resources as it was. Thus the stunning intelligence from Paris, which the French did not officially confirm for over a month, induced the British to consider a negotiated settlement with the Americans.[24]

Some members of Parliament had urged just such a course in the aftermath of Saratoga. With this diplomatic gambit, however, and with clear signs that France was preparing to join the war, the matter assumed real urgency. Concern about the French now prompted the British to offer significant concessions to their rebellious cousins. On 9 March Parliament repealed most of the legislation that had so upset the colonies since 1763, including the hated Tea Act and the Coercive Acts, while promising to refrain from further taxing the Americans. In effect, the mother country had offered the colonies virtual home rule within the empire. The proposed arrangement envisioned a relationship between Britain and America resembling twentieth-century Commonwealth status: Americans and Britons would share a common monarch but for the most part would be free to conduct their own affairs. In an era in which few governments entertained notions of divided sovereignties, Britain had taken a daring step in trying to heal the breach with its North American colonies. (Had Parliament extended such an offer in 1775, the American national anthem might well be a version of "God Save the Queen.")[25]

Parliament having acted, North's government moved quickly. Germain immediately dispatched copies of the repeal bills to America, hoping to forestall congressional ratification of the treaties with France. In order to explain the government's position personally, North sent a new peace commission. Led by Frederick Howard, fifth Earl of Carlisle, the "Carlisle Commission" embarked for America on 21 April.[26] Not all Britons wanted peace, objecting that blood had been spilled and the nation insulted and fearing that the kingdom's prestige as a major power was at stake; they still wanted the colonists brought to heel through force of arms. Others simply doubted that the Americans would agree to any measures short of full independence. Walpole, at his sarcastic best, was less than enthusiastic, commenting that Carlisle was the right man "to make a treaty that will not be made."[27] Nevertheless, Lord North and the King were serious about not fighting the French and the Americans at the same time if it could be avoided.

Yet even as efforts to end the war in American proceeded, Britain and France moved gradually toward open conflict. The implications were global. Both powers had interests in the Caribbean, the Mediterranean, India, and elsewhere, and both had to consider that hostilities might affect any or all of their far-flung possessions. In addition, the French were working to isolate Britain diplomatically and, eventually, to bring other European powers into the conflict. They were getting results. Spain would declare war against Britain in 1779, war with the Dutch followed in late 1780, and much of the rest of Europe maintained a hostile neutrality. What had begun as a colonial rebellion was drifting toward a world war. In the recent past Britain had fought its major conflicts in coalition with allies; now it faced the prospect of fighting alone against a coalition.

The alliance was a godsend for the patriots, but France was fighting in its own interest, having no particular love for the Americans. It had fought the then-British provincials in the French and Indian (Seven Years') War but assisted the Revolution because it offered an opportunity to bleed a long-time enemy and exact a measure of revenge for the losses suffered fifteen years earlier. Washington shared in the euphoric American reaction to the new alliance but, ever the realist, recognized French motives. "France appears to have acted with politic Generosity towards us," he wrote to Major General Alexander McDougall, "and to have timed her declaration in our favor, most admirably for her own interests and the abasing her ancient Rival."[28] But as the saying goes, "The enemy of my enemy is my friend." France would be a friend indeed.

The British and French finally exchanged shots in mid-June 1778, by which time the latter already had dispatched an army to fight alongside the Continentals. For North's government the timing could not have been worse. The American War had forced a vast deployment of men, materiel, and ships to the colonies to the detriment of imperial defenses in other quarters; in fact, much of the empire was now thinly guarded. London also kept a watchful eye on a steady resurgence of French forces, the army now well equipped and well trained, while the navy approached parity with the British fleet. In a worst-case scenario, the Admiralty knew that an alliance of the French and Spanish fleets (not to mention the Dutch) could tip the balance against the Royal Navy. This was not war as the British wanted it, and certainly not the one they had anticipated.

Soberly, London took a hard look at the new strategic situation. The government conceded that it lacked the resources to defend every inch of imperial territory and assigned military priority to the most important areas. London became convinced that the lucrative sugar plantations in the West Indies would prove irresistible to the French as would the growing Indian holdings of the politically influential East India Company. Lord North's ministers concluded that these possessions were too valuable to remain at undue risk. If Britain was to hold the Caribbean and India and defend the home islands, it would have to reduce or end military efforts elsewhere, specifically North America. Facing reality, the government admitted the disappointing results of the campaigns in the American middle and northern colonies; by early March 1778 new plans called for a major retrenchment of efforts there. The British would no longer seek a decisive military result in the North, instead redeploying forces from the army then in Philadelphia to other theaters.[29]

The plan made sense given the altered military context of 1778, but the timing could have been better for Howe. Orders for the redeployment, issued on 21 March, reached Philadelphia on 23 May. This was only a day before Howe sailed for home and less than two weeks after Clinton had taken formal command. Sir Henry, who had barely settled in, thus had little chance to discuss the new orders with his departing predecessor, who could not wait to be gone.

Change of Command

The new royal commander in chief faced a difficult situation. The political landscape presented some real imponderables, few of which Clinton could have anticipated when he accepted the top command. He had little idea of how Carlisle and his fellow commissioners would go about their business, nor could he predict how successful their efforts might prove or how they might affect the military situation. If Congress responded positively to Carlisle, should the general remain in Philadelphia? But if he remained, what of the reported French fleet? Might it close the Delaware and trap him in the city? Under the circumstances, Clinton decided that he had no choice but to move ahead with the evacuation, a matter that presented its own problems.

It was not a pleasant first assignment. Moving an entire army in the face of an enemy was (and is) an exacting operation under the best of conditions; to do so in conjunction with a change of command, however, was to compound the difficulty. The arrival of General Clinton added a new factor—and another dimension of chance—to the British military equation. Howe had been a popular commander, one who frequently charmed even his critics. Clinton was cut from different cloth. Not a gregarious man—he once described himself as "a shy bitch"—the general was reserved and less prone to be social with his subordinates. Yet he brought to his new command a long record of service, which included a reputation for personal bravery and a considerable familiarity with the Americans. Now he would need to draw on virtually everything he had learned as a professional soldier.

The career of Henry Clinton, who would retain his command until 1782, illustrates the means of ascent typical among the British senior officer corps.[30] The son of Admiral George Clinton, colonial governor of Newfoundland (1732–41) and of New York (1741–51), Henry also was related through marriage to the Duke of Newcastle. He spent his teenage years in New York City, where he held a commission in the New York militia. In 1751 the then-nineteen-year-old left New York when the admiral returned to Britain. Ambitious for a military career, Henry purchased a commission in the regular army and eventually a captaincy in the prestigious Coldstream Guards. During the Seven Years' War he distinguished himself in action in Germany; promoted to colonel, Clinton was badly wounded in 1762 at the Battle of Nauheim. During his service in Europe, the young man met two future rebel officers, Charles Lee and William Alexander, both of whom he would face at the Battle of Monmouth.[31] Opportunities for military distinction were meager after the peace of 1763, but the colonel was able to cultivate important social and political connections. A promotion to major general repaid his efforts in 1772, the same year he secured a seat in Parliament through the patronage of the Duke of Newcastle. Clinton was a brave and competent soldier, but he was a general also because he came from the right family and knew the right people.

Much was expected of Clinton when he went to America with Howe in 1775. He showed great bravery at Bunker Hill, but the next year the patriots foiled his attack on Charleston, South Carolina. Rejoining Howe in the North, Clinton did much better. In 1776 he led successful operations around New York, notably on Long Island, where he executed the flanking movement that precipitated the rebel defeat. The following year he did well at Newport, Rhode Island, which the British wanted as a base for foraging and naval operations, and then also on a limited strike up the Hudson River in a forlorn effort on behalf of Burgoyne. Yet Clinton served Howe without enthusiasm. He never warmed to his commanding officer and was free with criticisms of his leadership. In particular, he vigorously opposed the 1777 Pennsylvania invasion, urging instead a drive up the Hudson Valley to cooperate with Burgoyne. That Clinton was right does not change the fact that he could be a difficult subordinate with a very casual loyalty to his chief.

Indeed, feeling Howe regarded his opinion lightly, Clinton took leave in 1776 and seriously considered resignation. Germain disliked the general personally but respected his military reputation and political connections. Rather than risk a flap in Parliament, the American secretary assuaged the unhappy Clinton with a knighthood and a promotion to lieutenant general (although Sir Henry held the local rank of full general in America). Then Germain induced him to return to America as Howe's second in command; this grudging regard also induced the secretary to offer him the American command in 1778. On balance, Germain's decision was reasonable. Clinton had proved a capable soldier, and his American experience suited him for the top military command there.

When Clinton relieved Howe, he was forty-eight years old and in his professional prime. He was confident he could beat the rebels if the Americans ever committed to a showdown fight, and he cursed the luck that gave him the command along with orders to retreat. The thought of surrendering Philadelphia without firing a shot was humiliating; the only real victory of 1777 was being tossed aside. But the general was a good soldier, and he "consequently prepared with all diligence to obey His Majesty's commands to the fullest extent of my ability."[32]

The instructions from Germain revealed the gravity of Britain's new strategic position. Clinton's orders explained that because of the recent Franco-American alliance, Britain could not await events or lose the initiative; His Majesty's forces would strike first. Plans called for an immediate attack on the crucial French Caribbean island of Saint Lucia and reinforcing imperial positions in the Floridas. These operations required Clinton "to detach 5000 men to the West Indies" and another "3000 men to St. Augustine and West Florida." He noted that his "army would be much weakened by these detachments" and understood that his reduced numbers would preclude any major offensive operations against Washington. There was no further thought of crushing the rebellion in the North through force of arms. Rather, he was "commanded to evacuate Philadelphia and proceed by sea with the remaining troops and stores to New York," where he was to await the results of the Carlisle Commission's efforts to reach a peace with the rebels. If these talks failed and the subsequent military situation looked too perilous—that is, if the general felt that he could not hold New York—Clinton had the authority to pull back as far as Halifax.[33] The government did note the importance of Philadelphia and added that Clinton might try holding it if he was strong enough after redeploying his forces. But the general knew that this was impossible; he would have to leave the city.[34]

For the time being, Sir Henry did not share the import of his orders with anyone beyond Howe, who had not yet left for England, and a small circle of senior officers. He wanted to assess the task confronting him and to learn what he could of Washington's capabilities before committing himself to any course of action. Clinton did, however, make one quick decision: he would not evacuate all of his army by sea. In fact, he *could* not. A survey of available shipping disclosed a shortage of transports, and he could not afford to wait in Philadelphia while the Royal Navy assembled more. In another disappointing communication from home, word reached the city of the possible approach of a strong French naval squadron. The alarm was premature: the enemy fleet, under the comte d'Estaing, had sailed from Toulon on 13 April but failed to reach New York until 11 July. Unsure of d'Estaing's progress or whereabouts, however, British naval commanders wanted to quit Philadelphia while passage of the Delaware was still uncontested. Yet even without the French threat, Clinton still feared delay. He wrote Germain that if his army took ship and "contrary winds" slowed the voyage, there was no guarantee that Washington would not attempt a descent on lightly defended New York. Thus he would send what he could on the available ships and would get the rest of his command back to New York by "marching through Jersey."[35]

What remained was for Sir Henry to plan the evacuation and to explain it to the army and to the region's loyalists. It remained for General Washington to learn of his new opponent's plans and to formulate an appropriate response.

CHAPTER 2

A General under Fire

George Washington and His Critics

The Philadelphia campaign left George Washington no happier than Sir William Howe. One of the war's ironies was that both commanders came under fire for their respective performances in 1777: Howe for failing to beat Washington, Washington for failing to beat Howe. Sir William, of course, would go home to face his critics, but Washington would have to do so while still in command and trying to hold his army together at Valley Forge. Unlike Howe, he would have to confront criticisms that went beyond his performance in battle. True, Washington's defeats distressed many patriots and raised questions about his leadership, but the reversals in the field also gave rise to deeper concerns. Republican purists posed ideological objections to the general's vision of what the Continental Army should be and how it should fight the war. From whatever quarter the complaints came, however, it was clear that events had shaken confidence in the commander in chief. In the months following the close of the Philadelphia campaign, Washington faced a serious challenge to his command.

General Washington's War

For Washington and the Continental Army, 1777 had started well. In fact, the evident success of the early campaign season raised patriot hopes for the year. Justifiably, historians have credited the rebel commander in chief with rebuilding his army over the winter and spring of 1777. This was no easy task. The army had wintered in and near Morristown in northern New Jersey where, relatively safe from British attack, the general had supervised the creation of new regiments; the acquisition of animals, supplies, and equipment;

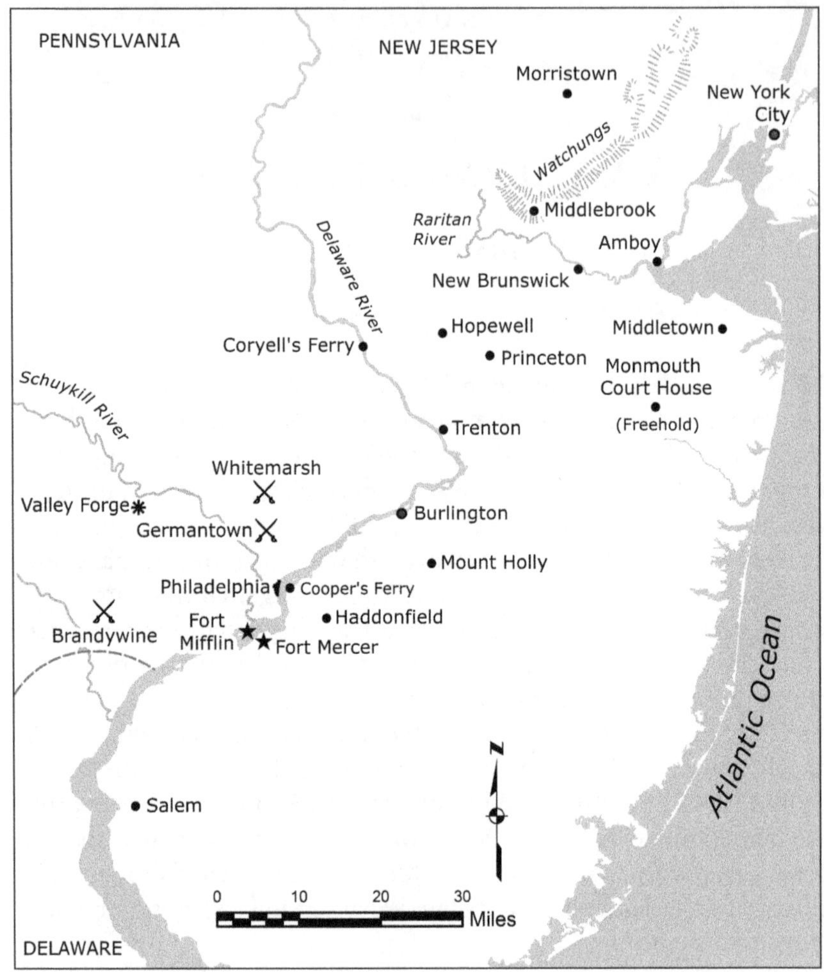

New Jersey and eastern Pennsylvania, the theater for the main British and Continental armies, 1777–78. Map by Garry Wheeler Stone. Copyright © 2016 by the University of Oklahoma Press.

and the organization of intelligence operations. He did all this while keeping Howe guessing as to his actual strength and intentions. By April Washington felt strong enough to move south, occupying the Watchung Mountains above Middlebrook, close to the advanced British post at New Brunswick. The American general had virtually rebuilt an army in a matter of four months—a stunning achievement.

From the Watchungs, Washington initiated small-scale combat operations. There were no major battles, but the rebel commander did not want any. Rather, he wanted his new units to gain combat experience, to learn to work with local militia, and to deny New Jersey's rich forage to the British. He also wanted to keep Howe off balance—and Sir William never did discern what Washington's real intentions were. In conjunction with New Jersey militia, the Continentals waged an active hit-and-run campaign against British foraging parties and patrols, effectively closing the countryside to Howe's army unless it sallied in strength. Throughout the spring, Washington refused to be drawn into a general action, although he posed enough of an offensive threat to make his counterpart cautious. Patriots took heart. In Congress Massachusetts delegate Elbridge Gerry expressed the opinion of many when he wrote, "Mr. Howe is maneuvering in the Jersies, but our Army is on so respectable a Footing, that he has not yet ventured to attack them."[1] Indeed, Washington was sufficiently menacing to convince Sir William that a march directly across New Jersey to Philadelphia would be unwise. In July Howe's final withdrawal left New Jersey in patriot hands, a signal achievement for the rebel cause.

Washington found it hard to take immediate advantage of Howe's departure. Intelligence reports were contradictory; speculation had the British headed for the Hudson to cooperate with Burgoyne or sailing to New England; Charleston, South Carolina; or Philadelphia. Washington simply had no way to tell. Only in late August did he learn that Howe was headed for Philadelphia via the Chesapeake. With the uncertainty resolved, the rebel commander in chief still had plenty of time to move the bulk of his men to the Philadelphia area; Washington also sent a significant detachment to Peekskill, New York, where it could react to British movements around New York City. Ultimately, he ordered units north to reinforce patriots gathering against Burgoyne, including Colonel Daniel Morgan's riflemen, who would play a key role in the fighting around Saratoga. Washington did all of this with an army only partly trained and with logistical and administrative support services barely up to the job. Arguably, he had done about as well as he could have under the circumstances. The general had maintained the Continental Line as a force in being—one perhaps not strong enough to defeat his opponent but too strong for the enemy to take lightly—and in so doing he had kept the Revolution alive.

Washington's performance in New Jersey also raised hopes. His new army now had experience, and patriots expected it to do well over the rest of the campaign season. The commander in chief shared this growing enthusiasm. In fact, he was itching for a fight as he deployed outside of Philadelphia.[2] This optimism reflected the general's success in rebuilding his army and its recent performance in New Jersey; it certainly was a break with his earlier posture, which had stressed a cautious approach to operations. The year before, in September 1776, he had outlined a strategy that governed his behavior on all but the most unusual occasions. "On our Side the War should be defensive," he explained to the president of Congress. "It has even been called a War of Posts. That we should on all Occasions avoid a general Action, or put anything to the Risque, unless compelled by a necessity, into which we ought never to be drawn."[3] But Washington was flexible. Despite considerable talk of the general as an American Fabius, the Roman general who shadowed and threatened Hannibal but never committed to a battle that might end in disaster, the patriot commander would fight when he thought he could win—or at least when he thought he must. The major battles around New York City and the smaller but crucial actions at Trenton and Princeton had demonstrated as much.

Yet the fighting that autumn belied Washington's optimism. Once the British army was ashore in Maryland, the initiative quickly passed to General Howe. The Continentals fought hard, but they had no effective answer for the aggressive enemy offensive. Washington lost on 9 September 1777 at the Battle of Brandywine, which led directly to the fall of Philadelphia. His October counterattack failed at Germantown, and by late November so had efforts to hold the Delaware River forts controlling maritime access to Philadelphia. These defeats evoked painful reactions from Congress. After Brandywine an angry James Lovell of Massachusetts grumbled that the battle was a lost opportunity, a wasted "day of Salvation offered by Heaven to us" unlikely to recur "in 10 campaigns." Gerry was furious to learn of the loss of the river forts: The army had failed to support them, he complained, and "Delays in the Councils of War" had lost a river that should have been "impregnable."[4] Even the skirmishing at White Marsh in early December left some rebels dejected. Cornelius Harnett, delegate from North Carolina, had come to expect the worst: Howe had sortied from Philadelphia, he wrote, "& by a precipitate March Out general'd us, as usual."[5] Lovell, Gerry, and Harnett were not alone in their frustrations, and an air of pessimism replaced the bright outlook of earlier in the year.

For many patriots the military setbacks around Philadelphia—bad enough by themselves—seemed to be part of a general malaise. In July in the face of Burgoyne's advance in upper New York State, Major General Arthur St. Clair had evacuated Fort Ticonderoga without a fight. The matter shocked patriots. Soon thereafter an appalled Congress relieved St. Clair *and* his immediate superior, Major General Philip Schuyler.[6] John Adams, not usually an especially bloodthirsty rebel, was furious and would have gone further. "Don't you pitty me to be wasting my Life," he wrote to his wife, Abigail, "in laborious Exertions, to procure Cannon, Ammunition, Stores, Baggage, Cloathing &c. &c. &c. &c., for Armies, who give them all away to the Enemy, without firing a Gun?"[7] Less delicately he moaned to Horatio Gates, "We shall never hold a post until we shoot a general."[8] Still venting, he wrote James Warren that the loss of the fort "Calls for Inquiry." The innocent should be acquitted, he insisted, but those guilty should "meet their Deserts. I see no Medium, I confess, between honourable Acquittal and capital Punishment."[9] Adams was perhaps the only member of Congress actually to suggest shooting someone (at least no recorded similar sentiments have come to light), but others shared his frustrations. Thus, even before the reverses around Philadelphia, many patriots were in a sour mood regarding the performance of their officers, and they were saying as much.

There was more. In October patriot troops, inhibited by poor weather and poor planning, bungled an attempt to force the British out of Rhode Island. Indeed, the Continental commander, Major General Joseph Spencer, cancelled the operation before anyone fired a shot. Once again Congress was aghast. An investigation exculpated Spencer, who resigned in 1778, but the entire affair was yet another example of a war effort that appeared stalled and incapable. Rhode Island delegate Henry Marchant could not contain his exasperation. "How long are we to be ruined by false Delicacy!" he wrote Virginian Richard Henry Lee. "I wish that Congress would in some self Evident Cases exercise the Sovereign Right of removing [incompetent officers]." "The public Good is sufficient Cause," he insisted. Marchant conceded that Spencer was a decent man—"a sober Man, a religious Man, and a Friend to his Country—but is this enough?"[10] For Marchant and many others, the answer was an emphatic no.

Still, in the face of these disappointments, civilian leaders called on Washington to keep fighting. They wanted the army to protect the countryside around Philadelphia from British patrols and raids, and if possible, they also wanted to recapture the de facto capital. Gerry wrote Adams that Congress was unanimous in its insistence on a winter offensive. When Washington demurred, on 28 November Congress appointed a committee at headquarters composed of Gerry, Robert Morris (Pennsylvania), and Joseph Jones (Virginia) to meet with the commander in chief to press the point.[11] What they found was an army without the numbers and supplies to open a new campaign; an officer corps upset over matters of rank, late pay, and congressional resistance to granting postwar pensions; and a pervasive sentiment in camp opposed to any venture against Philadelphia.[12] Certainly Washington had lost the fighting mood of September. "It would give me infinite pleasure to afford protection to every individual and to every Spot of Ground in the whole of the United States," he told Henry Laurens. "Nothing is more my wish. But this is not possible with our present force."[13] Nothing occurred before the spring of 1778 to make him change his mind. There was no winter campaign.

As patriots dwelled on the military situation, the condition of the army became increasingly dire. Rebel logistics nearly broke down under the trials of sustained campaigning, leaving the army in a desperately poor position to feed and supply itself. Foul weather exacerbated the situation. While the winter was warmer than usual, there were cold snaps and snow followed by rains that turned roads to mud and made rivers difficult to pass. Communications and deliveries of food, forage, and supplies suffered dramatically. The first days of January 1778 saw the army sheltered in what the young marquis de Lafayette called "little shanties that are scarcely gayer than dungeon cells."[14] Yet even these realities evoked criticisms. In a scalding letter to Samuel Adams, Lovell excoriated the army: "tis a Subject very sickening to even a strong Stomach." He was furious at the lack of a winter campaign, at the demands of the officer corps for pensions, at "the nakedness of the Soldiers," and at what he considered a disinclination to fight.[15] For Washington, 1777 had ended badly indeed, and things were only going to get worse.

The Chorus of Critics

The high expectations of the spring and early fall of 1777, as well as the success of Major General Gates at Saratoga, had put Washington's failures, and those of patriot arms generally, in bold relief. Pointedly, questions arose about the commander in chief's fitness for that rank: generals were selected to win, or at least not to lose, and Washington had disappointed on both counts. Yet understanding Washington's critics requires careful perspective—the perspective of 1777 and 1778, *not* the hindsight of historians generations later. Since the winning of independence, accounts of the struggle, scholarly and otherwise, have tended to view Washington and his detractors in something of a "good guys, bad guys" dichotomy.[16] To be sure, some of his critics were less than noble in their motives; some were stupid (more on them later). But much of the obloquy heaped on the general's critics has stemmed from the fact that Washington proved them wrong—he ultimately won the war. This was something patriots, friendly or unfriendly to the commander in chief, simply could not have known in late 1777 or early 1778. Under the circumstances, it would have been surprising if the patriot general's record had not evoked censure, or at least serious questions.

Understandably, many patriots had wearied of defeat and an expensive war effort that seemed to promise few results. Thus the commander in chief became the target of private and public doubts, which were not entirely new. As early as late 1776, after the loss of New York, questions arose about Washington's leadership. Among others, Adjutant General Joseph Reed and, most notably, Major General Charles Lee, the army's second-ranking officer, groused indiscreetly at Washington's performance. In the wake of the disaster at Fort Washington, they lamented the commander in chief's seeming indecision and a penchant (as they saw it) for listening to poor advice. Washington was aware of some of these complaints, having inadvertently seen one of Lee's letters to Reed.[17] Preoccupied with a deteriorating military situation, he chose not to make an issue of the matter. Lee, however, became even more trenchant in his criticism. Following orders only reluctantly, he had been marching his men slowly across northern New Jersey to join the main army across the Delaware, dawdling to the point of insubordination. Lee had wanted to remain in the state to threaten Howe's rear and despaired of Washington's orders. On 12 December 1776 he let loose on his commander in a letter to General Gates. "*Entre nous,*" he grumbled, "a certain great man is most damnably deficient." He protested that his orders promised either the ruin of his command or the final loss of New Jersey. "Our counsels have been weak to the last degree."[18] This letter, which Washington did *not* see, was a virtual indictment of the general's leadership. Had he seen it or become aware of it, or if Lee had become less discrete in his disparagement of his chief (he was wont to speak his mind), it is difficult to see how the two senior patriot generals could have avoided an open rupture. Lee's capture by a British patrol the following morning may have spared the rebel army a crisis of the first magnitude at a time when it most needed unity.[19]

Worse came in 1777. Despite the accolades garnered after Trenton and Princeton, Washington still drew the private skepticism of Samuel Adams, John Adams's cousin and fellow congressional delegate from Massachusetts. Samuel groused at what he considered the general's operational caution in New Jersey. While professing to "have no Judgment in military Affairs" (he was right in that respect), nevertheless, in a string of letters to various colleagues, he bemoaned what he saw as Fabian tactics and the failure to pursue a vigorous campaign. Adams wanted "decisive" action. "I am apt to be displeased," he wrote to Richard Henry Lee, "when I think our Progress in War and Politicks is Slow. I wish to see more of an enterprising Spirit in the Senate and the Field."[20] After the patriot defeat at Brandywine in September, Lovell, also of Massachusetts, queried "whether fortune alone is to be blamed, or whether [Major General John] Sullivan and the Chief should not share."[21] Days later, as Howe's army closed on Philadelphia, John Adams, ever critical of the commander in chief's judgment, called for divine intervention: "Oh, Heaven! grant Us one great Soul! One leading Mind would extricate the best Cause, from that Ruin which seems to await it, for the Want of it. . . . One active masterly Capacity would bring order out of this Confusion and save this Country."[22] For Adams, the man who had proposed Washington as commander in chief in 1775, the general no longer possessed that "masterly Capacity." Three months after Howe's occupation of Philadelphia, Virginia's Francis Lightfoot Lee, observing the scene from the congressional exile in York, sourly commented that "the campaign in this quarter has been very disgraceful."[23]

Outside of Congress, there were doubts in the officer corps as well. Brigadier General Anthony Wayne, who always preferred active operations (and who would play a prominent role at Monmouth Court House) and usually enjoyed Washington's regard, grew tired of losing battles. Like the Virginian's other critics, Wayne wanted to see more decisive leadership. Colonel Daniel Broadhead, another Pennsylvania Continental, reportedly told Gates that many officers were unhappy under Washington.[24] In short, patriots wanted victory in the field, and to those of an impatient temperament, that meant winning battles and knocking the British out of the war.

One of the most cogent (and stinging) critiques of the commander in chief came from the pen of New Jersey delegate Jonathan Dickinson Sergeant. Sergeant hated the British. Before sitting in Congress he had been an active whig, serving on local revolutionary committees and in the New Jersey Provincial Congress. In December 1776 he paid the price for his radical allegiance when the British burned his Princeton home, prompting him to transplant to Philadelphia. On 1 November 1777 Pennsylvania appointed him state attorney general, but he remained in Congress until New Jersey sent a replacement later that month. By then Sergeant had seen enough of Washington's leadership and vented in correspondence with Lovell, a kindred spirit when it came to the subject of the commander in chief:

> Things look gloomy here below. We want a General; thousands of Lives & Millions of Property are yearly sacrificed to the Insufficiency of our Commander in Chief. Two battles [Brandywine and Germantown] he has lost for us by two such Blunders as might have disgraced a Soldier of three Months Standing; and yet we are so attached to this Man that I fear we shall rather sink with him than throw him off our Shoulders. And sink we must under his Management. Such Feebleness & Want of Authority, such Confusion & Want of Discipline, such Waste, such Destruction will exhaust the Wealth of both the Indies & annihilate the Armies of all of Europe and Asia. Twenty Thousand Recruits annually would be absolutely necessary to maintain an Army of forty thousand. I believe this is the most moderate Calculation. In the mean Time People are so disaffected to the Service that no more Recruits can be got. In short, I am quite a Convert to [New Jersey delegate] Abraham Clarkes Opinion; that we may talk of the Enemy's Cruelty as we will, but we have no greater Cruelty to complain of than the Management of our Army.

Sergeant's was a voice of utter exasperation. He trusted his correspondent as "a Man of prudence" as to whether or not to share the letter with others, and it appears that Lovell sent it on to Samuel Adams.[25]

In and outside of Congress, then, the chorus of Washington's critics was growing.

The general's record as a combat commander, however, was only part of his problem. A circle of politically radical whigs also took aim at his broader vision of how to fight the war, their arguments going beyond questions of military operations and into the realm of republican ideology. Washington was adamant in his belief that only a professionally trained regular army could stand up to the British in the field; he just as fervently believed that this was the key to ultimate victory (discussed further in the next chapter). Most whigs conceded the need for a disciplined army, but some voices inside and outside of Congress questioned the general's emphasis on regulars, particularly the wisdom of efforts to develop the American regulars on a European model. Rather, they wanted more reliance on militia—theoretically, the citizenry in arms—which reflected the zeitgeist of their more radical republican political outlook. Free men fighting for their liberties, homes, and families, these patriots insisted, were infinitely superior to a professional army. Professionals, so the argument went, were often recruited from among the poorest elements of society, having fewer attachments to civil virtues and serving primarily for their pay.[26] But before dismissing these radicals as mere ideologues, it is well to remember that their beliefs were sincere, however misguided from a strictly military perspective. They meant what they said in an age when many Americans believed devoutly in republicanism.

Of the radical whigs, the most outspoken was James Lovell. But Lovell was no crank; in fact, he was highly intelligent. Born in 1737, he received a first-class education (for its day) at the prestigious Boston Latin School, of which his father, John Lovell, was headmaster. He afterward graduated from Harvard in 1756, finished a master of arts degree three years later, and taught at the Latin School. The coming of the Revolution tragically divided the Lovell family. John remained loyal to the King, while James took up the patriot cause. After Bunker Hill, Howe had the younger Lovell arrested and sent to Halifax, Nova Scotia; the father left Boston with the British Army when it evacuated the city. James was exchanged in November 1776, and in December Massachusetts sent him to Congress, serving diligently until 1782. Lovell was deeply involved in foreign relations—he had more experience in the area than any other delegate—and was a self-taught cryptologist, greatly concerned with the security of congressional communications; later in the war he actually broke British ciphers for the Continental Army.[27] That such a man came to question the ability and performance of Washington is testimony to how serious the doubts about the general had become.

Like the other critics, Lovell was disappointed in the string of Continental defeats. "The Spirit of Enterprize is a Stranger in the main Army," he wrote his friend Joseph Whipple of New Hampshire. "You may expect so long as the War continues that 3 times more men will be lost in the *main* army by marching and countermarching over hills and thro' rivers than in *battles.* I should deceive you greatly if I lead you to look for any thing favourable from the *main* army."[28] And by the "main army" he pointedly meant Washington's, rather than the Northern Army that Gates had commanded at Saratoga. But Lovell's anger (and he was a very angry man) had deeper roots than tactical success or failure. He was furious with Washington's determination to build a professional Continental Line on the European model. In particular, he denounced the general's advocacy of half-pay pensions for the officers, which he considered nothing less than extortion and a "mode of introducing into Society a set of haughty, idle, imperious Scandalizers of Industrious Citizens & Farmers." Lovell sought to remind all who "have not forgotten that this *was* in its beginning a *patriotic war*"; after its victorious conclusion, the officers could farm like anyone else. Lovell also objected to Washington's seemingly untouchable status in the army: the commander in chief had become "a Demi G——," the "one great Man, whom no Citizen *shall* dare even talk about say the Gentlemen of the Blade."[29] Lovell was a splendid ideologue.

Lovell was not alone. Indeed, the ranks of republican doubters contained some prominent names. Samuel Adams warned that professional troops were "apt to consider themselves as a Body distinct from the rest of the Citizens. . . . They have their Arms always in their hands. Their Rules and their Discipline is severe. They soon become attached to their officers and disposed to yield implicit obedience to their Commands. Such a power," he concluded, "should be watched with a jealous Eye." John Adams, whose patriotism was beyond reproach, took an equally dim view. A professional army would enlist "the meanest, idlest, most intemperate and worthless, but no more." The yeomen farmers and mechanics, the backbone of republican armies, would never serve in a standing army. "Was it creditable that men who could get at home a better living, more comfortable lodgings, more than double the wages, in safety . . . would" join Washington for the duration of the war? "I knew it to be impossible."[30] Major General Lee, perhaps Washington's most radical lieutenant, warned that "when the soldiers of a community are volunteers [that is, regulars], war becomes a distinct profession. The arms of a Republic get into the hands of its worst members."[31] Such an army was a whig nightmare. Benjamin Rush, one of the Revolution's most zealous republicans—he had signed the Declaration of Independence for Pennsylvania, did yeoman service as an army doctor, and yielded to no one as a vociferous critic of Washington's leadership—put the matter as a well as anyone: "I should despair of our cause if our country contained 60,000 men abandoned enough to enlist for 3 years or during the [duration of the] war."[32]

Other radical whigs insisted that the record showed that enough militia, ideally stiffened by regulars (very few patriots totally rejected the use of regular troops in time of war) but alone if necessary, could deny the enemy safe access to the American interior and overwhelm British forces that ventured there. There were actual militia successes in this regard: Lexington and Concord, the rising in New Jersey in late 1776, Bennington, and most recently the militia's role in the defeat of Burgoyne at Saratoga. In Congress Samuel Adams waxed almost rhapsodic about the prowess of militia when led by competent officers. If only this had been the case in New Jersey early in 1777, he mused, when "so great an Animation prevaild" among the militia, "who knows but that they w[oul]d have destroyd" Howe's army.[33] Some radical Pennsylvanians had the same notion. In December they asked the state assembly to muster the entire militia and end the war with an all-out assault on Howe's army in Philadelphia. The legislature actually endorsed the plan, which failed to even reference the Continental Army.[34] Gerry, pondering the loss of the Delaware River forts and the botched Rhode Island operation, wished the seat of war was in New England, where he was sure the patriot irregulars would overwhelm the British, instead of Pennsylvania. Lovell wanted the regular army to adopt the militia practice of electing officers; casting about for even better ways to organize local forces, he joined with Richard Henry Lee in asking the American commissioners in Paris to send "by the first opportunity a plan of the militia of Switzerland."[35] If events later proved them wrong, the militia partisans were articulate in pressing their case.

Yet with patriots barely able to support Washington's small band at Valley Forge, more-realistic whigs were skeptical of such ideological purity. How, they asked, could the struggling Congress or the new states afford to mobilize, feed, pay, and equip a massive militia army?[36] And if such troops had performed wonders during certain periods, what about their failures? The Pennsylvania militia had refused to rally during Howe's offensive against Philadelphia, and militia alone could not have stopped Burgoyne; indeed, in the major battles at Saratoga, Continental regulars had played the key combat role. Convinced republicans, however, casually ignored such questions. Again Rush said it best. "The militia began," he wrote John Adams, "and I sincerely hope the militia will end the present war."[37] And Rush, along with his like-minded friends, knew all such wishful thinking was anathema to George Washington.

By January 1778 the practical doubts about the commander in chief's generalship had become intertwined with the ideological critiques. The most glaring example of this development emerged in an anonymous pamphlet, "The Thoughts of a Freeman," dated 17 January; Henry Laurens reported to Washington that a member of Congress had "picked it up on the Stairs" in York.[38] The tract was a scathing analysis—"disparagement" is a better word—of Washington's leadership. "Freeman" wondered why the general had allowed Howe to march so unhindered from Head of Elk and why the British had outflanked the Continentals at Brandywine. He criticized the loss of the river forts and concluded "that the proper methods of attacking beating and conquering the Enemy has never as yet been adapted by the Commander in C—f." The army's medical and supply services, "Freeman" continued, were a disgrace. These were the author's practical concerns.

"Freeman" then turned to ideology. He warned "that the general contempt shown to the Militia by the standing forces is a dangerous Omen. That in every victory as yet obtained by the Americans the Militia has had the principal share. That the Liberties of America are safe only in the hands of the Militia." He called on Congress to recognize that the victory at Saratoga "was owing to a change of Commanders"—that is, the firing of St. Clair and the relief of Schuyler by Gates—and that a similar change would have allowed the main army to win around Philadelphia. His conclusion was utterly unambiguous: "That the people of America have been guilty of Idolatry by making a man their god—and that the God of Heaven and Earth will convince them by woeful experience that he is only a man. That no good may be expected from the standing Army until Baal and his worshipers are banished from the Camp—I believe that. Verte." This was strong stuff, a direct call for Congress to fire the commander in chief. And one doubts "Freeman" (whoever he was) would have written and distributed it without some confidence his message would find a fair number of favorable readers.[39]

General Washington had lost a lot of friends. Still, his critics have not fared well in the public memory of the Revolution or, for that matter, among historians. Their tone was strident and their assumption that they held some high moral ground still smacks of arrogance; the ramblings of such military naïfs as Rush were silly even at the time. The fact that events ultimately proved them wrongheaded has not helped their image. Yet they were still patriots. In their doubts about Washington, men such as the Adams cousins and Major General Lee, or even a busybody like Rush, never meant harm to the American war effort; indeed, they had risked their lives in declaring for independence. At least seven of them—John and Samuel Adams, Richard Henry Lee, his brother Francis Lightfoot Lee, Elbridge Gerry, Benjamin Rush, and Abraham Clark—were signers of the Declaration of Independence and had pledged their "Lives," "Fortunes," and "sacred Honor" to the cause; Sergeant too would have signed the declaration, but he had left Congress to return to New Jersey, where he was instrumental in drafting the new state constitution.[40] While Lovell and Samuel Adams criticized Washington, their sons served in the general's army—young Samuel Adams as a doctor and the junior James Lovell as an infantry officer (both would serve at Monmouth). Two of Clark's sons were Continental officers; both were captured and suffered cruelly while prisoners, one of them aboard the infamous prison hulk *Jersey* in New York harbor.[41] To suggest that these men had any desire to impede the patriot military effort is absurd. They wanted to win the war as badly as anyone else, but they had honest doubts about Washington's ability to produce victory. Their political views reflected the reality that even in the face of disaster, traditional republican fears of standing armies died hard.

Cabal?

After the defeat at Brandywine, Congressmen Thomas Burke of North Carolina, who could be as dramatic as Benjamin Rush on paper, despaired of the patriot military effort. He poured out his frustration in a long letter to fellow North Carolinian Richard Caswell, giving an account of the battle and reaching a dismal conclusion on affairs in the Philadelphia theater. "I have the Melancholy Conviction," he wrote, that Washington's "principle Officers are Incompetent, and I fear it is an Evil that cannot be remedied."[42] Others were as angry as Burke but disagreed with his conclusion. To the contrary, like "Freeman," they believed there was a remedy: Congress could find a new commander in chief.

That some patriots reached this conclusion should be no surprise. Historically, it is a truism that unsuccessful generals frequently lost their commands, and they just as frequently deserved the criticism they received. During the eighteenth century, the consequences of failure could be serious for the officers concerned, and patriot leaders certainly remembered the lessons of British military history. In 1757 the British shot Admiral John Byng on his own quarterdeck for failure "to do his utmost" to prevent the French capture of Minorca.[43] (Byng's execution was a sensation in the empire, and it is not too much to speculate that John Adams had Byng in mind when he wrote so scathingly of St. Clair's conduct at Ticonderoga.) The British were severe with underperforming generals as well, something Americans also knew from recent experience. During the French and Indian War, the ministry had sent John Campbell, Lord Loudoun, to command in North America after Edward Braddock's defeat and death on the Monongahela. When Loudoun failed to get results, the British replaced him with James Abercrombie; when Abercrombie failed, he gave way to Jeffery Amherst.[44] Amherst proved a war winner, but had *he* failed, another general would have replaced him. When it became clear that General Thomas Gage could not contain the growing colonial rebellion, Germain wisely concluded, "I must lament that General Gage, with all his good qualities, finds himself in a situation of too great importance for his talents."[45] The ministry recalled Gage and sent William Howe. Standard practice was clear: unsuccessful commanders could expect to be relieved.

Most historians have concluded that no organized faction or "cabal" in Congress or the army actually plotted to remove

Washington. That was true enough, though this did not mean that individuals were not thinking seriously about it and had ample precedents to guide them had they acted. Nor should the absence of a formal congressional resolution to relieve Washington or request his resignation mask the fact that the ranks of those discontented with him were, if not organized, then more extensive and determined than most modern historians have allowed.[46] For various reasons, some important patriot leaders thought that the general had failed the test of leadership and that it was time for a change. Certainly, Washington and his political and military friends believed his command was in jeopardy. They also believed that some of those in the anti-Washington "faction," "party," "junto," or "cabal"—the commander in chief's allies used all of these terms—had a mission: they sought to replace the losing Washington with the winning General Gates, the hero of Saratoga.

To the extent any single individual was at the center of this activity, Thomas Mifflin of Pennsylvania filled the role. He was a formidable man. Born in 1744 to a Quaker mercantile family with important political connections, Mifflin was well educated, well traveled, and urbane. In 1765 he formed his own trading house and became independently wealthy. Mifflin broke with the Quakers when he took an early and active role in the patriot cause, playing a distinguished part in leading Pennsylvania into rebellion. Active on whig committees before independence, Mifflin was a delegate to both Continental Congresses. With no prior military experience, he organized a volunteer militia unit and then served in significant quartermaster and field commands in 1775 and 1776. He fought well on Long Island, covering Washington's withdrawal from Brooklyn Heights, and had rallied volunteer reinforcements for the Virginian in the darkest days of late 1776. With a commission as major general, he had been close to Washington as an aide and then as the Continental Army's quartermaster general.[47] His dedication to the cause was beyond question.

But Mifflin's relationship with Washington soured as the patriot war effort faltered. The Pennsylvania general looked with dismay on the Virginian's successive defeats. But the motive for his subsequent actions was probably personal, for he nursed a growing resentment of Major General Nathanael Greene. Mifflin coveted his own role as an influential aide to the commander in chief, and he took umbrage as Washington turned increasingly for advice to the general from Rhode

Island. As Greene's influence overshadowed his own, Mifflin developed a venomous hatred of him, and his consequent disenchantment with the commander in chief grew apace.[48] It is too much to attribute the general's posture completely to personal pique, but his jealousy of Greene and anger at Washington certainly were intertwined. Pleading illness, Mifflin resigned as quartermaster general in early 1778, leaving his department in dire straits (a matter not entirely his fault) and crippling Continental supply efforts when the army needed them the most. Yet he remained a power in Pennsylvania politics, was a darling of the radicals in and out of Congress, and even maintained his major general's commission—all while convinced that the Continental Army needed a new commander.

Mifflin kept influential company, and he was in a position to share his dim view of Washington with others. John and Samuel Adams, Lovell, Richard Henry Lee, Rush, and kindred spirits were his frequent correspondents and guests at his country estate. Many of Mifflin's own attacks on Washington were oblique, heaping calumny on subordinate officers, especially Greene (the men now hated one another), but it was clear enough who his real target was. It was from the group around Mifflin that many, if not most, of the private letters, anonymous newspaper articles, and verbal jibes emanated. Certainly, officers around Washington saw the Pennsylvanian as their chief antagonist; Lieutenant Colonel John Laurens, one of Washington's closest aides-de-camp, was sure of it. In a letter to his father, Henry Laurens, president of Congress, the young officer charged that there was "a certain party, formed against the present Commander in chief, at the head of which is Genl Mifflin."[49] Washington had made some dangerous enemies.

If the various complaints about the commander in chief were just talk, from Washington's perspective it was dangerous talk. At the very least, it was a distraction he did not need while laboring to hold his stricken army together. Worse, however, was the fact that for the first time a seemingly credible alternative to Washington had appeared in Horatio Gates. Gates had not only triumphed but also was genuinely popular with the New England militia so beloved of the more radical whigs. In their eyes Gates had it all: he was a winner in battle *and* politically acceptable. There is no question the more ardent whigs wanted him. Samuel Adams had been singing his praises even before Saratoga: Gates "is *honest and true,* & has the Art of *gaining the Love of his Soldiers.*" Lovell was of the same mind. "We want you in different places," the zealous delegate wrote directly to Gates, lamenting the dismal state of military affairs in the Philadelphia theater.[50] Other patriots of a less radical persuasion—those simply tired of losing battles and a stalled war effort—would have understood a turn to a winning general. Nor was Gates bashful about making friends with the commander in chief's detractors. Without openly saying as much—at least that we know of—the radicals understood their hero was amenable to an appointment as Washington's replacement. There seems little doubt that the general wanted the job.

History has been unkind to Gates. His links to Washington's critics—indeed, he was one himself—and his disastrous performance in 1780 in South Carolina tarnished his reputation among contemporaries and among many historians. Yet his disappointments lay in the future. In late 1777 Gates was a genuinely and deservedly popular man among patriots. Born in Great Britain in 1727, his mother was the housekeeper of the Duke of Bolton (Horace Walpole was his godfather); in 1745 he secured a commission through the duke's patronage. He saw duty in the French and Indian War—like Washington, he survived Braddock's bloody defeat in 1755—and served competently in various posts in America, Europe, and the Caribbean. In 1769, frustrated at his lack of advancement, he sold his commission (he was then a major) and in 1772 settled on a modest estate in Virginia's Shenandoah Valley. Gates had declared early for the colonial cause, and Congress quickly commissioned him a brigadier general. During the first years of the war, he served ably (although in circumstances offering little chance for distinction), mostly in the northern theater.[51] No military lightweight, had Washington lost a broader base of support than he actually did, Gates was by no means an illogical choice as a successor.

After Saratoga Washington knew only too well that unflattering comparisons between himself and Gates were circulating. Subsequent events only heightened his suspicions of his fellow Virginian. Congress, led by delegates loudest in their criticisms of Washington's performance around Philadelphia, named the hero of Saratoga president of the reorganized Board of War. Although a civilian position, it technically made Gates Washington's superior. Adding to the commander in chief's discomfort was the fact that Gates, once ensconced in office, retained his commission as major general, continued in uniform, and lived in York with full access to Congress. Gates was politically influential and the commander in chief knew it, and with Mifflin on the board with him, he was in a position to intervene directly in army affairs and make Washington's life difficult.[52]

By the late fall of 1777, Washington understood that he had lost the trust of some disgruntled rebels, although he may not have appreciated the full bitterness and extent of their strictures. But what could he do about it? As no one had made an overt move in Congress to challenge his command, the general had little opportunity to confront his critics. This changed, however, when he received a letter dated 3 November from Major General William Alexander of New Jersey (or "Lord Stirling," as he preferred, claiming a lapsed earldom in Scotland, which the House of Lords never recognized). The letter was nothing short of explosive.

Stirling's communication was actually quite lengthy. The river forts below Philadelphia were still holding out at this time, and the general briefed Washington on the situation. He also wrote of forwarding men to the main army, supply matters, and his own health (Stirling had been wounded in 1776). It was not until the last sentence of his letter that he alerted the commander in chief to some astonishing news: "The enclosed was Communicated by Col. Wilkinson to Major MacWilliams, such wicked duplicity of Conduct, I shall alway's think it my duty to detect." The enclosure Stirling referred to was a quotation attributed to Major General Thomas Conway, supposedly an extract from a letter Conway had written to Gates probably in late October 1777 (the letter has not survived). The original message flattered Gates, extolling his generalship in effusive terms. It then supposedly took a swipe at Washington, which Stirling quoted as follows: "Heaven has been determined to save your Country; or a weak General and bad Councellors would have ruind it."[53] Anyone reading the passage could not have mistaken its meaning; Stirling certainly did not—and neither did Washington when he read it.

How did Stirling come by this inflammatory information? Lieutenant Colonel James Wilkinson, an aide to Gates, stopped in Reading, Pennsylvania, to visit Stirling, which resulted in an evening of convivial drinking leading to loose talk. When the general went to bed, Wilkinson stayed up drinking with Stirling's aide, Major William McWilliams. When McWilliams asked about rumors circulating in York to the effect that Conway had penned a note to Gates disparaging Washington, which Wilkinson allegedly confirmed—including the inflammatory quotation—the major told Stirling. The general wrote down the passage and sent it with his letter to the commander in chief. Wilkinson later admitted to being rather free with his liquor that evening, although he steadfastly denied doing anything to damage Washington's reputation.[54] But the proverbial cat was out of the bag.

Washington already had a frosty relationship with his fellow Virginian. Gates had pointedly bypassed the commanding general in communicating the news of the victory at Saratoga directly to Congress. Technically, he was correct in doing so, as he commanded a separate department. Washington, however, felt slighted and complained that a prompt confirmation of the victory at Saratoga might have influenced operations in Pennsylvania.[55] Under the circumstances, the commander in chief could hardly put an innocent construction on the Conway correspondence. Then there was Conway himself. An Irish-born soldier of fortune, Conway was a veteran of the French army, one of many foreign officers to offer their services to the Revolution. Commissioned a brigadier general, he seemed more useful than most of the others; indeed, he had led a division capably at Brandywine and Germantown. But as the British consolidated their hold on Philadelphia, his view of Washington changed. He openly harped on what he considered the general's demerits and gravitated into Mifflin's orbit (and hence to Gates). Washington knew the Irishman was no friend. Unsurprisingly, the commander in chief was furious with Conway and Gates and, breaking with his usual reticence, chose to confront them.[56]

Blunt letters from Washington to Conway and Gates followed. Both men, red faced at the situation, replied equivocally, claiming no animosity toward the commander in chief but unable to convincingly explain away the gist of the damning correspondence. As the matter became public knowledge, even some congressional radicals were disturbed. To snipe anonymously at Washington was one thing, but to have him return fire at two senior officers and have the controversy go public was entirely another. Two months later even Abraham Clark, a heatedly zealous delegate from New Jersey and no friend of Washington's leadership, was alarmed. Fervent whig that he was, Clark understood that "a dissention among the principle Officers of the Army must be very injurious to the Publick interest." And "a dissention," to put it mildly, was exactly what Conway's indiscretion had brought about. Clark knew what had to be done: "The Authority

& Credit of the Commander in Chief must be Supported."[57] Gates was thrown on the defensive. Publicly embarrassed, he tried to distance himself from the insulting letter, sending a conciliatory note to Washington in late January 1778 disclaiming any disloyalty. He insisted that Conway's letter was simply a normal and frank discussion between two senior officers (that is, between himself and Conway) on the conduct of the war that denigrated no one and essentially blamed Wilkinson for any misunderstandings. (While Gates was fretting, Mifflin warned him to be more careful with his correspondence.)[58] Washington accepted a "solemn" assurance that Gates was part of "no faction" and agreed never to bring the matter up again—but he never forgot it either.[59]

In turning the tables on Gates and Conway, the general had played a brilliant hand. He had assumed a pose of wounded innocence and forced Gates to dither as he lamely tried to explain away the incident. But the contest was not over. Indeed, even before the two Virginians had agreed to close the affair, Washington endured another reminder that Gates had powerful allies. In a move that he and other senior officers particularly resented, on 3 December Congress promoted the now intensely unpopular Conway to major general and named him inspector general of the army. Equally irritating, he had the authority to report directly to the legislators. To the circle of officers around the commander in chief, this seemed a calculated affront to Washington (although not all members of Congress intended any such thing) as well as an insult to brigadiers with seniority over Conway. Washington was livid. When Conway reported to Valley Forge in late December, Washington was barely civil, and the unwanted major general left camp within days (although for the time being he kept his title as inspector general).[60]

With this, what historians have tagged the "Conway Cabal" (a term never used during the Revolution) began to evaporate. By mid-January 1778 Henry Laurens, who had worked quietly as president of Congress to shore up Washington's command, believed that things were calming down. Whatever Washington's critics had attempted, he wrote the marquis de Lafayette, who was convinced a conspiracy had been afoot, it now "amounts to little more than tittle tattle." Yes, he admitted, there had been "parties" in Congress who had made "the Road rough but not impassible," yet they had done their worst. "The friends of our brave & virtuous General," he continued, "may rest assured that he is out of reach of his Enemies, if he has an Enemy, a fact which I am in doubt of." It was a soothing sentiment meant to ease the mind of the ardent young Frenchman, by now almost a son to Washington. Laurens, however, knew the reality: there had been enemies, and there still were, and this fact was well known; he said as much in correspondence with other patriots. Yet he thought that most delegates were beyond listening seriously to any "junto" hostile to the commander in chief.[61]

Laurens may have been too optimistic. In fact, delegate Robert Morris had a decidedly different perspective. Morris was a prosperous Pennsylvania merchant with interests in shipping, real estate, the slave trade, and other lines who had emerged as the most important financier of the patriot war effort. He served in Congress from 1775 to 1778 and worked successfully with delegates holding a wide range of views on how to conduct the war; he was, for example, a stalwart supporter of Washington while remaining friendly with Charles Lee.[62] In late January 1778, however, he genuinely feared that a "party" in Congress and the Board of War had targeted the commander in chief. On 25 January, in one of the most revealing letters dealing with the so-called cabal, he wrote to Richard Peters, secretary of the board, pleading Washington's case. He expressed his utter distaste for those criticizing the general, "for I really think it a horrid thing that mankind shou'd ever combine to support each other in unworthy attacks on Worthy Characters." Those who did so were "justly obnoxious to chastisement"; in Morris's view they were a combination of "Force & Arts of Malice, Envy, Hatred & destruction." Everyone needed to realize that to hurt the commander in chief was to injure the cause of independence itself, and it was time to quit complaining about past defeats and to focus on providing Washington with the army he needed "to shine with that Splendor he merits." Morris concluded, "His Enemies must then hide their Heads & silently witness the Triumph of that Virture which first excited their Envy."[63]

Others shared Morris's forebodings. Peters himself was concerned that camp rumors connected him to "a party against General Washington." Convinced that Peters was leagued against the general, Colonel Morgan challenged him to a duel (Morgan backed off when Peters accepted). The colonel thought that the secretary was "determined to keep myself clear of all these dirty Matters," but it was apparent that he thought "dirty Matters" existed. Benjamin Harrison of Virginia was certain they did. Harrison had served in Congress until October 1777, then returned home to sit in the House of Burgesses.

Before leaving, however, he had served on the Board of War and thus was well versed on who was thinking what in Congress when it came to military affairs. "It gives me great pain," he wrote to Morris in February 1778, "to be certainly inform'd that there are some in the Senate who dislike our General." Harrison had every confidence in Washington but reported that there were indeed "Cabals"—and that the general knew it. Those in the group sought to "prey on his [Washington's] Constitution, sink his Spirits," and apparently hope for the general's resignation. Who was behind it all? With Gates and Mifflin on the board, Harrison pointed a finger: *"Be Ware of your Board of War."*[64]

Even Laurens, who maintained good working relationships with some of the general's congressional critics (including Samuel Adams and Richard Henry Lee), tacitly admitted that his reassuring words to the young Lafayette may have been premature. As late as 11 June—only a week before the Monmouth campaign opened—he wrote to his son, Lieutenant Colonel John Laurens, "your antagonists [Washington's detractors] I find have not yet turned their backs, the more motions they make the more I suspect them. When they shall be fairly gone I will sing te deum, but 'till then my duty & my Interest dictate infidelity & command me to be watchful."[65] Critics of the commander in chief were less vocal, but critics they remained, and there was still plenty of tension in the air.

A Fate Deferred

Why, then, after castigating Washington for long months, did his critics never initiate a formal attempt to relieve him? There were four reasons. First, the general's opponents never constituted an organized group. Indeed, they were anything but organized. Some, such as Lovell and Mifflin, preferred Gates to Washington, while others criticized the commander in chief without a real idea of who might replace him or even if he should be replaced. Still others, such as Gates, Mifflin, and Conway, were professionally or politically ambitious. Then there were men like Charles Carroll, who questioned Washington but moved into his camp when they came to understand military realities. Radical whigs favored a war waged by militia, a view not all of Washington's critics shared. The Lee brothers, the Adams cousins, Gerry, and kindred patriots shared genuine doubts about the war effort and had serious questions about Washington's leadership, but they did nothing more about their concerns beyond writing acerbic private letters. Nor were the general's detractors always friends. Richard Henry Lee and Sergeant, for example, were bitter political enemies.[66] Under the circumstances, any organized conspiracy on the part of Washington's critics was impossible; they simply never thought or acted in concert. They were never a "cabal" in the sense having of any common goal but rather were a cacophony: they made *a lot* of noise, but very few of them hit the same note.

A second reason flowed from the first: without a common basis for their opposition to Washington, critics probably understood that they lacked the votes in Congress to remove him. Even the general's most vociferous detractors could count, and they recognized that any such motion, resolution, or similar action would fail. If the votes had been there, the vote would have taken place—it never did.

Washington himself provided the third strike against his critics. As historian Thomas Fleming has emphasized, the general was a deft politician—better than Gates, Mifflin, Lovell, Rush, and the others combined.[67] With the exception of his responses to Gates and Conway in the wake of the Conway letter affair, the commander in chief never publicly confronted his critics. Instead, he worked quietly through allies such as Henry Laurens and Morris who used their influence in Congress to keep any formal action against him at bay. In the army subordinate officers carried the fight, castigating anyone they suspected of disloyalty to their chief.[68] Washington deliberately tried to appear above the fray, successfully avoiding any stigma of partisanship. He even maintained whatever positive communications he could with Lovell, Samuel Adams, Richard Henry Lee, Gates, and others he knew were not his friends.

The conduct of Benjamin Rush was a glaring example of just how disorganized (or *never* organized) and politically inept Washington's detractors were. On 12 January, during the height of the general's concerns over the safety of his command, Rush wrote to Patrick Henry, then governor of Virginia. Why he did so has never been explained; perhaps he felt that Henry shared the circulating doubts about the commander in chief and thus was writing to a kindred spirit. If so, he was mistaken. In any event, the letter was another blistering assault on the general's military reputation, repeating many arguments of Conway and others. Rush failed to sign the letter but made no effort to hide his authorship; he certainly assumed the governor would know it was from him and would circulate the note. Henry did—he sent it to Washington, who already saw Rush as a troublemaker and was furious.[69] But the general issued no rebuke, realizing that another of his critics had stupidly overplayed his hand. Any true conspirator would have been more discreet or guarded in his communications; if Rush was a plotter, he was a rank amateur.

Finally, the grim conditions at Valley Forge compelled most delegates to recognize that the welfare of the army simply had to be their first priority. With that understanding was the realization that removing Washington would have convulsed the officer corps at a time the Continentals most needed stability. Radicals like Abraham Clark recognized as much, and even Conway was dismayed to find former friends in Congress supporting Washington.[70] Indeed, most of the delegates supported the work of a committee at camp, authorized on 10 January 1778 to report on army conditions and give the commander in chief every possible assistance in resolving supply and administrative problems. Recognizing the antagonisms between Washington and Gates and Mifflin, members agreed that the latter two would not accompany the committee to Valley Forge.[71] The committee proved of immeasurable help to the patriot chief, and for the time being common sense (and relative calm) prevailed.

Given the embarrassments surrounding the gaffs of Conway, Rush, and other critics as well as the need to address the army's dire situation, Washington's relations with Congress improved over the early months of 1778. Yet the calmer atmosphere failed to completely assuage the general's feelings. Always sensitive about his position and dignity, he would carry his resentments through the rest of the war. Moreover, his critics were merely muted, not gone. They still nursed their grievances and their doubts about his leadership. In fact, the commander in chief had yet to disprove them. Public opinion, including the opinion of Americans who wavered between sides as the fortunes of war changed, was sensitive to military developments, especially the performance of the Continental Army. Washington and his friends knew this, and so did his critics. The general had not won another battle, and his vision of a regular Continental Line was still only that—a vision. Much would depend on what happened in 1778, and those in Congress knew it.[72]

Important questions remained. Washington certainly was hoping for a winning campaign in 1778; military success meant political success, and he needed both. But what if he lost in 1778, or if his retrained battalions failed the test of a new campaign? Would support for the war effort further erode? Would critics be back with an even stronger case against him? And why should critics not multiply? Another disappointing outcome could allow the hitherto disparate strands of criticism to coalesce. In that case, what conceivable justification would patriots have for leaving an oft-defeated commander in chief in his post?

Lovell was willing to watch and wait on events. In June 1778 he still had little faith in Washington, and on the ninth he wrote General Gates a cryptic letter (by this time Gates had returned to the field to command in the Hudson River highlands). He advised the general to "be purblind to the Peccadillios of your Friends till this one Campaign more is over. And then we will settle who is jealous, fretful, mislead, waspish &c." After that the time would come to "conclude upon Paris or Rome."[73] Gates must have understood: forget about the likes of Conway and Wilkinson, see what happens in the new campaign, and then we will see who our commander in chief should be. Clearly, Lovell thought he knew.

CHAPTER 3

ANTAGONISTS

The British and American Armies

General Clinton's decision to lead a portion of his army overland to New York meant a march through almost seventy miles of enemy territory. This did not make a battle inevitable, but it did precipitate a campaign that carried the risk of battle. General Washington caould hardly stand by and watch the British simply march away; he would need to plan some kind of counteraction, if only to shadow the redcoats or prevent them from doing anything but retreat. Thus if the armies did not actually fight, they would be maneuvering in close proximity and be constantly on guard.

The opposing armies knew each other in many crucial respects. Both were veteran forces, having fought one another in actions large and small for two years. Thus they each had an appreciation of the other's capabilities, although the British, with some justification, considered their redcoats more than a match for the Continentals. The rivals had come to share some similarities of organization, aspects of drill and tactics, and, to an extent, the social composition of their officers and rank and file. By the spring of 1778, however, there were also a host of unknowns. Washington could only speculate on the effect of the British command change. He had fought Clinton before—indeed, Sir Henry was largely responsible for defeating him on Long Island—but never as his actual counterpart as an army commander. There was also no way to fully assess the consequences of the loss of Philadelphia on redcoat morale. Patriots generally agreed that giving up the city would be a blow to British pride, but Washington had to assume Clinton's regiments would remain in fighting trim. Perhaps a retreat would even make the enemy more dangerous; with their pride wounded, they could be spoiling for a fight. The only way to tell was to observe them in the field or in actual battle.

Washington, however, was not the only general looking for answers. Clinton had even more questions about the Americans. He was not oblivious to developments at Valley Forge and knew that the rebel army had been retraining, reorganizing, and reequipping. Yet no one knew the extent of Washington's success in these labors, or more important, what difference these changes might make in rebel combat effectiveness. Would the Continental Line of 1778 fight better than it had the year before? This was an open question. For that matter, Clinton had no idea whether Washington would offer battle at all.

Adding further to the uncertainty was the British route of march. Burgoyne's fate the year before hardly boded well for royal armies in the American interior. Clinton would have to go only a fraction of the distance traveled by the unfortunate northern army, but there were numerous indications that New Jersey would not be friendly territory. Like Burgoyne before him, Clinton would have to take his chances with local irregular forces. In 1776 the New Jersey militia initially had shown little fight, but by late in the year it had become a force to reckon with; it had done well in the spring of 1777. British officers had to assume that any march through the state would have to deal with some of the most experienced militia in the rebellious colonies. Who knew how well they might do on their own ground, especially if operating in conjunction with rejuvenated American regulars?

The opposing commanders therefore had much to ponder as they prepared for the 1778 campaign. Clinton based his plans on a proven army, though one facing a vastly different mission: it was no longer on the offensive. Washington worked with a force greatly changed from 1777 but as yet unproven. While he guessed correctly that Clinton was leaving Philadelphia, initially he was not sure where his rival was actually going. With all of their doubts, however, both commanders shared a common assumption: they had to assume that their enemy would fight and thus had to be ready to do so themselves.

The variables governing success in combat are complex. The element of chance is always in play, but commanders can do little about good or bad luck. Good luck is always welcome, but bad luck does not have to be a major blunder to be disastrous. It can be an accumulation of small things, what the Prussian Carl von Clausewitz, certainly the greatest military thinker of the eighteenth century, called "friction": the broken axle at the head of the wagon train that slows everyone, the subordinate who forgets a component of his orders, the unexpected rain that turns the roads to mud, the inaccurate map that leads a column into an ambush—the list is endless. But generals can try to limit "friction" and thus ill fortune, and the steps are basic. They can understand the nature of their commands and do their best to make sure their officers and men are ready. That means attention to training, food, forage, equipment and supplies, logistics, intelligence, organization, and morale—all the things affecting an army's ability to campaign, deal with adversity, and to stand the test of combat. How well Clinton and Washington dealt with these matters would be critical to their armies' performance at Monmouth.

The British Army, 1778

Clinton's command was a tested weapon, a part of one of the best professional forces of its day. It was also one of the largest in the empire. While available personnel returns offer only approximate strength estimates, it is clear that the British had a substantial corps under arms in the area. A return of late March 1778, with Howe still in command, noted 19,530 men in ranks in and around Philadelphia, 13,078 of whom were British regulars; the rest were Hessians and loyalists. By June 1778, while encamped at Monmouth, the numbers had changed only slightly: the rolls listed a total of 19,940 troops or noncombatant military personnel (excluding civilians with the army), of whom 12,604 were redcoats in combat formations.[1] The discrepancy is easily, if not precisely, accounted for: desertion, deaths from combat and illness, and unit rotation all changed the muster rolls. The 71st Foot, for example, a regiment reduced by illness, went back to New York in late 1777 to be replaced by another regiment of foot in March 1778, though unit rotations did not result necessarily in man-for-man replacements.[2] King George's army was not large by European standards. In 1775 the regular forces numbered fewer than 50,000 troops of all arms, although vigorous recruiting during the American War added new regiments—there were 70 at the beginning of the conflict, 105 at the end—and had increased total manpower to around 110,000 by 1781. Only half of these troops served in North America or the Caribbean, which means Clinton's command represented a sizable proportion of all British regulars.[3]

The basic unit of the army was the regiment. There were two kinds: line regiments, which composed the bulk of the army, and six household regiments, three infantry (foot) and three cavalry. The household regiments were elite outfits, the oldest and most prestigious in the service; they were composed of "picked men"—fit and well trained, with strong unit attachments—and usually posted in London as bodyguards to the monarch. Clinton's command had no household cavalry, and no complete foot guards regiment came to North America. But the army formed a Brigade of Guards by drawing fifteen men from each of the sixty-four guards companies (each guards regiment had twelve companies). Mustered in February 1776 under Brigadier General Edward Mathew, this brigade was a powerful unit. Having seen tough fighting with Howe in the campaigns of 1776 and 1777, it would serve Clinton equally well.[4]

The heart of the army, however, were the foot regiments of the line. Like the household regiments, each had a commanding colonel who seldom actually led the men in the field. Rather, colonels handled the business and ceremonial affairs of the regiment, usually in depot. Some colonelcies were honorary, often held by ranking nobles or general officers: Clinton, for example, while serving in America, was colonel of the 12th Regiment of Foot, then posted at Gibraltar; Burgoyne, while campaigning above Saratoga, was colonel of a cavalry unit then with Howe in Philadelphia.[5] The normal arrangement saw the lieutenant colonel, or even a major, in tactical command. Fortunately, lieutenant colonels generally knew their business.

In 1778 Clinton's army in Philadelphia had twenty British—English, Irish, Welsh, or Scottish—regiments of the line.[6] The terms "regiment" and "battalion" often were used interchangeably. Infantry (foot) regiments officially consisted of ten companies: eight of standard infantry—collectively known as the "battalion" companies—and one each of grenadiers and light infantry. At full strength a company consisted of three officers (a captain, lieutenant, and ensign), five noncommissioned officers (three sergeants and two corporals), three drummers, and usually between 70 and a 100 privates. Thus a regiment would muster between 700 and 1,000 troops.[7] But units were rarely up to official strength. In 1775 most regiments numbered only some 475 men; foot companies typically had about 47 men of all ranks, including officers, noncommissioned officers, the drummer, and some 38 privates.[8] Occasionally, regiments had more than one battalion. The 71st Regiment of Foot—one of the first new outfits raised after the start of the war—had two battalions (these were the troops returned to New York before the 1778 campaign).[9] At Monmouth the rosters varied widely, although all reflected the understrength norm. The strongest individual regiment was the 42nd Foot, Royal Highlanders, with 639 men in two field battalions; the weakest was the 10th Foot, with only 135 troops. Most mustered in the neighborhood of 360 redcoats.[10]

Whatever their numbers, troops in the foot regiments trained to fight in the linear formations of the day. Prior to 1775, this meant they usually fought shoulder to shoulder, and their training—generally at the hands of long-serving noncommissioned officers—emphasized volley fire and massed bayonet attacks.[11] At Boston General Howe changed the formation from three to two ranks, an innovation Clinton maintained when he took command in 1778. But the men remained almost elbow to elbow in the advance, and the solid lines proved easy targets at Bunker (Breed's) Hill. The debacle in that action led to a formation change. Howe ordered a spacing of eighteen inches between files, making for more-open ranks, which made for easier maneuvering through dense ground and for greater difficulty in hitting the line of troops. (Only the Hessian regiments retained the traditional close-order formation.)[12] In the open field these regiments were formidable, probably the best in the world in their day at what they did.

When serving with their regiments, light-infantry and grenadier companies generally deployed on the flanks and thus were referred to as "flank companies." The light infantry served as skirmishers and scouts and generally mustered the regiment's most physically fit men. They were trained to fight in open order, taking advantage of cover and aiming at individual targets. In the field they would take post on the left flank. The grenadiers were traditionally the toughest and tallest men in the regiment—a custom from the days when these men hurled grenades, a practice discontinued before the War for Independence. They took post on the right flank, often called upon for the most difficult combat assignments. With the light infantry, the grenadiers were the regimental elite. On campaign the army frequently organized these companies as separate light-infantry and grenadier battalions. In 1778 they did the same; marching from Philadelphia, Clinton had two battalions of light infantry and two of grenadiers.[13]

At the beginning of the war, Britain also had sixteen regiments of cavalry and would eventually field more. Horse regiments were much smaller than foot regiments, typically with six or eight troops, each with three officers, three noncommissioned officers, about thirty private troopers, and a trumpeter—some 280 men in all—plus attached light infantry, although strength on active duty could vary.[14] The British placed much less emphasis on their mounted arm during the Revolution. Long experience in North American warfare had demonstrated that the terrain was generally unsuitable for large mounted operations. Horsemen could be useful as scouts, in screening operations, and for skirmishing actions, raids, and other light duties, but there would be no massed cavalry charges so familiar to European battlefields of the period. Thus Clinton had only two horse units, the 16th and 17th Regiments of Light Dragoons. Both were veterans of the Philadelphia campaign, and in June 1778 both were stronger than most British horse regiments, with some 365 and 333 men respectively.[15] The 16th and 17th would play an active part during the march across New Jersey.

The balance of Clinton's force included loyalists and Hessians. Elements of three loyalist units had come with Howe to Pennsylvania. A detachment of the Loyal American Regiment, organized in New York in 1776, probably served as light infantry. These were veterans, but muster rolls for the period are missing, making it impossible to tell the strength of the detachment; it was not large. There were also four companies of veteran New Jersey Volunteers—129 men total—attached to the Royal Artillery.[16] More significant was the presence of the Queen's American Rangers, a combined-arms unit with dragoons and light infantry. The Rangers were a crack outfit, originally recruited in 1776 from among New York, Connecticut, and Virginia loyalists. They had performed well at Brandywine and Germantown and had been active in operations outside Philadelphia and in New Jersey. Commanded by the dashing and aggressive Lieutenant Colonel John Graves Simcoe, the unit added real striking power, especially in the mounted arm. With 454 men in June 1778, the Rangers were perhaps the best loyalist outfit in the army—and one of the best of its type on either side—and would play a key role in the coming campaign.[17]

Other tories took up arms during the occupation of Philadelphia. The British organized twelve loyalist units from Maryland, the Philadelphia area, and western New Jersey, varying widely in strength. Some quickly disappeared upon learning that Clinton was going to abandon the city; the men deserted into the countryside or tried to mend fences with patriots. Others merged into larger formations. The Volunteers of Ireland, for example, raised in and around Philadelphia, initially mustered several hundred men but had only sixteen at Monmouth; the Bucks County Volunteers numbered only forty and were attached to the Queen's Rangers.[18] More capable were the three battalions of Maryland, Pennsylvania, and West Jersey loyalists, which enrolled approximately 200–370 men each. In March 1778 loyalist strength stood at 1,250 men; but at Monmouth they totaled 2,054 troops, slightly more than 10 percent of British combatants. Aside from the veteran Queen's Rangers and the detachments of New Jersey Volunteers and Loyal Americans, many were new to the army, some merely raw recruits.[19] Yet a few of these soldiers were very good. Having left their homes to fight for the King, often given little choice by threatening local whigs, they had little to lose.

Clinton also had 5,202 Hessians in Pennsylvania.[20] Patriots denounced these soldiers as mercenaries, mere hirelings serving only for their pay (a calumny repeated by too many historians). They were not. Rather, the Hessians were troops from the armies of seven of the various independent German principalities and served under contracts between their princes (of various titles) and the British. Most of these units were from Hesse-Kassel and Hesse-Hanau, thus the general appellation "Hessians" for all German troops. Most had little or no personal stake in the war—although some had enlisted with the hope of remaining in America after the peace—but the majority were well trained, equipped, and led, having proven themselves effective in the field.[21] Some of their officers were among the best in the royal army. The commander of the German troops in Philadelphia, Baron Wilhelm von Knyphausen, stood second in seniority only to Clinton. Knyphausen was a proven European veteran, had served under Frederick the Great in the Prussian army, and was a lieutenant general in the army of Hesse-Kassel. He had fought in all of Howe's campaigns and commanded the right wing at Brandywine. Clinton trusted Knyphausen, who would play a critical role in the march across New Jersey.[22]

There were eight Hessian infantry battalions, organized roughly along British lines, on the New Jersey march. German soldiers carried an .80-caliber Prussian-style musket, similar to the British Brown Bess. In addition, there was a small detachment of German artillery and a fairly large corps of jaegers—a few dozen mounted and over 750 on foot. The jaegers were superb soldiers, carefully recruited, often from among woodsmen used to the outdoors and living rough. They were highly trained light troops, armed with short rifles and known for their marksmanship and skill in open tactics, who could meet patriot militia and light infantry on their own terms. Jaegers received better pay than ordinary German infantry and were exempt from manual labor.[23] The Hessian elite, they would be in action almost every day of the coming campaign. All the Germans, however, were critical to the British war effort. With London unable or unwilling to substantially reinforce Clinton from Britain, the Germans were an indispensable component of the army.

The redcoats, and some of the veteran loyalist units, were well equipped for the period. Most privates carried a .75-caliber Brown Bess musket, a smoothbore, muzzle-loaded weapon. But it was never officially known as the Brown Bess: the British Ordnance Office name for it was the Short Land Musket (New Pattern), first produced in 1768—"short" because it was four inches shorter than the previous model; troops in grenadier and guards units still carried the older Long Land Pattern muskets.[24] The Brown Bess with sling weighed about eleven pounds, came with a metal ramrod (some units still had wooden ramrods), and mounted a thirteen-inch bayonet. Troops carried a load of eighteen to thirty paper cartridges containing a one-ounce lead ball and black powder for priming and loading. A well-trained soldier could fire three to four rounds per minute (two shots per minute was the norm for less experienced soldiers), conducted generally by volley. At close range a Brown Bess volley could be devastating, but the musket was grossly inaccurate at ranges over a hundred yards, frequently much less. This meant that opposing combatants often exchanged fire at much closer ranges, thus casualties could be heavy. But even so, the Brown Bess was never a sharpshooter's gun.[25]

Some commanders preferred the bayonet for close combat. In the hands of trained regulars, it could be a terrifying and gruesomely effective weapon. After volley fire, tactical practice called for a foot regiment to charge with the bayonet. In his memoir of the war, Simcoe noted, "It was the object, to instil into the men, that their superiority lay in close fight, and in the use of the bayonet, in which the individual courage, and personal activity that characterise the British soldier can best display themselves."[26] This observation made for grim work. Early in the war most rebel units lacked bayonets, putting them at an often-fatal disadvantage in close-quarter fighting. This could be terrifying. Of this, there was no more graphic example than the action at Paoli Tavern, about twenty-five miles west of Philadelphia. On the night of 20 September 1777, Major General Charles "No Flint" Grey led five regiments in a surprise assault on the command of Continental brigadier general Anthony Wayne. Without firing a shot, Grey's men cut the stunned patriots to bits with cold steel. At the cost of four killed and seven wounded, the redcoats killed, wounded, or left missing at least 272 of Wayne's men, and some accounts put the toll higher. Even some British officers were appalled at the carnage.[27] It was a telling demonstration of what the bayonet could do. The rebels eventually adopted the bayonet effectively, but at least through late 1777 the advantage in this respect lay with the redcoats and their Hessian allies.

In addition to their weapons, soldiers carried packs containing spare clothing and personal items. Along with the pack came a blanket, canteen, a cartridge pouch, and a haversack with rations for one day or several, all slung over the shoulder or fastened to leather belts. This equipment added up, with the typical redcoat carrying a standard load of about sixty pounds.[28] Veterans got used to it, but there is no question that the burden placed a premium on physical fitness and made campaigning arduous in difficult terrain and weather.

The British also had excellent artillery. Officers of the Royal Regiment of Artillery generally had a better professional education than officers of foot or mounted regiments. By 1775 most had attended the Royal Military Academy at Woolwich. The academy, located southeast of London, was founded in 1741 to train "good officers of Artillery and perfect Engineers." Cadets, active-duty officers, and all other "inexperienced" members in the ordnance field were invited to attend. The curriculum stressed practical gunnery, but advanced classes delved into the scientific aspects of ballistics, powder, metallurgy, and advances in all facets of artillery development and deployment.[29] The regiment had four battalions of eight companies, with the 4th Battalion fully deployed to the American theater in 1775. Officially, a company roster carried 107 officers and men, commanded by a captain. But by 1777 the 4th Battalion had seen hard service and was woefully understrength. Unable to get timely reinforcements from Great Britain, the unit recruited some 300 men in New York—probably loyalists—in time for the

Philadelphia campaign. Howe took eight companies of artillery with him to Pennsylvania, bearing a mix of howitzers (for high-trajectory firing) and 1.5-, 3-, 6-, 12-, and 24-pounder guns (the "pounds" indicated the weight of a solid cannon ball). The artillery was in the thick of the fighting, losing five killed in action at Brandywine.[30] All eight companies were in or around Philadelphia when Clinton assumed command.

The British army had other components as well. Maintaining an army, especially in the field, was a complicated business. Troops needed to be fed, paid, their equipment maintained and transported, their medical needs attended, and at times their behavior policed. These were the jobs of the army's noncombatant services, generally small units or groups of individuals assigned specific technical or other support roles. Included were staff or servants within the suites of senior officers, various guards and inspectors, medical personnel, paymasters, civilian support staff for the artillery, 138 army engineers, and even a "Bridgemaster's Department" of twenty-one men. The quartermaster general, Brigadier General Sir William Erskine, had the largest department of noncombatants at 494 troops. There was also the Black Company of Pioneers. Recruited first in 1776 in South Carolina, these men were mostly escaped slaves who came north with the British army after the abortive attack on Charleston. They were unarmed and functioned as military laborers, building fortifications, clearing roads, and digging trenches; in occupied Philadelphia, where they recruited additional men, the company worked on city sanitation and military construction. Forty-nine pioneers, including their white captain, made the trek across New Jersey with Clinton. In aggregate, all of these support units added around a thousand individuals to Clinton's forces, all of whom would travel with the general.[31]

Military Culture: Soldiers as Society

In numbers, organization, and basic equipage, this was the army Clinton inherited from General Howe. Clinton maintained the structure as he found it, a military structure he had known for all his professional life and in which he was thoroughly at home. Typically, European armies tended to reflect the societies that raised them, and in this regard the British military was no exception. Leadership was the prerogative of an upper-class officer corps, much of which came from the aristocracy and the gentry. While there were prominent exceptions, the relatively few officers who rose from the ranks generally advanced no further than company grade (that is, up to captain). This had little to do with merit; rather, most officers could buy and sell commissions at market price (about two-thirds of commissions were purchased). This could vary over time and between units, with commissions in elite regiments such as the Coldstream Guards commanding a premium. The practical result of the purchase system was to exclude officers of modest means from field rank; they normally could not afford the asking prices.

A colonel's or general's commission were never for sale, though, and promotion beyond the rank of lieutenant colonel often required access to political patronage. Not infrequently, general officers had well-placed friends or relatives to advance their requests for promotion or for choice commands. Indeed, senior officers often acquired considerable influence themselves: Cornwallis, Howe, Burgoyne, and Clinton, for example, all with excellent social and family connections, held seats in Parliament while on active duty.[32] Thus the officer corps offered social mobility only to a narrow strata of British society.

A military career did not imply standards of professional conduct typical of a modern Western army. Rather, eighteenth-century officers actively mixed partisan politics with military affairs. They could be remarkably indiscreet in criticisms of brother officers, including their superiors, often relying on political patrons to deflect disciplinary action or other retaliation. Some senior commanders were quite indifferent to the chain of command and thought little of communicating directly with political and government officials. At one point Clinton even went home to look after personal and political matters, having first made some astringent comments on Howe's leadership. The government, including Lord Germain, not only knew about Clinton's criticisms but also, seeking to avoid a political flap, assuaged the general with a promotion and knighthood and persuaded him to return to America as Howe's second in command.[33] Howe, knowing the system, accepted the situation.

While officers might become professional soldiers over the course of a career, they generally came to the army as amateurs. With the exception of Woolwich, which dealt with artillerists and engineers, Britain had no formal system of military education, and the army required no specific training prior to the purchase of a foot or cavalry commission. Combine purchased rank with political influence, and it should come as no surprise that the system pinned epaulets on its share of fops and blockheads, though it also provided the army with generally competent leadership. Through practice, most officers learned to handle their units in the linear formations of the day, and most also took seriously the obligations of command. Many compiled impressive records under fire, and some were inspirational commanders. At Monmouth Lieutenant Colonel Henry Monckton, brother of Lieutenant General Robert Monckton, fell while personally leading a charge of his grenadiers battalion.[34] His courage was typical; most British officers were brave men, and few of any rank failed the test of combat.

Like their commanders, the British rank and file also reflected their social origins, and the gulf between commissioned and enlisted rank was considerable. Most enlisted personnel came from the lower end of the socioeconomic scale. Over the early eighteenth century, regular-army ranks traditionally included unemployed laborers, peasants, drifters, and at times the sweepings of the jailhouses. But the work of Sylvia R. Frey, a careful historian, has documented an evolution among the rank and file noticeable by the mid-1700s. While the overwhelming majority of the troops were still poor, there were fewer recruits with agricultural backgrounds. Most enlisted from urban areas, and some had roots in the middle class. Many were unemployed workers "possessed of occupational skills no longer in great demand." In particular, textile workers and shoemakers, having lost their jobs to the advancing mechanization of their industry, "enlisted in extraordinary numbers." So too did men from economically marginal seasonal trades.[35] Irish regiments and English units from rural districts still had firm roots in the land, but advancing economic change dictated that the British army would not consist largely of dispossessed peasants.

Over time, social origins probably mattered little to combat effectiveness. Most enlistments were for life, and recruits from all walks absorbed the fundamentals of drill and regimental traditions.[36] Unit pride was genuine, and in 1778 it had no real counterpart in the Continental Line. Some regiments (or detachments thereof) with Clinton had been on the army list for a century: the 1st and 3rd Regiments of Foot Guards dated from 1660. Others were of more recent, but still decades-old, lineages. The 42nd Foot—the Royal Highland Regiment, also known as the Black Watch—began as

Scottish militia in 1725. Organized in 1716, the Royal Regiment of Artillery also was a relative newcomer. Unit battle honors represented some of the most desperate engagements in the annals of British arms, and tradition as much as discipline or training provided a firm basis for group cohesion. Longstanding regional affiliations had links to the monarch—thus the *Royal* Welsh Fusiliers and the *Royal* Highland Regiment—and members of the royal family often held honorary colonelcies in these units, further reinforcing regimental identities.[37]

Under the circumstances, a soldier's regiment became his world. Training and promotion took place within the unit, and so did social life. When in garrison for long periods, troops often took odd jobs with local civilians during off-duty hours, and merchants and taverns in Europe and colonial America welcomed the soldiers' trade. But most of the socializing took place among the troops, and the regiments became small societies unto themselves. It was possible to serve twenty-five years with the same comrades in arms, sharing the same work and training routine, the same food and barracks accommodations, and the same campaign experiences. Even when quartered in an area for a substantial period, the troops retained an aspect of the alien and the insular.

Women and families were an integral part of the regimental world. In garrison, officers' wives were an important part of social activities and sometimes became involved with religious and charitable activities on behalf of the rank and file. The wives of enlisted men, like their soldier husbands or companions, were usually poor. Regiments normally allowed a number of wives, other women, and children to draw rations; women got half a soldier's ration, children a quarter. Frequently women supplemented family income by taking in washing, peddling, cooking, mending, and through other odd jobs in camp and in garrison towns. They foraged for extra food, sometimes stole it, and sometimes engaged in prostitution. If the eighteenth century was a hard time to be a soldier, it was an equally hard time to be a soldier's wife or female companion.[38]

A certain number of wives and other camp followers also accompanied regiments in the field. Officers with means could elect to bring their wives or mistresses with them; Burgoyne, for example, had his mistress with him on his ill-fated Saratoga campaign and several senior officers brought their wives. But campaigning was often rigorous, if not dangerous, which normally discouraged camp followers used to a more genteel lifestyle. Most women with the army accompanied the rank and file. Commanders often tried to limit the number of camp followers, but the task was thankless. This was especially the case when soldiers stayed more than briefly in a region and began to form attachments. In May 1777 an army commissary in New York reported that women and children with the army had become "numerous beyond any Idea of imagination." Howe's command, he noted, listed 23,101 men, 2,776 women, and 1,904 children; the Hessians did not count their children but listed 11,192 men and 381 women. As the war dragged on, the number of women and children probably doubled. In December 1777 another commissary return showed 1,648 women and 539 children attached to the forces in Philadelphia alone. By 1781 one New Jersey loyalist regiment counted a remarkable proportion of women: 582 soldiers accompanied by 179 camp followers.[39] An army on the move, then, was akin to a small mobile society.

The British regimental system, while it reflected virtually all the virtues of a force trained and led in the European tradition, did not produce an army without problems. Far from it. Desertion rates were frequently high, especially at the opening of new campaigns. Many soldiers left rather than leave wives or sweethearts behind. On the other hand, many women followed the army because they had no alternative means of support; if poverty drove them (and the men) to illegal foraging to sustain themselves, then discipline could suffer. Problem drinking and petty fighting, seemingly endemic to armies of the period, required considerable attention from the officers, and courts-martial generally convened whenever the troops made camp for an extended period. Both men and women could be flogged for infractions—although such punishment, along with being drummed out of camp, was reserved only for the most troublesome camp followers—and enlisted men risked execution if the army chose to crack down on pillaging. The lash was an integral part of the service, and civilians had good reason to refer to the redcoats as "the bloodybacks."[40]

Whatever the state of Clinton's army in physical terms, the looming evacuation of Philadelphia adversely affected morale. There was grumbling over handing the city back to the rebels. The prospect seemed a humiliation to some officers, a negation of the entire 1777 campaign. Simcoe, commander of the Queen's Rangers, had hoped the coming of spring would mean an advance against Valley Forge. With apparent irritation, however, he noted that "those hopes vanished" with the recall of General Howe.[41] Captain John Montresor, the army's chief engineer, was of a similar mind. Less than a week before the evacuation, he confided to his journal, "this army [is] rather discontented since the Departure of Genl. Sir. Wm. Howe and the new measures received from the ministry [that is, giving up Philadelphia]."[42] Jaeger lieutenant Heinrich von Feilitzsch wrote privately that the uncertainty of where the army would be going was trying. He longed to see home again, "but very much doubt, that things will change for us." The lieutenant was in a dour mood and noted rumors of an evacuation, which if true, "will give comfort to the enemy." In the meantime, Hessian "soldiers desert in large numbers.[43]

Nor was the dark outlook confined to junior officers. Quartermaster General Erskine, also a combat veteran, was furious and sought out Clinton to protest. He argued that the army should at least make one last thrust at Washington. Retreating without a fight would make Erskine "ashamed of the name of a Briton." Other senior officers, notably Major General Grey—whose bayonets had done such grisly work at Paoli—and Brigadier General James Pattison of the Royal Artillery, were equally disconcerted. They were convinced that a drive against Valley Forge would destroy the Continental Army or throw it across the Susquehanna River in two days.[44] Clinton would not change his mind yet was anything but upbeat himself. In his memoir he recalled taking command of the army just as events in Europe and America "had so clouded every prospect of a successful issue to the unfortunate contest we were engaged in that no officer who had the least anxious regard for his professional fame would court a charge so hopeless as this now appeared to be."[45] We may take this with a grain of salt, the statement of a general trying to justify his conduct after a losing war, but there is little doubt that Sir Henry was displeased with the strategic situation he faced. It was not a happy officer corps.

Many enlisted men had their own reasons for resenting the evacuation. Some shared the frustration of their officers at giving up the only real prize of 1777 without a fight. Elias Boudinot, the patriot commissary general for prisoners, was trying to negotiate an exchange when he learned of the pending evacuation. He wrote his wife, Hannah, that the news had sparked a riot among the light infantry. They had "mobbed" the Carlisle commissioners and "hung Lord North in Effigy. . . . They cannot bear the thought of Peace."[46]

Other soldiers, just as unhappy, reacted differently. As troops will do in a long occupation in an urban area, they had formed bonds with the local population. Some chose not to leave behind new wives, sweethearts, or other attachments, including economic opportunities.

Under the circumstances, their only real alternative to departing with the army was to desert. This they did. Precise numbers are hard to confirm, but desertions were significant. Irish soldiers found it relatively easy to blend into the Irish population of the city and its environs. So to did the Hessians, who found a large and welcoming German-speaking population in Pennsylvania; Congress even authorized the enlistment of Hessian deserters in a corps of German volunteers, promising bounties, including postwar lands, similar to those pledged to Continental troops.[47] Some of the best English units, including the guards, the grenadiers, and the rangers were hemorrhaging as well. A senior Hessian officer knew why: it was the result of "our long stay in Philadelphia and the many kinds of temptation, which need not be very alluring to blind the common soldier and make him break his oath."[48] Whatever the allure, some loyalist soldiers also had second thoughts about the war. In early June a court-martial dealt with one Richard Hilford, a drummer in the "Battalion of American Loyalists" (probably the Loyal American Regiment), for attempted desertion and for trying to induce others to come with him "with their arms and accouterments to the Rebels." The drummer was spared death but received a thousand lashes.[49] Hilford was just one such case as the army prepared to leave Philadelphia.

Yet even at less than peak morale, the British, including the Hessian and veteran loyalist regiments, could fight. They were anything but invincible, but no one questioned their courage. They had won the bitter respect of their antagonists at Valley Forge; in fact, the British regulars were examples of the kind of fighting men Washington wanted to command. In a piece of unintended flattery, one patriot later observed that the regiments under Clinton's command were "the finest troops in the service of his Britanick Majesty."[50]

Rebel Renaissance: Toward a "Respectable Army"

Bitter experience had convinced the patriot commander in chief that the enthusiasm of military amateurs had to give way to the cooler competence of regular soldiers.[51] In several strongly worded letters to Congress, Washington explained that the only way to defeat a professional force was to have one yourself. "Our Liberties must of necessity be greatly hazarded, If not entirely lost," he warned,

"If their defence is left to any but a permanent standing Army." His conviction grew after the disasters around New York, and he entreated the delegates to "Let us have a respectable Army, and such as will be competent to every Exigency."[52] A "respectable army" covered a multitude of military blessings: enough men to face the British in at least equal numbers, long-term enlistments to allow for proper training and discipline, and sufficient commissary and logistical resources to keep the army adequately fed, supplied, and mobile. Moreover, the general urged Congress to give up on simple virtue as a motive for enlistment. Instead, he wanted to offer bounties to fill the ranks, a practice fully in the European tradition; without them, he warned, the number of volunteers would be "no more than a drop in the Ocean."[53] In short, what Washington proposed was a "new model" Continental force organized and trained like the British professionals and capable of meeting them on their own terms.

But not everyone agreed with the general. The more strident whigs were not persuaded, yet most of Congress came around. The British threat was too powerful to ignore, and the rebel failures of 1776 too manifest; faced with choosing defeat or accepting Washington's new model army, the majority of the delegates saw the light. In legislation passed between September and December 1776, they voted Washington an army of 104 regiments (or battalions, the terms were interchangeable) of 738 officers and men each, with the recruits signing on either for three years or "for the war," meaning for the duration. Troop quotas assigned 88 regiments to the states by population, with the largest putting more men into the field; Washington was to raise 16 "additional" regiments on the authority of Congress. In filling the state quotes, tiny Delaware, for instance, would raise a single regiment, larger New Jersey four, and even larger Massachusetts fifteen. Beyond infantry, the new plan also called for units of artillery, cavalry, and support troops, all of which brought the total authorized strength of the new army to 75,000 men. Congress promised each recruit a bounty of twenty dollars and a clothing allowance, and those who enlisted "for the war" received an additional promise of a hundred acres of land after the conflict. Once in ranks, however, the men would find stiffened discipline. At Washington's request, Congress increased the number of capital crimes and allowed a freer use of the lash: instead of the old thirty-nine stripes, the army could now inflict up to a hundred in a single flogging. Now there would be American "bloodybacks."[54] Such was the new American army: larger, better organized, and better disciplined—at least on paper.

While Washington was gratified at the new legislation, he must have winced privately at some of its features. To propose an army of 88 regiments and 75,000 troops was an extraordinary exercise in wishful thinking. With perhaps three times the population of America, by late 1777 Britain mustered only some 60,000 men (probably a bit fewer) and would struggle to double that number by the end of the war.[55] The necessity of hiring Hessians was testimony to its manpower problems. How were patriots, without even the loyalty of much of the American populace, to enlist 75,000 Continentals? And if they managed that feat, how were they to pay, feed, clothe, and equip them? Through 1777, the 75,000 regulars never materialized, nor did they throughout the war.

Beyond the promise of greater numbers, however chimerical, one of the key benefits for the rebel military was long-term enlistments—the prospect of an army of disciplined veterans with more or less stable units. A smaller army of such men was probably better than a larger force of relatively untrained short-term soldiers. Still, numbers were important, and Washington did his best to encourage recruiting operations. It rapidly became clear, however, that volunteers would not fill the newly authorized regiments. In October 1777 rebel strength in all theaters peaked at just over 39,000 men, including militia attached to Continental formations. To meet their troop quotas, states began to offer supplemental bounties, to recruit illegally in neighboring states, and to exempt men from militia duty if they hired a substitute for Continental service. In some cases, they resorted to conscription: New Hampshire and Massachusetts led the way in 1777; New Jersey and Maryland followed the year after.[56]

The result was an American regular army resembling its British counterpart. As demands for manpower increased, the states dug deeper into their reserves. Propertied yeomen enlisted in only relatively small numbers, so recruiters accepted virtually anyone else healthy enough to serve. Quantitative studies of the Continental rank and file of at least four states have demonstrated that most of the troops enlisted after late 1776 were from the youngest and poorest quarters of society. Most were in their late teens and early twenties, but some were boys of fourteen and younger; few had property or other ties to the civilian economy. Moreover, poverty was not just a function of youth, as the majority of recruits also came from poor families. Many men were unemployed laborers, drifters, recent immigrants, and sometimes even criminals allowed to enlist in lieu of prison sentences or other punishment.[57] White indentured servants and free and enslaved blacks also served. Eventually, all the northern states, as well as Maryland and Virginia, either allowed such enlistments outright or permitted indentured servants and slaves to serve as substitutes for their masters. By the end of the war, a large proportion of the Continental Army was black or Native American; in some units the number was as high as 25 percent. Only the Deep South, fearful of arming any blacks, refused the services of such troops. While official army regulations forbade the practice, many recruiters also winked at Hessian and British deserters enlisting in American regiments.[58]

As the new army came into the field, the rank and file frequently brought their women with them. The American regulars, however, had fewer women in camp than the British. Rebel troops generally were younger than British enlisted men and were less likely to have developed long-term relationships. On the other hand, there were enough formal and common-law marriages between the men and local women, or enough soldiers bringing wives with them, to make women a familiar part of the patriot military. Washington occasionally expressed irritation over women riding army wagons or acting in disorderly fashion, and he never officially condoned their place in the army. But he recognized their role in maintaining army morale, and officers and men valued the contributions they made to camp life. The general personally asked regimental commanders to help army surgeons "in procuring as many Women of the Army as can be prevailed on to serve as Nurses." The army paid them "the usual Price" for any official duties and allowed them on regimental rations, generally at a ratio of fifteen men to one woman (about half the proportion allowed in British regiments).[59] Thus in the presence of women as an integral and functional part of army society, the Americans shared another aspect of military life with the redcoats.

The new Continental ranks were not particularly stable. When operations began in early 1777, Washington's units were mostly green. For many soldiers, the experiences of harsh discipline, the difficult aspects of camp life, long periods away from home, and losing in combat were too much. Men deserted in droves; it was not unusual for units to lose 20 percent of their men in this way over

1777, and some battalions recorded losses of 50 percent.[60] Nor were some officers any more dependable. Requests for leave and unexcused absences drove Washington to distraction. So did frequent resignations, which were often the fault, he believed, of thin regiments; without a full complement to command, too many company and field-grade officers lost interest in their jobs. The loss of good officers, he feared, "will shake the very existence of the Army."[61] It was quickly clear that legislating a "respectable army" was not the same as having an effective force in the field.

It is possible to paint too bleak a picture of the Continental situation, however, for there were bright spots. Significantly, even if the army lacked the hoped-for numbers, at least regimental organization was in place. There was also a cadre of officers who, though they still had much to learn, at least knew their men and had proven themselves under fire. Many of these rebel leaders came to the army with good educations or from successful backgrounds in agriculture and business. While they lacked the titles of their British counterparts, they were fully representative of the American middle and upper class. These men, or their families, were as prominent in society as they were in the military.[62] On the whole, the officers were a capable group who gradually brought discipline and stability to the Continental Line, having the potential to be every bit as good at their jobs as an officer in a British uniform.

A New Regimen

By early 1778 the officer corps looked forward to improving Continental training and battle drill (that is, standard formations and maneuvers in actual combat). Both officers and men understood that they lacked the tactical skill of the British; rebel officers could put their units through basic formations, but most were not yet good enough to adjust their lines rapidly or under pressure. Moreover, not all regiments learned the same drill, as different officers approached the matter differently, which made it difficult to combine units for maneuvers in large formations. What the army needed was uniformity in drill and field command, and many officers were willing to take advice from anyone who could help them. Lieutenant Colonel John Laurens, one of the young officers closest to Washington, was even willing to listen to the detested Major General Conway. "We want some kind of general tutoring in this way so much," he wrote his father, "that as obnoxious as Conway is to most of the army, rather than take the field without the advantages" of any "judicious exercise" that he might provide as inspector general, young Laurens was willing to tolerate the unpopular Irishman.[63]

Quickly, however, the situation took a turn for the better. The catalyst was the arrival at Valley Forge on 23 February of Friedrich Steuben. A pretended member of the Prussian nobility, Steuben had served as a captain on the staff of Frederick the Great. He had investigated possibilities for American employment with the patriot commissioners in France, and Benjamin Franklin probably was responsible for inflating Steuben's European record—which included a story that he had been a Prussian lieutenant general—in order to smooth his way with Congress. He made a good impression from the beginning, however, and the Americans never begrudged his assumed title of "baron." Whatever his background, the Prussian soldier-for-hire brought at least two major attributes to the army: he could train soldiers, and he knew how to deal tactfully with his American hosts. Unlike Conway and other Europeans in Continental employ, Steuben did not badger Congress for senior rank or other preferment. Rather, the "baron" agreed to serve as a voluntary inspector general. He left matters of a permanent post and rank for later discussion with the understanding that if he proved himself, appropriate emoluments would follow.[64]

As the absent Conway had not resigned his post as inspector general, Washington put Steuben to work in an "acting" capacity. The Prussian performed with a will, and he was as good as his word. His task was to bring uniformity to Continental training and tactical deployments and to make sure that all officers were competent to maneuver their commands. He succeeded in part because he did not slavishly copy European drill; instead, he modified old commands and procedures, simplifying them for American use. Equally important, Steuben knew how to motivate fighting men. He organized a model company, built around Washington's own guards and an additional one hundred picked men, which he drilled personally as an example for the rest of the army. He taught officers to teach their men, and breaking with European practice, he insisted that they do so personally. No longer would officers delegate training duties to their sergeants; henceforth, company commanders would be responsible for instructing their recruits. Steuben never said it would be easy. Dealing with recruits, he conceded, was "a service that required not only experience, but a patience and temper not met with in every officer." Colonels were "answerable" for making sure that their company officers were effective and for the overall performance of their regiments.[65] They would no longer institute different drill regimens.

Large-scale training operations began on 24 March, with regiments drilling individually. Each day the Continentals received another lesson from their Prussian taskmaster. They learned or relearned volley fire, movement from file into line and back again, and any number of other tactical evolutions. They learned to march to a "common" cadence of 75 steps per minute and a "quick step" of 120 steps per minute, in line with British practice.[66] Skirmishing operations received considerable attention. The men learned to move on the flanks of main formations in open order, keeping a hundred yards out to prevent enemy units from closing to within effective musket range by surprise.[67] There was also bayonet drill, teaching proficiency with the weapon the British had used to such deadly effect. This could be dramatic. At the command "March! March!" with bayonets already fixed, the battalion advanced at the quick step. Then with "Charge—Bayonet!" the troops would "quicken their step"—they would be virtually jogging at this point—and "the drums" would "beat the long roll" as the lines of infantry moved forward in dressed ranks.[68] Steuben taught a brutal trade.

The acting inspector general drove the troops hard, and even detached units followed the new drill. On 1 May Washington sent one of Steuben's aides to work with Brigadier General William Smallwood, whose troops were posted in Wilmington, Delaware. The commander in chief wanted Smallwood's command "perfectly acquainted" with the new training program. Across the Delaware River, detached New Jersey Continentals practiced "the Baron de Steubens Instructions" as well.[69] Steadily, the regimen took hold. As word filtered back to York, congressional delegates reacted with interest and approval. Henry Laurens wrote Steuben to express his joy at hearing "repeated Accounts of the great utility of your presence & aid" at Valley Forge.[70] The army was shaping up.

The applause Steuben received from the officers at Valley Forge was virtually unanimous—at least initially. He had earned it. Yet his success needs some important perspective. In the early months of 1778 the Continental Army was not a mob. Many of the troops were veterans and had picked up a working knowledge of maneuver and weapons drill over the previous year or two. Many officers familiar with European military ideas had read translations of the Old World military works, while some were veterans of the French and Indian War and had learned British drill. Indeed, several had begun to train their men in uniform drill, and only the pace of operations had prevented Washington from implementing a standard system in 1777.

Some of the more observant officers with the British recognized that the rebel army was changing. Among these was Johann Ewald, captain of the elite Hessian jaegers of the Leib Regiment. Ewald was born in 1744, the son of a post office bookkeeper. At age sixteen he enlisted as a cadet in the army of Duke Ferdinand of Brunswick and saw considerable action during the Seven Years' War. Gallant, he was wounded and won a commission for his bravery, yet he could also be foolhardy, losing an eye fighting a duel in a drunken stupor. But Ewald had a first-rate mind. He studied military science at the Collegium Carolinum at Kassel and published a well-received tract on leadership in the field. He knew his profession, and he arrived in America a tested veteran with an incisive understanding of eighteenth-century warfare.[71] The captain led his jaegers in action during the 1776 and 1777 campaigns, played a major part in Washington's defeat at Brandywine, and enjoyed the regard of both Howe and Clinton. Thus his judgment in military affairs carried weight, and his opinion of the Americans is noteworthy: "During these two years," Ewald wrote in his private journal,

> the Americans have trained a great many excellent officers who very often shame and excel our experienced officers, who consider it sinful to read a book or to think of learning anything during the war. For the love of justice and in praise of this nation, I must admit that when we examined a haversack of the enemy, which contained only two shirts, we also found the most excellent military books translated into their language . . . , and the *Instructions* of the great Frederick to his generals I have found more than one hundred times. Moreover, several among their officers had designed excellent small handbooks and distributed them in the army. Upon finding these books, I exhorted our gentlemen many times to read and emulate these people, who only two years before were hunters, lawyers, merchants, physicians, clergymen, tradesmen, innkeepers, shoemakers, and tailors.[72]

Coming as it did in December 1777, this was high praise and probably a more favorable assessment of patriot military leadership than Washington held at the time.

Thus Steuben did not have to start from scratch, nor did he have to convince anyone of the value of uniform drill. As a functional combat organization, the army was, as one detailed study has put it, on the point of "crystallization" before Steuben arrived. What it needed was a "knowledgeable, patient and pragmatic individual with the authority and credibility" to pull all of the loose ends together.[73] The "baron" proved to be the very man, but he had plenty of help. In virtually all he did, the inspector general enjoyed the unstinting support of the commander in chief. General orders at Valley Forge were replete with official thanks for Steuben's efforts, to which Washington assigned the utmost importance. The general directed that all units were to drill with scrupulous regard for the "written Instructions of the Inspector General" so "that the strictest Uniformity may be observed throughout the whole army." Any deviation from Steuben's instruction would not be tolerated; failure to conform, Washington warned, would "again plunge the Army into that Contrariety and Confusion from which it is endeavouring to emerge."[74] In great measure it did emerge, and with Washington's enthusiastic endorsement, on 5 May Congress confirmed Steuben's appointment as inspector general with the rank of major general. (Steuben compiled his drill and procedures in written notes, which eventually became the famous "Blue Book." The manual remained the standard army reference on drill until the War of 1812.)

The Continental Line as a Work in Progress

As Steuben labored to standardize infantry drill and training, Washington and his officers addressed a myriad of other organizational and functional issues. The tasks encompassed virtually every branch of the service, combat and support arms alike. In some areas, especially those requiring sophisticated technical or administrative skills, change came slowly. Field communications, for instance, would remain a problem, and Washington had to rely heavily on European officers for military engineering. Medical services never functioned at their best and frequently were the source of turmoil among feuding personnel.[75] In critical areas, however, the army made remarkable strides. Credit for these successes lay with a number of particularly able subordinates and with Washington himself for putting them in their posts and supporting them as they went about their assignments.

The commander in chief took a direct role in reorganizing the infantry. As in the British military, these regiments were the heart of the army, and Washington moved vigorously to improve their effectiveness. The first order of business was to bring in more men. He pushed state and army recruiters to enroll volunteers and draftees as quickly as possible, and over the spring the recruiting machinery established the year before slowly responded. In March the main army at Valley Forge counted fewer than 7,500 men of all arms fit for duty; by May this figure had climbed to slightly over 15,000. In June (after the Battle of Monmouth), the roster of the main army showed 15,336 men actually on duty.[76]

At the same time the patriot commander began reorganizing his battalions, paying particular attention to the consolidation of weaker units into a smaller number of stronger regiments. In May 1778 Congress responded to his request to reduce the number of Continental battalions. This step, he believed, would make it easier to control the army in the field; it also would bolster the morale of unit commanders who were dejected at dealing with regiments and companies far below authorized strength.[77] Instead of 104 regiments, the new arrangement called for only 80. Regiments now would consist of eight companies of sixty-four officers and men (fifty-three privates) each; including all staff, they thus would comprise 582 officers and men, down from the 738 authorized in late 1776.[78] Even this manpower goal was ambitious, but at least it was more realistic.

In the artillery Brigadier General Henry Knox fostered a growing competence in his branch. Knox, a Boston bookseller before the war, was a self-taught artillerist, learning the rudiments of his trade from his own books. Since 1775 he had done wonders in establishing an effective artillery arm in which technical competence was critical. Knox established armories and repair shops for his guns and carefully supervised the training of his gunners. At Valley Forge he quietly completed a reorganization of the Continental artillery so that by January 1778, having incorporated various state artillery companies, he had four regiments (or battalions). These units had no standard table of organization until 27 May, when Congress established artillery battalions of twelve companies and a staff, with a total of

729 officers and men.[79] Like the infantry regiments as well as their British counterparts, artillery units were seldom at full strength. Muster rolls for May 1778, on the eve of the Monmouth campaign, showed the strongest artillery regiments with only 289 officers and men and a total of 1,039 artillery personnel of all ranks.[80]

Knox made the most of what he had. Gun crews became expert at the labor-intensive tasks of loading and aiming their weapons, handling ammunition and related tools and equipment, working with the civilian teamsters who hauled them on the march (also a practice in the British artillery), and maneuvering their guns in the field. Artillery regiments seldom fought as units; rather, companies or individual crews could expect to accompany infantry units, often two guns to a brigade. (Monmouth would be something of an exception in that one regiment fought as a cohesive unit.) Learning to work with the infantry regiments was important as well. By late spring Knox's men were trained to a high level of proficiency, and esprit among the artillerists was among the highest in the army.[81]

They also were well equipped. In late 1777 Knox had thirty-nine guns, twenty-six of them 6-pounders, most of the others 3-pounders. But the capture of Burgoyne's army, including its forty-four-gun artillery train, plus a substantial number of imports and local manufactures augmented Knox's firepower. From Burgoyne alone, the rebels got eleven more brass 3-pounders, twenty-two 6-pounders, six 12-pounders, and two powerful 24-pounders; there were also two 8-inch mortars. Over the winter and spring, Knox arranged to have most of the captured pieces shipped to the main army, with a few assigned to various critical defensive positions along the Hudson River. Most of the lighter field pieces, however, ultimately joined Washington's men. Knox also had six 4-pounders at his command, probably French imports.[82] The artillery chief had done his job well, and when the time came, so would his guns.

The outlook for patriot logistics improved as well. Responding to the entreaties of Washington and the Committee at Camp, Congress agreed to strengthen the Commissary and Quartermaster Departments. The post of quartermaster general went to Rhode Island's Major General Nathanael Greene, who took up his duties on 2 March. Greene had emerged as one of Washington's more able lieutenants, and it was only at the urging of the commander in chief that he gave up his line command (although he kept his line commission). "No body ever heard of a quarter Master in History," he lamented. In early April Jeremiah Wadsworth, a Connecticut man with prior experience in military supply, accepted the position of commissary general of purchases. Wadsworth had no aspirations to military glory and never asked where commissary generals stood in history. Neither man, as events subsequently proved, had anything to fear from the verdict of posterity.[83]

Greene and Wadsworth wasted no time grasping departmental reins, and soon the formal channels of the logistics system began to function better at all levels. Deliveries to the army became more regular, and food, clothing, forage, camp implements, and munitions were no longer scarce by the early spring. Substantial shipments of French supplies, landed in New England, also began arriving in camp, allowing many of the patriot regiments to reequip with new muskets and much-needed entrenching tools. By mid-June, just in time for the spring campaign, enough of the excellent .69-caliber French Charleville muskets had reached Valley Forge to complete the rearming of a majority of the men. Other troops marched with Dutch weapons, and some with older British models, but they all had ammunition. Greene worked hard to improve army transportation facilities, and by June Washington's men had enough wagons and teams for the campaign. Greene and Wadsworth enjoyed significant help and good fortune. Congress and Washington had resolved certain administrative bottlenecks that had impeded earlier supply efforts, French aid was generous, and the weather moderated after February 1778. Even General Howe cooperated by not attacking Valley Forge. But the two department heads were diligent and competent, and they deserved considerable credit for the improved state of army logistics.[84]

There is a final point, perhaps more difficult to assess but still significant. By early 1778 the Continental Line was a seasoned outfit. The ranks were still too thin, but officers and men had shared at least one full campaign; by late spring all the rebuilt regiments had a core of veterans. As armies went, the Americans were lean and mounted operations in the face of logistical problems no professional European force could tolerate. The patriot regiments learned to make do with less of everything and found ways to get more out of what they had. This took time and experience, but coping with privation became part of army routine, a fact reflected in any number of small but cumulatively important ways. Over time, for instance, the army established regulations discouraging militia from walking off with arms and equipment when they concluded tours of duty. Other orders made soldiers responsible for the care of their weapons and accountable for any issued tools, even to items as small as tin canisters used in the distribution of liquor rations. To the extent it could, the army even tried to make key skills organic. At Valley Forge, for example, it baked some of its own bread in field ovens, artificers fabricated a range of gun and vehicle parts, and military tailors made better clothing than their civilian counterparts. The Continentals were never self-sufficient, but they learned to do a great deal to help themselves, an ability that marked the passage to veteran status and proved a continuing benefit to field performance.[85]

Even with these improvements, there was still considerable work to do. Washington never considered any area of army administration or performance as good as it could be, and he was under no illusion that the Continental regiments would emerge from Valley Forge as the professional equals of the Coldstream Guards or the Royal Highlanders. Rebel cavalry in particular remained a problem: equipment, weapons, and mounts were hard to find, and when they were available, they were expensive. If many of his riders and their officers were of high quality, Washington never had enough of them.[86] Yet by late spring 1778, the general nevertheless considered the Continental Line a substantially improved fighting unit. The pieces had come together only slowly, but he finally had a version of his "respectable army."

Washington's cautious optimism proved infectious. Regular rations, new equipment, improved training, moderating weather, and the prospect of new recruits lifted morale to its highest levels in months. It soared higher still when the army learned that America no longer was fighting alone. News of the French alliance reached Valley Forge on 3 May, and Washington correctly concluded that a French declaration of war was in the offing. He announced the happy development in general orders on the fifth, casting the French intervention in terms of divine intervention: "It having pleased the Almighty ruler of the Universe . . . to defend the Cause of the United American-States . . . by raising us up a powerful Friend among the Princes of the Earth to establish our liberty and Independence upon lasting foundations, it becomes us to set apart a day for gratefully acknowledging the divine Goodness & celebrating the important Event which we owe to his benign Interposition." The celebration followed the next day. The entire army paraded in honor of the occasion, cheered Louis XVI, fired repeated artillery and musket salutes, and ended festivities with a final thirteen-gun discharge "To the American States."[87] Major Joseph Bloomfield of the Third New Jersey Regiment, who witnessed part of the festivities in the company of "his Excellency Genl. Washington, his amiable lady & suite," wrote proudly that "Approbation indeed was conspicuous in every countenance, & universal joy reigned throughout the Camp." For the men in ranks, perhaps the best news of all from the general came last: "Each man is to have a Gill of rum."[88]

General Washington

Valley Forge had changed the army, but it had changed the commander in chief as well. Washington there was at his administrative and inspirational best. He had bent every effort to remedy an array of the army's most pressing shortcomings, doing so in the face of daunting obstacles, not the least of which was the heavy political fire from patriot radicals. All his experience and persistence, to which he added a full measure of patience and political finesse, now paid dividends. As historian Thomas Fleming has pointed out, the general had honed his political skills over the winter of 1777–78. Keeping his army together mandated routine, if often frustrating, dealings with all manner of civil officials and congressional committees, state governors, senior regular and militia officers, and individual civilians.[89] To make these contacts productive in behalf of the army, the general had to be at his diplomatic best. He also cemented his relationship with the rank and file. Washington was never a "soldiers general" in the sense of encouraging informal camaraderie with enlisted men, or even most junior officers; to the contrary, he insisted on the formalities of rank and kept his distance from the troops. Washington was no social leveler. But as Edward Lengel has correctly observed, the general made a point of sharing the Valley Forge winter with his regiments. He did not take leave, as many officers did, and it was common knowledge that he was doing his utmost to keep the men housed, fed, and warm. Indeed, the general publicly declared that he would personally "share in the hardship, and partake of every inconvenience." If he was aloof personally, his loyalty to his troops gained their attachment to him.[90] Having endured the Valley Forge winter, Captain Ezra Selden of the First

Connecticut Regiment probably spoke for many when he wrote to a friend: "I am content should they remove almost any General Except his Excellency. . . . [E]ven Congress are not aware of the Confidence The Army Places in him or motions would never have been made for Gates to take Command."[91]

The commander in chief also solidified the dedicated—indeed, even fierce—support of a coterie of junior staff officers and younger generals he came to refer to as his military family. These were his closest aides and confidants, and by June 1778 they included Alexander Hamilton, John Laurens, Francis Barber, James McHenry, Lafayette, Richard Kidder Meade, Tench Tilghman, Robert Hanson Harrison, John Fitzgerald, and several others. All of these men were young and accomplished, most having joined Washington between early 1777 and the spring of 1778. Thus they had been with the general through some of his most difficult trials and had stood firmly by him when other patriots expressed their doubts. They enjoyed his complete trust, drafted his voluminous correspondence, carried sensitive dispatches and orders, and even undertook special administrative assignments. In February 1778, in a prominent example, when the army was desperately short of rations, Tilghman coordinated emergency foraging operations that went far toward alleviating the problem.[92]

The "family" was also useful politically. Hamilton was close to New York governor George Clinton, a key Washington ally, and Laurens's father was president of Congress. Washington certainly spoke for himself in dealing with Congress and other patriots, but he did so almost always tactfully and, when necessary, even in tones of deference. Thus it was useful to have staff able to communicate with influential patriots in an informal and sometimes blunter capacity. As noted earlier, Laurens gave his father unvarnished accounts of events at Valley Forge, including his fears of a "junto" acting against Washington.[93] Hamilton, writing to Governor Clinton, was blunt in describing Conway's alleged machinations against Washington: "He is one of the vermin bred in the entrails of this chimera dire, and there does not exist a more villainous calumniator and incendiary."[94] Washington may well have thought something like that, but he never would have written it to a prominent political leader. His young family neither forgave nor forgot the slights he had endured, and in June they would carry their sense of grievance into the field.

Thus as the 1778 campaign loomed, Washington commanded a much-improved army, with the vast majority of his officers and men firmly attached to him. What remained was to see how all of these changes might translate into success in battle.

CHAPTER 4

Toward a New Campaign

In May 1778 the rival armies at Valley Forge and in Philadelphia watched one another with increasing wariness, each seeking signs of the other's movement or intentions. Washington, anticipating the British evacuation of the city, considered his own departure from Valley Forge in the event, as he fully expected, Clinton moved by land. He also had to consider what to do if he actually caught up with the British—or even if he *wanted* to catch up with them. Clinton's job was more complex. His orders not only compelled him to move but, in effect, to concede the initiative to the rebels. His army would begin the campaign with a retreat, a circumstance that all but invited Washington to look for an opening to attack. Whatever the imponderables, as the spring of 1778 advanced, both generals knew a new campaign was in the offing.

Valley Forge: April and May 1778

Washington understood that spring would bring renewed confrontation. He still felt that his army was not ready for major offensive operations since enough recruits had not come to camp and the supply situation, while improving, remained problematic. Even so, there was a great deal to consider, especially the mystery of British intentions. Washington accurately predicted that Clinton was likely to replace Howe, but he warned that either Howe or Clinton, alarmed by the empire's deteriorating global military position, might try to redeem the situation through a surprise strike at Valley Forge.[1] The rebels, in his view, could not discount an enemy offensive; he knew it was time to have some general plan of action in place.

Some two weeks before the army celebrated the French alliance, the general took preliminary steps toward spring operations. On 20 April Washington submitted a memorandum on potential operations to his generals and invited their comments. He saw three alternatives for a new campaign. The first was the most ambitious: to attack and destroy the British army in Philadelphia. If they attacked the city, "shall we endeavour to effect the purpose by Storm, by regular approaches or by blockade, and in what particular manner?" The second was also offensive in nature: to transfer the war north by a move against New York. Washington estimated the enemy garrison in New York at about 4,000 men. That being the case, he wrote, "shall we attempt to take New York, by a coup de main, with a small force, or shall we collect a large force and make an attack in form?" The final option called for remaining in Valley Forge, continuing to rebuild the army, and to await enemy movements. "Which of these three Plans," he asked his officers, "shall we adopt?" In his note Washington told his generals to plan on facing a British force of roughly 10,000 men, exclusive of naval personnel (a figure wrong by about half—there were closer to 22,000 troops). He wanted answers in writing, so "that I may compare one with the other—weigh and digest the whole—and take my measures accordingly."[2]

Between 21 and 25 April, twelve general officers responded, some briefly, but most at length and with considerable care. These responses reveal how divided American command opinion was on prosecuting the war; of equal interest, they also say a great deal about what senior officers thought of the state of the Continental Line. All the generals stressed that any new campaign would be particularly important, coming as it would after the disappointments of 1777. This was partly a political concern. They realized that much of the public had grown war weary and was hungry for better news from the front. Military success, the generals told their commander, was critical to maintaining support for the cause and discouraging loyalism. Brigadier General James Mitchell Varnum spoke for most of the others: "We must improve upon the remaining Sparks of public Virtue. . . . Without obtaining some capital Advantage, the [public] Mind may be too well prepared to receive Submission & Slavery."[3] No matter what plans it adopted, the army simply *had* to perform well. Washington had not specifically asked for advice on what was clearly a political matter, but the link between military and political affairs was too obvious for his senior officers to overlook.

Beyond this point of general agreement, opinions differed considerably. Not all of the generals came out decisively for one or another of the choices, hedging their preferences against British actions, the availability of supplies, political developments, and other conditions. But in broad terms, thinking broke down as follows: Three men, Brigadier Generals Anthony Wayne and John Paterson and Major General William Alexander (Lord Stirling), favored attacking Philadelphia. Stirling, however, while agreeing that Philadelphia was the best target, urged a more aggressive course, wanting to move simultaneously against Philadelphia *and* New York.[4] Plan two, a movement against New York, had the most support. Brigadier Generals Henry Knox, Peter Muhlenberg, Enoch Poor, Varnum, and William Maxwell and Major General Nathanael Greene all favored it. In varying degrees they thought that efforts to supply the army, rally militia support, and fight on favorable terms seemed more likely if the seat of war was moved away from Philadelphia. Those who urged offensive operations, no matter what the target, generally agreed that a defensive posture would not do; it would only invite constant enemy harassment and would surrender the initiative.[5] Indeed, as far as General Poor was concerned, the "plan of remaining Quiet in Camp I would Explode."[6]

Of all of the generals favoring plans one or two, the most bellicose was Wayne. He would play a leading role in the fighting at Monmouth, and as his aggressive leadership early in the battle would figure in the controversies that followed, his response to Washington is of more than passing interest. Wayne, a native of Chester County, Pennsylvania, was the son of a locally prominent family. Well educated (he had attended the Academy and College of Philadelphia, the modern University of Pennsylvania), he had established himself as a successful surveyor, landowner, and tannery operator. Declaring early for the Revolution, in 1775 Wayne recruited a volunteer militia unit and by 1776 commanded a regiment of Pennsylvania Continentals, gaining a reputation as a fighter. He did well in the ill-starred Canadian campaign, and his performance won him promotion to brigadier general in January 1777. During the fighting against Howe, he led the Pennsylvania Continentals in all of the major actions around Philadelphia. Stung by his bloody defeat at Paoli, Wayne wanted desperately to strike back. In two letters to Washington (dated 21 and 23 April), he argued for the offensive in the strongest terms. His brother officers had offered the commanding general more or less detailed explanations of how to marshal logistical and other resources necessary to support operations, but Wayne slighted these concerns. Rather, he stressed the redemption of the cause through battle. Defeating the British in Philadelphia, he enthused, would erase "the fruits of two hard Campaigns" and tarnish British "Glory forever." Such a victory would bring American arms respect at home "and Shine with Redoubled Lustre through the Courts of Europe." Even a movement against New York, Wayne assured his commander, would be beneficial. The effort would compel the British in Philadelphia to mount a relief of New York, which would leave the King's army vulnerable somewhere. "In all probability" this would lead to the "most happy and Glorious Consequences—for a Conquering Army finds no difficulties."[7]

In a thoughtful essay on the general, Hugh F. Rankin has called Wayne a "military romanticist" bent on seeking fame and glory in the field.[8] The general's recommendations to Washington easily reflected the "romanticist." His fighting spirit did him credit, and no one questioned his personal bravery, but he seemingly lacked the broader perspective on what it would take to sustain operations in a major campaign. Years later, in 1794, Wayne would combine his aggressiveness with meticulous planning and preparation to win the Battle of Fallen Timbers. But the more mature Wayne of Fallen Timbers was absent in 1778.

Three other generals advocated a more conservative policy. These were the Europeans—the marquis de Lafayette, Inspector General Steuben, and Brigadier General Louis Duportail—all of whom championed, however reluctantly, Washington's third plan: that is, they wanted to stay at Valley Forge, watch events, and continue to improve the Continental Army. In a long and rambling response, Duportail was having none of Wayne's (or anyone else's) enthusiasm. The Continentals, he argued, while improving, were not up to facing British and German regulars in major operations. It would be better for the patriot troops to remain where they were as they presently had the advantage "of obliging the enemy to march to our own ground to fight us."[9] Lafayette and Steuben agreed: the Continentals should continue to train and rebuild. "There are occasions in which a Nation is obliged to put her all at Stake," Steuben advised Washington, but under the present circumstances, "I cannot think this to be our case."[10]

In soliciting his generals' comments, Washington never intended to reach any firm decisions on future operations. He got what he wanted: the thinking of his generals at a point when the army was still trying to transform itself into an effective force. Perhaps he was surprised that his subordinates had delved so deeply into the political implications of a new campaign, but no one was more aware of the importance of such considerations than he. In any event, Washington concluded that plans one and two were beyond patriot capabilities. He thought the army could muster some 17,000 effectives by early June, although that number might not be enough to attack Philadelphia or New York (much less both at once). Nor did he think that militia support would be adequate, perhaps even draining resources from any major operation. Besides, offensives entailed risk—the British certainly would respond—and failure would deal another blow to already fragile civilian morale. Thus the commander in chief saw Valley Forge as the best alternative. Remaining on the defensive, he noted, made sense while the army was gaining strength and would afford time for vital training and reorganization.[11] The back-and-forth communications had allowed Washington to judge the temper of his generals, and these men now knew, if they had any doubts, that their commander was not going to rush into anything.

This was not the end of the matter. On 23 April the commander in chief informed President Henry Laurens that he would, as Congress wished, convene a full council of war to discuss a 1778 campaign; he was only awaiting the arrival in camp of Major Generals Horatio Gates and Thomas Mifflin.[12] (Mifflin had returned to duty, but unpopular with most officers, he would stay only briefly. In May Congress recalled him to York to defend his conduct as quartermaster general.) Of all the people in the army Washington wanted to see, it is easy to imagine these two men were near the bottom of the list. They were senior generals, though, and excluding them from such an important consultation would have courted needless acrimony. Besides, events soon made campaign planning imperative. From New Jersey, Washington received word of large-scale British foraging operations as well as the occupation and fortification of Coopers Point (modern Camden). The enemy had moved in force but with unknown purpose. In addition, the news of the French alliance, joyous as it was, left many patriots wondering what the implications would be for 1778. New Jersey governor William Livingston asked the general if he would be making "a grand push," while Greene wanted to know if the change in affairs would compel attention to new plans. Washington admitted that he had little idea what all these developments meant but promised a council of war to consider them.[13] It really was time to talk.

The meeting took place on 8 May. Ten generals attended, including Gates and Mifflin; Wayne was absent. Washington informed the officers of the congressional directive to meet in council and presented them with a written estimate of the situation. This he framed in generally optimistic terms. The status of the army was much improved. There were still supply shortages, but the situation was better, and he did not think the British could substantially reinforce their forces in Philadelphia. Yet he did not expect Continental strength in all quarters to climb much beyond 20,000 rank and file and had little faith in receiving significant militia support. Once again, he asked each general to respond in writing.[14]

This time they did not. Instead, they agreed on a joint statement that mirrored the caution Washington had displayed in April. With events making action seem more likely, the generals dispensed with the more aggressive suggestions they had mooted only weeks earlier. The consensus was that offensives against Philadelphia or New York promised more risks than rewards; moderation ruled the day as the officers recommended a continued defensive posture. Their written response was actually a sober, well-reasoned document. "By remaining on the defensive," the generals stated,

> we put nothing to the hazard. Our army will increase in number and improve in discipline. Our Arsenals and magazines will be more respectable and more adequate to the exigencies of the service. A large emission of public money will be saved, which will have a negative efficacy, in raising its value. We have the chance of events, resulting from the important treaties lately concluded between France and America, which may oblige the enemy, to withdraw their force, without any further trouble to us. If this does not happen, and they make a vigorous effort [in] the ensuing campaign, which seems to be a necessary alternative, we shall be in a much better situation to give them opposition. We can then rely on the aid and cooperation of the Militia, who having been left in a state of repose to cultivate their lands, and persue their other private avocations and domestic concerns will more cheerfully come to our assistance.

The council unanimously advised that the army "remain on the defensive and wait events; without attempting any offensive operation of consequence, unless the future circumstances of the enemy, should afford a fairer opportunity, than at present exits."[15]

Washington agreed; true to past practice, he saw no reason to risk his men without sufficient cause. Safe at Valley Forge, the rebel general could afford to bide his time. In Philadelphia the British could not.

Philadelphia: Rumor and Reality

On May 20, two days after his farewell Meschianza and four days before he boarded HMS *Andromeda* for home, General Howe met socially with one of Philadelphia's loyalist municipal officials. As the conversation turned to the state of the war, Howe, in so many words, confirmed the rumors of the impending evacuation of the city. Not surprisingly, the news leaked and quickly became, as one officer put it, "the whisper of the day." Two days later Howe sent one of his generals to officially notify Joseph Galloway. Rumor was now fact: the British army was leaving.[16]

The news met with general consternation among the city's tories. Watching developments from York, Congressman Oliver Wolcott wrote his wife that "a most dreadfull Anxiety excercises the Philadelphian Tories." The "less guilty" of them, he reported, looked to "the Clemency of their Country" to shield them from patriot reprisals. There was little more they could do, as even ranking British officers admitted. Just before his departure, Howe actually encouraged loyalists who chose to stay in the city to sound out patriot leaders on possible terms of reconciliation. When Clinton balked at the proposal, Howe advised him "to *consent* or *wink* at it." The new commander demurred, fearing that such a policy would play into rebel hands. Still, he realized that many prominent tories were understandably reluctant to trust in any patriot mercy.[17]

It took a few days for Philadelphia loyalists to grasp the full implications of what was happening. On 23 May Quaker diarist Elizabeth Sandwich Drinker noted the rumors of a British evacuation and the hopes of many that "tis not ye case."[18] The matter came to a head on 25 May, when a nearly frantic Galloway met twice with Clinton in a vain effort to avert the British withdrawal. The general, who had not revealed his orders from Lord Germain to evacuate the city, quickly found himself in a delicate position. He genuinely sympathized with the plight of the loyalists while realizing that unless he made public the fact that Germain had ordered him to retreat, he would bear the onus of the decision. The next morning the general sent word to Galloway that his orders were clear and his hands were tied, the best he could do was offer tories who wished to leave safe passage with the army or the fleet. Galloway (among others) accepted, convinced that he was doomed to "wander like Cain upon the Earth without Home, & without Property."[19] (Actually, Galloway went on to a comfortable, if sometimes lonely, postwar life in England.) He prepared to leave the province he had called home for most of his life and to assist fellow loyalists in preparing their departures.[20]

The evacuation was a classic example of British inability to arrive at a workable position regarding the tories. When royal forces left any region without sufficient military protection, local tories generally found themselves at the mercy of their (usually enraged) patriot neighbors. Such were tory fears in 1778, and the British were in no position to allay them. In May jaeger captain Johann Ewald noted sadly that so many "brave people who have rendered such good service to the King, are being left behind. They grumble and swear that the army will leave Philadelphia and would rather let them be hanged by the Congress than serve England. God alone knows what will happen to them!"[21]

The circumstances of loyalist soldiers were particularly dire. Clinton understood fully that the evacuation doomed the tory outfits raised during the occupation. They stood no chance alone against the rebel military, and the chances of patriots offering an olive branch to former loyalist troops was close to nil. On 8 May the Pennsylvania Council attainted hundreds of citizens for treason, including many who had enlisted with the British.[22] Contemplation of their probable fate in a "liberated" Philadelphia was anything but reassuring. Accordingly, Clinton's plans called for the tory units to march out with the British and Hessian regulars. These men now had lost everything, a bitter reward for loyalty.

Yet the tory dilemma did not end the chorus of woe. On 6 June the Carlisle Commission arrived in Philadelphia and sent word to Congress of Parliament's conciliatory acts. The effort came to nothing. With France about to enter the war, neither Congress nor other patriots were seriously interested in peace on terms short of independence. Moreover, Lord North had never informed Carlisle that Clinton had orders to evacuate the city. The commissioners were mortified. Lord Carlisle, utterly dismayed, lamented that the prime minister had made his entire effort "a mixture of ridicule, nullity, and embarrassments."[23] Nevertheless, the commissioners thought giving up Philadelphia would only further embolden the rebels and pressed Clinton to stay on; an evacuation, they pleaded, would make negotiations impossible. They also wrote to Germain. Preparations for the evacuation, they reported, had the city in an uproar, "so that we found ourselves, by this untimely removal of His Majesty's army and the readiness of the enemy to profit by it, likely to be deprived of all the advantages which we had reason to expect from the effect of the conciliatory bills."[24] Clinton was sympathetic (or at least said so) but insisted that his orders bound him. To patriots it made no difference. On 17 June, the day before Clinton pulled out of Philadelphia, Congress unanimously resolved not to negotiate without a prior recognition of independence. Washington spoke for many when he wrote President Laurens that any talks with Carlisle were "wholly incompetent to any valuable end."[25] The commission's mission was stillborn from the beginning, but the military situation ended it amid the gloomiest of circumstances.

Even as he dealt with disappointments over the pending loss of Philadelphia, Clinton moved ahead with his plans to pull out of the city. As a technical exercise, a major evacuation in the face of the enemy could be tricky. The last thing the royal general needed was a patriot attack while he was in the middle of packing transport ships or as he ferried his men across the Delaware River to New Jersey. Consequently, security was a prominent concern, and the British did their best to keep their intentions from Washington. Efforts to mask the evacuation had begun even before the change of command. In late April Howe ordered his chief engineer, Captain John Montressor, to construct a series of new defensive positions on the outskirts of Philadelphia. The intention was to give the appearance of digging in for a long stay; actually, Clinton would post his rear guard in these redoubts to cover the withdrawal. Improvements on these lines continued until the evacuation. Clinton also maintained active patrolling. Over May and June, British forces engaged in no fewer than fifteen small-unit or naval actions outside Philadelphia or in New Jersey as they sought to cover foraging columns, fight off rebel probes, destroy patriot shipping, or bombard patriot coastal positions.[26] If appearances counted for anything, Sir Henry did not look like a general on the run.

For a while, Clinton's deceptions managed to keep many patriots guessing about his intentions. Indeed, on 5 June Thomas Paine wrote to Washington that Clinton was not going to leave, arguing that the British would not give up a major city without first concluding some sort of formal treaty.[27] As late as 9 June Joseph Reed noted that all signs of an evacuation stopped with the arrival of the Carlisle Commission and that the British now seemed as likely to stay as to go. That same day James Lovell complained to Gates that "here we are still the Sport of Lyars. One Day we are told the Enemy are filling their Ditches and preparing to leave Philada . . . in the next we are informed of new Works & fresh arrived Troops." Lovell was sure that Clinton would try to attack somewhere. Another delegate commented that British activities had become "so various as to render it utterly impossible to guess what measures they mean finally to pursue."[28]

Yet the charade counted for little. Through spies, deserters, and other contacts in the occupied city, most patriot military and political leaders had a fairly good idea of what was going on within British lines. Other intelligence confirmed observations from in and around Philadelphia. Over the latter part of May, Governor Livingston and New Jersey militia general Philemon Dickinson reported that the British in New York were busy preparing emergency housing. The assumption was that it was for troops and refugees from Philadelphia. Washington agreed, informing Livingston that "from a variety of concurring circumstances it would seem, that the Enemy mean to evacuate Philadelphia." Other sources in New Jersey noted a general belief that the British would quit Philadelphia and march through the state. By mid-June Dickinson was positive the British were coming, and he feared they would burn Trenton on their way.[29] If some patriots still doubted that Clinton intended to give up Philadelphia, Washington was not among them. It remained for him to learn when and where his adversary would go when he did leave.

By the end of May, though, the commander in chief was still in the dark on these points. "Notwithstanding the most diligent pains," Washington wrote Henry Laurens, he simply could not determine whether Clinton would evacuate by land or sea. "Appearances favor either."[30] To be sure, the Virginian was concerned about a British retreat through New Jersey, but until he was absolutely positive, he felt that he could not safely detach a major part of the army to that state. Such a move, he feared, would leave the remaining troops and valuable stores at Valley Forge vulnerable to a last-minute strike. He would not take that chance, but the alternative was unpalatable as well. If he waited until Clinton actually crossed into New Jersey before dispatching a significant patriot force, Washington would risk never catching the British, "so that we must give up the idea of harassing them *much* in their March through the Jerseys."[31] He was uncomfortable, however, doing nothing at all and toyed with the idea of taking a major precautionary step. On 30 May he drafted orders for Major General Charles Lee, directing him to take three brigades—some 2,465 men—across northern New Jersey to the North (Hudson) River. In so doing he probably thought Clinton was going to New York by sea, and if that proved to be the case, no doubt the rest of the army would have followed Lee's vanguard; the Continentals would have concentrated at Newburgh to watch developments. But the commander in chief quickly had second thoughts, probably still too unsure of Clinton's intentions (although he left no record of exactly why), and there is no evidence that he ever sent the orders to Lee.[32] For the time being, Washington would watch and wait.

As patriots tried to discern his intentions, Clinton went about getting his army ready to leave Philadelphia. Troops began the arduous task of loading transport ships on 21 May. Gradually, the men dismounted the heavy artillery and loaded it aboard ship, replacing these guns in the defensive redoubts with field artillery. Packed away too were tons of stores and other weapons. By the first week in June, the British began dumping damaged ordnance and muskets, as well as surplus food, into the Delaware. They torched other supplies, including some four thousand blankets, and most shipping under construction in Philadelphia yards. Some troops gave forage and firewood to the poor, while others sold it throughout the city. British merchants packed up their merchandise and arranged to have it loaded aboard the transports, while loyalist and British civilians in government service boarded with their families and personal possessions. Discussions with Admiral Lord Richard Howe, Sir William's brother, revealed that the navy could marshal too few transports for the army and all the loyalist refugees. This revelation settled the issue of how Clinton would get to New York. He decided that the tories, heavy baggage, the women of the army, and the few troops who would fit, including three companies of the Royal Artillery, would go to New York by sea; the bulk of the army would march across New Jersey. By 3 June most of the loaded transports had dropped down the Delaware to a rendezvous near Chester, Pennsylvania. On 11 June the British put their sick and wounded aboard ships as well.[33] It would have been difficult to miss an evacuation in the making.

The troops sailing from Philadelphia included two Hessian units, the First and Second Ansbach-Bayreuth Regiments, which had come to America in 1777. Some historians have assumed that Clinton sent these units by sea because he considered them at risk for desertion, or at least the Americans believed as much.[34] While there seems to exist little contemporary evidence of this tale—Clinton never mentioned it in any of his known papers, and no other British or German officers attributed it to him—these regiments did have a problematic history. Before leaving Germany, they had mutinied over poor living conditions aboard the transport ships; put ashore at Ochsenfurth-on-the-Main, the Hessians engaged in widespread drunkenness and shooting at troops sent to bring them to order. It took the personal appearance of their prince, the Margrave Karl Friedrich of Ansbach, to address their grievances and restore discipline.[35] Yet the circumstances surrounding the departure of the Ansbachers from Philadelphia lent at least some credence to the story. After dark on 8 June (other accounts have it about 2:00 A.M. on 9 June) and without explanation, both regiments were marched to the waterfront. Stephan Popp, a young Hessian soldier, recorded, "the rumor was that Lord Cornwallis had come, by whom we were to be inspected."[36] But there was no inspection; instead, officers shepherded the men aboard small vessels that took them out to awaiting transports. If a sizable number of these troops had wanted to desert, they never got the chance.[37] The business certainly had a suspicious tone.

As signs of an imminent British departure clarified, congressional delegates planned a return to Philadelphia by the first days of June. Some spoke of recovering a trove of abandoned British supplies for Continental use. The president of Congress also looked forward to reoccupying the capital, but he remained suspicious. "I am still of the opinion that there is strategem in Mr. Clinton's proceeding," Henry Laurens wrote his son John, and he pointed out that the British remained in place even though rumors of an evacuation had now circulated for over a month. "In a word, 'tis impossible to trace minutely his designs—don't trust false fires—watch his motions & [be] double guarded."[38]

Essentially, this was the position Washington adopted at Valley Forge. Taking nothing for granted, the rebel commander had to anticipate that any move by Clinton would compel him to respond. Consequently, he increased his own security operations in an effort to watch British movements as closely as possible. Washington ordered his senior commanders to be ready to move quickly and even considered the possibility that he might have to link up with Gates along the Hudson River in order to confront a concentration at New York (probably the intent of the unissued orders drawn for Lee on 30 May). In the meantime he wanted strong outposts established near enemy lines and along probable routes of march. He also kept Greene and Wadsworth busy. The quartermaster general pressed his assistants to marshal supplies in Pennsylvania and New Jersey, with particular emphasis on securing wagons, teams, and forage. Even as the British were evacuating Philadelphia, Greene urgently wrote Moore Furman, his deputy in New Jersey, that there was "a great cry" for transport and forage for the Continentals. He wanted Furman to get them to Coryell's Ferry (modern Lambertville) in time to meet what he felt could be an imminent crossing of the army from Pennsylvania.[39] Greene also worked to preposition supplies across northern New Jersey at roughly fifteen-mile intervals. Like some other patriot generals, he anticipated that Clinton would head for South Amboy, so Greene placed the caches along a route likely to support a patriot march to intercept him.[40] Wadsworth was active as well. Doing his best to get food to the army, he was not sure he could provide everything necessary. "I shall leave nothing undone to Supply the Army," he promised, but he wished for better cooperation from civil authorities.[41] Still, by mid-June it appeared that the supply situation was about as good as it was going to be; there was at least enough to open a campaign.

Now all but certain that Clinton would try to reach New York via New Jersey, Washington's thinking turned more combative. He moved to augment patriot forces in the Garden State. A few Continentals already were there, namely the Second New Jersey Regiment, commanded by Colonel Israel Shreve. A Gloucester County farmer and justice of the peace, Shreve was a man of modest economic means but locally prominent. Although married in a Quaker meeting house and with many neighbors who were Friends, he eschewed their pacifist principles and took up arms for the patriot cause in 1775. His son, John, a junior officer in the regiment, recalled that during the war the colonel weighed over three hundred pounds. Still, he was spry enough to serve actively in the

Canadian and Philadelphia campaigns and was wounded in the thigh at Brandywine. The colonel quickly returned to active duty but had to endure family concerns. During the British occupation of Philadelphia, with enemy activity frequent in Gloucester County, for a time his wife and children fled to safe haven in Pennsylvania.[42]

Shreve had crossed into New Jersey on 19 March after Washington became concerned that the British were preparing a major foraging expedition in Salem, Cumberland, and Cape May Counties. He also worried that they might sail around Cape May and attack vital patriot salt works along the Atlantic coast. The general ordered Shreve to watch both shores of the Delaware and to discourage British and tory raids and foraging parties.[43] If the British did not land, Shreve was to conduct his own foraging operations. But the colonel and his men found plenty to do. The lower Delaware counties of New Jersey were in chaos: the British were foraging aggressively in Salem County, and in southern Gloucester County a loyalist rising had wrested control from patriot authorities. Shreve was diligent in pursuing his mission. When British foragers withdrew on 27 March, the colonel and local militia began restoring order. On 5 April this activity prompted a British raid that chased the Second New Jersey out of Haddonfield.[44] Yet Shreve persevered. He was a valuable source of intelligence to the patriot commander in chief, and his regiment stiffened rebel authority in the region. But it was clear that continued enemy operations in the state were increasingly likely, and the Second New Jersey could do little in the face of a major attack. Shreve asked for more men, but for the time being Washington had none to send.

But the general was fully aware of Shreve's circumstances, and as soon as he could sent help. By early May new recruits and returning veterans were filling the rosters at Valley Forge, and Washington felt better about his army's strength. Accordingly, on 7 May he sent the First New Jersey (under Colonel Matthias Ogden) to join Shreve. At this point the general was thinking about more than loyalist threats. He was still not sure of what Clinton was going to do, but he had to take seriously the possibility—the growing probability—that his opponent would take at least part of his army into New Jersey. If that happened, he understood that the two regiments could do little and would need reinforcement. On 25 May Washington therefore ordered Brigadier General William Maxwell to Mount Holly, an important road junction north of Haddonfield, with the rest of the New Jersey Brigade (the Third Regiment and the woefully understrength Fourth). Maxwell was to continue Shreve's mission and, if Clinton attempted to march through the state, to cooperate with the militia in harassing and slowing the enemy. Washington's orders to the brigadier were clear: "Every possible expedient should be used to disturb and retard their progress, by hanging on their flanks and rear, breaking down the Bridges over the Creeks in their route, blocking up the roads by falling trees and by every other method, that can be devised."[45] The brigade, with some 625 officers and men fit for duty, was in place by the end of May, giving the rebel army a key outpost squarely astride the likely path of any enemy incursion. To give Maxwell broader reach, Washington also detailed a dragoon outfit under Lieutenant Colonel Anthony Walton White and Captain Allen McLane. Both were capable officers, and White, a wealthy and politically prominent Jerseyman, was able to rally some militia horsemen to augment his command.[46] Thus while Maxwell was hardly strong enough to confront the British alone, his force was not inconsiderable.

The New Jersey Brigade's commander was a good choice for this assignment. Maxwell, a British veteran of the French and Indian War, had settled in Sussex County, New Jersey. He had raised a volunteer unit and marched to Boston in 1775, and the following year he led the Second New Jersey as colonel. Maxwell served competently in Canada and received his promotion to brigadier general in 1777. During the Philadelphia campaign, Washington put him in command of a unit of Continental light infantry, which skirmished with Howe as he advanced on the city. By 1778 Maxwell was known as a reliable if unimaginative brigadier (his troops called him "Scotch Willie," supposedly in reference to his Scottish brogue).[47] But the general put his time to good use. Convinced that his men eventually would have to confront Clinton, Maxwell mounted strong guard posts around Haddonfield and nearby towns, and his officers cooperated with militia in alerting civilians to possible trouble. Taking no chances, many residents began moving livestock and furniture out of harm's way. When not on other duty, Maxwell's troops spent their time at drill since many of the men were green recruits; brigade inspector Major Joseph Bloomfield put them through Steuben's maneuvers as often as possible.[48] Throughout his years in the army, Maxwell was more competent than he was brilliant, but by June he had his brigade ready for action. When the time came, Maxwell would not be caught unaware.

Not all rebel preparations went so smoothly, however, and one operation almost backfired disastrously. On 18 May Washington sent Lafayette with 2,200 men and five guns to establish an observation post at Barren Hill, about eleven miles outside of Philadelphia.[49] The deployment was foolhardy, and two days later the inexperienced Lafayette only barely escaped a British effort to trap him. It was a near catastrophe for the Americans, and if his men had not maintained a disciplined march as they moved away, the military career of their young and enthusiastic commander might have ended rather abruptly.[50]

Washington saw Lafayette's escape at Barren Hill as a humiliation of the British.[51] That was true enough, for there were recriminations among Howe's officers after the action. But there is something else worth noting. Barren Hill was the first time the commander in chief had entrusted the very young marquis—Lafayette was only twenty years old—with a significant independent mission. It almost ended badly, but Barren Hill would not be his last opportunity. The near fiasco in Pennsylvania was barely a month old when, on 25 June, Washington ordered Lafayette into harm's way a second time in New Jersey. And for a second time, the young general courted disaster, this time by advancing an inferior force dangerously close to the main British army near Monmouth Court House.

As May drew to a close, Washington turned his thoughts briefly from the immediate problems of military affairs. He took the time to write a long letter to his friend Landon Carter, a major plantation owner in rural Richmond County in northern Virginia (not to be confused with the future Virginia capital, the city of Richmond) and one of the wealthiest in the state. He and Washington had known one another for years. While Carter had come only slowly to the Revolutionary cause, the men remained on cordial terms, and during the war they occasionally exchanged correspondence until Carter's death in December 1778. The general dwelt on their friendship and mutual esteem—as gentlemen of the period were wont—and reprised for his fellow Virginian the state of the war. Significantly, he commented at length about reports Carter had received and reported to Washington (in a letter of March 1778) of a movement afoot among officers "from the Northward" (meaning New England) to replace him as commander in chief. There was nothing to fear, the general wrote. "That there was a scheme of this sort on foot last fall admits of no doubt but it originated in another quarter—with three men who wanted to aggrandize themselves—but finding no support . . . they slunk back—disavowed the measure, & professed themselves my warmest admirers."[52] The three men unnamed in the letter were certainly Gates, Conway, and Mifflin; one does not have to read deeply between the lines to grasp the contempt in which Washington held them.

New Jersey: The State of the State

As he tried to plan for every contingency, Washington also turned to state militias. He never expected the New Jersey irregulars to stand up to Clinton in pitched battle, but with Maxwell in place to offer support, he placed real hopes in their ability to slow the British enough for Washington's army to catch them. The general had grounds for optimism on this score. He had firm and competent allies in New Jersey, including Governor Livingston and Major General Dickinson. Livingston, scion of a socially and politically prominent family of New York, was born in Albany in 1723. He graduated from Yale in 1741 and subsequently moved to New York City, where he became a lawyer and journalist. Livingston was active in the factious local politics of the day, but in 1772, tired of the fray, he moved to Elizabethtown, New Jersey. There he built a large country retreat, Liberty Hall (now a museum), where he and his wife, Susannah French, raised a family that ultimately included thirteen children. Livingston rose quickly in patriot circles, serving as a delegate to the Continental Congress, a brigadier general of militia, and beginning in 1776, governor, a post he held until his death in 1790. He lived dangerously. Liberty Hall was close enough to New York to attract British raids, and the Livingstons frequently removed to the interior of New Jersey to be out of harm's way. But the governor was an effective administrator and held the state for the whig cause. He was in frequent communication with Washington, supplying a steady stream of intelligence and doing his best to support the war effort, including as a prolific essayist, pamphleteer, and propagandist.[53] In 1778 and again in 1780, he successfully pushed the state to conscript militiamen to reinforce New Jersey's Continental regiments.[54] As a war governor, Livingston was among the best, and probably none was closer personally to the patriot commander in chief. As the armies moved toward collision at Monmouth, the New Jersey governor would play an active role.

Livingston's job was seldom easy. By June 1778 New Jersey had been a military theater for two long and violent years. Prior to 1775, when the crisis with Great Britain deepened, the colony had not been a hotbed of revolutionary sentiment. Indeed, had its larger neighbors, New York and Pennsylvania, remained loyal, New Jersey probably would have as well.[55] Even after the break with the empire, loyalism was strong in parts of the province; in 1776 Continental troops had to help put down a tory rising in Monmouth County. In March 1778, encouraged by British incursions from Philadelphia, loyalists in Gloucester County rose in considerable numbers; only the dispatch of Shreve's Second New Jersey contained the situation.[56] British and loyalist activity kept parts of the state in turmoil. The first six months of 1778 (through 18 June) saw some fifty-seven engagements, mostly skirmishes or other small actions, either within New Jersey's borders or on its coasts.[57] Still, Livingston and other patriots at the state and local levels had managed to establish whig authority in most of the province. With some interruptions, commerce continued, courts functioned, taxes were assessed, the legislature met, and the war was supported. If loyalists remained a threat in certain areas, they remained just that—threats—not viable civil or military alternatives to patriot rule. Tories could raid, but they could never muster the strength to sustain a counterrevolution anywhere in the state.[58]

As Livingston struggled to hold the state against internal and external threats, he relied on no one more than Philemon Dickinson, New Jersey's senior militia commander. The men were not friends; in fact, Dickinson was an unsuccessful rival for the governorship. But they were united in waging the war and worked professionally as the feared British invasion loomed. Born in Maryland but raised in Delaware, the future major general graduated from the College of Philadelphia in 1759. In 1767 he moved to Trenton, New Jersey, where he became active in regional social and political affairs. As the controversy with the mother country flared, he was a cautious whig, more conservative than some of his fiery colleagues. But as a patriot, he had an impeccable pedigree. Philemon was the younger brother of John Dickinson, the "Penman of the Revolution" and author of the famous *Letters from a Farmer in Pennsylvania* (1767–68), which railed against the Townsend Acts. He also was cousin to John Cadwalader, major general of the Pennsylvania militia.[59] In 1776 Dickinson served prominently on patriot committees and sat in the Revolutionary Provincial Congress, then actively took the field in militia operations. He was promoted to major general in 1777. In this post he was an articulate proponent of a well-trained and effective militia and worked closely with Livingston to reform the militia laws. By 1778 Dickinson had emerged as one of the most capable militia generals of the war. As the British prepared to march across New Jersey, Dickinson and Washington corresponded regularly, the militia general becoming his single-best intelligence source on enemy activities on the east bank of the Delaware. Thus it was with a certain confidence that Washington asked Dickinson to rally his forces and link up with Maxwell.[60]

The New Jersey officer already had some men in the field, and he quickly went to work raising more. To assist in the mobilization, the *New-Jersey Gazette* notified all militiamen "to be particularly attentive to signals, as a movement of the enemy is soon expected." Following this alert, Dickinson asked Governor Livingston, whom Washington had contacted independently, to call out all of New Jersey's citizen-soldiers. The governor declined this extreme step, which would have left the rest of the state defenseless. He had to worry about British raids from the New York area, and many militia from the extreme northern and southern counties were too far away to respond effectively anyway. In addition, many units were in the process of drafting men for the Continental regiments, which delayed their availability for militia duty. Still, faced with what looked like eminent invasion, on 16 June Livingston called up half the local forces, ordering them to join those already with Dickinson.[61]

Sensing the urgency of the situation, the militia began turning out. While no rush to the colors, the citizen-soldiers moved into action in respectable numbers. By the time Clinton began his march, Dickinson commanded a thousand men, a number that would slowly increase.[62] No doubt the militia general wished for greater numbers. Yet there was a qualitative difference between these troops and those raised during the first years of the war. After two years of conflict, the New Jersey militia had seen considerable duty and were no longer the raw and unsteady force that had dissolved before the British onslaught of 1776. A core of the militia force consisted of genuinely seasoned campaigners, many of them having served repeated tours of duty as substitutes for their more reluctant neighbors.[63] Thus if the mobilization was far from perfect, in 1778 the state marshaled its military resources with relative efficiency, and the militia appeared ready to make a fight of it when Clinton made his move.

There is another point to consider. Washington's efforts to rebuild the Continental Army, and his personal trials with patriot radicals, have properly received considerable attention from historians. But the events of early 1778 in New Jersey and Washington's close relationship with Dickinson (and, for that matter, with several other senior militia officers, including Dickinson's cousin Cadwalader) point to a less appreciated yet critical aspect of the war. Washington's distaste for militia as a primary arm of the war effort is well documented, as is his preference for regular troops. Yet without being explicit on the point, at some juncture the general made certain assumptions about who should perform what military roles during the war. In his view the Continentals would be the force in being, always the main threat to the British; they would also do the bulk of the heavy fighting. As James Kirby Martin has emphasized, the regulars also would represent the legitimacy of American claims to independence to the world—something part-time soldiers, who would fade away facing British professionals, could never do.[64] But the Continentals were too few to occupy large swaths of territory and offer protection to local populations or even to undertake a range of local military tasks. Washington came to expect militia to handle these missions. Local forces would police the interior, cowing tories and providing muscle for local whig authorities; guard prisoners and stores; gather intelligence; conduct raids and harass enemy movements; build fortifications; and the like. Under favorable circumstances and backed by Continentals, they could fight in larger actions. In general, these roles lacked the drama of standup confrontations with the enemy line, but they nevertheless were essential, and Washington knew it. Competent militia officers such as Dickinson made these things happen—thus the commander in chief's appreciation of and dependence on them.

Dickinson earned Washington's respect through his effective work with Continental officers. When detached to New Jersey, Colonel Shreve and Brigadier General Maxwell dealt routinely with the militia general, trading intelligence, handling prisoners, shadowing British units on the Jersey side of the Delaware, and receiving enemy deserters. The regulars and militia cooperated in scouting and skirmishing operations. There was no major fighting, but both sides inflicted casualties.[65] The Continental officers often routed their intelligence to Washington through Dickinson; indeed, Washington also used Dickinson as a conduit to Maxwell and Shreve. On 15 June he asked Dickinson to inform Maxwell that the brigadier was "to keep his small parties close upon the enemy in order to discover their first motions and course" and to report anything he learned immediately.[66] As the British gathered their forces on the New Jersey banks of the Delaware, Captain Ewald noted that the tempo had picked up. His pickets were skirmishing "constantly" as patriot militia "received us with sharp rifle fire" and Washington's regulars "hung on our rear guard. The skirmishing continued without letup."[67] The New Jersey militia and the Continentals were learning to work together.

Historian Thomas M. Huber has called this "compound warfare," the "phenomenon of regular and irregular forces fighting in concert." The trick for a commander was to mobilize "the synergistic effects of conventional and irregular operations" as a coherent strategy.[68] The Continental Line forced the British to concentrate their resources in opposition, thus leaving the patriot militia room to operate. Active militia operations, however, compelled them to disperse their forces, which otherwise could have concentrated to confront Washington's regulars. If the redcoats went in force after the Continental Army, they then left the countryside open to the irregulars. Yet if a commander scattered his forces chasing militia, those detachments were prey to concentrated American regulars. The British never had the numbers to face both threats. Whether Washington pursued this regular-irregular brand of war by design or through serendipity is a matter of debate, but he did so routinely.[69] In New Jersey he would employ it in his pursuit of Clinton, who would have to deal with it as the pursued.

Evacuation and Response

In mid-June General Clinton readied his men for the move into New Jersey. It would be a phased withdrawal, with the army moving in stages to positions on the east side of the Delaware. By mid-May the general already had a loyalist battalion at Billingsport and had posted two regular regiments and two small loyalist units at Cooper's Ferry to protect woodcutters. When Maxwell and the rest of the New Jersey Brigade crossed the river, Clinton sent three more regiments across to protect his eastern footholds. In aggregate these forces totaled only slightly more than 2,000 men, but they would soon receive plenty of company. Knowing that he could not linger in New Jersey, Clinton also sought intelligence on regional road networks. He sent John Hills, a British engineer, over the Delaware to scout the area. It was a dangerous mission, as Hills had to avoid detection while making observations and taking notes; at best he had only a few light horse with him for protection. Upon his return to Philadelphia, he drew up a series of maps for the general.[70] In addition to Hills's maps, Clinton knew that he could also rely on tory guides, but he made it his business to know as much as he could about where he was going before sending his army into the state.

Activity intensified during the second week of June. Beginning 12 June the British began to move horses, wagons, and provisions to Cooper's Ferry. On the fifteenth the first major troop movements commenced. Later that day Stirn's and Loo's Hessian brigades crossed to Cooper's Ferry and marched about two and a half miles toward Haddonfield to secure the area.[71] On the sixteenth the last field artillery and the 17th Light Dragoons crossed along with more wagons and almost all of the remaining horses. The following day another three thousand men disembarked at Cooper's Ferry—the jaegers, Queen's American Rangers, Hessian grenadiers, and the last of the provincials. Directed by Lieutenant General Knyphausen, they marched almost to Haddonfield. Also shipped across the river were the packs of the troops remaining in Philadelphia. Thus in just four days, the British army and the Royal Navy had moved two regiments of light dragoons and the equivalent of ten brigades of infantry across the Delaware—about 11,000 men. It was no mean logistical feat, and it did not go unnoticed. "A Gentleman of Reputation who lives near Philada," General Dickinson reported to Washington, "sent me word last Evening, that the Enemy were very industrious, in transporting their Troops, Artillery, & Waggons, over to Coopers Ferry. The Intelligence comes so many different ways, & so well authenticated, that it does not admit of a doubt."[72]

When finally assembled, the baggage train consisted of some five thousand horses and fifteen hundred wagons, which at times stretched out twelve miles on the march. The horses had their work cut out for them. The wagons fairly bulged with food and forage for six weeks, army supplies and equipment, and the private soldiers' baggage and tents. Clinton rued his decision to allow the men to pack so many personal belongings, but he was fully determined to bring his train safely to New York. He assigned the thoroughly competent Knyphausen to get the wagons safely as far as Haddonfield. (After that the train divided between the two main columns of march until the army reached Monmouth Court House.) Working feverishly, the baron had the train organized and ready to roll before sunup on the eighteenth.

Clinton himself was still in Philadelphia. Late in the afternoon of the seventeenth, the royal commander marched the remaining troops (except the 33rd Regiment and a few small units left to police the city) to Captain Montresor's defensive works. They would serve as a rear guard in case the Americans made an effort to disrupt the evacuation. The men lay on their arms until early morning when, before daybreak, the 1st and 2nd Brigades filed out, marching west of the city to Gloucester Point. This was much farther than the city's ferry landings, but the low, level farmland would give no rebel assailants protection from the covering 24-pounders of HMS *Vigilant.*[73] At daybreak the 3rd and 4th Brigades followed and quickly behind them came the best troops of the British army, the battalions of grenadiers and light infantry. Included in the mix were at least some of the 16th Light Dragoons as well as the horses of Generals Grant, Cornwallis, Clinton, and their aides. By 9:00 A.M. all troops—about 11,000 men—had landed in New Jersey at Gloucester Town. It was a masterful evacuation, a revealing demonstration of what a professional military could do.

With the army in New Jersey, the last transports and men-of-war dropped downriver several hours later. Unknown to Clinton, the transports had lost a number of passengers. Unwilling to sail without their men, an unknown number of women had slipped ashore to join their consorts and husbands among the troops; they would march with the army.[74] Everyone else onboard watched Philadelphia recede into the distance as the ships sailed to rendezvous with the waiting fleet, after which over two hundred vessels made sail for New York. The King's army was gone, and Philadelphia, the only real prize of British arms in 1777, quite peacefully had become an American city once more.[75]

In and around the newly unoccupied city, word of the British departure spread quickly. Citizens who only days before had given no credit to "strange rumors about the British leaving" now found the streets empty of redcoats. "This Morn'g when we rose," wrote

Elizabeth Drinker, "there was not one Red-Coat to be seen in town." American patrols moved in cautiously to verify the reports, scooping up British stragglers as they probed through the city to the banks of the Delaware. According to Carl Baurmeister, among these captives were "a few British officers and their servants, who . . . were found in the houses of their tender acquaintances and taken prisoners."[76] Couriers rushed news of the evacuation to York, where delegates to Congress filled their letters to friends and relatives with happy reports of the event. Most began to pack for a return to Philadelphia even as they wondered what would happen next. And they *were* wondering, for few of them assumed that Washington would let Clinton go without trying to land a punch. Word of the enemy evacuation was coupled with speculation over the possibility of battle; there was no mistaking the excitement in the air.[77]

At Valley Forge word of the withdrawal met a mixed response of joy and caution. Despite some questions, there was no real concern that the enemy movement was a ruse, and Washington realized that, at last, he faced the prospect of chasing a retreating Clinton. Yet exactly what to do remained a question. He took two steps. In orders of 17 June he put his officers on notice: the army was going to move, and everyone should be prepared to break camp the following day. At this point Washington was still unsure of the route Clinton would take across New Jersey, but for the time being he thought it best to direct his troops across northern New Jersey and on to Newburgh, New York, on the Hudson River. He established an order of march that called for Major General Lee to move on 18 June, taking a vanguard of three brigades to cross into New Jersey at Coryell's Ferry (modern Lambertville). The plan called for the rest of the army to follow over the next two days, with divisions crossing at Coryell's Ferry, Sherard's Ferry (now Frenchtown, New Jersey), and Easton, Pennsylvania. Washington assumed that Clinton would head for South Amboy and instructed Lee to stop with the vanguard on the first good ground he found after his crossing. Lee was then to await further orders unless he learned that Clinton had indeed taken route to South Amboy, in which case he was to continue his march to the Hudson.[78]

With these orders issued, the patriot commander in chief convened yet another council of war. Frankly, one wonders why the general waited so long. For days he had all but known that Clinton was pulling out, and for weeks he had strongly suspected such a development. Even lacking specific information on what his adversary was going to do, there was enough intelligence to make some informed guesses about appropriate responses. Yet the British move still caught him and his senior officers without any consensus on how to respond. Be that as it may, faced with the prospect of immediate active operations, Washington again put several questions to his generals.

These were disconcerting questions. First, he wanted opinions on whether the Continentals should attack Philadelphia while the British were evacuating. The second query posited staying in Valley Forge until the British were gone or moving "immediately towards the Delaware." Washington also asked about reinforcing Maxwell and the New Jersey militia on the chance they might give the enemy some "material interruption." Or assuming the British would head for Amboy, should the rebels march to the North (Hudson) River to secure communications "between the Eastern and Southern states?" In addition, he wanted their thinking on how to deal with the camp's sick and wounded and on what to do with army supplies when and if the troops marched out. Finally, he asked them what to do if the army overtook Clinton on his march. Should the Continentals attack? If so, should they try to land a partial blow or bring on a general engagement?[79] All of this was a great deal to consider with an enemy already on the move.

If Washington was hoping for decisive advice, he was disappointed. Fifteen generals attended the council, and all of them, plus two others, responded in writing by the next day. Most of the answers were equivocal, and much of the caution voiced in the May council remained. No one wanted to move against Philadelphia during Clinton's withdrawal; several insisted that any British rear guard would make an attack too costly. But this question was already moot, for Clinton had his entire force into New Jersey the next day (18 June), before the officers even had a chance to respond. There was some sentiment for reinforcing Maxwell and hoping his New Jersey Brigade and the militia could cause some damage. Steuben was willing to send a detachment to northern New Jersey, with the rest of the army eventually moving to the high ground at Middlebrook, north of New Brunswick. Only Greene favored an immediate move to the Delaware to watch events. The prevailing view was that the Continentals, or at least the largest part of them, should remain at Valley Forge until Clinton's departure from

Philadelphia was confirmed and his intentions became clear. After that, a move to the Hudson River had broad support. Yet there was some feeling, notably on the part of Charles Lee, recently exchanged after sixteen months as a prisoner of war, that Clinton might not be planning a New Jersey march after all. Indeed, Lee already had written to Washington (on 15 June) that he thought the campaign would likely open in Pennsylvania or even in Delaware and Maryland.[80] There was also speculation that Clinton would march down the New Jersey side of the river and then embark on navy transports; even Washington was unwilling to rule out this possibility.[81]

On only one question did the council approach unanimity. A large majority of the generals—fifteen of the seventeen—opposed bringing on a general engagement. Knox noted the "general sentiment [of the council] that it would be the most criminal degree of madness to hazard a general action."[82] Lee strongly agreed, convinced that the Continental regiments were still no match for British regulars. Greene was willing to fight, though only under favorable circumstances, and even he saw no sense in provoking a general action.[83] No one imagined ending the war with a single bold stroke in New Jersey.

Almost no one, that is, because two officers *did* urge Washington to attempt a showdown with Clinton. Unsurprisingly, one was the ever-aggressive Anthony Wayne. He wanted the army to move quickly, carrying only essentials, and "take the first *favourable* Opportunity to strike the Enemy with Advantage." If the attack failed, Wayne discounted any effective pursuit by Clinton, plausibly arguing that the enemy general would be too burdened by his enormous baggage train to follow up any victory. He also was confident that the British soldiers would not be at their best, knowing they were retreating. On the other hand, an offensive would animate the patriot troops, and "we may Inculcate the Idea of Burgoyning Clinton . . . and you will more than probable Effect it."[84] This was Brigadier General Wayne at his most optimistic and romantic.

The other optimist was Major General John Cadwalader of the Pennsylvania militia. Cadwalader, a native of Trenton, New Jersey, moved with his family to Philadelphia in 1750. He and his brother established a successful mercantile business, and John took an early stance against imperial taxation policies. His whig activities brought him election as commander of the local volunteer militia. Over the course of the war, Cadwalader did as well as anyone in organizing and leading the often truculent and unpredictable Pennsylvania and Maryland militia. In 1776 only bad weather prevented him from crossing the Delaware as part of Washington's attack on Trenton, though he did fight at Princeton. Cadwalader stood firmly in the commander in chief's corner as criticisms of Washington's leadership mounted in late 1777 and early 1778. He twice declined offers of a Continental commission, preferring to stay with the Pennsylvanians.[85] Washington trusted him and valued his opinion, although the memorandum he received from the Pennsylvania general on 18 June may have surprised him.

Cadwalader's response was not only lengthy but also revealed an appreciation of the relationships between war in the field and domestic and international politics. Indeed, it was as much a political treatise as an estimate of the military situation, and no response from the other generals matched it in sophistication. Cadwalader urged Washington to pursue Clinton into New Jersey and bring him to battle. That combat, the Pennsylvanian argued, should be a general engagement in which the rebel army threw in everything it had. This was no quest for glory, and Cadwalader had no illusions about "Burgoyning" Clinton. Rather, he was convinced that the numbers and new discipline of the Continental Army offered the best chance patriots would ever have to "strike a decisive Blow." Moreover, in striking that blow, winning or losing was not the point. Even if the Continentals lost in a major action, Clinton would gain nothing; the general would be unable to subsist his army in the New Jersey interior. Cadwalader then proceeded to the heart of his argument. A victory for Clinton, if not actually a patriot disaster,

> might in their present Situation, prove very injurious—when we consider their Strength & without any Expectation of Reinforcements; & when we consider the Situation of their affairs in Europe—after considering all Circumstances relating to the War in America—the most important of which are, the great Reduction of their Force by frequent Actions, Defeats, Desertions, Captures & other Casualties; the immense Sum of money already expended, the little Territory acquired after a three years war; the Idea of Conquest extinguished even in the minds of the Ministry; the fall of Stocks & the injury done in other respects to public Credit; the difficulty of raising Troops throughout the Kingdom; the American War very unpopular in England & Ireland, & lastly the acknowledgment of the Independance of these united States by France &

> the Treaty entered into with that Nation—I am enduced to believe, I say, from all these Circumstances that their whole Force now in America will be drawn from these united States for the Defence of Canada, their W. India Islands & their Dominions nearer Home—Possessed of this opinion it appears to me we have every thing to hope & nothing to fear—A Defeat of our Army will be no essential disadvantage to us & cannot in the least serve their Cause.[86]

Cadwalader had virtually spelled out the British government's reasons for abandoning Philadelphia; Lord North could have put the case no better. The Pennsylvanian had given a plausible rationale for a bold offensive—probably too bold for Washington and certainly too bold for his brother officers.

Thus, with the exceptions of Wayne and the more thoughtful Cadwalader, it was a generally cautious and somewhat divided rebel command that learned of the full British withdrawal on the morning of the eighteenth. Confirmation reached Washington at about 11:30 A.M., and he found himself forced to act without his generals in concert and without a specific plan.[87] Given the timing of events, it is doubtful he even had a chance to fully consider the advice of his generals before deciding what to do. But events were now in motion, and remaining inert was not an option. Besides, the general now believed that he understood the situation: Clinton was virtually gone, and it was evident that he was going to march through New Jersey, even if his precise route and destination were unknown. Probably immediately after receiving confirmation of Clinton's final departure, Washington made a decision: The Continental Army would not march to the Hudson River, it would pursue the British. Seemingly in a more aggressive frame of mind than most of his generals, there is little doubt that Washington at least wanted to move within striking distance of Clinton—perhaps he had read Cadwalader's letter, or at least Greene's. In any event, the indecision of the last couple of weeks was gone, and the voluminous jottings of the council of war suddenly were rendered moot. Washington explained to Henry Laurens that he still was unsure of Clinton's route, but nevertheless the Continental Army "shall proceed towards Jersey & govern ourselves according to circumstances."[88]

If the Americans were going to catch the British, they had to move immediately. Nor could they waste time marching to three separate crossings on the Delaware. Washington abandoned any thoughts of moving to Easton or Sherard's Ferry; instead, he ordered the entire army toward Coryell's Ferry. This made sense: Coryell's was the southernmost of the three ferries and offered the shortest route to Clinton's possible lines of march. There were also concentrations of supplies and transport there, and a single crossing point would allow the army to concentrate quickly. Lee was to take the vanguard of three brigades out of Valley Forge at 3:00 P.M. on 18 June; Wayne would march two hours later with three Pennsylvania brigades; and the rest of the army would follow at 5:00 A.M. on the nineteenth. Both Lee and Wayne had orders to halt on "the first strong ground" beyond Coryell's and await further orders, or if Clinton had already gone too far toward Amboy or somewhere lower on the New Jersey coast, they were to proceed to the Hudson.[89]

While his officers prepared the troops to march, there were other matters for the commander in chief to consider. He issued orders placing Major General Benedict Arnold in command of a reoccupied Philadelphia and sent him Colonel Henry Jackson's detachment in support. Intelligence communications from Dickinson and other sources continued to reach Valley Forge, and Washington did his best to keep his subordinates informed of developments in New Jersey. He pressed his officers on matters of supply, dealt with routine courts-martial, kept in touch with Congress, and sent a dispatch to Gates, in command at Peekskill, on the Hudson, informing him of Clinton's movements and his own intentions.[90] On 18 June alone Washington sent or received forty-two communications (that have survived), and it is clear the pace at all levels at Valley Forge was near frantic.

With Lee and Wayne already in motion and hoping that Maxwell and the militia would slow the British enough for the Continentals to come up, Washington put the main army on the move. As scheduled, the troops broke camp before sunrise on Friday, 19 June. It rained for most of the day, but the departure from Valley Forge went relatively smoothly, testimony to the restored efficiency of the Continental Line. After camping for a night in Pennsylvania, Lee and Wayne completed their crossing into New Jersey on the twentieth. Washington, with the main body, stopped for the night near Buckingham, Pennsylvania, some two-thirds of the way to Coryell's. The troops were wet—drenched, actually—and tired, but morale was high, no doubt helped when the general ordered "a Gill of spirits" for each man.[91] Thus fortified, the army crossed into New Jersey over the next two days. The chase was on.

CHAPTER 5

The Matter of Major General Charles Lee

With the exception of Washington himself, no single individual was more central to the events surrounding the Monmouth campaign than the man who led the Continental vanguard out of Valley Forge on 18 June—Major General Charles Lee. He was a special case in the army. One of the Revolutionary generation's most complex figures, Lee was by turns erratic, vain, opinionated, quarrelsome, and even crude. But he was also intelligent, personally brave, scholarly, an able writer, and politically interesting—and because of a persistent inability to control his temper, his tongue, and his pen, he was his own worst enemy. His presence with the army would lend a complicating factor to Washington's campaign, sending it in directions no one could have predicted, and make the historical legacy of the Continental Army's second-ranking officer one of never-ending controversy. All of this has colored our views of Charles Lee. He has been tarred by his friendships with Washington's detractors, by a nineteenth-century revelation of supposedly treasonable correspondence while a prisoner of war, and by his court-martial. But in the spring of 1778 he commanded the respect of much of the officer corps; his views carried weight. That being the case, his relationship with General Washington before Monmouth requires some attention.

A Complex and Difficult Man

Charles Lee was born in 1732 near the city of Chester, Cheshire, in west-central England.[1] The Lee family was middling gentry of distinguished ancestry but of moderate economic status. Charles's father was Colonel John Lee, and his mother, Isabella Bunbury, was the daughter of Sir Henry Bunbury, baronet. Aside from his title, Sir Henry was a man of considerable influence: he variously sat in

Parliament, served as high sheriff of Cheshire, and was commissioner of the revenue for Ireland.[2] Charles had a difficult youth. He and his elder sister, Sidney, with whom he remained close throughout his life, were the only two of seven siblings to survive childhood, and his mother never warmed to her only remaining son. He grew into an ungainly and, in his own view, physically unattractive youth without the social graces normally associated with the English gentry. Charles seemed more attached to his dogs than to most people. Still, as the son of a family with political connections, he began life with considerable advantages. He was well educated, attending school locally at first, then in Switzerland, where he learned French, Greek, Latin, and Italian; in 1746 he enrolled in the famous grammar school in Bury St. Edmunds, Suffolk. Lee proved intellectually curious and developed a lifelong passion for reading. He loved the classics, especially Plutarch; was well versed in military history; read Shakespeare avidly; and became a devotee of the radical works of Jean-Jacques Rousseau. The future general was a man of the Enlightenment, comfortable in the realm of ideas.

Given his father's occupation and the fact that other relatives were army officers, Lee may have decided early on a military career. In any event, it began while he was still at Bury St. Edmunds, when Colonel Lee purchased his son an ensign's commission in the 55th Regiment of Foot, which the elder Lee commanded. It was one of the first ironies of the future patriot general's career (there would be others): in 1751 the 55th was renumbered as the 44th Regiment, which later would fight at Monmouth Court House.[3] In 1748 Ensign Lee reported to his regiment in Ireland. There he purchased a lieutenancy, and in 1754 he sailed for America when the 44th deployed for what became the French and Indian War. Lee saw rugged duty there. In 1755 his regiment was badly cut up during Major General Edward Braddock's disastrous defeat at Monongahela. Lee also served at Louisbourg (1757); Fort Ticonderoga (1758), where he was seriously wounded; Fort Niagara (1759); and the fall of Montreal. Finally, he commanded a mission west of Fort Pitt (1760). By this time Lee was a captain, a battle-hardened veteran with a service record the envy of any professional soldier.

When not on campaign at this time, Lee remained active. America fascinated him: he enjoyed the towns and the scenery awed him. He indulged his love of books. Lee briefly took a Seneca consort (whose name has been lost to history) who bore him twins; the

Indians called him Ounewaterika, a loose translation of which is "boiling water, or one whose spirit never sleeps."[4] If the Indian moniker derived from a reading of the officer's personality, he was aptly named, for Lee had emerged as a complex and volatile individual. He could be brusque, difficult, and arrogant, yet generous and genial with friends and those who agreed with him. Lee thought nothing of castigating what he considered the foibles of senior officers, and he cared little that his views became known. He quarreled with his regimental officers, and an army surgeon actually tried to kill him. John Alden, one of Lee's principal biographers, had it right when he noted that the captain developed a well-deserved reputation for "pugnacity and hotheadedness."[5] In 1760, when he sailed for home, Lee certainly ranked as one of the most—if not *the* most—unconventional junior officers in the army.

Upon his return to Great Britain, Lee sought promotion to major. He petitioned the King directly and had influential friends importune George III in his behalf. But promotion was slow in coming, no doubt in part because his acid pen had irritated too many ranking officers. Lee finally advanced when he transferred to the new 103rd Regiment of Foot. In 1762 the young major accompanied his command to Portugal, a British ally, to resist a Spanish-French invasion. It was here he met Brigadier General John Burgoyne. On 7 October Burgoyne gave him command of a mixed British-Portuguese detachment, including fifty men of the 16th Light Dragoons. In a daring night attack, Lee routed the Spanish at the Battle of Vila Vehla, an action that effectively stymied the invasion. (Lee would meet the 16th again during the War for Independence.) In gratitude for his service, the Portuguese made him a colonel, yet the campaign was Lee's last as a redcoat. In 1763, with the end of the Seven Years' War, the 103rd Regiment was disbanded and Lee retired on half-pay.[6]

With no place on the British roster, in 1764 the major sought opportunities in Europe. For the next eight years, Lee led the life of a gentleman adventurer and military vagabond. He spent much of his time in the service of King Stanislaus Poniatowski of Poland; the Englishman saw no fighting, but he was a friend and aide-de-camp to the king, who made him a major general in the Polish army. Lee's travels, for Stanislaus and otherwise, took him far afield. Among many stops along the way, his itinerary included Constantinople, the Russo-Turkish War of 1768–74 (he was an observer with the Russian army), Hungary, Austria, Italy (where he killed a man in a duel), and France. As he wandered through Europe, he endured a series of health problems and was prone to gout. His journeys also included periodic visits to England, where he vainly continued to seek a place in a British regiment. Lee was nothing if not well traveled.

His final return to Great Britain proved unhappy. Despite all entreaties, Lee found no place in the army, although in 1772 he was promoted to lieutenant colonel on the inactive list. His failure to advance left him bitter, and he allowed his resentment to overrule his judgment. Lee's political views only exacerbated his lack of self-control. Since the 1760s he had identified with Britain's liberal whigs, admired English radical John Wilkes, and had publicly approved of colonial resistance to the Stamp Act. Lee was openly pro-American. Hardly a republican, he did have private doubts about the wisdom of monarchy. In 1770, however, his politics blended with his frustrations. Furious that the King had not advanced his career—and George III had made promises—Lee published a biting satire of the monarch. It was hardly an act of a man hoping for preferment. Burgoyne, who had maintained "a certain style of friendship" with Lee since their service in Portugal, saw this inability to control his temper and his opinions as the major impediment to Lee's efforts to get back into active service. "His disappointments in preferment," he told Lord North, "arose from the indiscretion of his discourse and writings, which had not been bounded to Ministers, but had been daringly and unjustly leveled at the King himself."[7] In the land of his birth, Lee's career was finished.

Like many Englishmen with dimmed expectations at home, Lieutenant Colonel Lee (retired) looked to the New World for relief. He was not impoverished and had the means to make a new beginning. He briefly considered Bermuda, but in 1773 he chose America. The following year he purchased an estate of some three thousand acres with a modest house near the modern town of Leeville (named in his honor) in what is now West Virginia, renaming the estate Prato Verde (now called Prato Rio); he had found the property through the advice of an old army friend, Horatio Gates, who also had settled in Virginia.[8] Lee quickly made influential friends (or at least acquaintances), including Richard Henry Lee, George Mason, Thomas Jefferson, George Washington, and William Byrd and his son Otway, his future aide in the Continental Army. When he wanted, Lee could be good company; many Americans found the transplanted Englishman, with his grasp of ideas, radical sympathies, and well-traveled background, a fascinating character. Indeed, as historian Phillip Papas has observed, when Lee joined the patriot cause he was "perhaps the most cosmopolitan of the revolutionaries. No other American revolutionary, except maybe Benjamin Franklin, was as worldly as Lee."[9]

Lee was indeed a revolutionary. He quickly identified with the rising colonial resistance to Great Britain, and as the imperial crisis deepened, his was one of the earliest voices to call for the strongest possible measures against the mother country. In speeches, letters, and publications he denounced moderation, becoming among the first patriots to call for outright independence. In fact, Lee was something of a zealot.[10] No doubt some of this depth of feeling derived from the bitterness he still felt toward those who, in his eyes, had unjustly thwarted his advancement in the British army. Horace Walpole, ever the man with a pithy observation, was sure this was the case: "Lee was a gallant adventurer whom George 3d disgusted by an absolute breach of promise, and drove into the service of the colonies."[11] But Walpole was wrong. Lee's radicalism was sincere; his views were too consistent over time to admit of mere opportunism in his new country.[12]

After Lexington and Concord, Lee's rise in the patriot military is well known. His credentials as a patriot and accomplished soldier justifiably impressed Congress. The delegates commissioned him a major general, ranking only behind Washington and Artemus Ward. With Ward's subsequent resignation, Lee became second in command of Continental forces. There is reason to believe that he thought he deserved the chief command, but he largely held his peace and did well during the first eighteen months of the conflict. Lee worked capably with Washington around Boston, where he tried to reestablish contact with Burgoyne, then trapped in the city with the rest of the British. Nothing came of the effort, for Burgoyne now considered his former subordinate an "incendiary" driven by vanity.[13] After the siege of Boston, Washington sent Lee to Virginia and South Carolina, where he helped frustrate a British effort to take Charleston. He arrived in New York in time to assist in the losing defense of that city, although he was instrumental in staving off complete disaster on Long Island. After the Battle of White Plains, Washington left Lee in command of a detachment near the battlefield while the commander in chief led the main army on its retreat across New Jersey.

At this point Lee's volatility asserted itself. Critical of Washington's leadership—and the commanding general had made his share of mistakes—Lee unburdened himself in his now-famous letters to Joseph Reed and Gates. Those were private letters, and while Washington was aware of the one to Reed, they had no effect on operations (as discussed in chapter 1).[14] But in his intemperance, Lee crossed the line between criticism and insubordination. In early December, with his army moving toward the Delaware River, Washington urged his subordinate to join him as quickly as possible. Lee delayed, and when his commander sent preemptory orders to move, he refused to hasten—that is, he disobeyed.[15] Lee had a case: He was convinced that Howe was not going to drive on Philadelphia, as Washington feared, but would stop for the winter in New Jersey. Lee wanted to remain in New Jersey to rally the militia, then fall on Howe's rear.[16] That events proved him right—the British did stop, and the militia did rally—was no excuse for not following direct orders. Washington, trying to assemble enough men to hold his army together, was bewildered by the conduct of his principal subordinate. At this point, the last thing the patriot army needed was a showdown between its two senior officers.

Fate spared the patriots that trauma; in fact, the saving event was deus ex machina. On the evening of 12 December, with his troops encamped just west of Morristown, Lee rode some three miles to White's Tavern, near Basking Ridge. There he spent the night, attended only by a small guard (some accounts have insinuated that he was also attended by the Widow White, but the story is likely a calumny).[17] The next morning a mounted British reconnaissance patrol fortuitously learned of the general's presence and closed in on the tavern. Lee had no chance to escape. The horsemen were from none other than the 16th Light Dragoons, a detachment of which Lee had led to victory in Portugal.[18] War is riven with coincidence and irony, and it is doubtful this was lost on Lee as the dragoons led him away, supposedly in his nightshirt, a prisoner of war.

The Captive General

Lee was a prisoner for almost sixteen months, from mid-December 1776 to early April 1778, when he was freed on parole. He was effectively away from the army until mid-May.[19] Yet even in captivity he managed to be at the center of his share of drama. His capture delighted the British and alarmed patriots, who considered Lee a hero and feared the loss of his leadership. There was concern for his safety, and with cause. The British saw Lee as a half-pay officer taken in arms against the King—that was treason, a capital offense. The British sent him to New York in close confinement, but his circumstances improved. Congress demanded that Lee be accorded the status of a prisoner of war with the respect normally shown senior officers, failing which British and German prisoners in patriot hands would pay the price. Washington supported this position.[20] Howe relented, and Lee found himself comfortably accommodated, much of the time aboard HMS *Centurion* in New York harbor. He was even allowed to bring up his servant from Prato Verde and keep one of his beloved dogs, and he met occasional guests for tea.[21] Eventually, he was allowed the liberty of the city. It was a captive existence a world apart from the American enlisted prisoners and junior officers penned relatively nearby—and dying by the thousands—on the rotting prison hulks.[22]

His captors also allowed him pen and paper, a particular joy for Lee. The general's former aide-de-camp, Otway Byrd, knew how important this was, and once told him, "I know you would rather write than be idle."[23] Indeed, Lee could not stand to be idle, and he wrote frequently. He penned letters to Congress, Washington, and friends about his treatment in New York, about the possibility of exchange, and about offering himself as a go-between for peace negotiations (nothing came of that idea); to his sister, Sidney, assuring her of his well-being; to Robert Morris on his finances; and to others on various subjects. He wrote to his servant, Guiseppi Minghini, asking him to visit immediately and to bring fresh clothing as well as "Ainsworth's Dictionary & the six French books, l'histoire politique—if any of the Dogs are with you bring them."[24]

But Lee's most unusual missive—*extraordinary* is a better adjective—never reached patriot eyes. In the mid-1850s George H. Moore, the librarian at the New-York Historical Society, found a Lee manuscript dated 29 March 1777. The general had addressed the document to the "Royal Commissioners"—that is, to Lord Richard and Sir William Howe—and in it he described how the British supposedly could defeat the Revolution. The essential plan offered in this lengthy piece called for the Royal Navy to seal off a line of American ports stretching from Annapolis, Maryland, to Newport,

Rhode Island. Control of this line, Lee claimed, would encourage the loyalists to rise and end the rebellion in two months.[25] In 1858 Moore presented his findings in a paper, "The Treason of Charles Lee," the title of which sums up Moore's conclusions.[26] For decades, his findings colored prevailing views of Lee, although most modern scholars have dismissed any notions of treason. There is no evidence to suggest anyone took the plan seriously, or even any indication of who might have seen it—no British military or civil official mentioned it during or after the war. But the question remains: Why did Lee write such a document? John Alden has conjectured that it was a ruse, with Lee intending to send Sir William on his (eventually) pointless campaign into Pennsylvania. But John Shy may have hit closer to the mark: Lee did it "perhaps simply to become a participant again instead of a bystander."[27] And perhaps the Iroquois were closer still—maybe it was all another manifestation of the one "whose spirits are never asleep."

Of course, had Congress or any credible rebel source learned of the document, there is no question they would have considered the captive general a traitor. But none ever did, and the patriot concern for Lee was about getting him back. After months of wrangling, both sides agreed to a prisoner exchange. The British would recover Brigadier General Richard Prescott in exchange for General Lee. In anticipation of the transaction, the British sent Lee to Philadelphia, where he spent some cordial time with Sir William and other British officers, including Lieutenant Colonel Harcourt (Lee would meet Harcourt again, less cordially, at Monmouth). While the prisoner-exchange commissioners worked on final parole details, Lee inadvertently demonstrated how distant he had become from political realities. He again volunteered to act as go-between in peace negotiations with the Americans, even proposing terms. Howe showed some initial interest, but nothing came of the matter, while the blunt patriot refusal to deal with the Carlisle Commission the following month revealed how completely rebel sentiments had bypassed Lee. On 5 April he was released on parole. The major general was still technically a prisoner of war and so could not return to duty, but as long as he did nothing "contrary to the interest of his Majesty or his government," Lee was a free man.[28]

Paroled and Reproved

Lee's release from captivity was the first step on a path to professional oblivion and personal trauma. Things went wrong quickly, although Lee did not seem to notice. In fact, that was the problem: General Lee had little sense of how much things had changed since his capture in late 1776. He had missed the political attacks on Washington, the reformation and retraining of the army at Valley Forge, the new personnel in the "family" of the commander in chief, and the rise to prominence of such men as Lafayette, Steuben, Greene, and the combative Wayne. Significantly, he also missed the central importance many patriots in and out of the military now placed on the performance of the Continental Army and failed to appreciate the hunger and impatience for victory in the field. In short, the man lacked "situational awareness," or to use a modern military definition: "the ability to identify, process, and comprehend the critical elements of information about what is happening. . . . More simply, it's *knowing what is going on around you.*"[29] As to that, Lee seemed at a complete loss.

From this general problem, specifics accumulated. No one issue or action on Lee's part was necessarily worse than another, but in the critical weeks before the march from Valley Forge, his conduct was problematic on several counts—political, military, and personal.

Shortly before his release, Lee corresponded with Washington, who gave assurances that he was anxious to have his fellow Virginian back. The commander in chief's expressions of good will were sincere. If Washington held any hard feelings from 1776, he buried them; with a new campaign imminent, it was no time for discord. On 5 April, when Lee rode into Valley Forge, Lieutenant Colonel Richard Kidder Meade of the commander's staff met him with an honor guard of horse. That evening Lee dined with Washington, Martha Washington, and many ranking officers; the army generally seemed glad of his return.[30] In this cordial atmosphere the general, still barred from returning to active duty, left to visit York; from there, he wanted to go home briefly to Prato Verde. It was on this trip that the trouble started.

On the political front, Lee was especially obtuse. His inability to sense new political realities surfaced almost immediately. Apparently unaware of the extent of the criticisms Washington had endured earlier in the year—or not caring—Lee was again indiscreet.

Just before leaving camp he met with Elias Boudinot, a Washington loyalist and, as commissary general of prisoners, the man instrumental in the exchange negotiations that had freed him. He supposedly told Boudinot that "he found the Army in a worse situation than he expected and that General Washington was not fit to command a sergeant's guard."[31] This may be apocryphal, as Boudinot had come to loath the major general. But in York (either on his journey to or from Virginia) the note of discord continued. Lee met or corresponded with friends and members of Congress, probably including his own partisans Richard Henry Lee, Thomas Burke, and others.[32] Indeed, on 9 April, the very day Lee reached York, Burke wrote a long letter to North Carolina governor Richard Caswell. "We are many of us [in Congress] persuaded," Burke informed the governor, "that some Officers in the Army wish not for the release of General Lee because his enterprising disposition and martial genius will be a strong contrast to their want of both."[33] It is impossible to know (short of some new evidence surfacing) if the general was aware of or had a hand in the communication, but it has a Lee ring to it.

Lee did meet with President Henry Laurens, although the conversation left Laurens uneasy. He recalled that the general seemed ill at ease with Washington's leadership, hardly an impression one would want to leave with one of the commander in chief's strongest political supporters. On his way to Virginia, Lee followed up on the meeting with a letter. He politely expressed his gratitude to Laurens for all Congress had done to arrange his exchange, going on to note that his relationship with Washington was "well" and hoped it "always shall be well." Then, in an utterly tactless passage, he told Laurens, "I am persuaded (considering how he is surrounded) that he [Washington] cannot do without me."[34] That was an astonishing message to a man whose son—Lieutenant Colonel John Laurens—was one of those "surrounding" the commander in chief. In fact, in a letter of 17 June, Laurens directly stated to his son that he did not care for Lee's conduct.[35] If Lee had thought to make a friend of the president of Congress, he had failed miserably.

Lee's friend Benjamin Rush was not in York, and the general wrote to him only upon his return to Valley Forge, but it is worth noting that his correspondence continued in the same vein. Again, without ever mentioning Washington by name, his comments to Rush were disparaging of the commander in chief. It was "hard to say," Lee wrote, which side had blundered the most thus far in the war, and while he saw affairs looking up for the rebels, he added, "Upon my Soul it was time for fortune to interpose or We were inevitably lost."[36] Thus in York and after, Lee maintained his old habits: that is, he seemed unconcerned with the perceptions others might have of the company he kept or the thoughts he might express. The fact was that he was careless in his comments and openly consorted with some of Washington's most virulent detractors.

The paroled general also displayed dubious judgment in his dealings with Congress. He was in York twice, in April and May, while going and coming from Virginia. Both times he took it upon himself to lobby in behalf of army reforms and personal promotion. Lee wanted to be a lieutenant general, noting that when he joined the patriot cause, he had held that rank in the Polish army. Had he stayed in Europe, he claimed, the Poles, the Portuguese, or the Russians would have promoted him; besides, he insisted, no one in the Continental Army had as strong a resume. Lee also pointed out that during his captivity, many Continental brigadiers had advanced to major general, while he remained at that grade.[37] He probably understood that such a request solely on his own behalf would have seemed self-serving and thus may have advanced a rationale for the appointment of other lieutenant generals. It is a reasonable supposition, as he did think the army needed the higher rank. Major generals usually led divisions, and when the army organized formations of more than a single division—Lee referred to these as "wings" (the modern term would be "corps")—Washington would assign a major general from one of the divisions to the command. This meant that a division might go into action under someone other than its usual commander, another major general or a brigadier brought in to replace the man moved up to wing, someone who might not be familiar with the other divisional officers. Lee thought this invited confusion and wanted permanent lieutenant generals to handle wing commands, leaving division commanders in place. In a larger army with standing wings, or at least large enough to train with formations larger than a division, the idea would have made sense. Even Washington admitted it had merit.[38]

But Lee went further, which took him into murkier territory. He presented Congress with a plan for the reorganization of the army, one markedly different from that Washington had labored long and hard to convince the delegates to approve and then to implement. Congress was accustomed to dealing with the commander in chief on such matters, and to receive such an unsolicited proposal from a subordinate officer must have struck an odd note with some, especially since it warned against the offensive operations many patriots yearned for (see below). Lee warned delegates and others about the continued strength of the British army; Adjutant General Timothy Pickering recalled the general giving a glowing account of the fitness and morale of the King's forces.[39] Lee also suggested, however obliquely, that peace negotiations might still be possible. However sincere he was in advancing these views—and there is no reason not to credit his sincerity—he was overreaching. His conduct was inappropriate for a subordinate officer, especially one absent from the army for an extended period and acting without the authorization of the commander in chief. Congress was cool to his overtures.[40]

Lee also believed that Washington had misjudged British intentions for a 1778 campaign. In at least two long communications to his chief, the general insisted that Clinton would not march through New Jersey, but rather would leave Philadelphia for operations either in the Chesapeake or southwest toward Lancaster and on to the Susquehanna River. This would outflank the Continentals at Valley Forge and imperil vital stores at Head of Elk and elsewhere in the region. Lee claimed that Boudinot (of all people) agreed with him and that many British officers were incredulous that Clinton had not already ordered a move on Lancaster.[41] His final epistle to this effect arrived on 15 June, by which date Washington was virtually convinced of Clinton's intention to cross into New Jersey.

At this point Washington had had enough. While Lee did inform him of some of what he was going to do in York, and sometimes did mention to whom he had been speaking or writing, the commander in chief eventually found his subordinate's conduct more than a little annoying. Lee had not consulted with or sought Washington's permission before broaching his request for promotion and tendering his plan for army reorganization to Congress—that is, to Washington's political superiors. And why was he discussing possible military movements to Boudinot (and possibly others)? Having received Lee's letter of 15 June, the commander in chief responded the same day. He explained at length his efforts to work with Congress to have the army "properly organized" and stated that he already had asked for the appointment of lieutenant generals. But Congress had demurred on the new rank, and so the army would have to make do, which Washington thought it could. While he did not believe that Clinton was going to move toward the Chesapeake or the Susquehanna, he assured Lee that he had seen to the security of supplies in vulnerable areas. Then he got to the real point of his letter. Washington told Lee he would "always be happy in [receiving] a free communication of your sentiments upon any important subject relative to the service," but he begged that any such communications "come directly to myself." The implication was clear: no more ignoring your superior officer and vetting ideas or requests directly to Congress or other individuals. "The custom," he continued, "which many officers have, of speaking freely of things and reprobating measures, which upon investigation may be found to be unavoidable, is never productive of good, but often of very mischievous consequences."[42] It was a tactful reproof, but a reproof nevertheless, and certainly a reminder of who was commander in chief.

Lee's "Hobby Horse"

Lee pursued his travels for some six weeks. During that period, Washington completed the formal prisoner exchange, and Lee returned to duty at Valley Forge on 21 May. Two officers vacated their quarters to make way for the returning general, and as they had in April, most greeted him cordially.[43] Major General Greene, however, noting that Lee had arrived with "his usual train of dogs," sounded a private cautionary note.[44] He allowed that the Virginian was a fine officer and scholar, but he feared that the "junto"—the radical whigs, and Mifflin in particular—would try to "debauch and poison his mind with Prejudices" against Washington (as if Lee needed any help in this regard). Greene was uneasy and confessed that he thought "no great good" would come of the general's return.[45]

If Lee was aware of Greene's trepidation or similar feelings elsewhere in the officer corps, he did not let on. Indeed, his attitude upon his return to duty was a bit cavalier. In the aftermath of the debate over army reorganization and postwar officer pensions, Congress had ordered all commissioned officers to swear a new loyalty oath. On 9 June Washington arranged to personally administer the oath to Lafayette and Lee. The young Frenchman swore routinely, but not the former British officer. Instead, Lee gladly renounced all allegiance to George III but announced that he had some "scruples about the Prince of Wales." Most officers present took the remark as a joke or a typical bit of the general's irreverence. Nevertheless, Washington, who had worked long and hard with Congress in behalf of the army and the status of the officer corps, was anything but pleased with the behavior of his second in command.[46] Again, this was lost on Lee.

As was his wont, the general energetically involved himself in army affairs. Washington gave him one of the five divisions of the army—a highly responsible command—and he proved useful in other ways. In May Lee teamed with Lafayette in defusing potentially disruptive antagonisms between foreign and American-born troops. The foreigners, including various European nationalities and British deserters, often showed little respect for their American officers, and Washington feared that they were sowing insubordination among the rank and file generally. Lafayette and Lee suggested forming separate units for the problematic recruits (and some European officers as well), a solution that actually did some good.[47] On the other hand, Lee once again generated friction. In particular, he wasted no time in expressing reservations about Major General Steuben. Indeed, Lee wanted the inspector general's authority curtailed, and he looked askance at the baron's training regimen. He induced other officers to complain about the Prussian as well.[48] But by definition, this also meant that he disagreed with Washington's vision of the Continental Army as a regular professional force, which was no small difference of opinion.

Lee's disagreement was fundamental and longstanding, and Washington was aware of it. There is no record of the general having discussed army organization or training with the commander in chief earlier in the war (it would have been a logical topic), but in April 1778, after his release on parole, Lee made his views abundantly clear. In a letter from York dated 13 April, he explained to Washington his thoughts about "how to form an army in the most simple manner possible" and how such an army would best suit American needs in the war against Great Britain. He put his recommendations into a document with the fulsome title, "A Plan for the Formation of the American Army in the least Expensive Manner possible, and at the same Time for rendering their Manoeuvers so little complex that all the Essentials may be learnt, and practiced in a few Weeks."[49] This he enclosed with his letter. The plan was, Lee wrote, "a hobby horse of my own training," and he was wildly enthusiastic about it. "Indeed," he went on, his pen seemingly racing, "I am so infatuated with it that I cannot forebear boasting its excellencies on all occasions, to Friends or Enemies." Then he begged pardon: "You must excuse me therefore if I could not refrain from recommending the Beast to some members of the Congress."[50]

Washington received the letter and the plan about a week later, too late to suggest that such a presentation to congressional delegates was inappropriate—or to order Lee not to do so. On 22 April he wrote a cordial response to his subordinate (who already had left York for Virginia), assuring him that he looked forward to Lee's return to the army. Washington's comments on the "Plan for the Formation of the American Army" were brief and jocular. Upon Lee's arrival at Valley Forge, the proposal would be "the subject of conversation." In the meantime, he hoped that this "hobby horse" would not be "so limping a jade" as the nag Lee apparently had ridden to York.[51] It was clear that Washington had not taken the plan the least bit seriously.

What had Lee proposed, and why had Washington reacted so blithely? At first glance one would have thought the proposal would have infuriated the commander in chief. It began with a direct jab at Steuben. The elaborate tactics of Europe, Lee wrote, were impractical in action, "and it is to be lamented that America has servilely copied these defects." What the Continentals needed was simplicity in tactics and organization. Men "drawn from their Ploughs have little Time for dressing [in ranks]," and if they were "servilely kept to the European Plan, they will make an Aukward Figure, be laugh'd at as a bad Army by their Enemy, and defeated in every Recontre which depends on Manoeuvres." Instead, Lee wanted Americans to stand on the defense and wear down an enemy forced to come after them: "Harassing and impeding can alone Succeed." Taking the offensive against British professionals and fighting in the open, he warned, was "talking Nonsense"; it would be "Insanity" to try.[52]

To implement such a strategy, he called for new unit organizations. Regiments would comprise two battalions, each battalion having four companies; a regimental roster would carry 1,154 officers and men—larger than Washington's Continental regiments—with enough officers to assure that units could "with Ease change their Front, retire, advance, or rally." Ideally, each regiment would have two attached light-artillery pieces. Lee wanted "young Gentlemen" encouraged to raise horse troops that would operate with "Genius and Industry with as few Restrictions as are consistent with the general Rules of Subordination." He also wanted small units of regulars called "legions." These were mixed foot-and-horse formations capable of independent operations and suited to Lee's favored "harassing and impeding" tactics.

From a strictly military point of view, Lee's plan was not necessarily bad, and it had some interesting features. The implication was that the national army would be essentially a uniformly organized and trained militia organization. Lee probably would not have objected to a small corps of regulars—perhaps the legions he admired—but saw no need for this.[53] Nothing in the plan discouraged long-term militia troops, who could serve tours of six months or a year; such veterans could stiffen shorter-term militia called out at need. Thus constituted, the army could distribute regiments throughout the interior. If all else failed and British pressure became too great, his plan of operations called for a retreat beyond the Susquehanna River and the fortification of the river fords. Behind these fords, patriots could fight on indefinitely. His "Plan" was thus a recipe for defensive small-unit warfare, a strategy in which rebel troops would avoid set-piece engagements and whittle away the King's army over time.

Yet any theoretical merits of the "Plan" were beside the point. The entire proposal was completely out of step with Washington's vision for the army. Its talk of soldiers "drawn from their Ploughs," "Young Gentlemen" raising their own troops, the "Spirit of Partisans," and disdain for the tactics of Europe all harkened back to the days of republican ardor of 1775 and early 1776. That ardor, as Washington understood—and as bitter experience had demonstrated—was now dormant in most of the country. Lee's strategic vision, emphasizing the defensive and, if necessary, falling back into the interior to fight a protracted war, also fell on deaf ears. Most patriots now cared little about hit-and-run tactics; they wanted a Continental Army that could stand and *fight.* Lee's proposal was simply out of date, and if the commander in chief made light of it, it was a sign of how sure he had become of his footing in Congress, at least on this point. Congress also had invested in the reorganization and retraining of the army, most delegates having endorsed Washington's plans for the new regiments and waxing enthusiastic about Steuben's training program. No one at York, it seems, took Lee's proposal seriously, at least not publicly. If they had, Washington would have learned about it quickly enough; certainly Laurens would have told him. All the "Plan for the Formation of the American Army" accomplished was to signal the degree of difference between the thinking of its author and that of the commander in chief, most officers, and most of Congress. Some of Lee's contemporaries saw this clearly. In her history of the Revolution published in 1805, Mercy Otis Warren, who lived through the war and had met many leading participants, wrote with some sympathy for the general. Previous to his capture, she observed, "the American army was too justly considered by him, an undisciplined rabble." But upon his release, Lee never had time to appreciate the "great improvements in the art of war" achieved during his absence. John Shy summed it up: during his months of captivity, "the war seemed to have moved beyond Charles Lee."[54]

There were other things, less tangible perhaps, but still serving to distance Lee from many peers. One was his personal conduct, for he was not genteel in language or manners. Lee was famously careless about his appearance, once sitting down to breakfast with General and Mrs. Washington unshaven and bedraggled. His conduct the night before allegedly was worse, supposedly having secreted the wife of a British sergeant in his room—"a miserable dirty hussy," according to Boudinot. (As Lee's room was next to Martha Washington's sitting room, the situation was potentially very awkward.)[55] A correspondence with Horatio Gates reflected a similar casualness toward gentility. Gates, boasting of an exploit of his son, Robert, told him that in one encounter the youth had drunk himself silly and had caught a venereal disease. Lee thought it was splendid and bespoke a manly youth.[56] Lee was no reprobate, at least no more than many other officers of the era. But such conduct and sentiments were foreign to Washington; one cannot imagine the commander in chief applauding the exploits of Robert Gates. Nor did he expect those in his military family to feel differently in such matters. Like Washington, most of these men, as well as many other officers, were highly conscious of their dignity as officers and gentlemen. Lee frequently was not.

Armies are, and always have been, composed of disparate individuals; behaviors vary widely and personalities differ. So it was in the Continental Army. Officers frequently clashed over issues large and small, and some fought duels over points of honor. But those with differences could and did function as professional associates. Such was the case with Generals Lee and Washington. On important matters—personal, political, and military—the gulf between them was considerable, and despite mutual expressions of affection in their correspondence, they were never close friends.

At Valley Forge in June 1778, all of this was largely unspoken, and for the moment antagonisms were buried in the rush of events—the excitement of breaking camp and the pursuit of Clinton. But there is no question that potential flash points existed that made it easier for Washington and those around him to break with Lee when the crisis finally came. Few things are inevitable in history; perhaps none are. But it is not going too far to say there are things that are or were *likely.* And even without benefit of hindsight, a rupture between Washington and Lee was certainly one of them—it just was not *quite* time.

CHAPTER 6

The Roads to Monmouth I

Henry Clinton's March

The British evacuation of Philadelphia, and the subsequent Continental crossing of the Delaware, put two armies on the move in New Jersey. Neither knew exactly what the other was doing; indeed, Clinton had not even made up his mind where he was going. There was more than one way to New York, and early in his march circumstances had not compelled Sir Henry to make a final decision on which to take. On the other hand, Washington could not be sure of catching his adversary no matter which route the British commander chose; nor was he certain of what he could do if he managed to confront him. As they moved deeper into New Jersey, both generals tried to discern the other's intentions. Battle was not inevitable, but as the rival armies came into closer proximity, Clinton and Washington understood that at least some level of action was a probability. For different reasons, both men hoped for it.

The British army marched some sixty-seven miles from the west bank of the Delaware River to Monmouth Court House. It was a complicated undertaking, the details of which often have proved confusing to historians.

To Allentown: The First Forty Miles

With most of his army consolidated in and around Haddonfield (some units were still at Billingsport), Clinton took stock of the situation. Patriots had reconnoitered his landings in New Jersey but mounted no serious opposition. Crown forces suffered only a handful of casualties. On 13 June a party from the New Jersey Brigade killed or wounded several enemy horsemen scouting the Haddonfield Road. As Lieutenant General Wilhelm von Knyphausen pushed farther out of Cooper's Ferry on the seventeenth, a jaeger recorded seeing only eight enemy soldiers and encountering only occasional sniper fire. At Haddonfield a rebel shot wounded a Hessian picket; and on the nineteenth troops withdrawing from Billingsport met "a scattered and concealed fire," wounding two men and killing a horse.[1] These incidents were annoyances but indicated no imminent threat to Clinton's regiments as they prepared to march.

The British faced an overland trek of some ninety miles to New York, a bit more or less depending upon the route taken. For the time being, Clinton would head northeast, with the main army following a road network leading through Gloucester and Burlington Counties and eventually to Allentown in Monmouth County in central New Jersey, about forty miles distant. At Allentown Clinton would have to decide on the final leg of his journey. The roads were sometimes in poor repair, passing over sandy soil and through marshy terrain often cut by streams; easy passage depended not only upon the condition of the roads but also on a series of bridges and wooden causeways. While travel could be difficult, the existing routes were part of a long-established transportation corridor connecting Philadelphia and New York; even during the Revolution, the main routes were generally passable. The army was prepared for road maintenance—it even had portable bridging equipment—and would not be cutting its way through virgin wilderness.

Geography would be a factor in traversing the state. The march itinerary lay mostly within New Jersey's Inner Coastal Plain, a relatively narrow band of terrain fronting on the banks of the Delaware and arching northeast across the state. The region was composed of glacial deposits left with the retreat of the last ice age over 40,000 years ago. With some notable exceptions, the land was generally flat and not necessarily as scenic as the more varied geography of northern New Jersey. But the area boasted some of the richest farmlands in the world, and during late 1777 and early 1778, British and American foragers fought over the bounty of its agriculture and husbandry. There were also extensive woodlands and many small rivers and creeks, which frequently cut through defiles. The forests afforded excellent protection for lurking patriot snipers and patrols, and in a number of places the defiles and passes made for excellent defensive positions. Had Clinton marched to South Amboy, he would have completed his trip on the Inner Plain, but his diversion to Sandy Hook (described later) took him into the Outer Coastal

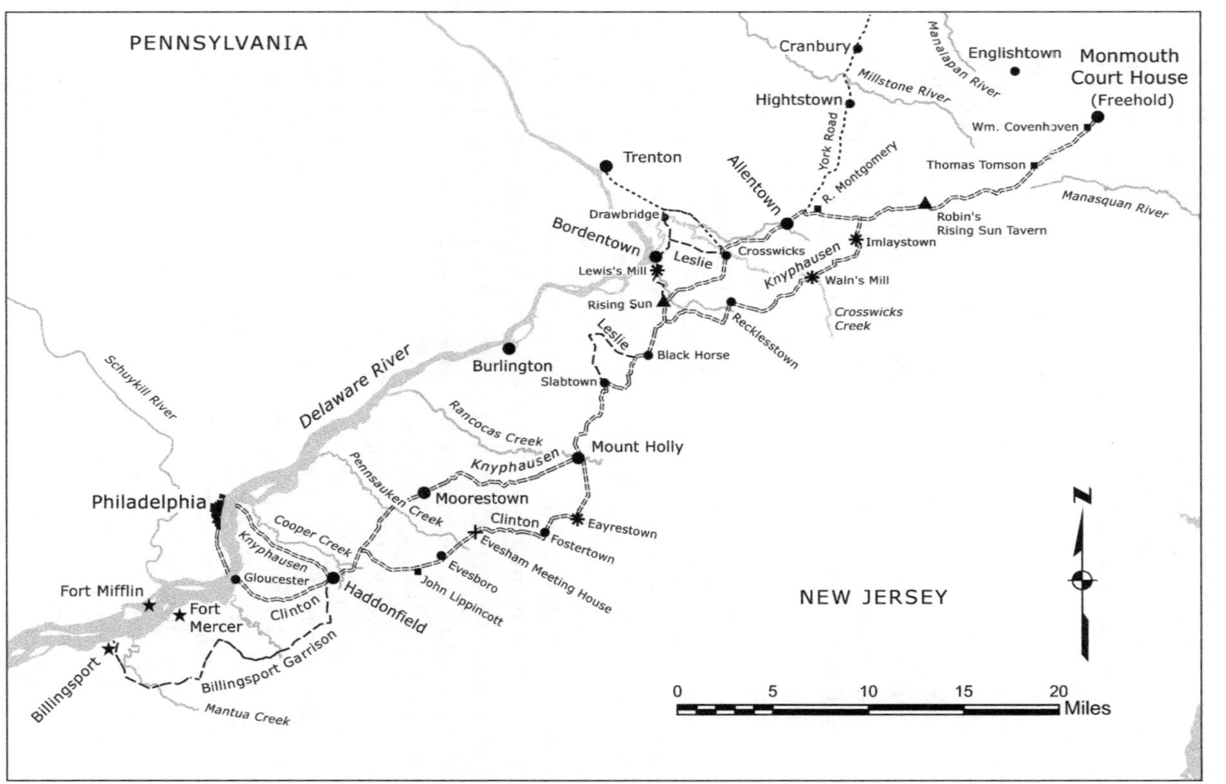

The British march routes from Philadelphia to Monmouth Court House, June 1778. Map by Garry Wheeler Stone. Copyright © 2016 by the University of Oklahoma Press.

Plain in Monmouth County. Much of the Outer Plain was pineland and, with the exceptions of acreage around Allentown and in Freehold Township, generally not as fertile.[2] It still featured many small streams and some rolling hills. Taken as a whole, Clinton's route was not overly difficult from a strictly geographical perspective, but neither was it suited to an easy or safe passage if patriots chose to dispute it.

Clinton wasted no time in organizing his army. Coordinating the movement of some 20,800 people, forty-six artillery pieces and ammunition stores, perhaps 5,000 horses, and 1,500 horse-drawn wagons packed with provisions for six weeks was no easy matter.[3] Security and efficiency mandated expectations of strict "Discipline and good order" on the march, and on 18 June general orders at Haddonfield charged officers with keeping a tight rein on their units. Looting and unauthorized "Straggling" risked execution "upon the Spot." All civilians with the army were to register their professions, former addresses, and who had recommended them for the march. Clinton also wanted a careful count of all women with the regiments and made arrangements for two per company to draw rations. Women were to march with the baggage of their respective corps, and the general issued orders to the provost marshal "to drum out any woman who dares to disobey this order." Hessian and British brigade commanders were to assure that all pickets were in order.[4] These were generally standard instructions before an eighteenth-century army moved, but Clinton wanted the rules understood from the beginning.

The army would move in stages and use most of the existing main roads; at least for the first week, this would be no march in single file. Fortunately for Clinton, the reconnoitering and cartography of John Hills, as well as assistance from the area's many loyalists, gave him a good understanding of the road network. This knowledge was vital if the march was to avoid devolving into a massive traffic jam, subject to crippling delays and patriot harassment. By 18 and 19 June, the entire army was in motion.

Clinton's forces marched in two divisions, each containing roughly half of the army. The 1st Division, commanded by Lieutenant General Charles Lord Cornwallis, which Clinton accompanied, comprised some 10,470 individuals. These included 10,020 combatant personnel, among them Clinton's servants and aides and roughly half of the artillery complement, as well as 448 or so noncombatants, 355 of whom were women. The 2nd Division marched under Knyphausen. The Hessian general had about 9,150 men and women in his column as well as three children. Some 7,696 were combatants, including all the loyalist units except the Queen's Rangers. Among the noncombatants were the support units: paymaster, quartermaster, engineer, medical, bridgemaster, and other specialized personnel. These numbers are not exact, as various units moved between divisions over the course of the march and artillery units were divided between the divisions. The Hessian jaegers, for example, operated with the 1st Division for much of the march, but by 28 June they were listed with the 2nd Division. A unit of loyalist horse, initially on the roster of the 2nd Division, sometimes marched with the 1st Division.[5] However approximate, though, these figures showed a preponderance of the army's combat strength in the 1st Division. Each column would take its share of wagons to support immediate needs, but the heavy baggage train, including provisions and stores, would be with Knyphausen.[6] Where possible, the two divisions marched on parallel routes for mutual security.

On the 18 June—as the last troops arrived in New Jersey—Clinton began moving. Knyphausen brought his division up to Haddonfield, while Clinton and Cornwallis arrived from Gloucester. From Cooper's Ferry, Brigadier General Alexander Leslie arrived with his brigade (the 5th) and its baggage, the 16th Queen's and 17th Light Dragoons, Major General Johann Stirn's German brigade, the artillery park, provisions train, pontoons, and army baggage. Bringing up the rear were three loyalist battalions and a loyalist horse troop. At Haddonfield Leslie rested for two hours. Then with the vanguard of the 1st Division—his brigade, the Queen's Rangers, the jaegers, and Captain Richard Hoveden's loyalist Philadelphia Light Dragoons—he marched out on the relatively good road toward the small Quaker village of Evesham, just on the Burlington side of the border of Gloucester and Burlington Counties. The Queen's Rangers and the Hessian jaegers screened the advance.[7]

As Leslie's vanguard marched east from Haddonfield, they entered a "very thick [wooded] Country" where the rebels could operate in greater safety. At the front of the column, the jaegers skirmished "constantly with an enemy scouting party, which slowly fell back, giving resistance at every defile, woods, or bridge, and tore up every bridge, and caused whatever other harassment they could." The harassment included a company volley from fifty men under

Captain John Ross of the Third New Jersey Regiment.[8] To Captain Johann Ewald, it seemed that militia and Continental light infantry "hung on our rear . . . without letup." A number of his men dropped dead from heat exhaustion.[9] But through it all, Leslie's contingent apparently suffered few (if any) combat casualties.

Leslie reached Evesham after a march of about seven miles and encamped near the farm of John Lippincott. The Lippincotts were a prominent local family, having farmed in the area for several generations (they also did some distilling and cider making). Lippincott and his wife had thirteen children, and the family apparently moved out of their home for at least two nights, with Leslie presumably using the house as headquarters. Aside from the Lippincotts, the British found the area mostly deserted, many locals having fled into the woods with their livestock and goods. Some villagers had cut their well ropes to prevent the soldiers from drawing water.[10]

The following day, 19 June, Leslie planned to move through Fostertown to the South Branch of Rancocas Creek, then link up with Cornwallis and Clinton at Mount Holly on the twentieth. As he marched from Evesham, however, shooting broke out between his men and the New Jersey militia. In the ensuing skirmish, historian William Stryker tells us, two village houses caught fire, the first of others that would go up in flames over the week. During the brief action, the jaegers suffered one man killed and several wounded, but they wounded several rebels in return, one shot bringing down Jonathan Beesley. Beesley was a captain in the Second Battalion, Cumberland County militia, and although his wound was serious—mortal, as it turned out—he managed to hide from Leslie's men. Advancing to Evesham later on the nineteenth, a party of Clinton's grenadiers found the wounded American. Pressed for information on the whereabouts and plans of his comrades, he refused to talk. This was conduct the British expected of their own officers, and the admiring redcoats gave Beesley all possible medical care. They left him in the house of Hinchman Haines (close to modern Mount Laurel), where he died later that night. "He was a brave man," Clinton said, "and should not be treated with indignity." He was not: the British buried Beesley with full military honors. (Much later, his body was reinterred in the Friends Burying Ground in Haddonfield.)[11]

The Beesley incident gave rise to an unearthly Evesham legend. As the tale went, 19 June 1778 did not end the patriot captain's war; rather, he remained on duty, even in death. The Haines home, where he expired, was his post. After his death "a phantom horseman was seen to emerge from the" house, "whose appearance always meant death to some of the British, if any were in the neighborhood, but this phantom apparently disappeared at the close of the Revolution, feeling its mission was ended after the country's freedom was gained."[12] Thus did the restless spirit of Jonathan Beesley earn its final rest.

However dire a threat a ghostly militia captain may have posed, more temporal problems occupied the British. Patriot sniping continued, and British screening forces were constantly on the move. On the nineteenth Ewald's men dispersed militia firing on them from a mill at Eayrestown. The next day the redcoats captured another wounded rebel, this time a horseman. Again the captive was a hard man. Andrew Bell, a tory diarist of the campaign and confidential secretary to Sir Henry, actually seemed offended at the rebel's silence. He was "so obstinate," Bell wrote, "as not to tell the Route his Comrades had taken."[13] What Bell saw was more than obstinacy. If he had looked closely enough, he would have seen a man indicative of many Major General Philemon Dickinson had brought into the field—men a world apart from the militia who had rushed to accept a King's pardon in the dark days of 1776. Dickinson may have wished for more men, but of those he had, many had come to fight. It was low-intensity combat, but it was enough to dispel the cavalier British attitude toward the rebels so prevalent in 1776. Clinton knew that Brigadier General William Maxwell (and by 25 June, Colonel Daniel Morgan) had disciplined regulars operating against him, and some of his lieutenants believed intelligence estimates putting Dickinson's strength alone at over two thousand men (it was more like twelve hundred).[14] It remained to be seen to what extent the patriot advanced forces could slow Clinton, but they were clearly doing their best.

While Dickinson and Maxwell were the sources of considerable British irritation, they could not match Clinton's strength and were incapable of doing much damage. Patriot snipers generally worked in small parties, often in twos and threes. (Captain Ross's fifty-man volley was an exception.) William Lloyd, a Monmouth County militiaman, participated in one such action. He and another comrade rode close to a British party, each holding the bridle of the other's horse while they took one shot apiece before riding for their lives.[15] This kind of thing was dangerous to individuals, but it was never enough to measurably slow a British column, even after Continental reinforcements under Colonel Morgan moved to join them (discussed below). Prudently, patriots avoided major confrontations while sending a steady stream of intelligence back to General Washington. Both sides took casualties by ones and twos.

The main body of the 1st Division, accompanied by Clinton and Cornwallis, marched from Haddonfield on 19 June, also moving toward Evesham. Once there, Cornwallis also used the Lippincott home as headquarters for the night, with Clinton using a house about two miles away (near modern Mount Laurel). Still beset by rebel sniping—Ewald complained that the head and flanks of the march "were constantly annoyed by the enemy"—but taking no losses, the column arrived at Mount Holly on 20 June.[16] It was a march of seven difficult miles, beset by alternating rain and brutal heat. Under the circumstances, Clinton was relieved to reach the town without serious opposition. He knew that the New Jersey Brigade had been in the town for some two weeks and had only left the day before; as the local terrain favored a defensive action, Clinton feared that a determined American effort might cost his exhausted men dearly.[17] But Maxwell, with only his brigade and some militia, pulled out to continue his mission of harassment and delay. As anticipated, Clinton and Cornwallis met Leslie's vanguard at Mount Holly. Clinton wanted to rest his men for a day and allow Kynphausen and the 2nd Division to catch up. The troops were grateful for the break—and for a gill of rum. Leslie, concerned that wandering troops might be swept up by rebel patrols or tempted to desert, ordered sentries to prevent anyone from straying beyond the lines.[18]

Small incidents continued, and one was particularly vicious. Just outside Mount Holly, a British detail was rebuilding a demolished bridge. In what may have been a planned ambush, militia waited until the repair work was underway, then opened fire from a nearby house. British covering forces attacked the building, causing the militia to flee—not all of them fast enough. The counterattack killed three "villains," captured two, and drove two more into the basement of the house, where they refused to come out. Unable to get at the militiamen in any other way, the British fired the building and "consumed them in it." Battles did not have to be big to be brutal. The next day (21 June), while most of the army rested, a jaeger detachment burned a small concentration of rebel shipping in the Rancocas Creek and confiscated flour from a local gristmill.[19]

General Knyphausen and the 2nd Division had an easier time marching to Mount Holly. On 19 June he had moved his wagons and artillery across Cooper Creek. Later in the day the 15th Regiment and Major John Van Dyke's loyalist West Jersey Volunteers arrived from Billingsport, escorted by the 28th and 55th Regiments (which had met the Billingsport garrison at Mantua Creek). The next day the whole force marched north. After a night at Moorestown, on 21 June Kynphausen rendezvoused with Clinton and Leslie, having encountered no opposition.[20] Thus between 18 and 21 June, Clinton's army had covered about twenty miles, a pace of roughly five miles per day.

Mount Holly had seen the British before. Hessian troops and the 42nd Regiment had occupied the village for several days in December 1776 after a tough skirmish with some 600 militia (known as the Battle of Iron Works Hill); Ewald's jaegers had participated in the fighting.[21] Mount Holly was an old farming village dating from 1677 and consisted of some forty dwellings and other buildings around a town center at a road junction. On opposite ends of town were Saint Andrews Church and a Quaker meetinghouse. It also boasted gristmills and sawmills, a library with a charter from George III, a brewery, and an important iron works. "The Mount," a modest but distinctive hill, rose just north of the village.[22] Major John André, on the staff of General Grey, drew a map of the British encampment. It showed the troops encamped in a rough quadrangle, with unit concentrations and artillery north of the Mount—the direction from which any real threat was expected—and approaches to the town covered to the south. Soldiers occupied all prominent terrain features. It was a thoroughly professional arrangement and typical of British encampments along the march. Other encampment maps show the same care for effective defense.[23] Thus arranged, the encampments did not invite attack from any but the most powerful enemy formations, which at this point the rebels could not bring to bear.

General orders at Mount Holly called for the army to be ready to march at 3:00 A.M. on the twenty-second. As usual, Clinton wanted to spare his command the afternoon heat. The 1st Division order of march is worth noting, as it demonstrates the premium Clinton placed on security and how he provided for it. Light security forces led: twenty mounted jaegers followed by "all the dismounted Queen's Rangers." Next came an officer and twenty black "Pioneers," who could do quick road or bridge repairs or clear obstructions. Then came the heavier components of the division:

the combat commands—infantry and mounted—interspersed special-purpose commands, baggage, various equipment, cattle, artillery, and more infantry (the 5th Brigade) as a rear guard. A battalion of the 4th Brigade would detach to provide flank security to the left of the train, the New Jersey Volunteers would march in the center of the baggage, and the Pennsylvania Loyalists would protect the right flank.[24] The rest of the baggage train would fall to Knyphausen's 2nd Division. Clinton was taking no chances with the safety of his vital provisions and other heavy baggage. Should any rebel sally break through the outer screening forces, the train would enjoy a considerable close-in defensive capability.

But Clinton had little to worry about. Either through deliberately planted false information or a rebel picket mistaking an evening patrol for a sortie, Dickinson had been spooked. He reported to Washington: "At one of oClock this morning [22 June], I received information, that the Enemy were endeavouring to surround us, with a strong detachment that marched last Evening from Holly." With Cornwallis's 1st Division advancing to the east, Dickinson pulled all militia back to the north side of Crosswicks Creek; Maxwell's Continentals did the same.[25]

The army divided again on the morning of 22 June. Leaving Mount Holly, Leslie took the jaegers, some loyalist horse, and three British regiments (the Queen's Rangers had detached from Leslie and were now the van of Clinton's main body). He diverged westward, following a road parallel to the Clinton-Cornwallis route, to screen the main column from any threat from the Burlington, Bordentown, or Trenton areas.[26] Clinton's men moved along a direct route through the rather inelegantly named Slabtown (now Jacksonville) to Black Horse (modern Columbus), named after the local Black Horse Tavern. British accounts mention no shooting on this march, but Dickinson wrote Washington that several houses in the area had burned.[27] There is no record of any fighting, and the fires may have been vandalism on the part of the soldiers.

Not every incident was destructive or tragic. On the advance toward Black Horse, a guide's mistake sent the Queen's Rangers down a wrong turn at a crossroad. Seeing this, a stranger called to them, "You are wrong, you are wrong." It turned out the man was a militia officer, probably taking the rangers for friendly forces. As the distance between them closed to a few yards, everyone discovered the error, and the rangers prepared to fire. They could not have missed. Lieutenant Colonel John Simcoe checked them and told the enemy officer "to keep at a greater distance." He promptly did so.[28] It was a small piece of gallantry but no doubt long remembered by the lucky American. After a difficult march due to rain and demolished bridges, Leslie rejoined Clinton and Cornwallis at Black Horse.[29]

It was now Tuesday, 23 June, and from Black Horse the British had another early start. At 2:00 A.M. Leslie's vanguard broke camp, with the rest of the 1st Division following "Punctually" an hour and a half later. Knyphausen had the 2nd Division, with the provisions train, moving as soon as Cornwallis had cleared away. The army was now in three columns, with Knyphausen on the right. He would take a track roughly parallel to the 1st Division. Clinton told him to be careful about security on his right flank, as the Americans seemed to be working their way in that direction.[30]

Historian William Stryker tells a curious story about the departure from Black Horse. As the troops broke camp on the morning of the twenty-third, the sight of the ponderous baggage train supposedly set Clinton to thinking. The train was a "terrible encumbrance," and protecting it forestalled any hopes of offensive action against Washington. But what if he burned it all? Doing so would free him for a lightning attack, but then another thought stayed his hand: destroying the train might seem an act of weakness to his army, the thought of which strengthened his resolve to push on through the state. Stryker carefully informed his readers that any truth behind the story "cannot now be determined," and he cited no source even for the legend. He did think, however, that Clinton cutting loose from his baggage to strike at Washington was a good idea. Had the British commander "possessed the great decision of character necessary to do such an act . . . , he might have punished the American Army so severely as to have secured an early peace."[31] Or, in an alternative outcome Stryker did not suggest, he might have been engulfed without supplies in the New Jersey interior—that is, "Burgoyned."

Nowhere in Clinton's papers is there a scintilla of evidence suggesting that he remotely considered burning his baggage. Nor do other army sources hint at the idea; surely Clinton would have discussed such a dramatic step with his chief subordinates. But as it happens, the story does have a contemporary source, an Englishman named Thomas Anburey. Not much is known of Anburey's background in Britain, other than he came from comfortable circumstances, apparently was well educated, had excellent social connections, and did not think highly of the Irish. He was also bored. Finding that "a dull inactive life neither suited my circumstances nor my inclination," he came to America as a volunteer with the 29th Regiment early in the war. He did well in the army and received a "free ensigncy" in the 24th Regiment, a distinction in an age of purchased commissions.[32] When the 24th surrendered at Saratoga, Anburey eventually found himself a prisoner with Burgoyne's captive army (the Convention Army) in Charlottesville, Virginia. As an officer, he traveled widely throughout the state under a flag on army business. As he did so, he continued a series of letters (actually a journal with entries in letter form) begun while still in Britain. Published in two volumes in 1789, Anburey's *Travels through the Interior Parts of America* was an instant success and quickly translated into French and German editions. The work is cited frequently today as a source on early American natural history, social mores, politics, economics, and ethnography. As a soldier, Anburey also commented on military affairs; one of his letters was almost certainly the source of Stryker's story.

In a letter to "My Dear Friend" of 12 May 1779, written from "Jones's Plantation, near Charlottesville," Anburey asserted that the day before the Battle of Monmouth, Clinton

> sat upon a stone for near an hour viewing the baggage as it passed along, and debating in his own mind, whether he should not give instant orders to destroy it. At length, as he concluded it would be a matter of great exultation with the Americans, and a disgrace to the British army, he determined to preserve it at all costs; therefore, on the day of the action at Monmouth, he sent the baggage, early in the morning, under the care of General Knyphausen, in order that it might proceed without molestation.[33]

Aside from the date and place of Clinton's "debating in his own mind"—Stryker had it on 23 June at Black Horse—the accounts are virtually identical. And what was Anburey's source? He was, after all, in Virginia, at least 250 miles away from the event he described. How could he have known? Anburey had his information third-hand, sourcing it to a commissary officer of the Convention Army, Jonathan Clarke. Sometime after the battle, Clarke had visited Clinton in New York on business, and according to him, the general asked him secretly to confide in Major General William Phillips, also captured with Burgoyne. (Unlike Burgoyne, who returned to Britain on parole, Phillips remained in America in command of the Convention Army.) Clarke then supposedly told the same story to Anburey.[34] Why Clinton should want to send such a message to Phillips is a mystery.[35] But there is no question on one count: Neither Phillips (if he actually received such a confidence) nor any other Briton ever confirmed the story, even after the postwar publication of Anburey's *Travels*. It all has the ring of army gossip, or perhaps Anburey's commissary friend was just kidding him. The fact remains that Anburey is the sole authority—if that is the word—for this implausible fable.

The events of 23 June, however, did not need a blazing baggage train to provide drama. In fact, that day would see more excitement than any other of the campaign except for the Battle of Monmouth itself. It began with General Leslie. Leaving Black Horse, he pushed toward Bordentown, where a drawbridge nearby spanned Crosswicks Creek; the move led some patriots to believe that the British were moving on Trenton, less than ten miles north. Leslie's move was anything but an advance. Rather, it was a feint designed to draw patriot attention from Crosswicks, less than four miles away. Clinton intended the division's main body to march through that village on the way to Allentown. But the road led over a bridge and through a pass, and British officers feared that the terrain would favor a patriot defense.[36] If Leslie's feint could fool the Americans into thinking the main effort would be against Trenton—or if it could at least tie down rebel troops at the drawbridge—it might mean less trouble at Crosswicks. It was worth a try.

The initial fighting, however, was not part of the feint. In the morning some of Leslie's men tangled with militia at Lewis's Mill on Black's Creek near Bordentown, though not at the target drawbridge. This was the family home and mill of Lieutenant Colonel William Lewis of the First Regiment, Burlington County militia. A foraging detachment from Leslie's column gained the mill, probably to seek provisions. Captain Ewald, with the party, knew the family. He had billeted with them during the British occupation of Bordentown in late 1776 and had found them good company despite their known patriot affiliation. On the twenty-third he assured a household servant no harm would come to the property, then rejoined Leslie to take part in the later action at the drawbridge. Ewald subsequently heard that there had been fighting around the mill, and both "the very beautiful plantation and mill of Mr. Lewis were burned." Having promised the family that their property would be safe, he was devastated at the news.[37] Such are the fortunes of war. Luckily, however, the jaeger captain was somewhat misinformed: the mill had indeed burned, but not the Lewis home. British troops did damage or destroy some furniture, so that the losses from the mill and household goods came to over £2,043, a huge sum for the day.[38] But unlike less fortunate patriots along the redcoat march, the Lewises still had a roof over their heads.

Leslie moved to his target in the late afternoon. Approaching the drawbridge, the jaegers found it partially dismantled—four or five planks were missing. Walking out to the gap, they hailed some men they took to be civilians on the other side. They were not civilians, but militia, who opened a fusillade of musketry and cannon fire on the Hessians. Miraculously unscathed, the jaegers scrambled to safety and returned the compliment. Leslie deployed his command, and the fighting went on until dark. Late in the day, after the shooting stopped, Continental light infantry under Colonel Morgan arrived from Trenton to reinforce the militia. For the rest of the night, both sides remained on opposite banks of the creek. The fight at the bridge had been a noisy but relatively harmless skirmish. Dubiously, Ewald reported ten of his men killed or wounded in the action. Dickinson thought his troops had killed six or seven British over the course of the entire day at both Lewis's Mill and the drawbridge; he listed no militia casualties. Dickinson's account is the more accurate, as Ewald tended to overstate losses. In fact, another jaeger journal listed only several men wounded and an ammunition wagon damaged. The rebels had "cannonaded us severely," Lieutenant von Feilitzsch wrote, "but without causing any harm. God be praised!"[39] Leslie broke off the action that night. Leaving a light guard across from the patriot forces, around midnight he moved on to Crosswicks, where he rejoined the rest of the 1st Division. The last of his men left the Bordentown area near dawn on the twenty-fourth.[40]

Leslie's feint at Bordentown fooled no one. At Crosswicks Maxwell saw the move against Bordentown for exactly what it was and wrote Washington that it was simply "a faint."[41] His New Jersey Brigade would be at Crosswicks to meet the main body of the 1st Division. On the morning of the twenty-third, Clinton and Cornwallis marched from Black Horse, passing by the Sign of the Rising Sun, a landmark inn. The 16th Light Dragoons and the Queen's Rangers led the column. Along the way they endured a harmless bit of sniping from some Monmouth County militia.[42]

Matters soon became more serious. Receiving a report that the rebels were preparing to stand at the Crosswicks bridge, Clinton sent the dragoons and the Queen's Rangers ahead in an effort to seize it. The road to the bridge led through the village, and as the British approached, they drew the fire of rebel pickets. The rangers and dragoons tried to cut them off, but the defenders eluded pursuit, running through Crosswicks and crossing the bridge, which lay just north of the village. Pushing through the town, Captain Charles Stephenson of the Queen's Rangers was hit in the chest and seriously wounded. A disgusted Simcoe thought the shot had come from a Quaker "with a long fowling-piece."[43] As the rangers cleared Crosswicks, they emerged at the top of a slope above the vital bridge. Below, patriot troops were removing bridge planks and hewing away at trees, hoping to drop them across the bridge timbers. The sight of the British sent the axe men scampering across the bridge stringers on the heels of the fleeing pickets. The trees were still standing.[44] Taking the village, however, meant little without securing the road to Allentown, and patriots still held the road beyond the bridge. Strongly posted on the opposite bank lay militia units and most of Maxwell's New Jersey Continentals, well over 500 men in all.[45] In addition to partially destroying the bridge, they had closed downstream sluices, damming the creek and rendering it too deep to ford. The redcoats would have to fight to cross the stream and open the road.

The skirmishing began dramatically. As the British main body came up, the dragoons rode down the slope toward the bridge. The rebels turned them away with a long-range volley that was more sound than fury—no dragoons were unhorsed. Simcoe then led a ranger company to the south end of the bridge while Clinton personally led another ranger company to Simcoe's left. (This would not be the only time on the campaign that the British commander displayed a penchant for leading from the front.) To the right, the 16th Light Dragoons dismounted and lined a fence.[46] While the British deployed, a young Burlington County militiaman, Job Clevenger, showing more courage than sense, rushed onto the span trying to further disable it. He was shot dead and fell into the creek.[47] Active firing then commenced from both banks of the stream. Clinton sent his engineers forward to repair the span, while Simcoe rode back up the hill to form the remainder of his corps "behind the [Quaker] meeting house, ready to pass the bridge."[48] The weight of the combined British fire was sufficient to suppress much of the rebel opposition, otherwise the engineers would have shared the fate of Clevenger. Lieutenant John MacLeod of the Royal Artillery played a key role in this effort. His two 3-pounders plied the Americans with case shot—metal canisters containing thirty-two (or more) 1.25-ounce iron balls. It was too much for the Continentals and militia, and they began to fall back. Some of the militia marched to the right along the York Road, while others and the New Jersey Brigade moved to the left.

Seeing the Americans pulling out, the British moved forward. Using the stringers of the bridge, Simcoe led dismounted Queen's Rangers to the opposite bank and launched a vain pursuit of the militia column to the right. Seeking a closer look at the action, Clinton came forward and for a moment was within range of patriot fire; his red uniform made him conspicuous among the green-coated rangers. In the meantime, the engineers finished their work, allowing the 16th Light Dragoons, a battalion of light infantry, and a battalion of grenadiers to cross the bridge. They joined the pursuit of the retreating Americans, chasing the militia and Continentals to the left. The British followed the rebels another two miles, until they found the Third New Jersey and an artillery company in position behind still another wrecked bridge (over Doctors Creek, a tributary of Crosswicks). The Continentals were strongly posted and seemed disposed to fight. Having had combat enough for the day, the pursuers returned to the main body.[49]

Clinton referred to the entire affair as "a trifling skirmish." Compared to major battles, of course, he was right. Captain Stephenson apparently was the only serious British casualty. The wounded ranger was left in the village with an army physician and two privates to attend him. Badly wounded ("through his left breast"), Stephenson was only able to give his parole verbally. The Americans had lost three militiamen killed, including Clevenger, and seven prisoners. Among the Continentals, Colonel Elias Dayton lost a horse shot out from under him. (Dayton, one of Washington's favorite regimental commanders, was a hard man on horses; he had lost another mount at Germantown in 1777.)[50] But small and brief as it was, the Crosswicks skirmish provided plenty of excitement while it lasted. For the 1st Division, 23 June had been a long day.

The brief affair assumed larger dimensions as word of the skirmish reached civilians far from the scene. In Philadelphia rumors of fighting in New Jersey had been circulating since the British evacuation, and anxious residents did not know what to make of the news from Crosswicks. Quaker diarist Elizabeth Drinker noted that some of her neighbors mistook the sound of thunder for distant cannon fire amid reports "that many were slain near Crosswicks." But "the truth of the matter," she cautioned, "is not yet come out."[51]

At Crosswicks the British were satisfied with the day's work. Having taken the town and opened the road, they camped for the night in and around the village. The Queen's Rangers and 1st Light Infantry stayed on the north side of the bridge at the junction of the Trenton and York Roads. South of the bridge, the Hessian and British grenadiers camped between the village and the creek, while the 3rd and 4th Brigades straddled the road to Black Horse and the guards covered the east flank.[52] Once more, the deployment protected all approaches to the town, securing key terrain should the patriots again prove troublesome.

The next morning, 24 June, the 1st Division stayed in their Crosswicks encampments until a messenger from Knyphausen informed Clinton that the 2nd Division was safely on the road. Then the 1st Division—including Leslie—began its march, though not without some last-minute excitement. As the troops began to move, an unwelcome guest appeared in their rear. About 10:00 A.M. Lieutenant Colonel Anthony Walton White arrived with a detachment of Continental and militia light dragoons, part of the Third New Jersey Regiment, and some militia infantry. White found British pioneers destroying the Crosswicks bridge—an attempt to impede patriot pursuers—and he sent Captain Ross with his company of New Jersey regulars and some militia to stop them. A spirited skirmish developed until the British rear guard ended it by opening fire from the north bank with their light 3-pounders.[53] With the rebels shaken off, Clinton crossed from Burlington into Monmouth County.

The rest of the march to Allentown did not match the drama of the previous day or even that morning. There was the normal skirmishing with militia and Continentals early, but the light infantry dealt with them without trouble. At Allentown itself, no one was surprised to find the local bridge torn up, with patriots waiting on the other side. Again the delay was minimal; Simcoe dispersed them with several cannon shots. After this the British marched into the village without further incident, picking up a few whig stragglers. The only real excitement of the day occurred shortly afterward. A rebel patrol on the road from Cranbury, probably seeking intelligence on the whereabouts of the British, mistakenly approached a ranger detachment, thinking them patriots. They soon realized their mistake and faded into the woods; a British search failed to find them.[54] Aside from the continued heat, it had been a relatively easy day.

While the 1st Division forced its way through Crosswicks to Allentown, Knyphausen's column again escaped all the excitement. From Black Horse, the Hessian general moved to Recklesstown (modern Chesterfield), some seven miles to the right of Clinton. Rebels had dropped trees across his route, and the obstacles, including yet another demolished bridge at Black's Creek (a branch of the Rancocas), were irksome; although he thought the patriots in the vicinity had upward of 700 men, there was no fighting. On the night of the twenty-third, his men encamped in a fallow field; it was one of only a few encampments on the march that did not result in serious crop damage.[55] The following morning Knyphausen moved another twelve miles to Imlaystown and camped in a wheat field. Although only about four miles from Clinton's main body at Allentown, his men were exhausted. On this leg the 2nd Division had seen many rebels, and while the Americans never engaged, they had caused plenty of trouble. Trees felled across the road had to be cleared, and at Waln's Mill the column waited five and a half hours as men repaired a sabotaged bridge. When Knyphausen finally crossed, he notified Clinton and then destroyed the bridge behind him. The 2nd Division reached Imlaystown only at 9:00 P.M.

An Assessment at Forty Miles

The British army was now concentrated in, or in Knyphausen's case near, Allentown. Clinton had marched some forty miles from Cooper's Ferry and had reason to be pleased. His command was deep in hostile territory, but his security measures had been effective. The jaegers, dragoons, Queen's Rangers, and light infantry were trained for roving flank and outer security missions, and they had performed superbly. The army had suffered few casualties, and patriot harassment never seriously threatened the main columns of either division. In the most serious skirmishing at Crosswicks, British troops had the best of the fighting. The baggage train, the most vulnerable element of Clinton's columns, was fully intact. Repair crews had mended bridges and broken equipment, the portable blacksmith kept horses shod, hospital services remained in operation, and army administrative functions went on more-or-less normally. Courts-martial convened to handle routine disciplinary problems (there appear to have been few), none of which ever compromised the effectiveness of the army.[56] If judged simply as an operational movement, the march was a model retrograde. The army was on the march, not on the run.

The British managed all this in the face of everything the patriots had thrown in their path. The small-scale stands and skirmishing efforts were more annoyances than threats, and the main rebel army was still too far away to menace Clinton directly. (On 24 June Washington was some twenty-four miles north at Hopewell.) The Americans had shown fight, and the relatively good cooperation of Dickinson's militia with Continental regulars was a development that probably did not capture much British attention at the time (it should have). But the fact is patriot operations had not substantially delayed the royal troops. Maxwell and Dickinson had done their best to close the roads. The bridges at Mount Holly and Crosswicks were only two of many the rebels pulled down; they also tore up causeways over sandy or swampy ground. Before reaching Freehold on 26 June, the royal army had to rebuild no fewer than five bridges or causeways, which sometimes entailed putting construction gangs to work under the threat of sniper fire. Patriots also felled trees across the roads and moved all of the food, forage, and other supplies they could away from the British line of march. For good measure, they even filled in local wells.[57] These steps hardly constituted a scorched-earth policy, and while some resulting delays were short, over time they were cumulative and irritating. Still, Clinton advanced.

The weather seemed to favor the rebels. Cool at the beginning of June, by the middle of the month a heat wave had set in with a vengeance. The British marched through temperatures frequently exceeding ninety degrees. It was exhausting, and accounts of men on the march uniformly lamented the toll the heat exacted. Sergeant Thomas Sullivan of the 49th Regiment recorded that some units were able to make only short marches, and those only in the cool of the morning. On the first day out of Philadelphia, Ewald wrote that many troops "lost their lives miserably because of the intense heat," and on 26 June, perhaps the worst day, the army lost as many as twenty men from the heat.[58] Torrential rains brought little relief from the horrid temperatures and made the already poor roads more difficult. Wagons often bogged down in the sandy soil or in fording the many streams that cut across the terrain. Worse, clouds of mosquitoes rose from the swamps to add yet another dimension of discomfort. The troops hated it.

Some accounts of the campaign have questioned the role of army uniforms and soldiers' packs as a factor in the march. Did heavy woolen uniforms and the weight of packs and other accoutrements actually contribute to deaths through heat exhaustion? A full load (not counting a uniform) weighed upward of sixty pounds and, under the weather conditions of June 1778, certainly would have been a health threat. There may have been something to this in some units, but the evidence is against it for the army as a whole. The regimental history of the Royal Artillery specifically noted that on the Monmouth campaign, artillery units marched only with their personal arms and ammunition pouches; they loaded packs, coats, and other equipment on wagons and carts. A Hessian sergeant recorded that he was forbidden to wear his knapsack.[59] Looking carefully at this question, historian John U. Rees thinks it more likely the troops "were wearing a campaign uniform more suitable to the rigors of active service." This meant "cut down hats, short coats and trousers with socks instead of breeches and stockings." Indeed, much of the troops' heavier clothing was packed aboard the navy transports at Philadelphia. Rather than knapsacks, a "tumpline"—a rolled blanket with a minimum of personal necessities—was slung over the shoulder.[60] The men still carried their arms and ammunition, but they were not loaded down as beasts of burden. The British were experienced campaigners and certainly understood the need to adapt to adverse weather conditions.

Clinton did not worry particularly about the torpid pace of his march or about being cut off and "Burgoyned." He was sensitive to the tribulations of his men, and the short marches were deliberate. So whenever possible were the early starts, taking advantage of the coolest hours of the day. The general also was satisfied with his tactical circumstances; he was confident he could fight his way through anything the rebels could send his way. Besides, he wanted to fight. When the general explained his decision to march through New Jersey to Lord Germain, he frankly stated that he would welcome a chance to draw Washington into a general engagement. While he recognized the cautious nature of his American counterpart, over the course of his march Clinton still looked forward to "a brush" with the Continentals.[61] A major action at least would redeem the humiliation of the retreat; at best it might deal the rebellion a serious blow. He would not turn from his route to go looking for the patriot army, but he never stopped hoping that Washington might come to him. At any rate, Clinton had largely determined the pace of his advance, not (try as they might) Dickinson and Maxwell. The New Jersey militia general knew it and told Washington as much.[62]

Yet there was a darker aspect of the march. Over its first forty miles, the King's army was on its own. While southern New Jersey was home to a considerable loyalist population, few citizens greeted the redcoats happily. Instead, the British found most inhabitants sullen and inhospitable if not actually hostile. By early June, Maxwell's regulars and Dickinson's militia largely had suppressed tory activity in areas the British had not directly garrisoned or patrolled heavily. Many Gloucester County and other South Jersey tories had enlisted in the West Jersey Volunteers (later merged with the existing New Jersey Volunteers); as they marched away with Clinton, they left their home counties securely in the hands of their erstwhile whig neighbors. After June 1778, regional incidents between rebels and royalists decreased dramatically—for several months they actually ceased altogether.[63] There were too few loyalists left to carry on the fight. In some areas the British found only women or the very young and very old; they did not have to ask where the young men were. It was patently clear that the majority of the populace did not wish them well; at one point Major André ruefully noted finding patriot broadsides warning Clinton "to beware of being Burgoyned."[64] Whatever else it accomplished, the withdrawal across New Jersey had effectively rung the death knell of loyalist hopes in the state's Delaware River counties.

Moreover, as they marched, the King's troops did little to court civilian respect, let alone affection. General Clinton did issue strict instructions against plundering. In general orders of 18 June, while still at Haddonfield, he announced that he was "fully determined to execute on the Spot any man detected in Marauding." And in fact many officers did their best to protect local property. Simcoe told the Queen's Rangers that an "abhorrence of plunder" distinguished the "truly brave from the cowardly ruffian," and he posted officers to guard against anyone breaking ranks to pillage. Others took similar steps.[65] Clinton's intentions were good. Aside from his concern for the honor of his command, he did not want plundering troops further alienating an already hostile population or driving neutrals into the patriot cause. To their credit, many of the soldiers obeyed orders, and there were instances of troops privately paying civilians cash for provisions. The army itself collected all cattle and sheep it could find, and the commissary general paid cash on the spot.[66]

Yet the British commander was fighting a losing battle in this regard, and matters quickly got out of hand. John Peebles, an officer with the 42nd Foot (Royal Highlanders), noted dryly, "contrary to orders and not withstanding all the precautions," there was "a good deal of plundering going on." At Evesham troops rifled homes of food, alcohol, clothing, poultry, and household items. Losses suffered by Joseph Hammitt were fairly typical. The estimated costs of stolen or damaged goods and possessions came to £29, a considerable but not normally devastating sum for the period. John Wilkenson of Burlington County took a harder hit, losing furniture, bedding, crockery, wine decanters, foodstuffs, and other household items totaling more than £154.[67] Losses of this nature were commonplace along the line of the British march, although some were much worse. The experience of John Andrews of Monmouth County was a case in point. In a memorandum of 25 June, he listed the "Particulars Taken from me" as follows:[68]

One Horse three years old	90=0=0
one yerling Colt	25=0=0
four Milch Cows and one Dry Cow	70=0=0
Eight acres of Wheat and Rie	24=0=0
fifteen fine Sheep	39=0=0
four hogs	12=0=0
Upwards of one hundred Wt of bacon	13=0=0
Axes Coper Tools Tee Kettle &c	05=0=0
	278=0=0

In 1778 £278 was lot of money for any individual, and certainly to a farmer who had to replace livestock and wait until the next spring to replant his fields. The damages in wheat and rye no doubt were attributable to troops camping in the fields. But Andrews was not the only New Jersey farmer to suffer such a loss. On 24 June, when the 2nd Division reached Imlaystown, a Hessian junior officer noted that they encamped "in a most beautiful wheat-field."[69] The beauty would have been less apparent in the morning.

One of the worst incidents of plundering occurred at Mount Holly. On 23 June arsonists torched the nearby homes of militia colonel William Shreve and Peter Tallman. Shreve and Tallman were marked men, both prominent Burlington County patriots: Tallman was chairman of the county Committee of Observation with a relative in the militia, and Shreve was well known to the British as commander of the First Regiment, Burlington County militia, and brother of Continental colonel Israel Shreve of the Second New Jersey. William Shreve was in the field with his command when the pillagers struck. In addition to his home, they burned or otherwise destroyed his barn and outbuildings, carried off his livestock, and plundered his wagons, farm equipment, and numerous household goods and furniture. The damages totaled some £1,355, a very considerable sum in its day.[70] Targeting these properties was clearly a political act. Whatever the motives of the perpetrators, Clinton was furious. He again threatened the "Immediate Execution" of anyone found committing acts "so Disgraceful to the army" and offered a reward of twenty-five guineas—a lot of money for a soldier—for the apprehension of the culprits.[71] It was never collected.

Officers issued similar warnings at the regimental level. Lieutenant Colonel Alured Clarke of the 7th Regiment of Foot (Royal Fusiliers) was thoroughly exasperated. Proud of his regiment's usual discipline, Clarke found himself "Mortif'd at observing the great Irregularity and excesses that have been committed within these few days." He told his command, "Nothing is more disgraceful in a Corps than such humiliating Proceedings" and threatened "to Punish with the utmost Severity any man or follower of the Reg't" caught "Marauding or Stragling."[72]

Such threats did little good. As the march progressed, it left a trail of vandalism: the ironworks near Mount Holly were destroyed, homes were looted, livestock were killed or stolen, orchards were laid waste, fences were burned, and forage was carried off. There is no tabulation of damages incurred by New Jerseyans during the first week of the British march. Residents were allowed to file damage claims with the state, and the claim records today are in the New Jersey State Archives, but to date no one has mined them for a full accounting of losses suffered during the campaign. Such an effort, however, would present only an incomplete picture, as there is no certainty that all damages were recorded and no way to assess the accuracy of those that were—it is enough to note that the damages were substantial. Clinton's march was not Sherman's March to the Sea, but inhabitants on the direct line of advance suffered major losses, or lived in fear of them. Carl Baurmeister, adjutant of the Hessian forces, was dismayed at the extent of the plundering. His observations confirmed Clinton's worst fears: "It has made the country people all the more embittered rebels."[73] (On the twenty-seventh at Monmouth Court House, things would only get worse.)

To explain conduct is not to excuse it, but army plundering does require a note of clarification. Counterproductive as it may have been to the royal cause, pillaging was often perfectly understandable from the perspective of the rank and file. It is a truism in war that troops in enemy territory, subject to frequent harassment, taking casualties, and hot, tired, and angry are wont to vent their frustrations on hostile local populations. The British soldiery faced all of these things and reacted accordingly. This was especially the case among the many loyalist soldiers, who had every reason to feel resentful toward local whigs, if not openly vengeful. Many had lost everything at patriot hands, and they were not sorry if rebel civilians experienced some of the same. It is difficult to see the burning of the Shreve and Tallman homes and the damage inflicted on the Lewis properties in any other light than political payback. That the offer of a generous reward produced no suspects in these acts speaks volumes on the attitudes of most soldiers. Nor were there many courts-martial for plundering—at least not successful ones.[74] Plenty of troops must have seen, if not participated in, these acts, but few witnesses were willing to testify.

Moreover, the pillaging was not always wanton or mindless. There was plenty of that, of course, but the plunder of cured meats, live hogs, and poultry doubtless improved the banal diet of the soldiers as well as the women and other camp followers with the army (who sometimes helped with the plundering). It was, in effect, a form of foraging. Some officers even condoned aspects of the practice. Comrades of Hessian subofficer (sergeant) John von Krafft received permission "to take cattle wherever they should find any and kill and slaughter it for the use of the regiment."[75] Stolen clothing replaced worn-out socks, shoes, shirts, and trousers; other items—razors, tools, crockery, and the like—could be sold later or put to personal use. The soldiers were generally poor men. Clinton's commissary and quartermaster departments were generally efficient, but in the field it was not unusual for rations or replacement clothing to be late. So as soldiers frequently did on campaign, they alleviated shortages and discomforts by living off the land.

There was also a fine line between plundering and legitimate acts of war. Patriots reacted to any acts of property destruction by assuming the most malevolent of British intentions. This was not always the case. The burning of the ships on Rancocas Creek, for example, and the destruction of the ironworks at Mount Holly were blows against the rebel war effort. If private property suffered, it was property used to support a military insurrection. This was also the case in the ghastly incident at Mount Holly when the two militiamen hid in a private home and refused to surrender. The British had no time to wait them out and had no other real choice but to burn the building. Faced with the discovery of flour in rebel-owned mills, the troops took it; should they have left it to feed enemy soldiers? It was a war in which patriot irregulars blended easily into the civilian population, and it should be no surprise those civilians paid a price.

Furious whigs reaped a propaganda coup. Clinton's men, they proclaimed, were little better than pillaging barbarians. In an anonymous essay published in the *New Jersey Gazette,* Governor William Livingston waxed indignant over the destruction in and around Bordentown and Mount Holly, citing specifically the Lewis, Tallman, and Shreve incidents. But Livingston had a wit as sharp as his sense of indignation and got in a sarcastic jab: "How much cheaper might his Britannic Majesty buy sheep and oxen in England, in the usual manner, than he gets them now, by employing an army to steal them in America."[76] Continental soldier Joseph Plumb Martin was equally angry but lacked the governor's sense of humor. As he shadowed the rear of the retreating British, he was appalled at the sight of "cattle killed and lying about the fields and pastures," some where they were shot, others with steaks cut from hindquarters. He saw orchards cut down and homes and workplaces ransacked. "Such conduct did not give the Americans any more agreeable feelings toward them than they entertained before."[77] There was nothing Clinton could do about these reactions—he was not about to get favorable press or kind thoughts from patriots anyway. But he must have known that the "hearts and minds" of most New Jerseyans, if not firmly with the rebels, certainly held little regard for the royal army.

There was another area in which Clinton could do little. From the beginning, he recognized that not all his troops shared his enthusiasm for any sort of fight. In fact, a fair number of the troops—mostly Hessians but also many British—chose not to march at all and deserted before the army left Philadelphia. Still others slipped away soon after reaching New Jersey, often to return to American wives and lovers. Even more might have followed had not many of their wives, whom Clinton had supposed safely aboard the navy transports, slipped back ashore at the last minute to join their husbands on the march. It was relatively easy for men to drop out of ranks. Von Krafft noticed that when troops moved through thickets, some men just did not come out. Search parties sent after them found their missions pointless and even dangerous with rebel patrols hovering around the columns. In one case a Hessian officer and two British grenadiers assigned to guard a rebel prisoner instead used him as a guide to desert to patriot lines.[78]

Some of the discontented deserted in groups, sometimes after carefully laying plans to slip away while on patrol or outpost duty. Thomas Sullivan may have been the most successful in this regard. Sullivan enlisted in the 49th Regiment in Dublin, Ireland, in 1775 and arrived in Boston the day before the Battle of Bunker Hill. From the beginning, he planned to escape into what he saw as a land of freedom. But he was literate and ended up doing a lot of the paperwork for his regiment and so found no opportunity to abscond. When the 49th went to Philadelphia with General Howe, Sullivan married Sarah Stoneman, a native of nearby Bucks County. Neither of them wanted to leave the area, and when Clinton evacuated the city, they planned their getaway. On 25 June, a day after the skirmishing at Crosswicks, he had Sarah hide and wait for him at a prearranged location beyond the British encampment. He then took a corporal and twelve privates on picket duty outside the lines; aware of the plot to a man, they did nothing as Sullivan entered the woods and simply kept going. (The assumption is that at least some of the others deserted as well.) Meeting his wife, Sullivan found local civilians willing to help them reach the safety of a rebel camp near Allentown.

There he sold his equipment for ready cash, and the couple eventually returned to Philadelphia. They found work as servants in the household of Quartermaster General Nathanael Greene.[79]

Most stories of escape to patriot lines were not as dramatic (or romantic) as that of the Sullivans. But if other tales were comparatively mundane, there were plenty of them. By the end of the march a chagrined Knyphausen admitted that over 230 of his men had gone over to the rebels, and these were over and above those who had deserted in Philadelphia before the evacuation. Beyond the German losses, Baurmeister thought the British probably lost upward of 100 deserters in New Jersey. Of those who left, some officers thought many, if not most, were exchanged prisoners of war; apparently they liked what they had seen while in American hands and took advantage of patriot inducements to desert.[80] Maxwell and Dickinson reported a steady flow of deserters seeking the American lines. By 26 June, when Clinton's column reached Freehold, there were persistent and, as it turned out, fairly reliable reports that as many as 500 men had gone over to the rebels.[81] These losses were serious, and the Americans acquired these victories without firing a shot.

Yet not all deserters got away and not all of their stories ended happily. John Fisher was one exception, and as far as we know *the* exception during Clinton's march. Fisher, a drummer in the 28th Regiment of Foot, had a checkered past. In April 1777 he had deserted to the rebels during skirmishing in central New Jersey. He lived for a time in Morristown and served with the local militia. On 19 June in the vicinity of Fostertown in Gloucester County, Fisher was badly wounded in the same skirmish that claimed the life of Captain Beesley. Captured and his identity discovered, on 21 June he went before a court-martial. He pleaded that he had only joined the militia in order to get close enough to British forces so he could then desert to his old regiment. It did no good. Found guilty of desertion and bearing arms for the enemy, Fisher was hanged the following morning.[82] A Hessian witness noted that the execution "caused a dreadful uproar" among the troops, as Fisher was still bleeding from saber wounds. Afterward the army moved on, leaving his body hanging from a tree next to the road.[83] Fisher was the only man executed on the march.

The Road from Allentown

On 24 June, as the army moved toward Allentown, troops now resigned to torrential thunderstorms and enervating heat experienced yet another demonstration of nature's ability to astonish. This was something completely different—an almost total solar eclipse. It was visible over most of North America and evoked comment throughout the theaters of war from the Carolinas to New England.[84] Loyalist Ambrose Serle, variously secretary to both Howe brothers, had sailed from Philadelphia with the departing British and witnessed the eclipse while becalmed in Delaware Bay. It "rendered the apparent Horizon so dark, that one cd. [could] not read," he recorded in his journal; "the Phoenomemon was very beautiful."[85] To the north, Private Martin was then moving to intercept Clinton's command. He was not as impressed as Serle but did observe that in "olden time" an eclipse "would have been considered ominous of good or bad fortune."

With or without the eclipse, the test of fortune was near for both armies. On the twenty-fourth both Clinton and Washington had decisions to make. The patriot general was at Hopewell, New Jersey, only some twenty-four miles from Allentown, almost within striking distance. At Allentown Clinton had reached a literal and figurative crossroads. Until then the British commander in chief had avoided a decision on which route to take across the rest of New Jersey. Two paths were open to him. One road ran northeast from Allentown through Cranbury and New Brunswick, across the Raritan River, and on to South Amboy; there his men could cross to safety on Staten Island. The other road was more southerly, proceeding through the village of Monmouth Court House in Freehold Township and on to Sandy Hook, from which the Royal Navy could ferry the army to New York. Now he had to choose which to take.

Each route had its virtues. If Clinton went north, following the road through Cranbury, he could cross the Raritan River at New Brunswick and probably be at South Amboy in three days. From there, it would be an easy crossing to Staten Island; it was also the shortest route to New York. Washington had long suspected South Amboy as his opponent's destination. But the route had problems. Marching north would quickly bring his army into Middlesex County, a whig stronghold. The first sizable village on the way was Cranbury, which was ardently patriotic.[86] While Clinton felt he could fight his way through any opposition, he also was aware that more militia and Continentals were moving toward him, and a march northward would make it much easier for the Americans to rally forces against his columns. More worrisome was the Raritan River. The general later explained that a crossing would have invited an attack on his baggage train. He was convinced the train was Washington's real target, and if patriots managed to attack while the wagons were in midstream, an effective response would be difficult. Clinton also had intelligence that Horatio Gates was marching from the Hudson Highlands to link up with Washington around New Brunswick. In this belief, Clinton's normally good intelligence failed him: Gates was not marching south; he and Washington would not join forces until after the campaign. But the British commander had to assume that a concentration of patriot regulars would be in the New Brunswick area and under the circumstances concluded that the encumbrance of "an indispensably enormous provision train . . . was a sufficient motive for shunning the difficult passage of the Raritan."[87] All things considered, the northern route entailed too many risks.

On the other hand, there was much to recommend the road to Sandy Hook. The route would continue through Monmouth County, which had a major loyalist population; a friendlier locale hopefully would offer good sources of intelligence and fewer harassments. It also promised a safer retreat, especially once the column gained the easily defensible high ground near Middletown, just short of Sandy Hook. The latter place itself, garrisoned by a mix of loyalist regulars and irregulars, would provide a safe haven until the Royal Navy could ferry the army to New York. In addition, Clinton also reasoned that the more favorable terrain along the southern route would be advantageous if, unexpectedly, Washington offered battle. The more-open terrain of Monmouth County would favor his cavalry, in which he was much superior to the rebels, and offer better fields of fire to the Royal Artillery. If Washington wanted to fight, Clinton wanted him to come down from the "hilly country" to a place where the British could get "a fair stroke at him."[88] Accordingly, Sir Henry ordered the movement toward Sandy Hook.[89]

The orders surprised some of Clinton's officers. Until Allentown they had assumed that they would march to South Amboy. Lieutenant Colonel Simcoe was taken unawares. He learned of the new route when Clinton asked if any of his men could serve as guides through Monmouth County. Simcoe, who knew where most of his men had lived before enlisting, was able to help but admitted that this was his first inkling that the army was not proceeding to South Amboy. Adjutant Baurmeister professed no surprise at the news, but he thought Clinton altered his route to avoid building opposition to the north; the implication was that the general had changed course from his originally intended path. Andrew Bell thought Clinton had "outwitted" Washington by marching to "a different quarter," but it seems the general's own confidential secretary was caught offguard.[90]

One man was not surprised, or perhaps not *as* surprised. This was Major General Charles "No Flint" Grey of Paoli fame. Grey was an intimate of William Petty, Earl of Shelburne (Lord Shelburne). The earl was a former officer and cabinet member; by 1778 he was in the opposition calling for an end to both the American War and the government of Lord North. (In 1782, following the untimely death of the Marquis of Rockingham, Shelburne became prime minister and successfully ended the war.) To say the least, Shelburne was well connected in British politics and society, although many contemporaries mistrusted him.[91] He and Grey corresponded during the war, and the general was candid in his observations on the situation in America. In a letter of 15 June 1778, Grey wrote to thank the earl for favors to his family before moving on to political matters. He expressed his dismay over the likely failure of the Carlisle Commission. For this he blamed Clinton's orders to evacuate Philadelphia. The prospect had deflated all loyalist hopes and dashed what Grey considered an opportunity to strike hard toward the Susquehanna Valley (much as Charles Lee suggested the British would do). Then, in discussing plans for the evacuation, he passed along an interesting piece of intelligence. Clinton, Grey said, would cross "over to the Jerseys, marching to sandy Hook, the army to be posted upon the heights of the Navisink," and from there cross to New York and Long Island.[92] Did Grey have advanced knowledge of some decision the commander in chief had made before leaving Philadelphia?

The answer is probably—if not certainly—*no.* When it became clear that the Royal Navy could not transport the entire army and traversing New Jersey would be necessary, no doubt Clinton and his senior generals discussed possible routes of march. Given that there were only two real alternatives, it is inconceivable that any conversation did not include Sandy Hook. But this is not to say Clinton had made up his mind. Far from it. It would have been irresponsible if he had. Common-sense security concerns would have argued against any final decision at this point unless some powerful reason compelled it. There was none. In fact, there were too many opportunities for an early decision to leak. (Grey's letter to Shelburne is a good example.) Moreover, it would have made little sense to determine a final route without understanding the situation in the field. Clinton explained his decision in precisely those terms, and there is no reason not to believe him. The weight of the evidence is that Clinton wisely kept his own counsel until the last minute.

The royal commander put the army in motion early on 25 June; general orders called for everyone "to be in Readiness to move" at 4:00 A.M. To keep Washington guessing as long as possible, the Queen's Rangers marched north on the York Road a short distance beyond the intersection with the road to Monmouth Court House. The deception's goal, as Ewald wrote, was "to make the enemy believe we meant to aim at his [Washington's] march to Princetown and attack him."[93] With the rangers moving, Leslie, with the 5th Brigade and the loyalist Philadelphia Light Dragoons (a total of some 1,060 men), led the 1st Division as it turned east toward Monmouth Court House. Both divisions were now on the same road since the local road network would not allow travel by two columns within supporting distance. Knyphausen moved out first. With the bulk of the army's provisions train and a large contingent of noncombatants, Clinton wanted the 2nd Division out of harm's way as quickly as possible. The men took to the march with the promise of a gill of rum at the end of the day.[94]

At Imlaystown Knyphausen's men also marched at 4:00 A.M. Starting over four miles farther east and only a mile from the Shrewsbury or Monmouth Court House road, the 2nd Division remained in front, though much encumbered by its train of provisions, equipment, and noncombatants. Leslie's detachment soon caught up with the slow-moving division. Thus Clinton had his combat-heavy 1st Division between his vital baggage train and the most likely direction of any patriot attack.[95]

The huge column made an inviting target. When fully formed, the combined divisions extended some twelve miles, moving no faster than the teams could pull the heavily laden wagons over what turned out to be a "remarkably bad" and sandy road. It also remained oppressively hot.[96] Worse, there were now even more rebels probing the line of march. In addition to Dickinson, Maxwell, and Morgan, the British faced militia and Continental reinforcements. Recent arrivals included a brigade of Middlesex County militia under Brigadier General Nathaniel Heard, Continental light dragoons, some 100 Pennsylvania militia under John Cadwalader, the Continental detachment of Colonel Henry Jackson, and a temporary brigade of "picked men"—about 1,500 light infantry drafted from the army's infantry regiments—under Brigadier General Charles Scott; Washington had sent Scott from Hopewell on the twenty-fourth (as discussed later).[97] The patriots were building mass, and with mass came boldness.

The 1st Division was slow to depart Allentown. With the greatest danger now behind it, Clinton reversed the order of march. The pontoons, baggage, and cattle followed the vanguard, with the brigades of guardsmen and grenadiers positioned at the rear just in front of the light infantry, rangers, and jaegers. The rearrangement took time, and by the time the jaegers were clear of the village, a "body" of the enemy had advanced through the streets toward the Hessians. "A shot or two from their 3-pounders" dispersed these rebels. A short way down the York Road, the column turned right on the route to Monmouth Court House and Shrewsbury. No sooner than they had passed Robert Montgomery's big house—Cornwallis's quarters the previous night—than patriot marksmen opened fire from the windows. The rebels and some bricks were "dislodged by a gun of the Light Infantry." This was a foretaste of the skirmishing over the next day and a half. That night the jaeger diarist wrote that they had been "severely harassed by the enemy, who pressed us vigorously. We laid an ambush which made them cautious." It was another warm day of marching, and Clinton halted the column "from twelve to three o'Clock, in order to refresh the Men & Horses."[98] After the much-needed rest, the column moved on to Robin's Rising Sun Tavern, some twelve miles west of Freehold on the Shrewsbury Road (now in modern Clarksburg on County Route 524).[99] Clinton established headquarters at the tavern while Knyphausen encamped in Freehold Township, some four miles from Monmouth Court House.

The continuing action kept nerves on edge, although one incident produced an element of farce. As the Queen's Rangers screened the advance from Allentown, two horsemen approached them from out of a wood. Seeing the green uniforms of the rangers, the men took them for Continental dragoons, who wore the same color. Simcoe played along, posing as Lieutenant Colonel Henry "Light Horse Harry" Lee. The two strangers, both rebels, were delighted; one of them had a son in Lee's dragoons. They proceeded to tell Simcoe all they knew about patriot military dispositions. At this point one of them wondered aloud what Clinton was doing. Simcoe glibly responded, "You shall ask him yourself . . . for we are British."[100] Presumably, the abashed whigs met the Sir Henry soon enough.

Some of the men harassing the jaegers and light infantry were Colonel Morgan's light infantry. At 11:00 A.M. he notified Washington that "he had sent some parties to scarmish with them," then after a mile he moved his battalion off to the enemy right, seeking to find a weak spot. Morgan was not hopeful, however, complaining to Washington that Clinton camped his men "in a body so compact that it is empossible to get any advantage of them." But if it was difficult to kill or capture the enemy, it was easier to deprive them of sleep. That evening Major Joseph Bloomfield (Third New Jersey) and Captain Peter Voorhees (First New Jersey), with fifty Continentals and forty militia, took post on a hill a quarter of a mile from Clinton's encampment. During the night, they fired down into the British "& alarmed them several times." An irritated jaeger lieutenant got little sleep—"the enemy had disturbed us during the night up until we marched."[101]

The next morning, Friday, 26 June, the Continentals and militia clung to the rear of the 1st Division. Over the course of the day, near-constant skirmishing cost the British almost forty men killed, wounded, or captured. The rebels also took their losses as royal troops beat back attacks and laid ambushes for American patrols. Both sides agreed that the heat was "unbearable." Some Hessians "fell on the road and were put on the officers' horses in order to be carried along with us." "It was an extremely tiring day," Lieutenant von Feilitzsch wrote. "Would to God it is the last one."[102]

One of these skirmishes briefly assumed a more serious dimension. For a few minutes early in the morning of the twenty-sixth, it appeared that Captain Ewald's jaegers might be overrun. Patriots, apparently in stronger numbers than usual, hit Ewald's picket line, forcing the jaegers back under pressure. The captain called for help—which by itself seemed to frighten off many of the enemy—and Simcoe came up. The lieutenant colonel ordered the Queen's Rangers to fix bayonets, divided them into two parties, and sent them to the flanks of the jaegers (whose rifles could not mount bayonets). The rangers and jaegers then made short work of the Americans and reestablished the picket line. The engagement was over quickly. Knyphausen noted the incident as a sharp but brief affair, and most other contemporary accounts of the day failed to mention it at all.[103]

Ewald saw it differently. To him it was a desperate fight, and he claimed the rebels maintained contact all the way to Monmouth Court House. In his diary he lamented heavy casualties: "I lost over 60 men out of 180 foot jaegers and 30 horsemen, among which may well be some 20 men who dropped dead from the great heat and fatigue." In addition, he complained the "intolerable heat" had cost the army another 200 men.[104] One suspects that the hard-working officer was feeling the stress of over a week of almost constant duty with periods of continuous skirmishing, as he was thoroughly mistaken about the scale of fighting that day. No other account of the action noted such a grim toll or combat of the magnitude Ewald reported. Certainly, Knyphausen and Baurmeister would have referenced such losses among an elite Hessian unit, but neither man did. The Americans would have counted such an engagement a victory, but they never claimed it. Yet Ewald was on the point of the patriot attack, no matter what its scale, and in the heat of battle people see things differently.

To Monmouth Court House

The British army was now deeply into Monmouth County. Knyphausen arrived at Monmouth Court House well before midmorning on the twenty-sixth, marching the 2nd Division through the village and stopping just east of the town center. The rest of the army marched in by 10:00 A.M., halting on opposite sides of the road they had followed into town. Clinton made his headquarters for most of that day at the home of Thomas Tomson, four miles west of the village; in the late afternoon he moved to the house of William Covenhoven, about two miles closer. The British had marched some nineteen miles from Allentown, moving northeast along the Shrewsbury and Old Burlington Roads through blistering heat that left the troops exhausted. By nightfall, their tents and campfires formed an arch curving for approximately four and a half miles between the western and northeastern approaches to the town.

Sir Henry had picked his ground carefully. An extensive road network converged at the courthouse, and Clinton's position covered the most important approaches to the town. The deployment, while complicated, was skillful. The 1st Division camped to the west, along the route from Allentown, while the 2nd Division occupied the village. Immediately east of the village, two infantry brigades on William Wikoff's farm covered the provision train, artillery park, and the road from Middletown and Shrewsbury. The 4th Foot and 17th Light Dragoons protected Knyphausen's quarters at the Wikoff house. West of the village, two brigades of German infantry camped on the high ground above the intersection of the Englishtown and Amboy Roads, while to the north on the Amboy Road, the 2nd Light Infantry covered the bridge crossing Spotswood North Brook; their picket was across the stream at Forman's Mill.[105] Clinton also liked the surrounding terrain. To the west the ground was fairly open in places, but a number of woods, marshes, streams, and ravines cut the landscape, and the general felt that he could easily stop any assault from that direction. If Washington chose to come after him, he thought the terrain would favor his redcoats in a counterattack. Thus it was another careful deployment, putting the army in a position to fight or to continue its movement toward Sandy Hook.

Clinton planned to rest his weary army for at least a day, but it is entirely likely the general also was looking for a fight. The increasing activity of Dickinson's men and Continental light horse alerted the royal commander to the possibility that Washington was coming up in strength. Had he wished to avoid battle, Clinton could have moved at any time to the more defensible high ground at Middletown, some ten miles to the east. As it was, at least through most of the following day, he continued to hope that "Mr. Washington might yet afford me an opportunity of having a brush with him." Such anticipation dimmed after a reconnaissance westward convinced him that the rebel chieftain probably would not venture an attack over such difficult terrain.[106] Yet hope sprang eternal.

The army did need the rest. Although the usual potshots came from the peripheries, for the moment the troops were safely encamped. With their current strength, the patriots were unable to strike the main British positions. Indeed, Colonel Morgan expressed his frustration at being unable to do any serious harm. "Thay keep in so compact a body," he told Washington, "that it is impossible to do them much damage."[107] Ewald and the jaegers, Simcoe and the Queen's Rangers, the light infantry, the 16th and 17th Dragoons, and other regiments as necessary had done their jobs. The British army had marched some sixty-seven miles and arrived safely at Monmouth Court House, the county seat, and would occupy the town for more than two days. They would be days few would ever forget.

CHAPTER 7

THE ROADS TO MONMOUTH II

THE CONTINENTAL ADVANCE

General Clinton's army, of course, was not the only one on the move. As the British moved northeast through New Jersey, George Washington's track would take him on a roughly converging course to the southeast. Like Clinton's march, Washington's advance would be in increments. The commander in chief would move with the Continental main body as he tried to grasp where Clinton was going and what his army was likely to do along the way. In the meantime, he would send detachments to bolster the militia and Continental troops already in action. Ultimately, as American strength began to build around the royal army and the rival forces operated in close proximity, Washington was confronted with two of the most important decisions of his career: Should he fight? And if so, how? Following the various patriot advances that prompted these questions makes for a complicated narrative—but war is always a complicated business.

To Hopewell Township

The last Continental elements crossed the Delaware River at Coryell's Ferry on 22 June. The regiments concentrated on high ground several miles inland from Coryell's in the area of Amwell Meeting House (modern Mount Airy, New Jersey). The various campsites were from three to six miles from the river in the locale selected by Major General Lee two days earlier. At the ferry Washington established a temporary headquarters at the home of a "Mr. Haises," where his Life Guards pitched their tents.[1] Dr. James McHenry, the commander in chief's secretary, may have been luckier. He stayed at "Holcomb's," where he found the company

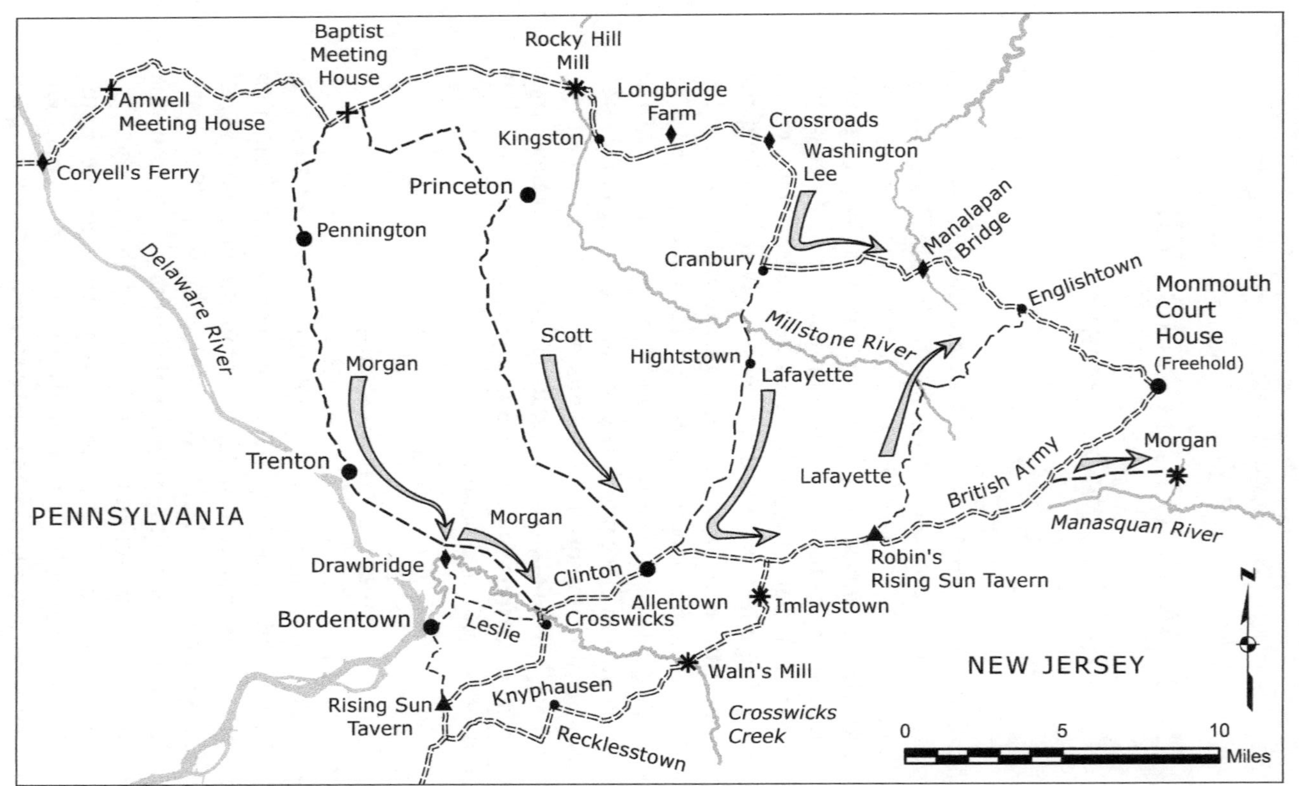

The Continental Army march routes from Coryell's Ferry to Monmouth Court House, June 1778. Map by Garry Wheeler Stone. Copyright © 2016 by the University of Oklahoma Press.

congenial. The young doctor was delighted to encounter "some charming girls," which he obviously appreciated after an unexpectedly difficult trip from Valley Forge.

The journey had been challenging. The crossing was neither easy nor fast. Since departing Valley Forge, the weather refused to cooperate, and the march was accordingly miserable. Periodic rains and sweltering heat slowed the main body. The general had wanted to get the whole army into New Jersey on the twenty-first, but a violent downpour impeded the crossing. Once across, he complained to Governor William Livingston and Major General Philemon Dickinson that the continuing rains had prevented any early movement, and even when the army marched, the "badness of Roads" and excessive heat had prevented a quick move inland. This was, of course, the same heatwave afflicting Clinton's men, and it killed Continentals as well as redcoats. Several rebel soldiers died even before reaching New Jersey.[2] By 24 June the rains had lessened, but the heat continued. Temperatures were likely in the middle to high nineties, "uncommonly hot weather" that would plague the army all the way to Monmouth.[3] As campaign openings went, the first several days were hardly auspicious.

Despite the weather, the army was moving on 23 June. The first scheduled stop was Hopewell Township, Hunterdon County, some ten miles south of Amwell and Coryell's Ferry.[4] Like the redcoats, the Continentals started early in the morning. The troops began to assemble at 3:00 A.M. and marched an hour later to avoid as much heat as possible. The Continentals left Amwell in detachments. The day before, Washington had divided the army into two wings. Lee commanded the right wing, consisting of six brigades with about 4,700 men; Lord Stirling, the next major general in seniority, commanded the left wing with five brigades, some 3,850 men. Major General Lafayette led the "Second Line" (reserve), with the First and Second Maryland and Muhlenberg's and Weedon's Brigades, with 3,687 of all ranks. (For administrative purposes, the same orders attached Brigadier General William Maxwell's New Jersey Brigade of 1,297 men, already deployed against Clinton, to the Second Line should it rejoin the main army.) Stirling's wing led off, followed by Lee and Lafayette, with Quartermaster General Nathanael Greene responsible for furnishing guides.[5]

Unlike the slogging pace of Clinton's army, the Continentals traveled relatively quickly. Terrain and planning had much to do with this. The road network in Hunterdon County was better established than the often sandy and boggy tracks in much of southern New Jersey; thus the route from Amwell lacked the impediments that so frequently plagued the progress of Clinton's men. Washington also sent his "Artificers and Pioneers" (maintenance and engineer troops) ahead to repair the roads, remove any obstructions, and mend bridges.

The Amwell-Hopewell area was (and remains) one of the most scenic regions of the state, and Washington's troops marched through rolling hills with ample woodlands and acres of carefully cultivated fields. It was a country of middling and generally prosperous farmers. As they marched, the troops—mostly farmers themselves—would have noticed that the rains had slowed more than their march. On the misty twenty-third, few men were working in the fields, and mown hay lay wet in some meadows. The next day was dry, and by noon men were mowing again. The more thoughtful soldiers may have wished them well while knowing it was unlikely that all the hay would be in before the wheat and rye harvest began in another week. With four regiments of militia out of the county, many Hunterdon farmers would be hard pressed to get their winter grain harvested before it was time to cut oats.[6] The season was too early for most fruit trees to be bearing, but cherries were ripe, and poultry roamed local farmyards. The fruit and birds were temptations for passing soldiers, who saw them as a tasty change from army fare. Even without filching a chicken or a hatful of cherries, many of the troops would have appreciated what they saw. Most had worked the land, and the rich countryside easily could have put the "for the war" men to thinking about the hundred acres of bounty lands promised to them.

Whatever they were thinking, the Continentals traveled light. Time was at a premium, and if the army was to catch the British, it could not afford the encumbrance of a lumbering baggage train. In order to speed the march, Washington ordered units to leave all heavy baggage and tents behind; officers and men were to carry only their packs, weapons and ammunition, and personal essentials.[7] Everything else went on wagons. The wagon train left the main army later on the twenty-third. Under the protection of a detachment of Life Guards, it arrived at Rocky Hill after a two-day march, remaining there until 1 July.[8] Over the course of the campaign, teamsters would shuttle supplies forward as the army advanced.

Thanks to Greene's efforts, essential supplies and transport were adequate—not abundant, but adequate. The major general had cached supplies at positions across northern New Jersey, anticipating that the British would march for South Amboy. In that case the Continentals would have taken a more northerly track as well. But Greene also had assembled wagons and teams, so when the time came, they were able to shift supplies from the northern caches to the army as it moved toward Monmouth County. There were occasions when advanced units would outrun the commissary wagons and go hungry for short periods, but with one brief exception, the main body had food and forage. In July Greene looked back on the campaign and gave his command (and himself) a pat on the back. The "great exertions" of the Quartermaster Department, he wrote, had underpinned the "success of the army in the operations through New Jersey." Washington fully agreed: Greene had done his job.[9]

As the army marched toward Hopewell, rumors abounded about what the British were doing—and for that matter, what was going on among patriot forces. One report had Clinton aiming at Trenton (sparked by news of Brigadier General Leslie's action at Bordentown), while another told of Governor Livingston personally taking the field at the head of 5,000 militia.[10] Whatever the reality—and no one really knew—hopes were running high. From Reading, Pennsylvania, James Abeel, one of Greene's efficient assistants, sent his chief a letter that captured the spirit of the moment: "God grant you Burgoyne the Enemy."[11] Even Congress, still at York, tried to monitor the action. Richard Henry Lee wrote Thomas Jefferson that Maxwell had successfully attacked part of Clinton's army, while Washington was over the Delaware and in "hot pursuit." If Washington could catch up, Lee was hopeful, "we may have a second edition of Burgoyne." Other delegates were just as enthusiastic, although President Henry Laurens still feared that Clinton was feigning a retreat.[12] The accuracy of any of these observations was beside the point: patriot morale in all quarters was high.

This included the soldiery. True, there was plenty of grumbling about the rain and the heat, but these are traditional soldiers' complaints. More important for the troops, however, was the prospect of action and the fact that they were on the offensive. There was an air of excitement, and some of the men were especially eager. One was Captain Walter Finney, formerly of the Pennsylvania Line. He had lost part of his skull to British fire earlier in the war, probably at Long Island, and a silver plate served to close the wound. On 23 June he left Philadelphia to join Washington "in the Jerseys as a volunteer, in order to convay my late Persecuters (the Brittish) out of that State."[13] Colonel Marinus Willett, having carried a dispatch to the main army from Major General Gates, then at Peekskill, did not want to return to Gates. He could sense an impending action and asked Washington's permission to stay on as a volunteer, joining Brigadier General Charles Scott as an aide and remaining through the rest of the campaign; Willet simply did not want to miss a fight. Private Joseph Plumb Martin of Connecticut noted widespread anger among the Americans as word filtered north of plundering and wanton destruction (as patriots saw it) along the British line of march. Other men were convinced they actually had the British on the run and Clinton was pulling away from them as fast as he could.[14] An army with the initiative, or at least *thinking* it has the initiative, can overlook a lot of bad weather.

Security measures were in place as the army moved. Orders provided for parties of infantry—bayonets fixed—and light horse on the flanks, in front, and in rear of the main column. Each battalion contributed a party of a lieutenant, two noncommissioned officers, and sixteen men, who marched eighty to a hundred paces from the main body. These precautions were prudent and were standard operating procedure, but they were not compelled by any real threat of enemy action.[15] While the British faced harassment, blocked roads, ruined bridges, and a hostile or indifferent populace, Washington's men marched through friendly country—a tory sniper or a wrecked bridge would have been a genuine surprise. In fact, Hopewell Township was very much a patriot locale, with many citizens playing active parts in the rebel cause. The main village in the township was Baptist Meeting House (sometimes just "Baptist Meeting"; known today as Hopewell, the still-charming town has homes and other buildings dating from the Revolutionary period, and the cemetery at its center contains the graves of Revolutionary veterans). By 1778 such tories as there might have been were long gone or cowed into virtual invisibility.

According to township antiquarian Ralph Ege (writing in 1908), Hopewell's war began with a flourish. Supposedly, a breathless messenger brought the news of Lexington and Concord during services at the Baptist church. Parishioner Joab Houghton, a local notable and landowner, stilled the excited courier. Following the service, Houghton climbed atop a mounting block (a stone used as an aide in mounting horses) outside the meetinghouse. As the congregation gathered, he regaled them with reports of the "cowardly murder at Lexington by the royal troops" and the patriot vengeance that followed the redcoat retreat to Boston. Pausing for full theatrical effect, he finally cried: "Men of New Jersey, the red coats are murdering our brethren of New England! Who follows me to Boston?' and every man of that audience stepped out into line and answered, 'I.' There was not a coward or a traitor in old Hopewell . . . that day."[16] One may doubt the specifics of the speech or even if Houghton actually delivered it, but Ege's telling captures the sentiments of the time and place. There is no questioning the commitment of Joab Houghton. The story may have some hazy basis in fact, as Houghton—eventually a lieutenant colonel—served honorably at the head of New Jersey militia or state troops for the duration of the war. His regiment would fight at Monmouth.[17]

There is no doubt about the story of another Hopewell resident, John Hart, one of the state's most prominent patriots. Hart was a miller and farmer, and with some six hundred acres, he was the largest landowner in the township. He had a fine stone home in Baptist Meeting House (named after the local church for which Hart donated the land). Hart had established himself in colonial affairs, serving variously as a county freeholder, judge, and member of the colonial assembly. He had raised New Jersey troops during the French and Indian War and personally led them to New York, but the outfit never saw combat. In 1775, unlike the majority of Jerseymen, he quickly embraced the Revolutionary cause. But he was then sixty-four years old, and his health was too fragile for field duty. Thus, while his sons served in the militia, Hart took up the political cudgels on the home front. He helped organize local committees of safety and correspondence, sat in the provincial congress, and in 1776 was elected to the Second Continental Congress; Hart reached Philadelphia in time to sign the Declaration of Independence. The British therefore knew who he was, and Hart was a marked man when General Howe swept through the state later in the year. A Hessian patrol descended on Baptist Meeting House looking for him, forcing Hart into hiding in the nearby Sourland Mountains. His home and farm survived but suffered some damage. Hart emerged from his sojourn in the mountains to serve in the new general assembly and as commissioner of the state loan office.[18] On 23 June he would lend his assistance to General Washington and the Continental Army.

The approach of some 12,000 soldiers and camp followers would have been difficult for any Hopewell resident to miss. When he learned of it, Hart sent two sons to intercept the army with advice on a possible encampment. At Baptist Meeting House, Hart's farm lay adjacent to that of Abraham Golden. The fields were planted but offered open camping ground large enough to accommodate the troops and a spring-fed pond, Lake Tommy, roughly in the middle. Washington gratefully accepted the invitation. The village itself had housing enough to put up at least the senior officers. This was a sacrifice for the Hart and Golden families, as an army bedding down in the open unavoidably trampled the crops; neither family would harvest in 1778. Despite Washington's explicit orders to the contrary, they also saw their fences disappear for cooking fires.[19] There is no record of Hart having asked leave of the Goldens before offering their fields as a campsite, but one doubts they objected: As a militia light horseman, Abraham Golden was captured in 1776, eventually sent to the dreadful prison hulks in New York harbor, and never seen again.[20] Like the Harts, the Goldens were committed whigs, and they had a personal score to settle.

The stopover at Hopewell was an important interlude in the campaign. Most of the army stayed two nights at Baptist Meeting House (23 and 24 June), and the troops got some badly needed rest. The meetinghouse itself became a temporary hospital. Washington probably dined with Hart on the evening of the twenty-third, but aside from that break, his time there was a constant swirl of activity. He set up headquarters in the home of a recently deceased militia captain, Joseph Stout.[21] With the property rented to a John Hunt, some headquarters correspondence carried the notation "Hunt's House." The commander in chief devoted himself to "digesting intelligence and deciphering the enemy's intentions." Those intentions were not clear, thus Washington wanted his army in a state of immediate readiness. General orders for 23 June called for the troops to "cook their Provisions and in every respect be in the greatest readiness possible for a march or Action very early in the morning."[22] He also arranged for camp guards and for the distribution of arms to units in need. Not yet knowing Clinton's intended route, Washington sent out reconnoitering parties to the Rocky Hill and Kingston areas in case the British decided to move north, striking for South Amboy.[23]

His correspondence those two days was voluminous as he received intelligence reports, kept in touch with detachments operating around Clinton's march, and dealt with army administrative matters. He wrote to senior commanders in other theaters to keep them abreast of developments, although he was unable to offer much in the way of concrete information. On the twenty-fourth Washington dispatched a short note to Major General William Heath, then near Boston in command of Burgoyne's Convention Army, informing him that the British had reached Allentown. But "whether they mean for Amboy, or Sandy-Hook," he noted, "is not evident."[24] His secretary and aides worked without letup.

Continentals and Militia

Washington's most immediate concern was the ongoing skirmishing against the British, less than twenty-five miles to the south of Baptist Meeting House. After departing Valley Forge, he wrote Henry Laurens that he would act "according to circumstances" in the pursuit of Clinton.[25] But Washington had no intention of allowing circumstances to be random; he wanted to be close enough to the retreating redcoats to seize any opportunity that might present itself. The Continentals would have to catch up with Clinton, however, and that meant slowing the British as much as possible—thus his various orders to Maxwell and his encouragement to Dickinson. Now he would reinforce the former and continue to encourage the latter.

Washington was anxious to get more Continentals directly involved in the fighting, hoping to dig harder at Clinton's flanks. He detached his first contingent to the south on 23 June; while the rest of the army encamped, he ordered Colonel Morgan to take some 600 light infantry to reinforce Dickinson and Maxwell. Morgan was a hard man. Working as a teamster during the French and Indian War, he received 499 lashes for striking an officer. This would have killed most men, and thereafter Morgan hated the British army with a passion. Still, he returned to duty then and finished the war as a rifleman against the Indians on the Virginia frontier. He became a prosperous farmer and militia officer in the years prior to the Revolution. When fighting broke out with the British, Morgan rushed to arms. He led Virginia troops from the first campaign of the war and emerged as one of the best combat leaders in Continental ranks. After a pivotal role at Saratoga, Morgan was renowned as a light-infantry and rifle-unit commander, and he was Washington's logical choice for the assignment.[26] The nucleus of the colonel's corps consisted of the rifle companies of the Fourth and Twelfth Pennsylvania Regiments and the Sixth, Seventh, Eighth, and Eleventh Virginia Regiments.[27] To add muscle, Washington attached most of his own company of Life Guards (the rest being sent to guard the baggage train) and a supplement of "picked men," comprising "an active, spirited Officer" and twenty-five men drawn from each of the army's infantry brigades. In choosing the men Washington was particular: he ordered the brigades to send their best marksmen. The commander in chief wanted Morgan to work with Dickinson, gain the enemy's right flank, "and give them every degree of annoyance in that quarter."[28] The pace of events was accelerating.

The Virginia colonel marched quickly. Shortly after 3:00 A.M. he left Hopewell, taking the road south toward Trenton, about fifteen miles away. The march was tiring. The weather remained hot, and in the early afternoon, Morgan sent a rider ahead to Dickinson at Trenton. The messenger reported that the light infantry were about three miles outside of town, that they were exhausted, and that Morgan intended to encamp in Trenton for the night.[29] But with Leslie's troops threatening near the drawbridge at Bordentown, the colonel decided to push on. His troops arrived too late to get into the action—the exhausted militia were glad of his arrival—and spent the night on the north bank of Crosswicks Creek while Leslie's men remained on the south bank. With the British departure early on the twenty-fourth, Morgan remained in place until the afternoon; his men had undertaken a punishing march and desperately needed some rest. He then set out along the north bank of the creek, following its course to the village of Crosswicks that night, then on to Allentown, where he arrived on the morning of 25 June.[30]

There Morgan finally closed with the enemy. Hanging on the British rear, the light infantry and Clinton's rear guard exchanged a few shots with "no harm done." The rivals then faced one another from opposite sides of the creek before both moved on, the redcoats heading east, while Morgan sent some skirmishers after them and rested his hot and tired main body. After a three-hour break, he led them around the enemy columns to gain their right flank, joining three small militia battalions sent by Dickinson, which brought Morgan's strength to about 800 men. The colonel inflicted no real damage, finding the British formations too concentrated to approach.[31] But Clinton now had Morgan on his right, Maxwell and Dickinson's militia on his left, and would soon have additional militia and Continentals closing on his rear.[32] The British army was now akin to a Royal Navy ship-of-the-line, deadly and unstoppable wherever it was for a given moment, but plowing through an increasingly hostile sea.

As Morgan shadowed the enemy, Dickinson labored to bring the militia to bear on the British. Indeed, of all Washington's correspondents while at Hopewell, he was in touch most often with Philemon Dickinson. Over the two days of 23 and 24 June, he exchanged eleven dispatches with the militia general, avidly reading intelligence reports and asking for more information. He wanted as much timely detail as possible, and he urged Dickinson to animate his men and impress on them the critical state of affairs.[33] Thus far, Washington had demonstrated a steady hand in coordinating Continental and militia operations, with Dickinson as his chief collaborator. In fact, he was dealing with the New Jersey militia general as he would with one of his own major generals, and Dickinson was functioning as such. There was no clear chain of command in the forward area—a region that shifted daily as Clinton moved—but the de facto command fell to Dickinson. Washington trusted the militia general to maintain an overall perspective on the unfolding situation.

The New Jersey general generally was not directly in combat, although he was close to the action at Bordentown. Rather, his role was that of an operational commander managing the scene: he ordered the stand at the Bordentown drawbridge, sent militia units into action as they moved into areas of active operations, distributed supplies to new arrivals, took charge of enemy prisoners and deserters, and was Washington's best single source of intelligence. Dickinson spent considerable time coordinating operations with Maxwell and other Continental formations as they arrived. He arranged local guides for the Continentals so they could find their ways in unfamiliar terrain and personally roved the British left flank trying to understand what Clinton was up to. When his cousin John Cadwalader arrived with a small contingent of Pennsylvania militia, Dickinson arranged for their resupply.[34] Through 26 June, when Lafayette arrived to take charge (as discussed below), it was Dickinson who knew the most about where the various militia and Continental units were and what they were doing. He was all the commander in chief could have wished in a militia leader. The Jerseyman was driving himself hard, and on the morning of the twenty-fourth, he apologized to Washington for a nearly illegible dispatch: "your Excellency will excuse this blotted scrawl, as I am rather sleepy."[35]

Militia strength was never as great as Dickinson or Washington wished, but it built to respectable numbers. On the twenty-third Dickinson told the commanding general that he had about 1,200 to 1,300 men in the field. This number was probably higher by the end of the campaign—perhaps as many as 2,000—as the militia general admitted that there were units operating out of reach of any headcount.[36] Ultimately, nine counties sent militia into action—Burlington, Cumberland, Essex, Hunterdon, Middlesex, Monmouth, Morris, Salem, and Somerset—all contributing infantry. Monmouth and Hunterdon also sent artillery companies, while Hunterdon, Middlesex, and Somerset dispatched light horse.[37] While some outfits fought independently, they never attempted major attacks. On 23 June, however, the defensive fighting at Bordentown was primarily a militia affair—and well remembered by those involved.[38] But militia operating alone usually did so in small parties. To get the most out of his men, whenever possible Dickinson tried to attach his units to Continental formations, giving the regulars much-needed reinforcements as well as equally needed confidence to the local troops. He sent 200 militia to Maxwell early in the campaign, and Morgan annexed another 200 or so (men Dickinson had sent) when he swung around Clinton's right. Still later, elements of the Somerset and Middlesex light horse would scout for General Lee as his command advanced on Monmouth Court House. Other Somerset riders worked with Continental dragoon lieutenant colonel Anthony Walton White, while Captain Joshua Huddy's Monmouth artillery was attached to Morgan's Continental light infantry. Nor was it unusual for Continental officers to take command of militia units on reconnaissance missions.[39] Whatever the exact numbers of militia may have been—and we will never know precisely—the run up to the Battle of Monmouth offered one of the best examples of militiamen and Continentals working in combination.

The local troops had their shortcomings, of course. Colonel Henry Jackson of Massachusetts was not impressed with the militia. He had arrived at Black Horse on 24 June (two days after the British had left), having marched his detachment of some 240 men from Philadelphia to join the main army. With him he had fifty dragoons under White. He found other Continentals in the vicinity but complained, "the militia do not turn out at all."[40] He was right *and* wrong. Coming through Gloucester County, Jackson would have seen few local forces. Two months previous, the county militia had suffered a near collapse in the civil turmoil convulsing the area. There had been no time to rebuild, and no organized Gloucester units were in the field.[41] The militia of other counties were fighting, but Jackson missed them simply because most had pursued Clinton and were no longer in the Black Horse area. Still, as he approached the theater of active operations, Jackson had expected to find more local troops in the field.

So did Dickinson. One of his biggest disappointments was the failure to bring a brigade of 800–1,000 militia into action. These men served under Brigadier General William Winds of Morris County, and Washington hoped these troops would cut in front of Clinton and substantially slow his progress.[42] Winds had marched south, passing New Brunswick and intending to cross the South River near Spotswood. On the way, however, he received intelligence that the bridges had been cut and he could not get his command across the river. Instead of waiting for verification of the report, Winds returned to New Brunswick, where he learned of a possible British threat to Elizabethtown, opposite Staten Island. Going first to Woodbridge and then on to Elizabethtown, there he learned to his mortification that the bridges at Spotswood were fully intact. Winds also found no looming attack on Elizabethtown. The best he could do was write embarrassed letters to Dickinson and Washington and beg "Your Excellency Will not Entirely Disapprove My Conduct." Dickinson was not pleased, and unsurprisingly there is no record of Washington having responded. The incident damaged Winds's reputation beyond repair, and he resigned under a shadow the next year.[43]

Council of War

Still in Hopewell, Washington struggled to understand what was happening to the south. By the evening of 23 June, intelligence from Dickinson made it all but certain that Clinton was approaching Allentown, about halfway across the state, although where he would go from there remained in question. Later that night Dickinson sent another dispatch, this time with a telling conclusion on Sir Henry's probable intentions. Writing at 11:30 P.M.—meaning that it reached Hopewell only in the very early hours of 24 June—he told the commander in chief that the militia and Maxwell had done all they could to delay the enemy march. They had destroyed bridges, dropped trees across roads, and, as mentioned in British accounts, caused the redcoats considerable annoyance. Yet they had not stopped the enemy for any length of time, and Dickinson was convinced that nothing his men (or Maxwell's for that matter) had done could account for the glacial pace of Clinton's army. Rather, the militia general had no doubt that the royal commander was deliberately lingering in the state for a single purpose: "to bring on a general action." He assured Washington that "intelligent" deserters from the British had confirmed his own conviction in this regard.[44] Not everyone at headquarters was convinced, but Washington had to take the possibility seriously. Indeed, less than twenty-five miles separated the two armies; they were almost within striking distance. Washington decided to talk to his generals: it was time for another council of war.

This would be the third council since May. The previous two had produced little in the way of concrete results; indeed, events had rendered the decisions of the 18 June council (such as they were) entirely moot. Still, Congress expected Washington to consult with his senior officers on important occasions, and the situation on the twenty-fourth was certainly one of them. In May and early June, the meetings had dealt with an enemy whose intentions were very problematic. Now those intentions remained hazy, but one thing was clear: if the Continental Army was to fight at all, it would have to do something quickly, otherwise Sir Henry was simply going to march away. At this stage of the conflict, that was unacceptable—it would be disappointing from a strictly military perspective and embarrassing politically. Thus for the army and Washington personally, the Hopewell council would be one of the most important of the war.

That morning the commander in chief convened his generals in the parlor of the Hunt house. Eleven officers attended: Major Generals Lee, Greene, Stirling, Lafayette, and Steuben and Brigadier Generals Knox, Poor, Wayne, Woodford, Paterson, Scott, and Duportail. The patriot commander began with a review of the situation as he understood it. He estimated British strength at between 9,000 and 10,000 rank and file—a serious underestimate, for Clinton had closer to 17,660 combatants of all ranks[45]—while the Continentals at Hopewell counted 10,684 plus Maxwell's advanced party of 1,200 and Morgan's light infantry; he also noted roughly 1,200 militia available, with more on the way. Washington then referenced Dickinson's contention that Clinton had deliberately maintained a leisurely pace, the implication being the British commander wanted to fight. All of this said, he wanted to know what his generals thought. Should they "hazard a general action?" If so, should they attack the whole or part of the British army or provoke an enemy assault and fight a defensive battle? If a general engagement was unadvisable, could the patriots at least "annoy the Enemy" as they crossed New Jersey? "In fine," Washington asked, "what precise line of conduct will it be best for us to pursue?"[46]

Rather than producing any consensus, however, the council served only to air the differences among the senior commanders. While there is no transcript of the meeting, it appears that Lee's was the dominant voice. Even if that concedes too much influence to him, the second in command certainly spoke his mind with his usual bluntness. At the council of 18 June, Lee had insisted that bringing on a general engagement would be "to the last degree criminal"; and his position had not changed.[47] He now argued for letting Clinton go, in fact, for doing nothing to slow the British exit from New Jersey. As Lafayette recalled after the war, Lee spoke "very eloquently" to "erect a bridge of gold for the enemy." Why risk the patriot regulars, Lee asked, in pointless action against the best-trained professional troops Europe had to offer when prudence would accomplish results equally important? Would it not make more sense to await the results of French intervention while conserving American strength? As it was, the general stressed that a rebel victory would probably do the cause little good, while a defeat in a general action could do it irreparable harm.[48] It should be noted that despite the unpopularity of Lee's views among some of the other officers, and the pall cast over this able but eccentric man's career after Monmouth, his arguments had some merit. The French alliance and the evacuation of Philadelphia had lifted patriot spirits to new heights and left the royal troops dejected and bitter. Clinton was looking for a chance—any chance—to redeem the honor of British arms, and a rash patriot attack could have played directly into his hands. So if Lee's conservative course would have brought no new laurels to the rebel army, neither would it have risked boosting British morale with even a partial victory over Washington.

Lee's argument for caution seemingly swayed the council, at least for the moment. According to Lafayette, four other generals—Stirling, Woodford, Scott, and Poor—agreed with Lee. The others wanted more forceful steps, with at least Wayne favoring the immediate dispatch of another 2,500 or 3,000 men to the south. Those with Lee were more interested in shadowing the British and watching events; the rest favored an attack if they could do so without undue risk. The only matter of agreement was on that of a general engagement: no one, not even the bellicose Wayne, wanted one. With opinions divided, a rough compromise emerged. The council wrote Washington that a general engagement would "not be advisable"; instead, they urged sending a detachment of 1,500 troops to "act as occasion may serve" in conjunction with the Continentals and militia already in the field. All the generals signed the statement except Anthony Wayne.[49] It was hardly a decisive recommendation. A disgusted Alexander Hamilton had attended the council as an aide and had the unpleasant (for him) duty of drafting its response. He had hoped for a more hawkish result and later denounced the entire proceeding. It "would have done honor," he wrote acidly, "to the most honorab[le] society of midwives, and to them only."[50]

It is not difficult to fathom Washington's thinking at this point. The commander in chief was disappointed at the council's tepid response.[51] But he was not bound by any council decision—it was only advice—and he quickly regained the initiative. The patriot chief was not about to risk his Continentals unnecessarily in any showdown fight, but he wanted offensive measures beyond the cautious recommendation of his generals. He first issued orders dispatching the additional 1,500 men against Clinton. He sent Brigadier General Scott, an old friend from Virginia and an ensign in the Virginia Regiment during the French and Indian War. Scott was to proceed "immediately" toward Allentown, gain the British left and rear, "and give them all the annoyance in your power."[52]

Like Morgan, Scott took "picked men" with him, and their morale was high.[53] As it marched, Scott's column found the public enthusiastic about the unfolding campaign; there was a perception that affairs were building toward a climax. As the troops passed though Princeton—a town that suffered its share of pillage in 1776 and 1777—residents gave the soldiery a warm welcome. As Private Joseph Plumb Martin recalled, they dealt out "toddy" to the men as they marched by, "which caused the detachment to move slowly at this place." Cheerful young ladies watched "the noble exhibition of a thousand half-starved and three-quarters naked soldiers pass in review." In this, the private's memory lapsed a bit: the troops were actually in reasonably good condition. But he remembered the "ladies" well enough. "I declare that I never before or since saw more beauty," he wrote. "They were *all* beautiful." With sectional loyalty, the Connecticut soldier allowed that "Yankee ladies" were perhaps smarter, but he insisted that "New Jersey and Pennsylvania ladies" were "handsome, the most so of any in the United States." We can never know if his comrades shared his infatuation, but his paean to the Princeton belles suggests that on that evening, they were as much concerned with Venus as with Mars.[54] Scott's troops slept rough that night in a field outside town, and the following day (25 June) they prepared to close with the British rear near Allentown. From then on, it was all Mars.

Yet even as Scott left Hopewell, Washington was considering additional and more belligerent steps. Quickly after the council adjourned (we do not know exactly how fast, but probably no more than an hour or two), his more aggressive generals gave their commander in chief an opportunity to act. In fact, it happened soon enough to raise a suspicion that Washington fully expected to hear from them and even knew what they were going to propose. At any rate, he received individual letters, and perhaps visits, from Generals Wayne, Lafayette, and Greene; all objected to the conservative recommendation of the council of war and argued for an augmented offensive movement.[55] It was exactly what Washington wanted to hear, and it is difficult to believe that these communications came as a surprise.

It was a subdued Anthony Wayne who wrote to his commanding general. The Pennsylvanian, having refused to sign the council's half-hearted statement, wanted a more vigorous course and told Washington as much. But his tone had changed. Perhaps the prospect of active operations had sobered him, but the former bravado that marked his letters of the previous April was gone—there was no mention of military glory, no "Conquering Army," no patriot renown shining "through the Courts of Europe."[56] Rather, in muted terms, "with all due Deference to Other Opinions," he pressed for the dispatch of 2,500 to 3,000 rank and file with appropriate leadership. He eschewed any rush to a general engagement but thought that such a reinforcement, with the troops already in action, could make "an Impression in force." The main body should move within supporting distance but engage only if the commanding general thought best.[57] Wayne's proposal would have resulted in the commitment of roughly a third of Washington's total strength.

If anything, Lafayette and Greene (doubtless encouraged by Hamilton) were even more insistent than Wayne on bolder measures. The Frenchman told Washington that he had signed the council statement only because other officers told him he should. Like Wayne, he wanted to send an additional 2,000–2,500 men into action, with the main army moving to supporting distance. He assured Washington that Steuben and Duportail were of the same opinion and had asked him to explain to the commander in chief in English how upset they were that a golden opportunity to hit Clinton might slip away. Lafayette agreed. It "would be disgraceful for the leaders and humiliating for the troops," he told Washington, "to allow the enemy to cross the Jerseys with impunity."[58]

Greene was the most emphatic of all. He was for hitting the enemy as hard as possible short of bringing on a general engagement, and he even liked American chances if a general action developed. But his reasoning was as much political as military and is worth quoting at length:

> If we suffer the enemy to pass through the Jerseys without attempting anything upon them, I think we shall ever regret it. I cannot help thinking we magnify our difficulties beyond reallities [*sic*]. We are now in the most awkward situation in the World. We have come with great rapidity and we got near the Enemy and then our courage failed us and we halted without attempting to do the enemy the least injury. . . . People expects [*sic*] something from us and our strength demands it. I am by no means for rash measures but we must preserve our reputation.
>
> I think we can make a very serious impression with out any great risque and if it should amount to a general action I think the chance is greatly in our favor. How ever I think we can make a partial attack without suffering them to bring us to a general action.[59]

This was a general who understood that wars are not won by battles alone; popular morale and political support are critical as well. Greene, having worked closely with Congress as he reorganized the Quartermaster Department, was fully aware of how anxious the delegates were for the Continental Army to prove itself. He knew how important it was for Washington to do the same. Greene had it perfectly: "People expect something from us," and the patriot officers had better deliver.

Washington, of course, shared precisely these concerns, and he needed no lessons in politics from his quartermaster general. He knew that if he was to silence his critics of the past winter, his chance was disappearing toward Sandy Hook. But he was no doubt pleased that some of his most talented and favored subordinates had spoken up (and one suspects, with his full approval), and he wasted no time in acting on their advice. Late on the twenty-fourth or early on the twenty-fifth (probably the latter), he ordered the deployment of another 1,000 picked men. Initial orders gave Brigadier General Poor the command, but Washington quickly changed his mind and put Wayne in charge. No documentation has survived to explain this decision; Wayne's orders may have been verbal. At the council of war, Poor had favored Lee's more cautious approach to the campaign, while Wayne very much wanted to fight. One suspects that the command change reflected a similar desire on Washington's part. At any rate, Wayne's 1,000 men would follow Scott's 1,500.[60]

Thus, if 24 June had begun with a lackluster council of war, within twenty-four hours the commander in chief had gotten what he wanted: an offensive movement that posed little undue risk to the army as a whole but strong enough to hit hard if opportunity arose. It was a sensible middle course between doing little more than harassing Clinton as he marched away and seeking a potentially disastrous general engagement.[61] Hamilton was delighted and years later still applauded Washington's decision. "It was happy for America," he wrote, "that the man, whose reputation could not be wounded without wounding the cause of his country, had the noble fortitude to rescue himself, and the army he commanded, from the disgrace with which they were both menaced by the characteristic imbecility of a council of war."[62]

Lafayette's Gambit

With Scott on the way south and Wayne preparing to follow, Washington faced a command question. He would remain with the main body, but there would be three brigadiers—Maxwell, Scott, and Wayne—operating around Clinton, as well as Colonels Morgan and Jackson, Continental horse detachments, and Dickinson's militia. If Washington attempted to manage their operations from a distance, the potential for confusion was enormous. The situation called for a clear chain of command, and the obvious solution was for a major general to assume overall charge of the forward elements. Washington turned to his second in command, the senior major general, Charles Lee. He may have offered the command to Lee before he ordered Wayne to follow Scott—the exact timing remains unclear—but in any case Lee demurred. He had opposed any strong forward movement and thought the nature of the assignment was appropriate to a more junior officer. In Lee's estimation, the size of the contingents headed south was not significant enough to serve under the army's second-ranking general.[63] With this, Washington offered the command to the twenty-year-old Lafayette, who accepted immediately. In fact, James McHenry found "the young Frenchman in raptures with his command and burning to distinguish himself."[64] Indeed, "the young Frenchman" was as much the military romanticist as Anthony Wayne.

By 25 June the main army had moved from Hopewell to Longbridge Farm, near Ridge Road in the modern town of Monmouth Junction (the site of this encampment also has been called Lawrence's Farm). It was a march of fourteen miles, with stops at Rocky Hill Mill and Kingston, where Washington issued orders to Lafayette. The French general was to march with Wayne's detachment, catch up with Scott, get his forces on Clinton's left and rear, and—in the now familiar phrase—give him "every degree of annoyance." Further, he was to take command of all forward Continental units—meaning Maxwell's, Morgan's, and any other forces in the theater—and cooperate with Dickinson. Washington also wrote to Dickinson, informing him of Lafayette's approach and that he (Lafayette) was to have overall command. Lafayette was to guard against surprise, but he had positive orders to attack: "you will attack them as occasion may require by detachment, and if a proper opening sh[oul]d be given by operating against them with the whole force of your command."[65] For the first time on the campaign, the commander in chief had issued unambiguous orders to fight.

Lafayette moved south from Kingston, arriving at Cranbury at 9:30 P.M. after a march of about ten miles. There he joined Lieutenant Colonel Hamilton, who would serve as the major general's aide (and who had been itching to get close to the action). Hamilton had gone ahead to the village to gather intelligence and establish headquarters. This he did in the home of Dr. Hezikiah and Mary Stites, where he and Lafayette would spend the night. The troops encamped in the fields and woods along Cranbury Creek; while no one expected trouble, the site was on good defensive ground.[66] Hamilton's intelligence briefing was not comforting. He reported that Clinton was headed toward Monmouth Court House and the British had a considerable head start; their rear already was six miles beyond Allentown. Morgan was skirmishing on Clinton's right, and Maxwell was at Hightstown, about three miles from Cranbury; but he did not know exactly where Dickinson and Scott were. Given the scattered dispositions of patriot forces, Hamilton recommended that Lafayette designate some rendezvous in order to concentrate.[67] Thus the newly arrived commander found the tactical situation murky. Consequently, although it was late and Hamilton already had had a hard day, sometime around midnight (perhaps a bit earlier), Lafayette sent him forward again for another look. If the Frenchman was to accomplish anything, he needed a better grasp of where friendly and enemy forces were and what they were doing.

After conferring with Hamilton, Lafayette was back in touch with Washington. He relayed the intelligence that Clinton was on the move and already had a considerable lead. Lafayette would have to march early and fast the next morning (26 June) if he was to catch the enemy column. Moreover, he found that he was short of supplies, especially "*provisions.*" He asked for food and liquor for 6,000 men and pleaded for Washington to "spur" the commissary personnel in their duties. But he assured the commander in chief that he was going to march.[68] If he was short on supplies, the young general remained full of enthusiasm.

Enthusiasm, however, will not feed men, and on 26 June this became painfully apparent. In his haste to catch Clinton, Lafayette had his command on the move by 5:00 A.M., not bothering to wait for new provisions, although he wrote Washington, "we want them extremely." Two hours later he learned that he was within seven or eight miles of the British and pushed his men hard to close the distance. Lafayette fully intended to attack, although he still felt the lack of resupply.[69] Upon receiving these reports from the major general, Washington became concerned. Shortly before 10:00 A.M., he sent a dispatch to the marquis informing him that the main army had arrived at Cranbury and he was doing his best to get fresh provisions to the forward units. He then cautioned his lieutenant that "giving the Enemy a stroke is a very desirable event, yet I would not wish you to be too precipitate in the measure or to distress your men by an over hasty march." Washington feared that a forced march through the intense heat would do little more than incapacitate Lafayette's troops.[70]

That was exactly what was happening. By noon of the twenty-sixth, Hamilton, having ridden through the brutally hot morning, had reached Robin's Tavern (where Clinton had made his headquarters the night before), and Lafayette's contingent arrived some four hours later. A weary Hamilton wrote Washington that they could go no farther without rations and that Wayne's men were "almost starving." "If we do not receive an immediate supply," he warned, "the whole purpose of our detachment will be frustrated."[71] Still, Lafayette was loathe to give up the chase. From Robin's Tavern he notified the commander in chief that he was within three miles of Clinton and only the want of provisions kept him from attacking. He had discussed the matter with his officers and was contemplating a night march to hit Clinton the morning of the twenty-seventh.[72] By this time, however, it had become obvious to Lafayette that commissary operations could not keep up with him—and that exhausted and famished patriot soldiers would have been no match for well-supplied redcoats.

Lafayette had pushed his men to the breaking point. His predicament, however, went beyond the want of provisions, for in his pursuit of Clinton, he had advanced well beyond Washington's ability to support him with the main army. The detachment was in harm's way—and on its own. On the afternoon of the twenty-sixth, Hamilton still hoped Lafayette might "do something clever" if the main body could support him, but he also complained "we are entirely at a loss where the [American] army is." Under the circumstances, he feared that an attack on Clinton would risk "the total loss" of Lafayette's forces. The British, he noted, were securely encamped near Monmouth Court House, so any movement against them without Washington's support "would be folly in the extreme."[73] But even before he sent his second letter, Hamilton was relieved to learn that the commanding general was every bit as alarmed for Lafayette's safety.

Washington and the rest of the army arrived at Cranbury about 9:00 A.M. that day. Like Lafayette, he made his headquarters at the Stites house. There he attempted to learn the status of the Frenchman while dealing with problems of his own. The main column had marched only seven miles from Monmouth Junction, but the men had struggled through the continuing heat and violent thundershowers.[74] And, if only briefly, they had outrun the commissary wagons. For the moment, the Continental main body shared not only the heat, wetness, and exhaustion but also the hunger of the advanced detachment. Intelligence continued to be contradictory. While the general was all but positive that Clinton was headed for Sandy Hook, even Hamilton warned that the British still might make a turn toward South Amboy. Various reports told of different British movements but presented no clear picture.[75] There was even a command problem. General Lee had reconsidered his decision of the twenty-fifth; he now wanted command of the advance forces. Thus Washington had a lot on his mind, mostly uncertainties.

With the general situation so murky, Washington had every reason to be uneasy over Lafayette. While he exchanged communications with his major general over the course of the twenty-sixth (he sent Lafayette four letters and received three), he had no real assurance that his subordinate was in control of the scattered units shadowing Clinton. As the day wore on, Washington's fears grew that his young friend was flirting with trouble and that his detachment would stand little chance in a real fight. Late in the day he decided that it was time to take control of the situation; he had waited too long. In a letter that reached Lafayette well after dark, the commanding general minced no words. Lafayette, with all forward Continental elements, was to move immediately to Englishtown, about eleven miles from his current position at Robin's Tavern. There, Washington told him, the main army could support him if he was attacked or cover him if he had to retreat. He could do neither of these things at Robin's Tavern. Also, Washington noted that concentrating at Englishtown would facilitate resupply—the wagons could bring provisions to one place rather than chasing across the countryside after different columns. He closed by warning Lafayette to stay in touch with Dickinson and to maintain march security, as he had intelligence that a British picket (probably only a patrol) was within two miles of Englishtown.[76] Washington obviously felt the need to put his subordinate on a shorter leash.

Any hopes Lafayette had entertained for a bit of martial glory had vanished. At 10:30 P.M. he wrote Washington that he had abandoned any offensive plans even before receiving orders to march for Englishtown. At this point he said that all he wanted to do was get to Englishtown; once there, he knew he would join General Lee, who had come forward to take command. He planned to march at 2:00 A.M. the next day, bringing everyone but Morgan and the militia, who would remain behind to protect the detachment's right and rear from any British attempt.[77] Yet even at this stage there were complications. Scott, who was not encamped immediately with Lafayette, did not receive orders to join the march to Englishtown. Instead, he evidently acted on the earlier discussions of a morning attack on the British; courting disaster, he marched to within a mile of the enemy before learning that he was to withdraw.[78] Obviously, an exhausted Lafayette had only a tenuous command and control of his forces. Scott made good his countermarch, however, and sometime before noon on 27 June linked up with Lafayette and Lee at Englishtown.[79]

Lafayette's gambit had been dangerous. The major general's intentions were good, but his leadership was questionable. He never fully consolidated his control over the widely dispersed patriot elements, especially Morgan's detachment, which was too far away. As a result, Washington's hope that a unified forward command could strike a meaningful blow was never realized. Perhaps it was asking too much of Lafayette. The lack of supplies, the dispersed nature of patriot operations, the distance from Washington, as well as the strength and care of Clinton's dispositions all discouraged American opportunities to strike. Thus Lafayette's two-day command accomplished nothing in the way of impeding the British. Indeed, Lafayette had been determined and rash; the episode was not his finest hour.[80]

What if the Frenchman had attacked? We can only speculate on the fortunes of war, but there are possible scenarios. The closest British troops to Lafayette were the elite grenadiers, and they would have been his likely target. It is doubtful the general would have made any attempt against them unless they were marching—but caught marching or stationary, the grenadiers would have been strong opponents. Reinforcements, probably nearby Hessian units, would have arrived quickly, and eventually Clinton would have sent the rest of the 1st Division. Lafayette's 5,000 hungry and tired troops would have faced some 9,000 relatively fresh royal soldiers (about the same odds Lee would face on the morning of the twenty-eighth). As the British pressed their inevitable counterattack, Lafayette could have retreated into the pine trees less than two miles from the grenadier encampment. If the Frenchman was lucky, Clinton, concerned for his baggage train, may not have pursued too far. But what if Sir Henry came on too fast for Lafayette to react or caught the young general in the open and without Washington close enough to offer support? In writing (after the war) of Lafayette's circumstances, Lieutenant Colonel Henry Lee observed, "nothing is more dangerous than to hang with an inferior force upon a gallant enemy, never disinclined to draw his sword, and watchful to seize every advantage within his reach."[81] The result could have been a patriot disaster, an outcome perhaps less likely than a successful Lafayette retreat, but still a real possibility. It was just such a grim scenario that prompted Washington to recall Lafayette to Englishtown.

For his part, General Clinton apparently never knew how close the Frenchman had come. Had he known, it is difficult to believe that he would not have reacted with as much force as he could bring to bear. And if Clinton had done so, it is worth wondering if the luck of Barren Hill would have held a second time for Lafayette. But these questions are academic. The reality was that Clinton and Lafayette would meet soon enough.

CHAPTER 8

General Lee's Orders

Expectations and Misunderstandings

The late morning of 27 June found the British and American armies in dangerously close proximity. Clinton's troops occupied Monmouth Court House and its immediate environs; they were strongly posted with excellent security. The main body of the Continental Army had arrived at Manalapan Bridge (also called Penelopen), about six miles from Cranbury and ten from Monmouth. Lafayette had joined Lee at Englishtown, four miles from Washington at Manalapan. Both armies had advanced pickets and other parties out to guard against and feel for the enemy. The weather remained hot. During the day, it was probably over ninety degrees in the shade, and the opposing forces shared the misery of the suffocating heat. Most of the British remained inactive, grateful for a day without a march in the sun. Among the Continentals, even the relatively short march from Cranbury proved fatiguing. To their great relief, they went no farther on the twenty-seventh; the men lay exhausted on their arms in the open and recuperated as best they could while enduring yet another thunderstorm.[1]

Washington had little rest. All the while, Philemon Dickinson's New Jersey militia, Continental horse, and other units maintained a flow of intelligence on Clinton's position, occasionally exchanging shots with the British. Washington therefore knew approximately where his enemy was, if not exactly what he was doing.[2] The patriot chief wanted to strike, but after Lafayette's premature thrust, he needed a moment to pause and take stock before, once again, sending his men toward the enemy. When he did, however, the vanguard now would belong to Major General Lee. But how did Lee came to the command, and significantly, exactly what did Washington expect of him?

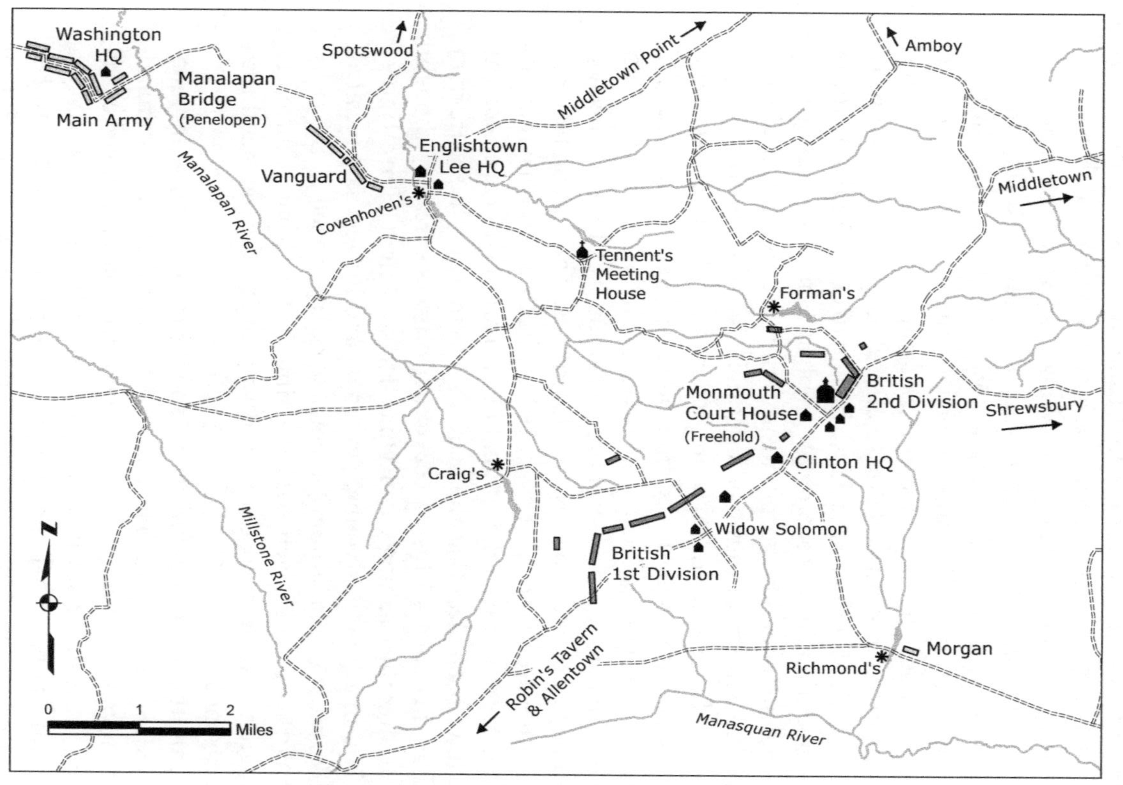

The rival army encampments, 27 June 1778. Map by Garry Wheeler Stone. Copyright © 2016 by the University of Oklahoma Press.

Lee Takes Command

The Manalapan encampment differed considerably from earlier stopovers in New Jersey. For the first time, Washington had to consider that his post might serve as a base for active combat operations. As he explained to Lafayette, Manalapan was close enough to British lines to support the movement of an advanced detachment or, if necessary, serve as a strong bulwark against attack. In fact, with Clinton so near, Washington was taking no chances. He had not neglected security at the earlier encampments, though at the same time he did not think a British attack was a serious possibility at those locations. But at Manalapan he had to consider that Clinton might come after him. Accordingly, he had Major General Stirling and Brigadier General Duportail inspect the surrounding terrain and place the encampment in the best possible defensive posture.[3]

Leaving Stirling to it, the commander in chief was free to think offensively. In this regard, the first order of business was dealing with Lafayette, whose recall to Englishtown had extricated him from a problematic tactical situation; it also afforded a much-needed opportunity to rest and reprovision his troops. There is no real evidence to indicate that the events of 26 June had shaken Washington's faith in Lafayette, but in the context of the Barren Hill experience, it should have been clear that the marquis was more enthusiastic than skilled at this stage of his career. Other officers certainly thought so, including the dashing cavalryman Henry "Light Horse Harry" Lee. "The marquis was young, generous, and brave;" Lee recalled, "and like most of his brother generals, yet little versed in the art of war."[4] Without other events intervening, it may have occurred to Washington that he needed a tactful way to put the vanguard into more seasoned hands.

But another event did intervene, and it turned out to be momentous: Major General Lee had changed his mind about commanding the advance troops. On the twenty-fifth, after Lafayette had marched from the main body at Kingston, Washington received a letter from his principal subordinate. While it explained why Lee initially turned down the command of the advanced detachment, in explaining his change of heart, it is best to quote the letter in full:

> When I first assented to the Marquis of Fayette's taking the command of the present detachment, I confess I viewd it in a very

> different light than I do at present. I considerd it as a more proper busyness of a Young Volunteering General than of the Second in command in the Army—but I find that it is considerd in a different manner; They say that a Corps consisting of six thousand Men, the greater part chosen, is undoubtedly the most honourable command next to the Commander in Chief, that my ceding it woud of course have an odd appearance. I must intreat therefore, (after making a thoushand apologies for the trouble my rash assent has occasion'd to you) that if this detachment does march that I may have the command of it—so far personally, but to speak as an Officer—I do not think that this detachment ought to march at all, untill at least the head of the Enemy's right column has pass'd Cranbury—then if it is necessary to march the whole Army, I cannot see any impropriety in the Marquis's commanding this detachment or a greater as advance Guard of the Army—but if this detachment with Maxwells Corps Scotts, Morgans and Jacksons are to be considerd as a seperate chosen active Corps and put under the Marquis's Command until the Enemy leave the Jerseys—both Myself and Lord Steuben will be disgrac'd.[5]

A cursory reading could reduce Lee's communication to a single issue: the forward detachment turned out to be larger than he thought, and as the army's second-ranking officer, he wanted the army's second-largest command. One also finds a sense of pique. This is exactly how Lieutenant Colonel Alexander Hamilton saw things. After the battle, when he was thoroughly hostile to Lee anyway, Hamilton wrote his friend Elias Boudinot that "General Lee's conduct with respect to the command of this corps was truly childish."[6] On 25 June, however, the matter was actually more complicated—*much* more complicated—and Hamilton probably held a minority view. General Lee was not alone in his reasoning or in his feelings of wounded honor.

The problem began on 25 June, almost as soon as the size of Lafayette's detachment became apparent. Hamilton again offers a perspective on the situation. "According to the incorrect notions of our army," he cooly observed, Lee's seniority "intitled him to the command." Not only that, other officers had queried Lee on his decision not to lead the vanguard; after learning of his refusal, Lord Stirling, the ranking major general behind Lee, had pressed a claim of his own. It was only after some discussion that both Lee and Stirling agreed to drop the matter.[7] All of this no doubt weighed on

Lee's mind when, later that day he decided that he could not stand aside and wrote to Washington. Lee may have seemed inconsistent to Hamilton, but to others his position was understandable. In the era's military culture, matters of seniority and status were bound inextricably to matters of personal honor and precedence. Indeed, disputes over seniority and related issues were common and frequently drove Washington and Congress to distraction.[8] However "childish" they seemed to Hamilton, for many officers, American or European, such "notions" were anything but "incorrect." There was no malice toward Lafayette in Lee's request; rather, under the conventions of the day, he sincerely believed that he and other officers with many years of experience (such as Stirling and Steuben) had a better claim to such a significant command.

It is difficult to discern Washington's initial reaction to Lee's about-face. Hamilton thought the commander in chief was irritated.[9] If so, his response to Lee avoided expressing it, and given the fact that other generals apparently agreed with Lee, Washington could hardly deny the justice of the request. If anything, his response to Lee—and for that matter, Lafayette's response when he linked up with Lee—was in keeping with prevailing views on seniority. On the twenty-sixth Washington noted his second's concern but felt that he could not fully allay it without "wounding the feelings" of the marquis. The commanding general offered what he hoped would be a workable solution. He would send Lee to Englishtown with two brigades to support the outfits under Lafayette, and there Lee would assume overall command when he joined forces with the Frenchman. If Lee found Lafayette in the midst of an engagement, he was to support the junior general and refrain from taking the reins; otherwise, the vanguard was his. The plan, Washington noted, was "not quite" the change of command Lee had requested, but he trusted it would satisfy him without insulting Lafayette. It was the best he could do under the circumstances. In a second letter Washington explained the situation to Lafayette and noted that Lee was satisfied with the arrangement; he assumed the marquis would not object.[10] Unspoken in either letter was the fact the plan would gracefully bring Lafayette under firmer control. (There was also another command change: with the detachment of Lee, Washington put Nathanael Greene in command of the right wing.)

Lee reached the Englishtown area on the afternoon of 27 June. With him were his adjutant, Lieutenant Colonel John Brooks of

Massachusetts, and aides Captain John Mercer of Virginia and Captain Evan Edwards of Pennsylvania. Colonel François Lellorquis, marquis de Malmédy, served as a volunteer aide. Lee also had a dragoon escort. Lafayette, to his credit, received Lee and his entourage cordially and professed his satisfaction at serving under so distinguished an officer.[11] Thus when the advanced corps (the vanguard, as it was usually called) went into action, it would be under General Lee.

Lee's force was not inconsiderable, although its composition of various detachments, regiments, brigades, battalions, and other units was confusing. Yet the vanguard's component organizations and their commanders would figure significantly in the action of the twenty-eighth, especially in the battle's critical morning phase. Lee brought the brigades of Brigadier Generals James Varnum and Charles Scott, though neither Varnum nor Scott commanded in person, and the "brigades"—supposedly outfits of two or more regiments—were such in name only. They were small, with rosters well short of even a full regiment. Varnum's, under Colonel John Durkee of Connecticut, numbered only some 300–350 men in four very understrength New England regiments. His able seconds were Lieutenant Colonels Jeremiah Olney of the Second Rhode Island and Giles Russell of a composite Connecticut battalion. About half the brigade had been detached earlier as "picked men" under Scott or Wayne, which had depleted regimental ranks. With Scott already attached to Lafayette, his brigade passed to Virginia colonel William Grayson. Grayson had no more than 300 men in three terribly thin Virginia regiments as well as two of the congressional "Additional Regiments," also quite lean. Wayne's detachment of 1,000 picked men were in battalions under Colonel Henry Beekman Livingston, Colonel James Wesson, and Colonel Walter Stewart. Scott's 1,440 troops composed four battalions of picked men under Colonels Joseph Cilley (First New Hampshire), Richard Parker (First Virginia), Richard Butler (Ninth Pennsylvania), and Nathaniel Gist (Gist's Additional Regiment). We know the most about Cilley's battalion. In a July letter to a friend, the colonel related that his "350 rank and file" were "detailed from Poor's, Glover's, Patterson's, Larnard's, and Varnum's brigades."[12] As there were a total of eighteen battalions in these brigades, it appears that Cilley had been sent one platoon-sized detachment from each regiment. Other units included Maxwell's Brigade, with up to 1,000 men in four New Jersey regiments and an unknown number of militia light horse (probably around forty), and the detachment of Colonel Henry Jackson (200 men in three skeleton Massachusetts and Additional regiments). Artillery companies with a combined twelve guns were distributed across the brigades. The senior artillerist was British-born Lieutenant Colonel Eleazer Oswald of Connecticut. Thus constituted, the vanguard totaled some 4,500 troops.[13] (See Appendix 2 for the vanguard's order of battle.)

This was the force Lee would take into battle. It was large enough to hurt an isolated or careless component of Clinton's army or to fight its way out of trouble if the British came after it in force. But it also reflected a problematic aspect of the Continental Army. At Valley Forge Washington had worked hard on army reorganization. Of the problems he faced in this regard, one of the most difficult was the many understrength regiments; his intention was to consolidate weaker units into fewer but stronger formations. But the opening of the campaign delayed the process, and as matters stood the advance force had elements of no fewer than thirty-one infantry regiments, albeit in relatively compact formations. Washington had consolidated many of the units on a temporary basis simply to get through the new campaign, so the situation was not as complicated as it looks on paper.[14] But the stop-gap amalgam of regiments and other organizations still brought together officers and men who may not have been familiar with one another. The arrangement was a potential administrative and tactical nightmare. Lee, having been absent from the army for so long, certainly knew few of the regimental commanders. And with so many units present, *any* officer in Lee's position would have been hard put to be sure of the strength of any one of them or even to tell one outfit from another—hardly a reassuring state of affairs on the eve of battle. But this was the state of affairs, and Lee would have to do the best he could with it.

What Were Lee's Orders?

If at all possible, Washington wanted Lee to hit the British the following morning, that is, on Sunday, 28 June. Any attack by the vanguard, however, would require the support of the main (or "grand") army, which Washington addressed in general orders on the twenty-seventh. "As we are now nigh the Enemy and of consequence

Vigilance and Precaution more essentially necessary," the orders read, "the Commander in Chief desires and enjoins it upon all Officers to keep their Posts and their soldiers compact so as to be ready to form and march at a moments warning as circumstances may require."[15] The tenor of the brief order—only a single sentence—was clear: Washington believed that some kind of action was likely, and soon. With that in mind, early on the afternoon of 27 June he rode the four miles from the main camp to Englishtown to confer with Lee. The meeting took place at Lee's headquarters in the Village Inn. At the army commander's invitation, Lafayette, Maxwell, Scott, and Wayne attended. There were no minutes of the meeting, and Washington issued no written orders or other instructions. In the absence of such documentation, whatever he said has remained a matter of controversy ever since. What did he actually say to Lee? And what did Lee and the others make of what they heard? Certainly, the commander in chief issued orders, but what was their nature? Until the day he died, Lee fervently believed that his orders were discretionary—that is, Washington had left in his subordinate's hands the decision of how or if to fight on 28 June. Others would as stridently insist that Lee was expected to attack Clinton come what may. Which was it?

Fortunately, even without written orders from Washington, the answer rests on a surprisingly large documentary foundation. The most important source is the sworn testimony given at Lee's court-martial; indeed, the first day of actual trial testimony (4 July) was largely devoted to establishing precisely what orders the general had received either on the twenty-seventh or subsequently. Aside from Lee, only Scott and Wayne testified on Washington's comments at Lee's headquarters. Scott recalled no "positive order" to attack, but he also had no doubt that Washington intended Lee to strike at Clinton the next morning. He "understood we were to have attacked the enemy at all events," and Washington wanted Lee to meet with his officers and formulate a plan. Wayne, an acknowledged hawk, had a similar but more detailed recollection. He stated that Washington issued no "particular orders for the attack." The only positive directive he recalled was the general's desire, in case of any patriot attack, that there be no disputes over rank. Maxwell, as senior brigadier, could have claimed the honor of leading the advance, but this was considered unwise because much of the New Jersey Brigade was composed of green recruits and draftees. Instead,

Washington wanted Lee to attack with a corps of picked men. In any event, Wayne said that the commanding general promised to support the vanguard with the main army. Under questioning from Lee, Wayne replied that while he "understood" Lee was to attack "at all events," he again conceded that he heard Washington give "no particular orders" and "knew of no restrictions in regard to your [Lee's] manoevres."[16] Whatever Scott and Wayne "understood," it is clear that neither brigadier ever heard the commander in chief give Lee unambiguous orders to attack or what to do should an engagement occur. If Washington had wanted an attack "at all events," he never explicitly said so. Frankly, it was no time for ambiguity, and the fact is Washington had left the meeting with his chief subordinates (however unknowingly) without any agreement on what their chief had said or meant. He returned from Englishtown having, in effect, left the coming battle to Lee. Under the circumstances, Lee's assumption that his orders were discretionary was reasonable.

It was now obvious to everyone that some kind of action was imminent. Clinton had rested his men for a full day, and no one could believe that he would remain stationary on the twenty-eighth. It was also clear that the best chance for a patriot attack would come when Clinton moved—presumably toward Middletown—which might leave the British rear guard vulnerable. But if he was to time his assault before Clinton actually got away, Lee would need to know exactly when the royal army would pull out of Monmouth Court House. With that in view, soon after Washington left his headquarters, Lee sent Captain Mercer to see Dickinson. The militia general had encamped part of his New Jersey troops at Tennent's Meeting House, about two miles from Englishtown. Mercer informed Dickinson of Lee's intention to advance as soon as he was sure that Clinton was on the move, but the Virginian did not have light horse to scout for him and the Continentals did not know the locale. Therefore Lee would have to depend "entirely" on Dickinson for intelligence on British activity. Dickinson promised full cooperation.[17]

Later on the twenty-seventh (around 5:00 P.M.), as Washington had requested, the officers gathered at Lee's headquarters. Scott missed the meeting (Lee spoke privately with him later), but for the others (Lafayette, Wayne, and Maxwell), Lee reiterated the commander in chief's injunction against any squabbles over rank and repeated what the generals already knew from the general orders of the day: they were to have their commands ready for action "at a moment's warning." Lee stressed that he expected any orders he gave the next day would be obeyed, but he offered no plan of attack. He saw no point, though, having little intelligence on Clinton's intentions and being unsure of enemy movements; for that matter, he lacked detailed knowledge of the terrain closer to Freehold. Efforts to gather better information from local residents had come to little. "The People here," he wrote Washington, "are inconceivably stupid." Thus Lee would not commit to any fixed plan of attack. He noted that the numbers and positions of the British "were mere conjecture" and the Continentals were unfamiliar with the terrain. Under the circumstances, he warned, forming "a precise plan" was unwise. "The least trifling, unexpected circumstance" could upset everything and "lead us astray," rendering a plan "invalid." All the vanguard could do was to stand ready to move quickly and govern itself according to events.[18] He assumed that everyone understood as much. If any of the other generals objected to the lack of a formal plan, they never said so.

Before this meeting adjourned, however, Lee and his officers again heard from Washington. Shortly after leaving them earlier—probably less than half an hour—the commander in chief noticed good defensive ground not far from the vanguard's current position. He thought a British preemptive attack was improbable, but considering how close the armies were, the general was still concerned that Clinton might strike first. Thus he sent one of his aides, Lieutenant Colonel John Fitzgerald, back to Lee with additional orders. Washington wanted him to take post on the better position in order to avoid any "risqué" and to have officers and men sleep on their arms, ready for any contingency. Lee agreed, telling Fitzgerald that he was personally acquainted with some of the British generals and conceded that they indeed "might turn about and make a stroke." The major general promised to reposition his command once his men were rested, a task he completed by about 7:00 P.M. Fitzgerald also informed the general that he was to let Dickinson and Morgan know what roles they would play the next morning. Lee already had sent Mercer to Dickinson, but he lacked any current information on Morgan's location.[19]

At Manalapan Bridge, Washington was spending a restless night. Having talked personally with Lee and his generals and having sent the additional orders via Fitzgerald, the commander in chief remained worried that Clinton might get away before the vanguard struck. Late that night he had Hamilton draft a letter to Lee. It again told him to coordinate operations with Morgan and to hit Clinton as soon as possible. Fearful that the redcoats would move out before the full vanguard could reach them, Washington directed Lee to send a party of 600–800 men forward to close with the British. If Clinton did march, this force was to skirmish and slow him enough for Lee to bring up his full command. Hamilton then had a light horseman carry the dispatch to Lee.[20] The message arrived sometime before 2:00 A.M., and the officer commanding the general's guard roused his aides Mercer and Edwards. Reading the orders, Edwards wrote to Morgan, Grayson, and Dickinson in behalf of Lee, dating his letters 1:00 A.M. Dickinson was to send an observation detachment toward Clinton and report any intelligence. Morgan was to attack the right flank of any British movement "tomorrow morning" (which the colonel unfortunately interpreted as the morning of the twenty-ninth, a lamentable miscommunication). Grayson was to lead the advanced party Washington had requested, taking Varnum's and Scott's brigades—about 700 men in all—to within three miles of Clinton, wait there, and send "repeated intelligence" of enemy movements. Grayson was to notify Lee when he was ready to move.[21]

The orders sent by Hamilton made it abundantly clear—if any clarification was needed at this point—that Washington expected Lee to fight. Those Edwards drafted seemingly indicated that Lee understood as much. Yet later at the court-martial, Hamilton made it equally clear that Washington's orders never touched on how Lee should conduct his attack or how to handle an ensuing engagement. Hamilton was sure the major general had the discretion to act according to circumstances. When asked if Lee had orders to "attack the enemy at all events," his answer was unequivocal: "I can't conceive that General Washington could mean to give orders so extremely positive, but that circumstances, which had been unforeseen, might arise, to leave the officer, who had the execution of them, liberty to deviate." Hamilton also confirmed that he understood that Washington wanted Clinton attacked and only "very extraordinary and unforeseen" developments should prevent it; he also admitted that he did not make this last point forcefully to Lee. Finally, he stated that he did not think Washington meant Lee to attack if confronted with "the enemy's whole army."[22] All of this was telling considering that Hamilton was among Lee's most bitter detractors.

At this juncture, we need to jump ahead of the narrative to examine two more perspectives on Lee's orders. On the morning of 28 June, as Lee was taking the vanguard into action, another of Washington's young aides rode to him. This was Lieutenant Colonel Richard Kidder Meade of Virginia, a member of Washington's staff since March 1777 and a close friend of Hamilton. He had come forward on Washington's behalf to see that Lee was in motion and to convey the commander in chief's desire that he make contact with Clinton as soon as possible. Before leaving Washington, however, Meade had suggested that some circumstances could make an attack "improper," and the general agreed that "powerful reasons" might prevent Lee from attacking. But Washington wanted to fight, and Meade told Lee as much, noting that the main army would come up to support the vanguard. Yet the aide did add, as he had discussed with Washington, "some very powerful circumstance" might "forbid" an engagement.[23] He offered no detail on what such a "circumstance" might be, thus the judgment would have to be Lee's.

A final account deserves mention. A letter by Major John Clark, who was an unimpeachable source, came to light only in September 1778, after the close of Lee's court-martial. A former aide to Major General Greene, Clark was a staunch Washington partisan. He had seen active duty since 1775, and despite a shoulder wound, at Washington's request he had established an elaborate spy ring in and around occupied Philadelphia. Over the course of the occupation, he was one of the most successful patriot secret agents, sending some thirty intelligence reports to the general and feeding false information on the Continental Army to the British. With his wound still unhealed after Clinton's evacuation, Washington arranged a desk job for Clark as an auditor of army accounts.[24] When asked to submit testimony by Lee, Clark reacted coolly, telling the general that he would declare himself "your Enemy" if he had "used him [Washington] ill." But Clark regretted not being asked to give evidence at the court-martial and felt that he had to give a candid version of his experience at Monmouth. He wrote Lee that early on the twenty-eighth he was about to return from Englishtown to Rocky Hill—Clark may have been attached to the baggage train—when he heard the firing from the direction of Monmouth Court House. The major stopped to see Washington, who had by then brought the main army to Englishtown, and volunteered to carry orders to Lee. The commander in chief accepted and, according to Clark, issued verbal orders as follows: "You will inform General Lee that 'tis my Orders that he annoy the Enemy as much as in his power, but at the same time proceed with caution and take care the Enemy don't draw him into a scrape." The orders also included intelligence that Clinton was moving and an assurance that Washington was marching quickly to support the vanguard. Clark said he delivered the orders to Lee in the field near "Monmouth Village" and fully believed the orders "*to be discretionary* and *as such he* [Lee] *received them.*"[25]

Washington himself thus seemingly confirmed the discretionary nature of Lee's orders. At 11:30 A.M. on the twenty-eighth, after speaking with Clark and while Lee was already in action, he wrote to Henry Laurens from his headquarters at Englishtown. He summarized the situation as he then knew it, mentioning that Clinton had moved out of Monmouth Court House earlier in the morning and that he (Washington) was bringing up the main army to support the vanguard. Lee, he said, had "orders to attack their rear, if possible." Whether the general could catch the British before "they get into strong grounds" was "a matter of question."[26] In a brief earlier (6:00 A.M.) letter to Horatio Gates, Washington related that the enemy was on the move but stated that the Continentals meant only "to harrass them as much as possible."[27] These letters were not from a general expecting his vanguard to initiate a major engagement or to fight at all hazards, nor did his orders to Lee reflect any such thing.

To summarize: While Scott and Wayne believed Washington wanted an attack "at all events," neither officer ever heard the general issue any orders to that effect. In the later meeting at Lee's headquarters, no one discussed a particular battle plan or any clear attack orders from Washington. Early on 28 June, when Lieutenant Colonels Hamilton and Meade passed on their general's orders, they did so in such a fashion that anyone could have interpreted them as discretionary. Finally, Major Clark emphatically stated that he had done the same and Lee had received them as such. As Lee was in action, Washington wrote Laurens that he had ordered the major general to attack "if possible," *not* "at all events," and in his letter to Gates spoke only of harassing Clinton. From all this, it is simply impossible to make out a case that Lee had unequivocal orders to bring the enemy to a major battle or that his orders were anything but discretionary.[28]

Lee certainly felt this was the case, and it seems clear enough in retrospect. But on 27 and 28 June, the situation was replete with misunderstandings. Lee could honestly say that at no time since the council of war on 18 June, including the Hopewell council on the twenty-fourth, did anyone ever argue in favor of a general engagement. Nor did anyone, including Washington, ever urge any sort of attack at all costs. There were always caveats: in so many words (or in the *exact* words), attack, *if possible*; attack, but do not get drawn *into a scrape*; attack, unless there were *very powerful* reasons to the contrary. There was to be no undue risk of any major element of the army. In any of his orders, Washington never said a word to the contrary. Lee not only understood all of this but also had argued for it as the army's chief voice of caution. As he led his men forward on Sunday morning, he had every reason to think that the coming battle was his to fight—or not fight—as circumstances determined.

But Lee had misread the commander in chief. While Washington certainly wanted to avoid a general action or any serious fight that might find his men at a disadvantage, his thinking had clearly turned toward the offensive. His progressive reinforcement of forward units operating against Clinton revealed his inclination to strike; he had no intention of letting the British march away unscathed. His final communications on the morning of the twenty-eighth, delivered via Hamilton's rider and Lieutenant Colonel Meade, emphasized this. Had the two generals been on better personal terms, Lee might have grasped this. But the men did not enjoy such a relationship, and differences in understanding were not communicated; instead, each officer assumed the other was in agreement. In all the mixed messages inherent in the attack orders, Washington was emphasizing *attack*, while Lee was hearing *if possible* and be careful to avoid *a scrape*.

In the end, however, responsibility for the ambiguity lay with the commander in chief. He was in command, and it was up to him—as it was (and *is*) up to any commander in similar circumstances—to make sure his subordinate officer understood his orders. This was especially the case as Washington dealt with Lee, for he was fully aware that his second in command repeatedly had cautioned against any overly aggressive operations. In all likelihood Washington's various orders to Lee meant something akin to "Do nothing rash, but I do expect you to hit Clinton hard and to engage him until I bring up the main body." But if that is what he really meant, Washington should have clearly said so and had Lee acknowledge as much. He never did.

The Eve of Battle

Charles Lee had a relatively sleepless night. As dawn approached on 28 June, he already had put in hours of work. He had awakened with the arrival of Hamilton's horseman, and within an hour the general had put Grayson's "party of observation" in motion—or at least he tried. About daybreak the colonel mustered his command at Lee's headquarters expecting to find militia guides waiting. They were not; unaccountably they had left. While Captain Edwards rode through Englishtown searching for them or for replacements, militia general David Forman fortuitously called on Lee. Forman lived in the area and quickly found new guides, but the delay prevented Grayson from marching until 6:00 A.M. He finally set out with six light horsemen in the lead.

The late departure may have been fortunate. Before the new guides reported, the enemy situation clarified somewhat. About 5:00 A.M. Dickinson sent word that Clinton was breaking camp, thus Grayson understood that he would be advancing on an enemy in motion. The same report prompted Lee into action. He had Mercer draft marching orders for Maxwell and Lafayette, who would command the Scott and Wayne detachments. All troops were to drop their packs and assemble at Englishtown on the road to Monmouth Court House. While Mercer sent off these orders, Lieutenant Colonel Brooks rode after Grayson with Lee's orders to press ahead and hit the British as quickly as he could. Lee intended to move shortly with the rest of his men in Grayson's support. As Lafayette's men assembled, the Frenchman stopped in on Lee to ask after new intelligence; he found a tired general resting with one of his dogs at his feet.[29]

One wonders what was going through Lee's mind at this point. He was about to commence operations with officers about whom he knew relatively little. The general, having been away from the army for so long, "hardly knew a single man or officer under" his command.[30] Moreover, he was fully aware that most of his subordinate generals had urged a more aggressive course than he had. Nevertheless, he did expect help. Lee counted on Dickinson to support the morning advance and expected that Morgan eventually would hit the British right when his own assault went in. But what of his own feelings? Was he now looking for a chance to show these men he could fight? Did he feel any obligation to erase, through combat, any embarrassment of having first refused the vanguard command? Or perhaps, because of Washington's orders for a limited attack, did Lee think he had moved his commander toward his own less hawkish perspective on the campaign? We have few clues on the general's state of mind; but he had set events in motion when he sent Grayson forward. As he prepared to put the rest of the advanced corps on the road, Lee gave every sign of determination to make the best showing possible.

CHAPTER 9

Battlefield and Village

It was after a later conflict that the Duke of Wellington made his oft-quoted observation on intelligence in war. "All the business of war," he wrote, "and indeed all the business of life, is to endeavour to find out what you don't know by what you do; that's what I called 'guess what was at the other side of the hill.'"[1] By extension, his quip implied knowing all you could about the hill itself. Thus place—location, the lay of the land—was (and is) critical in any general's planning. As much as his appreciation of enemy strength and intentions, it was a foolhardy commander who ignored the local terrain, road networks, and possible food, forage, water, and other useful resources. Knowledge of regional inhabitants was important too. What were their loyalties? Who could be trusted to offer intelligence or other assistance? Who might pose a security threat or actually shoot at you? Success or failure in battle could hinge on the ability to use such factors to advantage or to guard against any disadvantages they might pose.

Certainly, Generals Clinton and Washington understood this. They devoted considerable effort to gathering intelligence and otherwise informing themselves on these matters, seeking what information they could on key terrain and which local residents could offer reliable information or threaten their armies. That is, they wanted to know "what was at the other side of the hill."

Place names, family farms, prominent landmarks and terrain features, and even individual structures of the Freehold region would figure prominently in the events of 28 June, and it is well to examine them at this point. In addition to these is the village of Monmouth Court House itself—the town that lay in the heart of a landscape at war.

Farmers and Villagers

For the moment, the focal point of events was the village of Monmouth Court House, or simply Freehold, as it was also known by 1778 (it is now the Borough of Freehold). The first European settlers arrived in the area in the 1680s, mostly Scots with a few English and Dutch from Long Island. In the eighteenth century, Irish and more English immigrants joined the mix. The large majority of these men and women were farmers or farm laborers, but by the early eighteenth century, enough settlers were present in support trades, small businesses, or the professions to allow a village to take root. It was a small town—none of the southern New Jersey towns were large—little more than a hamlet fourteen miles from the Atlantic coast and twelve miles south of Raritan Bay. Monmouth grew slowly. When the British army moved in on 26 June, it found a village of less than a couple dozen structures. The most prominent were the Anglican church (still standing) and the courthouse from which the village took its name. Across the street from the courthouse was a large tavern. Immediately east was a tanyard—an industry that must have given the village a distinctive odor. Just outside town were a blacksmith shop and gristmill.[2]

Even before the arrival of Clinton's army, the war had had a profound effect on the village. The largest residence in town was for sale, owned by a lawyer who was now a refugee in New York City. At least two residents—former sheriff Thomas Leonard and John Longstreet, Jr.—were now members of loyalist battalions; their property was being confiscated by New Jersey.[3] At some point during the war, the Anglican church would be used as a warehouse for rebel arms.[4]

Other homes and buildings dotted the countryside and farms surrounding the village proper. About four miles west of town stood Tennent's Meeting House (now called Old Tennent Church; it remains on its original site). Built in 1751, the meetinghouse was a reminder of the evangelical Great Awakening that swept the colonies in the mid-eighteenth century and was a place of worship for regional Presbyterians, who were overwhelmingly loyal to the Revolution. In June 1778 the church lacked a parson, the Reverend William Tennent having died the previous year. The structure was at the intersection of the Englishtown, Middletown Landing, Upper Freehold, and Courthouse Roads. On 27–28 June Philemon

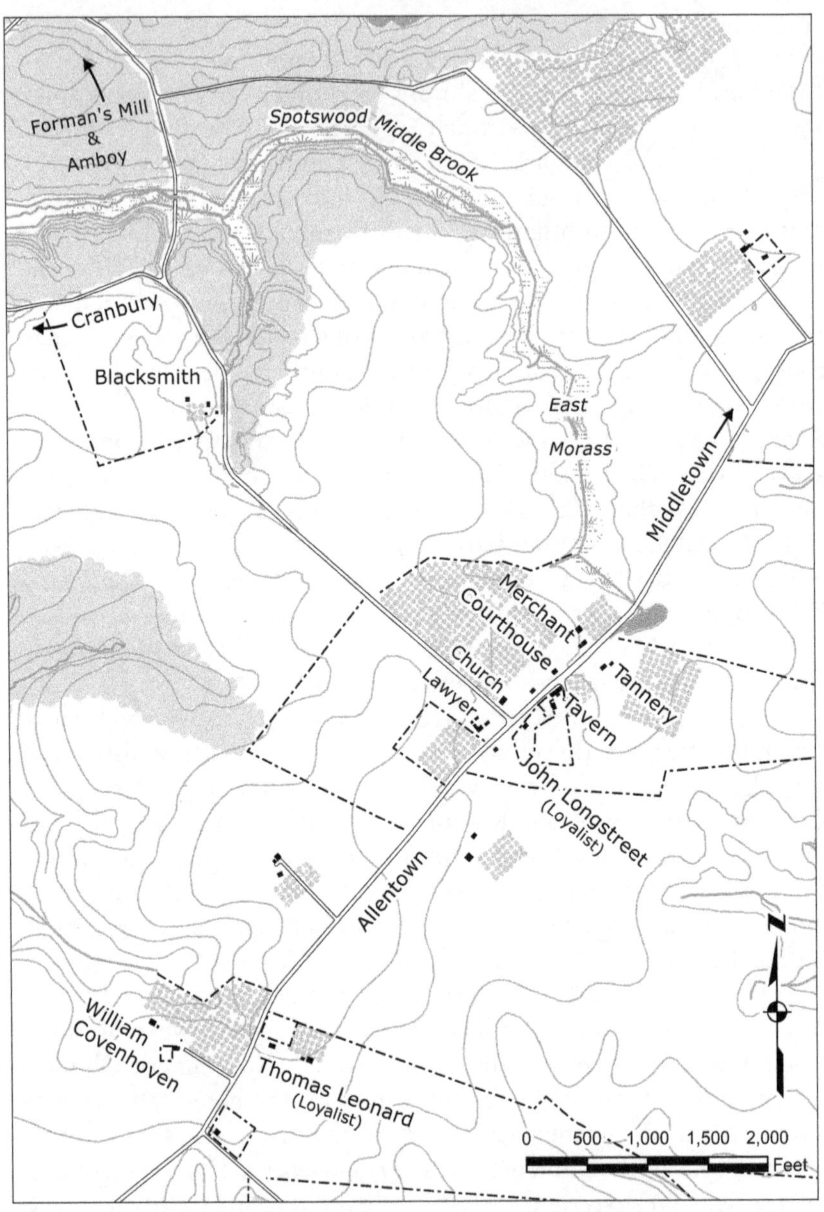

The village of Monmouth Court House (Freehold). Map by Garry Wheeler Stone. Copyright © 2016 by the University of Oklahoma Press.

Dickinson used the meetinghouse grounds as a staging area for militia operations.[5]

Despite its small size, the town was important, being the county seat. Middletown, some fifteen miles northeast, and coastal Shrewsbury also had wanted this distinction; but in 1713 John Reid, a prominent landowner and the first surveyor general of East Jersey, made land available for the courthouse at an attractive price, and the county freeholders accepted the offer. Local agriculture supported a relatively large population, which also had played a role in the decision to build the courthouse in Freehold Township. The county justices had stated that they wanted the courthouse "nearest of all to the middle of the good land and the whole inhabitants of the County."[6] The courthouse was erected in 1714, a modest, shingled frame building with jail cells in the basement and a steeple atop a peaked roof.[7] Monmouth Court House subsequently emerged as the administrative and political hub of the county. For local patriots, it became the center for militia operations as well.

Location also contributed to the importance of the village. Monmouth Court House lay astride or near one of the most important road junctions in the colony. Over time, colonists had widened and otherwise improved three prehistoric Indian trails; eventually, they evolved into significant thoroughfares. The most important of these was the Burlington Path (or the Great Path). For much of its distance, the road followed an old Indian track that ran northeast–southwest across New Jersey. In 1684 colonial authorities began improvements to make it a permanent route connecting the two capitals of the colony, Perth Amboy in the east and Burlington in the west. From these towns it was a relatively easy trip to the commercial centers of Philadelphia and New York. As roads of the era went, the Burlington Path was a relatively good one. Winter travel was very difficult, but by 1770 a one-way journey from New York to Philadelphia during the warmer months took four days. From Middletown to the edge of the pines south of Monmouth Court House, the old Burlington Path remained the main road, while north of the village, a branch of the path led east. This followed yet another old Indian trail moving toward Colts Neck, Tinton Falls, and on to Shrewsbury. The Burlington Path and its secondary trail formed a vital corridor; the road regularly guided travelers across the colony and literally put the small town on the New Jersey map. But it was also the route that brought the British to Monmouth Court

House and offered the King's army the way to safe haven, first on the heights of Middletown, then on to Sandy Hook.[8]

A third trail, also a Lenape track, began in the village and led west toward the former Native American villages of Manalapan and New Manalapan.[9] About a mile-and-a-half west of the courthouse a road led from the path to Tennent's Meeting House, Englishtown, and on to Cranbury. With no pretense to originality, the crossing of the Manalapan River was known as Manalapan Bridge (Continental headquarters correspondence called it "Penelopen").[10] Beyond Cranbury, the road was part of a network that led to Kingston and eventually Pennsylvania. This was the general route the Continental Army had followed as it converged on Monmouth Court House. Lee's vanguard would travel the stretch from Englishtown as it sought contact with the enemy on the morning of Sunday, 28 June. Thus it was location that brought converging armies to the country hamlet.

Freehold Township was something of an anomaly in Monmouth County, and this too made it significant. Monmouth, established in 1683, was one of the four original counties of colonial East Jersey. It was a large area. Its east coast ran from Egg Harbor in the south some ninety miles north to Sandy Hook; to the north was Middlesex County, while Burlington County (then part of colonial West Jersey) lay to the west.[11] The terrain varied, but much of the county struggled with marginal farmlands. North of Monmouth Court House lay the poor soils of the Barrens of Wickatonk. To the south are the large and sandy Pine Barrens (much of which survives today as a federally protected natural area), largely unfit for anything but the barest of subsistence cultivation. The barrens were sparsely populated as were the fishing villages along the southern coasts of the county. But the farms of centrally located Freehold, including those immediately around Monmouth Court House, were remarkably different. The hamlet was situated on the intersection of New Jersey's Inner and Outer Coastal Plains, and it was blessed with the excellent soil characteristic of the Inner Plain. Now classified as Freehold Sandy Loam, the rich ground supported a thriving and relatively highly populated agricultural economy. A census of 1784 found a population of 3,024 composed of 2,525 "White Inhabitants" and 499 "Negros." The population may have been somewhat higher before the Revolution—that is, before the exodus of tory exiles and others seeking respite from the turmoil of the war years.[12]

As the British army approached on 26 June, some observers were struck by how different the area was from the more hard-scrabble parts of the state they had seen. A jaeger commented in his journal after marching to Monmouth that the army "camped on a very beautiful plain." A British officer agreed, noting his encampment on "a very fine extensive plain in the Environs of the little Village of Monmouth Court House."[13] The plain stretched over four miles south of the courthouse along the Burlington Road and the watershed between the Atlantic and South River drainages. A crossroads tavern, blacksmith shop, and Baptist meetinghouse gave a focus to this neighborhood south of the courthouse, known as "Upper Monmouth Court House" as it was upcountry (farther from New York) than the courthouse. North of the courthouse the plain continued two-and-three-quarters miles as the "1,000-acre tract," land purchased in 1699 by a group of Long Island Dutch.[14] The buyers divided it into five farms; it was on these farms that the 28 June battle began. The Middletown branch of the Burlington Road ran along the east edge of these farms, just off the edge of the plain; this road location would influence the outcome of the morning action. A mile north of the courthouse, the Burlington Road forked, the left branch continuing toward Middletown and Amboy, the right branch toward the port of Shrewsbury.[15]

Croplands and pasturage dominated the regional landscape. While some craftsmen and laborer "householders" had small holdings, most farms ranged in size from 150 to 225 acres. The largest in the township (now divided between three of his sons) had been Captain Robert Rhea's 690 acres.[16] Most of these farmers produced for the market; the days of subsistence farming were generally two generations past, sometimes longer. Wheat for export had been the cash crop of the first two generations, but with soil fertility declining, wheat was secondary to less demanding rye and Indian corn. Corn, in the form of pork and fat cattle, was marketed to urban dwellers, the merchant marine, and the West Indies. Butter and cheese also sold well. Fallow fields were allowed to rest (sometimes as pasturage) or manured for subsequent planting. Beaver flats (former ponds) along the brooks were now hay meadows. Most farms devoted at least some acreage to orchards, and apples were especially popular; a few larger farmers operated commercial cider presses. Flax was cultivated for export and local textile production.[17] Before the Revolution, New Jersey was known as one of the bread baskets of colonial America, and the Freehold locale was one of the reasons. British foragers would "harvest" what they could from the local farms.

The farms of most interest here are those to the immediate east and west of the village: the Battle of Monmouth would be fought on or near them. Eight families owned these battlefield tracts. Northwest of the village, brothers John and William Craig worked adjoining farms north of Spotswood North Brook, while their nephew, John, Jr., farmed 200 acres between Spotswood North and Spotswood Middle Brooks. His neighbor to west was Derick Sutfin, with 265 acres; west of Sutfin was the large holding—535 acres—of farmer and tanner Henry Perrine. The Presbyterian parsonage had 150 acres south of Sutfin, while to the east the orphan sons of Captain Rhea held two plantations totaling 690 acres. Aaron Davis, Rhea's former brother-in-law, ran a blacksmith shop on 30 acres in the middle of the east Rhea farm. Finally, south of the parsonage, Thomas Combs farmed 260 acres of marginal soil, and west of his property, Deacon Craig's tenants worked still another tract. All these family names, and others, would figure in the action of the twenty-eighth. The light skirmishing that began just east of the courthouse gradually shifted west for some three miles, where the most serious fighting occurred. As the battle developed, British and American troops traversed these family fields, doing considerable damage to crops and structures.

Landowners built split-rail fences to divide and subdivide the farms, and some of them proved key landmarks on the day of battle. Constructed of stacked rails braced with "stakes and riders," these zig-zagged, or "wormed," their way across the landscape. Such fences used a lot of space and timber but were easy to build and move. While they would be a common sight over the course of the fighting, two received special note during the battle. While taking a volley, American light infantry would throw down a fence on Sutfin's land as they pursued the 42nd Regiment (Royal Highlanders). In the center of the battlefield, a "hedge fence" or "hedgerow" between the parsonage and Rhea farms would be central to the action. Indeed, it would be the scene of some of the day's most savage combat. Continental officers "described it both as a hedge and a fence," and British officers referred to "it as a 'strong' and 'high' fence."[18] It was probably a fence through which trees and shrubs had grown, and at various times during the fighting it was strong enough to serve

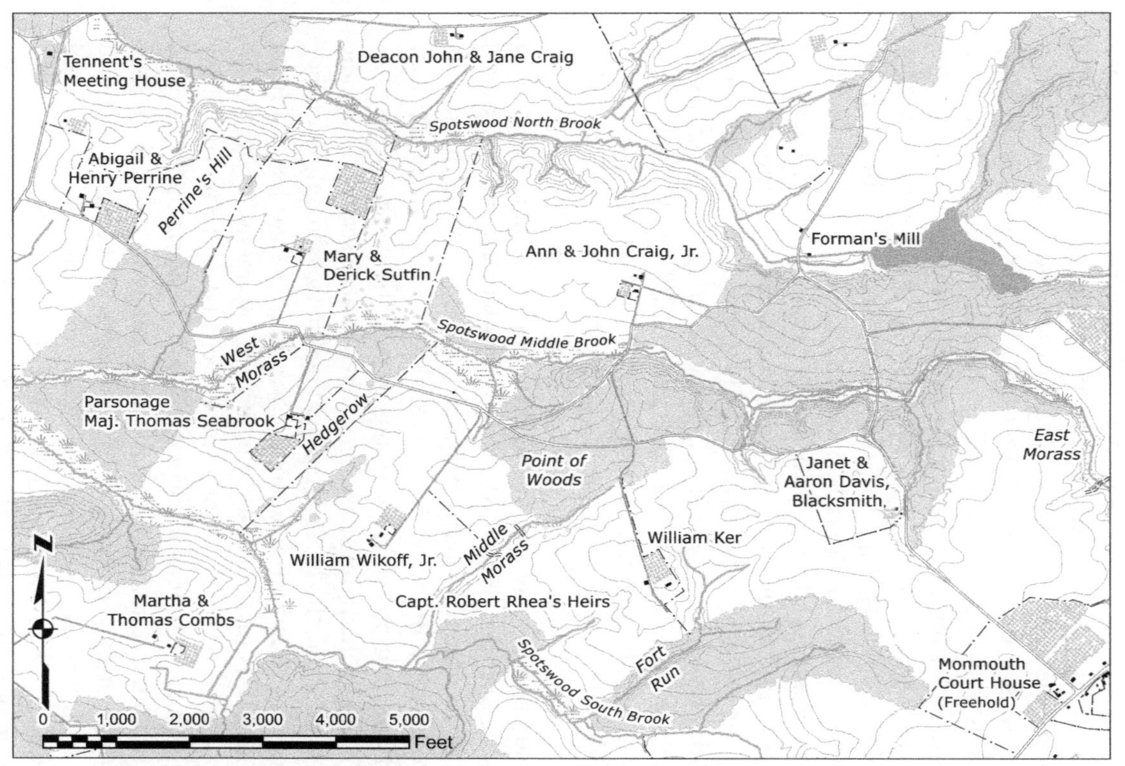

The farms on the western battlefield. Map by Garry Wheeler Stone. Copyright © 2016 by the University of Oklahoma Press.

as a substantial, if temporary, defensive position for patriot militia, Continentals, and redcoats.

The battlefield farms lay on open, rolling terrain with elevations between 100 and 165 feet above sea level. With few exceptions, the farmers had cleared their lands for cultivation; woodlots lay in scattered sections, with only a few sections of thick forest remaining. Thus vistas from higher terrain often extended well over a mile, with obvious military implications. During the battle, patriot and British artillery crews would have line-of-sight views of one another as they traded fire. Combs Hill (part of the Combs farm), on the southern edge of the battlefield, offered a sweeping view of the farms below and would prove an effective position for patriot artillery. There was also high ground on the battlefield's western edge, the land of Henry Perrine, one of the few tracts still heavily wooded. The rise lay about three miles from the village, just behind the bridge (or "causeway") over Spotswood Middle Brook. "Perrine's Hill" would anchor the Continental main line during the afternoon of the twenty-eighth.

Besides the farms and roads, the future battlefield had other distinctive features. It was well watered. While several creeks (known by various names over the years) intersected the land, four main streams are of chief concern. Spotswood South Brook and Spotswood Middle Brook joined to form Weamaconk Brook. To the north was Spotswood North Brook, which flowed through swampy ground that was difficult, but possible, for troops to pass, though nearly impossible for all but the lightest artillery. The western section of Middle Brook was deeper; the bridge that spanned it crossed a difficult bog that provided excellent defensive protection for men beyond it on Perrine's Hill. Four ravines—three termed "morasses" by the combatants—cut the terrain. Along the eastern edge of the village lay the beginnings of Spotswood Middle Brook. Heading in the tanyard pond, its course remained a shallow depression where it crossed under the Burlington Road. It then deepened into a substantial ravine, with wet hay meadows on the bottom and a steep, wooded west bank. West of Monmouth Court House, the ravines of "Fort Run" narrowed the upland. The "Middle Morass" lay farther west, about half-way across the battlefield. The "division ditch" between the east and west Rhea farms, it was better defined but was passable along its northern portion, with wooden causeways easing the way in places. The "West Morass"—often called the West Ravine in accounts of the fighting—was defined by Spotswood Middle Brook and was a true morass in that it constituted an extensive, boggy wetland. Each morass would have its influence on the battle.

The landscape between the village and the West Morass had an east–west bias; that is, the terrain generally sloped toward the west, and any given position on the higher ground to the east dominated any given position on lower western ground. This was true until one reached the West Morass, beyond which an extent of high ground on the Perrine farm afforded a commanding view of terrain toward Monmouth Court House. On the morning of the twenty-eighth, General Lee would learn all of this the hard way as he sought to counter Clinton's advance from the east.

An Army at Rest?

When it marched into the village, Henry Clinton's army had trekked some sixty-seven miles. Soldiers and civilians had endured scorching heat, torrential thunderstorms, wilting humidity, poor roads, swarms of mosquitoes, and exhaustion. Added to these miseries were frayed nerves born of constant rebel threats and active skirmishing as they advanced through a largely hostile countryside. One suspects that a fair number of redcoats and their Hessian and loyalist allies would have traded all this for a general engagement in good weather without insects. On the twenty-sixth Hessian lieutenant Heinrich von Feilitzsch summed up the feeling of many with the footsore and exhausted troops. He wearily noted that patriots had harassed them all the way from Allentown, and he was thankful for "a day of rest, which was very necessary."[19]

If not marching, however, 27 June still found officers and men busy. Troops received fresh and salted rations for two days, easily enough to get to Middletown the next day, perhaps all the way to Sandy Hook. Men cleaned weapons and checked equipment, mounted guard, reported for special duty, and did their laundry. Teamsters prepared fresh horses for the baggage train and artillery, getting ready to resume travel on the twenty-eighth. Courts-martial convened, and foraging operations continued.[20] Everyone had to cope with the continually disappointing weather. The heat remained at inferno levels, and some of the storms were actually alarming. Subofficer von Kraft recorded a "terrific thunderstorm" that caused a lightning strike "only 15 paces behind my hut," killing two horses and injuring several men.[21] Thus a day of "rest" was anything but a day of inactivity.

Although the army remained in and around the town to rest and refit, there was no point at which the troops could drop their guard. The skirmish Captain Johann Ewald found so alarming on 26 June was only one example of the low-intensity fighting that took place between then and the early morning hours of the twenty-eighth. In addition, Clinton's men were under almost continual observation and were well aware of it. A favorite patriot lookout was Longstreet's Hill, about two miles north of the courthouse, affording a good view of the countryside and serving as a point of departure for small scouting patrols. Colonel Stephen Moylan's Continental horse, as well as Major General Steuben, took advantage of the height to monitor British movements.[22] West of town, militia staged probing operations from the grounds of Tennent's Meeting House. There were few if any times that rebel eyes were not peering from cover at Clinton's pickets and encampments.

The rebels were shooting as well as looking. The twenty-seventh was an especially active day. Engagements came in rapid succession as patriots converged on British lines and both sides aggressively probed one another. Von Feilitzsch reported leading a patrol about a mile outside his lines but found nothing, although he understood that virtually all of the army's pickets had come under fire sometime during the day. Captain John Peebles of the 42nd Regiment reported capturing "half a dozen of the Sculking rascals" after several sniping incidents. Another rebel foray compelled Hessian pickets west of town to fall back until a few rounds of artillery forced the Americans to retreat.[23] In a larger action, a royal foraging party of some 200 men, who had just finished plundering the home of David Forman and driving his cattle back toward British lines, came under a spirited attack by Hunterdon and Somerset County militia. The men escaped, but the militia recovered the cattle. Later in the day Morris County militia drove off pickets of the British light infantry at Forman's Mill.[24] While the British were in and around the village, this persistent low-intensity combat was the norm; it was "rest" only inasmuch as the army was not on the march.

The most embarrassing (for the redcoats) incident of the twenty-seventh occurred south of the courthouse on one of the brooks flowing into the Manalapan River. Some fifteen grenadiers were doing their laundry—no doubt happy to relax and cool off in the shallow brook after their days on the march. But the men were too relaxed and had wandered too far from their lines; they were helpless when surprised and captured by a mixed party of militia and Continentals, Colonel Morgan's men. It was a coup that cheered patriots and chagrined the British.[25] Among the Continentals were some of the nicely uniformed members of Washington's Life Guards, having marched from Hopewell with Morgan; the encounter at the creek left their uniforms soaked and mud spattered. When the men brought the grenadiers before Morgan, the hard-bitten colonel, never one for spit and polish, saw the bedraggled Life Guards and thought it was hilarious.[26] No doubt the grenadiers disagreed.

The Sack of Monmouth Court House

In the village, however, no patriots were laughing. If Freehold Township was a geographical anomaly, it also differed from the rest of Monmouth County politically, being a generally whig locality. Early in the war, Monmouth Court House had seen considerable tory activity, but by 1778 patriots were in control. Much of the rest of the county, however, was in a state of civil war waged with varying degrees of intensity. In late 1776 and early 1777, a loyalist rising briefly took control of the county; patriot authorities called in the Continental Army to crush it. But that hardly ended active loyalism. Coastal villages traded more-or-less openly with the British in New York, and loyalist and free-booting "Pine Robbers" infested the Pine Barrens and sallied to pillage whigs—though often just anyone with something worth stealing. Sandy Hook sheltered a garrison of loyalist regulars as well as irregular raiders, some of them escaped slaves. The former slaves knew the county and were active in raids, sometimes against their erstwhile owners. The threat of incursions from the Hook and the Pines kept patriot families on edge, and real violence was common. Rhoda Sutfin, daughter-in-law of Derick Sutfin and whose husband, Joseph, was a Monmouth County militiaman, recalled the perils of the times. Joseph's company was always ready to muster at a moment's notice, she said, "to repel marauding excursions of the Brittish & Tories—who from their vicinity in the City of New York, & and their fastnesses in the pines & unfrequented parts of the county were continually harassing the inhabitants & committing robbery & murder whenever they could find the patriots unprotected."[27] At times patriot morale was so low that entire militia regiments became dysfunctional, at least as effective units.[28] For the duration of the war, active loyalism and the threat of violence were facts of life in the county.

Divided Monmouth loyalties offered some advantages to the royal army. Tories provided a stream of intelligence to Sir Henry; and the British commander had no problem finding guides who knew the county. In fact, he found them easily enough from among Monmouth County men in the ranks of the Queen's Rangers.[29] Others were glad to help as well. Of these, John Leonard of Upper Freehold was probably typical. Before the war, Leonard had farmed 380 acres, but when violence erupted in 1776, he left his family and marched "with near 100 of his Friends in a Body and Armed" to fight for the King. It was a costly decision, for the state eventually confiscated his property. Leonard saw action in late 1776 and during the Philadelphia campaign the following year. During the occupation of that city, he had guided British troops on foraging expeditions in New Jersey. After the evacuation, he was attached to Knyphausen's division, noting that he was "well acquainted" with the proposed British route of march and was able to render "many services" on the way to Monmouth Court House. Leonard was also at the subsequent battle.[30] His career with the British, and the state's response to it, was indicative of the bitterness that ripped the Monmouth County social fabric.

To put it mildly, Monmouth patriots resented the activities of Leonard and of his tory compatriots, who often were former neighbors and friends. Whigs retaliated vigorously. State and local authorities confiscated loyalist property and drove tory families into exile. Fines and imprisonment for loyalists were commonplace, as was blunt intimidation. Rebel militia—both organized units and extra-legal "Retaliators"—met violence with violence, harassment with harassment. Militia general and sometime Continental colonel Forman, the man who found local guides at the last minute for General Lee, was the mainstay of regional patriot military efforts. He wasted no sympathy on county loyalists. Indeed, some rebel violence was virulent enough to make moderate patriots wince. In his painstaking study of the war-torn county, historian Michael Adelberg has found "an estimated 50 percent of the county's families suffered tangible harm to person or property during the war." Among identifiable whig leaders, a full one-third endured some kind of suffering, while the same was true of two-thirds of loyalist leaders.[31] Those are sobering figures. Monmouth County was, in the words of Governor Livingston, "the theatre of spoil and destruction."[32]

In this sorry context Monmouth Court House, in the interior and away from the worst of the civil turmoil to the east and south, was actually a bastion of relative stability. By January 1777 Forman's Continentals had scattered organized tory forces in the Freehold area, and patriot militia had begun to rebuild. Of the three county militia regiments eventually organized, only the First Regiment, mustered from Freehold and Middletown Townships, was consistently reliable.[33] Its ten companies were instrumental in maintaining order in the central interior of the county. In April and May 1778, loyalist raids struck at coastal Manasquan, Middletown Point, and other locations. One of the worst incursions came on 27 May, when loyalists from Sandy Hook descended on Burrows' Mill, near Keyport and Shrewsbury. They burned the mill, killed two militiamen and wounded another twenty troops. But the various raiders did not push inland. By the spring of 1778, the civil courts in Freehold were open again, and rebel authorities used the full vigor of the law against loyalists unlucky enough to be hauled into the courthouse.[34] While the threat of violence was always present, to the extent any place in the county could be considered "safe" for patriots, it was the area around Monmouth Court House.

Still, by mid-June Freehold residents were leery as the track of the British march became clear. Living in a generally patriot township, they suspected the worst if the British reached the area and stayed for any length of time. Many began taking what precautions they could to protect families and property. Farmers drove livestock into woods and other areas they hoped would escape notice of British foragers. They buried valuables or hid them in wells. Some families took to the woods themselves or hurried to the protection of American units. Benjamin Van Cleave, the son of the village blacksmith, was just over five years old in June 1778. When his father and uncles had gone to join patriot forces, he recalled fleeing in "confusion" with women and children to the "pine swamps." They eventually reached Daniel Morgan's command and sheltered there with other refugees from the village and surrounding farms. On the twenty-eighth they listened to and wondered at the ebb and flow of the firing they could easily hear. In other instances men left to join American forces, trusting the British would respect the safety of wives and families who remained behind.[35]

While these precautions were wise, they were not available to many residents of the town itself. Homes, shops, outbuildings, and heavy tools and implements had to remain in place, with owners (even if they fled personally) only able to hope for the best. Frequently, they were disappointed. Problems began almost as soon as the King's army occupied the town. British troops perceived Monmouth Court House for what it was—a rebel center—and they acted accordingly. While the march already had seen serious instances of plundering and violence, it was not until reaching Monmouth Court House that troop discipline suffered a near collapse. Whatever respite the villagers had enjoyed from the violence that so troubled the rest of Monmouth County ended on 26 June.

The incidents of vandalism, plunder, and outright destruction were too numerous to mention individually, although contemporary accounts leave little doubt as to their scope. Hessian subofficer von Kraft's recollection of events is one of the best. In his journal entry for that day he wrote that he had arrived in "*Freholdt*" early in the morning, by which time things were already out of control. He found "almost all the inhabitants had fled," and "every place here was broken into and plundered by the English soldiers. The church, which was made of wood and had a steeple, was miserably demolished." He found troops "breaking and destroying everything" in the courthouse, "even tearing down the little bell in the steeple." English soldiers also had "set fire to a house outside of the town after having ransacked it, because it was said to be the property of a prominent Rebel."[36] Von Kraft was disgusted and made it clear that wanton behavior was rife among the soldiery.

Patriots who hoped that some sense of British chivalry or restraint would exempt women from the plundering were mistaken. When Rebecca Dennis, widow of a militia captain, objected to the looting of her home, the answer from one Hessian was a blow from his musket stock.[37] Even Clinton could not protect Elizabeth Covenhoven, who lived on the Burlington Path just west of the village center. She was seventy years old, and her husband may have left to join the rebels (there is no conclusive account of his whereabouts). Sir Henry made his headquarters in her home from the afternoon of the twenty-sixth until the morning of the twenty-eighth. He assured her that her household goods would be safe and even set a guard to watch them. "The following morning," however, Covenhoven found "most of her goods plundered and stolen." She saved only "some trifling articles" and was "turned out of her bedroom and obliged to lie with her wenches, either on the floor, without bed or bedding . . . or sit in a chair in a milk room." The widow Hannah Solomon fared worse: soldiers burned her tavern, which was also her home.[38]

In fact, Hannah Solomon was not alone in her misfortune. Between 26 June and the early hours of the twenty-eighth, eleven dwellings, assorted outbuildings, and at least two businesses were torched or otherwise destroyed. The first to burn was the homestead of Dr. Thomas and Rachel Henderson; the doctor was also a militia colonel. Their buildings were south of the courthouse, as were the homes and farm structures of Garret Vanderveer, George Walker, Benjamin Covenhoven, and David Covenhoven. All went up in flames, as did the Solomon tavern and the blacksmith shop and farm of Benjamin Van Cleave. Troops "tore and broke down" the house and barn of the Benham family "so as to make them useless." North of the courthouse, troops pulling out of town on the twenty-eighth fired the properties of Matthias Lane, Cornelius Covenhoven, John Antonidas, and the Emmons family.[39]

Vandalism, pillage, and destruction ranged for six miles along the Burlington Road. Years later Benjamin Van Cleave, son of the blacksmith of the same name, recalled the consequences for his family and neighbors. When the British left, they returned to Monmouth Court House and

> found, with some exceptions, the buildings around our neighborhood burnt, the naked chimneys standing, a great part of the trees in some orchards cut down, the woods burnt and property that had been hid destroyed or carried away. The earth was strewn with dead carcasses, sufficient to have produced a pestilence. My father had neither a shelter for his family, nor bread for them, nor clothes to cover them, save what we had on. He saved one bed with a looking glass only, which he carried with us, a yearling had escaped the enemy and a sow, whose back was broken with a sword, lived, and his anvil, I believe, remained among the rubbish of the shop.[40]

During the entire campaign, no other town was truly sacked. But at Monmouth Court House, the tragic proceedings revealed a major breakdown of army discipline and bespoke soldiery acting out of frustration and anger, and in the case of loyalist troops, rage and vengeance.

The worst of the violence was not random. When blacksmith Van Cleave fled, he left a partially rebuilt militia gun carriage in his shop. At Mount Holly the burnings of the Shreve and Tallman estates, as well as the Lewis mill and home near Bordentown, had targeted whig properties. The same was true at Monmouth Court House. While looting may have been indiscriminate, all the arson near the village was political in nature; only buildings owned by patriots were torched.[41] Rebels noted as much. Steuben, reporting to Washington after a scouting mission, told of seeing British detachments pillaging homes and burning two of them, including Colonel Henderson's.[42] Henderson himself had no doubt that patriot buildings were targeted. He claimed that the burnings stopped as the royal army left Freehold and moved east toward Middletown—that is, toward areas where loyalism remained entrenched. "They passed the houses of a number well-affected to *their* country," the colonel claimed, and "they never attempted to destroy one."[43]

Some officers were embarrassed by the conduct of their men and tried to distance themselves. Hessian officers in particular took a dim view of events. Adjutant General Baurmeister was disgusted, wistfully (and erroneously) recording, "there was no pillaging or plundering on the part of the Hessians." Sergeant von Kraft understood the need to take local cattle to feed his regiment, but these were authorized seizures, and he was aghast at the wanton behavior of the "English soldiers." No German soldiers were among the looters, he claimed, as the Hessian officers kept their men on a tight rein. Still, von Kraft conceded that some comrades did their share of plundering "secretly."[44]

British commanders never condoned the sack of the town. Indeed, Clinton issued orders to restrain pillaging. Guards were instructed to arrest anyone caught plundering and to open fire on anyone offering resistance. Orders for the twenty-eighth directed that women and "other strollers" with the army were to remain strictly within the line of march; they risked punishment if caught lurking around homes, barns, or other buildings.[45] But there was a half-hearted feel to these orders. Amid a genuine atmosphere of plunder and destruction, there were none of the earlier warnings threatening the "immediate execution" of looters or rewards offered for the apprehension of arsonists (of whom there were plenty). Most officers seemed not to care particularly about the mayhem or felt that they could do little to stop it. On 27 June the army did convene a court-martial. Five individuals were prosecuted for horse theft, arson, and looting; one woman was convicted of looting. None of the offences had taken place at Monmouth Court House.[46]

While it did not excuse the conduct of their men and their seeming lack of attention to it, British officers were working under pressure. If they were not on the lines, they were readying their commands to move on the morning of the twenty-eighth. On Saturday, preparatory to the final push to Sandy Hook, Clinton issued general orders for the march. At daybreak on Sunday, the baggage of the entire army again would march together, the train of the 1st Division following that of the 2nd Division. As on the march from Allentown, Knyphausen would command the whole along with the rest of the 2nd Division.[47] Clinton planned to wait for Kynphausen to be well on his way before following with the combat-heavy 1st Division. He was concerned that Washington would make an attempt on the baggage train and wanted the 1st Division in a position to head off any serious rebel thrust. If things went well, the entire army would be well beyond Monmouth Court House by midday; Clinton would be done with the encampment fields and the village with its still-smoldering buildings—if things went well.

Washington Rallying the Troops at Monmouth, by Emanuel Leutze. German American portraitist and historical artist Emanuel Leutze (1816–68) painted this dramatic rendition of Washington rallying the army in 1857, seven years after completing his iconic *Washington Crossing the Delaware.* The Monmouth painting depicts the battlefield confrontation of Washington and Lee and helped ensconce the popular view of Washington as hero and Lee as villain. Leutze took pains with detail. He captures the heat of the day, men collapsing from exhaustion, patriot artillery coming up, and even, one assumes, one of Lee's beloved dogs. The artist also took considerable license. The meeting of the two generals did not play out amid the throng Leutze depicts, Washington did not brandish his sword, and Lee, as Leutze seems to imply, was not immediately disgraced. Crestfallen in the painting, Lee quickly assumed command of the delaying action east of the West Morass bridge as Washington rode back over the bridge to organize the main rebel line on Perrine's Hill. (Courtesy Monmouth County Historical Association)

George Washington, by Charles Willson Peale. Philadelphia artist Charles Willson Peale (1741–1827) was one of the renaissance men of the Revolution. A fervent patriot, he fought at Trenton and Princeton, was active in rebel politics, and his many portraits of patriot officers are the best visual record of the Continental officer corps. During the Valley Forge winter, Peale was often at camp painting portraits, and this "Valley Forge" portrait of Washington shows the general as he appeared only months before the Battle of Monmouth. (Permanent Art Collection of West Chester University of Pennsylvania)

Sir Henry Clinton, K.B. A contemporary British engraving (1778) of Clinton (1730–95) as British commander in America, published by Fielding & Walker, London. (Courtesy Library of Congress Prints and Photographs Division, LC-USZ62-45262)

Charles Lee, Esq., Major General of the American Forces. There are no known portraits of Charles Lee (1732–82) from life. This one is an illustration from *An Impartial History of the War in America between Great Britain and Her Colonies, from Its Commencement to the End of the Year 1779* (London: Printed for R. Faulder, 1780), published when Lee was still alive and a figure of continuing controversy. (Courtesy Library of Congress Prints and Photographs Division, LC-USZ62-45253)

Charles Cornwallis, 1st Marquess Cornwallis, by Thomas Gainsborough. Cornwallis (1738–1805) sat for this well-known Gainsborough portrait in 1783, two years after his surrender at Yorktown. He commanded the British 1st Division during the Monmouth campaign; his counterattack against the patriot advance force on the morning of 28 June 1778 spoiled Lee's effort to cut off Clinton's rear guard and compelled Lee to retreat. (Copyright © National Portrait Gallery, London)

Philemon Dickinson. This etching is from Benson J. Lossing's *The Pictorial Field-Book of the Revolution* (1860) and shows Dickinson (1739–1809) as a New Jersey militia brigadier general and member of the Continental Congress. He was a major general of militia during the Monmouth campaign. (Emmet Collection, New York Public Library, EM4805)

William Livingston, Governor of New Jersey. Livingston (1723–90) was a close ally of Washington and one of the most capable of the war governors. During the Monmouth campaign, he did his best to turn out the state militia, and his able pen helped craft the victory narrative for Washington after the battle. (The John Kean Collection at Liberty Hall Museum, Kean University)

John Graves Simcoe (1791), by Jean-Laurent Mosnier. Simcoe (1752–1806) commanded the crack Queen's American Rangers from October 1777 until the surrender at Yorktown in 1781. On 28 June 1778 he opened the fighting at Monmouth in a heavy skirmish with patriot militia, during which he was wounded. After the war he was the first lieutenant governor of Upper Canada, where he actively tried to assist the settlement of exiled American loyalists. (Courtesy Toronto Public Library, 927-1 Fra)

Daniel Morgan, engraving after a painting by Alonzo Chappel. Morgan (1736–1802), the premier American light-infantry commander of the war, played a key role in shadowing and harassing the British advance to Monmouth. Poor army staff work and miscommunications kept him out of the fighting during the battle on 28 June 1778. Chappel (1828–87) was a prolific painter of historical themes, including many works on the Revolution, and probably is best known for his *John Smith Saved by Pocahontas* (c. 1865). (Courtesy Library of Congress Prints and Photographs Division, LC-USZ62-49177)

Richard Butler, by John Trumbull. The Irish-born Butler (1743–91), commanding a battalion of picked men, opened the fighting for the Continentals during the morning battle. He was a close friend of Daniel Morgan and served with distinction throughout the war. Butler was killed fighting the Indians in Ohio during Arthur St. Clair's catastrophic defeat on 4 November 1791. His Shawnee son, Tamanatha, fought for the Indians in the same battle. (Yale University Art Gallery)

Henry Laurens, by John Singleton Copley, engraving by Valentine Green. This image depicts Henry Laurens (1724–92) as president of the Continental Congress. He was an influential congressional supporter of Washington and the father of Lieutenant Colonel John Laurens of the general's staff. Following the Battle of Monmouth, Henry and John were key critics of Major General Lee's conduct and supported Washington during the controversies attending Lee's court-martial. (Courtesy Library of Congress Prints and Photographs Division, LC-DIG-pga-01421)

Eleazer Oswald, reproduction of a painting by Albert Rosenthal. Oswald (1755–95) commanded Continental artillery with distinction and played a critical role in opposing Clinton's counterattack against Lee's vanguard. Oswald staunchly defended Lee's conduct during the battle and resigned in disgust after the general's court-martial. (Courtesy Library of Congress Prints and Photographs Division, LC-USZ62-48941)

Tennent's Meeting House. The meetinghouse, now First Presbyterian Church, lacked a parson at the time of the battle, but it was one of the most prominent landmarks of the Monmouth campaign. New Jersey militia used its grounds as a staging area, and the churchyard served as a rebel medical site during the battle. British lieutenant colonel Henry Monckton, killed in the attempted grenadier advance over the West Morass, is buried in the churchyard. (*First Presbyterian Church, Tennent, Monmouth, N.J.*, photograph by R. Merritt Lacey, courtesy Library of Congress Prints and Photographs Division, HABS NJ, 13-TENT, 1-7)

Sir Charles Grey, K.B. (1797), by William Austin. Grey (1729–1807), 1st Earl Grey, was known as "No Flint" Grey after his devastating bayonet assault on Anthony Wayne's men at Paoli, Pennsylvania, in 1777. At Monmouth he led the 3rd Brigade in an effort to flank the American left. The major general was one of Clinton's most aggressive subordinates. (Anne S. K. Brown Military Collection, Brown University Library)

Anthony Wayne, etching by Albert Rosenthal, after a painting by Charles Willson Peale. Wayne (1745–96) was Washington's most aggressive brigadier and argued for offensive action throughout the Monmouth campaign. No admirer of Lee, the major general nevertheless had him command the leading elements of the patriot vanguard as the battle opened. Later in the day Wayne fought brutal actions against determined British attacks in the Point of Woods and at the Parsonage. He testified against Lee at the latter's court-martial. (Courtesy Library of Congress Prints and Photographs Division, LC-USZ62-56544)

CHAPTER 10

Morning at Monmouth I

The Opening Round

Sunday morning, 28 June, finally would see the main forces of the American and British armies come to blows. Major General Lee would send his advanced force—the "party of observation" under Colonel William Grayson—to locate the enemy and, if conditions looked promising, open the battle. He did so, however, through torrid heat and in the face of an operational context that had become exceedingly complex. Indeed, the situation was rife with possibilities for confusion. Beyond what the British may have been doing—and Lee's intelligence in this regard was hazy at best—the patriots had different units on the move, with varying degrees of command and control; some were outside Lee's command, and some were in it only nominally. Aside from Grayson's detachment, the general had authority over the bulk of Washington's vanguard, though he had minimal contact with Daniel Morgan, then hovering on the British right, and the locations of some major militia units were completely unknown to him. Scattered Continental reconnaissance and horse parties were in the field as well, or soon would be. Lee was unaware of when Washington intended to bring up the rest of the Continentals from Manalapan Bridge (Penelopen). Any of these units faced the possibility of going into action separately and without coordination with allied units; and in fact, some did. Of course, as the various patriot formations moved toward Monmouth Court House (Freehold), the different segments of Clinton's command were also in motion. It made for a complicated scenario, one even more uncertain because commanders moving toward contact with the enemy are seldom blessed with a clear knowledge of their rival's intentions or capabilities. Certainly Lee was not so blessed as he rode from Englishtown toward Monmouth Court House—and into a battle the very wisdom of which he had long questioned.

Prelude: The Situation and Its Problems

With combat looming, Lee understood the American situation as follows. By 6:00 A.M. on the twenty-eighth, with guides finally procured, Grayson was moving toward the enemy. Including Grayson's detachment, the vanguard consisted of some 4,500 men (perhaps somewhat less), enough to offer a stiff fight. If his forces ran into trouble, Lee had Washington's assurance that the main army would be within supporting distance. The main body then lay near Manalapan Bridge, about four miles from Englishtown, and mustered slightly over 7,800 men, including the bulk of the Continental artillery. Colonel Morgan's 800 troops were south of Freehold at Richmond Mills; Lee depended on him getting into any action. In addition, some 1,200 (perhaps as many as 2,000) militia continued to hang on Clinton's flanks, with a significant concentration forming on a prominent rise about two miles west of Freehold.[1] Thus, whatever happened when Lee made contact, he could be excused for assuming that plenty of help would be close at hand.

While the general could not have known it, several factors worked against rebel abilities to bring all their strength to bear around the courthouse. The first serious miscue involved Colonel Morgan. If ever there was a classic example of "friction"—as Carl von Clausewitz termed the accumulation of unanticipated mistakes, bad weather, difficult terrain, misunderstandings, conflicting intelligence, and other complications—the effort to bring the Virginia rifleman into action was it.[2] Unfortunately for Lee and for patriot operations generally, Morgan would never get into the fight. This was a serious command lapse for which Lee, Morgan, Washington, and others shared the blame. Morgan had done well enough in harassing Clinton and in providing the commander in chief with a flow of intelligence. But now the patriot army was preparing for a much larger operation, and Lee and Washington expected the colonel's troops to play a major combat role. Yet neither general knew exactly where Morgan was. Under the circumstances, Washington had left him out of touch with the main army too long. Now, with the storm gathering, a flurry of attempts to reach the colonel would breed only confusion.

As Washington had instructed early on the twenty-eighth—in the orders Lee received about 1:45 A.M.—the vanguard commander quickly sent a messenger toward Richmond Mills, where he thought

Morgan was encamped. The rider eventually found the colonel, probably around 3:00 A.M., although we do not know precisely when. But Lee's letter, drafted at the general's instructions by Captain Evan Edwards, apparently contained the seeds of misunderstanding. That letter is now lost, but in another dated 29 June, Morgan revealed some details of the communication from the general. Specifically, on the twenty-ninth he noted that Lee had written him "yesterday" and that the message carried a time notation of one o'clock in the "evening."[3] Did "evening" mean early on the twenty-eighth, that is, at 1:00 A.M.—when Lee issued the orders—or one o'clock in the afternoon? Had Edwards made a clerical error, as historian Samuel Smith has speculated, perhaps calling for an attack "tomorrow morning" rather than "this morning"? Without the missing orders from Lee, there is no certainty that the message was clear. Morgan evidently knew that Lee wanted a morning attack, but having received orders on the twenty-eighth, he apparently assumed the general meant the following morning—that is, Monday the twenty-ninth.[4] There is at least one important clue suggesting this was the case. Three weeks later, in his testimony at Lee's court-martial, another of the general's aides, Major John Mercer, said the letter sent to Morgan specified that Lee was going after Clinton's rear "the *next morning*" (italics added), which could well have implied 29 June.[5] This was "friction" indeed.

There was even more confusion. Shortly after midnight on the twenty-eighth, a rider from Morgan got through to Washington's headquarters. The message has not survived, but the colonel apparently was proposing action—perhaps a daylight attack on the enemy—that Washington considered risky, as both Lee's vanguard and the main army were too far away to support him. Nathanael Greene had already written Morgan to be cautious, but concerned that the colonel might not have received these orders, Washington sent Morgan's rider back to Richmond Mills with a short note. The commanding general reiterated Greene's message: Morgan was now too distant for the main army to support, so he was to avoid a serious action unless he was "tempted by some very evident advantage."[6] But Washington failed to mention his hope that the vanguard would launch an attack in the morning and that Morgan should stay in touch with Lee.

Concerned that these officers were not in communication, Washington dictated to Hamilton the order (discussed in chapter 7) that to prevent the enemy from escaping by a night or early morning march, Lee should send forward a party of observation and orders to Morgan. The colonel, if he could catch Clinton on the move, was to attack "in such a manner as might also tend to produce delay, and yet not so as to endanger a general rout of his party, and disqualify them from acting in concert with the other troops when a serious attack should be made."[7] These were the orders that Lee received just before 2:00 A.M. and that resulted in him sending the poorly dated instructions to Morgan. Coupled with Lee's communication, the colonel could easily have concluded that the senior patriot commanders did not intend to provoke a major battle on Sunday.

Morgan eventually did try to clarify matters himself. On Sunday morning, probably in response to Washington's message and certainly as a result of the firing he could hear toward Freehold, he sent another rider north. This time the dragoon galloped onto the battlefield itself looking for General Lee. Instead, he found Brigadier General Anthony Wayne, probably sometime after noon. When the horseman asked what instructions to carry to Morgan, Wayne, who was in the process of pulling his men back with the enemy in view, replied that the rider could see for himself how the battle was going, the clear implication being not well.[8] (Inexplicably and deplorably, Wayne failed to send the rider on to Lee.) If Morgan received this news, and one can only assume he did, he may not have known what to make of it. Told by Washington and Greene on the twenty-eighth to stay out of major fighting and by Lee that same day to be ready to fight on the twenty-ninth (or so the colonel apparently thought), he elected to stay put. Morgan, as one of his chief biographers has noted, generally was not a man "to exceed what he thought were his instructions," especially if they came from Washington.[9] His riflemen, who had played such havoc with Burgoyne at Saratoga, never fired a shot at Monmouth. Thus an order from Lee, unclear or misinterpreted (or both), complicated by messages from Greene and Washington and a battlefield report of dubious clarity, deprived the Continentals of the services of some of their best comrades in arms at a critical time.

Communications (or rather miscommunications) with Morgan were not the only problem. Contrary to Lee's expectations, the main army did not come up as quickly as anticipated. About 5:00 A.M.—that is, before Grayson had marched and after Lafayette had found the vanguard commander getting some badly needed rest—riders from Major General Dickinson reached Washington and Lee, notifying both generals that Clinton was moving out toward Middletown. This was news they had anticipated but only now had confirmed. Independently, the main body and the vanguard broke camp. Washington, perhaps not knowing Lee had received word of the British march, once more sent orders to his second in command. He ordered an immediate move against Clinton's rear, although he again emphasized that Lee was to use his judgment on whether or not to engage. (This was the message sent via Lieutenant Colonel Richard Kidder Meade.) He could desist if "there should be powerful reasons to the contrary," and he was not to provoke a general engagement.[10]

Well behind Lee, it took longer for Washington's main body to move. Encumbered as it was with more artillery and regiments, it was only about 10:00 A.M. that the long column filed slowly into Englishtown. The commander in chief was still in Englishtown as late as 11:30, when he wrote a brief note to Henry Laurens. He told Laurens that "the main body of the Army" was "pressing hard to come up with the Enemy," although the severe heat had slowed his march. The vanguard, he said, was trying to catch Clinton, but the success of this operation was still "a matter of question."[11] Yet even as Washington was writing—and unknown to him—Lee was fully engaged and well beyond the main army's immediate support. For the time being, then, without the assistance of either Washington or Morgan, the vanguard would have to look to itself.

It was advice Lee hardly needed. He had started long before Washington's orders reached him late in the morning, by which time the vanguard was preparing its final approach toward Freehold. It was not a smooth departure. Lee's men dropped their packs and began assembling by 5:00 A.M., the troops crowding into the few narrow streets of Englishtown. The previous day, when Washington had met with Lee and his officers, they decided that William Maxwell's New Jersey Brigade would stay to the rear of the vanguard, yet inexplicably the brigadier found himself at the head of the column. This miscue began a chain reaction of delays. The entire movement slowed as the New Jersey troops stepped to the side of the road to allow Brigadier General Scott to pass. Scott, however, was also out of order, and in turn he had to make way for General Wayne; Colonel Henry Jackson then inserted his men between Scott and Maxwell.[12] All the shuffling took time, and the vanguard's leading elements reached Tennent's Meeting House, some two miles from Englishtown, only shortly before 8:00 A.M. More friction—and the confusion and delays were only beginning.

By then Lee and his staff had ridden well ahead. Around 7:00 A.M., with the marching column only a quarter mile out of Englishtown, the major general rode toward Monmouth Court House to better understand his route of approach and learn what he could of the enemy situation. Even farther ahead, Captain Edwards was riding to Grayson with Lee's orders to close with the British as quickly as possible. On the way the captain met one of Dickinson's aides coming from the direction of Freehold. The militiaman carried alarming news: contrary to Dickinson's earlier intelligence, the enemy was not retreating toward Middletown, but rather had "arranged their whole army at Freehold" and appeared to be preparing to attack the Continentals. Edwards sent the messenger on to inform Lee while the captain hurried forward to warn Grayson. The militia courier probably reached the general within ten minutes, and his unexpected news jolted Lee. Worse, the militiaman warned Lee to advance no farther, for the British had an open road that would enable them to outflank him on the right and cut him off.[13] For all Lee knew at the moment, Clinton had made the first move, and if not his own troops, at the very least Grayson's advanced contingent was in real trouble.

However surprised he may have been, Lee reacted prudently. He told Dickinson's aide to ride toward Englishtown and halt the oncoming vanguard. The general then rode forward to overtake Grayson but quickly halted as a thought occurred to him. The colonel was a sound officer, but Lee did not know him personally. With the advanced party apparently marching into danger, Lee wanted a more senior officer in charge. To that end, he gave Captain Mercer orders for Brigadier General Wayne. Mercer was to ride back and "beg of General Wayne that he would come forward and take command" of the party of observation. Lee "looked upon it as the post of honor"—that is, of the greatest danger and concern—the place for a proven commander. He was less concerned with military etiquette than with the developing situation: After conferring with Wayne, Mercer was next to find Maxwell, supposedly in position at the rear of the column (the units were still jockeying for their correct positions). The New Jersey Brigade was to march on the road past Covenhoven's Mill toward Craig's Mill and take position at a fork where another road led toward the courthouse. Such a position would block the feared British move to cut off the vanguard; Maxwell was to move to the road junction and wait for either new orders or the British, in which case he would fight, green recruits or not.[14]

As Mercer rode back, he met one of Washington's aides, Lieutenant Colonel Meade, coming forward. Meade's ride in search of General Lee was discussed earlier, but it is well to put it into chronological sequence here. Carrying orders from Washington, Meade asked if Mercer "was going to order on the [vanguard] troops?" Mercer said no, in fact the British "were advancing." This exchange would have been the first inkling by anyone on the commander in chief's staff of just how unknown the situation was in front of Lee. Mercer then galloped backed to Wayne and relayed Lee's orders, at which the Pennsylvania brigadier hurried forward, while Mercer continued to the rear in search of Maxwell. The captain found the New Jersey Brigade still waiting by the side of the road, only half of Wayne's and Scott's detachments—now halted—having passed. Mercer gave Maxwell his orders and a "rough draught of the road" and hurried back east, only to encounter Meade again.[15] Meade was returning to Washington after having conferred with Lee.

While Mercer was riding to Wayne and Maxwell, Meade, well mounted, seems to have caught up with Lee and his escort just west of Tennent's Meeting House. Meade told the general that he had orders from Washington, "but as the enemy remained on the ground"—that is, given what he had just heard from Mercer—"it would be needless to deliver the orders." Lee complained about the confusing intelligence he and Washington had received and told Meade that he "had advanced a body of troops that he thought in danger [Grayson's]; and that he had sent back to General Wayne to take the command of them." While they were talking, the picture suddenly changed. Captain Benjamin Walker, aide to Major General Steuben, rode up. Walker had been on a scouting mission with Steuben (discussed below) and "informed General Lee that the enemy had left the ground." This information directly contradicted the report from Dickinson's courier, received only minutes earlier. The news caught Lee by surprise, and the general "did not seem to credit it till it was repeated frequently by Captain Walker." In fact, Dickinson's ominous report had it wrong: the enemy was not advancing on the Americans, the redcoats were moving away. With the situation seemingly clarified, Meade decided to deliver Washington's orders: Lee was to advance "immediately" and "bring on an engagement, or attack the enemy as soon as possible, unless some very powerful circumstance forbid it." He added that Washington "would soon be up to his aid."[16] Lee then asked Meade to send forward the rest of the vanguard troops as he rode back. So Clinton was not attacking, and Lee could resume his march. But if there were any signs of relief among Lee and his staff, they were likely matched by feelings of irritation and frustration. Reports on the enemy situation had been starkly contradictory: what *was* going on ahead of them?

With the false alarm behind him, Lee, joined by his adjutant, Lieutenant Colonel John Brooks, resumed his pursuit of Colonel Grayson. Coming to the militia encampment at the meetinghouse, the officers there confirmed Walker's information. They related that "the enemy moved from the Court-house at two o'clock, and only a light party of infantry and cavalry remained to cover their retreat."[17] Shortly after Lee left, Wayne, with his aides and escort, caught up to the general. They rode south toward Craig's Mill and Upper Freehold and then turned left toward the courthouse. Grayson, who had marched quickly once leaving Englishtown, was still out of sight, and Lee wanted to reestablish contact. But at this point they heard gunfire ahead.[18] Someone was engaged—but who?

The Militia Battle

As Lee (and well behind him, Washington) was getting his men on the road, Colonel Grayson, with at least an hour's head start, moved his "party of observation" steadily toward Tennent's Meeting House. After sunrise, the weather quickly turned hot, and as Grayson reached the meetinghouse his men were kicking up dust through high humidity and heat already above eighty degrees. About this time—between 7:30 and 8:00 A.M. and before the firing ahead reached Continental ears—Captain Edwards finally caught up with him. Just before, Edwards had passed "several" small groups of militia forming "in a very confused manner." Grayson had seen them as well, but apparently they provided no clear intelligence to either him or Edwards. Coming up with the colonel, Edwards found the advanced detachment emerging from a woodlot on the Sutfin farm and moving downhill toward a causeway and bridge that crossed the boggy meadows (the West Morass) and Spotswood Middle Brook.[19] They were about a mile beyond the meetinghouse. Grayson halted to talk, but Edwards, who had been sent to urge him to make haste, was now unsure what to do. The captain told the colonel "of the orders that I had from General Lee, but that I supposed General Lee was ignorant of the present situation of the enemy, and that I fancied he [Grayson] had better not move on."[20] It was at this moment the discharge of musketry occurred ahead of the column.

Grayson had walked into a very fluid situation; in fact, he had just missed the first serious fighting of the day. About half a mile forward, militia lining the Hedgerow between the Parsonage and Rhea farms had fired a battalion volley and then began retreating toward a fence closer to the West Morass bridge. The colonel had arrived just in time to watch the militiamen falling back, observing as a platoon or two kept "up an irregular retreating fire." If he had looked to his left, he could have seen green-jacketed hussars pursuing a running militiaman along the road while enemy infantry crested the hill. A militia officer hurried up to the Continentals with a request from Major General Dickinson for a regiment to support the men. Grayson obliged by forming his troops on a rise on the Englishtown side of the bridge. He then ordered a Virginia battalion (the combined Fourth, Eighth, and Twelfth Virginia Regiments) to follow him. Artillery lieutenant colonel Eleazer Oswald called for a field piece, and then Grayson, Edwards, and Oswald kicked their horses into motion and hurried forward to join a cluster of militia officers, including Dickinson. By the time they arrived, the enemy—a detachment of the Queen's American Rangers—had disappeared.

The incident, brief as it was, was the opening round of the Battle of Monmouth. Neither side had intended to fight this skirmish, which began early in the morning with three concurrent but unconnected rebel movements. The first to move was Major General (and Inspector General) Friedrich Steuben. Early that morning Steuben, his aide Benjamin Walker, a small dragoon escort, and Washington aide John Laurens crossed "Tennent's" bridge and rode to the high ground on the easternmost Rhea farm (occupied by William Ker), overlooking Monmouth Court House.[21] This was not Steuben's first such expedition. He had been out the previous morning as well and had pushed some scouts "so near [British positions] as to fire a Pistol at their Horsemen whilst feeding their Horses." He watched the burning of the Henderson and

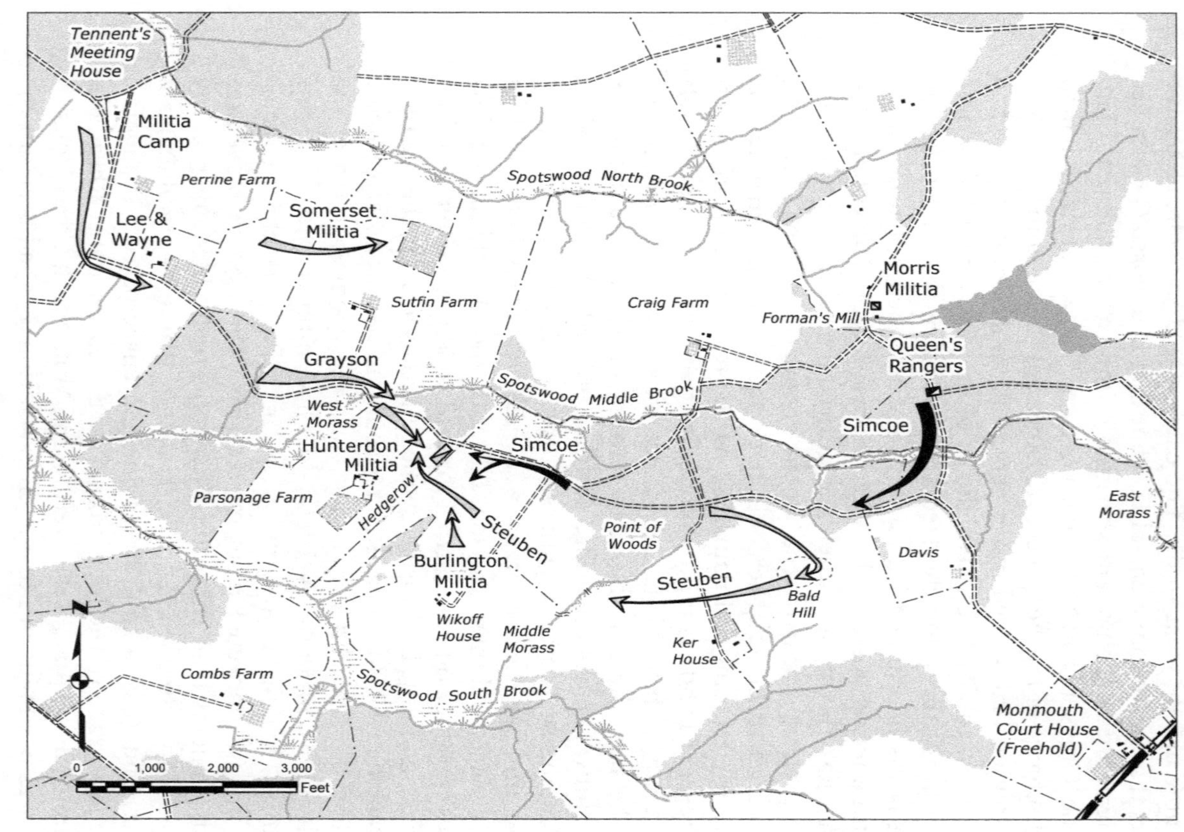

Steuben's escape: The Queen's American Rangers' pursuit of Steuben leads to a skirmish with New Jersey militia. Map by Garry Wheeler Stone. Copyright © 2016 by the University of Oklahoma Press.

Wikoff homes and reported to Washington that the British had "not the least appearance of moving."[22] But this morning was different. From a "bald hill" on the Ker farm, Steuben clearly saw the British army in motion—moving up from the south through the village toward Middletown. He sent Walker back to report to Lee and continued watching the marching redcoats.

If Steuben had a good view into the village, the British had even a better view of him. The sun was shining directly on the Americans and the baron's glittering star. Eventually, some sharp-eyed enemy soldier spotted the rebel party. The view was clear enough to allow the British to correctly conclude that senior patriot officers were present; they even mistakenly identified one as Lafayette. The party was a tempting and seemingly exposed target, and the British reacted. About 7:00 A.M. Lord William Cathcart—one of Clinton's aides-de-camp—brought orders to Lieutenant Colonel Simcoe, commander of the Queen's Rangers, "to take his hussars and try to cut off a reconnoitering party of the enemy, (supposed to be M. Fayette)."[23]

Knowing that he was about to venture into woods populated by rebel militia, Simcoe received permission from Cathcart to take some infantry with him. At the quick step, Simcoe marched south from his post on the Amboy Road with twenty hussars (the mounted rangers) and his grenadier company of forty rank and file. They turned west on the Englishtown, or Cranbury, Road, trying to get around the reconnoitering party and scoop up the lot. About half a mile, or ten minutes, into their march, the rangers encountered two "rebel Videttes" (mounted militia scouts) "who, galloping off, the cavalry were ordered to pursue them, as their best guides." Simcoe was wrong. Pursuing the scouts took the rangers well west of the bald hill. Yet as Steuben seems to have left his party to ride back and personally report to Lee (and perhaps to have some breakfast), he and Simcoe paralleled each other—Steuben riding through the fields, the rangers on the wood-fringed road—each unaware of the other.[24]

Simcoe was wise to be concerned about the militia. Even as Steuben ventured toward the village on his reconnaissance, Dickinson had about 700 troops posted at Tennent's Meeting House, and they were on the move. Not only had patrols been out all night, but before breakfast Dickinson was dispatching larger groups on a mile-and-a-quarter-long front between Spotswood North and South Brooks. To the south was Colonel William Shreve with Burlington County militia and the men of Captain Joseph Clunn's Hunterdon

County artillery (acting as infantry). In the center at the Hedgerow, Dickinson was personally with the First and Fourth Hunterdon Regiments and a few volunteers from the Third. To the north, marching directly east through the fields, was Colonel Frederick Frelinghuysen with men from the First and Second Somerset. Farther east, at Forman's Mill, Morris County's Colonel Silvanus Seely and a party of 200 had lain on their arms all night after driving a British light-infantry picket across Spotswood North Brook. Back at the meetinghouse, the Third Hunterdon and off-duty men were guarding the baggage. Farther afield, Dickinson had over 300 Middlesex and Monmouth militia to the north and at least 200 Monmouth and Burlington men to the east with Morgan.[25] Unknowingly, Simcoe risked being outnumbered in any serious clash.

At the Hedgerow Dickinson ordered another movement. He wanted a patrol to reconnoiter the road to the courthouse and assigned a sergeant and ten men from the Fourth Hunterdon. The patrol then asked for another volunteer, and Private Ralph Schenck stepped forward. While willing to go, however, Schenck had misgivings. He thought the mission too dangerous for a small patrol; in his view it called for at least a hundred men. Events would prove him right.

The men marched down the road, across a log causeway bridging a marshy rivulet, and into the woods. After traveling about three-fourths of a mile, the men heard a "rumbling noise ahead." Schenck's sergeant ordered his men to form behind trees, but the woods were too thin to offer any real cover; as the Queen's Rangers hussars bore down on them, the relatively small number of riders looked to the exposed militia like "a large body." The sergeant then ordered an every-man-for-himself retreat as the riders closed and the grenadiers joined the chase on foot. At the end of the patrol formation, Schenck and his right-hand man bolted down the road—a mistake. The two men made it out of the woods and onto the log causeway, with the hooves of the hussars' horses "clattering" behind them. Schenck heard an ugly sound and, glancing back, saw that his mate had been sabered in the head; the blow had brought the skin of his head "down over his ear." Schenck ran even faster, with the riders trotting behind waiting for him to falter. Then the hussars received a surprise. From behind the Hedgerow came a ragged volley from the First and Fourth Hunterdon.[26] This was the firing Grayson and the other Continentals heard.

To the militia behind the hedged fence, the Queen's Rangers looked like the van of a British column. Dickinson ordered his men to fall back to the next fence. The retreat was not precipitous and there was no panic, but when the rangers began to flank their left, the militiamen had had enough for the moment. Although they had the advantage of numbers, the aggressive action of the enemy horse and the advance of the grenadiers proved unnerving. Edward Taylor, another member of Schenck's patrol who had managed to join the militia at the Hedgerow, recalled "the British were too strong for the Americans." But even in pulling back, the militiamen were still dangerous; at one point they "wheeled upon the British and gave them a strong and brisk fire."[27]

Halfway to the new position, Lieutenant Moses Estey of the Fourth Hunterdon looked back and saw Schenck running from the hussars. He halted his company, evidently to offer cover for Schenck. The private made it back past the Hedgerow and, still carrying his musket, vaulted the fence along the road and ran into the field. Estey then shouted to him, "Take care, the horse is coming after you!" Schenck turned—a hussar had jumped the fence—brought up his musket, and pulled the trigger. Nothing happened—in his flight all his priming had shaken out. The hussar stopped, drew a pistol, fired, and missed. Miraculously, Schenck was able to reprime and shoot before the ranger could fire again or charge him. The hussar, badly wounded, fell off his horse. From the road, other hussars were firing at Schenck. The private dashed to the horse, mounted, and rode away in a volley of pistol shots. The horse received flesh wounds in the thigh and leg, and three pistol balls riddled the clothing roll tied behind the saddle.

Quickly, Schenck was out of pistol range and at the next fence. Captain Phillip Snook, Third Hunterdon (Schenck thought his name was "Smock"), saw him coming and pulled down a section of fence to let the fleeing militiaman through. At the time Schenck feared that he and the militiaman with the head wound were the only members of their patrol to escape. Initially, he thought he was the *only* man to escape, as he learned only later that the wounded man had crawled under cover and, badly bloodied, survived the fighting. The rest, he believed, "were all cut to pieces by the refugee horsemen [the Queen's Rangers]."[28] Most of the patrol had wisely not tried to outrun the hussars but had fled into the wetlands north of the road.

But Schenck's morning was not over. No sooner did he get through the fence than a cry went up that Captain Snook had been shot. "Return with the horse," a man behind him shouted, "the captain is wounded." Simcoe's grenadiers had arrived at the Hedgerow and were steadily pouring aimed fire into the militia's position as some of the hussars continued firing from the road. One of their shots had hit the captain. Schenck wheeled his horse to go back after the officer who had helped save his life. But when he rode up, Snook told him that he had suffered only a flesh wound and that he needed no help; gallantly, the captain told the private he should keep the horse and look after himself.[29] Trying to do just that, Schenck turned again toward safety when he came across a plainly terrified boy with a musket. With the action swirling around him, the youth was crying and paralyzed by fear. Now it was Schenck's turn to save a comrade. The private dismounted, put the boy on the wounded horse, and sent him off with instructions "to take good care of the horse until I came or sent for him." He never learned the boy's name and, for all we know, never again saw the horse. Now trudging past the fence on foot, Schenck rejoined the militia and was gratified to see Grayson's reinforcements coming up. With his new comrades in arms, he headed toward the approaching Continentals, still willing to fight. The private, fortunate to be alive, had had quite a morning.

Schenck's exploits were noteworthy, but others on both sides fought as gamely. Somewhere behind the lucky private, a British ball had caught Lieutenant Estey in the groin. The young officer remained with his command, however, and helped maintain discipline even as the militia fell back to safety; only then did he allow comrades to carry him from the field. Schenck credited him with preventing the rebels from being overrun as "the balls flew around . . . like hail." After the battle Estey's heroism brought him a promotion to captain. Simcoe also remembered a tough fight. The lieutenant colonel correctly believed that he had come up against "a large corps," and he had pressed home his attack aggressively in trying to keep his more numerous opponents off balance. He mentioned in particular one "Ellison, a very spirited Hussar," who jumped a fence chasing the rebels.[30] Although the militia had retreated, they had pulled back in reasonably good order and with enough of them stopping to fire to make things hot for Simcoe's men.

After posting his grenadiers along the Hedgerow, Simcoe was riding back toward his hussars when a militia ball hit him in the arm. "For some seconds, he thought it broken, and was unable to guide his horse, which, being also struck, run [*sic*] away with him, luckily, to the rear." Recovering the use of his arm, Simcoe returned to his hussars, and seeing two small parties of Burlington County militia, he led his men toward them at a gallop. The militia fled, leaving behind two men who had been in the advance. Simcoe sent two hussars to capture them and then rode back to extract the rest of his men and retreat.

The ranger commander was just in time. Men from the Second Hunterdon had joined Dickinson, and Continentals were starting up the hill from the bridge. The militia too were realizing how few enemies opposed them. Simcoe could see "some general officer, and his suite, advancing to reconnoiter"; this was probably Dickinson and his aides. Concerned that the militia might attack, Simcoe sent a hussar back on the road where it entered the woods; the rider then signaled with his cap to an imaginary force advancing on the road. When the lieutenant colonel got closer to the rebel officers, he shouted out to other imaginary men "not to fire till the main body came close." Slowed by his militia prisoners, Simcoe sent a hussar ahead to see if the grenadiers remained where he had posted them and if any wounded remained forward. When the rider reported that the grenadiers had withdrawn with their wounded, Simcoe turned from the fence, placing the shoulder of the hill between his riders and the militia, and joined the grenadiers. The engagement effectively was over.[31]

It had been a brief action. Although it probably seemed an eternity to those involved, from start to finish—that is, from the time Simcoe's men spotted and set out after the first rebel horsemen until the ranger commander called for a withdrawal—the affair probably lasted only twenty-five minutes. The skirmishing had elements of confusion, chance encounters, close-in fighting, terror, and heroism—a microcosm of everything that made combat brutal and unpredictable. It also demonstrated the effectiveness of an aggressive mounted arm—of which the patriots had little—as well as the fact that some militia units were willing to put up a stiff fight. It was also a strictly American affair; the skirmish pitted tories against rebels—other than Simcoe, there were no British or Hessian troops involved—a vivid reminder that a bitter civil war raged within the larger struggle.[32]

Except for Schenck's escape from the hussars, most of the action was at relatively long range, but both sides exchanged aimed fire and sustained casualties. Besides the sabered private, two militia officers were hit. Six rangers had been wounded: Simcoe, three grenadiers, and two hussars. The hussar Schenck shot died in the field hospital at Monmouth Court House. The other, Humphrey Cochran, was left at the courthouse with the surgeons when the army departed that evening. Years later, when Simcoe reworked his journal into a memoir, he still was angry that Cochran was left behind. Rangers were especially vulnerable to mistreatment since they were mostly loyalists, including "many deserters from the enemy." Simcoe himself was out of action for the rest of the day. In "excruciating pain," the tough ranger joined Knyphausen's baggage train, already on the move. He was convinced that there would be no more fighting that day.[33] But the rangers' day was only beginning. Without their commander, they would march miles farther, fight another skirmish, and suffer more casualties. But they were veterans—none of their casualties would be from fatigue.[34]

And where was Major General Steuben during all of this? He was, after all, the man Simcoe had set out to capture. Unmolested, the baron had arrived at the Hedgerow ahead of the hussars. He may have heard the commotion as Simcoe tangled with the militia patrol but was probably unaware that his mission had sparked the skirmish. In his haste to get through the Hedgerow, however, the general did suffer a loss. Simcoe happily recorded that "the Baron Stuben . . . lost his hat in the confusion," and it was taken prisoner.[35]

CHAPTER 11

MORNING AT MONMOUTH II

GENERAL LEE'S BATTLE

As Colonel Grayson brought up his detachment in support of the retreating militia, he saw the Queen's Rangers draw off. He could not have known the British party had not come looking for a serious fight; Simcoe's chief assignment was screening the withdrawal of Clinton's army. That operation began hours ago. Long before dawn, the British commander had Lieutenant General von Knyphausen prepare the baggage train and the 2nd Division for departure toward Middletown; the Hessian general was to march at 3:00 A.M. An hour earlier Clinton had deployed the Queen's Rangers northwest of Monmouth Court House (Freehold), blocking the Amboy Road to protect the wagons.[1] (Simcoe's action with the militia was actually a diversion from his primary mission.) Clinton always considered his baggage train the most vulnerable part of the army and took special pains to protect it. Indeed, at the last minute he ordered Knyphausen to march by a more easterly road to Middletown, via Polhemus Ford, rather than risk what he feared was greater militia activity on the more direct route. The train moved out shortly after 4:00 A.M., traveling under a heavy escort; over the course of the day, the Hessian jaegers would help beat back several militia attempts to break through the defensive cordon. By 5:00 A.M. Clinton's infantry were marching too, and the last British troops cleared Monmouth Court House by 9:15 A.M., moving under the cover of the 1st Battalion of Light Infantry and the 16th Light Dragoons.[2] Thus once Grayson had come up, Simcoe's rangers were the first British defense line west of the village.

At this time the colonel and those with him had little idea of what the British were doing. Based on the skirmish just concluded, they assumed that enemy mounted troops were patrolling aggressively. At the same time, Philemon Dickinson, who was then unaware that Steuben's reconnoitering party had confirmed that the main enemy columns were heading out of town, continued to urge caution. He insisted that "not a man" of the enemy "had stirred from their post at or near the Court-house." The militia general warned Grayson that the British might even send a column against his right. Taking no chances, the colonel pulled back across the bridge toward Tennent's Meeting House and took post on the opposite hillside.[3]

It was at this point that Major General Lee came up and informed Grayson that the rest of the advanced corps was on the way and that the British were marching out of the village. He was intent on closing with Clinton's rear, but upon crossing the bridge to meet Dickinson, the militia leader again warned him against an immediate assault. Once more Dickinson stressed his belief that the British were still in Freehold, which Lee found hard to credit in view of the report from Captain Walters. The two generals exchanged some sharp words, with Dickinson finally insisting, "you may believe or not, but if you march your party beyond the ravine now in your rear"—that is, over the bridge across Spotswood Middle Brook and the West Morass—"you are in a perilous situation."[4] Lee, more than likely convinced that the New Jersey general was wrong, nevertheless had no clear picture of what Clinton was doing.

If Dickinson was wrong about the enemy situation, he did have a point regarding the terrain toward Freehold. The view from the high ground offered a fine vista east toward the village. Despite the picturesque landscape, any move toward the town would take Lee through some deceptively difficult ground; indeed, it was treacherous ground for soldiering. What soon became the battlefield spanned some three miles of generally rolling terrain, running from the high ground just west of Spotswood Middle Brook eastward to about a mile northeast of Freehold. Northeast of town the ground was more open, and the fields rose toward a small hill (now called Briar Hill) astride the road toward Middletown and the fork to Shrewsbury. The three major ravines (or morasses) as well as several minor hollows cut the field; all had streams or marshy ground with woods or thickets. The Cranbury (or Englishtown) Road, which Grayson and Lee had followed from Englishtown, crossed the West Morass by a bridge across the Middle Brook, while a causeway took it across a small rivulet that flowed into the brook. The road then skirted just south of the courthouse as it reached Freehold itself, then turned north across the East Morass. Off the road, the ravines were passable only with difficulty; men could do it alone and in small groups, but any large formations of troops would have to break ranks and reform on the opposite side.

North of the Cranbury Road and east along the Middle Brook, a band of forest roughly paralleled the road. In places the road ran through the woods. Organized troops could move easily enough along the road, but men north of the creek would have trouble acting in concert with those in the fields and orchards to the south. A unit cut off on either side of the Middle Brook or pinned against one of the ravines or morasses could easily find itself in serious trouble. It was exactly such a possibility that weighed so heavily in Dickinson's warnings to Grayson and Lee. The same observation convinced Clinton that Washington would never risk a major action west of Freehold. "I could not entertain so bad an opinion of Mr. Washington's military abilities," the British general wrote, "as to suppose he would risk" his advanced guard "over those difficult passes without the support of his" main body, "or that he would even venture to support through such a country."[5]

Frustrated at the delay, but fearing that Dickinson might be right about the enemy holding at Freehold, Lee held his troops near the bridge. Conflicting reports came in telling both of British withdrawals and efforts to cut off the Americans by a thrust toward Englishtown. Lee sent regiments back and forth over the bridge as changing intelligence warranted. All reports of enemy threats proved false. At one point Captain Mercer took an entire brigade to investigate an apparently serious enemy movement to the north only to find that the mysterious troops were New Jersey militia, a Somerset County contingent under Colonel Frederick Frelinghuysen, who became lost trying to link up with Dickinson.[6] Another apparent flanking probe, upon examination, turned out to be local residents out to watch the troops.

Intelligence reports may have conflicted, but they were not necessarily inaccurate. Scouts relayed what they saw, or at least what they thought they saw. The problem lay in the fact that they reconnoitered the British from different perspectives and at different times. No one could see the entire situation, which was fluid anyway. Those who saw the Queen's Rangers in action, Clinton's covering units taking post, or stationary infantry columns reported possible enemy threats or that the redcoats were staying in or near Freehold. Rebels who saw the same British columns withdrawing reported that the enemy was pulling out entirely. Lee never lacked

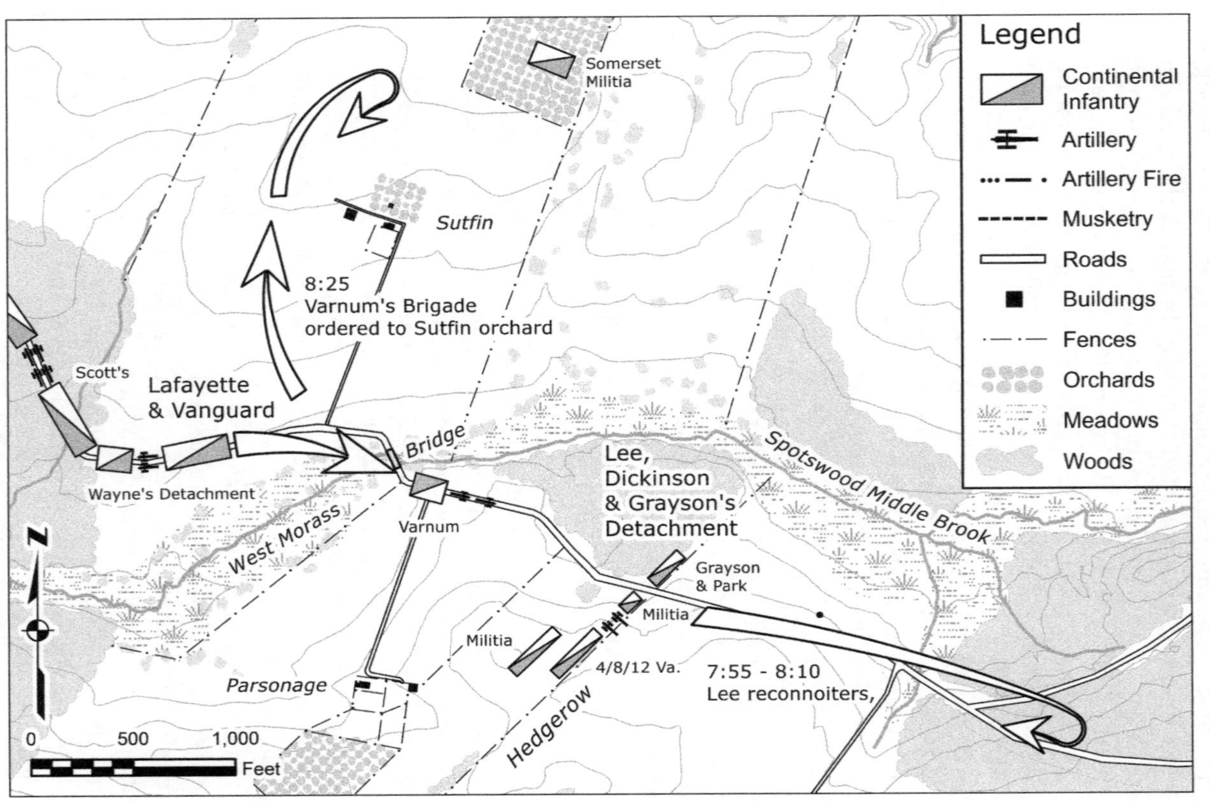

Lee's advance stalls at the West Morass between 7:35 and 8:55 A.M. due to conflicting intelligence. All times are approximate. Map by Garry Wheeler Stone. Copyright © 2016 by the University of Oklahoma Press.

for news of the British; his problem was trying to make sense of it. Finally, a plainly irritated Lee said that he would march anyway, see for himself what the British were doing, and form his plans accordingly. By then, however, Lafayette had brought up the rest of the vanguard, and Lee, having personally reconnoitered the woods beyond the Hedgerow, ordered his whole command to advance.[7] But he had lost a full hour.

Movement to Contact: Lee Attacks

At this juncture it seems that Lee's blood was up. Perhaps frustrations born of the repeated delays and contradictory intelligence were telling on the general, but when he crossed the West Morass bridge, any reticence he may have had about engaging had evaporated. Lee was clearly looking for a fight. Anthony Wayne had come up to assume command of Grayson's men, and Lee ordered him to advance. The two generals had disagreed over the campaign's goals in the various councils of war, but now Lee wanted the aggressive Pennsylvanian to find the enemy. In the lead was a battalion of picked men under Colonel Richard Butler, a veteran commander, followed by Colonel Henry Jackson's command. In all Wayne had some 550 men, and at the least Lee wanted him to hit part of Clinton's retreating rear guard.

Butler, following orders from Lee, took the general track of the Englishtown Road, moving under cover of woods whenever possible to conceal his approach. He put out small advance and flank parties for security and marched the battalion "in such a manner as I could form them [on line] immediately in case of an attack." Enemy light horse were now visible; as Butler steadily closed the distance, he finally stopped only to let Lee and Wayne reconnoiter. It was now about 9:30 A.M., and the rebel army was within minutes of engagement.

To this point, Lee had performed admirably. Acting as the eyes of Washington's army, the vanguard commander had executed a virtually flawless movement to contact: that is, he had set out with limited forces to clarify intelligence reports, find the enemy, and develop the tactical situation in the rebels' favor.[8] Lee had sent Grayson to guard against surprise and to locate the enemy for the rest of the advanced corps. The march to Freehold, conducted over unfamiliar terrain and against an opponent of unknown strength, deployment, and intention, had brought the Americans to the village essentially ready to fight. At the moment of contact, Lee had his best brigadier (Wayne) forward and his forces organized and firmly under control. He had the initiative, and it was his choice to attack or to hold his ground. To have brought up the vanguard in such fashion was no mean feat; under the circumstances, he could have done no better. So far, so good.[9]

Lee showed no hesitation in moving from approach to attack. His orders from Washington were to go for Clinton unless confronted with "powerful" circumstances to the contrary. As it happened, Lee's advance with Wayne to reconnoiter convinced him that circumstances favored an assault, and he quickly formed a plan. It was bold. The general estimated the British columns at some "five or six hundred cavalry and light infantry," probably a rear guard with a considerable gap between themselves and Clinton's main body. That gap was the key: Lee wanted to march a major part of his command rapidly to the left and circle behind the British columns. He was certain that, cut off from their main body and outnumbered, they would surrender. It would be a neat little victory, one that would sting Clinton without having to fight a costly battle.[10]

Exactly when Lee concluded that he could envelope the British rear is unclear, although it must have been within minutes of seeing the enemy near the courthouse. As he reconnoitered with Wayne, Lee had sent his aide Evan Edwards to scout the enemy; the captain quickly returned to confirm that the roads to the left not only led to the enemy rear but also would support artillery. Other officers must have realized what was afoot, as militia general David Forman then approached Lee with an offer to lead a column to the left. After the earlier dispute with Dickinson, the vanguard commander may have been leery of militia intelligence. At any rate, he curtly put off Forman, telling him that he already knew his "business"; but Lee promptly sent off another of his aides, Captain John Mercer, to have a second look at the route. Mercer's scout was also brief but informative. He confirmed that the road was passable as well as Edwards's opinion on the ability to haul artillery to the left. Equally important, he found a recently abandoned enemy encampment, about which a local resident stated that some two thousand men had camped there (these were the 799 men of the 2nd Light Infantry, replaced around 2:00 A.M. by the 455 men of the Queen's Rangers). This was a surprise to Lee, but he accepted this higher figure as the probable enemy strength. Still, he was confident that he could handle the apparently isolated detachment.[11]

While much would depend on the movement to the left, Lee also needed the continued, if unwitting, cooperation of the British. He wanted the targeted enemy columns, then at Freehold, to maintain position. He did not want the enemy main body moving to their support, nor did he want those two thousand to retreat to its protection. Thus Lee needed to control the movements not only of his own men but those of the redcoats as well. He thought he could do both. While Lee planned to lead the flanking column himself, he intended Wayne to attack in the center, although he wanted no pitched battle. Rather, he wanted the Pennsylvanian "to affect shyness rather than confidence, lest the appearance of vigor" should drive the British back on their main body or induce them to send a call for reinforcements. If Wayne's attack could simply fix the enemy troops where they were—not push them—then Lee could swing in behind them. Lee also assumed that the sound of the action would bring Daniel Morgan into play farther on the right, thus further complicating any British escape attempt or other response.

Wayne continued reconnoitering as Lee returned to the advanced force. The enemy light horse—well west of the village—prevented the brigadier from getting a good view of the enemy infantry, so he sent for Butler and Jackson to "drive their horse back." As Butler approached Freehold, his battalion drew "a small scattering fire" from the Queen's Rangers, at which he swung on line, ordered his men to hold their fire, and pushed on. The temptation to return fire was too much for some, however, and they let fly at the greencoats. At this the British marched off in good order up the road toward Middletown. (The Battle Monument in Freehold, erected in the nineteenth century, is close to the position of the British troops against whom Butler advanced.)[12]

The action now picked up pace. With the British withdrawing, Wayne had Butler swing to his left as he marched forward into the protection of some woods along the East Morass; his intention was to reinforce the picked men before fully committing them to an advance. Lee already had ordered Jackson's regiment to support Butler. Jackson, however, having joined the army after a brief stay in reoccupied Philadelphia, never had a chance to replenish ammunition. Lee had a team of sergeants collect a supply and get it to Jackson's men, but the delay kept the regiment from closing up with Butler.

More help was on the way. To provide Wayne and Butler with artillery support, Lee dispatched Lieutenant Colonel Oswald with Captain Thomas Wells's artillery company. Oswald was a hard man: Twenty-three years old during the battle, the British-born artillerist was a proven veteran. He had soldiered with Benedict Arnold during the attack on Fort Ticonderoga and the later invasion of Canada. Wounded and captured at Quebec, defeat only hardened his feelings of resistance. (Oswald was a partisan of General Lee, and he never forgave those who ruined the general after Monmouth.)[13] Realizing that Wayne's units had only some 550 men (including Jackson), Lee ordered the two battalions of Scott's Brigade (Grayson with the combined Fourth, Eighth, and Twelfth Virginia Regiments, and Lieutenant Colonel John Parke with Grayson's and Patton's Additional Regiments) detached to Wayne. In the meantime, Butler had the British in view and insisted that the Continentals strike quickly while the enemy was in motion and not formed defensively. The Pennsylvanian then led his regiment left, through the East Morass, to make room for other troops as they came up.

Wayne then rejoined Butler and noted that the enemy seemed to be forming on the hill by the fork in the roads. He sent two aides, Captains Benjamin Fishbourne and David Lenox, to warn Lee that he expected an attack. The general responded that such an enemy halt was simply part of a standard retreating maneuver and that Wayne need not worry. Still, he sent Mercer back with Lenox to make sure that Wayne understood his mission. Mercer stressed to the brigadier that he was not to drive the British back on their main body or provoke an enemy call for reinforcements. (Wayne later testified at Lee's court-martial that he was clear about this point.)[14]

This done, Lee and Wayne must have moved almost simultaneously. Lee had already sent Edwards to lead Varnum's Brigade, then under Colonel John Durkee, up the road toward Forman's Mill. There, if all went well, Durkee would turn right on a lane (a short-cut from the Middletown Road to the mill) and come out of the woods and drop down behind the unsuspecting rear guard. If he needed help, Lee was also bringing Wayne's detachment (now with Lafayette in command) and had the rest of Brigadier General Scott's command (and behind Scott, William Maxwell's New Jersey Brigade) moving up and within easy supporting distance. He did not tell Scott or Maxwell the details of his plan, considering that his personal leadership of the encircling column would be enough as long

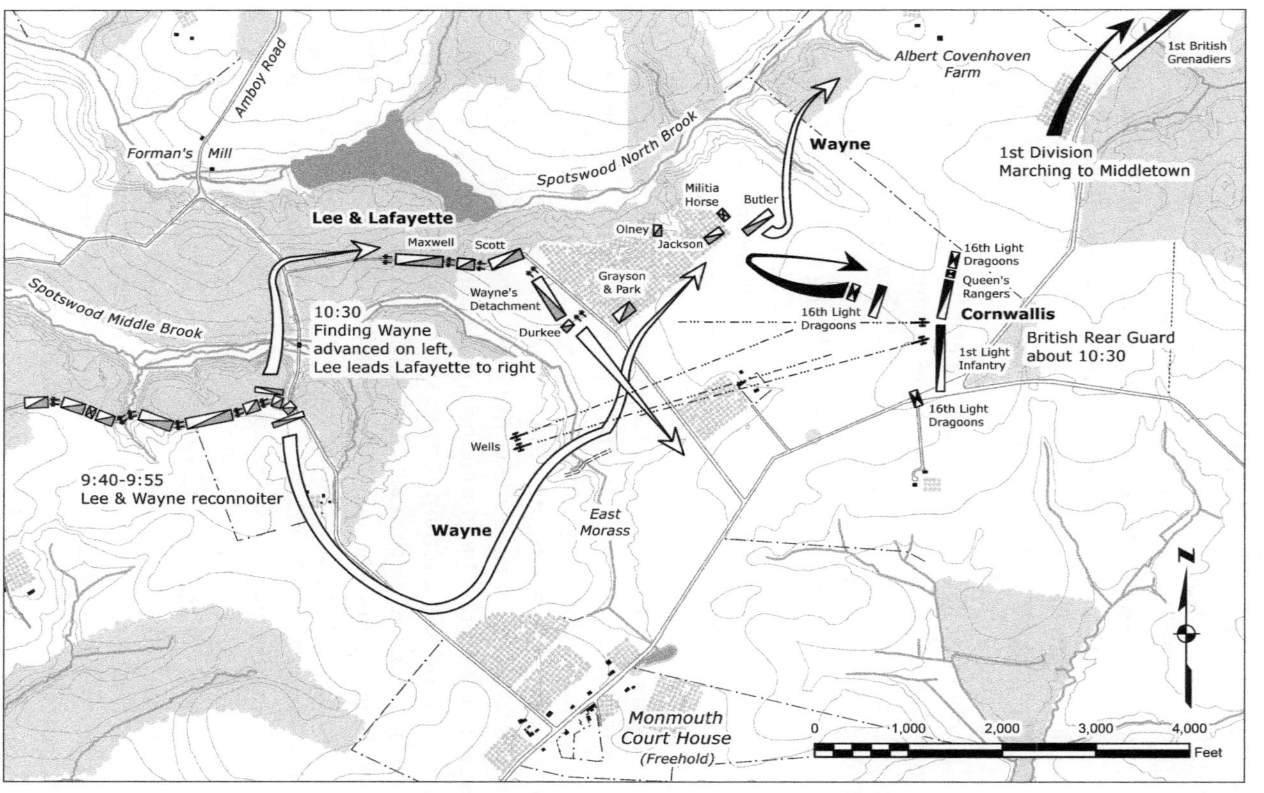

Lee marches to contact and attempts to envelop the British rear guard. Map by Garry Wheeler Stone. Copyright © 2016 by the University of Oklahoma Press.

as everyone kept their place in the line of march. But Lieutenant Colonel Brooks, Lee's adjutant, informed the regimental commanders of the major general's intentions.

With Lee in motion, Wayne pushed on. He did so with some critical help in the person of Lieutenant Colonel David Rhea of the Second New Jersey.[15] Rhea was an interesting man, and he figured repeatedly in the day's events. Three generations of Rheas had lived on the future battlefield. David was the sixth of seven children and the youngest son in a family that combined farming, milling, and business. His oldest brother, Robert, had purchased half his father's Freehold lands but spent more time at his store and mills in Allentown. David preferred the life of a merchant, dividing his time between Allentown and Philadelphia. The Rheas were rebels. By 1778 David Rhea was an experienced soldier who had seen hard service in Canada, skirmishing in New Jersey during the spring of 1777, and heavy fighting in Pennsylvania that fall. After the commander of the Second New Jersey, Colonel Israel Shreve, was wounded at Brandywine, Rhea led the regiment at Germantown and during the terrible first weeks at Valley Forge. In March 1778 Shreve, Rhea, and their men were sent to southern New Jersey to assist militia against loyalist and British activity. Shortly thereafter, Rhea returned to Freehold on furlough to help settle Robert's complicated estate.[16] He probably returned to his regiment just before the British evacuated Philadelphia, by which time the entire New Jersey Brigade already was in its home state. On 28 June he was detached to Lee, helping the general reconnoiter terrain toward the village and then guiding the Continental advance through the familiar countryside.

With Rhea leading the way, Wayne again turned to Butler and told him to keep going and try for the British left flank, then perhaps a half mile away. The brigadier sent Rhea to inform Lee of this movement, and the New Jersey officer quickly returned to tell him that Lee was in motion as well with militia general Forman serving as a guide.[17] By the time Rhea got back to Wayne, Butler and his picked men had advanced about a quarter of a mile. The colonel then saw a detachment of enemy horse form and appear to launch a charge directly toward him. These were the 16th Light Dragoons, who thought they were chasing away some American horse (mostly militia) on a scouting mission. Actually, they were victims of a ruse.

The trap for the 16th developed quickly. Riding from the right of Wayne's position—that is, from the right of Butler and Jackson—a patrol of militia light horse, part of Lieutenant Colonel Anthony Walton White's command (White himself may not have been with this group), reconnoitered the British rear guard on the Middletown Road. With Lieutenant General Cornwallis's infantry were the light dragoons, who heavily outnumbered the patriot horse. The British riders soon discovered the Americans and formed for an attack. At this point Captain Edwards, Lee's aide, rode up and suggested a plan. He told the militia "to let the British horse come as near as they could, with safety, and then to retreat off towards where General Wayne was."[18] In other words, the patriot riders were to decoy the 16th into the guns of the Continental infantry.

The British took the bait and chased the rebels. The 16th came hard after them, unaware until the last minute that rebel infantry were in the field. Colonel Jackson, then about a hundred yards behind and to the right of Butler and trying to close up, saw them coming. He recalled "a large column of dust" followed by one of the American light horse shouting, "For God's sake form, or we are cut to pieces." The light horsemen probably were galloping for the narrowing gap between Jackson and Butler. Jackson wheeled his platoons into line, ordering his men to hold their fire—even threatening to cut down the first man that fired without orders. Butler reacted just as quickly, and his men came smartly on line to receive the enemy charge. When the dragoons "got to within forty yards of us," Butler recalled, the riders fired their pistols at the Continentals while Butler's men replied with a full volley of musketry. The result gratified both rebel colonels: "They rode off as fast as they could ride," Jackson said; "they broke," Butler remembered, "and in their retreat from us broke through their own foot and disordered them."[19] Private Abraham Voorhees, one of the patriot horsemen, recalled that many fleeing British mounts "had no Riders." Four or five discharges from Captain Wells's field pieces added to the dragoons' discomfort.[20] The Continentals had started well.

This had been a typical mounted assault. Horsemen generally would not close with disciplined infantry unless the situation gave some promise of breaking and scattering them. Cavalry did their best and bloodiest work when riding down fleeing men, who were easy prey to saber and pistol; such was the case earlier in the morning with Simcoe's pursuit of Private Schenck's militia patrol. If the infantry held, however, as did Butler's picked men, about all the mounted troopers could do was to fire their pistols or carbines and hope they could ride out of harm's way without being blown out of their saddles. The 16th apparently got away with only a few casualties, some of whom fell prisoners, but riding through their own lines of infantry—probably their own dismounted men in porous open order—was ample testimony to their discomfort at Butler's hands.[21] Edwards's ruse and Butler's volley were a neat little victory for the Continentals.

Like so much of the Monmouth narrative, the incident gave rise to its share of postwar legends. In his old age Rhea embroidered on his role during the charge of the 16th Light Dragoons. He put himself in advance of the reconnoitering militia troop—and he may have been, as we do not know his exact movements, and he did send out militia patrols—upon which a dragoon dashed from the ranks of the 16th and gave chase. Rhea saw that his opponent

> was mounted on an elegant Horse, and as his own was an indifferent steed, he determined to possess himself of it. When within 50 or 60 yards, Ray [*sic*], who was an excellent shot, felt perfectly sure of the horse, and deliberately drawing a pistol, coolly aimed and fired at the rider, but without effect. He fired the other pistol, and that too missed. The trooper was now within a few yards, dashing at him at a furious speed, his eyes flashing vengeance, and sword uplifted for the fatal blow. There was no time for further ceremony. The colonel abruptly wheeled, put spurs to his horse, and galloped to a barn, the dragoon after him. Around the barn, and through one door and out at the other, went both pursuer and pursued. Ray galloped for safety to the regiment [Butler's], passed in front, the trooper still at his heels. More than 100 muskets were discharged at him. But he escaped unharmed, galloped back to his regiment, and was seen to take his place in line.

Rhea laughed in telling the story, gallantly conceding that he had never before seen "such a daring fellow."[22] He made no comment on the marksmanship of an entire infantry battalion that missed a single enemy rider. Yet of the men who fired the "100 muskets" at the brave dragoon, much less the troops looking on from Jackson's nearby command, not one ever told of the thrilling encounter (or at least left nothing for the historical record). But factual veracity has seldom stopped a good yarn from an old soldier.

With or without Rhea's apocryphal theatrics, the dragoons' precipitous retreat gave Wayne the perfect opportunity to implement the orders he received earlier from Captain Mercer: to keep the enemy halted with a feint, as Lee "did not wish that the enemy should retreat to their main body, or. . . . call for a reinforcement." He ordered Butler's picked men to attack the disordered British lines. The colonel's battalion advanced with fixed bayonets and, as one British witness recalled, "huzzaing."[23]

Lee was supremely confident. He had always considered himself a realist in assessments of American military capabilities, and from the beginning of the campaign he had argued that rash measures would invite disaster. As he set out to the left, however, the general was a portrait of enthusiasm. Amid planning the movement, he turned to Lafayette, who would march with him, and gestured toward the British. "My dear Marquis," he told the young Frenchman, "I think those people are ours." Two of Washington's aides, riding separately from the main army, received much the same message. One of them, James McHenry, relayed Lee's sense of confidence, telling the commander in chief that Lee had implied "the certainty of success." The other messenger, Lieutenant Colonel Jeremiah Gilman, rode back to Washington with an equally optimistic report.[24] These communications, accurate enough at the moment, raised Washington's expectations for the day. Advancing with the main army, he believed that his second in command had opened a winning battle.[25]

Lee's march was swift. The route was less than two miles, and by roughly 10:30 the maneuver force had begun to emerge in battalion columns from the woods well to the enemy's left. Of Lee's column, all but Maxwell's men emerged from the woods into the fields.[26] The rebel vanguard was advancing in force.

Yet Wayne's rapid advance along the Spotswood North Brook wood line led to confusion. Only minutes before the charge of the British dragoons, Lee emerged into the clear ground with Varnum's Brigade. By then Wayne's advance had carried him far enough along the tree line to make visual recognition from Lee's position difficult. At first glance the major general concluded that the infantry out in the open were British (he had spotted Wayne's rear battalions to his own right), and he promptly ordered Lieutenant Colonel Jeremiah Olney's Rhode Island Continentals to the attack. Olney was an aggressive and capable officer; luckily, he was also careful. "On a near approach" the Rhode Islander discovered that his intended target was in fact American—probably Butler's or Jackson's battalions.[27]

Almost at the same time, the light dragoons' charge and Butler's volley clarified the situation for Lee. As he watched Butler's men launch their bayonet "charge" against the British rear guard, Lee became concerned that Wayne might have misunderstood his earlier orders. Captain Edwards having returned, the general sent him back with orders that Wayne was only to make a feint since Lee was sending "a large column . . . to surround and take them." As Butler advanced, the British opened fire with the light infantry's two 3-pounders, and the rain of shot quickly gave Wayne an excuse to pull him back; Butler and Jackson took cover in the woods and ravines along the North Brook. There was every reason for this: before reaching the trees, a round tore the arm off of one of Jackson's infantrymen. At this point the Continentals briefly had no artillery support—Wells's two guns were then crossing the East Morass.[28]

Counterattack: Clinton Turns the Tables

With the rebuff of the dragoons and Jackson's or Butler's near brush with friendly fire, the intensity of the situation began to build. Lee, sensing that his right was vulnerable, halted Wayne's original detachment (now under Lafayette); these units would form the patriot right. He then started Scott's detachment along the wood line north of Lafayette's men to hold the left. As he did, Oswald and Wells appeared from across the morass, unlimbered in a grain field, and opened fire on Cornwallis's troops. Wells's gun crews quickly attracted intense counterfire from the enemy artillery: the light infantry's 3-pounders increasingly reinforced by the 6-pounders of the British and Hessian grenadiers. In the brutal heat Wells's gunners soon tired. Each time the cannons fired, they kicked back four or five feet, and the drag-rope men had to pull them back to their firing positions. Choking from powder smoke and dust that hung in the stifling air and dripping with sweat, they began staggering from exhaustion.[29]

After sending Scott to the left, Lee again rode forward to reconnoiter. He was surprised to find the enemy "force considerably larger than" the 2,000 reputed to have camped along the lane. Artillery, foot, and horse were in the center of the plain while a stronger column was marching toward the courthouse. He instantly understood that should the column gain the American right, it "must have put us into the most dangerous situation." Nevertheless, Lee still thought he could cut off the enemy rear guard. After checking with Oswald, he ordered Lafayette to lead three battalions east to form the south flank of the envelopment; the same movement also would block a British advance toward the patriot right. To conceal the Continental numbers as much as possible, Lafayette was to march along the wooded bank of the East Morass. When he responded that the artillery could not follow the wood line, Lee said the field pieces could proceed along the morass side of the fence along the road—the fence would partially conceal them.[30] The marquis put his units in motion.

After giving Lafayette his orders, Lee sent Captain Mercer to Brigadier General Scott. As the enemy was marching toward the courthouse, Lee saw no need for the Continentals to advance farther on the left. Scott was to halt his detachment, which along with Wayne's men (Butler, Jackson, and the others) would form the Continental left. When Mercer asked where he could find Scott, Lee pointed to the woods on Albert Covenhoven's farm. The captain could see other Continentals, less advanced, in Wikoff's cider orchard. He asked his commander who they were; Lee responded that "they were General Maxwell's brigade." But he was wrong. The only troops in Covenhoven's woods were Butler's; the troops in the orchard were Scott's. After sending off Mercer, Lee rode to the head of Lafayette's men to hasten their movement.[31]

As Lafayette advanced, rebel artillery fire briefly slackened. Wells's crews quickly had exhausted the round shot in the ammunition boxes on the gun carriages. Worse, enemy fire had killed two patriot gunners, and others were collapsing in the heat. Oswald ordered Wells back across the East Morass. Seeing the guns leaving, Lee, alarmed, rode up. The lieutenant colonel explained that their ammunition wagon was on the other side of the morass and that with men killed or exhausted, Wells could only work one gun. Lee understood and directed Oswald and Wells to Wikoff's cider orchard, where there would be some shade. The general instructed Oswald to form a battery with guns from Varnum's Brigade and Wayne's detachment, and by about 11:15 A.M., Oswald was back in action, cannonading the enemy with six guns.[32]

When Wells's artillery, descending downhill toward the morass, had dropped out of sight, the British and German gunners turned their field pieces toward the infantry (Lafayette's men) marching across their front. Within minutes, redcoat shot had killed two of Varnum's men and wounded two others. One of the wounded was

Colonel Durkee. A ball, probably from case or grape shot, struck one of his wrists and traveled up the arm, fracturing the bones as it went. In excruciating pain, Durkee was evacuated—he never recovered the use of the hand—and brigade command fell to Lieutenant Colonel Jeremiah Olney. According to Olney, the casualties had no effect on unit discipline, and the advance continued.[33]

After giving Oswald his new orders, Lee and Edwards rode back uphill. They could see the enemy continuing toward the Continental right. Some "gentlemen" rode up to the general to warn him that the enemy were trying to "gain our rear or the Court-house." As Lee rode at the head of Lafayette's and Olney's men, he became increasingly uneasy about the troops he had left along Spotswood North Brook. Worried that something might have happened to Mercer, he sent Edwards back with the same orders: Scott was to hold his position in Covenhoven's woods.[34]

Even before dispatching Edwards, Lee's force along the brook had become demoralized. From the protection of woods and the bank of Spotswood North Brook, Colonels Butler and Jackson watched a slow but steady advance of "a very heavy column" of enemy foot and "a considerable body of horse." These British troops were moving from the east, back toward the courthouse. Jackson thought he saw about three thousand men; in fact, not believing Clinton "could afford so large a rear guard," he considered—correctly, as it turned out—that the enemy had countermarched his main body, or at least a major part of it. Watching the same column march from a different position, Wayne saw the British force grow from an estimated 600 to perhaps 1,600 or 2,000 men. But if his estimate of enemy strength was accurate for the moment, that moment passed quickly. British numbers were building steadily, and the redcoats, whatever their exact strength, clearly had turned around and were moving in force down the road toward the American right. Jackson did not like his position. They were in the edge of the North Brook valley and protected from artillery fire, but a deep ravine isolated them from most of Lee's command. After some debate with his lieutenant colonel, Jackson decided to retreat. At this point it was anyone's guess as to who was the hunter and who was the hunted.[35]

Sir Henry had no doubt on this score: He had seized the initiative. As quickly as he learned that the rebels were probing his rear guard, Clinton elected to react in strength. Not knowing patriot intentions or numbers, some British officers saw the rebel approach as a major attack, while others thought Washington was mounting a general assault.[36] Clinton did not share the latter view, but he considered the matter serious enough. The royal commander was sure the attacking force, which he guessed was still small, was reaching for his baggage train. He consequently resolved to hit back "so hard as to oblige" the Americans to call off any flank attacks on the baggage and to concentrate to defend themselves. The patriot force, Clinton thought, was vulnerable; he astutely judged that Washington was not in supporting distance and that the ravines would make it difficult for the rebels to maneuver. Personally reconnoitering the American advance, he decided that the enemy right, then well north of Freehold, was itself open to a flanking movement.[37] Cornwallis, who commanded the British rear guard with some of the army's best units, was ready for action, and Clinton soon had the entire 1st Division turned around and headed back to Freehold. For good measure, he even ordered a brigade and some additional dragoons to return from Knyphausen's column. The gathering counterstroke would soon number in excess of 10,000 men. A move toward the town could turn the patriot right (as Lee feared); it was the British advance on Freehold that Butler and Jackson watched.

While Clinton advanced, Mercer "made what speed" he could to Scott's supposed position, but his horse was tired, and he had a deep ravine with a "very miry" bottom to cross. As he reached the other side of the mire, he was surprised to find Jackson's detachment beginning to retreat across the ravine. Jackson reported that Scott was not in the woods. Riding up the ravine toward the plain, the captain found Grayson's battalion, then climbing the hill, he saw Cornwallis's reinforced rear guard continuing toward the courthouse. Looking to his left at the north end of the plain, Mercer was appalled to see the head of what he took to be the "main body of the enemy" marching back. Returning to Grayson, he directed him to fall in behind Jackson and retreat. Mercer ordered Jackson to find Maxwell's brigade and form with them.[38]

As Lee began moving units to the right, there was an increasing feeling of isolation among the troops watching from the left—and not just by Jackson. Indeed, the patriot left had lost contact with the rest of the vanguard. In the rush of developments, Lee had failed to keep all of his key subordinates apprised of the changing situation.[39] As Lafayette began his move to the right, other American officers were not privy to Lee's orders and had no idea what to make of this new maneuver. Several observers thought another attack was in the making, which was a logical assumption. Lafayette's trek toward Freehold very roughly paralleled the course of the approaching British—the rival columns actually were within sight of one another for much of the time—with the roads gradually converging on the town.[40] If the opposing columns kept moving, they were bound to collide. But if they did, what should the watching officers do? Hold position? Move to the sound of the guns? They had no instructions from Lee.

More ominous was the possibility that Clinton's movement toward the American right might cut off the troops still in the woods north of town—or so some on the American left feared. Lee thought that Scott and Maxwell occupied highly defensible ground and that they faced no immediate threat; he was right. Nevertheless, the two brigadiers looked to their right with increasing apprehension. Lee had sent both Mercer and Edwards on separate missions to convey his intentions, but the aides never found Scott.[41] Without contact with Lee, Scott decided to pull back from what he increasingly considered an exposed position. At least two developments probably account for his action. First, Scott did not initially consider his movement a retreat; rather, he was shifting to ground he considered more defensible. When Scott moved, Maxwell quickly followed. In fact, the two brigadiers even agreed on a plan: Scott moved to the west side of the Middle Brook ravine, while Maxwell—with his own and Scott's two heavier guns—marched counterclockwise with the aim of coming in behind Lee and reinforcing him in the center.

The second, although probably less critical, incident occurred near Lee's position closer to Freehold. When Oswald and Wells moved their guns over the East Morass, the rebel troops on the left apparently mistook this retrograde for part of a retreat. For Scott and Maxwell, who never received word on Lafayette's move from the left, the seeming retreat of the artillery was the last straw. They too pulled back, which left Butler, Jackson, and part of Grayson's men even more exposed; they ultimately felt compelled to retire as well.

By the time that Mercer and Edwards got back to Lee, the general had arrayed Lafayette's troops along a quarter-mile front between the British and the village. The two captains found Lee amid a group of officers, reading a letter and preparing to ride left to command the enveloping column. When Edwards and Mercer reported that Scott and Maxwell were gone, Lee was dumbfounded; he could "scarcely

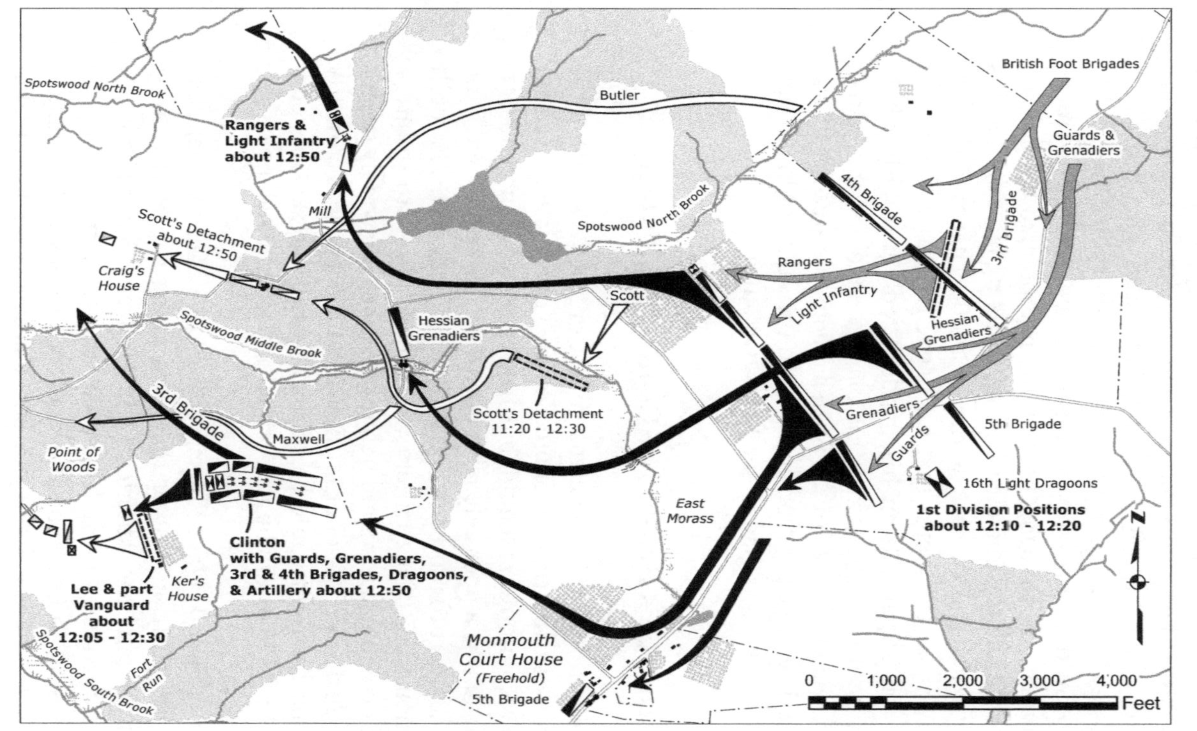

Counterattack: Clinton marches back the 1st Division in two columns, forms briefly at the East Morass, and then launches a three-prolonged attack to crush the Continental vanguard at the West Morass. Divisional positions at 12:10–12:20 based on a sketch by Capt. Archibald Robertson, Royal Engineers. Map by Garry Wheeler Stone. Copyright © 2016 by the University of Oklahoma Press.

believe it, and expressed in strong terms his disapprobation of it." Mercer's report that the enemy main body was advancing in a second column also "disconcerted" the general.[42] Looking toward the Middletown Road, Lee saw Colonel Henry Beekman Livingston's battalion, part of Lafayette's command, retreating. This retrograde came after Lafayette, losing men to British artillery fire, had rashly decided to storm the guns with Livingston's men; finding no troops following Livingston, though, the marquis had ordered the colonel back. At first this also astonished Lee. Now his right, as well as his left, seemingly had pulled back without orders. That was the last straw, and it was at this point that his battle fell apart. Command and control was slipping from his hands. Credit Lee with a bold attempt, but he now realized that his plan to envelope the British covering party had failed. With the British advancing steadily, it was time to find a defensive position and look to the safety of his troops. He admitted that he was glad to see Lafayette pulling back.[43]

To William Ker's House: The Continental Retrograde

Lee now thought of forming a defensive line on the west side of the East Morass, with his right anchored on the town itself. He sent Lafayette to reconnoiter Freehold, but his report was not encouraging. The village was a poor defensive position. The houses were too few and too far apart to protect an infantry line. They were also built of wood, which the Royal Artillery would have blown to splinters. Nor was the neighboring orchard helpful, its trees too widely spaced to afford any real cover. Under the circumstances, Lee was correctly concerned that his right could be turned. Grimly, he sensibly concluded that he could not fight at Freehold and that he had no choice but to pull back.

Brigadier General Wayne disagreed. The Pennsylvanian had maintained his position east of the town along the North Brook on what had become the American left. He wanted to fight it out behind the courthouse, or at least from the western edge of the morass. Wayne urged Lee to recall the patriot troops and to make a stand. In this Wayne was brave but not necessarily smart. In addition to holding a poor position, a patriot stand at the ravine would have contended against vastly superior numbers. It was clear by now that Morgan was nowhere in view and that Washington was not at hand with the main body; in fact, the commander in chief was still several miles away. In addition, Lee was under the impression that most troops on the left were marching out of action. He did not know what Scott, Maxwell, and the men with Butler and Grayson were doing. He *did* know that his immediate command was now reduced to fewer than 2,500 men—too few to stand against the powerful British units moving steadily toward them. Like it or not, then, Wayne followed the rest of Lee's units across the ravine.

Other officers, Scott in particular, may have agreed with Wayne, but there were good reasons for Lee's decision. The retreat made perfect sense to one junior officer in the Second Rhode Island. Captain Stephen Olney—eight Olneys served as officers with Rhode Island troops during the war—felt that Lee had no choice but to pull back. Washington had not come up with the main army, the British were coming in strength, and Lee was conducting an orderly withdrawal. All things considered, the captain believed, the major general "was justified in his retreat."[44]

Besides, Lee was not retreating blindly. When he realized that any line based on Freehold was untenable, he sent a brigadier general of engineers to find better ground to the rear. This officer was Louis Le Bèque du Presle du Portail (or Duportail), a Frenchman who brought crucial professional skills to the young American army. (He is now remembered as the "father" of the Army Corps of Engineers). Duportail did his best and found what looked to be a defensible line about a mile west of the village. The proposed position ran along rising terrain roughly between the Craig family house on the north (which still stands) and the William Ker home to the south.[45] The Ker house was the most prominent landmark west of the village, and it became the focus of the new concentration. Lee quickly started his units toward the new line, hoping, however vainly, that Scott, Maxwell, and others from the left would link up again.

There was no major fighting during the retreat. Lee probably arrived in the vicinity of Ker's house about noon, bringing a substantial number of men with him. Other detachments came up independently, some dropping back in stages to cover the artillery, which continued to fight with genuine gallantry. Oswald and the other artillery officers performed superbly; they were not strong enough to stop Clinton, but they gave him something to worry about as his forces came on. Indeed, the guns did the only real fighting as the Americans pulled back toward the Ker house. From the start of the retreat, the patriots had suffered only about a dozen casualties from enemy fire (others had collapsed from the heat), virtually all of them victims of the Royal Artillery. While individual soldiers may have fired scattered rounds, there were no infantry volleys discharged after Butler's initial blast at the 16th Light Dragoons. Further infantry fire was likely only if the patriots stood and waited for the British infantry to close up and engage.

Lee himself was now in a funk. Over the course of the morning, he had acted with enterprise and bravery, and he remained cool as his command fell back. Even his later detractors gave him credit for remaining in control of himself. Anything but happy about developments, Lee saw no alternative to the retrograde. There seemed no chance to reorganize for another stab at Clinton, although the general remained at Ker's house for about half an hour looking vainly for a way out of his dilemma. Lieutenant Colonels John Fitzgerald and Richard Kidder Meade, both of Washington's staff and riding on separate intelligence missions, each found the major general about this time. They reported that the main body was still some two miles away and asked what estimate of the situation they should take back to the commander in chief. With blunt honesty, Lee replied to each "that he really did not know what to say."[46] This response should have alerted Washington that his subordinate's earlier optimism was now problematic; certainly, it should have signaled the need to bring up the main body at speed.

Chief among Lee's difficulties in trying to organize a stand was the inability to communicate effectively with his subordinates. Despite the many improvements in the patriot army, field communications remained a glaring deficiency. The Americans had fifers, drummers, and buglers who were useful in sending commands at close quarters, but they were of limited use over longer distances, in broken terrain, or in the din and smoke of combat. The rebels lacked the signal flags common to many European military establishments, which facilitated communications over an extended battlefield. Lee also noted the lack of regimental uniforms or "distinguishing colors." Regimental or brigade flags, so much a part of European military tradition, and uniforms of different cuts or colors had practical origins, for they allowed commanders to identify units at a distance. Under the circumstances, Lee was compelled to send his aides—Mercer, Edwards, Brooks, and other junior officers—on horseback with orders or merely to confirm which units were which. Given the demands of the morning, he did not have enough aides, and those he had eventually suffered badly from the heat. Two lost their horses and were themselves "almost dead with fatigue"; two others had mounts so tired as to be almost useless. Thus, while there was a sizeable American force within sight of the Ker house, the general could no longer maneuver all of his units as a unified organization.

The retreat, if disconcerting to Lee, was at least generally orderly. The various units usually moved in columns, with a few outfits stopping to rest in the shade of convenient woods. Regimental officers knew their business and kept their men under control. Bernardus Swartwout, a "gentleman volunteer" with the Second New York Regiment, recalled that the Americans "retired in great haste but in good order."[47] Swartwout was right about the "good order" but exaggerated the pace of the withdrawal, which was deliberate but not hasty. Brooks, who saw most units at one time or another as he carried orders for Lee, noted that the regiments marched "in a very easy, moderate and regular way" as they moved toward Ker's house. Oswald, whose safety depended on a disciplined withdrawal as he worked his guns, credited Lee with providing infantry protection for the artillery every step of the way. The general himself thought he had conducted a model "retrograde manoeuver in the face and under the fire of an enemy"; his troops, he claimed, moved with "order and precision."[48]

Not everyone agreed with such favorable assessments, however. No one reported panic or men running away, but over the course of the morning, some riders from Washington and officers with Lee reported considerable "disorder" among the troops. At different times some regiments did break ranks, and some soldiers, given the heat, may well have appeared dazed or ill disciplined. Lieutenant Colonel Alexander Hamilton thought some of the columns marching away from Freehold were too close to one another to allow deployment on line; Scott thought he saw artillery horses trotting along with cannon and limbers bouncing out of control; Duportail worried that enemy grape shot would play hell with some bunched-up columns.[49] Such reports would later haunt General Lee.

Upon examination, though, most of these criticisms were quibbles or simply inaccurate; certainly they did not characterize the general state of the troops with Lee. It is a rare engagement that does not produce some confusion or throw off some stragglers, and Lee's retreat was no exception. But the general or other officers, especially at the regimental level, seem to have corrected most of the really dangerous situations during the move. Some instances of disorder were apparent only: One outfit, in an experience probably typical of the day, attracted Lee's unfavorable attention by breaking ranks. But as the officer in charge explained, the seeming confusion was only a scramble to pass a ravine quickly; the men immediately formed up on the other side. If some columns were too close together for efficient deployment, they still moved to safety. Below Ker's house, the hardworking 16th Light Dragoons again chased a small body of patriot horse that, as before, ran for the cover of the infantry. A patriot regiment came on line, and the 16th, already bloodied at Butler's hands, veered off before any exchange of fire.[50] Significantly, during the course of the retreat to the Duportail line and later during the subsequent withdrawal to the West Morass, there was no panic, and no American regiment broke.

There was a certain irony in the success of Lee's retrograde movement. Much as Lee had looked askance at Steuben's efforts at Valley Forge, the discipline and drill learned earlier in the year paid dividends in an orderly withdrawal. By June there was no doubt that American tactical proficiency, at least in most units, could not measure up to British standards. Many patriot regiments had only a few weeks under the "baron's" tutelage, while many new recruits entered battle at Monmouth without much formal instruction at all. But Steuben's work had helped, especially through the efforts of brigade inspectors and the regimental officers who kept the troops drilling even while on detached duty. When they did get to Valley Forge, even privates were impressed enough with the baron's efforts to record their impressions in journals and diaries.[51] Steuben worked no miracles, but at Monmouth the field- and company-grade officers marched into battle and deployed with considerable expertise. Thus, if the American battalions were hardly examples of a crack drill team, they were better prepared than ever before.

The ground near Ker's house offered an excellent view of the field toward Freehold. The British, having halted briefly in the village itself, struck westward. Lieutenant Colonel Laurens remembered his spectacular view of their advance: From the Ker house, he saw the red uniforms in two columns, with cavalry and artillery moving between the infantry.[52] Advanced units probed ahead, and it was clear that the British meant business. Shortly, Lee would have to stand and fight at the so-called Duportail line or retreat even farther.

Clinton in Front

As Lee pondered his options at Ker's house, he may have guessed that his opponent had decided against half measures. Clinton's concern for the safety of his baggage train, then strung out on the road to Middletown, was real enough. But launching the flower of his army, Cornwallis's 1st Division, at what he knew to be a rebel vanguard suggested that he had something more in mind. If a defense of his baggage was all that Clinton intended, there were alternatives to a full-fledged counterattack. A strong blocking force somewhere around the East Morass, coupled with strong flanking parties and a careful retrograde, would have sufficed. Sir Henry was a good enough general to know that, but he knew two other things: First, he was sure that Lee (or whoever the American commander was; initially he did not know) was on difficult terrain. If a counterattack could throw the rebels back against the ravines west of the village, the redcoats stood a fair chance of cutting their opponents to pieces (just as Dickinson had warned Lee). Second, the British commander had discovered that Washington had not brought up the main body of the Continental Army. As the 1st Division collected at Monmouth Court House and the troops caught their breath, Clinton reconnoitered Lee's position at Ker's House.[53] For the time being, the patriot vanguard would have little or no support and would have to fight alone. Under the circumstances, Clinton thought he could destroy them: as he wrote to the Duke of Newcastle after the battle, he felt that he could protect his baggage train while knocking out a significant portion of the Continental Army.[54] It was not the general engagement he longed for, but it would be a significant victory nevertheless. Certainly, it would take the sting out of having to give up Philadelphia and retreat.

The general planned accordingly. Moving toward the patriots (that is, facing west from the village), the bulk of the 1st Division formed in two strong columns. Their advance carried them toward the Middle Morass and the high ground beyond, where the militia had defended the Hedgerow from Simcoe earlier in the morning; beyond lay the bridge over the West Morass. The Brigade of Guards was on the right, and marching roughly in parallel on the left were the British grenadiers. The guards and grenadiers were the elite of the royal army, perhaps the best infantry any European military could boast. Ahead, around, and between the columns rode various elements of the 16th Light Dragoons, under Lieutenant Colonel William Harcourt, ready to ride down American stragglers or isolated units, exploit any infantry breakthrough, or take advantage of any perceived weakness in American positions. Also in the center, teams pulled the guns of the Royal Artillery. The 3rd Brigade, almost 1,600 strong, followed under "No Flint" Grey; behind them came the men of the 4th Brigade. Brigadier General Leslie's 5th Brigade halted in reserve, covering the roads at Monmouth Court House. It made for quite a spectacle, and the Americans were duly impressed.

Behind the columns, Clinton posted the brigade of Hessian Grenadiers in reserve. (André's map shows them guarding the Amboy Road flank, but most accounts place them on a hill on the farm Ker was renting.) They would not engage and spent the day watching the fighting ahead of them. After the battle, this led Governor Livingston to charge that they had refused to fight; his account had the Germans complaining that it was too hot for combat.[55] This is nonsense. Rather, following standard procedure, Clinton had ordered them to remain in place to serve as a strong defensive line in case the attack went badly and the forward troops had to retreat. Besides, as historian Matthew Spring has observed, the Hessians would have been unable to keep pace with the swiftly moving British, who so far were conducting a textbook advance.[56]

As Clinton neared the Middle Morass, he could see several enemy battalions on the near side and others just climbing the far bank. Less than a mile ahead was a bridge over the West Morass. Could he outflank the bridge and cut off some rebels? He had just the men to attempt it—"No Flint" Grey and his 3rd Brigade, whose largest regiment, the 42nd (Royal Highlanders), was as fleet-footed as light infantry. Clinton dispatched Grey on a slant across the Middle Brook to race to the bridge. As the Royal Highlanders reached the woods along the stream, they dropped their packs, "dash'd thro' that wood & a deep swamp," and emerged in the fields of the Craig farm.

At this point the 3rd Brigade unexpectedly made contact with the enemy. The British found three battalions of Scott's picked men still retreating west. Near the rear of the column, some infantrymen were helping artillery horses haul two guns across a swale. At the head of the 3rd Brigade, the Highlanders jogged to overtake Scott—the 1st Battalion to the right, the 2nd to the left. As the 2nd Battalion closed with Scott's rear, Continental marksmen began skirmishing, backing up as the Highlanders pushed them. As the

Americans' lead battalion crossed the last swale into Derick Sutfin's cider orchard, Colonel Butler formed his men to cover the retreat of Colonels Richard Parker and Joseph Cilley. Parker and Cilley's men kept ahead of the Highlanders, and all three battalions reached the safety of a strong Continental line, including artillery, on Perrine's Hill—Major General Stirling had arrived in the nick of time. (The fortuitous arrival of Stirling on the Perrine property is discussed in the following chapter.)

As the Highlanders passed through the cider orchard, they found "the Enemy in force" on Perrine's Hill, cannonading "briskly." The 2nd Battalion backed up into the orchard. There they remained, inactive for the time being, as grape shot tore through branches and leaves above them. Exhausted from their march in the brutal sun, the British were allowed little rest by the Continental artillery.[57] While the 2nd Battalion hunkered down in the orchard, the 1st Battalion—followed by the 44th Regiment—swung to the right and crossed Spotswood North Brook to outflank the Americans.[58] Probing closer, however, the 42nd and the 44th soon found rebel cannon fire too much to endure. They pulled back across the brook to the Sutfin farm and rejoined their brigade.

Even farther on the right, the Queen's Rangers (without the wounded Simcoe) and the 1st Battalion of Light Infantry were swinging in a wide arc heading beyond the American left.[59] The lights and rangers had a combined strength of over 1,000 men, and their commander this day was the capable Brigadier General Sir William Erskine. Clinton had sent Erskine to get on the Continentals' flank, probably assuming that he would advance through the open farmland between the Middle and North Brooks. Instead, Erskine moved up the Amboy Road, which, however, never touched the open fields of the Craig farm. The brigadier reached farm fields only after crossing the North Brook. The rangers and 1st Light Infantry then turned west. Their march slowed by several deep ravines, they reached the Continental left after the 42nd and 44th Foot, probably just after the 42nd had its brush with Scott's retreating detachment.

The light troops, like the men of the 3rd Brigade, were exhausted and thus in poor condition to fight.[60] Even had they been fresh, their probable combined strength was too little to attack the American line. Any British assault would have to cross a wide, treeless morass; the rebels would have seen them coming in plenty of time to concentrate defensive fire. Behind Stirling's position, a patriot reserve moved to face the light troops, probably hoping they would come within range.[61] Wisely, the British did not. But rebel batteries spotted them and took Erskine's men under fire with grape shot. Seeking cover, the lights and rangers cautiously retreated across Spotswood North Brook onto the Sutfin or John Craig, Jr., farms, where they came in on the right of the 3rd Brigade. There the tired men of both forces got what rest they could. One American 4-pounder continued to fire on them, but most rebel cannon were now busy with the Royal Artillery across the ravine. Both corps had lost men to heat exhaustion and enemy fire, and once under cover, the fire of one cannon may have seemed preferable to continued maneuvers in the scorching heat.[62]

From the vantage of Stirling's position, this enemy activity looked suspiciously like the start of an attack on the rebel left. Concerns lifted as the British took cover, but Stirling kept a wary eye on the Sutfin farm and, to keep British heads down, kept the 4-pounder firing on the orchard. The Americans probably did not know it at the time, but their fire was effective. The Highlanders were close enough for the artillery to engage with grape and canister, and the British took several casualties, later found by the patriots sprawled among the apple trees.[63] American small-arms fire added to these troops' distress. Armed with rifles and smoothbore muskets, marksmen—probably trailing elements of Scott's detachment—fired from behind a fence west of the 42nd. Modern archaeology has unearthed over two dozen patriot projectiles in and around the Sutfin orchard, and it showed that some Americans were not "fighting fair": some of the bullets were cut or otherwise modified to do greater than normal damage (which was bad enough) on impact. "These soldiers," archaeologist Daniel M. Sivilich has noted, "meant business."[64]

Busy directing his counterattack, Clinton was unaware that Grey and Erskine had stalled against the American left. For all Sir Henry knew, the flanking movements were part of what had become a major effort against the rebels. Strong as his attack was, Clinton had intended it to pack an even harder punch. As quickly as he ordered Cornwallis to strike, he sent to the 2nd Division for additional troops. The general wanted Knyphausen to detach "the nearest British brigade" and the 17th Dragoons, and he detailed his adjutant general, Lord Rawdon (Lieutenant Colonel The Hon. Francis Rawdon), to remain behind and form these units as they came up.[65] At the same time he had an aide, Lord Cathcart (William Schaw

Cathcart), send the necessary orders to Kynphausen. Cathcart did so via Lieutenant Forbes Champagne.[66] Riding to Knyphausen, the lieutenant first saw Major General James Grant, then at the head of the 2nd Division. Champagne informed Grant of Clinton's request and then rode on to the Hessian general to deliver the orders. At this point there was some miscommunication. Perhaps Knyphausen thought that Grant would deal with the matter—but as it turned out, no one did. Afterward, Clinton blamed Grant, who was not one of Sir Henry's favorite subordinates anyway (many in the army blamed his uninspired performance at Barren Hill for Lafayette's escape).[67] The British commander complained of Grant's "very reprehensible inattention," noting that officers with the major general vainly pressed him to be detached to Clinton. Had the requested reinforcements arrived, Clinton thought he might have remained on the field to fight on the twenty-ninth.[68]

Unaware of the failure of Lieutenant Champagne's mission, Clinton pushed ahead. The general was fully confident that the troops of the 1st Division could deal with any Americans who stood against them. But first his troops had to reach the enemy, which was no easy mission in itself. Indeed, it was a difficult task. From the point at which they turned to confront the rebels, many of the British had marched some five miles. One young officer complained that they had to move over "a road composed of nothing but sand which scorched through our shoes with intolerable heat; the sun beating on our heads with a force scarcely to be conceived in Europe, and not a drop of water to assuage our parching thirst." Several men died and others went delirious in the sun; "two became raving mad," while others fell out of ranks "wishing for death." It was "the most shocking scene" the man had ever witnessed.[69] This had been as brutal a march as any British army had undertaken to that point in the war.

As the royal troops climbed from the Middle Ravine, Clinton and Cornwallis rode ahead. In front, two Continental artillery batteries—guarded only by a troop of light horse—were firing on the advancing redcoats. Behind the rebel guns, a battalion was marching toward the Hedgerow. Time was running out—the bridge was just beyond the Hedgerow. The Continentals would escape unless Clinton struck quickly.

To the West Morass

Lee watched as the British columns inexorably bore down on him. What to do? The major general elected to retreat again. He had little choice as, upon full examination, the line near Ker's had a fatal flaw. Just to the east, a knoll offered a commanding view of the position Duportail had selected; whoever held that knoll, if they set up enough artillery, would command the ground from Ker's house to the north. In this instance Lee was fighting geography. A force from the west could not hold the knoll, as a ravine separated the knoll from the main position. But a force coming from the east—that is, from Clinton's line of march—could hold the key terrain. Lee also did not think that he could hold his flanks against the roving enemy cavalry. Faced with these disadvantages and badly outnumbered in the bargain, Lee was in no position to slug it out. He needed ground that would compensate for his inferior numbers and where he could stand until Washington came up with the rest of the army.

At this point Lee probably had little idea what to do next. He had examined the local terrain and found all possible defensive positions wanting. It may have been the first time that morning events found him at a total loss. As Lee cast about for alternatives, luck intervened in the person of Peter Wikoff. A local militia officer and farmer, Wikoff rode up unannounced to the general and explained that he was "perfectly acquainted with the country" and offered to be of any service he could. The timing could not have been better for the vexed rebel commander—almost the military equivalent of divine intervention. "I thought myself extremely fortunate in the reconter," Lee recalled, "and begged that he would inform me where a [defensible] position was to be found."[70] Wikoff pointed out Combs Hill. It lay south of where Lee and Wikoff stood and was a commanding eminence with marshy ground at its base; positioned on the hill, Lee's men, or even a small portion of them, would have been hard to dislodge. With the British steadily advancing, however, Lee felt that his troops could not get across the morass in front of the hill quickly enough. The militia captain then suggested the high ground in back of the bridge over the Spotswood Middle Brook; that is, on the Perrine property beyond the West Morass, the very heights down which the vanguard had marched to battle over three hours earlier. It was good ground, and Lee determined to stand there.

The general then moved quickly. He asked Wikoff to ride to the ravine, "make use of" his name, and to lead the first regiment he found to the new position and post them "as a point of halt for the whole." The general knew that Wikoff was not the best messenger since he was unknown to the regimental officers; indeed, Lee barely knew them himself, and given that the various units had few distinguishing uniforms or colors, he could not tell Wikoff which regiments he might meet. Such a vital mission properly belonged to one of the general's aides, but by this time Edwards and Mercer were either without horses or suffering from heat fatigue. The same was true of Lieutenant Colonel Brooks and Colonel Malmédy, his French volunteer aide.[71] Wikoff would have to do.

Having sent the militia officer on his way and confident that his retreating regiments would stop and form on the rise beyond the morass (Perrine's Hill), Lee set about getting his men across the bridge and safeguarding their withdrawal. In this he found some more unexpected help. Soon after Wikoff's departure, Lee met Major John Clark, the army auditor who had come from Englishtown carrying Washington's message to "annoy" the enemy without falling "into a scrape." Taking the opportunity to reinforce Wikoff's mission, the general "beg'd" Clark to "hurry the Troops over" the morass and tell any artillery officers he could find to post their guns "on the heights" to cover the ravine. Anticipating a possible withdrawal over the bridge, Lee earlier had ordered Maxwell (who was now back in contact) to take post in the woods and cover the vital route over the creek and morass. But he worried about a possible cavalry attack on his right (as one faced the morass)—elements of the 16th Light Dragoons were in sight and harrying American stragglers—and with Clark's quick return from the artillery, Lee gave him another job (Clark was now acting unofficially as an aide to Lee). The general tasked him with finding a regiment to form along a fence covering the American right flank. It was at this point that a moment of real confusion occurred.[72]

The first unit Clark found was Colonel Jackson's detachment, which consisted of Jackson's own "Additional" Continental regiment as well as the small Additional regiments of Colonels William Lee (commanded on 28 June by Lieutenant Colonel William S. Smith) and David Henley (led by Major John Tyler). These were Massachusetts men.[73] Clark passed along the order from Lee, though to little avail. Jackson had no idea who the major was and felt no obligation to follow any order from him. Besides, he protested that his men were so fatigued, they were incapable of forming; he continued his retrograde toward the bridge. Clark then appealed to other officers, and Smith, Jackson's second in command, formed about half the detachment along the Hedgerow—only to move off again when Jackson countermanded the order.[74] This caught Lee's attention, and it looked to him like yet *another* unauthorized withdrawal. "Where is that damned blue Regiment going," he shouted (many of Jackson's men had blue uniforms). Unlike the cases of Scott and Maxwell, Lee was close enough to Jackson to intervene directly. When Smith told the major general that he was pulling back on Jackson's orders, the furious Lee rode to the colonel and, brandishing his sword, bellowed, "by God, you are not commanding officer here, I am."[75] Hurriedly, Jackson tried to get his men to form, only to find himself in the middle of a series of contradictory orders. The angry general quickly ordered him to form behind a different fence, then countermanded the order and told him to form in the open to cover the retreat of the vanguard. Smith, caught between Jackson and Lee—who at one point had issued separate orders for Smith to form—was unsure of what to do. Rather than leave the field, he wanted to pull back to a woods to rest his men (unbeknown to Lee, Washington himself, coming up to meet with his senior subordinate, spoke briefly with Smith and approved this move).[76] Ultimately, however, the lieutenant colonel followed his regimental commander toward the West Morass bridge when the heat-dazed Jackson decided to pull out.[77] It was a brief incident—a matter of minutes—and while Lee had not lost control of the situation, he had clearly lost control of his famously volatile temper.

As an aside to this incident, while Jackson's exhausted command marched down the road, the colonel apparently called a brief halt to rest the men in the Sutfin woodlot. At this point, however, his trailing elements became aware that other detachments of the rear guard were coming along the road after them—any halt would bar their way. From the rear of his column, the regimental commander heard shouts of "Colonel Jackson, march on! march on!" He did, although an aide to Washington tried once more to get him to form. By this time Washington had come up, and it was the general himself who now saw that Jackson's troops were in no condition to fight and sent them on their way. "I don't recollect that I halted the men again until I got in the rear of English-town," Jackson later stated.[78]

By the time of the confrontation with Colonel Jackson, Lee's nerves may have been fraying. He had been under pressure for hours and was anything but happy with the performance of some subordinates. While he was in no position to investigate matters, he must have wondered at the conduct of Scott and Maxwell, and even whether Wayne's early morning decision to strike the British had exceeded his orders to feint while Lee attempted his envelopment. In addition, the major general clearly was distressed at the lack of support from the main army. Where was Washington? The stress told in his next assignment for Major Clark. He told the officer to ride to the commander in chief and inform him "that by *too much precipitancy in one of his Brigadiers & false intelligence his Troops were thrown in confusion & that he was retiring.*"[79] (Lee did not name the brigadier in question, although after the battle he would blame Wayne.) This was hardly an accurate statement of affairs. Aside from the incident with Jackson, no doubt fresh in Lee's mind, there was little confusion at this stage. But the general's message to Washington was clearly an appeal for help.

With the dispatch of the busy Clark—who one imagines had as much battlefield experience that day as any auditor in American military history—Lee devoted himself to completing the retrograde over the West Morass. The maneuver was well underway and should have taken no more than twenty minutes or so. Lee rode across the field, generally trying to be wherever his presence would do the most good. Clinton was within half a mile, but once on line above the morass, Lee looked forward to fighting him on favorable terms. At least this was his plan.

Yet it was not to be. With part of his command over the West Morass, Lee was monitoring the withdrawal of his rear units across the Middle Morass when Washington's aide-de-camp, Robert Hanson Harrison, arrived. Lee asked the aide where Washington was—Harrison answered that he was coming up. Lee, joined by Mercer, rode west to meet the commander in chief. The two generals met on the hill between the Hedgerow and a soon-to-be-notorious patch of trees called the Point of Woods. It was about 12:45 P.M., perhaps a few minutes after, and it was the end of Charles Lee's battle.

CHAPTER 12

Commanders in Conflict

The Washington and Lee Affair

During the late morning of 28 June, the columns of General Washington's main body marched toward Monmouth Court House (Freehold). By 11:30 A.M. lead elements were past Englishtown and approaching Tennent's Meeting House, and virtually everyone in the ranks suspected that they were moving toward a fight. Word had spread that Lee's men were engaged, and the leading regiments "could hear the Firing Distinctly towards Monmouth Court Hous [*sic*]."[1] Other signs were impossible to miss. Over the course of the morning, riders from headquarters had galloped to Lee's command and returned with reports of the action. Militia and local residents also were in contact with the advancing Continentals, and rumors and speculation must have traveled up and down the line of march.

There was no rush to glory; the march was a plodding affair. The army's heavy units traveled encumbered with artillery, ammunition, and supply wagons, all accompanied by at least a few women (most, though, remained with the baggage at Rocky Hill). Under the best circumstances the army would have moved slowly, but the blistering weather made things worse. By late morning the temperature had climbed to well over 90 degrees; it would soon reach 96 degrees, and back in Philadelphia a thermometer reportedly read an astonishing 112 degrees.[2] It was poor weather for soldiering, and Washington noted that the "intense heat" had "greatly delayed" his advance. A few men collapsed and died from heatstroke.[3]

All the same, there was a surprising lack of urgency to the patriot advance. Washington reached Englishtown by 10:00 A.M., and while there he took the time for breakfast at the home of Dr. James English. After this the general lingered a while longer to write a short letter to Henry Laurens, in which he mentions that Lee already was in the field and notes the probability of a wider action later that day. This was at 11:30, for the general noted the precise time on his letter.[4]

Afterward, with Dr. English riding next to him, Washington rejoined his men, most of whom had pushed through Englishtown and down the road toward Monmouth Court House.[5]

Had Washington known of General Lee's perilous situation, perhaps he would have eaten faster or urged his men to quicken their pace. As it was, no reports came from Lee for some time, and there seemed no reason to hasten the already hot and tired columns. The result was that even by noon the bulk of Washington's main force was still some four miles from the courthouse and thus only approaching supporting distance of Lee's retreating vanguard. All of this speaks to Washington's confidence, though not to his understanding of the situation or, frankly, his performance in restoring contact with Lee. The commander in chief was a veteran, and he knew from experience how fickle were the fortunes of war. He should have brought up his men faster, and he certainly should not have interpreted an absence of word from Lee as a positive sign.

In Dubious Battle

Riding ahead, Washington's outlook was positive; he was hoping to develop any opportunity the vanguard had created. Shortly before reaching Tennent's Meeting House, he stopped to converse with Alexander Hamilton, who just had returned from a forward reconnaissance. Unfortunately, the lieutenant colonel had left the advanced corps before Lee fully committed to a retreat, and his discussion with Washington dealt only with supporting the vanguard's assumed offensive. But Hamilton had surveyed the ground ahead, and he made a useful and, as events developed, fortuitous suggestion. He advised against sending the Continentals forward as a single body; rather, he proposed splitting the troops into two columns, with the largest detachment proceeding directly across the West Morass bridge toward Freehold to support Lee. At the same time, a smaller second column would move from the meetinghouse toward Craig's Mill to protect the American right. Hamilton was worried that the British might attack the Continental flank or rear, and his concern was well founded. If any of Clinton's 1st Division troops had remained in their encampment, they could easily have flanked the patriots by taking the road toward Craig's Mill and then turning north toward the meetinghouse. Moreover, the Americans were well aware that Clinton had designed the movement that had outflanked the Continentals on Long Island. Toward the end of the discussion, Brigadier General Henry Knox rode up and supported Hamilton's advice "in very strong terms." Persuaded, Washington put the second column under Nathanael Greene with orders to march toward Craig's Mill and then turn east toward Widow Solomon's tavern. He was to block or slow any oncoming British detachment.

With Lee's assignment to the vanguard command on the twenty-seventh, Washington had placed Greene in charge of the army's right wing. The major general, who had fretted over historical obscurity as a quartermaster, was delighted to be in the field with a line command and headed for battle. He was soon on his way, taking with him the Virginia brigade of Brigadier General William Woodford, then numbering less than 475 officers and men. Greene also had two artillery companies, a total of four guns, probably 3-pounders or French 4-pounders. Including gun crews, drivers, a few staff officers and militia vedettes, his column totaled somewhere in the neighborhood of 550 troops.[6] This was not a force sufficient to handle a large component of Clinton's army in open combat; but Greene would have strength enough to play a critical role later in the day. At the fork in the road south of the meetinghouse, Greene marched toward Craig's Mill and then turned east. As it turned out, no British were marching these roads; rather, Clinton had sent the 3rd Brigade circling to the north to get behind Lee.

Almost at the instant of Greene's departure, matters took a disconcerting turn. A militia officer hurriedly rode up with the first intelligence of Lee's retreat. Caught off guard, the rebel commander had to credit the source of the report. Lieutenant Colonel Tench Tilghman remembered the officer as "a countryman," but Stryker has insisted it was Thomas Henderson, a lieutenant colonel of the Monmouth County militia and a respected local physician.[7] If it was Henderson, he was a man with a serious grudge: Only two days before, the British had pillaged and torched his house when they sacked rebel homes and buildings near the village; the furious doctor had been in the field ever since, burning to even the score. When the surprised commander in chief asked Henderson how he had come by this astonishing information, the colonel pointed to a young fifer just coming up the road. The boy was so bedraggled that at first Washington failed to recognize him as a soldier and had to ask if he was part of the army. The obviously frightened boy replied in the affirmative, repeated what he had reported of Lee's withdrawal, and added that his regiment had been one of the first units to pull out. This news was as completely unsettling as it was unexpected. Still not knowing what to believe but not wanting rumors of a patriot reversal to spread through the ranks, Washington ordered a dragoon to keep the fifer quiet while he investigated further.

If Washington's march toward Freehold had been less than aggressive, the interview with the panicked boy was the equivalent of a wakeup call. The rebel commander moved quickly to ascertain the truth, and from this point to the end of the day, he acted decisively and capably. Immediately, he sent two trusted aides, Lieutenant Colonels Robert Harrison and John Fitzgerald, riding toward Lee to find out what they could. This was about 12:35 P.M. As the young officers galloped down the road in search of Lee, Washington continued his own advance and quickly began to find additional ominous signs. Within minutes he met scattered groups of men coming toward him who corroborated the fifer's report of retreat. Even winning battles produce stragglers, however, and Washington jumped to no conclusions on hearing their stories. But it was an anxious general who approached the top of the rise overlooking the West Morass.

While the patriot chief still had no clear picture of what was happening, by now he certainly realized that his earlier optimism had been ill founded. Washington was no longer riding past stragglers but entire units marching in good order back toward the meetinghouse and Englishtown. The first organized troops he met were from Grayson's command, then another outfit of Virginians. Washington heard the same story from virtually every officer: Most thought they were pulling back under orders (a point anything but clear), although they did not know why or even where they were going. Neither were they aware of the tactical situation; they knew only that most of their men were utterly exhausted and desperately needed rest and water. As he rode toward the bridge, the general ordered the junior officers to keep their men together, rest them in the shade, and issue rum rations. This last measure was intended to restore their energy (although in reality it would do anything but, especially in the intense heat), and the commanding general probably hoped it would do something for morale. He expected that he was going to need these men shortly.

Washington then rode across the bridge, passing more units as he went. The next regiment trudging down the hill toward the brook was Israel Shreve's Second New Jersey, the lead element of Maxwell's New Jersey Brigade. Shreve, all three hundred pounds of him, was sweating profusely and dead tired—so, one assumes, was his horse. The colonel calmly told the general that the entire vanguard was retreating, though without orders he knew of or where to go or what to do. Washington, now fearing the worst, told the fatigued colonel to get his men over the bridge, up the hill, and to rest them; he then spurred his horse up the east side of the ravine. It was now shortly after 12:45 P.M., and all of this had transpired within ten or so minutes of the general having heard the first warning of a patriot reversal from Dr. Henderson (or whoever the "countryman" may have been).

Lee had no idea that any of his men had marched over the crest of the West Morass, much less that they were continuing toward Englishtown. When he learned the truth, the general was appalled. His intention had been to form on the slope across the morass, and he had assumed that his plan, conveyed through Peter Wikoff, had been clear to his regiments. The general believed that any of his regimental officers, hearing Captain Wikoff's message on his (Lee's) authority, would comply. Wikoff swore that he had approached a regimental commander—Colonel Shreve—and that he even started to guide the New Jersey Brigade to the proper position. No doubt the captain had tried to do just that, but it was equally true that he was unable to make Lee's order sufficiently clear or convincing. Somehow, Shreve thought the directive had come from Lafayette, and Maxwell, not speaking with Wikoff or getting an adequate explanation from Shreve, did not take kindly to the colonel putting the New Jersey Brigade in motion without its commander's permission. The brigadier thereupon countermanded Shreve, kept the New Jersey regiments east of the ravine for some time, and then put them on the march again when he decided independently that they should move over the creek. The entire business was a major calamity. Clear orders from Lee to his subordinates would have avoided the situation. But the general (as noted previously) insisted that he was without means to send those orders other than through Wikoff, and he never accepted responsibility for what in fact was a tragic blunder. Lee had fully intended to properly confirm the decision to stand west of the morass and would have done so as soon as a staff officer became available for messenger duty. Indeed, he had sent

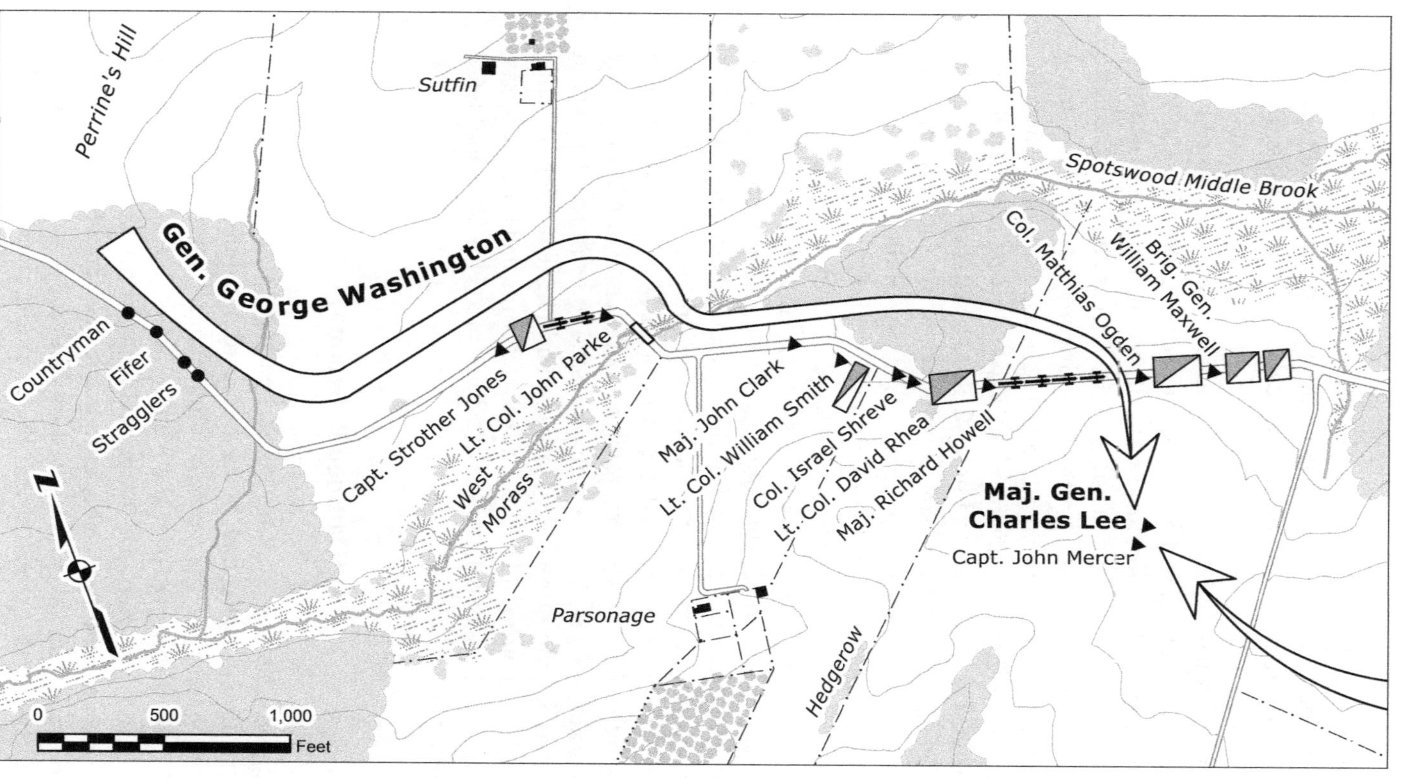

Washington encounters the retreating vanguard and confronts Lee. Map by Garry Wheeler Stone. Copyright © 2016 by the University of Oklahoma Press.

Major Clark on the same mission (to little avail), and his intention was to send Captain Mercer as well. Only the arrival of Washington himself at the front prevented Mercer (who had finally managed to find a mount) from leaving on the critical errand—by which time it was too late.[8]

Ahead of Washington, Fitzgerald and Harrison were every bit as alarmed as their chief, and for the same reasons. Crossing the West Morass, they found Lee's columns in full retreat. There was no panic and the units were under control, but the retreat continued, and no one seemed to know when or if Lee, having no means of informing them, intended to make a stand. In the absence of orders, some officers expressed their disgust to Washington's aides, convinced that the vanguard should turn and fight. Colonel Matthias Ogden, commander of the First New Jersey, was furious. "By God!" he shouted to Harrison, "they are flying from a shadow." Riding on, Harrison then encountered Mercer. "For God's sake," he asked the captain, "what is the cause of this retreat?" Mercer, not in the best of humor after a difficult morning, responded sharply. "If you will go further," he retorted, "you will see the columns of the enemy's foot and horse and that was reason enough for the retreat." Harrison replied in kind, reminding him that the British were no stronger than they were in Philadelphia and that the American army supposedly had come to fight. Events were improving no one's mood. After meeting several other officers, all of whom professed to be in the dark about the reasons for the retrograde, Harrison and Fitzgerald finally came upon Lee. The commander of the advanced corps had nothing to say, except to ask the whereabouts of Washington.[9] This he would learn soon enough.

A "Damned Poltroon"?

Washington was just coming up as Lee rode away from the two younger officers, who had headed toward Freehold to scout the British advance. As the commanding general left Shreve's men marching for the bridge over the Middle Brook, he still saw no sign of the enemy, but there was ample evidence of his vanguard giving way. Now in an understandably grim frame of mind, Washington had gone no more than several hundred yards to the top of a hill, where he found Lee with several other officers riding toward him. As the two senior generals of the army met, Lee fully expected a comradely greeting from a brother officer. The major general saw matters in hand; he had regained his composure after dealing with Colonel Jackson and sending off Major Clark. Now at long last, the main army had come up, and the vanguard, retreating in generally good order, could regroup with proper support. "Flattering myself," Lee recalled later, he thought that his conduct would draw Washington's "congratulation and applause."[10] Charles Lee was a man of long and varied military experience, but this assumption may have been the biggest mistake of his career.

Washington quickly dispelled any possibility of a friendly reunion. Ignoring pleasantries, and "with some degree of astonishment," the commander in chief asked Lee "what was the meaning" of the retreat? "I desire to know, sir," was Lee's recollection of Washington's words, "what is the reason—whence arises this disorder and confusion?" Now it was Lee's turn to be caught off balance. Stunned and "confounded," he felt himself accosted and was momentarily lost for words, something of a novelty for Lee. He found himself "incapable of making any coherent answer to questions so abrupt and in a great measure to me unintelligible." Indeed, it was less the question itself than Washington's tone and manner, which as Lieutenant Colonel Brooks noted, displayed "considerable warmth." All Lee could manage was "Sir, sir," until Washington repeated himself. The general then recovered and explained that the retrograde was the only real choice open to him. Intelligence had been faulty; officers, especially Scott, had pulled back without his orders; and consequently he chose not to "beard" the British under such conditions. Besides, he added, holding his ground would have tempted disaster: the risks were not worth any possible rewards. When Washington remarked that he thought the British force was only a strong rear guard, Lee retorted that they might be, but they were still stronger than the Continental vanguard.

If Lee was satisfied with his answer, the commander in chief was not. Officers close enough to hear the exchange recalled Washington insisting, in so many words, that his subordinate still should have obeyed orders—that is, he should have pushed his attack. Lee, who by this time was hearing well enough, was more specific in his recollection. "All this may be very true, sir," was the answer Lee remembered from Washington, "but you ought not to have undertaken it unless you intended to go through with it." Whatever the commander's exact words, it was clear that he was disappointed Lee had not landed a blow. That Washington had *never* issued any specific orders to attack and that a stand near Freehold or anywhere east of the West Morass would have been suicidal and could have cost patriots a large part of their army made no difference now. Washington's blood was up, and nothing Lee could have said in defense of his retreat would have sufficed. The rebel chief wanted a fight, and he rode forward on the Rhea farm to look for one. While Washington never said so specifically, Lee believed that the commander in chief had relieved him; Brooks thought so as well.[11] In something of a daze, the bewildered Lee rode after Washington at a distance, having no idea what to do next.

It had been an astonishing exchange. Such a battlefield collision between the two chief generals of an army was, and remains, unique in the annals of American arms. The incident became part of the folklore of the Revolution, with various witnesses (or would-be witnesses) taking increasing dramatic license with their stories over the years. The late-nineteenth- and early twentieth-century historian John Fiske, who hated Lee, offered what he claimed was the eyewitness account of Sergeant (later Major) Jacob Morton of Virginia:

> "My God! General Lee, what are you about?" General Lee began to make some explanation; but General Washington impatiently interrupted him, and with his hand still raised high above his head, waving it angrily, exclaimed, "Go to the rear, sir," spurred his horse, and rode rapidly forward. The whole thing occurred as quickly as I can tell it to you.[12]

The recollections of Lafayette and General Scott were similar, and they recalled Washington in a perfect fury. The Frenchman quoted the commander in chief as calling Lee a "damned poltroon," while Scott's version was eloquent in its flamboyance. Washington "swore on that day," the old brigadier insisted, "till the leaves shook on the trees, charming, delightfully. Never did I enjoy such swearing before or since. Sir, on that memorable day, he swore like an angel from Heaven."[13] But all such recollections were apocryphal; in fact, they were nonsense. Fiske gave Morton's account thirdhand; it derived from a dinner conversation in 1849, when Morton was eighty years old. Scott was nowhere near Washington and Lee on the field—about three-quarters of a mile away actually—and could not have overheard their exchange. Besides, like Morton's, his account and Lafayette's came years after the event (forty-six years after in the instance of Lafayette), when the fullness of time had ripened and expanded memories; neither man made any such claim during the war or while Washington was alive. Certainly Lee, who would have known and who would have broadcast the fact, never made any accusation of profanity or of his being ordered to the rear. This was true even during his embittered final years. Indeed, careful scholarship has conclusively demonstrated that Washington was angry but not profane at Monmouth, and he never ordered Lee off of the field.[14] The court-martial transcript, a veritable oral history of the event (and the basis for this account), remains the best source on the matter. It reflects the affair as it was: a heated contretemps between two of the most important military figures of the War for Independence. As such, the drama of the occasion needs no embellishment.[15]

"We Will All Die Here on This Spot"

At the point Washington rode from Lee, what had been an extended period of maneuver for both armies drew rapidly to a close; a genuine bloodletting was about to begin. Approaching the Middle Morass—the ravine dividing the east and west Rhea farms—Washington met his aide, Harrison, returning from his forward scout. The young officer brought alarming news: Clinton was now driving his men hard (discussed in the following chapter), and Harrison estimated that the enemy columns were no more than fifteen minutes away. He was right: the redcoats were no more than a half mile from where Washington stood. This put the Americans in awkward circumstances, as the vanguard was still retreating over the West Morass and the main army, while coming on steadily, was still not in position to help. Washington had to buy some time here, east of the West Morass, to organize a proper defense farther back. Moreover, he now had less than fifteen minutes to do the job. Dr. James McHenry, serving as another of the general's aides, recalled vividly the circumstances confronting the commander in chief. "The enemy, who were advancing rapidly," he wrote, "elated by our retreat, were to be checked—the most advantageous ground to be seized—The main body of the army to be formed—The enemy's intentions and dispositions to be discovered—and a new plan of attack to be concerted—and all this too in the smallest interval of time—But it is in these moments of a battle," McHenry observed, "that the genius of a general is displayed, when a very inconsiderable weight determines whether it shall be a victory or a defeat."[16] It was fulsome praise, but nevertheless true.

Washington rose to the occasion. He quickly pulled two of Wayne's battalions of picked men out of the retreating column and personally directed them into a wooded patch north of the Rhea fields. (This would have been just a few minutes after 1:00 P.M.) This was near the position in which Lee had earlier posted the New Jersey Brigade to secure the route to the West Morass bridge. Commanding these battalions were Pennsylvania colonel Walter Stewart and Maryland lieutenant colonel Nathaniel Ramsey, the brother of Revolutionary politician and historian David Ramsay.[17] Wayne, who was on the scene and avid for a fight, took overall command and, along with a composite Virginia battalion (comprised of the small Fourth, Eighth, and Twelfth Regiments), led the men into the woods to set up a line. (Contemporary battle accounts generally referred to this position as the Point of Woods, as part of the tree line jutted south from the main wood line.) Wayne's units were on the American left and offered some hope of covering the bridge and impeding the enemy approach. His infantry could be expected to sting the King's foot soldiers, but the rebels, who numbered only slightly over 900 men, would be standing against long odds: the Brigade of Guards and other regiments bearing down on them counted well over 2,500 troops.[18] The American rear guard, for that is what they now were, would simply have to do the best they could with what they had.

The commander in chief, however, could not be in two places at once. He could either deal personally with the impending enemy threat east of the ravine or fall back to organize the approaching main body somewhere west of the ravine. Having detailed Stewart and Ramsey as blocking units and ordering artillery brought back, Washington's attention shifted to the rest of the army. What to do? For a moment, Lieutenant Colonel Tilghman remembered, "the General seemed at a loss" as to where his gathering regiments might stand. Seeing this, the young aide ventured a suggestion. Tilghman had been present when Washington met Colonel Shreve at the top of the West Morass only some ten minutes earlier. With Shreve was none other than Lieutenant Colonel David Rhea, who knew the ground well and already had seen considerable action earlier in the day. He explained to Tilghman that the slope above Middle Brook, the very ground Peter Wikoff had pointed out to General Lee, was defensible terrain. Rhea had offered to help the commander in chief arrange the troops there if he chose to make a stand. Hearing this, Washington ordered Tilghman back over the morass with instructions to find both Shreve and Rhea. The general wanted Rhea to show Tilghman the ground, and he wanted Shreve, who had moved past the crest of the rise as he rode toward Englishtown, to countermarch and post his regiment so as to cover the road up the hill from the brook. The colonel was also to post the smaller regiments of Grayson and Patton in the same place. Thus the Second New Jersey, along with Pennsylvania regiments coming up quickly, would be the anchor on which the retreating units would take post and on which the advancing main body could align.

Even as he issued these orders, Washington was running out of time. British guardsmen and grenadiers were marching rapidly down the hill toward the Middle Morass, and enemy guns on the hill behind the infantry were pounding the rebels west of the morass. Unless the Continentals could slow the enemy advance, there would be too little time to organize a defensive line on the Perrine land. At this point Washington hailed General Lee. The commander in chief may have calmed down somewhat since the incident with his subordinate, or he may have overlooked it entirely when confronted with the need for an experienced man at a critical moment. At any rate, the former vanguard commander, who had remained close to the action as Washington arranged the rear guard, responded with alacrity. Would Lee command here, the commander in chief asked, while he (Washington) rallied the rest of the army? Or would Lee prefer to ride to the rear and organize the main body? Stung by his commander's biting remarks only moments before, Lee, never a man to brook slights lightly, jumped at the chance to redeem himself. He would *not* ride to the rear: the major general chose to remain on the spot. To the departing Washington's admonition to check the British, Lee replied that he would "be one of the last to leave the field." Satisfied with this, Washington " then galloped off to the rear." Lee quickly conferred with Henry Knox, sent word to other officers that he was back in command, and began organizing a hasty defense.[19]

As Washington rode toward the bridge, there remained a final, semicomic act before the serious fighting began. Alexander Hamilton, who had come up with Washington, quickly approached

Lee. To put it mildly, the men were not friends. Hamilton had scorned the general's cautious advice at the previous councils of war, and Lee, if he wasted any thoughts at all on Washington's young aide, probably considered him arrogant and conniving. But whatever he thought, the general clearly was surprised when the young lieutenant colonel, learning that Lee was going to stay on the hill and fight a holding action, suddenly lapsed into melodrama. Hamilton, "Flourishing his sword," began exclaiming, "That's right, my dear General, and I will stay, and we will all die here on this spot." Hamilton was possessed of one of his country's most remarkable and brilliant minds—maybe *the* most remarkable and brilliant patriot mind of his generation—but at this moment that mind was rattled. Lee saw as much and thought Hamilton "in a sort of frenzy of valor." Turning to the colonel, he asked if he (Lee) did not seem in complete control of himself, a fact Hamilton readily conceded. In that case, Lee told him, they should get about their jobs, buy the time the rest of the army needed to get into position, and then added drolly, "I will die with you on this spot, if you please."[20] As historic squelches go, Lee's was a good one.

Time was now measured in minutes, and events moved quickly on both sides of the morass. Having left the rear guard, Washington was just starting down the hill toward the Middle Brook when he met Tilghman coming up with Lieutenant Colonel Rhea. From his horse, Tilghman already could see patriot infantry deploying. The commanding general next sent his hardworking aide off with another officer to identify a unit spotted moving on their left (he mistakenly thought a British outfit might have flanked them; it turned out to be friendly). Then with Rhea, he crossed the bridge and rode hurriedly to the crest of the opposite slope.

Washington liked what he found. As Rhea and Wikoff before him had promised, the position atop the ravine was excellent. The road over the bridge below was in full view, as was much of the terrain east of the morass. Massed infantry and cannon on the west slope could play hell with approaching formations. This was the ground on which Lee had wanted to fight, and had he not met Lee east of the bridge, in all likelihood by 1:15 P.M. or shortly thereafter, much of the vanguard would have stood there. Indeed, had Washington lingered several more minutes over breakfast with Dr. English or added a few more sentences to his letter to Laurens, he may well have come up to find his second in command already holding a stabilized line. Timing had decreed otherwise, and Washington, who never knew Lee's intentions, nevertheless would act in a similar vein.

Perrine's Hill

Washington worked feverishly to establish a new American line on Perrine's Hill (also called the Perrine ridge or Perrine's heights). Time was of the essence: The British showed no sign of stopping their drive, and the commander in chief had to assume that Clinton's attack would continue across the West Morass. Fortunately, the patriot leader found the regiments of the main army coming up steadily, marching through the choking dust and heat toward the sound of the guns. They moved past the exhausted vanguard, although the sight of their bedraggled comrades trudging wearily in the opposite direction apparently had no effect on morale. Some of Lee's men did, however, get in the way of the advancing troops. Colonel William Irvine, leading the First Pennsylvania Brigade, complained that the retreating column "so impeded" his march that he threatened "to charge through them" to reach the front.[21] Like most officers coming up, Irvine was a man in a hurry.

The scene on the heights was one of intense activity. The fresh regiments immediately went into position, although "fresh" is a relative term because most of them had just marched at least five miles through the heat. Still, they were better rested than the redcoats they were moving to engage. The deployment of thousands of men in the face of the enemy was never easy, but it was the job for which officers and the rank and file had trained at Valley Forge. Officers shouted orders, couriers rode between commands, cannon fire echoed, arms and equipment rattled, horse hooves pounded the ground, artillery fire boomed as new guns arrived, and the 4-pounder kept firing at the British in the Sutfin orchard. Washington himself rode through the mix of men, equipment, and animals, taking advantage of every minute to make his deployment. Yet accounts of the day mention no real confusion as all this took place. The columns came forward and went on line smoothly in the face of what the rank and file believed to be an imminent plunge into combat.

Washington had plenty of senior help in arranging his deployment. In addition to his line commanders, three other general officers were on hand. Continental major general Arthur St. Clair served as an aide. After evacuating Fort Ticonderoga in 1777, he never again held an independent command; but he had done good service at Trenton and Princeton, and Washington trusted him. Militia major general John Cadwalader, who had marched from Pennsylvania with a small contingent, had attached himself to the general's staff; from the opening of the campaign, he had advocated a showdown with Clinton, and now he would see the fighting at Washington's side. Then there was also Joseph Reed, Washington's former adjutant general, Pennsylvania politico, and a man who had traded doubts about the commander in chief's abilities with Lee in the dark days of 1776. But when Clinton left Philadelphia, he had served loyally with Colonel Stephen Moylan's horse, shadowing the British across New Jersey, and would brave enemy fire as an aide to Washington on Perrine's Hill; he would even lose a horse in the action (his third of the war).[22] In an army that frequently faced a dearth of manpower, on this day at least, there was no shortage of brass.

All indecision behind him, Washington was a now a determined man. He was seemingly everywhere along the forming line, and it was one of the general's finest hours. Lieutenant Colonel Henry Dearborn, then of the New Hampshire Continentals and later Thomas Jefferson's secretary of war, was inspired. At first, Dearborn recalled, the general appeared "to be at a Loss whether we should be able to make a stand"; but with his decision made to hold the high ground above the ravine, Washington never wavered.[23] His conduct imparted a mixed sense of urgency and confidence, and it was at this critical juncture Washington may have received his highest marks for personal leadership. His subordinates were emphatic on the matter. As one colonel noted, the general's "presence inspired universal ardour along the line." "Our brave Commander-in-chief," recalled Major Shaw, "by his gallant example, animated his forces" as he rode the lines to position and encourage the men. The whole time, Lafayette wrote, "General Washington seemed to arrest fate with a single glance. His nobility, grace, and presence of mind were never displayed to better advantage."[24] Dr. McHenry thought it was the general's best day, and what he saw on the occasion left him genuinely emotional: "I do not think, for my part, the general ever in one day displayed more military powers, or acquired more real reputation. He gave a new turn to the action. He retrieved what had been lost. He was always in danger—examining the enemies manoeuvres —exhorting the troops—and directing the operation of his plans.

He unfolded surprising abilities, which produced uncommon effects."[25] Such praise, of course, came from men fully devoted to their chief—but it was through conduct of this sort that Washington had earned their devotion. Whatever his other faults as a general, the commander in chief was steady when he most needed to be and was unquestionably an inspiration to his troops. With the vanguard pulling back and redcoats fully visible across the West Morass, seeing a determined firmness in their general was no small thing to the gathering Americans.

Command of what became the patriot left fell to Major General Stirling. When the commander in chief rode ahead to assess the situation across the West Morass and to meet Lee, Stirling remained with the main body and shepherded the regiments forward. On Washington's orders (Major Clark claims to have conveyed them), the rebel aristocrat lined up the brigades of Huntington, Glover, Learned, and Conway along with the Second Pennsylvania Brigade.[26] When fully established, the patriot line curved gently from its right, anchored just off the Englishtown Road above the ravine bridge, to a left flank on ground about a half mile away on a hill above Spotswood North Brook close to and overlooking the Sutfin farm. For infantry, it was good defensive ground.

It was a good position for artillery as well. Stirling wasted no time in placing a ten-gun concentration of 4- and 6-pounders roughly in the center of his line. The number of cannons grew as the guns of Lieutenant Colonel Oswald and other elements of the vanguard pulled back from the fighting east of the morass. The guns went into action virtually as soon as they took position. It was a telling fire, and the gunners played a significant role in covering the withdrawal of Scott's battalions as they retreated before the Royal Highlanders. Indeed, the artillery and supporting infantry checked efforts by Generals Grey and Erskine to flank the patriot left.

The new American position was thus well-nigh invulnerable to any frontal assault. But even as the line was forming, patriot troops heard heavy firing open across the ravine: Lee, Wayne, and their Continentals were fighting for their lives.

CHAPTER 13

BUYING TIME

THE POINT OF WOODS AND THE HEDGEROW

Back in command and having restored the ardent Lieutenant Colonel Hamilton to his senses, Major General Lee prepared to make his first real fight of the day. He had only minutes to plan and relied heavily on his aides, Captains John Mercer and Evan Edwards, to carry orders. He also looked to Brigadier General Henry Knox, who stayed behind at Washington's request to assist with the artillery. Lee needed their help; the British were closing in, and he could not afford to have any more orders miscarry.

Lee's initial concern was for artillery support—and support for the artillery. He ordered Eleazer Oswald, hastened by Knox, to post his guns in the field overlooking the Middle Morass, roughly on line with Wayne's infantry in the Point of Woods. The intrepid artillerist, whose cannon had harried the enemy for some three hours, was dead tired. Oswald already had returned six guns to Brigadier General Maxwell and Colonel Grayson, and he now had only four. He asked Knox to bring up fresh guns, but there would be no opportunity; already, Stirling was posting the fresh artillery pieces coming up with the main army on Perrine's Hill. Oswald also wanted infantry support, as he had unlimbered on an open hill above the Middle Morass. Lee immediately tried to help. Pointing to the battalion of Colonel Henry Beekman Livingston, he ordered Edwards to bring the unit up to protect Oswald's guns. Livingston saw the necessity of the move, but his heart was not in it. He put his battalion in motion only "With the Greatest Reluctance," as his men were "weak and faint." Wayne also was concerned about the safety of the artillery *and* of the men he was leading into the Point of Woods.[1] Just before entering the woods, the brigadier passed the small brigade under Lieutenant Colonel Olney (Varnum's Brigade). Wayne told Olney to post his men along the Hedgerow. From there, he hoped, Olney could support the artillery—and Wayne. Accordingly, the Rhode Islander put his troops on the move.

Meanwhile, Oswald fought on with his four guns. These were the two-gun companies of Captains David Cook and Thomas Seward (Oswald remained with Seward). On the height above the Middle Morass, the artillery crews had a clear field of fire over 200 yards. Seward, with two 6-pounders to the left, was hitting the guardsmen and grenadiers with 4-ounce grapeshot and 2-ounce case shot. To his right, Cook's two 3-pounders were firing solid shot and 1.5-ounce case shot. Despite the "heavy fire of Grape," the grenadiers hurried up the slope "in excellent order."[2] Then the cannon fire stopped. Colonel Livingston, dazed with the heat, had formed his men not to the right of Oswald, but directly in front of the guns. Lee quickly "ordered the troops to open to the right and left, to give the artillery an opportunity of playing on the enemy."[3] The addled Livingston, still unable to follow orders, instead led his men farther west toward the Hedgerow; eventually, the battalion formed behind that prominent landmark.

Even as he set Oswald to work, Lee tried to reach Wayne. The Pennsylvanian had led Stewart, Ramsey, and the small composite battalion of the Fourth, Eighth, and Twelfth Virginia into the Point of Woods before learning that Lee was back in command. The major general sent Mercer after the brigadier with orders to hold the left until the bitter end. Mercer found Wayne, who shrugged off the orders and the news that Lee was in charge. He already had orders directly from Washington, and no one had to tell Anthony Wayne to put up a stout resistance. Never fond of Lee, after the experience of the morning, he was hardly glad to hear from the major general again in any case. Nor did it matter, for Wayne's men would have to look after themselves. Lee, although in titular command, was in no position to help him or direct his movements. Lee and Wayne would have to fight their battles independently.

Even if Lee had reinforcements to send, there was no time. No sooner had Mercer departed after delivering his message than firing exploded along Wayne's front. (This was at about 1:10 P.M.) The captain could hear the shooting as he rode down the hill to find Colonel Matthias Ogden's First New Jersey, then drawn up in a woods at the north end of the Hedgerow to cover the vital bridge over the West Morass. Mercer told the colonel that Lee wanted the bridge held at all costs. Ogden recalled replying that the First New Jersey would hold fast as long as its flanks were secure; Mercer, however, later insisted that Ogden already feared the British were on his left and said he would not sacrifice his men. The Jerseymen remained in place for the time being, but Mercer rode off muttering that the regiment was in no "more danger than those in front." But with more and more British visible north of the Middle Brook, Ogden foresaw a potential disaster at the bridge—the disaster of which Major General Dickinson had warned. Prudently, the New Jersey colonel led his men over the bridge to safety.[4]

By the time Mercer returned to Lee, now posted at the Hedgerow, the rebel position was already grim. The captain had taken less than ten minutes carrying the general's orders to Wayne and Ogden, and as he rejoined his chief, it was clear that the Americans were in trouble. On the left, Wayne's position in the woods had collapsed.[5]

The Point of Woods

As he led his men forward, Clinton probably had no idea that he was closing in on a blocking force buying time for a main line beyond the West Morass. With Lee on the hill crest, the royal commander could not see the Perrine farm, Ogden's regiment, or even Livingston and Olney marching for the Hedgerow. Nor did he see the Americans concealed in the Point of Woods; they had slipped into position only moments before the British could have noticed. Clinton's focus was on the Americans he could see, and they were directly ahead. To get at them, however, his men had to march past Wayne's position—that is, past Stewart, Ramsey, and the Virginians.

The American battalions had no time for a parade-ground deployment, which would have been impossible anyway. The woods and brush offered a fair degree of concealment but prevented the troops from forming coherent lines. Instead, they were strung out in small bodies, probably with gaps between platoons or whatever-size groups of men could shelter behind or next to a patch of trees. Contact between units would have been difficult, and officers would have enjoyed little direct control over events. This was especially true after the fighting began, with its confusion, noise, and smoke making effective communications virtually impossible. For this fight, there would be no formations learned from Steuben; it would be a fluid affair, with men fighting in small groups and individually, taking cover when they could, and confronting opponents eye to eye and hand to hand.

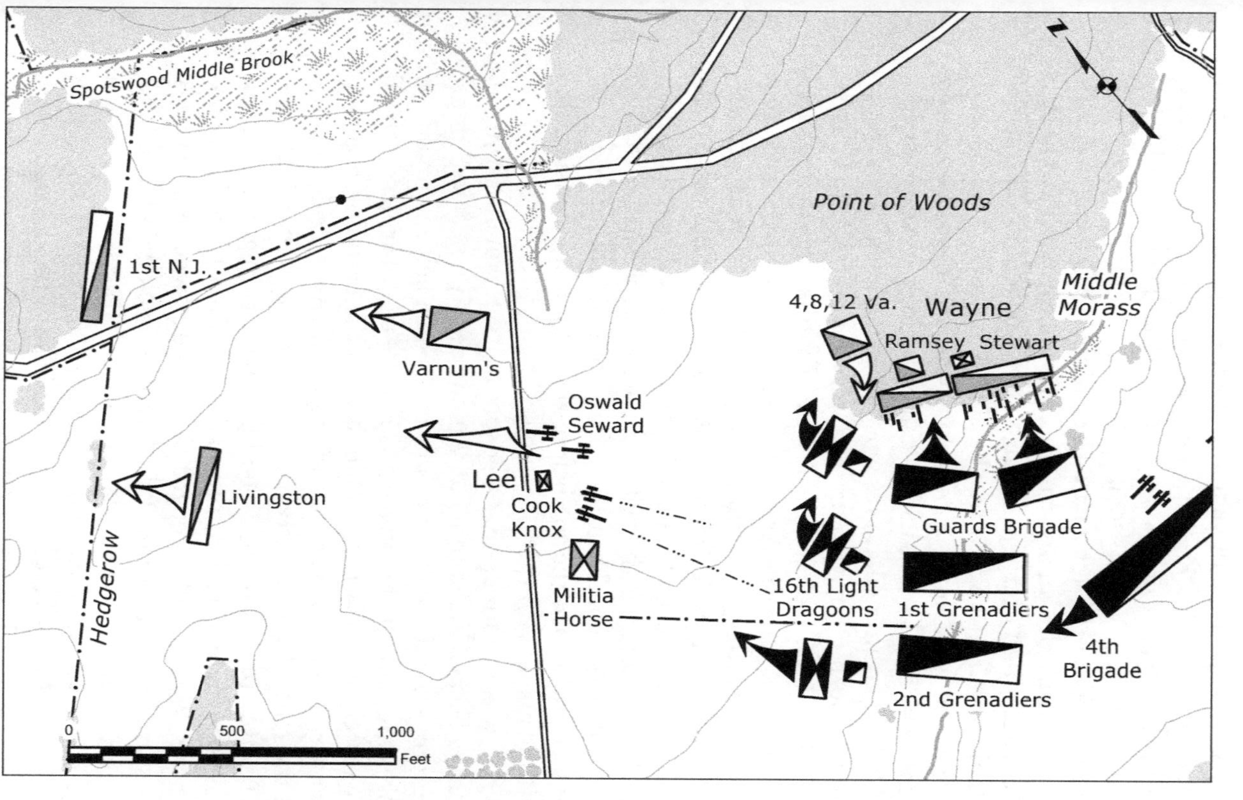

Melee at the Point of Woods: Under heavy artillery fire, the British cross the Middle Morass only to be ambushed by Wayne. Facing to the right, guardsmen, grenadiers, and dragoons charge and rout the Continentals. Map by Garry Wheeler Stone. Copyright © 2016 by the University of Oklahoma Press.

The shooting began as the guards climbed the hill from the Middle Morass. Ahead, Oswald's four guns were firing case, grape, and solid shot at them, and behind the guns Continental infantry was marching west. The British were probably paying little attention to the outcropping of woods on their right. They should have. As they moved past, Wayne's men opened fire, pouring a ragged volley into the flank of the 1st Guards Battalion. No Continental officer ever took credit for an order to fire; the volley may have been a spontaneous reaction of troops seeing enemy soldiers in the open at point-blank range. At any event, the shooting caught the redcoats by surprise, and guardsmen went down, ambushed by the unseen Continentals.[6] The guards quickly regained momentum. British doctrine called for an immediate response to an ambush, with troops not waiting to form; they were to turn toward the attack and charge en masse. The Brigade of Guards did exactly this, and their charge crashed full force into the Americans. All contemporary accounts agree that the fighting was vicious but short.[7] Guardsmen and elements of the 16th Light Dragoons struck virtually at the same time, quickly followed by several companies of the 1st Grenadier Battalion. The shock carried them through the porous rebel line, such as it was. The redcoats "pour'd in their fire," one officer recorded, "& dashing forwards drove the foe before them for some considerable time, killing many with their Bayonets."[8]

No one was in formation. Opposing units became intermixed, and fighting became hand to hand. Among the Americans, Colonel Stewart took a musket ball, and some of his men helped him off the field; his replacement, Lieutenant Colonel Lewis Farmer, stepped in immediately but was barely able to keep the battalion together. Not far away, Ramsey was fighting for his life. As the tide of battle pushed the rebels from the woods, they were attacked by light dragoons. Ramsey turned to fight the horsemen, killing one with his sword. As he fought a second, a third dragoon fired a pistol at point-blank range. With a bullet-gouged cheek and powder-burned eyes, Ramsey surrendered. Hearing of the lieutenant colonel's bravery, Sir Henry released him the next day on parole.[9] One British account claimed that five other patriot officers fell to bayonets and that of seventeen prisoners taken, eight had been "run through" with cold steel. The British were hurt as well. As the King's men pushed through the woods, they found "scarce a bush that had not a fellow under it," with those fellows putting up a stiff fight. Some forty guardsmen (perhaps more), including their commander, Colonel Henry "Harry" Trelawny, fell dead or wounded to the initial patriot fire or in the subsequent melee.[10] A rebel buckshot grazed Sir John Wrottesly, commanding a guards company, on the neck, while another American round blew the bayonet off the fusee (light musket) of Lieutenant Colonel Cosmo Gordon.[11] It was combat at its most desperate and grisly as men fought with musket, pistol, sword, and bayonet.

One account of the savagery is particularly graphic and probably reflected the experience of any number of soldiers in these woods. Solomon Parsons was drafted out of the Fifteenth Massachusetts as one of Colonel Stewart's picked men. His story of battle and survival is as remarkable as it is chilling. Parson began his narrative as the guards moved past the Point of Woods.

> I beheld the red-coats within eight rods. I was loaded with a ball and six buck-shot. I took aim about waistband-high. I loaded the second time, and made attempt to fire; but my gun did not go. I jumped into the rear, where I saw Major [John] Porter. I told him my gun would not go off. He said, "Take care of yourself: the enemy are just upon us!." I stepped into the front rank, and discharged my piece, the enemy within six rods. I loaded the third time. As I returned my ramrod, I found our men four rods distant, and the enemy the same. I wheeled to the left, and observed that the enemy had flanked our men which were out of the woods. I then ran out of the woods. I got ten rods, and the enemy came out of them, and fired a platoon upon me. One ball struck my heel, which much disabled me. The next platoon on the left fired on me, and broke my thigh. I then raised myself upon my right arm, and looked toward the enemy, and saw a man coming towards me. He came upon the run within a rod of me. I begged for quarter. He came within four feet of me. He says, "You damned rebel, I have none for you!" He drew back, and stabbed me through the arm. I *twitched* back my arm and seized the bayonet, one hand by the hilt and one hand by the point, and *twitched* it to the ground. Then he went to twitching it, and twitched it five or six times. He twitched me off the ground, and tried to stab me with the bayonet a number of times. I defended my body. He then drawed me about fifteen feet. I then began to faint. I looked over my shoulder, and saw the flourish of a cutlas, which was by a British officer, who said, "Why ain't you in your rank?" I let go of the bayonet, and they went off.

> I then was beset by two men. One took my piece, and said, "I will blow your brains out with your own gun!" He snapped it at me; but, not being loaded, he run upon me like a mad bear. A man standing by says, "Let him alone: he has enough." One cut away my canteen of rum and my time-piece. I had three days' provision and thirty rounds of cartridges, which I had in my blanket. The cry of all was, "Damn the rebel! Why don't you kill him?"
>
> Here there came a man, and demanded my money. I told him I would not; but, if he would help me to a shade, I would give it to him. He took towards eight dollars. He took hold of my arms, and took me up on my feet; and my *bones grated,* and I fainted; and he laid me down in the same place.

Remarkably, despite several more attempts to kill him, Parsons survived a horrific afternoon. Many others did not.[12]

With key officers down and the enemy pushing hard, it was time for the Americans to pull out of the woods. They had done all they could in the face of a savage assault. Apparently no regimental officer issued a retreat order, and neither did Wayne, who made his way out unscathed. The troops understood the situation; the choice was between getting out or being cut to pieces. As they broke from cover, enemy soldiers continued to harry them. Mercer recalled that "the enemy's infantry and light-horse came out of that wood seemingly mixed with our troops."[13] Maintaining as much order as possible, which was difficult (if not impossible) in most cases, battered groups of rebel survivors left the woods and started west on a perilous flight across a hayfield. Behind them pursued guardsmen, dragoons, and grenadiers from the 1st Battalion.

As Wayne's men cleared the trees, the disintegrating right wing of the 2nd Grenadier Battalion joined the chase. A lieutenant of the 49th Foot's grenadier company cut down one rebel with his sword. Jogging ahead, Lieutenant Hale of the 45th led a dozen or so men after "a battalion running away with their colours, . . . but to my unutterable disappointment they out ran us in a second." Later, Hale was just as glad. Had the rebels realized the small number of men chasing them, the British would have been in real trouble.[14] As it was, Hale and his men had run just under half a mile in the blazing heat, and they were probably incapable of going farther.

Having reached the Hedgerow or the Parsonage woods, the picked men retreated down the road or through the trees toward the West Morass bridge. Crossing the span, most of Wayne's shattered command finally reached safety on the slope leading up to the American line on Perrine's Hill. The British had won a tactical victory in the Point of Woods, but they had paid a stiff price.

The Hedgerow

Lee was terribly distressed with the withdrawal from the Point of Woods, for it also spelled the beginning of the end for American resistance on the right. That fight too was measured only in minutes, although the flow of events was a bit more tangled.[15]

As the Point of Woods exploded with gunfire, it was not only the Continentals in the woods who were in danger. The British were more than halfway up the slope from the Middle Morass. Lieutenant Colonel Oswald—"distressed for the preservation of his pieces"—again feared that he would lose his guns "as he had no infantry for their support."[16] Again, he was directed to Knox. The brigadier agreed that "they were in a very dangerous condition," but as the guns were still needed to slow the British advance, he "applied to General Lee in strong terms for a party on the right." Lee concurred and told Knox to take the first troops that he could get. He asked for Colonel Jackson's detachment, and Lee agreed, forgetting that he had placed Jackson west of the Hedgerow to cover the retreat to the bridge. Knox ordered Major Shaw to find "Harry Jackson."[17] But time was running out. Oswald would have no infantry on his right, only Lieutenant Colonel White's troop of militia horse.[18]

Oswald fought skillfully and stubbornly, directly in front of demanding generals. As the British neared the top of the hill, Captain Cook limbered up and began to pull back his two guns, but Lieutenant Colonel Hamilton and others intervened. Afraid the British would wrap around the Point of Woods and cut off Wayne's retreat, they asked Cook to return and continue firing. Only after firing twelve to fifteen rounds from each gun did Oswald order Cook to retire to a low rise about a hundred yards in front of the Hedgerow. To Cook's left, Seward's men fired more than twenty-five rounds from each gun, perhaps fifteen minutes work. Then, having covered Cook's retreat, they pulled back as well.[19]

From the high ground in front of the Hedgerow, Lee, Lafayette, and Knox watched grimly as Wayne's men fled from the woods, slower soldiers being bayonetted or sabered. Knox, near one of Cook's guns, spoke to his captain-lieutenant, John Cumpston. Pointing to the pursuing British, he ordered Cumpston "to give the enemy a shot." The artillerist objected, "fearful of injuring our own people." Knox replied to "fire over their heads or to their right." Cook's two 3-pounders kept firing until the running British were almost upon them. Then they limbered up and dashed for the Hedgerow.[20]

To the left, Seward's bigger guns were pounding the attackers. Had the British been approaching in formation, their casualties might have been hideous, but the running mob of grenadiers and guardsman made a poor target. As the enemy began to get dangerously close, Lafayette (who had remained forward near Livingston's battalion) told Seward to retreat. Lee immediately countermanded the order and told the captain "to keep up the fire, as it was of service."[21] Finally, after each of his guns had fired twenty more rounds—probably around twelve minutes work—Knox ordered Seward off of the field. As Cook's guns neared the Hedgerow, the foremost grenadiers were almost upon them—easily within a hundred yards. The guns passed through a breach in the fence, and Knox directed them to a knoll behind the south end of Livingston's battalion.

Along the road Olney, having concluded his conversation with Wayne, was still marching Varnum's Brigade to the Hedgerow. En route he had met Major Shaw, vainly searching for Jackson; Shaw gave up on Jackson and urged Olney to hurry. Finally reaching the Hedgerow, he found Hamilton. Washington's aide was now waving his sword in a more useful cause, urging Olney to form his troops lest the artillery be overrun. With Hamilton's assistance, Olney deployed the brigade behind the Hedgerow on a line from the road to Livingston's flank. As the New England troops took position, he looked over the Hedgerow to see the British already "within good musket shot"—that is, within sixty yards—and Oswald's guns withdrawn almost to the Hedgerow.[22] As Cook's gunners passed behind the fence, the Continental infantry began firing. A volley warded off the 16th Light Dragoons. Then the rebels concentrated on the enemy infantry. Despite heavy losses, the grenadiers came on, some stopping only twenty yards away to open fire on the defenders ahead.[23]

Having chased the rebels all morning, Clinton was sparing no effort now that he had almost caught them. This was the time to strike, fast and hard. Personally leading some of the 16th Light Dragoons, the general plunged after Wayne's fleeing Continentals. Disregarding the hail of shot from Oswald's field pieces, Sir Henry

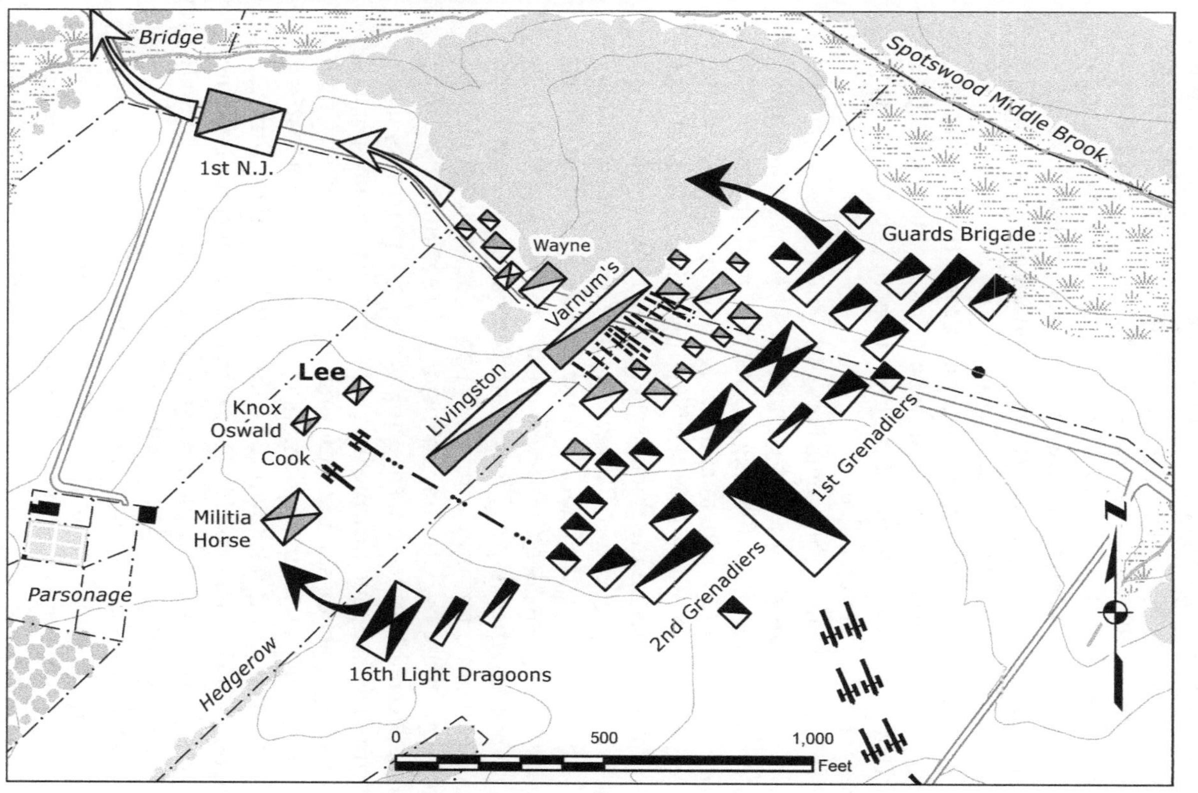

Bloody action at the Hedgerow: A mob of grenadiers and guardsmen storm the Hedgerow. Lee's men fire eight to ten volleys (three to four minutes) before, flanked to the north and south, they retreat. Map by Garry Wheeler Stone. Copyright © 2016 by the University of Oklahoma Press.

galloped across the grenadiers' front "like a Newmarket jockey," Lord Cornwallis and their aides trailing behind.[24] The British commander wanted the fugitives to screen the dragoons' approach to the Hedgerow and allow an easier breakthrough. It was a bold idea, with Clinton acting the part of a junior cavalry officer. But the attempt failed; the Continentals, the general later reported, threw "in upon us a very heavy fire through their own troops, [and] galled the cavalry so much as to oblige us to retreat with precipitation upon our infantry."[25] Yet as the Continentals had fired over the heads of Wayne's men, little damage was done to the light dragoons. In remembering the battle, Washington's military secretary, James McHenry, gave the dragoons credit for charging "with great impetuosity" in the face of "a cool and well directed fire."[26]

At the same time, the grenadiers bore in frontally on the Hedgerow. The guards and a few companies of the 1st Grenadiers had borne the brunt of the fighting against Wayne, but now it was the turn of the 2nd Grenadiers and the rest of the 1st to take the lead. They advanced in the face of blistering artillery and musket fire. Clinton remained in the thick of the action, riding up and down the line with a dragoon escort. The general nearly paid dearly for his bravery. In the midst of the fight, an American officer suddenly fired at Clinton from point-blank range. The rebel missed and then paid for his poor marksmanship as Lieutenant Thomas Lloyd, one of the general's adjutants, ran him through.[27] With Cornwallis and their aides-de-camp close by, Clinton, flourishing his sword and spurring his horse, cheered his men on, shouting "Charge, Grenadiers, never heed forming."[28] Anyone hearing him above the din did not need to be told to forget about staying in formation. The attack was now a mad rush to get at their tormentors. "We rushed on amidst the heaviest fire I have yet felt," wrote Lieutenant Hale, then with the 2nd Battalion of Grenadiers. "It was no longer a contest for bringing up our respective companies in the best order, but all officers as well as soldiers strove who could be foremost."[29]

As Clinton rallied his men, the engagement raged to a climax. It did not last long. Olney remembered his men firing about ten volleys before pulling out, several minutes work for trained infantry. One of Oswald's battery commanders thought that he fired only two or three rounds of grape from behind the Hedgerow before limbering and that the infantry stand lasted not much over two minutes. However long it lasted, it was costly enough. The British had been losing men all the way in, and as some of them reached the rebel line, American fire reportedly "did much execution" among the redcoats.[30]

Behind the Hedgerow, British fire took its toll as well. Hamilton's horse stopped a bullet and fell, badly roughing up the young lieutenant colonel; he was evacuated to Washington's position across the ravine. Another shot killed the horse of fellow aide-de-camp John Laurens.[31] Livingston took a musket ball through the thigh and reported a third of his command killed or wounded. Two men in his battalion color guard were killed, and a musket ball pierced the hat of the lieutenant carrying the flag. Later, when the lieutenant examined the flag, he found "sixty three bullet holes" (the flag had been hanging in folds).[32] Of the forty picked men in Captain William Watson's company, five were killed or wounded. To Livingston's left, Olney, who had no time to count, was sure that losses were "considerable" on "both sides."[33]

Lee and Knox, with the artillery on a knoll just behind the line, followed the action closely, finally concluding that the Continentals would not be able to hold. As the British closed on the Hedgerow, Lee saw both flanks in danger. On the left, some of the redcoats who had forced Wayne from the Point of Woods had taken advantage of the gap left by the retreat of Ogden's First New Jersey, threatening Olney's flank, and scattered firing had already begun. On the right, Lee's prediction that the absence of rebel horse would prove crippling was all too accurate. A large body of Harcourt's dragoons finally broke through the Hedgerow—and the militia horsemen were gone. Anthony Walton White pulled his troopers back in the face of superior numbers, leaving Lee, Knox, and the artillery exposed. Lee shouted, "where are our horse," and outflanked, realized the game was up.[34] It was time to leave, and he ordered the men and guns out. Knox sent the guns off. Once safely on Perrine's Hill, most of Cook's men collapsed from heat and fatigue.[35]

This was no rout. There was only minimal confusion as the troops disengaged, and many men were so intent on getting in a final shot that their platoon officers had to force them away from the Hedgerow. If they had to leave, Olney and Livingston did so, as one officer put it, "with great dignity," although Livingston thought that they left "with the Greatest Precipitation and Confusion."[36] But the Continentals clearly did not panic and run. By staying compact, with a perimeter of glittering bayonets, they warded off the

British light horse. The troops maintained their order as they rapidly moved down the heights and crossed the bridge. Testimony to the success of the retrograde was the fact that Captain-Lieutenant Cumpston saved both of Cook's guns. The captain, though, went out on the ammunition wagon, shot through the lungs. Oswald felt that "had the enemy pushed on with spirit they must have taken the two pieces," but Continental volleys had taken some of the spirit out of the pursuing dragoons.[37] Marching off rapidly, several of Livingston's and Olney's men died of heat and dehydration. Probably the last officer across the bridge was Charles Lee.

Monckton's Charge

This was not the end of the fighting. Thinking that they could still catch the retreating rebels, the British pushed on. In hot pursuit of Lee, the 2nd Grenadiers, or at least a major part of the battalion, moved over the bridge. Clinton never mentioned this advance in his memoir, but sending the grenadiers across may have been his last chance to come to grips with Washington's main force. There was some logic to the move. In the heat of battle, Clinton likely had no idea that efforts to flank the American left had failed. So as far as he knew, Grey and Erskine were hitting the rebel left while the grenadiers crossed the West Morass to strike the patriot right.

The grenadier venture, however, was as foolhardy as it was gallant (and it was certainly both). As they crossed the bridge, the British seemed unaware of the strength of the American position on Perrine's Hill, the high ground to their front. What they could not miss, however, were the reassembled (or reassembling) elements of Wayne's command that had retreated from the Point of Woods. They had crossed the bridge only some fifteen minutes before and were perhaps 350 yards from the bridge on a low rise, about halfway to Stirling's line. Confronted with a clear target, the grenadiers formed, or tried to form, to press their attack—and quickly paid the price.[38]

Archaeological evidence has made two things clear. First, a substantial if unknown number of grenadiers got across the morass, either by wading through the muck or, in most cases, crossing the bridge. The wealth of recovered American case- and grape-shot artifacts, especially in the area west of the bridge, indicates that the Continental guns engaged a considerable body of men. The same

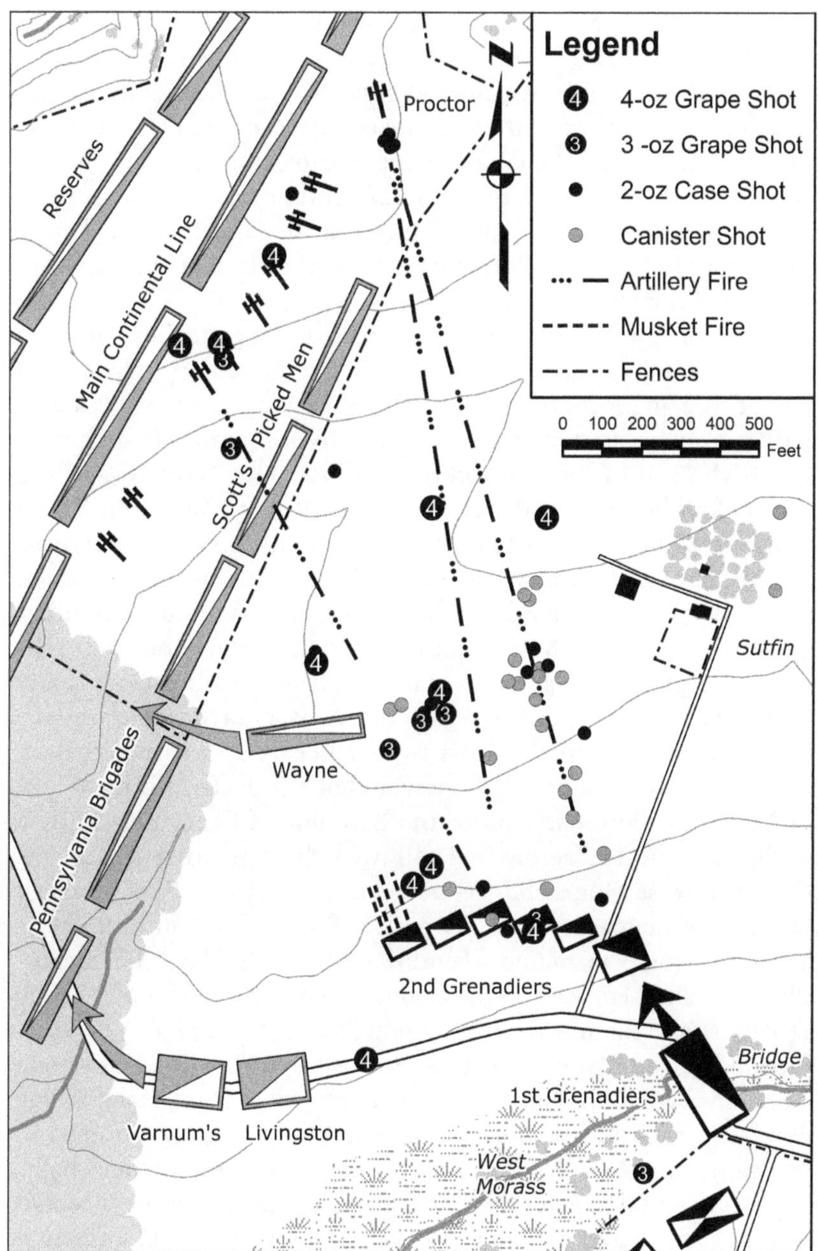

The grenadiers cross the bridge and attack Wayne's position only to be driven back by Continental artillery. Archaeology by the Battlefield Restoration and Archaeological Volunteer Organization. Map by Garry Wheeler Stone. Copyright © 2016 by the University of Oklahoma Press.

evidence confirms a second point. For about two hundred yards west of the bridge, the rise on which Wayne was positioned sheltered the grenadiers from the Continental artillery. But as soon as the grenadiers started up the rise, they advanced into the face of a terrifying hail of cannon fire.[39] Once again the patriot gunners could hardly miss; their targets were in the open. The British effort to form crumbled quickly. Lieutenant Walter Finney of the Fourth Pennsylvania noted that "by a few well directed shot on the Head of thire Collom they ware broke in Disorder."[40]

The officer leading the attack was a hardened grenadier. This was Lieutenant Colonel The Honorable Henry Monckton, who would become the highest-ranking British officer to die at Monmouth. Hailing from an aristocratic and politically influential Irish family, he was the son of John Monckton, 1st Viscount Galway, and the younger half-brother of Lieutenant General Robert Monckton. These connections did his career no harm, nor did his ability to purchase commissions with family wealth. He bought an ensigncy in 1760, and in 1769 he purchased a major's commission from none other than Horatio Gates.[41] Monckton was a popular and competent officer. He led grenadiers at every major engagement from Long Island through Germantown, compiling a record as a brave and aggressive leader. He was wounded at least twice and eagerly returned to duty as soon as possible. His gallantry would be the death of him.

Monckton commanded the 2nd Battalion of Grenadiers as they fought past the Hedgerow and followed the retreating Americans across the West Morass bridge; he led from the front. Forging ahead through the increasingly deadly patriot fire, legend had him cheering with a gusto to match Clinton's. "On to the day," he supposedly cried, and "Forward to the charge, my brave Grenadiers."[42] If he actually spoke them, they were among his last words. As the grenadiers advanced toward Perrine's Hill, a grape shot fired from one of Stirling's guns hit him full in the chest. Lieutenant Hale, seeing Monckton fall, could do nothing with the combat raging, but later in the day he ordered a detail to recover the lieutenant colonel's body. They never found it. After the battle and before the British detail could attempt their search (which would have been perilous), Continental soldiers (likely Pennsylvanians, but we do not really know) found the mortally wounded Monckton and carried him back to Tennent's Meeting House. He lingered painfully and died the next day. The Continentals buried him with military honors in the churchyard, his death noted in particular by the Americans and lamented by many of his brother officers. Hessian adjutant Baurmeister sadly recorded Monckton's death as "a great loss indeed." "The loss of the gallant Colonel Monckton," Hale wrote to his parents, "is one of the greatest misfortunes that could befall our regiment: no man was ever more sincerely and generally regretted."[43]

Monckton's fall may have signaled the futility of pressing on. The volume of patriot fire was simply too great, and a continued attack would have been disastrous. Even without the galling artillery fire, the redcoats were suffering from exhaustion. "The excessive heat," one British army journal recorded, "prevented the advantage being pursued." Thus with men wounded, tired, and confronted by a strong new rebel position, Clinton chose not to continue across the morass. He ordered his units "to retire till more troops came up to their Support."[44] Still under fire, they pulled back to the ground around the Hedgerow, where the reverse slope protected them from the Continental artillery. For a brief moment, there was a lull in the fighting.[45]

"Sir, Here Are My Troops"

Lee's rear guard had done its job. It had not taken long; once Washington put the major general back in command, the fighting in the Point of Woods and along the Hedgerow took no more than some twenty-five or thirty minutes; Lee himself probably crossed the bridge about 1:30 P.M. This may have seemed a short enough time for Washington as he hurried to position the rest of the army, but it must have seemed forever for those on the firing line. The senior officers directing the action knew they had done well. McHenry, Washington's secretary, thought the fighting "did Olney great honor" and that Livingston had been "very powerful in his fire."[46] Wayne wrote to his wife in gallant terms of his fight in the woods, but of course his account said not a word of Lee.[47] It hardly mattered, as Lee was more than satisfied with himself. Over the early morning he had retreated in good order without losing a cannon, and on the heights he had fought hard against superior numbers and an enemy with the advantage of cavalry. Again he had come off in good order and without the loss of "a single Platoon."[48] Most important, Lee had accomplished his mission: he had delayed Clinton long enough to allow

Washington to organize a strong new line. It was a proud general who presented himself to the commander in chief and reflected on the course of the day's action:

> So far at this time from conceiving ourselves as beaten or disgraced, that I really thought, taking into consideration all circumstances, the various contradictory and false intelligence, disobedience or mistakes in some officers, precipitancy in others, ignorance of the ground, want of cavalry, that it was the flower of the British army we had to deal with; considering all these circumstances, I repeat, so far was I from conceiving ourselves beaten or disgraced, that I really thought the troops entitled to the highest honor; and that I myself . . . had merited some degree of applause from the General and from the public.[49]

While Lee naturally put the best possible face on his conduct, it is difficult to fault his conclusion. He had saved the vanguard, and thus the army, from disaster. Had he not retreated in front of Clinton's advance, the patriot general could easily have lost most of his troops. Sir Henry said as much, writing later that Lee's "whole corps would probably have fallen into the power of the King's army" had any stand taken place between Freehold and the West Morass. Clinton had effective cavalry, but Lee had virtually none other than some militia horse. The patriot troops were outnumbered and, given the nature of the retreat, not massed for an effective defense; the more numerous British, with the initiative, were moving their troops in supporting formations. Under the circumstances, Clinton in all likelihood could have polished off a stationary Lee long before Washington arrived to lend any support. Charles Stedman, British commissary and postwar historian and a man critical of both Washington's and Clinton's handling of the battle, had only praise for Lee. "The conduct of General Lee on this day," he wrote, "which was so severely arraigned . . . by the Americans, was worthy of applause and admiration."[50]

While it was never the Continental plan, Lee's initial retreat had drawn Clinton into what amounted to a patriot defense in depth. The British counterattack began with an enervating march that left many troops exhausted before serious fighting began. Lee dropped back slowly, which drew the King's soldiers into the open and ultimately to the guns of the Continental delaying forces in the Point of Woods and at the Hedgerow. The Americans enjoyed excellent fields of fire and, in the case of Stewart and Ramsey, the element of surprise. The resulting actions were terribly costly, especially to the guards and grenadier battalions, which suffered the bulk of the British casualties for the day (a subject addressed in detail in chapter 16). Even some patriot observers were shocked at the damage they had inflicted.[51] The royal units, many of which were now thoroughly disorganized, stood no chance of assaulting Washington's line behind the West Morass. Clinton lost the initiative, and it was now up to the American commander to decide whether the Battle of Monmouth would continue. Had patriots deliberately planned a defensive battle, it would be difficult to imagine a better one than the unplanned action they had fought through necessity. As it was, it was one of the most important defensive operations of the war.

Upon crossing Spotswood Middle Brook, Lee once more rode to the commander in chief. Washington now had the main line more or less formed, and Lee needed to position the men he had brought over from the east side of the ravine. "Sir," he announced to Washington, "here are my troops; how is it your pleasure that I should dispose of them?" At first, the Continental chief formed the retreating units near the artillery, on the left of the new line. Considering the exhaustion of the men, however, he ordered Lee to march them to Englishtown, where the commanding general wanted an organized reserve.

In his decision to place the reserve so far back, Washington ignored a suggestion from Lee that the men form closer to the rear of the main line, perhaps near Tennent's Meeting House. Historian Theodore Thayer has pointed out that Washington's decision deprived the army of a veteran reserve closer at hand, a force that might have allowed the rebels to assume a more aggressive posture later in the day.[52] Perhaps there was something to this. But the packs of the vanguard, and the supplies and camp facilities necessary to rearm, feed, and properly rest the men, were at Englishtown. There also was good defensive ground west of the village, and if the fighting at Monmouth went badly, Washington wanted a prepared reserve position ready. He also wanted a place to organize troops arriving from other sectors, and Englishtown was the most convenient rendezvous. Besides, there was no gainsaying the fatigue of Lee's troops. They had been on the move since before daybreak, had marched with scant rest and in brutal heat for hours, and some had fought a bruising action. Whether at Englishtown or the meetinghouse, it would be some time before these battalions were ready to fight again.

Lee rode slowly toward Englishtown at the head of his tired column. Behind him were two battalions of the New Jersey Brigade, some of Scott's detachment, and a collection of other units from the old vanguard; half of Scott's men and most of Wayne's remained at the West Morass with Washington. Lee was in what he later described as a "ruffled" state as he rode toward Englishtown. Now that the pressure of battle was off, he had time to ponder his encounter with Washington and the insinuation that he had retreated unnecessarily. He sought assurances from junior officers that he had been "cool and firm" in the field, while repeating his earlier doubts about the wisdom of bringing on a general engagement. He reprised his old theme to anyone who would listen: the American cause, he insisted, was likely to gain little from a major battle; the British withdrawal from New Jersey and the French alliance would produce wonderful results without a fight. He repeated these sentiments on the march at least to Dr. David Griffith, a chaplain with the Third Virginia, and to several other persons in Englishtown.[53]

Lee would regret talking to Griffith. The chaplain, who also helped out with regimental medical duties, was destined to play a secondary but interesting role in later efforts to discredit the general. To Lee's disgust, Griffith related their conversation at Lee's court-martial, which the general denounced as a gross breach of privacy. Besides, Lee fully admitted that he was not at his best when he spoke with the chaplain; he was tired and anxious over his words with the commander in chief.[54]

All of this, however, was in the future, and Lee still had no idea if his labors were over for the day. He arrived at Englishtown about 3:00 P.M. and was still on horseback when Steuben rode up. Washington had sent the Prussian back with new orders for the reserve, which also put him in command in place of Lee. The Virginian was glad to hear it, telling Steuben that he was exhausted. With that, the general rested while his aides replaced their wounded horses. After this, however, Lee made his way back toward the fighting, meeting Washington near the meetinghouse. He offered his services to the commander in chief but had arrived around 7:00 P.M., too late to play a further role in the battle.[55]

At Englishtown Steuben established two defensive lines. He had Maxwell's New Jersey troops and Scott's men form behind Weamacock Creek; behind them, on higher ground, he placed the four brigades led here by Brigadier General John Paterson (Paterson's,

Muhlenberg's, Weeden's, and the Second Maryland). These were units that had marched from the main army and arrived soon after Lee's column. They had seen no action, but evidently Washington wanted some fresh troops with the reserves as well. Steuben also posted a battery on his right, near the Maryland regiments. All told, the reserve held over three thousand men, three-fourths of them rested.[56] They were positioned well enough to support a retreat by the main army, but too far from the battlefield to reinforce Washington quickly. They could not have known it at the time, but their role in the battle was over.

CHAPTER 14

The Great Cannonade

For a critical interval, elements of the battle unfolded simultaneously, not sequentially. While Lee and Wayne fought on the heights east of the morass, and as the British light troops and 3rd Brigade swung around the American left, Washington already had opened a new phase of the action. Arriving Continental troops rapidly moved into position on Perrine's Hill. Rebel artillery went into action quickly. From the western side of the morass, Knox's guns stopped any British advance on the American left and galled the British chasing Wayne and Lee; then they hammered Monckton's grenadiers. At that point, however, the frantic pace of events slowed, and the battle evolved into one of the most spectacular episodes of the entire war, "the Great Cannonade."

"A Most Furious Cannonade"

The lull in combat was only relative. As infantry action ceased, opposing cannon fire only slackened as infantry targets went to cover. Around 1:30 P.M., however, the tempo quickened. Patriot guns, which had never let up, increased their volume of fire. Riding the American lines, Henry Knox, who had retreated with Lee, now took personal charge of the growing cannonade. Over the previous winter he had labored to bolster the effectiveness of his artillery regiments and had emphasized the use of his guns against enemy infantry. In this role artillery deployed with infantry units, usually two guns with each brigade.[1] This was how the Continental artillery deployed during the morning of the twenty-eighth. Now, however, while cannon played on any redcoats bold enough to advance, guns attached to the infantry units were gathered along Major General Stirling's line.[2] It was one of the largest such concentrations of the war. As British infantry attacks petered out, Knox and his officers prepared for a much different fight. The massed Continental artillery would duel directly with the professionals of the Royal Artillery.

With the exception of the sieges at Yorktown, Charleston, and Fort Mifflin, it would be the largest single day's artillery action of the war, and although it attracted thousands of witnesses, we know surprisingly little about key aspects of it.[3] On the patriot side, the names of the tactical commanders (that is, the officers reporting to Knox and commanding the companies) have remained elusive. Nor are we certain of exactly which artillery units were involved. All four Continental artillery regiments had elements in the fray, along with two independent companies. But there is little certainty of exactly which units were present from each regiment or of where in the line they deployed. Only one regiment was present with its full complement, Colonel Charles Harrison's regiment—later (1779) designated the First Continental Artillery Regiment—which came up from Virginia and joined the army at Valley Forge in late April and early May. Lieutenant Colonel Oswald commanded as many as five (probably four) companies of Colonel John Lamb's regiment as well as the two independent companies, while Colonel John Crane's regiment had at least four companies in action, perhaps as many as nine. There was one company from Colonel Thomas Proctor's regiment, commanded by the colonel's younger brother, Captain Francis Proctor, Jr.[4] As he established his line, Stirling initially brought ten cannon into action; but more arrived as the fighting developed. During the battle Knox's total strength was something under 900 men of all ranks on all parts of the field (including reserves), with some twelve to sixteen guns in action on Perrine's Hill.[5]

Harrison's Regiment was one of the first outfits to come on line with Stirling, and it brought the bulk of the patriot guns. Harrison took command of the unit in 1776. The regiment had its origins in two Virginia State Artillery companies, but eight new companies (also Virginians) and the later addition of two from Maryland completed a Continental regiment of twelve companies. Harrison's had operated in Virginia through early 1778, seeing no major action before Washington called it north. Monmouth would be Colonel Harrison's first real fight.[6] The same was true for his second in command, Lieutenant Colonel Edward Carrington, another Virginian who turned out to be one of the army's best artillery leaders. Although previously not involved with any major operations, Carrington quickly impressed Knox and Nathanael Greene as an efficient officer. He actively directed Harrison's guns above the West

Morass, and his performance, like Oswald's, was testimony to the strides Continental gunners had made under Knox's leadership.[7]

Across the morass, Knox's likely opponent was his equal in rank and his senior in experience. This was Brigadier General James Pattison of the Royal Artillery, commandant of artillery in British North America.[8] He was a veteran and a professional in every sense. He enlisted in the artillery in 1740 at age seventeen, attended the Royal Military Academy at Woolwich, and since 1742 had been on active duty in combat and administrative assignments. Pattison received his promotion to brigadier in 1777 along with his orders for America.[9] At Monmouth the brigadier commanded the guns of the 4th Battalion of the Royal Artillery Regiment. The British artillery train had forty-six pieces of various sizes and types; to face the rebels, the general brought up twelve 6-pounders, two 12-pounders, and two howitzers. Thus the two sides slugged it out with an approximately equal number of guns, with the British throwing heavier shot.[10]

The guns dueled without interruption for approximately two hours. Sustained fire lasted from roughly 1:30 P.M.—that is, shortly after the rebels abandoned the east side of the morass, and after the Highlanders had moved to shelter (such as it was) in the Sutfin orchard—to about 4:00 P.M. It was time enough to send thousands of pounds of hot metal blasting through the already torrid air.

For the troops, it was all quite a show. The firing was "*the brisket Cannonade on both sides* that I Ever heard," wrote Lieutenant Colonel Henry Dearborn. "If any thing Can be Call.d Musical where their is so much Danger, I think that was the finest musick, I Ever heard." Yet "the agreeableness of the musick was very often Lessen.d," he observed, "by the balls Coming too near."[11] Dearborn, it seems, kept his sense of humor under fire. On the other hand, Israel Shreve saw nothing funny in the situation. The colonel was a stalwart but not brilliant officer; still, he was smart enough to know that flying metal was dangerous. "The Cannonade was heavyer than Ever known in the field in America before," he wrote to his wife the following day. Posted with Lafayette in the second line, he noted candidly that as the "Cannon Ball flew plentyfully, my horse Squated, and I Cowardly Doged, which Saved my head." But "a miss of an inch," he concluded, "is as Good as a mile."[12] In a more clinical observation, Surgeon Samuel Adams, with Crane's Continental Artillery, noted succinctly that the rival gun crews embarked on

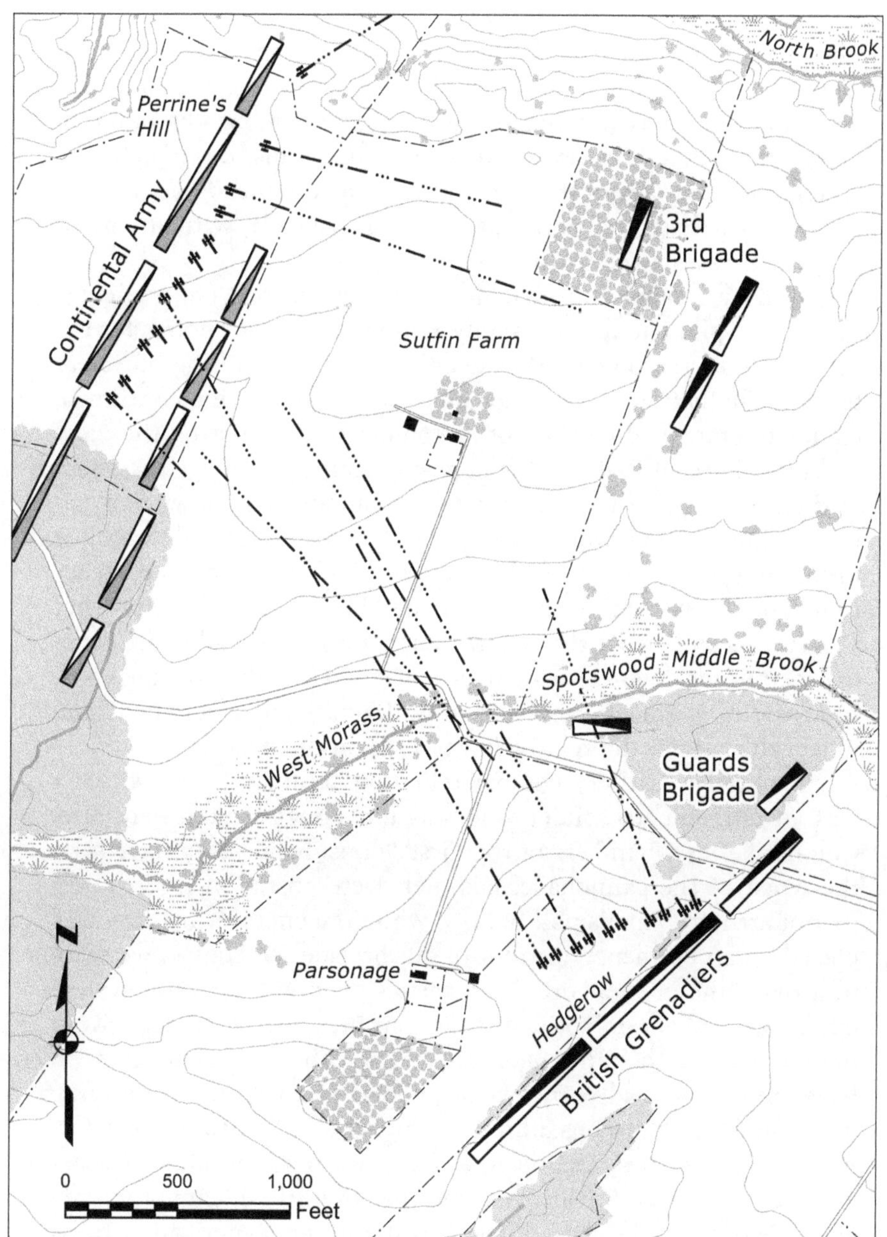

The Great Cannonade, a noisy but largely ineffectual duel that takes place between artillery deployed on hills two-thirds of a mile apart. Map by Garry Wheeler Stone. Copyright © 2016 by the University of Oklahoma Press.

"a most furious canonade . . . equal perhaps to any ever known in America." Colonel Joseph Cilley of the New Hampshire Line was sure of it. On the twenty-eighth he was commanding a battalion of picked men, and as he watched the crashing guns, he thought the barrage was the "severest . . . as was ever in America."[13] For a time, then, the battle offered participants a real spectacle, with any number of witnesses awed by the experience.

With awe came considerable incomprehension. The exchange of fire took place at approximately 1,200 yards, close enough for the gun crews to see one another over the generally rolling but clear terrain. The batteries could not hide. Still, as the firing continued, clouds of smoke filled the hot air, sometimes obscuring the view and making it difficult for the opposing gunners to judge the effect of their fire. The British, working their cannons and howitzers gallantly, thought they were scoring heavily. Lieutenant Hale watched in fascination as the crews, he thought, "did most horrible execution" among the Americans on Perrine's Hill.[14] Yet Hale, like other observers trying to see through the dust and smoke—all while keeping their heads down—was wrong; sound and fury did not equal positive results. Spectacle, no matter how dramatic, is seldom fatal, and in fact the barrage did relatively little serious damage.

Long-range artillery combat relied on solid shot, and while it was an unfortunate soldier who was hit, direct strikes were rare. Colonel James Chambers of the First Pennsylvania may have seen the worst of the cannonade. His men were posted in front of the patriot artillery "in a small hollow, while the enemy's artillery was placed on an eminence in front of our brigade. Of course, we were in a right line of their fire, both parties playing their cannon over our heads, and yet only killed two of our men, and wounded four of my regiment with splinters of rails."[15] No other regiment seems to have suffered as badly; most Continental infantrymen were lying down, making the troops difficult to hit.[16] Indeed, until infantry formations moved into the open, gunners on neither side had especially good targets. Stirling insisted that the British cannon blazed away "with out the least Effect," and another American witness wrote home, "we Cannonaded each other the whole time but without effect." Once shielded by the terrain on the Freehold side of the Hedgerow, the British infantry reduced their losses as well.[17]

Nor did the opposing gun crews score well on each other. Material damage was light. There are no accounts detailing artillery pieces knocked out of action by enemy fire during the afternoon barrage. On the American side, an artillery wagon lost a wheel to a British round shot, hardly a disaster. There were some personnel losses. While both sides lost artillerymen over the course of the day, few apparently fell to long-range fire during that cannonade. Washington reported Continental artillery losses at nine killed, fourteen wounded, and one missing, with six horses killed and two wounded.[18] In proportion to the number of artillerists engaged, these were not insignificant casualties. But most of these men went down during the morning fighting, when the gunners frequently fought in the open. British gun crews seem to have suffered comparably. Brigadier General Pattison reported the death of only one artillery lieutenant, and although he mentioned no figures for wounded (there must have been some), he was surprised that his men had escaped greater harm. The losses among the gun crews were "but small," he noted, "considering the heavy fire they were under."[19] The only memorable additional casualty was (at least supposedly) a civilian watching the action from the seemingly safe vantage of the Tennent's Meeting House graveyard. Struck by a bounding British ball, the poor fellow died hours later. If the story is true, then likely the man had the dubious distinction of being the only patriot civilian killed during the battle.[20] The real artillery killing would come later, when the infantry once again moved out of cover and into the range of grape shot and canister.

None of this is to suggest that the artillery fire was not dangerous. If casualties during the cannonade were few, they could be grisly. Unless a witness saw a particular individual fall, it is difficult to say precisely when a specific casualty occurred. Such cases were relatively rare, but there were some. Ebenezer Wild, a Massachusetts sergeant, noted several men killed or wounded in his regiment during the cannonade, a fire severe enough to cause the troops to move farther into the shelter of some woods.[21] Battas (or Baltis) Collins of Captain Gibbs Jones's independent Pennsylvania company was wounded in the left leg so badly that he was discharged as unfit for duty the following year.[22] Presumably, Collins was hit by a rock or wood splinter or only grazed by a cannon ball; a direct hit by a round shot likely would have cost the sergeant his leg, if not his life. And round shot did cost lives. Several days after the battle, Colonel Shreve wrote to his wife, Polly, with a graphic account of the death of a local tory, one Sam Leonard. Only days earlier, the home of Shreve's brother, William, had gone up in flames, torched during the British occupation of Mount Holly. Thus the colonel was in no mood to waste any sympathy on a dead loyalist—especially one who was probably with the enemy at Mount Holly. Shreve took grim delight in describing how "Leonard was Laying down" and was "took with a Cannon Ball in the Left Shoulder," which passed through his body and "Come out in his belly."[23] The nature of the fatal wound suggests that Leonard was hit while lying prone, probably trying to avoid cannon fire overhead—which was no defense against a shot that came in low.

Among the gun crews, weather was probably a bigger killer than enemy rounds. The heat and humidity remained a vivid memory for veterans of this fight, and the artillerymen had as much cause for complaint as anyone. They got little rest, and the black powder of the day (this a century before the advent of smokeless powder) only made their situation more miserable. With each round, the clouds of smoke got thicker—trapped longer in the high humidity—making it hard to see, breathe, or even stay on one's feet. Since midmorning Oswald had noted the effects of the heat and smoke on his men; during artillery action in the afternoon, other officers found the conditions just as trying. If few gunners fell to direct enemy cannon fire, any number of them collapsed from exhaustion or heatstroke. Casualty figures from heatstroke are incomplete, and many men who gave out subsequently rallied. One cannot doubt, however, that British or American artillerists ever fought as tirelessly or gallantly—or under conditions more trying—than the crews who dueled on this Sunday afternoon.

While the gunners labored in the heat, the infantry of both armies got what rest they could. Everyone was happy for even a small respite. "Our men being very much beat out with Fateague & heat," recalled Lieutenant Colonel Dearborn, "which was very Intence, we order.d them to sit Down & Rest them Selves."[24] Cilley's men looked on with "great fortitude" as they tried to catch their breath. Private Joseph Plumb Martin and his comrades lay in the grass behind the roaring guns and watched the gunners work. They also had a good view of the British guns, which Dearborn (Cilley's second in command) inaccurately estimated were only "60 rods of our front"—about 330 yards.[25] The noise must have been deafening, and clouds of smoke periodically made it hard to see anything, but no doubt braver souls lifted their heads to try to watch the action and to catch a glimpse of their opponents. Across the ravine, redcoats did much the same. One anonymous officer, probably with the 3rd Brigade, noted, "a violent cannonade from the enemy, gave the troops time to recover." Lieutenant Hale, having found cover, was unwilling to risk crawling beneath the cannon fire to the Middle Brook for water; instead he paid a more intrepid (or foolish?) artillery teamster to try. The man made the potentially fatal trip unscathed—and earned a Spanish dollar.[26]

The cannonade gave rise to a number of incidents long embedded in the public memory and folklore of the battle. Decades after the war, George Washington Parke Custis, step-grandson and adopted son of the commander in chief, was the origin of one of the best known. According to Custis—and retold over the years in other histories—"Billy" (or "Will") Lee, Washington's slave and personal body servant, had led a party of other officers' "valets" onto the battlefield. Like his master, Billy Lee was a superb horseman, and at the head of the group, he supposedly paused in the saddle beneath a large sycamore tree. Taking out a spyglass, Lee proceeded to "reconnoiter" the enemy. At this point Custis brought Washington himself into the narrative. The general,

> having observed these manoeuvres of the corps of valets, pointed them out to his officers, observing, "See those fellows collecting on yonder height; the enemy will fire on them to a certainty." Meanwhile the British were not unmindful of the assemblage on the height, and perceiving a burly figure well-mounted, and with a telescope in hand, they determined to pay their respects to the group. A shot from a six-pounder passed through the tree, cutting away the limbs, and producing a scampering among the corps of valets, that caused even the grave countenance of the general-in-chief to relax into a smile.[27]

Was the story true? Billy Lee accompanied Washington throughout the war years (and through his presidency), and there is no reason to believe that he was not at Monmouth. But it is curious that no one else recorded what would have been a striking incident, a "ludicrous occurrence," as Custis called it, whether or not anyone considered it humorous. Nor did any British account mention aiming a shot at a particular group of supposed senior patriot officers. Perhaps it was a tale told by the general to amuse the young Custis, but one doubts it. Custis makes Lee the butt of a clownish episode, a cartoon figure, and it strikes the wrong note. While the record on the slave is hardly voluminous, surviving accounts make it clear that Washington respected the man and accorded Lee a measure of dignity that does not fit an insulting "ludicrous occurrence."[28] Besides, sycamores grow near wetlands, not on heights. Custis was a storyteller, and his tale of Billy Lee was nothing more.

A second incident is more probable. The account comes from English-born Dr. William Read. Read grew up in Georgia and trained as an apothecary, in 1774 traveling to Philadelphia to train under (and live with) Dr. Benjamin Rush. Under Rush's tutelage, Read took up the patriot cause. He reached the field at Monmouth in the afternoon, seeking Brigadier General Wayne and hoping to be of service to the Pennsylvania troops. Read rode toward the frontline during the cannonade, his servant all the while (quite sensibly) protesting any approach to the front. Arriving at the American position, he saw "Washington riding to and fro along the line, sometimes at full speed, looking nobly, excited, and calling loudly to the troops by the appellation of brave boys." At one point the doctor saw a British cannonball "strike a wet hole," splattering dirt on the general. Two officers, whom Read thought were John Laurens and Brigadier General Jedediah Huntington, then took hold of the bridle of Washington's horse and asked him to move on, insisting that he had become too conspicuous a target. "The General, coolly standing in his stirrups," Read remembered, "was said to say to the officers who urged that that was no place for him, he being observed by the enemy, 'that he was admiring the manner in which Proctor was handling their right.' Dr. Read was near enough to hear the word Proctor, and was told what the General said." The commander in chief and his entourage then moved down the line.[29] Custis, likely writing of the same incident, characteristically added a dash of melodrama. When a British shot landed harmlessly and bounded away, he attributed an exclamation to Major General Steuben, then with Washington: "Dat wash very near."[30] Actually, Steuben was nowhere near the commander in chief; he was back at Englishtown.

The artillery exchange also gave rise to one of the most (if not *the* most) enduring and endearing legends of the war. It was during the cannonade that a young woman of the army entered American tradition as "Molly Pitcher." There are various claimants to the title, and the stories of women in battle during the Revolution are not confined to Monmouth. The exploits of Deborah Samson and Margaret

Corbin are well established, as are the many contributions and tribulations of the women with the patriot and British armies. Indeed, efforts to find the Molly Pitcher of Monmouth often combines the heroine of 28 June with the stories of these other women.[31] The individual traditionally accorded the role at Monmouth was almost certainly a young woman from Carlisle, Pennsylvania. She was either Irish or of Irish descent, although there is no reliable information on her parents or even her maiden name. She entered history first as the wife of one William Hays, an Irish immigrant who settled in Carlisle, eventually working as a barber. He was a man of modest means, but (at least after the war) he owned a cow and two small houses, one of which he rented. When war came, Hays enlisted as a private in the Pennsylvania State Artillery in 1777; this unit subsequently passed into Continental service under Colonel Proctor as the Fourth Continental Artillery Regiment, a company of which was in action at Monmouth.[32] Like many other women of the war years, particularly those who lacked the means to live independently, Mary followed her husband into the army. In 1778 she was probably around twenty-four.

In fact, there is little direct evidence of Mary Hays's exploits during the battle, and the documentation that does exist is contradictory. Joseph Plumb Martin, a Connecticut infantryman who actually watched a woman in action at Monmouth, insisted that whoever she was, she served next to her husband on a gun crew. Indeed, Martin, who told his story more than a half century after the battle, remembered some astonishing details:

> One little incident happened during the heat of the cannonade, which I was eye-witness to, and which I think would be unpardonable not to mention. A woman whose husband belonged to the artillery and who was then attached to a piece in the engagement, attended with her husband at the piece the whole time. While in the act of reaching [for] a cartridge and having one of her feet as far before the other as she could step, a cannon shot from the enemy passed directly between her legs without doing any other damage than carrying away all the lower part of her petticoat. Looking at it with apparent unconcern, she observed it was lucky it did not pass a little higher, for in that case it might have carried away something else, and continued her occupation.[33]

One is tempted to dismiss Martin's account as an old soldier's tale. Supposedly there were other witnesses to the miraculous cannon shot and the young woman's unflappable response; if it actually happened, Martin's comrades must have seen something—but no one else mentioned it (at least no one that we know of). On the other hand, his narrative of the Monmouth campaign is fairly lengthy and remarkably accurate except for obvious embroidery; other evidence corroborates virtually every important aspect of it. At least Martin was in accord with the popular notion that the woman was attached to the artillery, and his story comports with the service record of Private Hays. But again, there is no way to connect Martin's female artillerist with Hays, and the infantryman never called her Molly, much less Molly Pitcher.[34]

During the nineteenth century, the artillery connection received considerable embellishment. In its most polished version, Mary, or as the legend has her, "Molly," was not a gunner, sweating and working alongside the men. Rather, she had the slightly more genteel role of carrying water—thus Molly "Pitcher"—to the gun crews. Assuming for the moment that Molly was Mary Hays, the story has it that sometime during the cannonade, William was hit or fell temporarily through heat exhaustion. (The latter is more likely, as William's name never appeared on a rebel casualty list.) With her husband out of action, Molly supposedly picked up his rammer and helped keep the gun in action. At least there was an element of truth to the scenario. Keeping the gunners (and horses) supplied with water was an unsung but important job; normal cannon fire required swabbing between rounds, and at Monmouth the gunners themselves needed to drink in order to avoid dehydration in the brutal heat. For a woman to serve the artillery by providing drinking water was no rarity in eighteenth-century armies.[35] But the role Martin described—carrying ammunition from the box to the loader—is far more plausible than the myth of Molly wielding a rammer. As historian John Todd White has correctly observed, at least Martin expressed no surprise at seeing a woman with the guns or on the battlefield.[36]

There could easily have been more than one Molly Pitcher at Monmouth—there probably was. If Martin saw a woman working a gun on the left, local legend holds that a young woman either carried water or helped crew a gun on the right. New Jersey historian Frank R. Stockton, writing in the late nineteenth century and repeating an anecdote from even earlier sources, spun an apocryphal but persistent tale of a woman fighting with the artillery of Nathanael

Greene; this would have been in Du Plessis's crews on Combs Hill. After the battle Greene supposedly presented her to Washington, who made her a sergeant and had her formally review the troops.[37] There is no factual basis for any of this, and any public presentation of a woman gunner to the commander in chief would have received some reliable mention. The story (and it is no more than that) at least conforms with prevailing views that women were present and more than bystanders during the battle.

There is better evidence for yet another woman in the center of the line. On 3 July Dr. Albigence Waldo, surgeon for the First Connecticut Regiment, wrote his wife of a remarkable story told him by an infantry officer:

> One of the camp women I must give a little praise to. Her gallant, whom she attended in battle, being shot down, she immediately took up his gun and cartridges and like a Spartan heroine fought with astonishing bravery, discharging the piece with as much regularity as any solder present. This a wounded officer, whom I dressed, told me he did see himself, she being in his platoon.

This anonymous woman most likely fought during Wayne's late-afternoon attack on the 1st British Grenadiers. Another memory of her may be preserved in a pension application. In 1840 one Rebecca Clendenin, the widow of Sergeant John Clendenin, swore in her pension application that her husband spoke frequently of a "Captain Molly" at Monmouth; he told of seeing her carrying canteens to the troops. Sergeant Clendenin was a survivor of the Third Pennsylvania Regiment, one of the units that Wayne led against the British grenadiers later in the afternoon (discussed in the following chapter).[38]

The presence of other "Mollies" with the troops, however, if not verifiable through documentary evidence, would not have been unusual in an army that brought women on campaign.[39] Indeed, one can ask why Mary Hays or any other woman should have been the only one on the field. If Mary Hays was *one* of the Molly Pitchers of Monmouth fame—and there seems little doubt she was—it is at least possible to conclude her story. She ended her days back in Carlisle. Widowed about 1788, she remarried to a John McCauley (variously spelled "McCalla," "McCawly," and others). She lived with her son, John, and his family, poor but not impoverished. Mary was something of a local celebrity, and her neighbors accepted the prevailing belief that she had been on the field at Monmouth. Those who knew or spoke about her during her later years recalled her delight in spinning tales of serving a cannon during the battle; there was no mention of her telling of carrying water or a pitcher. Neighbors insisted she swore as well as any soldier, smoked, and enjoyed a chew of tobacco—all of this with a generous nature and kind heart.[40] In 1806 Mary received title to the bounty lands due William Hays, which she promptly sold, and in 1822, without requiring a great deal of proof, Pennsylvania granted her a pension of forty dollars per year on the basis of her Revolutionary War service without any specific mention of Monmouth. Not everyone in Carlisle believed her story, but most did or at least wished it to be true. Mary died in 1832; the citizens of Carlisle later (over forty years later) supplied a grave marker proclaiming her "Renowned in History as 'Molly Pitcher,' the Heroine of Monmouth."[41] Mary Hays McCauley was certainly at Monmouth, although her role in the battle is anything but clear, and she certainly was not the only woman there. Any new monument would properly have it "Molly *Pitchers*"—plural. Until then, Mary (or Molly, if you will) must stand in for all of the women with the armies, and she should be remembered in that light.

By the late afternoon the cannonade had blazed through its second hour. Spectators and participants—legendary and actual—had witnessed something they would remember for the rest of their lives. But they had seen little else beyond cannon fire. While the guns roared, neither side had attempted anything significant with infantry or cavalry. Washington successfully had established his defensive line, and Clinton had decided not to attack it. Thus, from roughly 1:30 P.M. to shortly after 3:30 P.M., the Battle of Monmouth was essentially a standoff. That, however, was about to change.

CHAPTER 15

Death in the Afternoon

The Battle of Detachments

The furious artillery duel was something of a respite for Clinton. Unlike Washington, he had no need to make rapid deployments, and after pulling his leading elements back from the West Morass—he had a strong force posted near the Hedgerow to cover the grenadiers as they retired over the bridge—he was content to wait out the cannonade. With the fighting seemingly stabilized, he rode to the rear "to attend to matters in that quarter."[1] No doubt he took the opportunity to assess the condition of his army, as he knew his men were exhausted, and to learn what he could of Lieutenant General Knyphausen's progress. Thus from his perspective, the lull in the battle was no bad thing. Every minute that Washington stayed west of the morass was a minute more Knyphausen had to move the baggage train out of harm's way. It also appeared that the rebel commander, safe on his high ground, was not about to commit to a larger fight. Under the circumstances, Clinton made a relatively quick decision not to renew any infantry assault. There was no point. Any movement against the American center would only meet withering artillery fire and result in massive losses, and while his 3rd Brigade and light units had flanked the American left, options there seemed at a dead end as well. The royal commander in chief considered a further attack anywhere would be unprofitable given his opponent's strength and the abominable weather.

Clinton also understood Washington's position. The American would not have to accept a fight to the finish even if the British launched a full-scale attack. Indeed, while Clinton could not have known it at the time, Washington's disposition of his reserve at Englishtown reflected just such a reluctance for a showdown. If necessary, the rebel commander easily could back away from any real trouble. With more men and without the brutal heat, Sir Henry later wrote his sisters, he might have attempted a major blow. "But with the thermometer at 96—when people fell dead in the street, and even in their houses—what could be done at midday in a hot pine barren, loaded with everything that [the] poor soldier carries? It breaks my heart," he concluded, "that I was obliged under those cruel circumstances" to do any fighting at all.[2]

Yet those "cruel circumstances" would oblige the King's weary soldiers to fight again. The renewed struggle would be a contest of detachments. Different units would engage consecutively on the British right and, in the center, then would come under attack from the far left. For the Americans, of course, the sequence was the same but the directions reversed. The Continentals would fight initially on their left, then the center, and finally would stage a dramatic artillery attack from their right. In all, this phase of the battle would last little more than an hour—but time enough to inflict some of the heaviest casualties of the day.

The Hedgerow and Combs Hill

Clinton had chosen to end the battle and now sought to get his forward units safely away and catch up with Knyphausen. Sir Henry feared that the light troops and the 3rd Brigade on his right were too far from the support of his main body. Accordingly, he ordered them to retire to the relative safety of his position in the Hedgerow area. Receiving his orders, Major General Grey put his units in motion. A battalion of the 42nd Foot remained in the Sutfin orchard to discourage any enemy initiative, while the departing troops were glad to leave the heat and patriot fire they had endured.

Brigadier General Erskine's command—the 1st Battalion of Light Infantry and the Queen's Rangers—was with Grey as well. Erskine, "a Cool, Penetrating officer," appreciating that Clinton's attack had stalled and that his men were vulnerable, led them south to join Grey.[3] It was a short march, although anything but uneventful. As they crossed North Brook, a sudden thrust by militia light horse caught a company of lights by surprise and threatened to cut them off. The lights' commander, Captain William Dansey, had to lead his men "up to our middle [waist] in a Bog to get away." He lost one man prisoner but no one was killed or wounded before the militia retreated.[4] Crossing the same brook, one of the "grasshoppers" with the retreating British became mired and risked falling into

American hands. Lieutenant Aeneas Shaw of the Queen's Rangers quickly wheeled his kilted Highland company about and secured the artillery piece in a brief charge.[5] The patriot irregulars failed to interrupt the retreat, but they were troublesome—and bold.

While Erskine and Grey were in motion, the Hedgerow, opposite the American center, became a key position. The bulk of Clinton's artillery was there as well as the two grenadier battalions. These were the survivors of the 2nd Battalion of Grenadiers who had crossed the West Morass with Monckton, as well as the troops of the 1st Battalion, posted at the Hedgerow to cover the withdrawal of the 2nd after Monckton's repulse. Now the grenadiers would hold the position against any American foray across the morass that might threaten the retreat of Erskine and Grey. Clinton had no reason to expect any real trouble—an expectation quickly shattered by a nasty surprise from his left. The Hedgerow had come under artillery fire from Combs Hill.

The British commander owed his sudden discomfort to none other than the indefatigable Lieutenant Colonel Rhea, who probably saw more of the battlefield on 28 June than anyone else. Having finished guiding the Continentals to Perrine's Hill, Rhea quickly pointed out to Washington the possibility of establishing patriot guns on Combs Hill; the position would anchor the extreme right of the American line and provide a commanding field of fire across the rolling terrain. This was only minutes after 2:00 P.M., and the commander in chief immediately agreed. He sent Rhea galloping after Major General Greene, who already was marching to the right with four guns and enough infantry (Woodford's Virginians) to cover them and almost three miles away by the time the officer started after him. Rhea caught up with the major general around 2:45 P.M., and Greene ordered the march for Combs Hill. The column arrived about an hour later, and Rhea sent a brief note to Washington announcing that patriot cannon were minutes from opening "upon their left flank hoping soon to silence them near your Senter."[6] The guns roared at about 3:45 P.M., roughly the time the rest of the cannonade was beginning to lift.

Indeed, the fire from Combs Hill helped end the cannonade. The man commanding Greene's artillery was a Frenchman, Brevet Lieutenant Colonel Thomas Antoine, chevalier de Mauduit du Plessis. Trained at a French artillery academy, he had journeyed to America with other French volunteers and joined the Continental

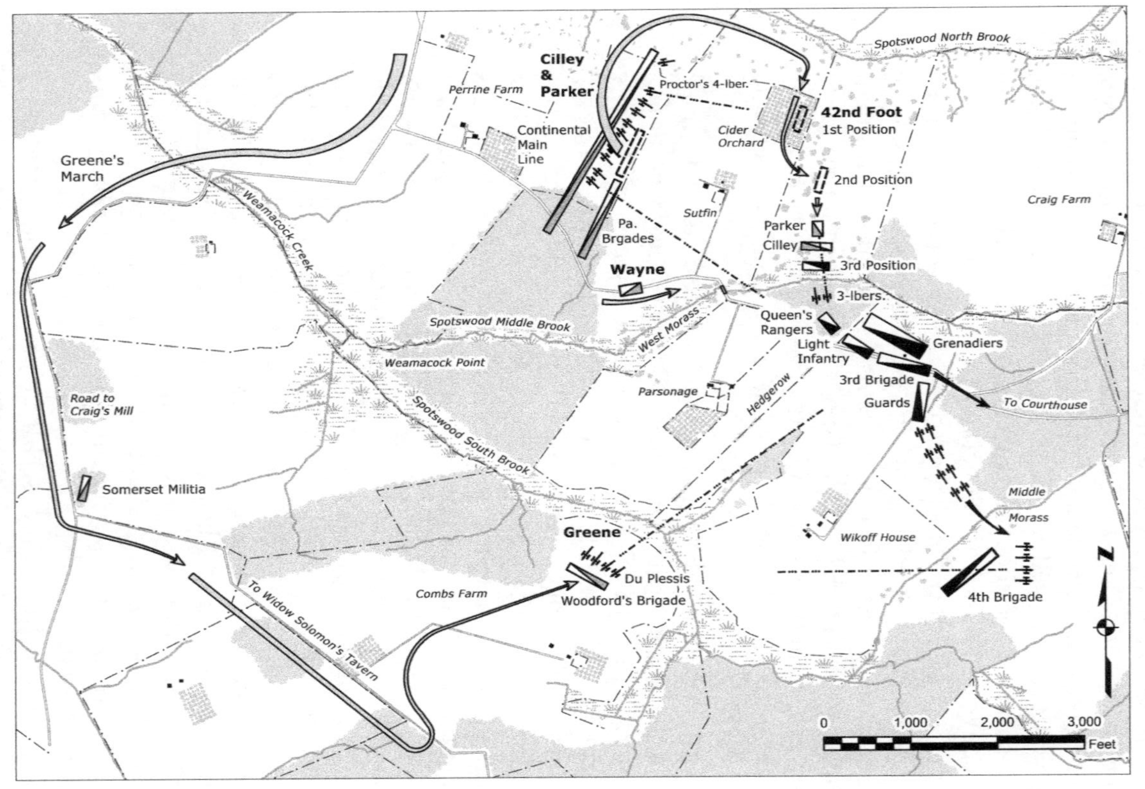

Washington resumes the offensive: Outflanked by Greene's appearance on Combs Hill, the British begin withdrawing, while Washington sends Cilley, Parker, and Wayne to harass Clinton's rear units. Map by Garry Wheeler Stone. Copyright © 2016 by the University of Oklahoma Press.

Army as a captain in April 1777. Du Plessis proved a first-class soldier. He fought well at Germantown and Red Bank, earning his brevet rank. At Valley Forge he capably assisted in retraining the Continental artillery and earned the respect of Knox, Washington, and Steuben.[7] At Monmouth he again demonstrated his worth. From Combs Hill the French artillerist had a clear view of the British artillery and grenadiers near the Hedgerow, and his four guns quickly made things intolerable for them. Even if he had wanted to open a new assault, Clinton had no way to respond. Combs Hill had open marshy ground in front, and an uphill charge would have been suicidal; a flank attack would have entailed a march of some five miles. Under the circumstances, the best alternative for the redcoats was to move to safer ground. Clinton repositioned the grenadiers on the north end of the Hedgerow in the barrack meadow, where the reverse slope shielded them from du Plessis; then, about 4:00 P.M., still intent on breaking off the action for the day, he pulled out all but one of his artillery pieces. With nothing left to shoot at, the patriot guns on Combs Hill fell silent.

"You Are the Boys I Want": Colonel Cilley and the 42nd Foot

Clinton had solved his problem at the Hedgerow, but he still had to complete the withdrawal of units on his right. The Americans were just as concerned with the same troops. While the redcoats on the patriot left made no aggressive moves for over two hours, Washington had no sense of their intentions. Some officers remained concerned that an attack on the left was a real possibility.[8] To the commander in chief, however, the British appeared to be relatively isolated, perhaps even vulnerable (he shared Clinton's thinking on this). With the rest of the field apparently stable and British artillery fire slackening (this was around 4:00 P.M., as Clinton's guns began pulling out), the enemy troops around Sutfin's seemed an opportune target. But the general needed to know more about their situation. At this point (probably around 4:10 P.M.) Washington turned to Major Aaron Ogden, adjutant of the First New Jersey. The major had spent the afternoon detached as an aide to Stirling, carrying orders through what he remembered as "a heavy and destructive cannonade from each side." The commander in chief asked Ogden if his horse was still serviceable—the heat being as hard on animals as on men—and when he answered in the affirmative, the general sent him across North Brook to reconnoiter. The major, who earlier had worried about a British threat on the left, now saw the enemy withdrawing and within fifteen minutes or so reported as much to Washington. Immediately, Ogden recalled, the general announced, "We will advance in our turn."[9] It was not quite 4:30 P.M.

Washington's statement was simple and direct, yet it represented one of his most important decisions of the day—he was going on the offensive. It was a choice he did not have to make. His army already had fought well, having (from their perspective) stopped Clinton's westward drive and inflicting damaging casualties on some of the enemy's best units. Washington reasonably could have remained on the defensive inviting a new British attack, one he would have welcomed. Or he simply could have waited for Clinton to leave. Either way he could claim credit for a good day's work. Instead, Washington acted on the aggressive intent he had harbored since the Continentals closed within striking distance of Clinton (the intent he failed to impress on Lee). He had no thought of bringing on a general engagement, but he wanted to hit the withdrawing 3rd Brigade. He would venture a limited attack, but it would be the first patriot offensive action since Lee's advance some six hours earlier.

Initially, the Continental movement would pit a battalion of New England "picked men" against the 2nd Field Battalion of the vaunted 42nd Foot (Royal Highlanders). The event would be more of a skirmish than a pitched battle, but it set in motion a chain of events that would bring truly savage fighting later in the afternoon. These actions would say a great deal about the capabilities and morale of both armies.

Under Washington's eye, Stirling organized a limited counterattack.[10] He chose two battalions of picked men from Scott's detachment, those who had remained after Scott's two other battalions moved into reserve at Englishtown. Commanding the lead battalion was Colonel Joseph Cilley of the New Hampshire Line. Cilley was an early patriot and had been in the field since 1775; by 1777 he was colonel of the First New Hampshire and a hardened veteran.[11] On the twenty-eighth he commanded a unit of some 350 men drawn from five of the army's brigades, with roughly twenty officers and men "picked" from eighteen different battalions—probably their best platoons or ad hoc collections of their best men. The other battalion was under Colonel Richard Parker of the First Virginia. Parker had 250 men, although their composition remains unknown. As events transpired, Parker would not get into action.[12]

Cilley received very general orders. The colonel remembered being told "to go and see what I could do with the enemy's right wing."[13] Given the mixture of regimental contributions to his unit, however, Cilley was not familiar with all his officers and men and had trouble finding some platoons of the improvised battalion. Some forty years later, Private Martin recalled the colonel's search for his troops: Cilley "passed along in front of our line, inquiring for General Varnum's men. We answered, 'Here we are.' He did not hear us in his hurry, but passed on. In a few minutes, he returned, making the same inquiry. We again answered, 'Here we are.' 'Ah!' said he, 'you are the boys I want to assist in driving those rascals from yon orchard.'"[14] His men found, Cilley led them to the attack. Behind the northerners came Colonel Parker with his battalion. They moved from Stirling's line shortly after 4:30 P.M., perhaps a half hour after the worst of the cannonade had lifted.

The Continentals advanced to take the Highlanders in the flank and to avoid screening them from the guns on Perrine's Hill. Cilley led his column north into the North Brook valley, the slopes of which were occupied by rough pastures. Concealed behind the hill crest and bushes, the Americans advanced in column to within less than 200 yards of the orchard. Then, no longer able to remain concealed, Cilley swung his platoons into line and advanced on the British. It was a good beginning and a tactical surprise, executed without confusion or delay, a maneuver that illustrated the maturing discipline and tactical capabilities of the Continental Line.

The surprised Highlanders responded like the professionals they were, moving from behind the apple trees and forming to meet Cilley's men. But they were bluffing. While their numbers almost equaled those of the advancing Americans—about 275 to 325—the Highlanders were in an indefensible position. As soon as they saw that the Americans intended to close, the battalion commander withdrew his men south through the orchard.[15]

Infantry action began at this point. Cilley, his advance impeded by the orchard fences, sent a platoon or two from his right to skirmish with the withdrawing Highlanders while the rest of the battalion advanced in formation. The skirmishers raced after the Scots, pursuing "in no order," harassing them with musket fire. Private

Martin, part of the rebel advance, passed through the orchard and noticed a number of enemy dead, killed earlier by artillery fire. Well-led veterans, the Highlanders were not flustered by a few skirmishers. South of the orchard, they filed east through the fence and a swale separating the Sutfin central and east fields. Battlefield archaeology has revealed the British commander reformed his battalion about two-thirds of the way up the opposite slope, giving his men the advantage of height and concealing them from Stirling's artillery. As the Continentals neared this position, Cilley wheeled his line up to a rail fence and began dismantling it. In the few seconds required to down the stacked rails, the 42nd fired a long-range volley and filed off from their left toward the Middle Brook and the rear of the retreating British column.

Equally coolly, Cilley's men advanced with shouldered arms, marching east across the swale, then wheeling south toward the brook. Ahead of them jogged the skirmishers. Martin recalled being so close to the retreating enemy, "I could distinguish everything about them." He drew a bead on one man, aiming "directly between his shoulders," but failed to see him fall because of the "fire and smoke." "I took as deliberate aim at him as ever I did at any game in my life," Martin recalled. "But after all, I hope I did not kill him, although I intended to at the time."[16] So far the rivals had engaged in largely bloodless movements in which both sides had taken advantage of topographic and manmade features. At the brook, however, maneuvering was over, and the fighting intensified.

The 42nd reformed along the north edge of the Middle Brook meadow, a bushy pasture. Their position was strong. Some British light infantry, with two 3-pounder "grasshoppers," covered them from a bluff south of the brook.[17] Down the gentle slope toward the Highlanders marched Cilley's picked men. Soon the 3-pounders began plying them with case shot, then the 42nd began crashing volleys of musketry. Undeterred and unwilling to slow their advance while under artillery fire, the picked battalion advanced in formation with shouldered muskets. "We had got within 4 rods of them," recalled Lieutenant Colonel Dearborn, "when our men dressed very coolly and we gave them a very heavy fire from the whole battalion."[18] The attack then continued, the men advancing between volleys with "charged bayonet." When one Continental checked his cartridge box afterward, he found twelve rounds missing—he had been firing furiously.[19] But the Continentals took losses as well.

Martin graphically described the deadly results of a ball from one of the British 3-pounders: "The first shot they gave us . . . cut off the thigh bone of a captain, just above the knee, and the whole heel of a private in the rear of him." The unfortunate officer was Edmund Munro of Massachusetts; the wound was mortal.[20]

At this point the commander of the 42nd saw no point in continuing the contest. His battalion had completed its mission, buying time for the light infantry and the rest of the 3rd Brigade to pull back safely toward Clinton's main position near the Hedgerow. Sacrificing men in further point-blank exchanges with the New Englanders would have served no purpose. Thus, about 5:00 P.M., the Scots withdrew across the brook in a fighting retrograde. The Continentals came on. Martin remembered Cilley shouting, "'Come, my boys, reload your pieces, and we will give them a set-off.' We did so, and gave them the parting salute, and the firing on both sides ceased." Cilley later regretted not pursuing the British farther but explained, "the extreme heat of the weather was such that several of my men died of the heat." Private Martin recalled, "[we] laid ourselves down under the fences and bushes to take breath, for we had need of it. I presume that everyone has heard of the heat of that day, but none can realize it that did not feel it."[21]

The brief action was over. For those engaged, however, it had been no game. Presumably the Continentals, as the attackers, suffered the heaviest casualties, but the subject is sketchy. We have only Martin's recollection of the crippling cannon shot and Cilley's report on fatalities from the heat. No doubt other men were hit, but regimental muster rolls do not identify where losses occurred. We have more knowledge of the 42nd's losses. In addition to the dead Highlanders lying in the apple orchard, Martin remembered other enemy bodies being plundered along the brook.[22] Yet with all sources considered—including Clinton's initial casualty return and the regimental history of the 42nd—it appears that the engagement with Cilley's command probably cost no more than three or four Highlanders killed or mortally wounded.[23] The officers had maneuvered expertly and brought the battalion out of trouble; the unit had paid a price, but it was relatively small.

Colonel Cilley had fought boldly. His men had advanced against one of the most feared regiments in the British army at roughly even odds and had seen it retreat. In so doing, the Americans had risked little. If the second battalion of the 42nd had stood to fight, Parker would have brought his battalion of 250 picked men on line and taken the British in the flank. Had Cilley waited for Parker to come up before closing with the Highlanders, it is likely there would have been no contact as the additional delay might well have given the redcoats time to withdraw unopposed. Even if the patriot foray had little direct military significance, the Continentals still had reason to be pleased with themselves. To have one of the best units of the King's army turn their backs on them was a psychological victory of the first magnitude.

British reactions were less dramatic—indeed, almost dismissive. Major André, for example, commented only that the rebels were "unsuccessful in endeavoring to annoy" the retreating column. A grenadier officer, noting the action on the British right, thought Erskine had brought off his men "in good order" before superior numbers. Captain John Peebles recorded only that the British thought it "improper" to push farther on the left and simply retired.[24] Clinton admitted, however, that the retreat of the 3rd Brigade and the light infantry had been challenging, impeded by the difficult terrain, rebel batteries, and the burden of their wounded.[25] As the retreating units struggled to reach Clinton, Washington kept track of their progress—the rebel commander was not necessarily done with them.

"Pick out the King Birds": The Fight in the Center

As his lights and the 3rd Brigade were disengaging, Clinton felt that he could pull back with mission accomplished and honor intact. There was no point in staying on the field longer. Accordingly, he issued orders for a general withdrawal toward Freehold. It should have been a relatively simple retrograde. Yet as if to demonstrate that even the veteran British army could botch a routine maneuver, the withdrawal misfired. Clinton wanted a phased withdrawal: the grenadier battalions were to stay in position near the Hedgerow until the 3rd Brigade and light troops were completely out of danger. Instead, as the general later explained, "from my instructions not being properly understood, or some other cause," all units but the 1st Grenadiers Battalion got out right away. The premature departure posed an immediate danger by leaving the still retreating 3rd Brigade farther forward than Clinton's main body and lagging behind on the British right.[26] It also left the 1st Grenadiers isolated near the north end of the Hedgerow. Here Washington may have seen an opportunity.

With Cilley's men still engaged and emboldened by their apparent success, the patriot commanding general looked for another opportunity. The view from Perrine's Hill allowed only glimpses of British troop movements, but it was clear enough that the redcoats had retreated on the rebel left, and patriots certainly knew that the enemy artillery had pulled out. Were the British vulnerable near the Hedgerow? Despite his lack of any solid intelligence, Washington ordered another limited advance. Through Stirling, he ordered Anthony Wayne to lead a detachment of Pennsylvanians *back* over the West Morass bridge.[27] There is no reason to believe the commander in chief had any specific target in mind, and Wayne's instructions probably were as general Cilley's. If so—and to paraphrase Cilley's orders—they were as simple as: "Go and see what you can do with any British you can find across the morass." That is, Wayne was to advance from the Continental center and pursue any opportunity.

This time, however, it was the turn of the patriots to make a hash of things. Wayne had intended to take with him a command considerably larger than Cilley's. In fact, he wanted three Pennsylvania brigades, which would have given him something over 1,300 men. In his view, this was strength enough to close with the British and then to "improve the advantage" in the event of success. But the mission suffered from confusion at the outset. Wayne's fellow Pennsylvanian, Major General Arthur St. Clair, then serving as an aide to Washington, quite fortuitously overheard the request for the three brigades. St. Clair promptly ordered the three brigades not to advance and allowed only one brigade to join Wayne. The two generals were not friends, and Wayne (in a letter intended for Washington) later put down St. Clair's action to either "ignorance" or "envy." As an aide to the commander in chief, the major general actually had no place in the chain of command. As far as Wayne knew, St. Clair was not acting on any instructions from Washington but merely pulled rank to deny the brigadier his requested number of troops. Furious, the aggressive Pennsylvanian never forgave St. Clair, but he had no time to argue the matter at present.[28]

If Wayne was disappointed in the size of his strike force, his ire was misdirected. St. Clair was no genius—his military career, which stretched well beyond the Revolution, was checkered—but he would not have intervened in an operation Washington had initiated without sufficient cause. And the "sufficient cause" was almost certainly the commander in chief. In ordering the new advance, Washington was *not* courting a major action or the possibility of damage to a substantial part of his army. The modest size of Cilley's party was more indicative of the general's thinking. An attack by three brigades was something else, quite contrary to an effort to strike Clinton without incurring unnecessary risk to the Continentals. An assault in such strength would have invited a major response, with Wayne too far forward for Washington to support adequately even if, as the brigadier put it, there was an "advantage" to "improve." In all likelihood St. Clair did nothing more than act on instructions from Washington. Wayne evidently realized as much after the fact because he never sent the letter in which he vented his spleen at his fellow Pennsylvanian.

Making the best of what he considered a bad situation, it seems Wayne took only the Third Pennsylvania Brigade and put it on the road toward the bridge. The brigade was made up of the Third, Sixth, Ninth, and Twelfth Pennsylvania Regiments (or at least elements of them) as well as Oliver Spencer's and William Malcolm's Additional Continental Regiments. Both Additionals were brigaded with the Pennsylvanians; Malcolm's, composed mostly of Pennsylvanians, was commanded this day by Lieutenant Colonel Aaron Burr. Spencer's troops were mostly Jerseymen, and Spencer led them personally. In all, Wayne's force was not much larger than Cilley's, probably around 400 men of all ranks—far fewer than the force he wanted.[29]

Wayne was his aggressive self even with only a brigade. He marched about 5:15 P.M., just after Cilley stopped pursuing the Highlanders. His men were relatively fresh and their advance was swift, although at this point the exact movements of the Continentals troops are conjectural. Without question, they crossed the West Morass bridge unopposed. Wayne probably left his men marching east on the road while he, his dragoon escort, and a fellow officer or two rode ahead to reconnoiter. As they moved up the hill, they found a battalion of British grenadiers marching south, heading for the Middle Morass causeways. No other enemy unit was west of the Middle Morass.

The 1st and 2nd Battalions of Grenadiers had remained, hunkered down, in the hay meadow along the Middle Brook. There

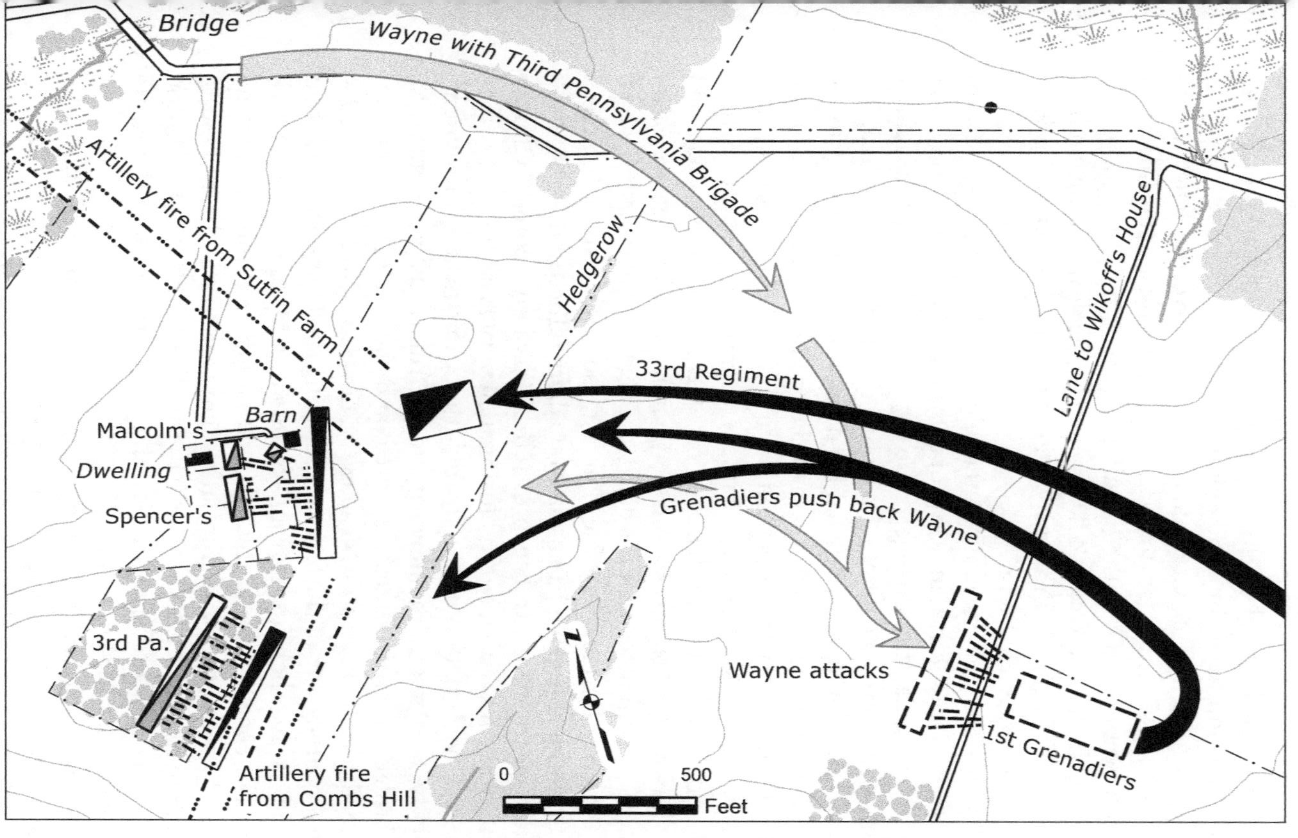

Wayne attacks the British rear unit, the 1st Grenadiers, and is pushed back until rescued by the Continental artillery. Map by Garry Wheeler Stone. Copyright © 2016 by the University of Oklahoma Press.

they were safe from du Plessis's guns and could cover the retreat of Erskine's detachment and the 3rd Brigade. After Grey's rear unit was safely on the road to the courthouse, the 2nd Battalion of the Grenadiers followed. In the hayfield Lieutenant Colonel William Meadows held his 1st Grenadiers, either to give the lengthy column time to escape or (as noted earlier) from a misunderstanding of Clinton's orders.[30] Then the battalion began to move south, probably along the lane to young Wikoff's house. Meadow's intention may have been to join and withdraw with the troops of the 4th Brigade. If so, he never reached them.

Before Colonel Meadow's grenadiers could turn east toward the ravine, Wayne's men were upon them. The grenadiers were slow to recognize their danger, probably assuming that the smaller Continental unit was merely shadowing them off the battlefield. But Wayne wanted blood, and he led his detachment of Pennsylvanians straight into the grenadiers, perhaps before they could form. In the first minute or so, the rebels fired three volleys into the British. The battalion, badly shot up earlier in the day, was now unsupported. The 2nd Grenadiers had marched off, and the Royal Artillery had withdrawn, leaving only a single 6-pounder. (In fact, one grenadier officer was convinced that the departure of the artillery had triggered the American attack—untrue, but a reasonable assumption from the British perspective.) The 1st Grenadiers rallied and fought back gamely, but patriot fire began to tell. "This brave corps," Clinton wrote of the battalion, began "losing men very fast."[31]

Sir Henry had not anticipated the Continental movement. Quickly, he sized up the new threat: the Americans had come over the bridge "in great force," he noted, and their advance found him alarmed for the safety of Meadows. The 1st Grenadiers formed—probably along one of the fences paralleling the lane—and held their ground, taking their losses from Wayne's fire. Meadows was a tough and experienced officer, a grenadier with a superb combat record and whose performance won him an assignment as a military aide to George III by the end of the year.[32] Riding close to the scene, Clinton realized that his orderly withdrawal was threatened, and he saw no alternative but to stand and fight.

In some anxiety, the general searched the field for potential reinforcements. Fortuitously, he spotted the 33rd Foot moving up. Luckily as well, the 33rd was a unit with an excellent reputation; its colonel was none other than Lieutenant General Charles

Earl Cornwallis.[33] The regimental commander, Lieutenant Colonel James Webster, apparently was heading for the sound of the guns on his own initiative. The 33rd pressed on, and a relieved Clinton sent Webster's troops immediately into the fray. The subsequent action may have been the bitterest of the day. The numbers, though, were against the Continentals; Wayne was now facing in the neighborhood of 1,000 redcoats. The grenadier battalion had a prebattle muster roll of approximately 760 men, and even after losses from the heat and the fighting earlier in the day, there were probably still some 650 to 700 Grenadiers in the field to go after Wayne. The 33rd Foot probably added another 300 to 350 men to British strength.[34]

Wayne was in his glory. Having had a taste of combat earlier, he was now in a classic showdown with some of the best soldiers in the British army. Quickly, however, the larger numbers and spirit of the grenadiers began to tell. Formed in semi-open order, their line threatened to flank Wayne's, and the Americans began backing up. (North of young Wikoff's house today, a scatter of impacted musket balls has helped locate the action. One ball from a British grenadier's musket bears the impression of coarse linen fabric from a Pennsylvanian's pack.) In a vivid recollection of the action, Pennsylvania lieutenant Alexander Dow saw men in his own company and in other units go down around him. These included some important officers. In the Third Pennsylvania, Lieutenant Colonel Rudolph Bunner took a lethal hit; he was the highest-ranking rebel fatality at Monmouth. One of Washington's favorite junior officers, former schoolteacher Lieutenant Colonel Francis Barber was wounded in the side. Late of the Third New Jersey and a talented light infantryman, Barber was serving as Stirling's adjutant general; his own impetuosity, not any requirements of his office, brought him to the frontline. Aaron Burr tumbled to the ground with his horse shot from under him.[35]

According to traditional accounts, as the British advance gathered momentum, Wayne remained cool. Watching the developing enemy charge, he told his men, or at least those near enough to hear him, to hold their fire. He wanted the grenadiers and the 33rd to get within range of a sure kill, then have the Continentals go for the enemy officers. "Steady, steady," the general called down this line, "wait for the word, then pick out the King birds."[36]

Lieutenant Dow, on the Continental left, may or may not have heard Wayne, as he had a more immediate concern. The lieutenant had three of his men killed and found his platoon "close pressed" as the enemy closed in. It was terrifying. Through the smoke he saw a mounted British officer—a man he mistakenly took to be Lieutenant Colonel Monckton—shouting "com on my brave boyes for the honour of Great Britain." Dow feared that the horseman was actually going to ride him down. Ordering his platoon to aim at the rider and the men with him, the Pennsylvanian gave the order to fire. The volley crashed and the target "droped," shot dead, or so Dow believed. British casualty reports, however, listed no senior "King birds" lost in the late afternoon's fighting, and no one knows who the platoon brought down, if anyone. The smoke and confusion easily could have left Dow mistaken; he certainly was mistaken regarding Monckton.[37] The most likely casualty of the volley was the officer's horse. Dow, grateful to be alive, saw the British charge slowed, and Colonel Spencer ordered him to fall back.

Slowed, the redcoats nevertheless maintained their advance. Pushed back through the Hedgerow, Wayne's formation began to disintegrate as Continental units hurried to take cover in the buildings and enclosures of the Parsonage farm. As they fell back, an enemy ball tore through the throat of Adjutant Peter Taulman. Bleeding and dazed, he crawled behind the barn thinking that he had but moments to live. Two soldiers came to his aid. They were carrying him farther back when a musket ball blew the hat off of one of them; he fled. The other remained and helped Taulman off the battlefield.[38]

The grenadiers pursuing Dow and Taulman were sheltered from the Continental artillery by the ridge to their left and the Americans in front of them, but they had no shelter from the Continentals who had taken refuge in the Parsonage buildings and yards. Behind fences and walls, Malcolm's and Spencer's men were safe from a bayonet charge. A grenadier officer reported that his men "lost Considerable from a Firing from a Barn & a House."[39] Just to the south, the Third Pennsylvania, moving toward the safety of the Parsonage apple orchard, slowed to get over a rail fence. The pursuing grenadiers knew better than to let the men take cover behind it. Before the Continentals could reform, the British were on them, loading and firing, forcing Colonel Craig's troops back into the orchard. Now it was the grenadiers who had the advantage, but it was short lived.

Indeed, the British advance came to a quick and deadly halt. A round of case shot landed just short of the fence corner, scattering 1.5-ounce iron shot along the edge of the orchard.[40] It was the first of many such rounds. Caught in front of the Parsonage on open ground, the redcoats were now sitting ducks for patriot artillery on Combs Hill. Du Plessis sent a withering rain of shot ripping through the British left flank. It is worth considering what the grenadiers and the 33rd faced. Du Plessis had four guns. Based on the small-size iron case shot they were firing, the guns were most likely 3- or 4-pounders. With excellent crews, they could fire two or three aimed rounds per minute. A 4-pounder case round using 1.5-ounce iron shot contained about forty-four shots; a canister of lead musket balls would contain many more.[41] With all four guns firing at a rate of three rounds per minute, at any given minute over 500 pieces of hot metal were hurtling downrange. Aimed at formed infantry in enfilade (that is, from the side), multiple hits were as likely as not. One *unlikely* tale had a round shot traveling the length of a platoon line, knocking the muskets from the grip of every soldier without doing further harm. Reality was much worse. The storm of artillery staggered the redcoats, who were powerless to reply. The American guns "quailed them so much," one Continental recorded, that the enemy simply had to withdraw.[42] Virtually every account of this action, American and British, bore testimony to the terrible effectiveness of the fire from Combs Hill.[43] The British attack was over almost immediately. The grenadiers "Run Back," and once east of the Hedgerow, the vegetation and topography hid them from du Plessis's gunners. As the gap between Wayne's and Clinton's men opened, the gunners on the Perrine and Sutfin farms may have been able to fire a few solid shot at the retreating troops before they disappeared from view.[44]

In a technical sense, Clinton had won the fight with Wayne—the Americans had retreated—but his grenadiers and the 33rd Foot were licking their wounds as they moved out.[45] The weary troops withdrew just over a mile to high ground near Ker's house. They arrived shortly before 7:00 P.M. for some much needed rest, safe from the galling rebel artillery. It had been a trying afternoon, and the British withdrawal from the Parsonage area marked the end of the day's longest period of sustained infantry action.

The Final Gambit: Washington Probes and Clinton Retreats

For Washington, however, the day was not over. Clinton's retrograde invited a response, and he laid plans to strike a final blow. Around 6:00 P.M. the commander in chief sent a rider to the reserve with orders for Steuben to send what troops he could from Englishtown. Lee's men were assembled there, although they were in questionable condition after their long day in the sun; the timely arrival of Brigadier General John Paterson had augmented the reserve with four more fresh brigades (Paterson's, Brigadier General Peter Muhlenberg's, Weedon's, and the Second Maryland)—a large force of over 2,200 men—and the inspector general personally organized and led these units toward the front.[46] They arrived too late to do anything on Sunday but were at hand if fighting resumed the following day. Simultaneously, elements of the Pennsylvania units that had fought near the Parsonage held their position; the gore of the fighting lay all around them as they looked out over the now-quiet field. The British, sheltering at Ker's, knew Wayne was still around the Parsonage, but the royal army was not looking for another fight.

But across the West Morass, Washington was doing just that. Shortly before 7:00 P.M. the general ordered two detachments to go after Clinton's flanks. The first was under Brigadier General Enoch Poor of New Hampshire, who took his own brigade and a picked body of light infantry. Also along was a detachment of North Carolinians under Colonel Thomas Clark. Poor had done well at Saratoga the year before, but he had shared Lee's caution about any major confrontation with the British in New Jersey. He had a reputation as a steady officer, however, and had been part of Stirling's left wing during the earlier fighting that day. The general was to follow the road across the morass bridge to go after Clinton's right. Moving in concert with Poor would be the small Virginia Brigade of Brigadier General William Woodford, whose men had been with Greene and had supported the guns on Combs Hill. Now he would advance from the hill and try for the British left. Knox limbered guns to accompany Poor and "gall" the enemy's front.[47]

The two forces moved at about the same time. Poor crossed the bridge and left the road. He moved carefully through fields and patches of woods, seeking to conceal his advance toward the British left. Woodford picked his way through the boggy terrain at the base of Combs Hill, going for the enemy right.[48] Once across the West Morass bridge, the artillery, with a small supporting detachment, kept to the road. Unsure of how far they could go before the British saw them or what the redcoats would do if they did, caution ruled the patriot approach. In fact, the pace was too slow. Soon sunset made a continued advance impractical, and Washington called off the effort before either Poor or Woodford closed. He had these advanced troops lie on their arms near the Wikoff house, close enough to keep an eye on the enemy at Ker's. Behind Poor and Woodford, Stirling's brigades from the Perrine farm also moved up and took position, perhaps near the Hedgerow, the troops "lying down on the field amongst the dead."[49] On Perrine's Hill, the fresh troops Steuben brought from Englishtown replaced Stirling's men. Washington, who fully intended to renew the fighting on Monday morning, slept under an oak on a cloak he shared with Lafayette.[50]

The infantry of the two armies rested within a mile of each other, but their only contact during the evening was when Colonel Parker sent a company of his picked men to disturb the royal army's sleep. The Virginians probed forward until they found an enemy picket, fired three volleys, and returned unscathed.[51] Other than return fire from the pickets, the only opposition Washington's troops met as they moved forward were a few bursting shells from British 5.5-inch howitzers. In an ineffectual effort to keep the Continentals at a distance, Clinton had his artillerists randomly fire at the ground he had abandoned.[52]

The British commander had no intention of staying to fight on the twenty-ninth. There was no reason. He had ensured the escape of his baggage train, and with no prospect of inflicting a major wound on the rebels, he saw his job as the completion of his planned evacuation to New York. Clinton let his exhausted units rest for the time being, secure in their temporary camp. But about 11:00 P.M. the general began preparations to move out. His intention was to join Knyphausen, who by 6:00 P.M. had marched the baggage train and its escorts to a defensible encampment at Nut Swamp, some three miles from Middletown. Around midnight, Clinton quietly broke camp, slipped into the night, and left the battlefield to Washington.[53]

Poor's men never heard him go. In fact, the withdrawal was skillful and efficient (every bit as good as Washington's escape from Cornwallis after Second Trenton), but the exhausted and sleeping rebels could have done little to stop him had they noticed his departure.[54] Not all the redcoats left. "The wounded were brought into Freehold," Major André noted, "and those whose cases would admit of it, brought away when the Division marched." But some men were too badly injured to move; Clinton left four wounded officers and forty men in the village. As their comrades marched away, they remained under the care of several surgeons and medical personnel who volunteered to stay behind. It was galling—"mortifying," in the view of one officer—to leave the wounded to the Americans, but there was nothing else to be done; even if the men were in condition to travel, there were not enough wagons to carry them. Clinton trusted, rightly, to their humane treatment by Washington.[55]

At Nut Swamp Knyphausen awaited his chief. The Hessian general had done well on Sunday, losing no wagons and offering patriot militia and light horse no chance to strike a telling blow. There were some anxious moments, as local units made several attempts to penetrate the British security screen. John Hills, the British engineer who had risked his life to provide route intelligence for Clinton before the campaign opened, noted three incidents with the militia on a map of the march.[56] Two appear to have been only brushes with the dragoon escort. To escape the Continentals as much as possible, Knyphausen avoided the direct road to Middletown that crossed the upper branches of the Navesink River at Van Mater's and Van Doren's Mills. Instead, he marched farther east to take the road from Tinton Falls to Middletown. The next day Colonel John Neilson, First Middlesex Militia, wrote from Van Doren's Mill to excuse his failure to intercept the enemy baggage. He explained that the enemy had marched "Along the most private Roads in this part of the Country by which means they Evaded the Sharpest lookout. . . . [H]ad they come along the Road that no Person Doubted but they would come, great part of their Baggage must have fallen into our hands."[57]

But Knyphausen was up against a local man, Joshua Huddy, captain of the Monmouth County militia artillery company. Huddy kept an inn at "Jewstown"—now Colts Neck—just south of the road that the general's column was following. That morning Huddy had been southeast of Monmouth Court House at Richmond's Mill with most of the Monmouth militia and Daniel Morgan's light infantry. When Huddy learned that the British had marched and Colonel Morgan had no orders, the captain called for volunteers and hurried north with fifteen or sixteen men. About six-and-a-half miles east of the courthouse, Huddy found a gap in Knyphausen's flank guards and launched a wild bayonet attack on the baggage—stabbing horses, beating drivers with musket butts, and even overturning a few wagons. Quickly, the 40th Foot and some dragoons arrived. In the confused firing, two women marching with the baggage were killed, one of whom had been carrying her baby. The baggage guards

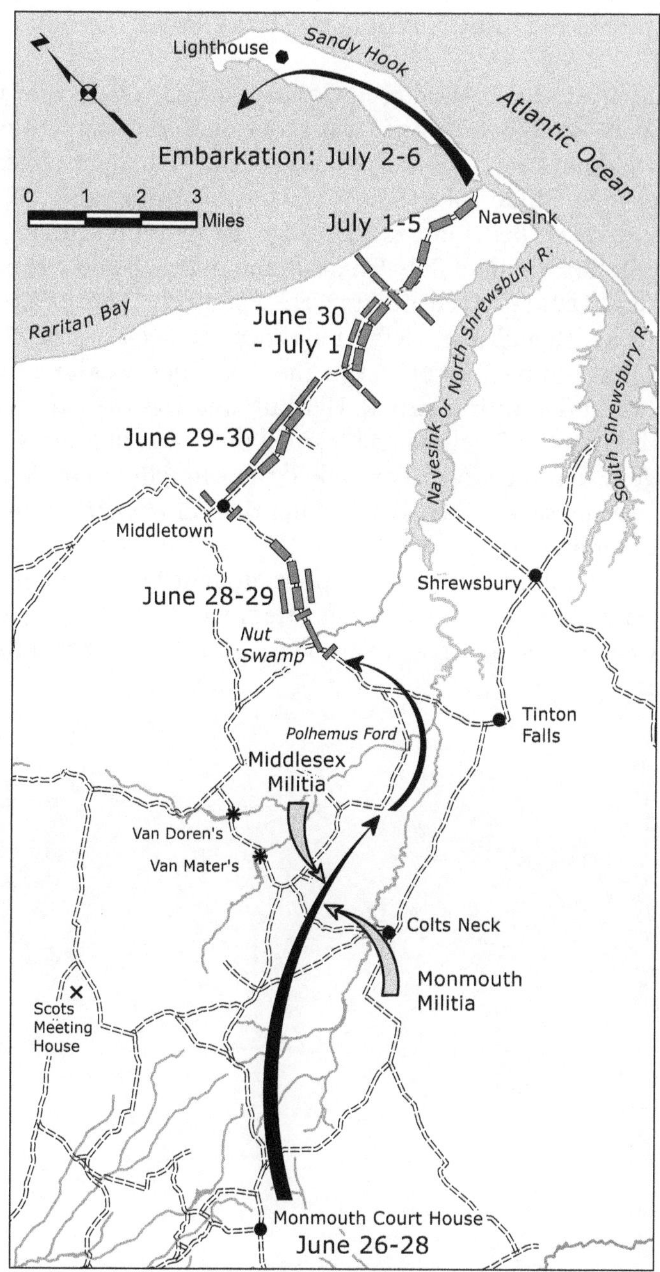

The British march route to Sandy Hook and encampments, 28 June–6 July. Map by Garry Wheeler Stone. Copyright © 2016 by the University of Oklahoma Press.

quickly routed the militia, killing two and chasing the others into a swamp.

While most of the Middlesex County militia was farther west, one company-sized detachment was scouting to the east and ran to the gunfire—and straight into the sabers of the 17th Light Dragoons. The horsemen killed John Boise, Harmanus Laing, and Michael Field, those men "being cut to pieces by the light horsemen of the enemy." Stelle Fitz Randolph "was cut and mangled and left on the field for dead" but survived; others were wounded.[58] These were pinprick attacks, though harrowing for those involved. Mary Inman, wife of George Inman, an officer in the 26th Foot, was in a nearby carriage when the militia struck. Her husband was then engaged in the fighting west of Freehold and learned only later of Mary's brush with tragedy. George fervently thanked the Almighty that "My dear Mrs. . . . was preserved." He reached her the following morning and "restored her drooping spirits."[59]

The raiders driven off, Knyphausen brought his command successfully out of harm's way. Clinton, after marching all night, joined him between 8:00 and 9:00 A.M. on 29 June. The Battle of Monmouth was over.

CHAPTER 16

Aftermath of Battle

The Living and the Dead

Daybreak on Monday, 29 June, offered the patriot army an exhilarating yet ghastly prospect. The British were gone, and the rebels held the battlefield; it was one of the few times over the past several years they could make such a claim, and they made the most of it. The enemy had "retired in a great hurry in the Night," Chaplain David Griffith wrote to his wife, leaving the field and their wounded to the victorious Americans. "It is Glorious for America," Colonel Israel Shreve exulted, "the Glory of the Day was Doubtful," but at last "the Enemy was Drove off the Ground." In "all the actions hitherto," Brigadier General William Irvine wrote a friend, "the Americans never took the field." They did this time and left "the pride of the British Tyrant" in decline. "Our little boys," another jubilant officer wrote his wife, drove "their Gigantic Grenadiers."[1] There was an element of sweet revenge in some reports, for the rebels had (in their eyes) beaten the very men who had defeated them the year before on the field at Brandywine and elsewhere. Certainly, Shreve saw just retribution in the hideous death of the tory Sam Leonard, and Anthony Wayne took a perverse delight in asking a friend in Philadelphia to inform the young "Ladies" of the city that the British officers who had so recently courted them had "humbled themselves on the Plains of Monmouth."[2] Whatever else it was, in patriot eyes the Battle of Monmouth was payback.

With the battle over, however, new tasks began; as they had during the frantic hours of 28 June, they took place roughly in parallel. In fact, so many things transpired at the same time or in rapid sequence that it is difficult to place them in any strict chronological order. Within days the army dealt with issues of redeployment, and within weeks it confronted matters of resupply, reorganization, and even international affairs. On the field of Monmouth, there were dead to be buried, wounded to treat, casualties to count, and prisoners and deserters to process. There was even looting; the aftermath of combat is never pretty. While all this was in progress, patriots and loyalists tried to interpret what had happened at Monmouth. In addition, Washington and his military family did their best to shape a politically acceptable version of events—an undertaking with momentous implications for the general personally, the army generally, and the Revolution at large.

Again, these matters all unfolded roughly in parallel. Yet bearing this in mind, we need to consider them individually, beginning with matters touching on two of Washington's most immediate concerns: dealing with the residue of combat—the dead, the wounded, and others left behind on or near the battlefield—and the redeployment of the Continental Army.

The Immediate Aftermath of Battle

With Clinton gone and the chance of catching him slim, on 29 June Washington decided to pull his men back to Englishtown. He sent the picked men (except for Colonel Morgan's) back to their original regiments, and the army marched from the battlefield at 5:00 P.M. On the high ground west of Englishtown, the troops could catch their breath, recover their packs, reorganize, and draw rations. Not everyone came, though. Woodford's Brigade remained near Freehold to cover a fatigue detail of two hundred men; over the next two days, they would count and bury the dead of both armies, recover the wounded, and secure any equipment, prisoners, and deserters.[3] On Tuesday, 30 June, the general allowed the men a full day of rest. The troops were to wash and make themselves "appear as clean and decent as possible." In the evening the army united "in thanksgivings to the supreme Disposer of human Events for the Victory which was obtained on sunday over the Flower of the British Troops."[4]

Washington's decision not to chase Clinton was well founded. The British position near Middletown was strong, and the route to Sandy Hook was easily secured. Reports from local patriots and army patrols indicated no opportunities to hit the redcoats decisively; the best Washington could do was have Clinton shadowed. William Maxwell's New Jersey Brigade, Morgan's light infantry (the colonel having finally linked up with the main army on 29 June), and local militia, including horse under Anthony Walton White, all followed the withdrawing British. Colonel Stephen Moylan's dragoons were still in the field as well, and on the twenty-ninth the colonel clashed briefly with the retreating enemy column; he took several prisoners and thought he had killed a few other British troops.[5] After this, however, the next few days saw only scattered shots exchanged.

Indeed, there was little the rebels could do. Consequently, the forces trailing the British soon dwindled. Maxwell's men were so exhausted that the brigadier marched them back to Englishtown.[6] Militia support evaporated as well. Washington and Major General Dickinson had hoped the local forces could jab at Clinton's retreat, keeping the field at least until the British were clear of New Jersey. It was not to be. A disheartened Dickinson found his numbers decreasing hourly; his men worried about their crops and considered the threat they had rallied to meet had passed. By 30 June the militia general counted less than 150 men near Middletown and perhaps a similar number near Tennent's Meeting House. None had any enthusiasm for pursuing the redcoats.[7] This left American shadowing operations mostly to a vastly outnumbered Morgan; with Moylan's departure, the Virginian had no effective horse and had trouble staying close to the British. Thus Morgan resigned himself to a relatively passive role.[8] Washington expected little more. He wanted only to keep track of Clinton, not have the unsupported light infantry provoke a real fight.

Without the immediate prospect of further action, the commander in chief still wanted to build on what he saw as the success of Monmouth and keep pressure on Clinton. That meant bringing the rebel army within striking distance of the British garrison in New York City. Washington elected to post most of his troops around White Plains, New York, which offered a good vantage of the city and the chance to interrupt British foraging. On 1 July the Americans marched northeast from Englishtown.

The Dead, the Wounded, and the Others

The onerous work of clearing the Monmouth battlefield began even before Washington marched toward the Hudson. The Americans had won a gory field. Men lay where they had fallen, some of them horribly mutilated by bayonet and saber wounds, musket fire, and all manner of artillery projectiles. Most bodies were bloated in the heat, some with their faces almost black. Scattered among the dead, the wounded awaited help, some dying before it arrived. "I Viewed the field of Battle," Shreve wrote his wife, "where many British Grenadier[s] and Light Infantry Lay Weltering in their Gore." Lieutenant Colonel Samuel Smith, with Richard Parker's battalion of picked men, was aghast at what he found that Monday. "The stench from the woods was intolerable," he recalled, "they being filled with dead men and horses."[9] If the apparent victory was sweet, there were soldiers who appreciated its grim cost. One French volunteer, "even in the midst of the pride and pleasure of victory," took no comfort in surveying the enemy dead. Massachusetts surgeon Samuel Adams, Jr.—son of *the* Samuel Adams—visited the field on the twenty-ninth and found it "shocking."[10] Certainly, the sight of the hundreds of slain must have sobered all but the most callous; Monmouth had been a bloody piece of work.

It was not all blood and gore, though. The Americans dealt easily with most enemy prisoners of war and deserters. There were relatively few of the former. Standing mostly on the defensive, patriots had few opportunities to make captures. John Laurens thought a lack of cavalry prevented the rebels from taking "but a very inconsiderable number of prisoners."[11] Most British falling into rebel hands probably were stragglers or those wounded too badly to get away. Of the 60 or so men taken during the battle, the wounded left at Freehold and on the field accounted for the majority. The rebels had taken another 70 or so prisoners along the British march to Monmouth Court House (including the grenadiers caught doing their laundry), and the few taken during the enemy movement to Sandy Hook brought the total to no more than 150 prisoners, if that many. Some were sent to Princeton, but most went to the Trenton "gaol," where they were held prior to exchange or transfer to locations in the Philadelphia area.[12] There were many more deserters—some estimates stated as many as a thousand over the course of the campaign. Roughly half of them were sent to Philadelphia; the others seem to have disappeared into the New Jersey and Pennsylvania interiors. Rebel authorities cleared British prisoners and deserters, wherever their destinations, from the area quickly. This was important. Prisoners and other extraneous personnel are a burden to an army on the march; at the least they require security and rations, sometimes even transport and medical care, all of which can slow a force on the move.[13] Washington's army never labored under this impediment as it moved out of Monmouth County.

The dead and wounded posed more difficult challenges, although the army dealt with them quickly. On the twenty-ninth patriot search parties swept the woods, fields, and bogs looking for anyone, friend or foe, dead or alive. The dead would be buried and counted for official reports, the wounded cared for if possible. It was a grisly undertaking. Colonel James Chambers, who had seen some of his own Pennsylvanians killed and wounded during the cannonade, rode over the field to find "our fatigue parties collecting the dead in piles." Lieutenant Colonel Cornelius Van Dyck of the First New York was in charge of the body count. He divided the two-hundred-man work party into thirteen groups, each group laboring in the hot and now stinking air under an officer or sergeant and assisted by "Different Inhabitants." A Connecticut sergeant wrote of the grim labor, "our next order of business was to gather the dead together in order to bury them which we did going about in wagons, loading them up . . . , and burying about twelve or fourteen in [a] whole." Over the course of the day, the detail recovered and buried 217 British and twenty-nine American bodies.[14] Other officers thought this count was low, stating that patriots buried closer to sixty of their own.[15]

Whatever the exact figure, the bodies of enlisted soldiers went into common burial pits. This happened without ceremony, without official or public remembrance. If anyone said a prayer or stood for a solemn moment, it was unrecorded—and unexpected. This was fully in accord with the socially accepted norms of the period: the anonymity of the common grave simply (if brutally) reflected popular attitudes toward the lower-class origins of most rank and file. Any grieving among surviving comrades in arms was done privately. This may seem heartless today, but there are no indications anyone thought so at the time.

It was different for fallen officers, though. Commissioned ranks were generally the military counterparts of the social betters in civilian life. As historian Caroline Cox has reminded us, Continental officers were men with aspirations to traditional "gentlemanly honor"; it was this sense of officers as gentlemen the army relied on to "maintain the distinctions of rank under all circumstances."[16] These distinctions held in such matters as living conditions, training, furlough opportunities, and even funerary arrangements.

Whenever possible, officers received individual interments with some formal observance—the "honors of war." It was a practice Washington fully approved, and so it was after Monmouth. In general orders of the twenty-ninth, the commander in chief informed the army: "The Officers of the American Army are to be buried with military honors due to men who have nobly fought and died in the Cause of Liberty and their Country."[17]

The Continental Line lost eight officers at Monmouth, just over 11 percent of the patriots killed in action. In their accounts of the battle, officers frequently mentioned their dead comrades by name and recalled the circumstances of their deaths, and there was some genuine mourning. Captain Walter Finney, Tenth Pennsylvania, wrote that American losses were "inconcedarable" except for the "brave officers that fell like Romans" (which begs the question of how the enlisted men fell).[18] Officer fatalities left Lieutenant William Watson deeply affected. Watson had fought under Colonel Livingston at the Hedgerow and may well have seen Major Edmund Dickinson fall. "We have lost a Number of Brave officers," he wrote home to Massachusetts, "Some of Whitch I had a Perticular Aquaintance and Regaurd for thay are dead But May thair Memories and Virtues Be Imbalmed With My Tears and Still Live in the Chambers of my Hart." Watson's letter reveals him to be a ferocious hater of slackers in the cause; he despised "them and all their Spitefull Things as the Scarlett Whore & I know of no Whore that tryes more to Corrupt the Earth with thair Fornications than those of that Denomination."[19] But his affection for his brother officers was as deep as his loathing of his enemies. There is no similar account of tears shed over enlisted dead, so the gulf between officers and men remained as wide in death as it was in life.

The ghastly death of artillery lieutenant James McNair, who lost his head to a British cannonball, evoked a response similar to Watson's. The event moved "Pericles" to a heartfelt and archetypical republican tribute. Laced with the classical elusions so dear to whigs, the eulogy bore echoes of the famed Athenian's "Funeral Oration." "*Tears like the dew shall fall on the memory of Heroes,*" the pseudonymous Pericles grieved. The author was certainly a brother officer, as he wrote of McNair with intimate detail. The lieutenant was loved by the officers and "loved and feared" by the enlisted men. "He was cool, attentive to his duty, intrepid and brave, undisturbed by the hottest engagement, and commanded with the firmness and courage of a Roman." McNair had "died fighting bravely for his country against slavery and tyranny. Not less than a cannon ball separated his noble soul from his body."[20] The emotional distress of Pericles was genuine, and his lament reflects the self-image of an officer corps that saw itself as the Revolution's pillars of courage, sacrifice, and honor. The army rendered honors accordingly: On the twenty-ninth Marylander Colonel Otho Holland Williams informed a friend that while writing his letter he could hear the "volleys that are discharged over the gallant Dead."[21]

The search parties that buried the dead also did what they could to recover the wounded. Military medicine, however, had severe limitations—it was still in its infancy—and for injured soldiers, medical treatment could be an ordeal unto itself. The quality of medical staff varied; some were well trained, some had little or no formal training. Knowledge of infection was rudimentary, and medical techniques were primitive and often did more harm than good. There was little anyone could do to recover many of the wounded quickly enough to help them, and army hospitals could offer only basic care when a patient arrived. Most were improvised affairs: A regimental hospital near the lines could be a tent or a convenient barn.[22] Farther to the rear temporary hospitals, or a "flying hospital," could be set up in public buildings, private homes, churches, or collections of such structures. Sanitary conditions often were appalling, and crowded conditions bred contagion. It was a fortunate casualty who survived a combat wound *and* an extended hospital stay. When Virginian John Allgood was hit at Monmouth, he insisted on remaining with his regiment rather than chance a hospital admission. He knew only too well that army hospitals posed risks as great or greater than the battlefield.[23]

While it was never a good time to be wounded, Monmouth was better than most. The army's Medical Department, long the scene of internecine squabbles and bitter personal rivalries, had solved some of its worst problems by 1778. The department had improved operations by the end of the Valley Forge encampment: most of the troops had been inoculated against smallpox, medical chests were generally full, supplies were adequate, and hospital administration greatly improved. As the British began their march across New Jersey, Dr. William Shippen, Jr., Continental director of hospitals, was aware a fight was likely, although with the rival armies on the move, he was at a loss as to where to preposition temporary hospitals.[24] Still, the numbers and quality of medical personnel were better than previously, and when the time came, numerous New Jersey towns were close enough to accommodate temporary medical facilities.

Treatment of the wounded began on the field or just behind the lines, a dangerous business while the fighting still raged. There is no mention of regiments establishing hospitals during the battle, but individual doctors and surgeons were at work. Dr. William Read reached the front on the afternoon of the twenty-eighth and briefly attended the mortally wounded Lieutenant Colonel Bunner; there was nothing the doctor could do for the poor man amid the sound of battle and "the groans and cries of the wounded." Dr. Adams also worked close to the front—he slept on the battlefield the night of the twenty-eighth—dressing wounds and bleeding "a number that were overcome with the heat."[25] (Bleeding was a highly detrimental practice, of course, but widely applied in the era.) No doubt other medical personnel rendered what assistance they could in similar circumstances, as regimental surgeons were supposed to remain as close to their units as possible. (These physicians would fall back to larger field hospitals when those facilities became overcrowded with casualties.) If they were lucky, the walking wounded could make their way to a hospital; those with more serious injuries could only hope comrades would assist them in finding help. During the battle, the grounds of Tennent's Meeting House filled the role of a field hospital, and surgeons and surgeon's mates dealt with a steady flow of wounded during the course of the day. Private Joseph Plumb Martin, having helped transport the mortally wounded Edmund Monro to the meetinghouse, watched in grim fascination as doctors performed emergency amputations.[26]

The agony continued the next day. Surgeons and mates in and around Freehold (including Englishtown) worked under the direction of Dr. John Cochran, the senior medical officer on the scene. An experienced physician, Cochran had campaigned with the army since 1776 and emerged as the most capable American medical administrator of the war. Washington directed him to take charge of the sick and wounded, and he did his best.[27] By the twenty-ninth, with the assistance of quartermaster personnel, he was able to get medical supplies distributed and was working to find shelter for patients evacuated from the field. Teamsters plied the battlefield, recovering and carrying wounded to whatever makeshift aid stations were available.[28]

The fates of the wounded varied. Some were beyond help, and for others help came too late. Lieutenant Colonel Rudolph Bunner was among the latter unfortunates. Corporal John Wilkins and Matross (artillery private) Thomas Price, both of Harrison's artillery, lived through the battle but succumbed to wounds a few weeks later. John Kelly, a matross in Lamb's artillery, died in mid-July as well.[29] They had fought in the open with their guns and probably fell victim to British artillery fire. Soldiers with less serious injuries fared better. Private Jacob Anderson of the Eighth Virginia, already wounded at Brandywine and Germantown, was hit again at Monmouth, probably in the Point of Woods. Up on his feet quickly, he remained with the Continentals until 1782.[30] Colonel Henry Livingston, struck in the thigh near the Hedgerow, and Lieutenant Colonel Francis Barber, hit later in the afternoon while with Wayne, had flesh wounds and soon returned to duty. Others took longer to recover. Colonel John Durkee, gravely wounded in the arm during the morning fighting, was still recovering late in the year and had lost the use of his right hand; he managed to return to active duty in 1779.[31] Massachusetts colonel James Wesson was hit by a cannonball, probably during the cannonade. He was bent over at the instant, and the round struck him in the neck, "raked along the spine, tearing away clothing, skin and integuments, and muscles, to its extremity." Miraculously still alive, he lay on the field all night before a party carried him to Englishtown the next day. He was reported mortally wounded, but Read and a Dr. Hunt treated him; the colonel recovered within a month and served until January 1781.[32] Equally astonishing was the recovery of Captain David Cook, shot through the lungs while commanding a company of Oswald's guns. No one expected him to live, but after a long convalescence at Englishtown, by late August he had returned to the artillery and served for the duration of the war.[33]

Others survived their injuries but were lost to the army. Lieutenant Colonel Nathaniel Ramsey, painfully wounded and partially blinded in the Point of Woods, recovered slowly while on parole; formally exchanged only in late 1780, he retired without seeing any further service.[34] Henry Anderson, who fought in Scott's Brigade, contracted asthma from the smoke of the battle, and it plagued him for the rest of his life. Sergeant Baltus Collins, an artilleryman, was hit in the leg so severely he was unfit for further duty. Samuel Leonard of the Third New Jersey was hit in the foot and spent eight months in hospital before being discharged; for nine years the wound "suppurated and discharged a number of small bones."[35] Pension applications of Monmouth veterans are replete with similar stories; wounds ended their military service and marked the rest of their lives.

The British experience was equally grim. They hastily buried around sixty of their dead on the field and felt compelled to leave behind wounded too badly hurt to move. In doing so Clinton was fully justified in his belief the Americans would look after them. They did indeed, but patriots often found the plight of wounded redcoats tragic. Dr. Read, unable to help Lieutenant Colonel Bunner, did his best in behalf of Bunner's enemies. Crossing the West Morass on the morning of the twenty-ninth, the doctor found several grenadiers "mired to the waist"; they were all dead. Just across the bog he found a wounded officer "nearly cut in two by a cannon shot." The dying man asked to be leaned against a tree so "that he might die easy." The officer thanked him, then bled to death. Close by, Read found several dozen other dead and injured grenadiers (these were in addition to the British casualties left in Freehold). It was a wretched scene: the wounded men—those still conscious—desperately gasped out cries for help and water as they lay in the baking heat and air fouled by the odor of shattered bodies. The doctor did his best, tearing the shirts off of the dead to make bandages for the living and hiring local civilians, white and black, to assist; one of these civilian helpers (working either with Read or other medical personnel) was Margaret Houck, a slave whose owners lived close to the battlefield. Read amputated when he had to. By the end of the day, he had moved over twenty grenadiers into the courthouse, where he established a temporary hospital. (Read was working as a volunteer, but senior officers noted his efforts and on 2 July he was formally commissioned into the Medical Department.)[36]

On Wednesday, 1 July, the day most of Washington's army departed the area, British medical assistance arrived from New York. General Maxwell was still at Englishtown where, to his amazement, one of Clinton's aides-de-camp suddenly appeared at his headquarters. The man, a Captain Murray, had come from Sandy Hook, riding all the way in without discovery by Morgan's light infantry. (So much for the American security screen.) An irritated Maxwell informed Washington that Murray brought Clinton's compliments, thanking the Americans "for their polite behaviour to the Prisoners that fell into our hands."[37] Traveling with Murray, or arriving close behind him, were two "gentlemen," presumably surgeons, who relieved Dr. Read from his "arduous duty" at the courthouse. As he explained the condition of the wounded to the "gentlemen," Read found their reactions "cool." They acknowledged his efforts but said the American had only "given so many subjects to the Chelsea Hospital"—the home for invalid veterans in London.[38] Four days later the British sent another doctor and two wagons of supplies for their wounded officers; there was no mention of their enlisted wounded.[39]

Facilities for extended medical care were unavailable near the battlefield, and enlisted men who could not be treated and returned to duty quickly had to go elsewhere. Princeton had the largest general hospital (probably in the colonial-era barracks) within reasonable distance, and general orders of the twenty-ninth directed casualties who could be moved, including the sick left behind as far back as Coryell's Ferry, be collected and sent there under the care of Dr. James Craik.[40] Men too injured to move remained for the time being at Freehold or Englishtown; they were sent on later. Princeton, however, could not handle the volume of patients. With one exception, all artillery casualties went there, but this was not the norm. More typical was the situation of Colonel Henry Jackson's wounded, who were scattered across nine towns in New Jersey and Pennsylvania. Presumably, this was the case with casualties of other battalions as well, because Morristown, New Brunswick (in the colonial barracks), Trenton, and probably other New Jersey towns also had makeshift hospitals (including private homes), as did Philadelphia, Lancaster, and other towns in Pennsylvania. William Hampton, a private in the Second Virginia, ultimately ended up in a hospital as far away as Danbury, Connecticut.[41]

Such a dispersal of the wounded was a logistical and administrative challenge, but it had a positive side: it minimized the spread of contagious disease. Camp diseases—notably typhus, dysentery, smallpox, and diarrhea—plagued armies of the day and killed vastly more men than combat. Earlier in the war, patriot sick and wounded died by the thousands in crowded and unsanitary medical facilities. Thus it is no surprise Dr. Adams expressed similar concerns after Monmouth. He feared that Englishtown, fouled by days of army encampment, would breed "fever and ague."[42] Yet there was no widespread calamity there. The smallpox-inoculation campaign at Valley Forge and the relatively quick evacuation of the wounded and burial of the dead prevented any serious contagion in the village. But the story was different at Princeton. There the general hospital was crowded, and almost predictably an outbreak of typhus occurred. Of the twelve members of the medical staff, about half died; others simply left, fearful for their lives. Read, ordered to Princeton, reported "five or six" patient deaths per day, with remaining staff often refusing to attend the sick. Read himself fell ill, and on his own authority—and "in a state of delirium"—he had all patients removed from the hospital and "deposited" in barns outside town. This stopped the outbreak.[43] Fortunately, none of the other hospitals reported a similar experience. But the incident at Princeton was a grim reminder of the difficulties confronting the sick, the wounded, and those tasked with their care.

The outlook for wounded officers was better. Here again was a military reflection of prevailing social norms. Most Americans with means avoided hospitals, seeking treatment at home; hospitals were for the indigent and homeless. Army doctors, most (if not all) of whom had practiced as civilians, either accepted this view or could do nothing to counter it while in the service.[44] Thus enlisted men went to the various hospitals, while officers, generally coming from higher social strata, would receive the individual care they would have expected as civilians. Accordingly, Colonels Wesson and Durkee, Lieutenant Colonel Barber, Captain Cook, and the others convalesced in private homes or other accommodations in and around Englishtown and Freehold; they also received the personal attention of Doctors Read, Adams, and others. This is not to say privates received no individual treatment; they did. Regimental surgeons served that role, and even more-senior doctors would visit the regiments on occasion.[45] But injury or illness that required long-term care meant commitment to a hospital, a risk few officers faced—and none did that we know of after Monmouth. Thus in the wake of the battle, patriot arrangements for medical care once again affirmed the distinctions between officers and men as well as the military hierarchy implicit in the regular army Washington had forged.[46]

Efforts to bury the dead and treat the wounded, however, shared the battlefield with other activities. There was also looting of the dead and wounded as well as scavenging of goods and livestock kicked loose in the violence of 28 June. This was not unusual, and it involved soldiers and civilians, American and British. In the aftermath of combat, soldiers saw little wrong with taking useful items—clothing, rations, and personal arms and equipment—from enemy casualties or simply found strewn on the field.[47] Some pillaging was entirely practical. After fending off Monckton's foray across the West Morass, Continentals took the opportunity to toss aside their Charleville muskets and replace them with the Brown Besses of the killed and wounded grenadiers (a soldierly comment on the perceived quality of the respective firearms).[48] It is a safe assumption the Americans also collected as much British ammunition as they could find. But there were less seemly activities as well. During Cilley's attack on the Highlanders, Private Martin had seen Captain Edmund Monro's leg torn off by a shot from a British grasshopper. When the firing stopped, he found three soldiers detailed to help the wounded officer neglecting their charge. Instead, to Martin's disgust, they were plundering British casualties. Dr. Read, treating the wounded on the twenty-ninth, watched with dismay as the servants of a dying British officer openly bargained over the man's personal effects.[49] Days after the fighting, owners of property lost on or near the battlefield hoped someone would report a find. One militia colonel advertised a reward for the return of a distinctive "brass mounted" pistol lost during the action. Similar advertisements reported horses "strayed or stolen" during or soon after the battle—hardly evidence per se of deliberate theft, but an indication that a fair number of mounts apparently found new "owners" in the fighting's aftermath. Someone even filched the pocketbook of the hard-working Dr. Adams. When local residents tried to recover valuables hidden from the British, they were dismayed to find that patriot troops had pilfered them.[50]

There was also some traditional souvenir hunting. Pennsylvania captain William Wilson claimed to have recovered Lieutenant Colonel Monckton sword as well as the battalion colors of the unfortunate grenadier commander. The colors supposedly remained in the Wilson family for generations. This is myth, as the grenadiers carried no colors at Monmouth; but the story certainly reflected the age-old desire of soldiers to carry off trophies of battlefield valor.[51] No doubt many American regulars and militiamen marched away with mementoes gleaned from the field. Combat leaves all manner of clutter in its wake, and someone is usually there to pick up anything useful or interesting. The Battle of Monmouth was no exception.

Whether souvenir hunting or pillaging, Washington was infuriated. He ordered unit commanders to conduct a search of all packs and to turn over any suspicious items to the adjutant general.

Whenever possible, looted goods were to be returned to owners and the looters themselves to be "discovered & brought to condign Punishment." Now it was the commander in chief's turn to make draconian threats. "Marauding," he insisted, "will henceforward be invariably punished with instant Death."[52] Washington knew the value of good civil-military relations and that the safety of private property was critical in maintaining such relations. But there is no evidence his warnings against pillaging had any greater effect than Clinton's.

The Cost of Combat: Counting Casualties at Monmouth

In the days following the battle, the rival armies totaled the costs of battle as they counted their own dead and wounded and tried to estimate the losses of their opponent. There was a practical reason for this. Commanders needed to know what their losses were for operational reasons. But there were also the political and public-relations aspects of the body count: the attempt to minimize your own losses while inflating those of the enemy. It was the age-old practice of using (or manipulating) casualty figures to assert victory claims or otherwise justify the results of an action.

Both sides made some widely divergent claims. "Tis generally thought the Rebels have lost 2000," wrote loyalist Andrew Bell, and that "Lee is killed and a French General."[53] On the other side, Surgeon Samuel Adams thought Clinton had left 800 dead on the field. Jeremiah Greenman, one of Lieutenant Colonel Olney's men, wrote of British losses numbering 1,000 killed and wounded; he put patriot casualties of all kinds, including heat exhaustion, at 200 men. Henry Dearborn's count was similar, holding that Clinton lost 327 killed in action, another 500 wounded, and 95 prisoners. Wayne thought the enemy's numbers were 1,500 casualties, with 300 killed. Other American estimates of British losses were comparable.[54] No two sources agreed.

Misinformation and wishful thinking shaped these numbers. The official tallies were quite different and, at least on the American side, more realistic. In his official return, Washington reported to Congress a total of 69 dead, 161 wounded, and 140 missing. Of the total dead and wounded, 29 (or about 10 percent) were in the artillery, which also lost six horses killed and two wounded. Of the missing, the general noted that many had dropped out of ranks temporarily because of the heat but "have since come in."[55] There is little corroborating evidence for these figures. At least one field report, possibly compiled by burial details, differed only minimally from Washington's count, listing the number of wounded at 144 and the missing at 127. Shortly after the war, historian David Ramsay, brother of the gallant Lieutenant Colonel Ramsey, generally agreed with the official numbers, accepting a slightly higher combined total of 250 killed and wounded. Surprisingly, Clinton also lent credence to Washington's report, noting 69 American dead and 159 wounded in his narrative of the battle.[56] Thus the reported number of rebels killed in action or lost to the heat seems about right. Even if there was serious undercounting of the dead, or if wounded or missing who died later went unreported, Americans killed in action were no more than 100 men.

But the reported ratio of wounded to killed, roughly two to one, seems too low. Instead, the more usual eighteenth-century ratio of three or four wounded for every man killed offers a safer estimate. If we use a figure of 90 dead (which would not be unreasonable, supposing about 20 of the 131 missing were fatalities), we could then estimate about 360 wounded.[57] This would bring the total of American killed and wounded to around 450 men, a fairly realistic figure given the grim nature of some of the fighting. A grimmer scenario would assign more missing to the dead and wounded (Washington never did say how many missing turned up alive or hurt), in which case a casualty total would reach slightly beyond 500 men. This was certainly plausible if those with minor wounds preferred to avoid the hospitals and stay with their units.[58] Yet even this higher estimate would put American losses at Monmouth far below those of the King's army.

Even with inaccuracies in the body counts, it is clear the British suffered far more than the Americans. Clinton admitted only to 65 killed, 59 dead of fatigue, 64 missing and 170 wounded. Shortly afterward, however, the loyalist *New York Gazette* published a total of 338 British casualties, including 110 killed in action or dead from the heat.[59] Washington made an effort to count enemy dead, which he reported to Congress as 249 officers and men. In addition, he noted that the British had buried some of their own, and he supposed a few others might still be lying undiscovered in the woods. There is little reason to suspect the commander in chief's figures were very far off. Lieutenant Colonel Van Dyck had reported 217 enemy buried on 29 June, and several days later Washington wrote of finding more British dead, which (if the counts were accurate) put the total a bit over 300 burials.[60] And at least some British reports tended to support the American estimates. Accounts reaching London stated that "several hundreds were slain," and a senior Hessian officer conceded that the royal army had suffered 174 fatalities. All this makes sense. The British were attacking and thus more frequently out in the open, which made them better targets more often. Rebel artillery hit them particularly hard. Moreover, the heat also took a heavier toll on the British. By the afternoon they had been marching for hours, while Washington's men (at least those from the main army) were still relatively fresh. In an exaggeration Bell claimed that more British fell to the weather than to enemy action, but it does appear upward of 60 died from exhaustion.[61] Thus Washington's count of British casualties may have been conservative.

Indeed, Major Samuel Shaw, who served with such distinction on the twenty-eighth, believed that and more. He was convinced the British had "never been handled so roughly in America"; to make his point, he made an interesting comparison to enemy losses at Bunker Hill in 1775. There, he noted, the redcoats had over 160 killed out of 1,053 total casualties, a wounded-to-killed ratio of "more than five" to one. Following the same rule, and accepting Washington's figure of about 250 British dead at Monmouth, Shaw concluded that enemy wounded were on the order of 1,235. Even if the wounded were only two-thirds that number, the major argued, Monmouth had been a bloodbath for the royal army.[62] If imprecise, Shaw's calculations fully reflect an honest American conviction that they had hit Clinton hard.

Shaw's estimates, no matter how thoughtfully contrived, were too high. Of the roughly 250 British dead, we simply do not know how many fell to patriot fire as opposed to succumbing to fatigue or heat exhaustion. But assuming American musketry and artillery accounted for at least half the redcoat dead—about 125 men—then the typical eighteenth-century wounded-to-killed ratios of three or four to one would have produced some 375–500 wounded.[63] If patriot fire caused more of the fatalities—say 160 or so, which is a reasonable assumption—then the number of wounded could have been somewhere between 480 and 640. These numbers were smaller than

Shaw's but still constituted substantial losses. Thus if we include deserters, it is safe to assume the British army paid a toll in the neighborhood of 2,000 men (including wounded) for their march through New Jersey. In fact, this was exactly the conclusion of the jaeger Captain Johann Ewald.[64] It was no small loss, and it appears the disparity in casualties between the armies was greater than most previous studies have allowed.[65]

To White Plains

While the rival forces counted their losses and dealt with their dead and wounded, the patriot army continued its march to the northeast. Progress was unhurried. There was no reason to rush, which was fortunate, as the weather allowed nothing faster than a snail's pace. Washington found the march as hard as any the army had undertaken on the campaign. He wrote Major General Gates that the trek "from English Town was inconceivably distressing to the Troops and Horses." During the first day on the road (1 July), the army moved less than ten miles, stopping at Spotswood. The rest of the march to New Brunswick was no better, as the columns had to move "thro' a deep sand, without a drop of Water, except at south River, which is half way. This, added to the intense heat, killed a few and knocked up many of our Men, and killed a number of our Horses." At one point so many men were overcome by the heat—one lieutenant thought it was a full third of the army—that the march had to stop until the cooler evening hours. Even then some of the stricken soldiers "were obliged to be conveyed in wagons." Early the next day the Continentals straggled into New Brunswick, where Washington decided to rest his men and animals for three days. The stop also would allow Major General Greene, resuming his quartermaster duties, to bring up necessary supplies.[66]

With rest came restored spirits. The men bathed in the Raritan River, drew new clothing and shoes, and were sternly warned against foraging among local fruit trees—meaning some of them were doing just that.[67] John Laurens loved every minute. "We are now arrived in a delightful country," he wrote his father, "where we shall halt and refresh ourselves—bathing in the Raritan, and the good living of the Country will speedily reestablish us." He wished his father "could ride along the banks of this delightful rivers [*sic*]."[68] It was the longest break from marching and fighting the troops had enjoyed since leaving Valley Forge.

On 4 July the army played the role of conquering heroes. As if to emphasize the ostensible triumph at Monmouth, Washington staged a huge Fourth of July celebration. At 5:00 P.M. the entire army formed on the New Brunswick side of the Raritan, the troops wearing "Green-Boughs" in their hats "to make the best appearance possible." Henry Knox thought the double line of infantry and gun crews stretched for two miles. On signal, thirteen cannon fired a salute, followed by a running fire of musketry and cannon down the entire line. The official celebration ended with three cheers for "Perpetual and undisputed Independence to the United States of America." The triumphant salutes were loud enough for the British to hear on Sandy Hook. It was grand public theater, and it put an exclamation point on Washington's claims to victory the previous week—exactly the point he wanted to convey to a war-weary public. The day ended with the men receiving a double ration of rum.[69] One assumes morale was especially high that night.

The march resumed on 5 July. The heat remained unrelenting, so the army rested on alternate days; when it moved, the heat made it necessary to put many weaker men in the wagons.[70] The troops reached the Hudson at King's Ferry only on 17 July, and the last units crossed the river only on the nineteenth. The army finally reached White Plains on 24 July. Once in place, the army turned to dealing with some loose ends of the campaign. Resupply was an immediate priority. Quartermaster and commissary personnel were busy getting new arms to camp and shipping out arms and munitions damaged at Monmouth for repair. The fighting had badly depleted stocks of artillery ammunition, and by mid-July shipments of three-, four-, and six-pound shot were in transit.[71]

Army reorganization, interrupted by the campaign, continued. As early as 1 July, the small Fourth New Jersey and three weak Pennsylvania regiments were dissolved, their men distributed among stronger units. By late summer three Virginia regiments had suffered the same fate.[72] For rank and file, unit consolidations meant continued service among new comrades. Some officers, however, lost their jobs, among them Lieutenant John Kinney of the Third New Jersey. He had enlisted as a private, had come up through the ranks, and had fought at Monmouth. With the influx of officers and men from the Fourth New Jersey after the battle, however, Kinney was no longer needed and went home.[73] His was one of many similar stories among the junior officers.

There was no fighting to speak of while the army changed base and refitted, so Washington turned his attention to future operations: notably to the situation on the Pennsylvania frontier (which had deteriorated in the face of Indian attacks), the arrival of the French fleet (a fruit of the new French alliance), and the possibility of an offensive against the British in Rhode Island. For the troops, it was a time to recuperate after a trying season in the field. "Here we lay till September," noted Lieutenant Thomas Blake of the New Hampshire Line, "and nothing remarkable happened."[74]

If the lieutenant's observation was somewhat blasé, Washington's outlook was anything but. The general believed the recent campaign had been quite remarkable. Almost a month after arriving at White Plains, he sent a letter to fellow Virginian Thomas Nelson putting the entire campaign in perspective. "It is not a little pleasing," he wrote his friend,

> nor less wonderful to contemplate, that after two long years Manoeuvring and undergoing the strangest vicissitudes that perhaps ever attended any one contest since the creation both Armies are brought back to the very point they set out from and, that that [*sic*], which was the offending party in the beginning is now reduced to the use of the spade and pick axe for the defence. The hand of Providence has been so conspicuous in all this, that he must be worse than an infidel that lacks faith, and more than wicked, that has not gratitude enough to acknowledge his obligations, but, it will be time enough for me to turn preacher, when my present appointment ceases.[75]

Before putting his army on the road to Monmouth, the general had seen divine intervention at work in the advent of the French alliance and on other auspicious occasions, so it is no surprise to find him discerning the "hand of Providence" guiding what he considered a victorious campaign. But there was also an army to thank for one of its grittiest performances of the war. Washington would do so, effusively, and so would many other Americans.

CHAPTER 17

The British and the French

Departures and Arrivals

As the Continental Army trekked toward White Plains, the campaign moved into its final phases in other quarters. Clinton was as busy as Washington. His immediate concern was to get his army out of harm's way. From Nut Swamp the road led to Middletown. His army would move next to the Navesink Highlands overlooking the New Jersey seashore, then to Sandy Hook, and finally across the waters of New York Bay to positions around and in New York City. The Royal Navy, of necessity, would become a factor in the campaign for the first time since the fleet sailed from Philadelphia. At the same time, and unbeknown to Clinton (and for that matter, initially to Washington as well), a third force entered the equation. A French fleet under the comte d'Estaing carrying 4,000 troops arrived in American waters. The event marked the beginning of an active French operational role in the war. Thus a campaign fought on land would end with a demonstration of the importance of sea power.

To Sandy Hook

The British completed their march to Sandy Hook without serious incident. The troops remembered it as a brutally hot but generally safe and quick passage. With Clinton having joined Lieutenant General Kynphausen at Nut Swamp early on 29 June, the King's army was reunited. It moved some two and a half miles to Middletown later in the day and, by the afternoon of the thirtieth, had reached the Navesink Highlands. As usual, the British security screen ranged protectively between the redcoat columns and the shadowing Americans. Daniel Morgan could do little to annoy, much less hurt them; scattered shots were exchanged, but no one inflicted any real damage. The speed of the march was revealing.

The journey from Philadelphia to Monmouth Court House took nine days to cover some sixty miles; the twenty-four miles from Nut Swamp took only two.[1] The difference? Between Philadelphia and Monmouth, Clinton was hoping for a fight; after Monmouth he was not. The general simply wanted to finish the march.

The view from the heights of the Navesink was (and is) breathtaking. The elevation offered a vista of New York Bay, with Long Island visible across the water; a bit to the northwest lay Staten Island. Directly below was Sandy Hook itself, the peninsula jutting north from the New Jersey mainland. At the tip was the heavily fortified lighthouse that guided mariners into the bay, the gateway to New York harbor and the city itself. The troops could easily see Royal Navy transports riding at anchor in Sandy Hook Bay; those ships were the army's lifeline to New York and the end of their long retrograde. Once on the Hook, the army would be safer than at any time since leaving Philadelphia. Sandy Hook was a loyalist stronghold. The chief garrison comprised tory regulars, but the position also held large numbers of irregulars. Most were refugees from New Jersey, driven out by patriot authorities; some were escaped slaves, mostly from Monmouth County. The number of refugees was always indeterminate but considerable, and thus contemporaries often referred to a section of the Hook as "Refugeetown." By whatever name, the place was an armed camp, serving as a base for loyalist foraging, intelligence, and punitive incursions into New Jersey; it would remain so until the end of the war. Here the army could rest and see to the tasks of embarking for the trip across the bay. Ordinarily, such a time would have found any army vulnerable—equipment was unavailable or packed; troops were scattered between ships and shore; and rear guards and security troops, separated from the main body, were subject to attack. But with its location and garrison, Sandy Hook was safe and secure.

Clinton began the move onto the Hook on 1 July. A security screen of jaegers and light troops probed to the west, while most of the infantry remained on the highlands to cover the embarkation. The position spanned the highlands in a semicircle from Sandy Hook Bay on the north to the Shrewsbury River on the south.[2] The British expected no trouble from the Continentals, but they were strong enough to handle anything that the rebels might venture. The rest of the army—including accompanying civilians—wound its way down the heights toward the seashore. Earlier in the year a violent storm had breached the base of Sandy Hook, and a channel some sixty yards wide now separated the peninsula from the mainland. Thus flat-bottomed boats ferried personnel, cattle, artillery, baggage, and equipment across; most of the horses swam the channel. By the end of the day, the difficult task of loading the waiting transports was well underway.[3] After its long march, the British army remained nothing if not efficient.

Transfers to the Hook continued over the next several days, often through heavy rains, and the ferrying process was slow and difficult. The troops and civilians embarked in stages. By the evening of 4 July, the army had completed the embarkation of most of the artillery, heavy baggage, horses, and provisions. Finding a lack of adequate transport and forage, Clinton ordered the army horse herd culled. Brigadier Pattison released seventy of the weakest artillery horses to roam in the woods, and the quartermaster general did the same for upward of four hundred more.[4] Units waiting their turns to load got what rest they could, but the weather remained hot, and mosquitoes made life miserable. On 4 July Johann Ewald was still part of the security screen on the highlands above Sandy Hook, and he had no fond memories of the area: "I did not know whether I would not rather skirmish with the enemy than spend one day longer here. We were so terribly bitten at night by the mosquitoes and other kinds of vermin that we could not open our eyes." Some men were "unrecognizable," the captain miserably recalled, and most looked like they had "measles or smallpox."[5] There are no such reports from the Hook itself, where the sea breezes presumably helped keep the insects somewhat at bay—and where it *was* preferable to dodging musketry and artillery fire. On 4 July the British heard heavy firing to the west: at New Brunswick the Americans were celebrating Independence Day.[6]

To Clinton's relief, on 4 July the navy stepped in to speed the embarkation. Sailors built a temporary bridge of flatboats and planks and assigned two armed galleys to cover the structure. Finally, on the fifth, the remaining troops descended from the highlands. The floating bridge proved too narrow for troops in column, so the infantry crossed single file. The crossing took some four hours, after which the British dismantled the bridge. By evening, in a driving rain, the last major units boarded the transports. Near the end the evacuation had become a bit more of a scramble, and an annoyed Captain Peebles of the grenadiers called it "very irregular."[7] The last security troops followed on the sixth. The crossings, escorted by men-of-war, were unopposed, the patriots having no naval forces to speak of in the area. The guards, dragoons, various loyalist corps, and Hessians sailed directly to New York; the 1st and 2nd Brigades landed on Staten Island; and the 3rd, 4th, and 5th Brigades disembarked on Long Island in the area of modern Queens. Clinton made his headquarters in the city.[8] Thanks to the Royal Navy, the Monmouth campaign was finally over for the tired men and women of the British army.

The British Reaction

Back in New York, British reaction to the campaign varied. Clinton had brought his army through a hostile province, fought off all efforts to stop him, and reached safety without the loss of a wagon. He was pleased, and most of his senior officers agreed with him. Pattison rightly believed that his artillery crews had done well and issued a congratulatory order upon his return to New York.[9] At the same time, there was a widespread understanding the Americans had done well. Andrew Bell, Clinton's confidential secretary, admitted that "the Rebels stood much better than ever they did." An officer in New York, reflecting on the battle in a private letter home, hoped his regiment would get a long rest: "the Enemy were very troublesom[e]" at Monmouth, he noted, and had left his unit "a good dale [*sic*] cut up."[10] One grenadier company, badly shot up, had lost its captain, the fourth killed during the war, which prompted a drummer to quip: "Well, I wonder who they will get to accept of our Grenadiers now. I'll be d—d if I would take them!"[11]

Perhaps the most revealing observation was attributed to Brigadier General Sir William Erskine—the man who had commanded the light infantry opposite the patriot left at Monmouth. After the battle, when Erskine learned that Charles Lee had described the action as a "handsome check" of the British, his retort was pithy indeed: "Lee may call it what he pleases, but by —— I call it a handsome flogging. We had not receiv'd such an one in America."[12] If the remark was true, it was high praise indeed. The Continentals had won grudging respect, but respect nevertheless.

Other matters left much of the British officer corps equally dejected. Even men who accepted that the march across New Jersey had been a success understood the war in the North was over—and they had not won it. A grenadier officer who fought Wayne near the Parsonage and maintained a low opinion of rebel fighting prowess conceded that the British war effort had come to little: "I much fear it [the Battle of Monmouth] will be the last Effort we shall make against them by Land." Another officer, Thomas Davies, not involved at Monmouth but trying to discern its consequences, did not like what he saw. A week after the battle, Davies expected no further trouble from the Americans; what bothered him was a radically changed military situation: "this then is a War with France."[13] War with France, Captain William Dansey knew, meant new strategic priorities. He told his mother, "I believe the war is over in this Country by Land and we shall be wanted at home." His outlook on the future was glum, and his verdict on British leadership scathing: Had the King's generals been up to the job, "we shou'd have had no French War and our turbulent [American] Bretheren, wou'd have been sensible of their Error, Armies can't conquer without [good] Officers." Dansey dismally recounted that he had "fought hard for Peace" for three years and sadly predicted that he probably would have to fight for another seven over very little, perhaps just a "few Acres the Armies occupy."[14] His implication was clear: What was it all for?

Aspects of the planned redeployment also raised concerns. Prominent among them were Clinton's orders to "reduce" the grenadier and light-infantry battalions—that is, to send the flank companies back to their home regiments (in the same manner that Washington sent "picked men" back to their original units). Redeployment meant that various regiments would be sent to different locations, some of them hundreds of miles apart. Administratively, it made sense to deploy complete regiments, including their flank companies, but officers of the elite battalions hated the idea. Peebles sourly noted the orders were "not relish'd." Another grenadier officer was utterly depressed: "I had so long served with the Grenadiers, that I really do not think being Reduced on Half Pay would have afflicted me more. . . . I have now joined My Regimt which is almost as much unknown to Me as when I first joined it."[15] Lieutenant William Hale, who had served with Monckton, was no happier. "Dismissing the flank companies to their respective regiments," he wrote, "gave no small disgust."[16]

The mood was such that even Clinton's official congratulations to the army on the success of the campaign struck a dull note with some subordinates. The British commander was lavish with his praise. The "long and difficult retreat in the face of a greatly superior army," he proclaimed, concluded happily "without being tarnished by the smallest affront." For this he thanked his generals and senior commanders, "whose conspicuous zeal, activity, and professional knowledge" had made it all possible.[17] Among some junior officers, however, such comments sounded hollow. "After lightly thanking us for the ardour we had shewn," Hale dryly recorded, "he repremanded us for disorder and plundering . . . and sent us about our business." A more complimentary message from Clinton followed but failed to lift the lieutenant's spirits. The campaign left him grousing at London over the state of affairs in the army and wishing the worst for Lord North's government. Peebles, less melancholy than his fellow grenadier, also noted the reprimand from Clinton, and it was clear the end of the campaign found the captain discontented as well.[18] It was not a happy officer corps.

Across the Atlantic, Britons did not receive news of Monmouth as glad tidings. In London the *Public Ledger* published Washington's letter to Congress of 1 July proclaiming the success of patriot arms without offering any rejoinder.[19] What was the public to think? The Earl of Abington drew a grim interpretation. "The news [is] terrible," he wrote to his friend, Lord Harcourt. "Clinton, in his march from Philadelphia through the Jerseys to New York, was exceedingly harassed, and at length attacked in his rear; the conflict was bloody, and the victory with the Americans." Abington feared that the French fleet's arrival in America, on top of the defeat in New Jersey, meant the war was all but lost.[20] Reality, of course, was hardly so dire, and George III later (in December) sent his "Royal Approbation" to the "officers and soldiers of the Army that marched through the Jerseys from Philadelphia."[21] The tribute was well deserved, although it could not mask the fact that some prominent Britons had reacted to the news of Monmouth with alarm—speaking volumes on the effectiveness of American arms and the waning confidence in the British war effort.

The difference between British and American reactions to Monmouth is striking. As Clinton boasted, the royal army indeed had accomplished its mission with professional skill and had fought well under trying conditions. Yet it had done so in a retreat that left an unbeaten enemy behind it and had abandoned everything it had won the previous year. Worse, the war appeared no closer to being won, and now hostilities with France only promised greater hardships. The entire situation was hardly one to boost morale. On the other side of the coin, every factor contributing to British gloom appeared a godsend to the rebels. However optimistic official British announcements on Monmouth may have been, the campaign had left the army and country with little sense of accomplishment or solace.

Enter the French

As Clinton made his way across New Jersey, he had not maintained contact with his Royal Navy counterpart, Admiral Lord Richard Howe (brother of the general). Howe's fleet had sailed from Philadelphia with its transports full of evacuees on 18 June, just as Clinton departed the city. As far as Sir Henry knew, as the army approached Monmouth Court House, Lord Howe was well on his way to meet him at Sandy Hook, if the admiral was not already there. In fact, Howe's passage was no faster than Clinton's. Contrary winds, or *no* winds, kept the fleet bottled up in the lower reaches of the Delaware River for ten days; Howe's vessels did not even clear the river until the twenty-eighth. The fleet arrived at Sandy Hook on the thirtieth, about the time Clinton was taking position on the Navesink Highlands. It had been a frustrating trip for the admiral, not to mention for the sweltering crews, passengers, and animals. It was also a more dangerous passage than he realized, for as his ships struggled to leave the Delaware, a French fleet was nearing American waters—heading directly for Delaware Bay.

France had openly entered the war, and the dispatch of a fleet to America was one of the first overt acts in behalf of the new Franco-American alliance. Vice Admiral Jean Baptiste Charles Henri Hector, comte d'Estaing, commanded; he had sailed from Toulon on 13 April with twelve ships-of-the-line and six frigates.[22] It was a force larger than anything the Royal Navy could match in America. D'Estaing's orders were to blockade Delaware Bay in support of any patriot effort against British-occupied Philadelphia. The British learned of his destination only on 5 June, and while they quickly dispatched a squadron to reinforce Howe, the relief would arrive only in mid-August. In the meantime Howe was unaware of the impending French threat, and it was just as well since there was little he could have done. Only as the navy was in the final stages of ferrying Clinton's men from Sandy Hook did the admiral and the general learn that d'Estaing was in the area, although they did not know exactly where. The situation clarified on Wednesday, 8 July, when word arrived that HMS *Andromeda*—the ship that had carried General Howe from Philadelphia—had spotted d'Estaing's ships off the Delaware capes. Admiral Howe had to consider that having missed the British to the south, the French would come looking for them around New York. He was right. After a difficult voyage of some three months, d'Estaing arrived off Sandy Hook on 11 July and anchored about four miles south.[23] The stage was apparently set for a naval showdown.

It never happened. Anticipating a fight, Howe worked feverishly to get his outnumbered squadron ready. Volunteers from merchant transports brought his crews up to strength, and the 15th and 44th Foot, as well as the light-infantry and grenadier companies of the 17th and 42nd (Royal Highlanders), joined the fleet as marines. Shore batteries targeted the approach to New York Bay, and Howe laid plans to contest the French as they sailed over the sandbar extending north from Sandy Hook.[24] Yet D'Estaing did not come. Fearing that his heavier ships would not clear the bar (he was wrong, at high tide and with favorable winds they could have passed over), instead the French blockaded the bay from outside the bar. For the next eleven days, the rival fleets watched one another. D'Estaing, wrote a grenadier officer, "resolved Not to Let us Out," and Howe resolved "not to Let him In." All the while the British expected Washington would do something by land in conjunction with the French.[25] This did not happen either—the Continental Army was still in transit to White Plains. When Washington did communicate with d'Estaing, the two officers finally settled on a joint (and ultimately unsuccessful) venture to drive the British from Newport, Rhode Island.[26] In a genuine anticlimax, on 22 July the French fleet sailed away; the British in New York were safe.

Washington recognized that Clinton had been lucky. If d'Estaing had made a more normal transoceanic crossing—say, a voyage of two months—he would have had a real chance to catch Howe's outgunned fleet at the mouth of the Delaware. In that case Clinton's haven at Sandy Hook would have been a prison. Without Howe's ships, the army would never have reached New York. If, per chance, Clinton learned of the Royal Navy's misfortune before reaching Sandy Hook, he could have diverted his march to the north, striking overland for New York. But this would have been problematic. Washington would have stood in his way, the passage of the Raritan posed a danger (a factor in convincing Clinton to head for Sandy Hook in the first place), and he would have been marching through largely patriot territory. Assuming Sir Henry was able to complete such a march—which assumes a lot—his troubles would have been far from over. With no fleet to protect New York, an unopposed d'Estaing could have blockaded the city, cutting off any hope of relief. Surrender would have been a matter of time.

Washington was sure that d'Estaing's inability to clear the bar into New York Bay was another lost opportunity. If the French had attempted to force their way in, Admiral Howe could have hurt them; he had cleverly positioned his ships to rake any attacking vessels. But could he have stopped d'Estaing? Probably not. Ultimately, the heavier French numbers would have told.[27] The result, Washington thought, would have been "one of the greatest strokes . . . that ever was"; the blow would have "reduced to moral certainty, the ruin of great Britain . . . as both army & Fleet must, undoubtedly, have fallen."[28] Whether the British could have absorbed the loss of two armies in consecutive years and still marshaled the political will to continue the war is an open question. If so, their military options would have been limited. As Brendan Morrissey has pointed out, with the loss of New York City, the British would have had no troops to speak of between upper New York State and Florida; the likeliest result would have been a patriot victory later in 1778.[29]

Of course, this is all speculation. D'Estaing arrived too late to prevent Clinton's escape, and the war went on. But it was a different conflict now. If he had thought about it, Sir Henry, with his campaign over, might have found himself in partial agreement with Washington. After two years of fighting, as the American had observed from White Plains, the campaign had left the rival armies in roughly the same places they had occupied in late 1776. Yet there were important differences. Now the rebels were celebrating, and the British found themselves down in the mouth. The King's troops certainly were not defeated, but they found little reason for satisfaction. There was another reversal as well. In late 1776 the British fully believed (however mistakenly) that the conflict was in its final stages and that the patriots were all but finished. In the summer of 1778, however, it was the Americans who believed that the British were in extremis. Monmouth also signaled that the nature of the struggle had changed. The campaign had opened with the British reacting to new strategic realities, and it ended with a French fleet casting those realities in concrete form. The American struggle for independence was now an international war. France would be an active belligerent in America, and for the armies that had fought at Monmouth, the conflict would never be the same.

CHAPTER 18

Constructing Victory, Settling Scores

The question of who won the Battle of Monmouth is largely academic; both sides claimed satisfaction with the results. In claiming victory, patriots pointed to Clinton's casualties and American possession of the field. Any number of them considered that Clinton had received a real "Drubbing."[1] The British ridiculed the American view. Sir Henry noted he had marched through the whole of an enemy province without losing a single wagon. Captain Johannes Ewald, with his usual penchant for exaggeration, considered the British campaign a marvel. "The retreat of Xenophon and his Ten Thousand Greeks," he wrote, as well as the most noteworthy fighting retreats of European armies, "could not have had more hardships on their marches than we endured." Splitting the difference, Mercy Otis Warren later concluded, "After the battle of Monmouth both parties boasted their advantages, as is usual after an indecisive action."[2]

Warren had it right. The Battle of Monmouth was a tactical triumph for neither side; the fighting revealed strengths and weaknesses in both armies (discussed in the next chapter). It did not alter the strategic balance of the war. The British did not cripple the Continental Army, while the patriots never came close to "Burgoyning" Clinton or stopping him from redeploying his army. The war would go on. Thus for Sir Henry, the results at Monmouth were acceptable. For Washington, however, they were *not;* he had needed a more decisive outcome.

Here we come to the heart of the matter: Washington needed a victory for reasons as much political as military, perhaps more political. No matter how well his army had performed—and it had performed well—what he got at Monmouth was a hard-fought draw. Ever the realist, Henry Laurens knew as much. Amid patriot rejoicing, he congratulated his son John on the "partial Victory" at Monmouth.[3] If Washington was to have the major triumph he wanted and felt he needed, it would have to come from somewhere other than this New Jersey battlefield.

Washington's objective in sending an advance force to attack the British rear never had been just military. He had politics in mind as well—to do the "something," as Nathanael Greene had put it, the people expected.[4] The patriot chief wanted to accomplish this with minimum risk to his army, and however unintentionally, Clinton had helped. When Sir Henry lunged for victory—and missed—the American responded with brilliant military theater. The spectacular cannonade, the small detachment actions to harass the British withdrawal, followed by moving forward to occupy ground that the British had abandoned all seemed the stuff of victory. Where Washington expected a small battle at a distance led by Lafayette then Lee, Clinton had given him the opportunity to preside over the largest sound-and-light show of the war. He *had* to make the most of it.

The Victory Narrative

If Clinton actually was not routed in the field, Washington and his partisans would have to defeat him in the battle for public opinion. That is, no matter what the actual tactical result at Monmouth, the public would have to perceive the engagement as a clear-cut victory for patriot arms and for Washington personally. It is impossible to overstate the significance of this point. Those around the commander in chief were determined to fashion a propaganda triumph for their leader. To this end they waged a campaign in Congress, within the officer corps, in the press, and in the public at large—and that campaign was masterful.

Washington took the first steps in this direction. Reporting to his political masters, he moved judiciously in shaping perceptions of the battle. On 29 June he sent an initial account to Henry Laurens. It was a brief missive—one short paragraph—positive in tone but without overtly claiming victory. The general related having "forced the Enemy from the Field" and promised further details as soon as possible.[5] His full report followed on 1 July. This was an important communication, and Washington must have realized it. The dispatch was his first detailed report from the front since his disappointments of 1777, and he made the most of his opportunity. The document was measured, detailed, but decidedly favorable in its conclusions on the battle. The commander in chief informed Congress of the circumstances leading to the action, the battle itself, the appalling heat, the bitterness of the fighting, the army's gallantry and skill, and the fact that the British had left the field to the Americans. He was generous in his praise: The "officers of the Army in general," he wrote, "seemed to vie with each other in manifesting their Zeal and Bravery." The general singled out Brigadier General Wayne for "particular commendation," and he lauded the performance of the artillery and the troops generally. He never claimed too much, and he mentioned the cloud hanging over Major General Lee, but the tenor of the report was absolutely clear: Monmouth was a win, and an important one.[6] The string of defeats was over, and the rebuilt Continental Army (and thus Washington's leadership) had proved itself in battle.

The effect in Congress was all the general could have wanted. Ignoring the restraint of Washington's dispatch, few delegates had any doubt Clinton had been smashed. Based only on the short note of the twenty-ninth, John Hancock wrote home that Monmouth had "discompos'd" and "Ruin'd" the British, knocking them out of the war for at least a year. Only days later, and with the benefit of having seen the general's full report, Connecticut delegate Titus Hosmer sent letters to friends announcing the supposedly calamitous state of the enemy and the fact that only accident (a veiled reference to General Lee) had prevented Clinton's complete destruction, adding that even tories were predicting Sir Henry would have to quit America entirely. Such effusions were typical of letters from delegates to correspondents throughout the colonies. Samuel Adams of Massachusetts, John Banister of Virginia, John Mathews of South Carolina, Elias Boudinot of New Jersey, and Thomas McKean of Delaware were among those spreading the joyous news. Recipients could hardly be blamed for concluding that Clinton had barely escaped the fate of Burgoyne.[7] To make the rebel claim to success completely unambiguous, on 7 July Congress voted a formal thanks to Washington and the army in honoring "the important victory of Monmouth over the British grand army."[8] Only the total overthrow of Clinton could have raised the level of congressional satisfaction with Washington's performance.

It would be difficult to imagine a more complete victory in shaping official perceptions of the battle. Alexander Hamilton in particular would have been appalled to learn otherwise. In fact, no one had worked harder than Lieutenant Colonels Hamilton and John

Laurens to make sure Monmouth received what today would be called a favorable "spin." Both men were intimates of Washington's military "family," and both held an abiding grudge against the general's critics. They neither forgave nor forgot the slights of 1777, and after Monmouth (in which they had both fought admirably) they quickly picked up their pens on their commander's behalf. Their goal was twofold: to support Washington's version of events while shaping a favorable public understanding of what the army and the commander in chief had accomplished; and to use the events of 28 June to silence potential critics or threats to Washington's position as commander in chief.

The young officers went to work almost as soon as the guns fell silent. Laurens wrote two quick letters to his influential father praising Washington and implying the worst about General Lee. The major general's "indecision" during the morning battle, the first letter claimed, was "calculated to ruin us"; the vanguard was caught up in a "disgraceful" retreat. Worse, Lee had replied "indecently" when Washington had expressed "his astonishment at this unaccountable retreat." The commander in chief then brought order out of the chaos. He rallied the troops, and the end of the day found the patriots "Masters of the ground" with "the Standards of Liberty . . . planted in Triumph on the field of battle."[9] A second letter (2 July) again praised Washington while taking an even more damning posture toward Lee: Clinton's "whole flying army," the lieutenant colonel wrote, "would have fallen into our hands" but for the conduct or the lack of "good will" on the part of Lee.[10] The claim was preposterous, of course, but it reflected young Laurens's loyalty to his chief and his hatred of the chief's detractors.

Hamilton's tack with Congress was similar. "You know my way of thinking about our army," he told Boudinot after the battle, "and I am not about to flatter it. I assure you I never was pleased with them before this day."[11] The glory was all due, of course, to Washington's leadership and dimmed only by Lee's questionable conduct. The message was the same as Washington's official communication, but Hamilton and Laurens aimed effectively at influential personal connections and told their story without any of the commander in chief's tact.

Other Washington loyalists helped. On 30 June Major General Stirling wrote his friend and South Carolina delegate William Henry Drayton with news of the battle; Drayton promptly penned a note to Washington expressing "my little tribute of thanks for the important Victory of Monmouth." Wayne sent a similar message to Richard Peters, secretary to the Board of War, boasting of defeating "the flower" of the British army.[12] Congress got the message, and Henry Laurens, as president, drove the point home. After a congressional dinner celebrating the Fourth of July, he offered thirteen toasts, variously honoring independence, the country, its allies, the American people, the Battles of Trenton and Saratoga, freedom, and union. Among the toasts, however, two loudly echoed the excitement that followed the Battle of Monmouth: "The Commander in Chief of the American Forces," and "The 28th of June, twice Glorious, 1776—1778."[13]

If amid the tumult of patriot self-congratulations there were any in Congress who questioned why the British had reached New York successfully, they wisely held their peace. Delegates Samuel Adams and James Lovell, no partisans of Washington, obligingly noted the importance of events at Monmouth, though without attributing any credit to the commander in chief.[14] While these less-than-enthusiastic sentiments were conveyed in private letters, the guarded applause by Washington's former critics apparently was public knowledge. Supporters of the general loved it. Replying to Hamilton, Boudinot sensed the uneasiness of the likes of Adams and Lovell. "The General I allways revered & loved," he told his friend, "has rose superior to himself." Then, in a direct slap at the erstwhile critics of the commander in chief, he went on, "Every Lip dwells on his Praise for even his pretended friends (for none dare to acknowledge themselves his Enemies) are obliged to croak it forth."[15] Sweet revenge.

The patriot officer corps overwhelmingly endorsed the Washingtonian victory narrative. Monmouth veterans told tales in vivid terms. Dr. James McHenry boasted of the army "conquering the culled and picked, the very flower of the British army, their light Infantry, guards, and grenadiers."[16] It was the same from other officers. From Colonel William Irvine: "Thus the pride of the British Tyrant is lowering. . . . [T]he 28th was a most Glorious day for the American arms." From Major Samuel Shaw: "The fortune of the day was great,—great in itself, and much more so will it be in its consequences; the superiority of the American arms was never so apparent." From Colonel Thomas Clark of North Carolina: "Our independence is now I think firmly established by which Britain has lost her right hand. . . . We charge[d] them with Bayonets and with smaller numbers drove them before us, this is a fact." And from Lieutenant Colonel Dudley Coleman of Massachusetts: "The enemy gave way & left us compleat masters of the field retreating with great precipitation."[17] Officers not at Monmouth had similar reactions. In Philadelphia Colonel Lewis Nicola was astounded at the number of British deserters coming in as a result of the campaign. Adjutant General Pickering thought Clinton's losses and the new political realities "will remove" the British "from the United States." Based on patriot reports, Major General John Sullivan, then at Providence, Rhode Island, concluded, "victory Declared in Favor of the American Arms." From White Plains, even Horatio Gates was gracious enough to send Washington a congratulatory note on the "glorious News."[18] The guiding hand behind all of this, of course, was that of the commander in chief.

Feelings ran high in the officer corps, and for some the occasion seemed opportune to settle scores from earlier in the year. As Washington marched northeast from Englishtown, two militia commanders, Pennsylvania major general John Cadwalader and his cousin, New Jersey major general Philemon Dickinson, rode to Philadelphia. Their intention was to provoke a duel with former inspector general Thomas Conway, the man central to the "cabal." They succeeded. After whatever words passed between Conway and Cadwalader—what exactly was said remains unknown—the former challenged the latter. Dickinson served as Cadwalader's second, and the Pennsylvanian's fire hit Conway through the lip. Initial accounts of the duel reported a mortal wound, but Conway quickly recovered.[19] His career in America, however, was over, Before returning to France, he sent Washington a letter apologizing for any offence he may have given; the general did not reply. There is no record of any officer censuring the actions of Cadwalader and Dickinson (other than Lee, as noted below). Indeed, Greene was positively gleeful and was sure others shared his view. Well after the event, he wrote Cadwalader: "Your duel made a great noise in the American World. Most People rejoiced at Mr. Conway's fate."[20] It is difficult to imagine the affair taking place, much less the approving reactions to it, outside of the afterglow of Monmouth.

But not everyone approved of Cadwalader. Thomas McKean, simultaneously a Delaware congressional delegate and chief justice of the Supreme Court of Pennsylvania, was one of them—perhaps the only delegate to leave a record of his disapproval. He thought the general's action reflected "weaknes and vanity." But McKean could read the sentiments of the day and took no action against the officer. Any move to bring Cadwalader into court, the judge thought, "might be attributed by uncharitable persons to resentment rather than justice."[21] McKean was right in questioning whether the duel served justice, but it clearly illustrated that Washington's loyalists were never bolder in defending his reputation than they were in the aftermath of 28 June.

The American press reflected the same euphoria. The press was not large, but most major population centers had a weekly newspaper, and readers regularly followed war news when it appeared, usually in the form of letters, official announcements, or reprints from other papers. If Monmouth was a resounding victory in Congress and the officers corps, it was equally so in the rebel press. Reports on the battle were electrifying—and sometimes quite fanciful. Patriot correspondents wasted no time in getting accounts into print, and newspapers produced the decisive victory that had eluded American arms in the field.

In the propaganda vanguard was New Jersey governor William Livingston. The governor was an active Washington partisan who stood solidly with the general against his critics. Livingston also was one of the most effective pamphleteers of the war. His anonymous account of the battle came out in the *New Jersey Gazette* only days after the fighting. It was stunningly effective. Writing as a witness to the action (he was no closer than Trenton at any time during the campaign), he depicted the British as little better than pillaging barbarians, slowed by the militia and finally thrashed by Washington's Continentals. The Americans "did amazing execution," he assured readers, and the enemy "line of march from the Courthouse was strew'd with dead, with arms, knapsacks and accouterments, which they dropt on their retreat." Clinton's march through New Jersey, Livingston's account proclaimed, cost him at least half his army. "How much cheaper might his Britannic Majesty buy sheep and oxen in England, in the usual manner, than he now gets them, by employing an army to steal them in America!" And who was responsible for these glorious events? Livingston had the answer: "Our success under Heaven, is to be wholly ascribed to the good disposition made by his Excellency," with the support of his officers and men.[22] So there it was: Clinton soundly defeated; Washington the hero. Credit Livingston with knowing how to make an unambiguous point.

This was not the end. The *New Jersey Gazette,* together with rebel papers in Philadelphia, the *Pennsylvania Packet* and the *Evening Post,* continued to print Monmouth-related items well into August. By mid-July the battle was a prominent feature in the Boston press as well. All the writers seemingly took their cues from Livingston and treated readers to British casualty reports (inflated, of course), tales of Continental valor, and Washington's gallantry.[23] The media view, which fully reflected the glowing official assessments of the battle, was consistent and articulate: Monmouth was a major triumph.

While it is difficult to assess clearly the results of this early "media blitz," it was at least partially effective. Those Americans who relied on newspapers for their information, or on any other official patriot versions of the battle, could be excused for believing that the rebel army had won a smashing triumph. On British-occupied Long Island, for instance, the wife of a Continental officer noted in her diary that local patriots were delighted with the battle. The redcoats, she had learned, were beaten and inactive after the fighting, not to mention deeply troubled by the French fleet's arrival. By 9 July news of the battle had traveled to New Haven, Connecticut, where Ezra Stiles, president of Yale College, recorded in his diary, "God gave us the Victory" at Monmouth. In Philadelphia, amid the rejoicing over the events of 28 June, Esther Reed, wife of Joseph Reed, shared congratulations with friends over "our success at Monmouth."[24] Thus General Clinton could think what he liked of the encounter at Monmouth Court House: Patriots believed they had won the day. For Washington's partisans, especially Hamilton and Laurens, the pen had proved at least as mighty as the sword.

There is another dimension to this. While it was not evident at the time—that is, in the weeks and months following the Battle of Monmouth—Washington's partisans had "oversold" their victory scenario. In 1776 patriots understood that the Battle of Trenton, followed closely by Second Trenton and Princeton, had breathed new life into the faltering struggle for independence. In 1778, in the aftermath of Monmouth, many patriots were convinced the war effort had turned a decisive corner—that in fact the victory at Monmouth spelled the doom of British sovereignty in America, that the war was as good as won. Certainly, this was the conclusion of some congressional delegates. "It is the Common opinion," Josiah Bartlett of New Hampshire informed his wife, the British "will Soon quit the United States." Connecticut's Hosmer was more cautious in his hopes—"a little Time will discover the Truth"—but he reported that tories in Philadelphia fully expected Clinton "is directly to leave the Continent and draw off his Myrmidons."[25] In July the Reverend William Gordon sent an adulatory letter to the commander in chief congratulating him on his success at Monmouth. Gordon hoped that with the French now in the war, the British would be gone by the end of the year. That being the case, the minister asked if the general would allow him to visit Mount Vernon in the autumn to study his (Washington's) papers in order to write a planned history of the Revolution. To crown the victor, a patriotic young woman surprised Washington with the gift of a laurel wreath. The general promised to wear it "with great pleasure in remembrance of the fair giver."[26]

Of course, these predictions were wrong: The war did not end, and some of the darkest days of the Revolution lay ahead. It would be almost five years before the last of the "Myrmidons" left America, before Gordon could say how his history would end, and before the commander in chief could don the victor's laurel. But Monmouth, indecisive as it was from a strictly military perspective, was a decisive tonic for patriot morale. The influence on popular opinion was every bit as dramatic as that of the Battle of Trenton two years earlier. Monmouth had restored faith in American arms—and in General George Washington.

Court-Martial

In this exuberant atmosphere the matter of Major General Lee came to a head in one of the most notorious courts-martial in American history. The event settled once and for all the sanctity of Washington's position as commander in chief, and it is time to consider how this came about.

Lee had not shared in the rejoicing following the battle. Exhausted after the morning action, at Englishtown he gladly had relinquished command of the reserves to Major General Steuben. Over the course of the afternoon, Lee had lost touch with events at the front; indeed, he reportedly was skeptical when told the Continentals had repulsed the British grenadiers.[27] Late on the twenty-eighth Steuben led the reserves back to the front. When Lee, sufficiently rested in the evening, again offered his services, Washington had no job for him.

Thus it was that the fighting by Washington on Perrine's Hill and then by Colonel Cilley, Brigadier General Wayne, and Major General Greene had established the basis for American victory claims. Lee had no part in it. No matter that his handling of the vanguard had drawn Clinton to Stirling's guns and that his efforts before the West Morass had bought the time necessary for the commander in chief to make a stand. When Clinton recoiled and withdrew, Lee was not there. Among the hosannas sung after the battle, his name was not among those celebrated. Indeed, the case was quite the reverse.

What had happened? An entry in the journal of Major Joseph Bloomfield is instructive. Bloomfield, a young major in the Third New Jersey, had been with Maxwell's New Jersey Brigade during the morning retreat; by the end of the day, his regiment was in reserve at Englishtown. On the evening of the twenty-eighth, he made a lengthy entry in his war journal. He described the early retreat and Washington's arrival with the main army, then added this:

> Drove the proud King's-Guards & haughty British Grenadiers, & gained Immortal-honor, to the Shame & infamy of Genl. Lee who acted the part of the base [word omitted] in not engaging the enemy when he had received positive orders to attack them. But History I expect will give a full account of this memorable action, justly censure Lee for his scandalous behavior & give credit (if possible for the pen of a writer) to Genl. Washington's bravery & merit.[28]

This was strong stuff from a devoted Washington partisan, and his praise of the commander in chief was fully in line with the all-but-official version of the battle previously described. But it begs the question of how Bloomfield could have taken such a decided position so early. He was a junior officer and not part of Washington's family, and he was not privy to any orders Lee may have received from their commander. Bloomfield had left the field before Washington confronted the general, and the only action he had seen was the relatively orderly retrograde of the vanguard. So how could he have so quickly drawn such pronounced conclusions?

Bloomfield had no personal experience or direct evidence on which to base an opinion on Lee's conduct, much less on any orders Washington may have issued. The fact that he could write in such strident terms the evening of the twenty-eighth is testimony to how quickly and effectively Washington's lieutenants put out their version of events. In other words, the tacitly "official" version was in place *before* anyone really knew the battle was over and two days *before* Washington ordered Lee's court-martial. It is important to note that the story had two parts. The tributes to Washington went hand-in-hand with the denigration of Lee. On 30 June, when John Laurens wrote to his father in praise of the commander in chief, he pointedly included an unflattering account of Lee's performance, doing so prior to the general's arrest later in the day. Hamilton did the same in writing to Boudinot, as did McHenry in a letter to his friend George Lux; McHenry also wrote *before* learning of Lee's arrest.[29] On the thirtieth as well, Brigadier Generals Charles Scott and Anthony Wayne sent a joint letter to Washington blaming Lee for the morning retreat and claiming (by clear implication) that he had robbed the army of a "most glorious and decisive victory."[30] Short of accusations of perfidy or outright treachery (most of those would come *after* the court-martial), these charges constituted as dark a portrait of Lee as fellow officers could paint. Bloomfield's account was actually nothing more than a faithful repetition of what already had become the pro-Washington and anti-Lee narrative, and it is inconceivable the major had not taken his cue from the officers closest to Washington. By 30 June Lee *already* was anathema to much of the officer corps.

Lee certainly was aware of all this, and he was deeply wounded. Late on 28 June (or early on the twenty-ninth) he vented in a letter to Richard Henry Lee. "What the devil brought us into this level country (the very element of the enemy) or what interest we can have (in our present circumstances) to hazard an action, somebody else must tell you, for I cannot." The bewildered officer told Lee that he had attacked as ordered but retired in good order in the face of superior numbers and effective enemy cavalry. He insisted that had he not done so, the army and "perhaps America, would have been ruined." But "the thanks I received from his Excellency were of a singular nature."[31] That, of course, was an understatement. The major general, however, did nothing else until 30 June, when he reacted to the accumulating atmosphere of censure by writing directly to Washington—another colossal error of judgment.

In a letter reflecting his truculent personality, Lee sought an apology for what he considered Washington's pointed words on the battlefield. Lee stated that while he held Washington in "the greatest respect and veneration," in this case, "I must pronounce that he has been guilty of an act of cruel injustice towards a man who certainly has some pretensions to the regard of every servant of this country." The commander in chief took umbrage, informing Lee that he considered the tone of the letter "highly improper" and that he recalled making no statements to Lee on the field other than those duty required. Rather than an apology, the major general would get an official inquiry into his conduct at Monmouth, which the rebel commander thought highly culpable. At this Lee asked, in clearly insolent terms, that any hearing be a full court-martial at which he would seek to clear his name of rumored misconduct. Washington promptly complied and had him placed under arrest that evening.[32]

The general was aware many officers harbored ill feelings toward Lee, especially since those in the commander in chief's "family" were so active in propagating and encouraging those feelings. But the depth of Lee's anger seems to have taken the general by surprise. True enough, Washington was not happy with him. Yet after the battle, he was probably willing to forget his battlefield exchange of words with Lee, or at least to drop the matter. As of 30 June, the commander in chief had kept his second in command in the normal rotation of administrative duties, hardly a sign of official disapproval.[33] William Gordon noted that Washington put Lee back in command on the twenty-eighth to fight the holding action east of the West Morass; having done so, why would the general take any formal action against him? Rather, Gordon was convinced Washington "meant to pass by what had happened"—the battlefield contretemps—"without further notice."[34] Long after the trial, Washington insisted he arrested Lee only because Lee himself had "solicited" it and only had brought "him to tryal at his own request."[35] That being the case, had Lee swallowed his pride and not acted as he did, the relationship between the two men probably would have returned to its former cool but professional correctness.

Yet with Lee's demand for court-martial, there was no turning back—and Lee did not think he was tempting fate. Such a request was a fairly normal practice among officers who felt their honor impugned; a trial would allow them to clear their reputations of alleged misconduct or poor performance. The goal was acquittal "with honor"—a formal recognition that charges against an officer were false, unfounded, or even malicious. After the debacle at Fort Ticonderoga in 1777, both Major Generals Schuyler and St. Clair faced courts-martial; both were acquitted "with highest honor." Accused of negligence that led to the bloody surprise at Paoli, Wayne demanded a court-martial; he also was acquitted "with honor."[36] There were cases in which the demand for a court-martial alone was enough to make an accuser withdraw an accusation.[37]

Lee sought a similar result, and he liked his chances. And why not? He sincerely believed his conduct on the twenty-eighth had been meritorious. True, there were times when he failed to communicate effectively with subordinates (although he never admitted as much), but he had done well enough in the face superior numbers, on adverse terrain, without effective cavalry, and with the Continental main body beyond supporting distance. He had done no worse than St. Clair at Ticonderoga and certainly better than Wayne at Paoli. (What Lee seemingly overlooked was the fact that in these other high-profile trials, the defendants were not pitted against the commander in chief.) Besides, Lee also thought other officers would support him. In his second letter to Washington of the thirtieth, he was impertinent enough to remind the general that all in the army were "not my friends, nor all your admirers."[38]

News of Lee's arrest stunned the army. Those who had maligned the major general certainly had taken aim at his reputation; they also had struck at him as one of those who had personally criticized the commander in chief and was friendly with others who had done the same. There is no evidence, however, that anyone had actually tried to goad Lee into demanding a court-martial. Hamilton, at the head of the phalanx of his detractors, was glad to find Lee in trouble but feared that a court-martial would do little to hurt the major general—it might even allow him to exonerate himself. "A certain preconceived & preposterous opinion of his being a very great man will operate in his favour," Hamilton warned Boudinot. "Some people are very industrious in making interest for him."[39] Wayne, who detested Lee and had done his share attacking the general's performance at Monmouth, was surprised matters had gone as far as a court-martial. He wrote successive letters to Richard Peters at the Board of War, Colonel William Irvine, and his fellow Pennsylvanian Sharp Delany saying he was "sorry for the Occation of it."[40] Other officers were appalled at the discord the trial might bring and earnestly hoped to avoid involvement. Henry Livingston, who had fought so stoutly at the Hedgerow, plaintively wrote his brother that he wanted nothing to do with the proceedings (he would end up testifying at length). Nathanael Greene thought Lee would receive only a "Slight censure" but feared the affair would "create many Divisions in the Army."[41]

Junior officers reacted as well, though not all of them were as certain of their feelings as Bloomfield. Major Shaw, Knox's gallant adjutant, saw the affair in terms akin to Greek tragedy—a tale of the high and mighty brought low. He probably captured the confusion that gripped many patriots when they learned of Lee's arrest. The major's bewilderment, expressed in a letter to his friend the Reverend John Eliot, is worth quoting in its entirety:

> I am sorry to write a piece of news which must grieve every good friend to his country. You will be surprised, but it is true;—General Lee, the second officer upon the Continent, is in arrest! The charges against him are high; *disobedience of orders* and *making an unnecessary and shameful retreat in face of the enemy*, are among the catalogue. A court martial sat this day for his trial; a more interesting one, perhaps, never came before a court. What will be its decision, God knows. Alas, the condition of humanity! That General Lee, a character known and regarded, not only in America, but in Europe, and ranked in the first class of military fame, should have such matters laid to his charge, is melancholy. Indeed, my dear friend, it affects me exceedingly; I feel more on the occasion than I am able to express. How precarious is reputation! On what a slender thread does it depend! 'It breaks at every breeze'! These charges against General Lee respect his conduct while with the detachments of which he had the command, when they came up with the enemy, as already mentioned. It would be presumptuous in any officer, much more so in a young one, to give his opinion in an affair of so much delicacy and importance; it is now before a court martial,—the members are gentlemen of approved abilities, integrity, and honor,—there let us leave it.[42]

The "gentlemen" Shaw wrote of were the four brigadiers and eight colonels who comprised the military court. Major General Stirling sat as president. To the extent one can discern the state of army politics, earlier in the year all these officers had stood by Washington against his critics, although there is no evidence Lee gave much thought to the matter.[43] After two days of delay, the court convened at New Brunswick on 4 July. Following Washington's orders, the judge advocate charged Lee on three counts. The first was in disobeying orders in not attacking on the morning of 28 June "agreeable to repeated instructions"; the second alleged "an *unnecessary, disorderly,* and *shameful retreat*"; the third charged Lee with disrespect toward the commander in chief in two of his letters.[44] The trial, which most historians now concede did no credit to the army, lasted until 12 August, the court meeting twenty-four times as the army moved through New Jersey (at New Brunswick, Morristown, and Paramus) and then settled at Peekskill, New York, near White Plains.

Lee conducted an articulate defense. Given the circumstances of the battle, the first two charges against him were absurd. Undeniably, however, he had been disrespectful to Washington, and therein lay his downfall. While Lee had his partisans, most of the army stood solidly with the commander in chief. "Under the circumstances," historian John Shy has observed, "an acquittal on the first two charges would have been a vote of no-confidence in Washington." But after Monmouth, the commander's stock soared; people no longer expressed reservations about his ability (or, as Boudinot implied, none dared). Given Lee's unpopularity, the verdict of guilty on all counts was not surprising. Yet the court tacitly conceded that some of the charges were too severe. The verdict deleted the word "shameful" from the second charge and found the retreat had been "disorderly" only "in some few instances."[45] The court suspended Lee from the army for a year—a ridiculously light sentence if members actually believed him guilty. Washington sent the verdict to Congress for confirmation, which considered the matter off and on until December. In the meantime, everyone involved lobbied to sway the congressional decision.

The treatment of Lee excited considerable public comment and even sympathy. Prominent South Carolina patriot and physician David Ramsay was shocked at the general's fate. The doctor was a great admirer of Washington, and his brother, Lieutenant Colonel Nathaniel Ramsey, had been wounded and captured in the Point of Woods, but Dr. Ramsay took exception to the court-martial verdict. In a letter to Benjamin Rush, subsequently published anonymously in the *Pennsylvania Packet,* Ramsay condemned the verdict and the later congressional vote to sustain it (discussed below) as gross injustices. He argued that the country owed Lee considerable thanks.[46] As late as 1789, when he published his *History of the American Revolution,* Ramsay had not changed his mind. He recalled "many were displeased" with the sentence and noted the existence of real skepticism over the court's insistence that the general should have stood and fought on the morning of 28 June. There was some popular understanding that Lee's orders were discretionary, that his lack of cavalry on open ground put him at a disadvantage, and that

Washington was not close enough to support the vanguard in a major action. If Washington had left an attack to Lee's discretion, then how could the army charge him with disobeying orders? Those who questioned the verdict, Ramsay concluded, felt "a suspension from command, was not a sufficient punishment for his crimes, if really guilty. They therefore inferred a presumption of innocence from the lenient sentence of his judges." The only agreement was on the charge of disrespect to Washington.[47] Ramsay's account may be trusted, for it fully reflects the import of comment in the press and in private letters and conversations.[48]

Indeed, feelings were such that had Lee not attacked Washington, Congress may have sought a compromise between the two generals. But Lee did attack. In defending himself, the major general was as casual with the record as those who attacked him. He denigrated the contributions of the commander in chief, which recalled his criticisms of 1776. "G. Washington saw, knew, and was almost as little concern'd in the affair of the 28th," he wrote to Rush, "as he was in the battle of Philippi." "I am taught to think that equity is to be put out of the question," he told Aaron Burr, who had lost a horse leading Malcolm's Additional Regiment at Monmouth, "and the decision of the affair to be put entirely on the strength of party."[49] He was right in fearing "party" but wrong in disparaging Washington's leadership. Lee insisted that his withdrawal in front of Clinton was never a retreat; rather, it was a "masterly manoeuvre" designed to draw the British into the maw of Washington's main force.[50] Of course this was nonsense. Until late in the action, Lee had no idea where Washington was or when he was going to arrive, and while he generally kept his command under control, he made up his movements as he went along. Lee's friends warned him not to make the contest a personal faceoff with the commanding general, which would compel delegates to see the case as a matter of public policy rather than a judgment of performance.[51] As a matter of policy, they would have to choose Washington no matter what the merits of Lee's position; to find for Lee and discredit the commander in chief would be to throw the army into turmoil.

In the absence of any timely congressional decision, the Lee affair reignited the simmering resentments of 1777. While the wounded major general raged, the commander in chief remained cool, disclaiming personal animosity toward his second in command while quietly professing disgust at what he saw as Lee's efforts to lead a partisan attack on him. Washington was furious. He later claimed that he never disliked Lee because the major general had been privy to "a party against me," or because he saw the commander in chief as an obstacle to his own advancement, or because Lee sought "to lessen me in the esteem of my Countrymen." Rather, he disliked him because "his temper, and plans, were too versatile & violent, to attract my admiration." Washington only marveled that he had avoided Lee's "venom" for so long.[52] The commanding general was being clever—and *disingenuous* is not too strong a word—in his disclaimers: He had known exactly where Lee stood in relation to his critics, and his catalogue of his subordinate's transgressions comprised exactly those that had enraged the general's loyalists. Deft politician that he was, Washington publicly remained above the controversy, but privately he must have known what his military family was doing.

Wisely, Washington let his inner circle carry the fight. The "family" included Hamilton, John Laurens, Lafayette, McHenry, John Fitzgerald, and several others. They had stood by Washington during the dark days of 1777 and early 1778, and they detested those who had schemed (as the young officers saw it) to humble or displace the commander in chief. None of these talented young men were close to Lee, most having joined Washington's staff or found their present positions while the major general was still a prisoner of war. Upon Lee's exchange in 1778, they certainly were aware of his jaundiced view of the increasing professionalization of the army. They also took particular notice of the company he kept. Lee had renewed his ties to Thomas Mifflin, Benjamin Rush, and Washington's other critics, some of whom had been party to the alleged Conway Cabal. And it was striking, Washington's lieutenants thought, that the commander in chief's previous critics now rallied to Lee's defense. Therefore, in attacking Lee, these younger officers, notably Hamilton and Laurens, aimed at bigger game. Just as they had shaped popular perceptions of Monmouth in order to credit their chief with a victory, they would use the matter of Lee to settle the score with Washington's detractors—permanently.

Buoyed by the decision to court-martial Lee, the inner circle worked openly to vilify him. They hinted broadly that his conduct had been responsible for Clinton's escape and may have involved actual treachery. Laurens and Hamilton said as much in their correspondence. McHenry felt the same. Lee's conduct, he noted, should be "well inquired into," as it had cost patriots "the fairest opportunity this war has afforded to destroy the British army." In a note to Boudinot, he was more pointed: "Had matters been conducted that morning agreeable to the system for attack, it is more than probable that their whole army would have been routed. Everything was in a fine temper for a total defeat."[53] Beyond implying treachery on Lee's part, McHenry and other officers of the "family" linked the accused general to the earlier critics of Washington. Laurens was convinced the same "junto" involved with Conway and Gates were again out to embarrass Washington, and he warned correspondents against their machinations. Hamilton got in a clever shot at Gates, noting that at Monmouth, Washington had no Benedict Arnold on hand to win his laurels for him.[54] These attacks were assiduous and insidious; they were also effective. Lee may have been quarrelsome and even disagreeable, but he was no traitor. Yet the persistent campaign of character assassination planted doubts about his loyalty, if not a conviction of his treason, in the public mind. His reputation never recovered.

Lee thought he saw the situation clearly: "A most hellish plan has been formed (and I may say at least not discourag'd by Head Quarters) to destroy for ever my honor and reputation."[55] Attempting to fight back, Lee played right into the hands of his critics. Turning to friends such as Rush and Richard Henry Lee only confirmed accusations that he was part of the old "Junto of last Winter," as Pennsylvania president Joseph Reed put it. "Gen. Lee is making his Court, & I believe successfully," Reed told Greene, "to the same Interests."[56] Lee also vigorously objected to the triumphalist narrative of the battle. The action was a "handsome check" of the British, "which did the Americans honor," but he insisted that calling it "a complete victory would be a dishonorable gasconade."[57] The message made no headway with euphoric patriots. In addition, Lee persisted in his ad homonym attacks on the commander in chief. He called Washington's official account of the battle "from beginning to end a most abominable damn'd lie," and he published the lengthy and cogent "Vindication to the Public," in which he vigorously defended his conduct at Monmouth and his attachment to the American cause.[58] Such efforts did nothing to bolster sympathy for his position; nor did attempts by anonymous Lee allies to smear Washington. Reed reported rumors charging the rebel chief with "great cruelty to his Slaves in Virginia & Immorality of Life." The attacks, he thought, bordered "upon frenzy."[59]

To the end, some officers remained unsure how the congressional decision would go. Finally, however, on 5 December Congress voted to sustain the court-martial verdict. It had no real choice in the matter: despite the injustice to Lee, it could not risk the effectiveness and reputation of the army to save one man. Still, almost a third of the delegates—seven of twenty-three—opposed the motion to vote on the verdict, clearly implying that Lee had been wronged.[60] In London, news of the verdict was no surprise. "When a dispute had been carried to so great a height," a sanguine Briton observed, "between an officer on whom the Americans reposed there chief consequence, and one subordinate less popular, it is not difficult to devine where the blame will be laid."[61] *C'est la guerre.*

Lee did not disappear gracefully. If anything, the congressional vote increased his fury and despair. His anger was such that he even rose to the defense of Conway. Near the end of the debate, a Baltimore newspaper published a lengthy tract on Conway's behalf. It accused Washington of mistreating Conway and argued that the French officer had committed no crime in privately criticizing the commander in chief. Private comments, the author pointed out, were common in armies of the day (he was correct in this), and they violated no article of war and generally evoked no retribution. Washington was mortal, the writer cautioned, and it would be a sad day if an officer could not privately say so. Lee disclaimed authorship (although the tone was his), but if he did not write it, he agreed with it. On 18 December he sent a copy to Gates and urged him to encourage its publication in New England.[62] Under the circumstances, the difference between a man who writes such a tract and one who endorses it and urges its publication is only a matter of degree. In any event, the public attributed the tract to Lee, further alienating him from the patriot mainstream. Few were now willing to defend him publicly.

The disgraced general would not quit. He sent vituperative and desperate correspondence to Congress and all who would listen, and in a pathetic episode in late December, he fought a duel with John Laurens. The lieutenant colonel issued the challenge, enraged at what he considered Lee's unwarranted attacks on Washington's character. In the resulting exchange of fire, Lee was slightly wounded. Steuben also issued a challenge, although that duel was averted.[63] Thinking anyone who had slighted Washington was in danger, if not literally, then figuratively, Lee sent a warning to Gates: "For God's sake take care of yourself there is a mine laid under your feet, and the train [of gunpowder] ready laid, the materials heap'd up from self conceit arrogance ignorance and mean jealousy."[64] Later Congress, reacting to an angry letter from Lee, closed the book on the major general, resolving it had no further need of his services. He was an embittered man. In 1792 Lee's first biographer, former Georgia congressional delegate Edward Langworthy, wrote, "The affair at Monmouth, several pieces of scurrility from the press, and numerous instances of private slander and defamation, so far got the better of his philosophy, as to provoke him in the highest degree, and he became, as it were, angry with all mankind."[65] (Lee retired to his modest estate in Virginia, sold up, and took a room in Philadelphia, where he died on 2 October 1782.) Lafayette, harshly but accurately, summed up most reactions to Lee's departure from the army: "he was not missed."[66]

Lafayette spoke for most of the officer corps, though not all of it. Lee still had army partisans. Captain John Mercer, the general's aide-de-camp at Monmouth, was furious. After Congress confirmed Lee's sentence, Mercer decided to resign from the army at the first opportunity. He did so the following year and studied law under Thomas Jefferson while serving in the Virginia militia. The captain made it clear that his resignation stemmed from what he considered the unfair fate of General Lee.[67] Major John Skey Eustice did not resign, but he nevertheless stood by Lee. He had served as the general's aide-de-camp in 1776, and the major had no doubt the court-martial had wronged Lee. A year later he was still willing to defend his former commander in print.[68]

Eleazer Oswald did not wait a year. The gallant artillerist's court-martial testimony had strongly defended Lee—perhaps too strongly. Passed over for seniority within his rank as lieutenant colonel, in the autumn of 1778 Oswald angrily tendered his resignation after exchanging correspondence with Congress and Washington.[69] The commander in chief finally agreed to his request, and Congress accepted his resignation on 2 January 1779. Oswald's politics then became as radical as Lee's, and he did not give up on him. The former soldier traded his sword for a pen as a left-leaning journalist. He went into partnership with printer and publisher William Goddard of Baltimore, publishing the *Maryland Journal and Baltimore Advertiser,* and on 6 July 1779 caused a sensation when the *Journal* printed an incendiary essay by Lee. Entitled "Some Queries, Political and Military, Humbly Offered to the Consideration of the

Public," the piece was a frontal assault on Washington. The tone and content of the "Queries" was fully reminiscent of the objections to Washington's status voiced during the "cabal" by the likes of John and Samuel Adams, Benjamin Rush, and other radical republicans. Among twenty-five pointed questions, Lee asked, "Whether it is salutary or dangerous, consistent with, or abhorrent from the principles and spirit of liberty and republicanism, to inculcate and encourage in the people, an idea, that their welfare, safety, and glory, depend on one man? Whether they really do depend on one man?" He then went on to castigate Washington's generalship throughout the war and to denounce the conduct and verdict of his court-martial.[70] One assumes Oswald agreed with every word.

His defense of Lee, however, endeared Oswald to few patriots. That battle was lost, although the journalist found new ones. He returned to England to settle some family affairs, but with the advent of the French Revolution, he removed to France and took up the revolutionary cause there, fighting gallantly as a colonel in the French army. Then he again faced Cornwallis in Ireland while fighting on the side of Irish revolutionaries.[71] Oswald seemingly loved a good fight wherever he went.

Other than Mercer, Eustice, and Oswald, however, perhaps the only officer to speak up for Lee was another of his aides, Captain Evan Edwards. The court-martial verdict left the captain "shock'd, confounded, and exceedingly chagrin'd." He told Lee, "I have been almost mob'd in defending you," and "ten thousand infamous lies have been spread that I never heard before to bypass the minds of People against you." He lamented, "In the name of God, what are we come to?—So much for our republicanism."[72] Edwards survived his loyalty to Lee (he even served as his second in the duel with Laurens) with his army career intact; but he was lucky to have important connections: the captain was the younger brother of Dr. Enoch Edwards, prominent Pennsylvania politician and sometime physician to none other than George Washington.[73]

Lee claimed other military friends. Before publication, he vetted his "Vindication" to some fifty "gentlemen" and officers and insisted he had received their blessing. He retained the friendship of Burr, who thought the public disgrace of Lee was part of an effort to exalt the commander in chief. Young Major James Monroe, Stirling's aide at Monmouth and future president, privately remained compassionate. Two years after the battle he wrote the former major general expressing his anxiety for Lee's welfare. Monroe "most sincerely lament[ed] that the temper of this continent should be" so unfavorable to Lee. As late as 1781, Edwards assured Lee that some officers remained sympathetic to him, but they dared not say so.[74] This was hardly surprising; openly supporting the disgraced general would have been a poor career move in the Continental Line.

Lee's removal and the virtual silencing of those who would defend him was the stuff of army politics at its highest. As he had during his difficult days at Valley Forge, Washington had taken the high road in choosing not to confront a critic frontally. He never resorted to the press or uttered a public word about Lee. Indeed, after the congressional vote sustaining the court-martial verdict, the commander in chief averred that he never mentioned Lee's name except when duty demanded, and then only in neutral terms.[75] Of course, he never had to. Blessed with his talented staff officers, he was able to go about his business while they took care of Lee. The entire episode once again revealed Washington as a master politician—*and this is no criticism.* Political finesse was (and is) necessary in any commander in chief. Washington needed to balance personalities and interests in behalf of the army and, frankly, to defend himself and his policies without throwing the army into turmoil.[76] He was at his best in this role, and in this case his victory was complete.

The disgrace of Lee eliminated Washington's last significant critic within the officer corps. By the spring of 1778, neither Lee, Gates, nor any other officer were serious rivals for Washington's position, but the departure of the second-ranking Continental general removed the last real alternative. A humbled Gates now professed his loyalty, Conway was gone, and Mifflin, while still active politically, was left with his military reputation in tatters. Lee's dismissal also excised the only credible opponent to Washington's goal of building a traditional regular army. When Lee left, he took with him his conception of an American army based largely on a popular militia, and his fate served as an object lesson to those who would criticize the commanding general. Washington had proved his political mettle and again routed his critics. Thus if Monmouth revealed a newly "respectable" American army, it also confirmed the advent of Washington as the unchallengeable "indispensable man."

CHAPTER 19

A Campaign in Retrospect

Assessments and Legacies

It is worth stressing again that General George Washington's Continentals never defeated Lieutenant General Sir Henry Clinton's army. Once Clinton determined he could not bring on a general engagement, he had no interest in prolonging the contest west of Monmouth Court House. The only hazy point in this regard is when Sir Henry realized the game was up: when Major General Grey and Brigadier General Erskine failed to turn the patriot left, or when Lieutenant Colonel Monckton's advance across the West Morass came to grief? Or when the Royal Artillery failed to silence the Continental guns? Colonel Cilley's clash with the Royal Highlanders, no matter how satisfying to the Americans, was a push against troops already retiring. The 1st Grenadiers and the 33rd Foot suffered cruelly at the hands of Brigadier General Wayne's infantry and the guns of Lieutenant Colonel DuPlessis, but the redcoats prevented the Continentals from disrupting their withdrawal. British superiority in cavalry and their excellent light infantry, including the German jaegers, provided outstanding protection for the major troop formations and the baggage train. The high order of British professionalism was evident throughout the campaign.

Washington, of course, made the most of the performance of his army. He never sought a general engagement, only a limited blow with political import. On the whole, he got more than he expected. Washington was proud of his army, which had fought well and showed its mettle in brutal defensive actions and in limited offensive forays. In the end, however, there was no case for deeming the campaign or the battle itself a military turning point in the war.[1] Initial patriot hopes that Monmouth would force the British out of the conflict proved ephemeral. The war in the North devolved into a strategic stalemate as Washington hovered around New York and the British shifted their efforts to the South and other theaters. That is, the British did exactly what they had set out to do after abandoning Philadelphia.

Yet if Monmouth was not a decisive encounter in a strategic sense, it raised questions in other quarters. The campaign was the first patriot effort after the Valley Forge winter, which invites comment on the state and effectiveness of the Continental Army, including its leadership. To what extent was its training under Major General Steuben and Brigadier General Knox (who supervised the training of the artillery) and its reorganization reflected in the field? How capable were its leaders, including the commander in chief? There is also the matter of the New Jersey militia. What did the performance of the local troops reveal about the nature of the wider patriot war effort? How effective was militia cooperation with the American regulars? The fighting across the center of the state also raised political questions. What was the effect of the campaign on New Jersey loyalists and on the grip of rebel authorities on a society amid continuing civil strife? What, finally, did the campaign mean for General Washington? All these questions point to a larger one: What were the results and meanings of the longest single day of combat of the War for Independence?

The Continental Army: A Post-Monmouth Assessment

There is no question the army that fought Sir Henry at Monmouth was much better than the army that had fought Sir William Howe the year before. A number of historians have seen the Battle of Monmouth as a "coming of age" of the Continental Line, the first engagement in which the results of accumulated rebel experience and training were clearly in evidence. This point deserves scrutiny.

Patriot infantry did well. Courage had never been a problem for the rebels, but they experienced trouble with field maneuvers and in deploying in large units. After Monmouth, few contemporaries argued that the Continentals could match British tactical finesse, but there was general agreement the American regulars had performed like professionals. Even the British conceded as much. Loyalist Andrew Bell, Clinton's secretary, candidly recorded, "the Rebels stood much better than ever they did."[2]

There is less agreement, however, on the reasons for the improvement. Specifically, some historians have questioned the extent to which Steuben's reforms were responsible.[3] Did Monmouth reflect the accumulated experience of two years of war, or was the tutelage of Steuben the key factor? There is no simple answer, and it is not even an "either-or" question. At Valley Forge, the "baron" certainly improved morale and successfully introduced uniform drill; his regimen also improved movement at the brigade and division level. But Monmouth presented few opportunities for the classic linear deployments integral to Steuben's instruction. In the morning Lee could have lined up his units for a formal slugfest with Clinton and Lord Cornwallis, but the heavier British regiments and slashing dragoons would have overwhelmed his Continentals. The major general wisely retreated. Cilley's men formed on line and traded volleys with a British line, but it was a brief action involving a single Continental battalion. Most American infantry combat on 28 June was defensive and from cover. The rebel position in the Point of Woods was not suitable for a formal line; the fighting there was a melee after an ambush. Colonel Livingston's and Lieutenant Colonel Olney's battalions fought from behind the Hedgerow, and Wayne later waged his desperate fight from the cover of the Parsonage outbuildings. The bulk of Washington's army remained in position either on Perrine's Hill or with Major General Greene on Combs Hill and were never directly engaged.

Thus the Americans gave a good account of themselves, but they fought a largely defensive battle. The limited attacks planned or mounted by Lee, Cilley, and Wayne involved relatively small units, and except for Cilley's action, even these engagements ended with the Continentals parrying enemy attacks. (Indeed, the only general who mounted a major offensive operation on 28 June was Clinton.) Washington let the British come to him, and rebel artillery accounted for many redcoat casualties. The commander in chief never considered fighting a major engagement against Clinton in the open field. Steuben's influence on any contest between full brigades or divisions maneuvering against one another must remain an open question. Would the regulars have performed better than they did at, say, Brandywine? We can never really know. The Battle of Monmouth never tested the American regulars in that kind of engagement.

Yet the results of the Valley Forge training *were* visible. True, no general action demonstrated improved Continental prowess, but the proficiency of the regulars was evident in any number of smaller details, mundane individually but critical in aggregate. At least two points are important in this regard, both involving the nature of rebel personnel engaged at Monmouth. The first is the matter of the "picked men." The majority of the Continental infantry under Lee were picked men and officers, drawn from any number of regiments and organized in temporary battalions.[4] Many—and as far as we know, *most*—of these officers and men had never served together previously. Veterans had the skills acquired over time, but their only common bond was the drill and training experience under Steuben. Officers needed to know the proper commands at the proper times, and they needed to know that men they had never drilled or even met could understand those commands and react promptly. The alternative to this common understanding was compromised unit performance, if not actual chaos.

There was no chaos. Lee's morning advance on Freehold had units shifting routinely from column to line and back again—key elements of Steuben's drill—and making the proper use of flanking skirmishers for security. Colonel Butler deployed effectively and dealt easily with the charge of the 16th Light Dragoons. With the British closing in on the Hedgerow, Olney men's responded with disciplined volley fire, and Lee managed an orderly disengagement. Even most criticisms of Lee's morning retreat were backhanded compliments to the proficiency of the troops; the complaints dealt less with confusion in the ranks than with columns marching too closely together to swing easily on line. It was a given the units knew what the proper maneuvers were. The same can be said of Cilley's ability to mount his afternoon attack on the Black Watch. It was an advance only in battalion strength, again with picked men, but the Americans displayed considerable competence. Thus it is not too much to credit Steuben's training regimen with enabling officers to maintain control of their commands in difficult circumstances—no mean feat.

A second matter points to the same conclusion. The army that marched from Valley Forge contained a large proportion of new recruits. In January 1778 Continental infantry of all ranks present and fit for duty numbered 7,538; in June, before the battle, the number had climbed to 15,336 troops.[5] Some of these men were recent conscripts drafted from militia to fill Continental regiments. Integrating recruits into any army is seldom easy; doubling the size of the patriot infantry under the adverse conditions at Valley Forge was daunting. Of course, the collective experience of the army was critical in this effort—recruits learned from the veterans—but so was Steuben. Uniform drill gave the newcomers a common experience, and the constant practice allowed them to bond with the veterans. While it is impossible to measure, the common training certainly contributed to unit cohesion. As much as he hated Major General Conway, Lieutenant Colonel Laurens admitted that *any* common drill and training regimen was better than none, whatever system Conway may have tried to establish.[6] But as we know, he never did. It was Steuben who dealt with the task; and it is fair to say that Continental performance at Monmouth owed a great deal—not everything, but a great deal—to his success.

The Continental artillery was the province of Henry Knox, and certainly the American gunners were a force to reckon with at Monmouth. Colonel Harrison and Lieutenant Colonels Oswald, Carrington, and du Plessis, as well as their subordinates, were crucial to the battle's outcome. Knox was justifiably proud of his corps. Their fire was lethal, and they demonstrated a proficiency for quick deployment, company-level *and* massed-battery operations against infantry and the Royal Artillery, and, in Oswald's case, courage and discipline in conducting maneuvers in the open. It was quite a performance. "My brave Lads behav'd with their usual intrepidity," the brigadier wrote to his wife, "& the Army give the Corps of Artillery their full proportion of the Glory of the day." Lee, who fought next to Knox, was unrestrained in his praise for the guns, "from General Knox and Colonel Oswald down to the very driver." On this point Washington, who by now had little in common with Lee, agreed wholeheartedly. The commander in chief was unstinting in his praise of the artillerymen, specifically mentioning their valor and effectiveness in general orders. "No Artillery," he told the army, "could be better served than ours."[7] He was right, for at Monmouth, and for the rest of the war, the patriot gunners were easily as good as their counterparts in the Royal Artillery.

Less visible, but hardly less important, was a sterling rebel logistics effort. Here the work of Nathanael Greene and Jeremiah Wadsworth paid major dividends. The two officers spared no effort (or expense) purchasing what the army needed, and Greene labored unceasingly to get the supplies to Washington. It was a challenge. "I had the whole machinary of the Army to put in motion," Greene recalled, "Supplies of all kinds to attend to; Camps to look out; Routes to f[ind] orders of march to furnish the General officers."[8]

Yet from the time the army broke camp at Valley Forge, the troops seldom wanted for food, forage, munitions, or other necessary items (the major exception was during Lafayette's ill-fated advance on 26 June, when provisions failed to reach advance units). Greene and Wadsworth also spent money lavishly to keep their departments running, but they got what they paid for. Rarely, if ever, had the supply services worked so smoothly in support of the combat arms.

Leadership

During the campaign, senior Continental leadership earned mixed marks. The army was fortunate in its commander in chief, however, for on balance Washington did well. We have faulted him for bringing up the main body too slowly on the morning of 28 June. As events transpired, however, that was no bad thing, as it allowed the general to fight defensively from a position of strength. There is no question that Washington took firm control when he arrived at the front. He issued orders quickly but decisively, and he used his subordinates effectively: Lee and Wayne to fight the delaying action east of the West Morass, Major General Stirling to establish the main line on Perrine's Hill, and Greene to occupy the key terrain on Combs Hill. His demeanor on the heights inspired confidence as he moved up and down the line, fully visible to his men as he surveyed the fighting below and watched the cannonade. His decision to send Cilley and Wayne forward imparted a sense of Continental aggressiveness while risking little. Ordering Brigadier Generals Woodford and Poor to advance at the end of the day allowed him to claim the battlefield and a morale-building boast of victory. Washington managed all this without theatrics. His defensive battle required steadiness, not daring, so he never assumed a dual role as commander in chief and tactical commander; that is, he presided over and managed the battle, rather than feeling the need to personally lead men into the fray. The general had sought a limited engagement that would enhance his stature and pay political dividends; that is just what he got.

Washington's conduct was in stark contrast to that of his opponent. Clinton was leading an attack, one he hoped would shatter a major part of the Continental Army. He led from the front, exhorting his troops, fully exposed to enemy fire, and bringing Cornwallis along with him. One easily imagines Anthony Wayne in such a role. If any rank and file did hear Clinton crying out to them, perhaps they admired the fact that he asked no more of them than he risked himself. "No Flint" Grey thought the general's performance was splendid; no doubt other redcoats of all ranks did as well.[9] But some officers were less impressed. "Sir Henry Clinton showed himself the Soldier," one of them wrote, "but not the wise General, on this occasion, exposing himself and charging at the head of a few Dragoons."[10] Lieutenant Hale remembered being "astonished at seeing the Commander of an Army galloping like a Newmarket jockey." It was not a compliment. In fact, Hale thought the general's behavior dismayed his fellow officers and the rank and file, taking particular offense at Clinton's "expressly forbidding all form and order."[11] Another account was less astringent but still skeptical: during the fighting, "many instances of bravery was shown, perhaps too many by S[ir] Henry in person."[12] It was not unusual for a British general to come under fire; without benefit of modern communications, they often had to be close to the action to maintain any control of a usually chaotic situation.[13] Clinton was no exception. He had been under fire before—in fact, he had distinguished himself at Bunker Hill and Long Island. But in those instances he had been a subordinate commander. At Monmouth, as Lieutenant Hale so acidly noted, he was an army commander, and his bravado imperiled his command at a critical juncture. On Perrine's Hill there was no reason for Washington to do anything similar.

Among the American major generals, Lee, Stirling, Lafayette, Greene, and Steuben were all in action or played a role. Despite the controversy that has dogged his reputation since Monmouth, Lee did not perform badly. He handled the vanguard competently in his movement to contact, and he conducted a professional retreat across adverse terrain while facing superior numbers and aggressive enemy cavalry. In the early morning he did well to withdraw intact, as he did after the fighting at the Hedgerow. And he fought well at and near the Hedgerow. Like the trained British officer he once was, he variously took post at vantage points from which he could observe the action, took an active role in ordering artillery and supporting infantry dispositions, and finally issued timely orders to pull back across the West Morass.[14] His mission had been to buy time for Washington to position the main army, and the major general had done so. Lee also made his share of mistakes.

Earlier in the day, failure to make his intentions clear to Brigadier Generals Scott and Maxwell, as well as not maintaining contact with them (not to mention Colonel Morgan), was problematic. Lee's problem with Scott and Maxwell, and shortly thereafter with Lafayette on the patriot right, stemmed partly from the poor state of Continental field communications, but Lee simply assumed his subordinates would act according to his intentions without ensuring they understood those intentions. (The situation was analogous to Washington's assumption that Lee understood how badly he wanted the vanguard to strike at Clinton.) Still, once Lee realized the precariousness of his situation, he did about as well as anyone could have under the circumstances. Certainly, he was wise in ignoring Wayne's insistence on making a stand near the East Morass. Lee's entire experience during the morning at Monmouth was a demonstration of the maxim that once the shooting starts, generals have only limited control over events.

It is easy to disparage Lee; he was a not a likeable individual. But did his conduct at Monmouth deserve the obloquy so many historians have heaped upon his reputation? It is worth pausing to focus briefly on Charles Lee and his historical critics. Like most of Washington's senior lieutenants, Lee was a competent general but not a great one, and his abrasive personality, penchant for sarcasm, and lack of social graces left him with more enemies than friends. Unlike Washington, he was not an inspirational leader, and unlike Wayne, he saw little romance in war. His criticisms of the commander in chief rankled not only many contemporaries but also many historians. Yet among the historians who have faulted Lee's performance at Monmouth, including some of the most recent, few (if *any*) have suggested what the general might or should have done differently. Should be have devised a specific plan before advancing? *How,* given the frequently changing intelligence of the enemy situation?[15] Did Lee fail to gather sufficient intelligence on the British before attempting his advance? If he had waited until Clinton's movements were fully clear, the redcoats would have been long gone—well beyond range of the blow Washington so badly wanted Lee to strike. Should he have maintained better control of his command during the morning? Of course. But *how,* given the terrain and distance realities of the battlefield, the necessity of making decisions on the spot, and the state of field communications? *How,* given that Scott, Maxwell, and others had marched away from the action and that Clinton was advancing with vastly superior numbers? Should he have stood and fought near the East Morass as Wayne wanted? This would have been suicidal. Was there another viable line he could have held east of the West Morass? No historian has remotely suggested where or how. Had Lee tried to fight somewhere between the East Morass and the Hedgerow, Sir Henry would have been delighted. With few exceptions, critics have ignored these questions, as well as the fact that Lee's early retreat kept the vanguard in reasonably good order, allowing major components of it to fight effectively at the Point of Woods and the Hedgerow. Nor have most historians credited him with buying the time Washington needed to position his main line on Perrine's Hill. They have uniformly glossed over the fact that Lee retained the respect of many excellent officers. To dislike him is one thing—there were plenty of reasons—but to demean his conduct on 28 June smacks more of the armchair general than the historian. It was only Lee's intemperate and foolish (*idiotic* is not too strong a term) insolence to Washington that led to the court-martial that doomed his reputation, *not* his performance on the battlefield.

The other major generals played roles of varied importance. Stirling did well, largely under Washington's eye. Once Washington ordered the stand on Perrine's Hill, the rebel "lord" deserved credit for getting the main army posted as the regiments came up and then taking the initiative in opening artillery fire. His timely action blunted British efforts to turn the American left and shattered Monckton's grenadiers. Stirling's performance required little imagination, and he served largely as a conduit for Washington's orders (although in private letters he saw himself as a major influence on the day's events); Monmouth marked his last real combat experience. He was solid in the heat of battle, and other officers noted as much. Greene showed himself as the versatile officer he was. Shifting from his role as quartermaster, he was delighted to assume a combat command. He executed Washington's orders to occupy the high ground on the American right, and from Combs Hill his guns played havoc with the British on the plains below. Steuben spent most of the campaign as an aide to the commander in chief, devoting considerable time to gathering intelligence. Monmouth never tested him as a line commander, his final role limited to relieving the exhausted Lee as reserve commander and bringing up those units late in the day.

The Monmouth campaign found the marquis de Lafayette still maturing as a leader. His problematic advance on 26 June did not result in a near catastrophe similar to his adventure at Barren Hill—but it certainly could have. His enthusiasm lacked the balance of more experienced senior officers. But Lafayette was brave. After Lee resumed command of the delaying force east of the West Morass, the marquis had no real role to play but remained forward as Lee held the Hedgerow, posting himself with Livingston's picked men. He wrote vividly of that fight in his memoirs, pointedly (and pettily) omitting any reference to Lee. Lafayette did not retire to Englishtown, but instead held a small reserve behind Perrine's Hill and maneuvered to discourage the British from moving on the patriot left. He was a willing warrior, but the Monmouth campaign was not his best performance. Lafayette was young, and with a long war in front of him, his best days in command lay ahead.

There is little to say of most of the army's brigadiers. Woodford played a supporting role on Combs Hill and was part of the late-day advance during the battle. Like Poor, he moved forward but did not engage. Maxwell and Scott saw little action, although some of Scott's men had a brush with the Black Watch as they retreated. After the battle both officers would complain of Lee's lack of communication. Neither man, however, showed particular initiative in maintaining contact with the vanguard commander, and their fears of being cut off on the patriot left had (and have) a hollow ring. Maxwell at least showed some initiative in getting his command back in contact with Lee as the vanguard retreated westward. Scott's repositioning was advantageous—likely what Lee would have wanted—he just failed to inform his superior, thus leaving Lee at a loss as to what was happening on the left.

Of the infantry brigadiers, only Wayne commanded in serious combat. His record was mixed. Wayne's penchant for fighting, usually an admirable trait in a combat officer, clouded his judgment near the East Morass, where a Continental stand would have invited disaster. He also played a role in the confusion that left Colonel Morgan out of the fight altogether. Why did he not send Morgan's rider on to Lee? He should have, and his failure to do so was a dereliction of duty. Wayne's men fought hard in the Point of Woods, but the brigadier's role is obscure. Once the guards, light dragoons, and grenadiers crashed into the woods, Wayne's ability to control events was virtually nil, and in the confusion leadership probably devolved to the company and platoon levels—if even that was possible (yet another example of how little a general could influence events amid close combat). He did better later in the day. In the withdrawal toward the Parsonage, he kept his command in good order when faced by a determined British attack; in this instance Wayne's leadership matched his dramatic personality. He exposed himself to enemy fire, shouting instructions as the British closed in. It was leadership akin to Clinton's or Monckton's, an attempt to rally the rank and file through personal example (which turned out better for Wayne than it did for the grenadier officer).

Regimental officers performed well. These were the men, colonels down to ensigns, who commanded the army's basic tactical units—the regiments and battalions, the companies and platoons. In his study of the British army during the Revolution, Matthew Spring identified four key responsibilities of regimental officers in battle: the motivation of the enlisted men, directing them in action, maintaining order in the ranks, and engaging in personal combat.[16] The fighting on 28 June indicated that American officers assumed identical duties.

Motivation came in various forms. In the opening stages of the fighting, Colonel Jackson, forming to meet the charge of the 16th Light Dragoons, threatened to kill any man who opened fire without orders—which was motivation of a kind. More frequently, officers exposed themselves to enemy fire or remained on the line after being hit to inspire their men. Steadying his battalion at the Hedgerow, Livingston held his post after a musket ball smashed through his thigh. Cilley was a rousing leader, hailing his picked men as he gathered them for the attack on the 42nd Foot, then cheering them on for a final shot at the retiring Highlanders. While not formally attached to any regiment, staff officers Alexander Hamilton and John Laurens stayed at the front for all to see, conspicuously on horseback, Hamilton also waving his sword. Both men lost their mounts to enemy fire; so did Aaron Burr as he led Malcolm's Additional Regiment later in the day. These were all brave men who took troop leadership seriously and realized (or thought) their personal conduct was a motivating factor for the rank and file. There is every reason to suppose many other officers did as well.

Most Continental officers also met the challenges of directing their units and maintaining order. At various times the Continentals met the British with disciplined volley fire: under Butler in the morning, at the Hedgerow with Olney and Livingston, with Cilley on the patriot left, and with Wayne later in the day. Volley fire implies firing on command, which in turn implies officers directing and maintaining control of their men. Lieutenant Dow, ordering his platoon to aim and fire at a specific target—the mounted British officer—was a perfect case in point. Even in retreat, the Continental infantry generally remained under control. At one point Jackson, dazed with the heat, seemed confused as he maneuvered just east of the West Morass, but even he was able to form his command and move out of harm's way. Other officers kept their units in formation, with an occasional break in ranks to pass an obstruction; in later court-martial testimony and in private letters, unit commanders made a point of noting that withdrawals on the twenty-eighth were orderly. The only major exception during the battle that took place in the Point of Woods. In that case the sheer weight of the British charge overwhelmed the Americans, although even in this instance most of Wayne's men regrouped across the West Morass.

Such competence among the regimental officers was the product of long experience. Working with Steuben probably sharpened their skills in tactical command and small-unit control, but by mid-1778 all these men had seen considerable active duty. A look at the colonels and lieutenant colonels (along with three majors and a captain) commanding the regiments or battalions of Lee's advanced force makes the point. We know the names of twenty-four of them (two others cannot be identified with certainty): ten received their commissions in state or Continental units in 1775, twelve in 1776, and two in January 1777. At least four of them had served in the French and Indian War. Thus even the shortest-serving regimental or battalion commanders had at least a year and a half of active duty; most had well over two years.[17] These were veteran officers, the majority of whom already had seen combat before Monmouth, and they acted the part.

Probably because they were veterans, available records reveal few of these men engaging in personal combat. Commanding a unit in the heat of battle—issuing orders (probably screaming them) and maintaining formation—demanded constant attention; joining the fight with blade or firearm was usually antithetical to maintaining a wider sense of what was happening amid sound, smoke, and confusion. In fact, Washington expressly forbid officers to carry firearms: "firearms when made use of" diverted their "attention too much from the men."[18] The voluminous testimony at Lee's court-martial, the best single source of detail on the battle, makes no mention of regimental officers, including junior officers, using personal weapons against enemy soldiers; the pension applications of most officers are silent on the matter as well. Yet there were instances when some had no choice. In the Point of Woods Lieutenant Colonel Ramsey, sword in hand, defended himself gallantly. There were probably other, similar, cases when officers had to confront a direct attack. What we know of those killed and wounded at Monmouth, however, also suggests that most officers in the thick of the fight concentrated on directing their men, not in personally trying to kill the enemy. Even Ramsey fought only in self-defense. Available evidence indicates that most of their wounds were from musket and artillery fire, not the close-combat cuts and stabs of sabers and bayonets.

Thus the battle revealed a competent patriot officer corps. Among Washington's generals, the test of combat produced examples of excellent leadership, though it also saw examples of mediocre performance. Over the course of the day, Lee and Wayne would display instances of both. In a long day of combat, it is the rare general who makes no decisions above criticism. The important point is that senior American leadership was able to stabilize the situation and then fight a solid defensive battle. In this, they relied on a corps of regimental officers able to couple a grasp of command and control with the personal courage expected of combat leaders.

Challenges Ahead

Thus the Continental Army displayed many positive qualities at Monmouth. It would be a mistake, however, to see the campaign as a major watershed in the history of the army as an institution. It was better than before, but hardly a flawless engine of combat. If the battle revealed the army's attributes, it also reflected its faults. Some of those faults were serious.

Beyond question, field communications remained a crippling disability. The inability to identify units from a distance or to relay orders expeditiously very nearly brought Lee's vanguard to grief in the morning; certainly communications problems made the retreat more difficult. Throughout that initial phase, too many regimental or battalion commanders lacked orders and, worse, lacked the means of getting them. In a battle of fixed positions or over limited ground, the lack of uniforms, colors, or enough staff officers to carry orders might not be a source of major problems; they were not for Washington in the afternoon, when the rebels fought from compact lines and sent out maneuver groups of manageable size. But large maneuvers over time and space, as the morning battle demonstrated, were a different matter. In his "Plan of an Army," Lee had foreseen the problem. Without the ability to readily identify units, a field commander was in trouble. "Colours, Colours," Lee wrote, quoting the French marshal Maurice de Saxe, "are the Life and Soul of Manoeurvering, and if ever Simplicity was necessary it certainly is for the Americans." As we know from the pension application of Lieutenant Ichabod Spencer, there were American colors at Monmouth, though hardly enough to materially assist command and control of units across an expansive battlefield.[19]

Cavalry was another problem. The Continentals had barely enough horse to handle scouting duties, and in their numbers and training, the American horse could not stand against the British. With no effective cavalry of his own, enemy light dragoons were among Lee's greatest worries. Fears of being flanked by British light horse compelled several shifts in position during the morning retreat, and at the Hedgerow the inability to counter the 16th Light Dragoons was instrumental in forcing the American withdrawal. Nor did the rebels concentrate their available horse for the campaign. The Continental dragoons of Major Henry "Light Horse Harry" Lee, perhaps the most capable rebel horsemen, were foraging during the battle and never got into the fight.[20] Certainly, General Lee could have used them at the Hedgerow, or they might have bolstered patriot attempts to hit Clinton's ponderous baggage train. Wayne believed Major Lee could have done some real damage had he been on hand to pursue the enemy dragoons retreating from Butler's volley.[21] The cavalry was the weakest American combat arm in 1778, and it would remain so throughout the war.

Ironically, however, Monmouth may have been the last time this really mattered in the North. Much of the ground near Freehold was relatively open and thus suited to cavalry operations in the European fashion. In this sense, Monmouth was something of an aberration; the rugged and wooded American terrain generally was not conducive to large cavalry operations, at least not against massed infantry. Monmouth demonstrated that volley fire could stop a horse charge, as Butler's fire did, and that infantry fighting from cover, as Colonel Stewart's and Ramsey's men had fought, had more to fear from enemy infantry. Cavalry was most dangerous when it caught light or disorganized troops in the open, as Lieutenant Colonel Simcoe did early on Sunday morning, or when it could flank an infantry position, as Lieutenant Colonel Harcourt did at the Hedgerow. After 1778, the development of the patriot cavalry arm emphasized partisan operations rather than heavy combat, with units composed of dragoons and infantry (very much like Simcoe's Queen's Rangers).[22] It was just as well, for over the course of the war, neither side ever broke a well-organized infantry line with cavalry alone.

Finally, important weaknesses in Continental staff work were evident at Monmouth. The chief problem lay in the control of detached corps, and the failure to bring Daniel Morgan's riflemen into play was the most serious case in point. Conceding the difficulties inherent in eighteenth-century military communications, this entire business was still a major gaff. Once the rebels determined on some kind of an action, there was no excuse for not clarifying the assignment of this important detachment. Despite the flurry of disjointed correspondence between Washington, Lee, Greene, and Morgan, no one on Washington's staff thought to straighten out the matter. Nor, initially, did anyone pay a great deal of attention to what Lee's vanguard was doing on the morning of 28 June. Washington received the reports of various officers, but the flow of intelligence broke down, leaving him stunned to find the vanguard in retreat. Lee, in turn, was not really sure how closely Washington intended to support him; in fact, until the commander in chief actually confronted him during the retreat, Lee was unsure of whether the main army would come any closer than Englishtown.[23] Command and control of detachments is one of the most difficult tasks in the military catalogue, and over the years Washington and his lieutenants honed their skills. Three years later, for example, in the Yorktown campaign, the army had corps moving separately but effectively over considerable distances. At Monmouth, however, the staff capabilities necessary for such results were not yet in place.

On balance, the Monmouth campaign found the Continental Line formidable. Its fighting qualities and support services were improved, and its officers were more confident than in years past. In these crucial respects, if the American regulars had not come of age, at least they were *coming* of age. Washington was aware that the army still had critical weaknesses, but the commander in chief finally had a force approaching the "respectable army" he had wanted for so long. The army's proficiency would grow over the years. For the American regulars, Monmouth was not so much a high-water mark as it was part of a continuing evolution as a professional military.

That evolution was never smooth. Anyone arguing Monmouth as a high-water mark must also concede the tide quickly ebbed. Around New York, the patriot army gradually fell on hard times. Retaining veteran officers became a persistent problem. Lack of regular pay imposed significant hardships on many of them. Worried about personal and family finances and angry at seeming civilian indifference to their plight, many officers with excellent records resigned in disgust. The leadership that had proved itself at Monmouth eroded steadily.

The distress of Continental finances also had grave consequences for army supply. Within months of the battle, Maxwell was complaining bitterly that a lack of clothing and rations had reduced the New Jersey Brigade to a perilous state; dismayed at conditions, many conscripts who had swelled its ranks simply walked away. In the First Pennsylvania, Colonel Chambers found his troops reduced to pillaging local White Plains residents.[24] Wadsworth and Greene did the best they could, but it was never enough. They cared more about buying what the army needed than what they spent, and Congress, which had only a limited ability to raise money, focused more on the proverbial bottom line. Frustrated, by 1780 both of these exceptionally able officers had quit, and the army was never again as capably supplied.[25] For several years after Monmouth, then, by which time the French alliance and further reorganization restored a measure of Washington's striking power, the patriot army was probably not as potent a weapon as it had been on that blistering Sunday morning in June 1778.

Fortunately, the expansion of the war partially discounted Continental weakness. French troops eventually arrived in strength. And the British, preoccupied with France, then successively with Spain, Holland, and an increasingly hostile diplomatic scene in the rest of Europe, shifted much of their strategic focus and resources away from America. The last major fighting in the North came in June 1780 at Connecticut Farms and Springfield, New Jersey, and at New London, Connecticut, in September 1781 (not, as is commonly mooted, at Monmouth). But the Monmouth campaign closed an important chapter of the War for Independence: Britain never again sought a military solution to the war in the northern colonies.

New Jersey

The campaign left an indelible mark on New Jersey. By no means did it end the civil war that raged there between loyalists and patriots, but Monmouth clearly redirected it. While the British held Philadelphia, the Delaware River counties of the state—Burlington, Salem, Cumberland, Gloucester—were in turmoil. Politically motivated violence, British foraging expeditions, and militia and Continental operations combined to make life dangerous and unpredictable for residents of all political inclinations. Yet the consequences of the British evacuation for regional tories were devastating. Without military protection, they were vulnerable to patriot reprisals and vengeful justice. Hundreds of families joined the retreating British army and left the state. After June 1778, active loyalism in the river counties was virtually dead.

The career of militia colonel Joseph Ellis, colonel-commandant of the South Jersey militia, confirms the point. He had led his militiamen against tories on the east bank of the Delaware prior to the campaign. Ellis was in the field through June 1778 but thereafter saw no action; with the British and loyalists gone, there was no occasion. The colonel spent the rest of the war recruiting for the New Jersey Brigade and guarding Egg Harbor on the Atlantic side of Gloucester County.[26] Along the Delaware, the next military incident occurred only in March 1780, when British privateers took a number of prizes in Delaware Bay and the Maurice River in Cumberland County. The final confrontation took place over a year later. On 20 August 1781, a band of tories (origin unknown) tried to capture a small ship at the mouth of the Maurice River, but militia chased them off; the event was the last of its kind in southwestern New Jersey.[27] Patriots had won the civil war decisively in this formerly volatile section of the state.

But they had not won it in eastern New Jersey. In the immediate aftermath of the Battle of Monmouth, there was a brief hiatus in the civil conflict there as local tories either went to cover or left with the British army. Any loyalists that patriots discovered risked rough justice. In mid-July Dr. Samuel Adams rode to Freehold from Englishtown hoping to see two tories hanged; to his disappointment, he arrived just too late to witness the executions.[28] With the British in the midst of redeployment, loyalists had no immediate prospect of help; the best they could do was shelter on Sandy Hook or in British-occupied areas in and around New York. Off the coastal sections of Monmouth County, patriot privateers took advantage of the situation and took a heavy toll on enemy shipping. Little Egg Harbor became a booming port supporting the American privateers. For a time, whigs seemed firmly in control of the region.

All of this collapsed, however, with the end of British quiescence. Indeed, the end came abruptly. On 5 October 1778 British captain Patrick Ferguson led 1,200 troops, including New Jersey loyalists, in a raid against Little Egg Harbor. Guided by patriot deserters, Ferguson caught the Continental troops of Colonel Casimir Pulaski completely by surprise, killing about fifty of them.[29] Thereafter, the civil war returned with a vengeance. In the Pine Barrens of Monmouth County's coastal and southern sections, the depredations of the "Pine Robbers" were a source of frequent terror. Given time to regroup on Sandy Hook and Staten Island, dispossessed New Jersey tories again became dangerous. By early 1779 they were mounting small and large raids. Central Monmouth County remained safely in patriot hands, but the coastal sections were contested ground. The deteriorating situation finally compelled Washington to send a detachment of Continentals to bolster whigs there and to combat a flourishing illegal trade with the British. It did little good, and a low-intensity local conflict simmered well after Yorktown.[30] The civil war, quashed in western New Jersey, had moved with greater intensity to the east.

Slavery's bitter legacy haunted Monmouth County throughout this violent period. Escaped slaves, some of whom had fled with Clinton's army as it passed through the county, became major combatants in the irregular warfare. Rather than enlist them in loyalist regiments, the British organized a Black Brigade (which probably never counted more than sixty men at any given time). Living in Refugeetown on Sandy Hook, its members, sometimes in cooperation with white loyalists, mounted hit-and-run forays against coastal communities. These intensified in 1779 as the brigade found a capable and daring leader in "Colonel Tye." Tye was a Shrewsbury slave named Titus, who in 1775 escaped from his owner, a John Corlies, and participated in some of the earlier tory raids on the county. He never held a British commission, but his exploits earned him the honorific of "colonel." By mid-1779 he was leading more-ambitious operations, and his successes demoralized many militiamen, some of whom had fought at Monmouth the previous year. One, William Tallman, had fought in the battle and subsequently in "several skirmishes with the Refugees with Col. Tye and his party." Benjamin Van Cleave served under Philemon Dickinson and Daniel Morgan during the Monmouth campaign and in June 1780 "was in quite a smart engagement with a Band of refuges headed or said to be by [a] Negro Called Colnl Ti."[31] On 31 August 1780, in an effort to capture militia captain Joshua Huddy—the same man who led the militia strike against Knyphausen's baggage train—Tye received a wrist wound, and a subsequent infection killed him. The Black Brigade maintained operations until the end of the war, and whatever its military significance, its actions demonstrated that the fight for freedom was never confined to white patriots.[32]

Monmouth County was not alone in its civil misery. All areas of the state close to New York were vulnerable to British and tory forays. Bergen and parts of Middlesex Counties in particular saw considerable violence. Yet the events of June 1778 did reveal a clear trend in favor of the rebel war effort. The loyalists could raid, but nothing more. As in Monmouth County, they could keep the militia off balance and cause considerable property damage, but they could not reestablish control over any part of the state with the exceptions of Sandy Hook and Paulus Hook (in modern Jersey City).

The key factor was the New Jersey militia. Even with its local failures, it provided the muscle for whig political authority. In the immediate aftermath of Monmouth, Major General Dickinson had expressed frustration at the militia's quick dispersal, but with almost a written shrug, he told Washington, "your Excellency knows the nature of *Militia*."[33] Still, the militia left Monmouth, *not* the war. Like the Continental regulars, the patriot locals had learned a lot in more than two years of conflict. Moreover, state authorities—however haltingly—gradually improved New Jersey's militia laws. Thousands of Jerseymen were carried on militia rosters, and local officials began to compel service. Consequently, more residents served their tours of duty, or at least hired substitutes to serve in their places. The militiamen gained in experience and confidence.[34] By June 1778 a solid core of part-time soldiers knew their business, and over the course of the campaign, they demonstrated that the militia had become vital elements in the military equation. While they still preferred not to face redcoats in open battle, they were effective in local operations. They had learned well the arts of harassment, bushwhacking, and intelligence gathering; just by hovering on Clinton's flanks, they had forced the general to commit resources to security operations. Some militia also fought heroically in open battle beside American regulars. They contributed vitally to Washington's ability to keep tabs on Clinton's movements.[35] Clearly, if Monmouth showed the Continentals coming of age, it did the same for the militia.

The ability of the Continentals and the militia to coordinate their activities also deserves comment. This was compound warfare. The increased effectiveness of the joint militia-regular war effort became a visible sign of revolutionary society. It showed clearly how an insurrectionary citizenry, embodied in the militia, could, once its activities were linked with the regular army, overwhelm and defeat an enemy.[36] The British received a taste of this at Saratoga in 1777, and patriots would have been delighted "to Burgoyne"—a verb the rebels invented for the occasion—Clinton in New Jersey.[37] This, of course, did not happen. Burgoyne had marched to his defeat over hundreds of miles through relatively difficult country; Clinton went less than a hundred miles over an established (if difficult) road network. Yet Monmouth showed that the Americans could credibly threaten to repeat their New York performance. Even with his advantages on the march, Clinton had a hard enough time, and one can only speculate on his fate if his journey had extended another hundred miles beyond Freehold. It was abundantly clear that New Jersey was dangerous territory for the King's army.

The militia performance at Monmouth was not an isolated incident. Rather, it was an example of what any major British force could expect if it pushed into the state. This was amply demonstrated two years later. In June 1780 during two weeks of on-and-off action, New Jersey militia and Continentals—including some regiments that had fought at Monmouth—faced a strong British raid into Essex County. Led by Lieutenant General Knyphausen (and later joined by Clinton), the probe crossed from Staten Island to Elizabethtown on 7 June. The redcoats then pushed inland, probably aiming for the patriot military depot at Morristown. They never came close. The rebels fought the raiders to a standstill at Connecticut Farms (modern Union) and Springfield.[38] At times the fighting was brutally intense, and the Continentals stood up well under some of the bitterest close-range combat of the war; the British now had no doubt that local militia were among their chief tormentors. Captain Ewald, once more leading his jaegers, made no secret of his grudging respect for the local soldiers. He complained of "daily" skirmishing and noted that Knyphausen "ran into enemy parties which made his every step troublesome."[39] Frustrated, the British left the state on 23 June. In effect, Springfield (as the 1780 action became known) was a smaller-scale repeat performance of Monmouth.

These improvements in the rebel war effort—which to again emphasize, went far beyond the increased efficiency of the Continentals—were matters of signal importance when viewed in the broader military context of the Revolution. The King's army could still handle the relatively few crack Continental outfits, but to face a war-wise populace at the same time was another matter. The New Jersey interior, with its hostile population and experienced militia, had become part of the quagmire that engulfed British armies whenever they strayed far from the American coast and Royal Navy support. Monmouth illustrated the danger, and if any confirmation was necessary, Springfield provided it. It was a problem the British never solved.

General George Washington

Washington gave an able and inspirational performance at Monmouth. Courage under fire, steadiness in command, intelligence, decisiveness, and resolve are attributes of an effective general, and the patriot chief displayed all of them. There is nothing new in this observation. But Washington was more than a general—he was commander in chief. This role entailed additional qualities: tact, patience, an ability to balance or reconcile conflicting personalities, and especially in Washington's case, the subtlety and skill to deal with civilian authorities on behalf of his army. That is, to do his job, Washington had to be a politician—and a good one. A comparison to Dwight Eisenhower as supreme allied commander is apropos.

Washington was no stranger to politics. John Ferling's incisive exploration of the young Washington's involvement in the affairs of colonial Virginia has revealed an often underappreciated side of the future general. He took his role as a member of the gentry seriously, serving in local offices and in the House of Burgesses, and learned early in his career to maneuver between frequently clashing political interests, to cultivate the friendship and patronage of the influential and powerful, and frankly to get what he wanted through very practical (and sometimes hardball) political dealing. If Washington preferred the image of a leader above partisan frays, he was no naïf; he had a healthy ambition and was not reticent about pursuing it.[40] Without this experience, it is difficult to imagine his success as commander in chief. The position demanded someone with precisely this experience as well as the talents of military command.

The general never hesitated to use his political talents to assure his position as commander in chief. This was to be expected: There is no question that Washington believed his vision for the Continental Army offered the best prospect for the success of the Revolution. There is also no doubt he took personally the criticisms he endured over the Valley Forge winter. He effectively struck at the supposed "cabal" in a skillful political counterattack. The Battle of Monmouth allowed him to complete and consolidate that effort. It was a wide-ranging political campaign: the humbling of Horatio Gates, Thomas Conway, and Thomas Mifflin; the carefully orchestrated effort to portray the tactical draw at Monmouth as a major victory; John Cadwalader's duel with Conway; the virtual silencing of Washington's radical republican critics; the court-martial of Lee; and finally, the congressional vote to sustain the court-martial verdict. These events were all of a piece. Washington's lieutenants and political allies waged the offensive in behalf of their chief, and it is inconceivable that he was unaware of most of their activities. (One doubts Washington even knew of Cadwalader's intention to challenge Conway, although he never publicly reproved the Pennsylvania general.) The Monmouth campaign was the success Washington needed to affirm his grip on the army and free himself from serious public criticism for the rest of the war. As a personal victory for the general, Monmouth was complete.

What kind of action was the Battle of Monmouth? In retrospect, it emerges as one of the more important engagements of the war. From a narrow tactical view, both armies could argue that they had the better of the fighting, although the rebels sincerely believed they had fought well. But it was on the political front that Monmouth had the greatest significance. There, the victory was decisive. If one accepts that the fortunes of the Revolution were inextricably linked to the personal fortunes of George Washington, then by definition, any event that significantly affected the commander in chief was crucial to the wider war effort and to the success of the emerging new nation. Monmouth was all of that.[41]

EPILOGUE

MONMOUTH! All hail forever
That made despairing foes recoil
Disgusted with the ungracious soil.

—*Thomas Ward, ca. 1906*

On the Fourth of July, 1823, James Stryker, scion of an old and distinguished New Jersey family, stood before the citizens of Woodbridge, New Jersey, delivering a stirring oration in commemoration of American independence. He was full of praise for the "citizen soldiers" who had secured victory in the Revolution, and he reminded his audience no state had been more forward in the cause than New Jersey. There was much to be proud of. "When the fate of our land hung upon a single blow," Stryker proclaimed, "that blow was struck in Jersey; two of the proudest days of America were witnessed here. As long as the history of that contest or of the heroes who shared in it, shall live in the annals of fame, so long shall the triumphs of Trenton and Monmouth be celebrated by a grateful posterity."[1] It was rousing stuff, the triumphal narrative of Revolutionary victory and glory at its best.

The Woodbridge audience was appreciative enough of Stryker's remarks to have them printed, and there is no question that most Americans shared the patriotic orator's view of the Revolutionary struggle generally, and of the Battle of Monmouth in particular. Indeed, the public memory of Monmouth was distinctly American. For the British, that campaign was only a successful retrograde preparatory to redeployment, a step along a march that led to bigger and better things—a southern campaign that recovered Georgia and that witnessed in 1780 the capture of an entire patriot army at Charlestown (Charleston), South Carolina. They had little reason to dwell on the engagement. Patriots, however, and especially Jerseymen, embraced the victory narrative crafted on behalf of Washington in the aftermath of the battle. Following the war, popular memory honored service at Monmouth as a heroic and glorious reflection of the nobility of the Revolutionary cause. Public recollections and celebration of the battle became a vehicle for maintaining the patriotic narrative of the young Republic, a narrative in which "martyrs and heroes," as other early New Jersey Fourth of July speakers enthused, confronted "savage foe-men, and the fiend-like Hessian," bearing it all with "fortitude," "patience," and "vigor and perseverance."[2] Much of this popular perspective has endured into the present, and its evolution and persistence is worth a closer look, for this narrative, so deeply seated in the public memory of the Revolution, is one of the most indelible legacies of that fatal Sunday, 28 June 1778.

We can begin with an incident involving two veterans of the 1778 fighting, men who, in the early morning hours of 28 June, were on the field as the initial shots of the Battle of Monmouth sounded. On 2 October 1835, former militia private Roelof (also spelled Ralph) Schenck walked to the Delaware and Raritan Canal dock in New Brunswick, New Jersey. He intended to catch the 8:00 A.M. boat to Millstone, about ten miles upstream. Upon arrival, he found that he was late—the boat had left—and while making inquiry with a canal agent about the next available departure, he looked up to see "an old gentleman coming down toward us." The "old gentleman" asked about the next boat to Philadelphia. The question answered, he and Schenk left the dock together and got to talking. They seemed of a similar age, and Schenck asked his elderly companion if he had fought in the Revolution. When the man answered yes, Schenck followed up: Where were you from? Hunterdon County was the response. "In what regiment?" Schenck pressed. The stranger said he was with Major General Philemon Dickinson's men. In what battle? And the answer was astonishing: the gentleman explained that he had fought at Monmouth, and he remembered "seeing a Brittish horseman make an attack upon Ralph Schenck and Schenck shot the trooper and made off with the Brittish troopers horse."

Briefly, Schenck was speechless. Then it was his turn to amaze his new acquaintance. He told the equally astounded old soldier, "I was the man you saw in that combat." The stranger was his old lieutenant, Moses Estey of the Hunterdon County militia. Estey had warned Schenck that the enemy hussar, one of the Queen's American Rangers, was closing in. The warning saved Schenck's life, but Estey never knew it. Painfully wounded himself, he never saw Schenck again and believed the private had died later in the fighting: "How can it be possible that you have escaped after the balls flew around us like hail?" Both men had been lucky that day, and both had fought heroically—fifty-seven years and three months before their chance meeting at the New Brunswick canal dock.[3] Despite the years, the elderly veterans recalled the battle as vividly as something that had happened the week before.

The reunion of the former militiamen suggests that two narratives grew from the fighting at Monmouth. They existed in parallel, sometimes intertwining, but quite distinct. The first was the veterans' story as told in the recollections of men like Roelof Schenck and Moses Estey. The chance meeting of the old soldiers certainly was remarkable, but thousands of other veterans also held memories of the battle. Their pension applications, filed after successive pieces of state and federal pension legislation through the 1830s, recalled the brutality, confusion, and excitement of that long-ago Sunday. These were accounts of the war at the individual level: wounds, deaths, bravery, the unrelenting heat, narrow escapes, occasional glimpses of Washington or Lee, advances, retreats, thirst, terror, exhaustion. They were the memories of old men—usually well into in their sixties or beyond—and they were the stories these veterans passed down to generations reaching well into the nineteenth century. In aggregate, their accounts depicted the proverbial "face of battle," candid and not pretty. Schenck and Estey had marveled at their escapes but gave no hints they looked back on the war as something romantic or thrilling. They had done their duty in a just cause, and they had survived—that was enough.

The second narrative was that of popular memory. While the veterans applied for their pensions and lived out their final years, time began to soften the memories of Monmouth. As so often happens in the aftermath of a successful war, a storyline of victory and military glory parallels and frequently obscures the discourse of brutality and pain. Ultimately, the victorious narrative subsumes the veterans' accounts, cloaking the horrors with an aura of heroic endurance, nobility, and sacrifice. In this view the old soldiers actually were lucky for the tribulations they had endured—the envy of a younger generation. "Oh! with what feelings do you recall the memory of such events!" James Stryker had declaimed in his speech. "In the circle of youthful friends, whilst relating the story of days that are past, whilst every tongue is mute, and every ear open, how do your bosoms swell, and how do your eyes glisten as recollection traces the scenes of former times, as you dwell upon memories of the companions of your youth."[4] Such romantic sentiments colored the public memory of the dreadful winters of Valley Forge and Morristown, and the same was true of Revolutionary battlefields throughout the new nation.

Monmouth was no exception, and veterans occasionally contributed to the sanitized public memory of the conflict. These accounts picture the battle as dramatic, thrilling, and even humorous: there was Lieutenant Colonel David Rhea's dash through the barn to escape the British dragoon, and the dragoon's miraculous escape from the musket fire of an entire rebel battalion; Joseph Plumb Martin's tale of the unflappable woman near the artillery, unfazed as a cannonball tore off the bottom of her petticoat; General Scott's fanciful rendition of Washington's confrontation with Lee; the admiring recollections of Washington's calm during the spectacular cannonade. The list could go on. Fact was embroidered with rose-colored memories to fashion a storyline of martial glory and patriotic heroism (not that there were no actual heroics).

Over the nineteenth century and into the early twentieth, several generations of romantic nationalist and patriotic historians "improved" the Monmouth story. Doubtless the most creative was the commander in chief's step-grandson (also his adopted son), George Washington Parke Custis, who simply invented tales of Washington's valor and patriotic derring-do during the battle. We have dealt with some of Custis's fantastic anecdotes of Washington, Billy Lee, and Steuben during the cannonade, but there were others just as dubious, colorful, and even delightful. Two will set the tone for the whole of the Custis account of the battle. The first was cut from whole cloth. It had Washington's senior officers meeting on the eve of battle, proposing to send a petition to the general begging him not to expose himself to British fire on the morrow. But Dr. James Craik, chief physician of the army and an old Washington friend, told them there was no need: long ago in the Ohio country, an Indian chief had prophesied the rise of a great leader, "spirit-protected" such "that the enemy could not kill him." Craik assured his nervous colleagues that he believed the "tawny prophet of the wilderness" was speaking of the commander in chief, and that while Washington "lived the glorious cause of American Independence would never die."[5] The outcome at Monmouth, of course, proved the "prophet" right.

The second tale borrowed from an actual incident. This was Alexander Hamilton's "frenzy of valor" (as Charles Lee put it) in which he offered to die on the spot with Lee in the delaying action near the Hedgerow. Custis simply removed the major general from the scene, substituted Washington, and had a paternal general sooth the nerves of a gallant but frantic young aide:

> Lieutenant Colonel Hamilton, aid to the general-in-chief, leaped from his horse, and, drawing his sword, addressed the general with—"We are betrayed; your excellency and the army are betrayed, and the moment has arrived when every true friend of America and her cause must be ready to die in their defence." Washington, charmed with the generous enthusiasm of his favorite aid [*sic*], yet deemed the same ill-timed, and pointing to the colonel's horse that was cropping the herbage, unconscious of the great scene enacting around him, calmly observed, "Colonel Hamilton, you will take your horse."[6]

In his lengthy account of the battle, Custis of course mentioned General Lee in only derogatory terms. The major general was a bungler whose mistakes threatened the army until Washington's timely arrival turned the tide of battle; Lee's just reward was the commanding general's sending him to the rear in disgrace.[7] Custis perhaps may be excused for his flights of historical fancy; he was more storyteller than historian. But more-serious historians followed a similar line with Lee. Washington Irving, in his multivolume *Life of George Washington* (1855–59), wrote a remarkably good account of the Battle of Monmouth, including a sympathetic narrative of Lee's difficulties in the morning combat. But Irving also put a sinister construction on Washington's reaction to the vanguard's retreat: "A suspicion flashed across Washington's mind of wrong-headed conduct on the part of Lee to mar the plan of attack adopted contrary to his counsels." George Bancroft was blunter in his assessment of the major general. His magisterial *History of the United States, from the Discovery of the American Continent* (1854–78) found Lee deliberately slow in his movements and confused at Monmouth, with "no disposition to retrieve his character" after his confrontation with Washington, who rightly dismissed him from the field.[8] In 1878, at a centennial celebration of the battle in Freehold, a speaker devoted over ten pages of his address to "General Lee's Incompetency." Still later (1916), a New Jersey historian was even more virulent in his denunciation of the fallen general: "Charles Lee was utterly without principle. Let it be clearly understood concerning this man that there was not an hour during day or night after he put on the Continental uniform when he was not a potential traitor, when he would not have sold out to the British for gold."[9] A harsh judgment indeed, and indicative of views that had hardened into an anti-Lee orthodoxy.

This hostile view of Lee had its uses, for as he appeared the blackguard, Washington's historical stock soared in comparison. There was a parallel during the War for Independence. With the discovery of Benedict Arnold's treason, whig leaders used the occasion to rekindle flagging support for the Revolutionary cause. Orchestrated denunciations of Arnold reminded patriots of the virtue of their struggle and its high-minded purpose.[10] In the first century of the Republic, the Charles Lee of Monmouth became the foil for Washington's valor and nobility. Indeed, in the popular view, the villainy of Lee easily equaled and probably exceeded that of Arnold: "was he," a poet asked of the foreign-born Lee, "Our Benedict Arnold from o'er the sea?"[11] Lee's fall from grace was a continuing reminder and reinforcement of the patriotic view of Washington as the savior at Monmouth and, by extension, the lynchpin in the success of the Revolution itself. Without Lee, how would the commander in chief have found glory on the fields of Monmouth?

All of these things—the infamy of Major General Lee, the fame of Molly Pitcher, the various stories of Washington in action, the devotion of the commander's aides—became fixtures in the collective memory of the battle and part of the accepted popular history of the Revolution itself. And there is no question of the vitality of the public memory. The battlefield remained largely intact through the 1840s, most of the land remaining in fields, orchards, and woods. In 1853 the Freehold and Jamesburg Agricultural Railroad opened service on a line through the battlefield, cutting across the Point of Woods, the West Morass, and the Perrine property.[12] Yet even traversed by rails, the Monmouth battlefield became a patriotic tourist destination, featured on maps and in magazine articles. For decades after independence, visitors walked the landscape as oldtimers pointed out locations where the rival troops clashed.[13] In 1854 a member of the prominent Forman family, who heard the cannon fire as a boy, clearly recalled the Hedgerow. It was "partly rails, and partly young lopped trees," he wrote from his home in Syracuse, New York, and reminded readers that it was at the Hedgerow that "Gen. Washington gave Sir Henry Clinton the first check." The Tennent Parsonage, whose outbuildings Anthony Wayne's Continentals defended and Clinton's redcoats attacked with such tenacity, was a favorite attraction until its demolition in 1860. In 1858 Tennent's Meeting House itself hosted a religious camp meeting that included an excursion to the battlefield.[14] One visitor, having walked the terrain repeatedly, had the temerity to suggest that Charles Lee was a military genius, that he deliberately lured Clinton into a trap; another concluded Lee was badly served by his subordinates and had no choice but to retreat.[15] The battlefield, cleansed of its gore, continued to fascinate and kept alive the controversies surrounding the battle itself.

The battlefield attracted more than tourists. In 1828 it hosted its first battle reenactment—probably the first such event in the state.[16] The occasion was not without controversy and involved the "campaign" of yet another general. On the fiftieth anniversary of the battle, New Jersey Democrats, promoting the presidential candidacy of Andrew Jackson, sought to connect the victor of the Battle of New Orleans with the glory of the Battle of Monmouth. It was an overt attempt to use the victory narrative for a political end (Hamilton and Laurens would have understood). Organizers invited the militias of New Jersey, Pennsylvania, and New York to participate, although in 1778 Philemon Dickinson had better luck in calling out the citizen-soldiers than the reenactment organizers did in 1828. Only 130 handsomely uniformed militia showed up and performed routine drills in front of some 1,200 spectators, then retreated to a Freehold church for a patriotic oration before departing for a celebratory dinner. At least one veteran of the original battle, his curiosity peaked by a circular announcing the event, "was induced, once more to visit the battle ground." He was less than impressed. "The whole affair . . . seemed to be an abortion," merely a Jacksonian political stunt. "Having fought in that field in the days of my youth . . . [I] was chagrined to find so brilliant a battle, so badly celebrated."[17] Jackson, of course, won the election anyway.

The following generation of reenactors did little better. In 1854 Monmouth County prosecutor and future New Jersey governor Joel Parker organized a "sham fight" in celebration of the battle. Preparations were elaborate: A "committee of arrangements" invited militia from New Jersey, New York, and Pennsylvania to participate; Senator Stephen A. Douglas and General Sam Houston agreed to speak; the Freehold and Jamesburg Railroad arranged a special excursion schedule to shuttle spectators to the battlefield; hotelkeepers and restaurateurs "laid in an extra supply of liquors and provisions"; and organizers asked residents in and around Freehold to take in militia participants and invited local "ladies . . . to set a table upon the field of battle to refresh the troops." ("It certainly is a very ludicrous idea," was the response of one of the "ladies.") "By mutual consent the whole country looked forward to it [the reenactment] as a grand gala day," recorded the *Monmouth Democrat*, "when business should be laid aside, and patriotism have the largest possible vent."[18]

The celebration was perhaps more realistic than Parker intended. Some 2,000 New Jersey and New York militia gathered to take part, and they found the weather as uncooperative for them as it was for the troops of Washington and Clinton. The heat forced the cancellation of the mock battle, and several militiamen actually collapsed from heat exhaustion. Eliza Smith, one of the "ladies" who boarded a reenactor, wrote a friend that her guest and his fellows "look'd precisely as if they had been in the *War.* Sure enough, their faces were burnt to blisters, tir'd & worn out with fatigue." While they rested, some men "had to pay one shilling for a glass of water"—shades of Lieutenant Hale paying a Spanish dollar to the artillery teamster who crawled through the cannonade to bring water from a battlefield creek. Things only got worse. Douglas and Houston cancelled at the last minute, and when the militia attempted to fire an artillery salute to Governor Rodman Price, the cannon exploded, costing gunner Private Abram Coles of Newark his hand.[19] More realism? "It is reported," one less-than-impressed resident observed, "that not one of the officers was able to command the troops & set them in order."[20] Major General Lee did better. No matter, the entire affair devolved into a grand picnic attended by thousands, many of whom then "returned to Freehold, very tired, very red, and very thirsty. The demand upon buckets, pumps, and bar-rooms was sudden, and continued seemingly unabated until a heavy thunder shower . . . relieved the drouthy world."[21]

By this time, the vision of the battle as a romantic chapter of the Revolutionary past had largely (if not fully) replaced the brutal realities of 1778. The veterans' narratives had disappeared.

Emanuel Leutze's justly famous *Washington Rallying the Troops at Monmouth* (1857) epitomized the transformation. The painting was all drama: an inspired and inspirational Washington, his loyal and immaculately uniformed aides, the humbled Lee, the exhausted troops rallying to their commander in chief, and the outcome saved for the patriot cause. Historical accuracy did not stand in the way of a powerful patriotic image. The same was true as the legend of Molly Pitcher reached iconic stature. The Pennsylvania legislature had granted Mary Hays McCauley a pension in 1822—without calling her "Molly Pitcher" and without any mention of Monmouth. No matter, the public imagination did the rest. Between the 1850s and 1870s, well-known artists Dennis Malone Carter, Alonzo Chappel, illustrators Currier and Ives, and many others committed the heroine to canvas, parlor prints, and product labels. By the 1870s a Mount Holly journalist could justifiably ask, "what school-boy has not heard of Molly Pitcher?"[22] In New Jersey, at least, one reasonably assumes most schoolboys had.

Patriotic poets, steeped in the romantic sentimentality of the Victorian age, added to the celebration of the battle. In 1906 the New Jersey Sons of the American Revolution assembled a collection of mostly nineteenth-century verse, all of it having a familiar ring. Again, Molly Pitcher stood heroically to her cannon, the heroic commander in chief blazed to the front to rally his retreating army, and Charles Lee—predictably—was the villainous cartoon character the public loved to hate. One sample speaks for the rest:

> But what can a band of true men do,
> If he who commands them prove untrue?
> And how can a loyal fight be made,
> If under the rule of a renegade?
> Oh wise psychologists, picture me
> The heart, that day, of General Lee![23]

There was a curious aspect to these memories and celebrations of Monmouth, including the poetry, one consistent from the late eighteenth century through the early twentieth. For an engagement that according to some historians saw the Continental regulars come into their own as professional soldiers, these same regulars were conspicuously absent from the popular narrative of the battle. By the nineteenth century, most Americans had embraced the myth of the "Embattled Farmer" as the hero of the Revolution. This was the virtuous citizen of republican ideology who rushed from his plough to confront the British tyrants and secure American liberty and independence. The Continental professional, very much the social counterpart of his British opponent, did not fit the popular image of the patriotic citizen-soldier.[24]

Those who celebrated Monmouth were fully in tune with the national myth. In "The Longest Battle," New Jersey poet Will Carleton of course feted Washington but devoted chief praise to the state militia: "Phil Dickinson, Jersey's noble boon, Will give you some Jersey lightning, soon!" And like Carleton, other poets of the genre gave scant mention to the Continentals, if any at all.[25] Orators also sang the praises of the militia, and some of them did so while warning against standing armies with an eloquence that would have impressed Benjamin Rush, James Lovell, or any of Washington's fiercest critics. As early as 1794 Isaac Watts Crane celebrated the Fourth of July in Elizabethtown (modern Elizabeth) by celebrating the militia as the victors in the Revolution and as the guardians of liberty. "In free governments," he proclaimed, "where the principle is virtue," there was no need for a standing army: "An army which consists of the people, and is actuated by the same interests, which consists of men who have certain rights to protect, will act with more spirit than an army composed of men, who neither know, nor think any thing of the cause in which they are engaged—with the same discipline, therefore, they [may] be supposed to excel standing troops."[26]

This was distilled republican cant, an expression of fond popular memories of Lexington and Concord and other militia triumphs, the *rage militaire* of the first year of the war. And Crane was not the only Jerseyman to share this rose-colored view of the struggle for independence. Others followed the same thread, reminding fellow citizens that "citizen soldiers," imbued with Revolutionary spirit, had "impregnated, with military ardor, the minds of thousands" who had "stopped, drove back, and ejected from their borders, the tyranic monster with all his hideous and devouring legions."[27] The attempted reenactments of the Battle of Monmouth reflected similar sentiments. They were militia affairs, and a *New York Herald* report of the attempted "sham fight" of 1854 stressed that spectators represented "the honest-hearted yeomanry of the country, worthy descendants of Washington and his companions."[28] No one mentioned that the bulk of the general's "companions" at Monmouth were anything but middle-class and could only aspire to the American yeomanry through grants of bounty lands after the war (much less that most such aspirations came to naught).

Like the Continental regulars, the vernacular storyline also deleted the loyalists. Celebrations of the Battle of Monmouth were festivals of patriotic American unity; there was no place for a tale of internecine strife. This was especially true in the aftermath of the Civil War, when the nation tried to emphasize reunification and reconciliation. Tories such as Sam Leonard—he of the unfortunate cannonball—or the hundreds of exiled Monmouth County residents who took up arms for the King, much less the slaves who fled Monmouth owners to join the British, were entirely absent, erased from the history of the period.

Popular mythology was literally set in stone in 1884. As early as 1846 Joel Parker had urged the construction of a battle monument, but the project languished as the nation approached the Civil War. After the war Parker, by now governor, had better luck. In 1877 the Monmouth Battle Monument Association began raising funds, and the following year the Schanck family donated property for the monument in front of the modern courthouse, close to where Colonel Butler's men had tangled briefly with the Queen's Rangers. Some six years and $36,000 later, the battle monument was dedicated on 13 November 1884. A statue of "Liberty Triumphant" stood atop a granite column ninety-four feet high. Around the base, five brass bas reliefs by well-known New York sculptor James Edward Kelly commemorated scenes from the campaign and battle. They included the Hopewell council of war, Lieutenant Colonel Ramsey in combat with a British dragoon in the Point of Woods, Washington stemming Lee's retreat, Molly Pitcher taking the place of her fallen husband at his cannon, and Anthony Wayne's afternoon fight near the Hedgerow.[29] The monument did exactly what it was supposed to do—narrate the story of the victorious and glorious battle the public wanted to remember.

Reenactments of different kinds and other celebrations of the battle occurred periodically. Historians Joseph Bilby and Katherine Bilby Jenkins have traced them: an 1894 tour of the battlefield by Sons of the American Revolution from New Jersey, Maryland, Pennsylvania, and Delaware; a National Guard parade, political speeches, and festivities in Freehold in observance of the 125th anniversary of the battle; and a parade, a battle reenactment, and related celebrations attended by thousands in 1928 to mark the battle's sesquicentennial. On a smaller scale, commemorations continued as the twentieth century advanced. The tone of most of these activities was the familiar victory narrative, although there were some variants. Joel Parker used battle commemorations to urge national unity after the Civil War, and in 1903 Governor Franklin Murphy warned sesquicentennial celebrants to beware radicals, labor unions, and supposedly dangerous immigrants.[30] But in all cases Monmouth was a symbol, a patriotic victory from the past used to rally patriotic sentiments in the present.

Most of the Monmouth battlefield that saw fighting during the afternoon of the engagement is now within the bounds of Monmouth Battlefield State Park. During the 1930s the Great Depression thwarted efforts to acquire battlefield properties for a park, and key battlefield terrain was almost lost to development in the late 1950s. But after strong lobbying by a coalition of state officials, private Monmouth County citizens, the Monmouth County Historical Association, and the Monmouth County Chapter of the Sons of the American Revolution, by the early 1960s, legislation and financing were in place to support preservation efforts. In 1963 New Jersey purchased a 200-acre farm, the first section of the battlefield to become state land. Over time, further acquisitions added more than 1,600 additional acres (as of 2015), incorporating virtually all key properties of the afternoon battlefield. The state park was dedicated in 1978 on the bicentennial of the Battle of Monmouth.[31]

Establishment of the state park quietly led to a significant reinterpretation of the Monmouth campaign. Park staff initiated efforts to broaden public understanding of the battle. Research for new exhibits was immensely aided by avocational and professional historians who volunteered their research on the subject. The additional information helped correct many of the myths and legends embedded in memories of the campaign. Battlefield archaeology offered new understandings of how and where the armies fought, research clarified where a Molly Pitcher might have drawn water, and careful surveys of the terrain confirmed or modified contemporary accounts of how the action unfolded. Park interpretation also addressed the issue of loyalism, at long last bringing the bitter civil war that traumatized Revolutionary New Jersey back into popular view. Also, the Continental regular—largely absent for so long—returned to the narrative of the battle. During the park dedication in

1978, tens of thousands of visitors watched a large reenactment of the battle, which prominently featured recreated Continental regiments (as well as some actual regulars from the U.S. Third Infantry). Reenactors have returned every year. Indeed, at least among most modern historians, the performance of the Continental Army at Monmouth has become a central point of interest.[32] Joseph Plumb Martin and his longsuffering comrades would be pleased.

Monmouth Battlefield State Park, with its fine visitors and interpretive center on Combs Hill, miles of hiking trails, and annual reenactments, attracts thousands of visitors each year. It is one of the best preserved of the Revolutionary battlefields. To appreciate it most, however, consider avoiding the often-crowded weekdays and reenactments. Choose an evening when most people are gone, when you can walk alone where de Plessis deployed his guns, near the Hedgerow fence where desperate Continentals and redcoats clashed, or the fields that saw Lee retreat and Clinton and Cornwallis pursue. You can wander the ground where Stirling marshaled his artillery on Perrine's Hill and look across the rolling landscape to where the Royal Artillery planted its guns to return patriot fire. And you can pause to look at the ground on which Washington rallied his army. There is a special feeling that comes from being alone where, long ago, thousands of men, and the Molly Pitchers with them, clashed in the June sun. It is the best way to see them.

APPENDIX A

Monmouth

A Campaign and Battle Chronology, 16 June–6 July 1778

This is a brief chronology of the Monmouth campaign and the fighting on 28 June 1778. It offers a frame of reference for the chief movements of American and British forces, with an emphasis on the battle itself. With certain exceptions, entries detailing the campaign before 28 June are day by day, while the battle chronology deals in hours.

Roads to Monmouth Court House

3 May 1778	British establish a post at Cooper's Ferry to protect wood cutters.
14 May	British begin packing heavy baggage to ship to New York.
30 May	Two regiments sent to Cooper's Ferry to reinforce garrison.
1 June	British begin moving wagons and provisions to Cooper's Ferry.
14 June	British destroy unserviceable equipment and stock, burn unfinished ships.
15 June	More baggage, cavalry, and two German brigades cross Delaware River, camps extend well beyond Cooper's Ferry.
16 June	Baggage, 17th Light Dragoons, and last of artillery cross river.

17 June Last of sick taken aboard shipping. Remaining German and loyalist units cross river. Camps extend to edge of Haddonfield, New Jersey. Two English regiments sent to Gloucester Town to cover landing of army on the eighteenth. At Valley Forge, American council of war decides to await British movements.

18 June Clinton completes evacuation, concentrating about 20,000 troops and the baggage train in and around Haddonfield. Royal Navy, with other troops, invalids, tories, and heavy equipment, drops down Delaware. Small New Jersey militia attack near Gloucester Point costs British several prisoners. Near Haddonfield, Continental forces under Brig. Gen. Maxwell harass British. About noon, lead elements of patriot main army under Maj. Gen. Lee depart Valley Forge, heading north toward Coryell's Ferry. Brig. Gen. Wayne follows with second contingent about 3:00 P.M.

19 June British 1st Division moves north toward Mount Holly; Jaegers kill militia captain. Lt. Gen. Knyphausen sends two regiments to cover the evacuation of the Billingsport garrison; their column harassed by a detachment of Continentals and militia. Knyphausen moves baggage across Cooper Creek. Early in the morning, Washington's men continue breaking camp at Valley Forge, with troops under Maj. Gen. Lafayette, Maj. Gen. Alexander ("Lord Stirling"), and Maj. Gen. DeKalb departing for Coryell's Ferry.

20 June Rebels skirmish with British near Mount Holly; no serious fighting, but Americans actively try obstructing British march by felling trees, destroying bridges, and hanging on flanks of march. Knyphausen reaches Moorestown.

21 June Knyphausen joins Clinton at Mount Holly; jaegers burn shipping in Rancocas Creek. Washington reaches Coryell's Ferry and crosses into New Jersey with balance of Continental Army. Rebels still unsure of direction of British march, but Washington moves south in effort to position his forces to intercept Clinton.

22 June Washington orders Col. Morgan's light infantry and Col. Moylan's horse to reinforce harassing operations under Maxwell and militia. British reach Black Horse; rebel and British patrols exchange fire.

23 June Washington establishes headquarters at Hopewell, learning that the British are approaching Bordentown. Knyphausen and Clinton separate. At Crosswicks Creek rebels and British skirmish, with Americans giving way after holding briefly.

24 June Clinton reaches Allentown. British fire on American patrol near Allentown; rebels flee without returning fire. Clinton decides to move toward Monmouth Court House (Freehold) and to cross to New York from Sandy Hook. Knyphausen camps at Imlaystown. At Hopewell council of war, Lee speaks for a majority of generals in warning against a general action. Washington decides to avoid major fight while detaching 1,500 men to hang on British rear and left with orders to act "as occasion may serve."

25 June Upon learning of British move toward Freehold, Washington strengthens advance detachment to about 4,000 men, with command to Lafayette. Detachment moves south, with Washington cautioning Lafayette against rashness. Main army moves from Hopewell toward Cranbury. Clinton marches east on Monmouth Road. Rebels harass rear of British column all day, at night, fire on encampment at Rising Sun Tavern. Knyphausen now farther east on Monmouth Road.

26 June After difficult march through intense heat, British arrive in Freehold. American army reaches Cranbury. Lafayette decides to attack Clinton's rear on the twenty-seventh. Learning (from Lt. Col. Hamilton) of Lafayette's situation—he is short of supplies and out of supporting distance—Washington orders Lafayette to Englishtown to await Lee, who will assume vanguard command.

27 June Clinton rests his men for the day in and around Freehold; troops loot a number of area homes. Lafayette arrives at Englishtown. Lee assumes command of advanced units (roughly 5,000 men) and meets with Washington and his brigadiers. Lee's orders are discretionary; he is to attack if possible, but not if, in his judgment, circumstances are unfavorable. Washington moves main army to Manalapan Bridge (Penelopen). About 2,000 New Jersey militia under Maj. Gen. Dickinson are on Clinton's flanks. Morgan has 800 men on the British left but is out of contact with Lee and Washington.

March of the 2nd Division

28 June

2:00–4:00 A.M. Knyphausen prepares for marching: column includes the provisions train, artillery park, pontoons, and baggage of both divisions. Column extends six to seven miles.

4:00–8:00 A.M. Knyphausen's column begins march, moving out the Middletown Road. By about 8:00 A.M. all wagons are moving and the rear guard can march. Rather than the direct route toward Middletown, Clinton, fearing the Americans are at Scots Meeting House and will outflank them, orders the column to take the easternmost road to Middletown. When they reach the forks of the road outside of Freehold, they are to turn east toward Shrewsbury.

8:00 A.M.–noon	Late in the morning, Monmouth and Middlesex militia attack the baggage train but are repulsed. The 2nd Division reaches Polhemus Hill about noon, stops to rest.
2:00 P.M.–midnight	Knyphausen's column resumes march, crosses Hop Brook at Polhemus Ford. The head of the column arrives at Nut Swamp (about three miles outside of Middletown) around sunset and encamps for the night.
29 June	
Midnight–5:00 A.M.	The column continues to arrive through the night. There are many stragglers; the jaegers bringing up the rear arrive after dawn.

Battle of Monmouth

28 June

March of the 1st Division

2:00–8:00 A.M.	At 2:00 A.M., the Queen's Rangers march north to guard the Amboy Road crossing of Spotswood North Brook. At 5:00 A.M. the remainder of the 1st Division begins march toward Monmouth Court House. There they wait for the 2nd Division to move out. The column resumes marching sometime between 8:00 and 9:00 am.
10:00 A.M.	The rear guard begins marching.

Continental Advance Force Marches from Englishtown

1:45–3:00 A.M.	Lee receives Washington's orders to send a party of observation to watch British. Col. Grayson receives order to command these troops about 3:00 A.M.
4:45–5:00 A.M.	Lee receives word that the British are marching. Main advance force begins assembling.

6:00–7:00 A.M.	After delay to find guides, Grayson leads "party of observation" toward Freehold; Lee follows with main advance force about 7:00 A.M. Maj. Gen. Steuben and aides already reconnoitering British encampments at Monmouth Court House. Washington puts main army into motion from Manalapan Bridge, approximately three miles west of Englishtown.
7:15–7:30 A.M.	Clinton sends Queen's Rangers to capture Steuben. Rangers stumble into Hunterdon County militia at Hedgerow; Grayson arrives just in time to see resulting skirmish. Rangers retreat.
7:40–8:55 A.M.	Lee arrives at Hedgerow. Dickinson warns him not to bring his troops across West Morass, as Clinton may attack. After hesitation due to conflicting intelligence, Lee orders advance toward Monmouth Court House.
9:45–10:00 A.M.	Continental advance force arrives at Amboy Road. Lee and Wayne reconnoiter; British rear guard (Lt. Gen. Cornwallis) marches out of Monmouth Court House on Middletown Road; Capt. Edwards sent to reconnoiter roads to left.

Lee Attempts to Envelope British Rear Guard

10:00–10:25 A.M.	Wayne with Cols. Butler, Grayson, and Jackson and Lt. Col. Oswald ordered to right to fix British in place while Lee and remainder of vanguard circle left to get on enemy flank.
10:30–10:35 A.M.	Enemy rear guard halts. British 16th Light Dragoons charge militia horse and are ambushed by Butler. Oswald opens fire with two guns; Wayne feints an attack on enemy. British open fire with 3-pounders.

10:35–10:45 A.M.	Clinton learns of Continentals threatening his rear guard, rides back, ordering 1st Division to follow.
10: 35–10:50 A.M.	Lee reconnoiters, finds Wayne on enemy flank. He intends Brig. Gen. Scott to follow Wayne. Enemy advancing toward courthouse on road, so Lee and Lafayette lead troops to block this advance. British 6-pounders in action.

Clinton Foils Continental Envelopment

10:55–11:30 A.M.	Second British column appears; Lee sends aides to Scott to direct him to hold position in woods along brook; aides cannot find Scott. Lee leads troops back to defensive position in Freehold; Scott sees Lee apparently withdrawing. Scott and Maxwell withdraw toward woods on west side of East Morass, Oswald with six guns cannonades enemy from Wikoff cider orchard (11:15–11:25 A.M.).
11:25–12:10 P.M.	Lee—his numbers reduced by absence of Scott—retreats to Ker farm. Oswald covers retreat with six guns from west side of East Morass (11:40–11:45) and then with ten guns from a hill west of road (12:00–12:10 P.M.).
11:30–12:20 P.M.	British troops begin arriving at East Morass and village. Clinton reconnoiters, then orders forced march to overtake Continentals. Light infantry and rangers sent north to outflank bridge.
11:35 A.M.–12:30 P.M.	Washington, after late breakfast in Englishtown, rides after troops. Meets Hamilton at crossroads south of meetinghouse. Hamilton warns of danger of being outflanked. Washington orders Greene to march down roads to right.

12:25–1:00 P.M.	After briefly resting at Ker's farm, Lee resumes retreat. Maxwell to cover road, while Lee forms troops west of Middle Morass to cover rear units. Meets Harrison (12:45 P.M.), then Washington.

Continental Delaying Actions

12:20–12:55 P.M.	Except for light infantry and rangers circling to north, British advance in three columns, with light dragoons and artillery in center. Approaching Middle Morass, Clinton sends 3rd Brigade across Spotswood Middle Brook to outflank bridge.
12:30–1:10 P.M.	Washington meets retreating troops, then Lee. He reconnoiters, sends Wayne with three battalions into Point of Woods, returns command to Lee, and rides back to array troops arriving on Perrine's Hill.
1:10–1:40 P.M.	Wayne fires on Brigade of Guards and is routed. British storm Hedgerow, outflanking it to right (infantry) and left (light dragoons). 2nd Grenadiers cross bridge and are beaten back by Continental artillery.

The Great Cannonade

1:45–3:45 P.M.	Clinton opens fire on Continental guns with 6-pounders, 12-pounders, and 5.5-inch howitzers. Continentals respond with over a dozen guns.
1:10–3:00 P.M.	British 3rd Brigade pursues Scott's picked men across Craig and Sutfin farms; Continental artillery stops British advance. Two British battalions cross Spotswood North Brook to outflank Perrine's Hill; shortly they are joined by rangers and light infantry. Washington sees threat to his left and counters by repositioning Lafayette and Continental second line.

3:45–4:00 P.M. Greene's artillery opens fire from Combs Hill. Clinton shifts his grenadiers and withdraws his artillery. British north of Spotswood North Brook begin withdrawing.

Continentals Harass Withdrawing Enemy

4:10–5:10 P.M. Washington sends officer to reconnoiter north of Spotswood North Brook, then orders two battalions of picked men to attack the battalion of 42nd Foot covering the British withdrawal across Sutfin farm. After skirmishing, last of British flanking force fords Spotswood Middle Brook and marches for courthouse.

4:30–5:00 P.M. Clinton orders British grenadiers guarding rear to join Hessian grenadiers and artillery on Ker farm. Washington sends Wayne with three regiments across the bridge to attack British rear.

5:15–6:00 P.M. Wayne attacks 1st British Grenadiers. Grenadiers, joined by 33rd Foot, push Wayne back into Parsonage buildings and enclosures. Greene's artillery drives back British, who withdraw to hill on Ker farm.

Clinton Retreats, Washington Moves Forward

5:30–9:00 P.M. Washington sends message to Steuben to bring Englishtown reserves to battlefield. Orders Brig. Gens. Woodford's and Poor's brigades to advance on enemy's flanks; troops on Perrine's Hill move forward to Hedgerow; reserves take position on heights. Darkness prevents contact. After dark one company fires on enemy picket.

6:00–11:00 P.M. At the Ker farm and Monmouth Court House, Clinton rests his men until 11:00 P.M., then prepares to march to join Knyphausen's column at Nut Swamp.

The Campaign Closes

29 June At midnight Clinton moves, leaving behind more than forty of the most seriously wounded. His column marches through the night, arriving at Knyphausen's camp between 8:00 and 9:00 A.M. British push on to Middletown, where they spend the night. Washington, finding the enemy gone, returns to Englishtown, leaving behind parties to bury the dead and assist with care of wounded from both sides. Morgan's light troops and the New Jersey militia sent forward to shadow the British withdrawal toward Navesink and Sandy Hook.

30 June Washington rests the army at Englishtown. Clinton marches to secure positions in the Navesink Highlands, overlooking Sandy Hook. Light troops screen the British positions and patrol toward Middletown to prevent American raids; Clinton starts organizing his sick, wounded, horses, and equipment for embarkation to New York. For several days, most of the British army gets badly needed rest.

1–6 July American army marches before daybreak toward New Brunswick, arriving on 2 July. After resting and celebrating the Fourth of July, most of the army marches early on 6 July toward the Hudson River Highlands. On 5 July the bulk of Clinton's men move onto Sandy Hook, where they board Royal Navy vessels for New York City. By the sixth, all troops have embarked, arriving at positions on Staten Island, Long Island, and Manhattan. American troops assigned to shadow the British withdrawal move to rejoin the main army, while the New Jersey Brigade takes up positions in Elizabeth, Woodbridge, and Newark.

APPENDIX B

Continental Army Order of Battle

CONTINENTAL ARMY FORWARD UNITS

Morning, 28 June 1778
(strength estimates are approximate)

CONTINENTAL ARMY VANGUARD

Advancing from Englishtown
(ca. 4,540 men of all ranks)

Maj. Gen. Charles Lee, Advanced Force Commander
Lt. Col. John Brooks, Acting Adjutant
Capt. John Francis Mercer (3rd Va.), Aide-de-Camp
Capt. Evan Edwards (Hartley's Additional), Aide-de-Camp
Col. François Lellorquis, marquis de Malmédy, Volunteer Aide-de-Camp
Brig. Gen. Louis DuPortail, Engineer
Jean Baptiste, chevalier de Ternant, Deputy Inspector
Brig. Gen. David Forman, New Jersey Militia, Guide/Adviser
Lt. Col. Eleazer Oswald (Lamb's Artillery Regiment), Senior Artillerist

Scott's Brigade*	Col. William Grayson	600
Combined 4th, 8th, 12th Virginia	Col. William Grayson	
Grayson's and Patton's Additionals	Lt. Col. John Parke	
One company, Crane's Artillery Regiment (two guns)	Capt. Thomas Wells	

*Brig. Gen. Charles Scott was detached to lead a detachment of picked men (below), leaving Grayson in brigade command.

Varnum's Brigade	Col. John Durkee (Lt. Col. Jeremiah Olney)	300–350
Combined 4th, 8th Connecticut	Col. John Durkee	
Combined 1st, 2nd Rhode Island	Lt. Col. Jeremeiah Olney	
One company, Crane's Artillery Regiment (two 3-pounders)		
	Capt. David Cook	
	Capt. Lt. Jonathan Cumpston	

Wayne's Detachment (Picked Men)	Brig. Gen. Anthony Wayne	1,000
Maj. Gen. the marquis de Lafayette, Acting Commander (after Wayne detached to lead morning advance)		
Livingston's Battalion	Col. Henry Beekman Livingston (4th N.Y.)	
Stewart's Battalion	Col. Walter Stewart (2nd Pa.)	
Wesson's Battalion	Col. James Wesson (9th Mass.)	
One company, Crane's Artillery Regiment (two 6-pounders)	Capt. Thomas Seward	

Scott's Detachment (Picked Men)	Brig. Gen. Charles Scott	1,440
Cilley's Battalion	Col. Joseph Cilley (1st N.H.)	
Parker's Battalion	Col. Richard Parker (1st Va.)	
Butler's Battalion	Col. Richard Butler (9th Pa.)	
Gist's Battalion	Col. Nathaniel Gist[1]	
Two unknown Continental Artillery companies (four guns)		

Jackson's Detachment	Col. Henry Jackson	200–300

(Jackson's detachment was composed of three understrength Additional regiments of mostly Massachusetts men: Jackson's, Henley's, and William Lee's. The three regiments were formally reconstituted as one regiment on 22 April 1779.)

New Jersey Brigade	Brig. Gen. William Maxwell	1,000
1st New Jersey	Col Mathias Ogden	
2nd New Jersey	Col. Israel Shreve	
3rd New Jersey	Col. Elias Dayton	
4th New Jersey	Lt. Col. David Brearley	
Independent artillery company, attached to Lamb's Artillery (two guns)	Capt. Thomas Randall	
New Jersey Militia Light Horse	Lt. Col. Anthony W. White	
Somerset County Light Horse	Capt. John Stryker[2]	
Middlesex County Light Horse	Capt. Robert Nixon	

DRAGOON DETACHMENT

(Middletown Road at rear of British 2nd Division)

Col. Stephen Moylan (4th Light Dragoons)

Detachments drawn from 1st, 3rd, and 4th Light Dragoons	Unknown

RIFLE & LIGHT INFANTRY DETACHMENT

Richmond's Mills

Morgan's Corps (Picked Men)	Col. Daniel Morgan	600*

Rifle Companies from the 1st, 4th, 12th Pennsylvania

Rifle Companies from the 6th, 7th, 8th, 11th Virginia

Light Infantry Companies from 1st & 2nd North Carolina

Washington's Life Guards (partial)

NEW JERSEY & PENNSYLVANIA MILITIA

At Richmond's Mills with Col. Daniel Morgan

New Jersey militia		224
1st Monmouth County	Col. Asher Holmes	
2nd Monmouth	Col. Samuel Forman	
2nd Burlington	Lt. Col. Joseph Haight	
Monmouth County Artillery	Capt. Joshua Huddy	

Operating from Tennent's Meeting House

	Maj. Gen. Philemon Dickinson	500+
	Maj. Barzillai Newbold, Aide-de-Camp	

Hunterdon Light Horse (Maj. Gen. Dickinson's guards) Capt. Israel Carle[3]

1st Burlington	Col. William Shreve
1st Cumberland	Lt. Col. Samuel Ogden
2nd Cumberland	Maj. Thomas Ewing
1st Essex	Col. Samuel Potter
2nd Essex	Col. Philip Van Courtland
Hunterdon Artillery (as infantry)	Capt. Joseph Clunn[4]
1st Hunterdon	Col. Joseph Phillips
2nd Hunterdon	Col. Joseph Beavers
3rd Hunterdon	Col. David Chambers
4th Hunterdon	Col. John Taylor
3rd Middlesex	Col. Jacob Hyer
1st Salem	Col. Samuel Dick
1st Somerset	Col. Frederick Frelinghuysen

2nd Somerset	Col. Hendrick Vandike	
Pennsylvania militia volunteers (50–60)	Brig. Gen. John Cadwalader	
	At Forman's Mill	
Eastern Morris and other militia	Col. Sylvanus Seely[5]	200

Operating from the vicinity of Scots Meeting House and Van Doren's Mill

1st Middlesex	Col. John Webster
2nd Middlesex	Col. John Neilson[6]
3rd Monmouth	Col. Daniel Hendrickson

* Militia units identified in Auditor's Accounts, Abstracts of Payrolls, Revolutionary War, Book B, NjTSA. Elements of these militia regiments were in the field, not entire regiments. Precise numbers from each regiment are unknown. Militia from other counties were also at and around Monmouth, probably intermixed with the units noted above. There were troops from the 2nd Salem County Regiment, which probably did not fight as a unit. Strength estimates based on Dickinson's troop dispositions, 25 June, in *Lee Papers*, 2:413; and Dickinson to Washington, 27 June 1778, 10:00 P.M., *PGW*, RWS, 15:562. At that time, Dickinson noted that more militia were arriving.

CONTINENTAL FORCES, MAIN BODY

Midafternoon, 28 June 1778
Gen. George Washington, Commander in Chief
(strength estimates are approximate)

Perrine's Hill

Gen. George Washington, Commander in Chief
Maj. Gen. William Alexander, Lord Stirling

FORWARD SCREEN

Scott's Detachment (partial)	Brig. Gen. Charles Scott	720 +/–
Battalion of Picked Men	Col. Joseph Cilley (1st N.H.)	
Battalion of Picked Men	Col. Richard Parker (1st Va.)	
1st Pennsylvania Brigade	Brig. Gen. Anthony Wayne	429*
	Col. William Irvine (in Wayne's absence)	
1st Pennsylvania	Col. James Chambers	
2nd Pennsylvania[7]		
7th Pennsylvania	Col. William Irvine	
10th Pennsylvania		
2nd Pennsylvania Brigade	Commander Unknown	487*
1nd New York	Col. Goose Van Schaick	
4th Pennsylvania	Lt. Col. William Butler (detached, picked men)	
5th Pennsylvania	Col. Francis Johnson[8]	
11th Pennsylvania	Col. Richard Humpton[?][9]	

3rd Pennsylvania Brigade	Col. Oliver Spencer (probable)[10]	438*
3rd Pennsylvania	Col. Thomas Craig	
6th Pennsylvania	Lt. Col. Josiah Harmar	
9th Pennsylvania	Col. Richard Butler (detached, picked men)	
12th Pennsylvania	Commander Unknown	
Malcolm's Additional Regiment	Lt. Col. Aaron Burr	
Spencer's Additional Regiment	Col. Oliver Spencer	

MAIN LINE

Learned's Brigade	Col. John Bailey (probable)	373*
2nd Massachusetts	Col. John Bailey	
8th Massachusetts	Col. Michael Jackson	
9th Massachusetts	Col. James Wesson (detached, picked men)	
Glover's Brigade[11]	Commander Unknown	636*
1st Massachusetts	Col. Joseph Vose	
4th Massachusetts	Col. William Shepard	
13th Massachusetts	Col. Edward Wigglesworth	
15th Massachusetts	Col. Timothy Bigelow	
Huntington's Brigade	Brig. Gen. Jedediah Huntington	632*
1st & 7th Connecticut	Col. Heman Swift	
2nd & 5th Connecticut	Col. Philip Burr Bradley	
Poor's Brigade	Brig. Gen. Enoch Poor	754*
1st New Hampshire	Col. Joseph Cilley (detached, picked men)	

2nd New Hampshire	Col. Nathaniel Hale	
3rd New Hampshire	Lt. Col. Henry Dearborn (detached, picked men)	
2nd New York	Col. Philip VanCortlandt	
4th New York	Col. Henry Beekman Livingston (detached, picked men)	
Artillery	Brig. Gen. Henry Knox	Unknown

Ten to twelve guns, including Capt. Francis Proctor's company, Proctor's Artillery Regiment

RESERVES

(Shadowed British flanking column, then rested in Perrine woods)

Maj. Gen. the marquis de Lafayette

North Carolina Brigade	Col. Thomas Clark	425*
1st North Carolina	Col. Thomas Clark	
2nd North Carolina	Col. John Patten	
1st Maryland Brigade	Brig. Gen. William Smallwood	790*
1st Maryland	Col. John Hawkins Stone	
3rd Maryland	Col. Mordecai Gist	
5th Maryland	Col. William Richardson	
7th Maryland	Col. John Gunby	
Delaware	Col. David Hall	
New Jersey Brigade (partial)	Commander Unknown	c. 500
2nd New Jersey	Col. Israel Shreve	
1st New Jersey (on extreme left)	Col. Mathias Ogden	

Right Flank Detachment

(Dispatched to Solomon's Tavern, then ordered to Comb's Hill)
Maj. Gen. Nathanael Greene
Lt. Col. David Rhea (2nd N.J.), guide

Woodford's Brigade	Brig. Gen. William Woodford	475* +Art.
3rd/7th Virginia	Lt. Col. Holt Richardson (7 Va.)	
11th/15th Virginia	Lt. Col. John Cropper (11 Va.)	
Four guns	Lt. Col. chevalier du Plessis-Mauduit	
Militia videttes		

Left Flank Detachment

(Harassing British column north of Spotswood North Brook)

Unidentified Continental/Militia Units	Maj. James Monroe (Aide-de-Camp, Lord Stirling)	c. 70
	Lt. Col. B. Bassett (14th Mass.)	

Morgan's Corps

(Richmond Mills)
Col. Daniel Morgan (11th Va.)

Morgan's Corps (Picked Men)	Col. Daniel Morgan	800*

Rifle Companies from the 1st, 4th, 12th Pennsylvania
Rifle Companies from the 6th, 7th, 8th, 11th Virginia
Light Infantry Companies from 1st & 2nd North Carolina
Washington's Life Guards (partial)

New Jersey Militia Regiments/Units

1st Monmouth County	Col. Asher Holmes
2nd Monmouth	Col. Samuel Forman
2nd Burlington	Lt. Col. Joseph Haight
Monmouth County Artillery	Capt. Joshua Huddy (detached)

*Includes ca. 200 New Jersey militia from units noted above.

Dragoon Detachment

(Middletown Road at rear of British 2nd Division)

Col. Stephen Moylan (4th Light Dragoons)

Detachments drawn from 1st, 3rd, and 4th Light Dragoons	Unknown

Heights of Englishtown

Maj. Gen. Freidrich Wilhelm von Steuben

RESERVES

Paterson's Brigade	Brig. Gen. John Paterson	485*
10th Massachusetts	Col. Thomas Marshall	
11th Massachusetts	Col. Benjamin Tupper	
12th Massachusetts	Col. Samuel Brewer	
14th Massachusetts	Col. Gamaliel Bradford	
2nd Maryland Brigade	Commander Unknown	602*
2nd Maryland	Lt. Col. Thomas Woolford	
4th Maryland	Col. Josias Carvil Hall	
6th Maryland	Col. Otho Holland Williams	
Muhlenberg's Brigade	Brig. Gen. Peter Muhlenberg	711*
1st, 5th, and 9th Virginia	Col. Richard Parker (detached, picked men)	
1st Virginia State	Col. George Gibson	
2nd Virginia State	Col. Gregory Smith	
German Battalion	Lt. Col. Ludowick Weltner	
Weeden's Brigade	Brig. Gen. George Weeden	587*
2nd Virginia	Col. Christian Febiger	
6th Virginia	Col. John Gibson	
10th Virginia	Col. John Green	

14th Virginia	Col. William Davies	
13th Pennsylvania	Col. Walter Stewart (detached, picked men)	
Artillery	Commander Unknown	
Unknown companies		

ADVANCE FORCE UNITS
(Lee's Vanguard, reforming after retreat)

Scott's Brigade	Col. William Grayson	300 +Art.
4th/8th/12th Virginia	Col. William Grayson	
Grayson's and Patton's Additional Regiments	Lt. Col. John Parke	
10th Company, Crane's Artillery	Capt. Thomas Wells	
Varnum's Brigade	Lt. Col. Jeremiah Olney (2nd R.I.)	300–350 +Art.
1st/2nd Rhode Island	Lt. Col. Jeremiah Olney	
4th/8th Connecticut	Lt. Col. Giles Russell (4th Conn.)	
11th Company, Crane's Artillery	Capt.-Lt. John Cumpston	
Scott's Detachment (partial)	Commander Unknown	720+/–, +Art.
Battalion of Picked Men	Col. Richard Butler (9th Pa.)	
Battalion of Picked Men	Col. Nathaniel Gist (Gist's Additional)	
Two companies artillery		

Wayne's Detachment	Commander Unknown	1,000 + Art.
Battalion of Picked Men	Col. Henry Beekman Livingston (4th N.Y.) (380)	
Battalion of Picked Men	Col. Walter Stewart (13th Pa.)	
Battalion of Picked Men	Commander Unknown	
Wounded colonel, captured lieutenant colonel[12]		
6th Company, Crane's Artillery	Capt. Thomas Seward	
New Jersey Brigade, Part	Brig. Gen. William Maxwell	400+/–, +Art.
3rd New Jersey	Col. Elias Dayton	
4th New Jersey	Lt. Col. David Brearley	
One company, Lamb's Artillery	Capt. Thomas Randall[13]	
Jackson's Detachment	Col. Henry Jackson	200
Jackson's Additional Continental Regiment		
Henley's Additional Continental Regiment		
William Lee's Additional Continental Regiment[14]		

* Entries marked with asterisk are from a brigade-by-brigade field return taken at Manalapan Bridge, 28 June 1778, reproduced in Stryker, *Battle of Monmouth*, 120. Brigade structure is based on Lesser, *Sinews of Independence*, 72–73. Brigade commanders are taken from John U. Rees, "'What Is This You Have Been about To Day?' The New Jersey Brigade at the Battle of Monmouth," http://revwar75.com/library/rees/monmouth/MonmouthD.htm.

APPENDIX C

British Army Order of Battle

CROWN FORCES, 28 JUNE 1778[1]

Lt. Gen. Sir Henry Clinton, Commander in Chief

		MEN	WAGONERS	WOMEN[2]	CHILDREN
Servants to the commander in chief		34	10	—	—
Servants to Capt. William Crosbie, aide-de-camp		5	—	—	—

2nd Division

(In the van with the baggage)

Lt. Gen. William Knyphausen

		MEN	WAGONERS	WOMEN	CHILDREN
Knyphausen's suite		69	—	2	—
Jaeger Corps	Lt. Col. Ludwig J. A. von Wurmb				
Hessian Jaegers	37 mounted; 664 foot	701	8	12	—
Anspach Chasseurs		92	1	6	—
		793			

CROWN FORCES—*2nd Division* (continued)

		MEN	WAGONERS	WOMEN[2]	CHILDREN
17th Light Dragoons	Lt. Col. Samuel Birch	333	5	12	—
2nd Battalion Light Infantry	Lt. Col. Hon. John Maitland	799	5	30	—
1st Brigade	Maj. Gen. James Grant?[3]				
General Grant's guard and suite		12	3	—	—
4th Foot The King's Own	Lt. Col. James Ogilvie	321	4	16	—
23rd Foot Royal Welsh Fusiliers	Lt. Col. Nesbitt Balfour	432	5	16	—
28th Foot	Lt. Col. Robert Prescott	313	4	16	—
49th Foot	Lt. Col. Sir Henry Calder	372	3	16	—
		1,450			
2nd Brigade	Maj. Gen. James Grant				
5th Foot	Maj. George Harris?	367	4	16	—
10th Foot	Lt. Col. Francis Smith	135	4	12	—
27th Iniskilling Foot	Lt. Col. Edward Mitchell	340	5	16	—
40th Foot	Lt. Col. Thomas Musgrave	322	3	15	—
55th Foot	Lt. Col. Cornelius Cuyler	268	5	14	—
		1,432			

		MEN	WAGONERS	WOMEN[2]	CHILDREN
Stirn's Brigade	Maj. Gen. Johann Daniel Stirn				
Gen. Stirn's suite		12	—	—	—
Leib Infantry Regiment	Col. Friedrich W. von Wurmb	573	—	14	6
Infantry-Regiment von Donop	Col. David E. von Gosen	580	—	12	—
		1,165			
Loos's Brigade	Col. Johann August von Loos				
Fusilier Regiment von Alt Lossberg	Col. Johann August von Loos	276	—	18	—
Fusilier Regiment von Knyphausen	Maj. Johann Friedrich von Stein	253	—	8	—
Grenadier Regiment von Woellwarth	(Divided between the Alt Lossberg and Knyphausen battalions)	257	—	12	—
		786			
Provincial Infantry					
Guides and Pioneers	Capt. Simon Fraser	206	—	8	—
Roman Catholic Volunteers	Lt. Col. Alfred Clifton	207	2	10	—
Maryland Loyalists	Lt. Col. James Chambers	370	3	14	—

CROWN FORCES—*2nd Division* (continued)

		MEN	WAGONERS	WOMEN[2]	CHILDREN
Pennsylvania Loyalists	Lt. Col. William Allen	168	2	8	—
New Jersey Volunteers	Lt. Col. John Van Dyke	211	—	6	—
Bucks County Volunteers	Capt. William Thomas	76	—	—	—
		1,238			
Provincial Horse					
Philadelphia Light Dragoons	Capt. Richard Hoveden	116	2	4	—
Bucks County Light Dragoons	Lt. Walter Willet	60	—	2	—
		176			
Provincial Recruits					
3rd Battalion of N.J. Volunteers		17	—	—	—
Caledonian Volunteers	Capt. William Sutherland	9	—	—	—
Volunteers of Ireland	Lt. Col. Francis Lord Rawdon	16	—	—	—
Emmericks Chasseurs	Capt. Christian Huck	11	—	—	—
		57			

		MEN	WAGONERS	WOMEN[2]	CHILDREN
Noncombatants					
Black Pioneers	Capt. Allen Stewart	49	—	2	—
Paymaster's guard and suite		10	1	1	—
Adj. Gen. Lt. Col. Francis Lord Rawdon's guard and suite		3	—	—	—
Deputy Inspector Gen. of Provincial Forces, Capt. Henry Rooke		3	—	—	—
Quartermaster Gen. Sir William Erskine's Department		494	—	—	—
Engineer's Department		138	—	—	—
Bridgemaster's Department		21	—	—	—
Royal Artillery (Civil Branch), Company of Conductors & Artificers		51	—	—	—
Surgeons, etc.		19	—	—	—
Sick and attendants of general hospital		134	6	—	—
Provost Martial, guard, prisoners, and criminals		57	1	—	—
Refugees		91	—	—	—
		1,070			
(Divided between the divisions)					
Royal Artillery	Brig. Gen. James Pattison	634	—	—	—
Royal Artillery drivers		261	—	26	—

CROWN FORCES—*1st Division* (continued)

		MEN	WAGONERS	WOMEN[2]	CHILDREN
2nd Battalion of N.J. Volunteers, 4 companies (matrosses)		129	—	4	—
Hessian Artillery		39	—	4	3
Anspach Artillery		34	—	—	—
		1,097			

1st Division

(Defending the rear)

Lt. Gen. Lord Charles Cornwallis

Queen's American Rangers*	Lt. Col. John Graves Simcoe	454	6	24	—
16th Queen's Light Dragoons	Lt. Col. Hon. William Harcourt	365	4	13	—
1st Battalion Light Infantry*	Lt. Col. Robert Abercromby[4]	730	8	30	—
1st Battalion British Grenadiers	Lt. Col. William Meadows	761	4	30	—
2nd Battalion British Grenadiers	Lt. Col. Hon. Henry Monckton	737	5	30	—

*During the afternoon, Brig. Gen. Sir William Erskine commanded the rangers and light forces.

		MEN	WAGONERS	WOMEN[2]	CHILDREN
Hessian Grenadiers	Col. Henrich Julius von Kospoth				
Linsing	Lt. Col. Otto Christian von Linsing	411	7	8	—
Minnigerode	Lt. Col. Friedrich L. von Minnigerode	427	6	9	—
Lengerke	Lt. Col. Georg Emanuel Lengerke	453	5	8	—
		1,291			
Brigade of Foot Guards	Brig. Gen. Edward Mathew				
1st Battalion Guards	Col. Henry Trelawny	502	5	10	—
2nd Battalion Guards	Lt. Col. Thomas Howard	480	5	10	—
		982			
3rd Brigade	Maj. Gen. Charles Grey				
General Grey's guard and suite		17	3	—	—
15th Foot	Lt. Col. Hon. Joseph Stopford?	352	3	16	—
17th Foot	Lt. Col. Charles Mawhood	330	3	16	—
42nd Foot Royal Highlanders	Lt. Col. Thomas Stirling	639	8	27	—
44th Foot	Lt. Col. Henry Hope	334	4	16	—
		1,672			

CROWN FORCES—*1st Division* (continued)

		MEN	WAGONERS	WOMEN[2]	CHILDREN
4th Brigade	Maj. Gen. Charles Grey				
33rd Foot	Lt. Col. James Webster	365	3	16	—
37th Foot	Maj. James Cousseau	386	3	16	—
46th Foot	Lt. Col. Enoch Markham	319	3	16	—
64th Foot	Maj. Robert McLeroth	426	3	16	—
		1,496			
5th Brigade	Brig. Gen. Hon. Alexander Leslie				
7th Foot Royal Fusiliers	Lt. Col. Alured Clarke	333	3	16	—
26th Foot	Lt. Col. Charles Stuart	314	3	16	—
63rd Foot	Col. James Paterson?	305	—	12	—
		952			
Totals		**19,940**	**180**	**709**	**9**
Grand Total		**20,838**			

Courtesy Todd W. Braisted, James L. Kochan, Donald M. Londahl-Smidt, and Garry Wheeler Stone.

Notes

Abbreviations

Whenever possible, we have cited the locations of manuscript collections using the location symbols from the *MARC Code List for Organizations* of the Library of Congress and *Symbols of American Libraries*, 12th ed. (Washington, D.C.: Library of Congress, 1980).

2BtnBrGrenOrBk	Second Battalion of British Grenadiers Orderly Book, 1778, ser. 68, Captured British Orderly Books, Vol. 5, GWP, Microfilm Reel 118, P37437
Bell, MS Diary	Andrew Bell, "MS Diary from Philadelphia . . . and the Battle of Monmouth . . . 1778," Andrew Bell Papers, MG 45, NjHi
DeHi	Historical Society of Delaware, Wilmington
DLC	Library of Congress, Washington, D.C.
DNA	National Archives and Records Service, Washington, D.C.
GW	George Washington
GWP	George Washington Papers, Manuscripts Division, DLC
JCC	Continental Congress, *Journals of the Continental Congress, 1774–1789*, ed. Worthington C. Ford et al., 34 vols. (Washington, D.C.: Government Printing Office, 1904–37)
LDC	Paul H. Smith, ed. *Letters of Delegates to Congress, 1774–1789*, 26 vols. (Washington, D.C.: Library of Congress, 1976–2000)
Lee Papers	Charles Lee, *The Lee Papers, 1754–1811*, 4 vols., Collections of the New-York Historical Society (New York: New-York Historical Society, 1871–74)
LRuL	Louisiana Technical University, Ruston
MBSP	Monmouth Battlefield State Park, Freehold, N.J.
MHi	Massachusetts Historical Society, Boston
MiU-C	William L. Clements Library, University of Michigan, Ann Arbor
NN	New York Public Library, New York

NHi	New-York Historical Society, New York
NJA	Archives of the State of New Jersey, *Documents Relating to the Colonial History of the State of New Jersey*, 33 vols. (Newark, 1880–1928).
NJA 2	Archives of the State of New Jersey, *Documents Relating to the Revolutionary History of the State of New Jersey*, 2nd ser., 5 vols. (Trenton, 1901–1907).
NjFrHi	Monmouth County Historical Association, Freehold, N.J.
NJHC	John Warner Barber and Henry Howe, *Historical Collections of the State of New Jersey: Containing a General Collection of the Most Interesting Facts, Traditions, Biographical Sketches, Anecdotes, Etc. Relating to Its History and Antiquities, with Geographical Descriptions of Every Township in the State* (New York: S. Tuttle, 1844)
NjHi	New Jersey Historical Society, Newark
NjMoHP	Morristown National Historical Park, Morristown, N.J.
NjRV	Special Collections and University Archives, Rutgers University Libraries, New Brunswick, N.J.
NjTSA	New Jersey State Archives, Trenton
PAH	Alexander Hamilton, *The Papers of Alexander Hamilton*, ed. Harold C. Syrett and Jacob E. Cooke, 27 vols. (New York: Columbia University Press, 1961–87)
PaVfNHP	Library, Valley Forge National Historical Park, Valley Forge, Pa.
PCC	Papers of the Continental Congress. DNA.
PennArch	*Pennsylvania Archives.* 5th ser., 5 vols. Harrisburg: Harrisburg Publishing, State Printer, 1906.
PGWde	George Washington, *The Papers of George Washington Digital Edition*, ed. Theodore J. Crackel et al. (Charlottesville: University of Virginia Press, Rotunda, 2007). Available online at http://rotunda.upress.virginia.edu/founders/GEWN.html.
PHi	Historical Society of Pennsylvania, Philadelphia
PHL	Henry Laurens, *The Papers of Henry Laurens*, ed. David R. Chesnutt and C. James Taylor, 16 vols. (Columbia: University of South Carolina Press, 1968–2002)

PLCM	Charles Lee, defendant, *Proceedings of a General Court Martial, Held at Brunswick, in the State of New Jersey, by Order of His Excellency Gen. Washington . . . for the Trial of Major-General Lee. July 4th, 1778. Major-General Lord Stirling, President* (New York: privately printed, 1864)
PMHB	Pennsylvania Magazine of History and Biography
PNG	Nathanael Greene, *The Papers of Nathanael Greene*, ed. Richard K. Showman, Robert E. McCarthy, and Margaret Cobb, vol. 2, *1 January–16 October 1778* (Chapel Hill: University of North Carolina Press, 1980)
PPFR	Rosenbach Museum and Library, Philadelphia
PRO CO	Colonial Office 5, vol. 96, Nation Archives of Great Britain (Public Record Office), London
PRO WO	War Office 4, Nation Archives of Great Britain (Public Record Office), London
PWacD	David Library of the American Revolution, Washington Crossing, Pa.
RWPBLW	Revolutionary War Pension and Bounty-Land-Warrant Application Files, DNA

Preface

1. Israel Shreve to Polly Shreve, 29 June 1778, Israel Shreve Papers, Buxton Special Collections, LRuL.
2. William Irvine to John Davis, 30 June 1778, *PMHB* 2 (1878): 148.
3. David Griffith to Hannah Griffith, 2 July 1778, Griffith Letters, Miscellaneous Manuscripts Collection, NjFrHi; Anthony Wayne to Richard Peters, 12 July 1778, Anthony Wayne Papers, PHi.
4. Clinton, *American Rebellion*, 97, 89; Clinton to George Germain, 5 July 1778, in Davies, *Documents of the American Revolution*, 16:161; Clinton to the Duke of Newcastle, 11 July 1778, Newcastle Collection, NeC 2645, Nottingham University Library, copy in PaVfNHP.
5. Ewald, *Diary*, 138–39.
6. Warren, *Rise, Progress, and Termination of the American Revolution*, 2:96.
7. Mark Edward Lender, "The Battle of Monmouth in the Military Context of the American Revolution," in Murrin and Waldron, *Conflict at Monmouth Court House*, 18.
8. Wallace, *Appeal to Arms*, 190.
9. Joseph Reed to Charles Lee, 21 Nov. 1776, in Reed, *Life and Correspondence of Joseph Reed*, 1:255–56; Reed to Lee, 21 Nov. 1776, in *Lee Papers*, 2:293–94; Lee to Horatio Gates, 12–13 Dec. 1776, ibid., 348.

10. John Adams quoted in Ketchum, *Saratoga*, 335. The revolutionary French could be especially tough on losing, or even questionable, officers. See Brace, "General Dumouriez and the Girondists," 493–509; Michael Glover, "Jourdan: The True Patriot," in Chandler, *Napoleon's Marshals*; and Ireland, *Fall of Toulon*.
11. Lengel, *General George Washington*, 277–78.
12. Mark Edward Lender, "Logistics and the American Victory," in Ferling, *World Turned Upside Down*, 103–105; Lengel, *General George Washington*, 275–78.
13. "A Plan for the Formation of the American Army in the least Expensive Manner possible . . . ," [13 Apr. 1778], *Lee Papers*, 2:383–84.
14. Flexner, *Washington*.
15. John W. Shy, "Charles Lee: The Soldier as Radical," in Billias, *George Washington's Generals*, 51n50.
16. For example, William S. Stryker's *The Battle of Monmouth* has long been considered the best account of the campaign, and most subsequent authors have followed him closely. Stryker was New Jersey's adjutant general and is largely responsible for assembling the superb collection of New Jersey Revolutionary manuscripts. He was a fine historian but died before the completion of his study of Monmouth; William S. Myers, a family friend but not a historian, edited the manuscript from Stryker's drafts and notes. The most recent account is Bilby and Jenkins, *Monmouth Court House*; see the bibliography for additional titles. With few exceptions, previous authors have worked from the same sources, with their narratives differing mostly in matters of operational detail. Other than some arguments over the conduct of Maj. Gen. Charles Lee, the political implications of the campaign have received scant attention.
17. Greenman, *Diary*, 102. For a similar view, see Boatner, *Encyclopedia of the American Revolution*, 719–20.
18. *PLCM*.

Chapter 1

1. O'Shaughnessy, *Men Who Lost America*, 83; Washington quoted in ibid., 89.
2. On Howe's decision to quit, see Anderson, *Command of the Howe Brothers*, 305; and Gruber, *Howe Brothers*, 252–56, 260–61.
3. On Howe's departure, see Jackson, *With the British Army in Philadelphia*, 251–64. On Howe's command in America, see Gruber, *Howe Brothers*.
4. Quoted in Stryker, *Battle of Monmouth*, 33. Stryker's work, written from a local-history perspective, remains an excellent source of detail on the Monmouth campaign.
5. Gruber, *Howe Brothers*, 236–38.
6. Jackson, *Pennsylvania Navy*; Lender, *River War*, 34; Gruber, *Howe Brothers*, 252; Anderson, *Command of the Howe Brothers*, 290. Unless cited otherwise, this account of the British campaign in Pennsylvania

relies on Gruber and Anderson. Estimates of Howe's losses are in Symonds, *Battlefield Atlas of the American Revolution*, 53–60.

7. The best biography of Galloway is Ferling, *Loyalist Mind.*
8. The best study of the occupation is Jackson, *With the British Army in Philadelphia.* For Galloway's efforts, see ibid., 98, 150–51, 165, 168. See also Ferling, *Loyalist Mind*, 35–44.
9. Quoted in *NJHC*, 421.
10. Stedman, *Origin, Progress, and Termination of the American War*, vol. 2; Jackson, *With the British Army in Philadelphia*, 197–218.
11. See, for example, Stryker, *Battle of Monmouth*, 18.
12. Franklin quoted in Symonds, *Battlefield Atlas of the American Revolution*, 59.
13. Howe's proclamation, 27 Aug. 1777, in André, *Journal*, 38–39.
14. McCormick, *New Jersey from Colony to State*, 138.
15. Quoted from photograph of original in Katcher, *British, Provincial, and German Army Units*, 78.
16. Jackson, *With the British Army in Philadelphia*, 99–101. The twelve loyalist units, with strength estimates, are listed alphabetically in Katcher, *British, Provincial, and German Army Units*, 83–101.
17. Anderson, *Command of the Howe Brothers*, 311–12; Jackson, *With the British Army in Philadelphia*, 99–101.
18. Lender, "Small Battles Won," 33–35.
19. Gruber, *Howe Brothers*, 290.
20. Stryker, *Battle of Monmouth*, 24.
21. H. Lee, *Memoirs of the War*, 1:32.
22. Gruber, *Howe Brothers*, 295; Stryker, *Battle of Monmouth*, 25; Ewald, *Diary*, 123, 401n13.
23. Gruber, *Howe Brothers*, 294.
24. The French decision to enter the war is explained in Bemis, *Diplomacy of the American Revolution*, 58–69.
25. Brown, *Empire or Independence*, 244–48; Reich, *British Friends of the American Revolution*, 121. Leland G. Stauber thinks the patriot failure to grasp the offered accommodation with Britain was a missed opportunity for peace—with profound and adverse political and social consequences for America's future development. See Stauber, *American Revolution.*
26. On the composition and dispatch of the peace commission, see Brown, *Empire or Independence*, 244–48.
27. Walpole quoted in Ferling, *Almost a Miracle*, 270.
28. GW to Alexander McDougal, 1 May 1778, Washington, *Papers*, Revolutionary War Series, ed. W. W. Abbot et al. (Charlottesville: University Press of Virginia, 1987–), 15:5–6.
29. The above account has been drawn from Willcox, "British Strategy in America," 97–102; Gruber, *Howe Brothers*, 300–302; Henry Clinton to George Germain, 5 June 1778, in Davies, *Documents of the American Revolution*, 15:132–33; and Clinton, *American Rebellion*, 86.
30. Unless noted otherwise, we have relied on the following sources for biographical information on Clinton: Willcox, *Portrait of a General;*

William B. Willcox, "Sir Henry Clinton: Paralysis of Command," in *George Washington's Opponents: British Generals and Admirals in the American Revolution*, ed. George Athan Billias (New York: William Morrow, 1969), 73–102; Selesky, *Encyclopedia of the American Revolution*, 1:219–22; and O'Shaughnessy, *Men Who Lost America*, chap. 6.

31. Willcox, *Portrait of a General*, 22–23.
32. Clinton, *American Rebellion*, 85–86.
33. Ibid., 86.
34. Mark Edward Lender, "The Battle of Monmouth in the Military Context of the American Revolution," in Murrin and Waldron, *Conflict at Monmouth Court House*, 10–11.
35. Clinton to Germain, 5 June 1778, in Davies, *Documents of the American Revolution*, 15:132–33.

Chapter 2

1. Elbridge Gerry to Thomas Gerry, 17 June 1777, in *LDC*, 7:201. For a similarly buoyant perspective, see James Wilson to Arthur St. Clair, 3 July 1777, in ibid., 287.
2. Lengel, *General George Washington*, 224.
3. GW to John Hancock, 8 Sept. 1776, *PGWde*, RWS, 6:249.
4. James Lovell to Joseph Whipple, 21 Nov. 78, *LDC*, 8:303; Gerry to James Warren, 12 Dec, ibid., 403–404.
5. Cornelius Harnett to Thomas Burke, 16 Dec. 1777, ibid., 425.
6. A formal inquiry cleared St. Clair of wrongdoing, but he never held another important command during the Revolution. The loss of Fort Ticonderoga brought a dispute between political partisans of Schuyler and Horatio Gates to a head, with Congress replacing Schuyler with Gates. John G. Pell, "Philip Schuyler: General as Aristocrat," in Billias, *George Washington's Generals*, 68.
7. John Adams to Abigail Adams, 18 July 1777, *LDC*, 7:350–51.
8. John Adams quoted in Ketchum, *Saratoga*, 335.
9. Adams to James Warren, 12 Aug. 1777, *LDC*, 7:460.
10. Henry Laurens to the Rhode Island Expedition Commissioners, 15 Dec. 1777, ibid., 8:415; Henry Marchant to Richard Henry Lee, 15 Dec. 1777, ibid., 416.
11. Elbridge Gerry to John Adams, 3 Dec. 1777, ibid., 373; *JCC*, 9:972.
12. Committee at Headquarters to Henry Laurens, 6, 10 Dec. 1778, *LDC*, 8:380–81, 399.
13. GW to Henry Laurens, 22 Dec. 1778, *PGWde*, RWS, 12:669.
14. Lafayette quoted in Martin and Lender, *Respectable Army*, 100.
15. James Lovell to Samuel Adams, 20 Dec. 1777, *LDC*, 8:450–51.
16. See, as a prominent example, Flexner, *Washington*, 113–18.
17. Lengel, *General George Washington*, 168.
18. Lee to Horatio Gates, 12 Dec. 1776, *Lee Papers*, 2:348.
19. On Lee's increasing skepticism with Washington's leadership, and on Lee's capture, see Papas, *Renegade Revolutionary*, chap. 12.

20. Samuel Adams to James Warren, 18 June 1777, S. Adams, *Writings*, 3:374. See also S. Adams to Nathanael Greene, 12 May 1777, ibid., 370–71; and S. Adams to Richard Henry Lee, 15 July 1777, ibid., 386–87. For more of the same, see S. Adams to James Warren, 23 June 1777, ibid., 376.
21. James Lovell to William Whipple, 17 Sept. 1777, *LDC*, 7:687.
22. J. Adams, *Diary and Autobiography*, 2:265.
23. Francis Lightfoot Lee to Samuel Adams, 22 Dec. 1777, *LDC*, 8:459–60.
24. Hugh F. Rankin, "Anthony Wayne: Military Romanticist," in Billias, *George Washington's Generals*, 269; Fleming, *Washington's Secret War*, 92.
25. Jonathan Dickinson Sergeant to James Lovell, 20 Nov. 1777, *LDC*, 8:296, 297n1.
26. For a full discussion of Washington's views on the matter, see Martin and Lender, *Respectable Army*, chap. 3.
27. Lovell lacks a full biography. We drew this sketch from Jones, "James Lovell in the Continental Congress," esp. 80–100 (for Lovell's antagonism toward Washington); "Lovell, James (1737–1814)," *Biographical Directory of the United States Congress*, accessed 1 May 2014, http://bioguide.congress.gov/ scripts/biodisplay.pl?index=L000463; and "The American Revolution's One-Man National Security Agency," *Cryptologic Almanac—NSA/CSS*, accessed 1 May 2014, http://www.nsa.gov/about/cryptologic_heritage/center_crypt_history/almanac/.
28. James Lovell to Joseph Whipple, 21 Nov. 1777, *LDC*, 8:302–303.
29. James Lovell to Samuel Adams, 13, 20 Jan. 1778, ibid., 580–81, 618.
30. Samuel Adams to James Warren, 7 Jan. 1776, S. Adams, *Writings*, 3:250; J. Adams quoted in *JCC*, 4:360n.
31. Charles Lee to James Bowdoin, 30 Nov. 1776, in Force and St. Clair, *American Archives*, 3:933–34.
32. Benjamin Rush to John Adams, 1 Oct. 1777, Rush, *Letters*, 156–57.
33. Adams to Richard Henry Lee, 15 July 1777, S. Adams, *Writings*, 3:386.
34. Fleming, *Washington's Secret War*, 86–87.
35. Elbridge Gerry to James Warren, 12 Dec. 1778, *LDC*, 8:404–405; Lovell to Samuel Adams, 20 Dec. 1777, ibid., 8:451; Committee for Foreign Affairs to the Commissioners at Paris, 2 Dec. 1777, ibid., 8:367. Lovell and Lee wrote the letter to Paris in behalf of the committee.
36. Committee at Camp to Henry Laurens, 5 Feb. 1778, ibid., 9:23.
37. Rush to John Adams, 1 Oct. 1777, Rush, *Letters*, 157.
38. Henry Laurens to GW, 27 Jan. 1778, *PGWde*, RWS, 13:364–65.
39. "The Thoughts of a Freeman," ibid., 13:364–66n1. No one ever claimed authorship of the tract, although it was likely a member of Congress. It has the tone of James Lovell's pen, and Lovell was expressing thoughts similar to the "Freeman" in lengthy letters to Samuel Adams at about the same time—but this is only a guess.
40. Lurie and Mappen, *Encyclopedia of New Jersey*, 732.
41. Heitman, *Historical Register of Officers*, 64, 358; Smith, "Abraham Clark," accessed 29 Apr. 2014; Goodrich, *Our Lives, Our Fortunes, and Our Sacred Honour*, 232.

42. Thomas Burke to Richard Caswell, 17 Sept. 1777, *LDC*, 7:680.
43. Daniel A. Baugh, "Byng, John (bap. 1704, d. 1757)," in Matthew and Harrison, *Oxford Dictionary of National Biography.*
44. Anderson, *Crucible of War.*
45. Germain quoted in Hallahan, *Day the American Revolution Began*, 278.
46. A notable exception is Fleming, *Washington's Secret War*, esp. chaps. 3–4.
47. Wright and MacGregor, *Soldier-Statesmen of the Constitution*, 109–10.
48. Golway, *Washington's General*, 149, 155–58.
49. John Laurens to Henry Laurens, 8 Jan. 1778, Laurens, *Army Correspondence*, 103.
50. Adams to Richard Henry Lee, 15 July 1777, S. Adams, *Writings*, 3:388; James Lovell to Horatio Gates, 27 Nov. 1777, *LDC*, 8:329.
51. The best biography of Gates is Nelson, *General Horatio Gates.* Unless otherwise noted, this sketch of Gates is drawn from Nelson.
52. Perhaps the most irritating (for Washington) example in this regard was the Board of War's plan to invade Canada. Conceived in early 1778, the venture was "ill-conceived" and, given available resources, had no chance of success. The board wanted Lafayette to command, with Conway as his second. From the beginning, Washington considered the idea foolish, and Lafayette, furious at Conway's slights of Washington, decided to have nothing to do with the effort, which quickly died. Higginbotham, *War of American Independence*, 220; Gouverneur Morris to Henry Laurens, 26 Jan. 1778, *LDC*, 8:658–59.
53. William Alexander (Lord Stirling) to GW, 3 Nov. 1777, *PGWde*, RWS, 12:110–11.
54. Wilkinson, *Memoirs*, 1:382–411. Wilkinson tried to exculpate himself in letters to and from Washington, Gates, Henry Laurens, and Stirling. The matter of who actually saw a copy of the now-missing letter is complicated and beyond the ken of this study; the key fact is that Washington saw the damning extract.
55. GW to Richard Henry Lee, 28 Oct. 1777, *PGWde*, RWS, 12:41.
56. Fleming, *Washington's Secret War*, 117–19.
57. Abraham Clark to William Alexander, 15 Jan. 1778, *LDC*, 8:597. On Clark's earlier criticism of Washington, see Rossie, *Politics of Command*, 183.
58. Horatio Gates to GW, 23 Jan. 1778, *PGWde*, RWS, 13:319–21. Thomas Fleming has interpreted this warning as evidence of a conspiracy. *Washington's Secret War*, 118. This is probably taking the point too far, but the matter did show that Mifflin thought there was something to hide in the issue of the Conway letter.
59. GW to Horatio Gates, 24 Feb. 1778, *PGWde*, RWS, 13:654–55.
60. Unless otherwise noted, this account of the "Conway Cabal" is based on Martin and Lender, *Respectable Army*, 110–14.
61. Henry Laurens to the marquis de Lafayette, 12 Jan. 1778, *LDC*, 8:571–72; Laurens to Isaac Motte, 26 Jan. 1778, ibid., 8:655.

62. Rappleye, *Robert Morris.*
63. Robert Morris to Richard Peters, 25 Jan. 1778, *LDC*, 8:649–50. Morris's sentiments were sincere, but one should note that he did have an ax to grind as he expressed them. In Congress he clashed bitterly with Richard Henry Lee and Samuel Adams in the Silas Deane affair (Morris stanchly supported Deane) and over access to western lands. Morris had business interests in western-land ventures, while Lee and his allies defended Virginia's longstanding claims to the same lands. This congressional infighting led historian Thomas Abernethy to suggest that Morris circulated rumors connecting Lee and Adams to Washington's opponents as a political smear. Patrick Henry, without naming Morris, warned Richard Henry Lee that such rumors were afoot. Abernethy, *Western Lands and the American Revolution*, 186–87. While it is true that Morris lost no love on Lee, Adams, and others who supported them, this is no proof that he did not genuinely believe Washington was in danger and knew who the general's enemies were. Lee and Adams were part of no organized group of Washington critics, but (as already noted) the commander in chief's failures left them gravely concerned, and neither man publicly expressed confidence in him after the loss of Philadelphia or during the Valley Forge winter.
64. Richard Peters to Robert Morris, 21 Jan. 1778, ibid., 8:650–51n1; Benjamin Harrison to Robert Morris, 19 Feb. 1778, ibid., 651n2.
65. Henry Laurens to John Laurens, 11 June 1778, ibid., 9:74.
66. Lee and Sergeant (a political ally of Robert Morris) were on opposing sides of the western-lands question. See McGaughy, *Richard Henry Lee*, 154.
67. This is the main thrust of Fleming, *Washington's Secret War*, but see esp. chaps. 3–6.
68. Higginbotham, *War of American Independence*, 220.
69. David Hawke fully discusses the Rush letter to Henry as well as Washington's reaction to it. See *Benjamin Rush*, 215–17.
70. Abraham Clark to William Alexander [Lord Stirling], ibid., 8:597–98; Thomas Conway to Horatio Gates, 7 June 1778, Horatio Gates Papers, NHi.
71. *JCC*, 10:39–41. Initially, Gates and Mifflin (as well as Timothy Pickering) were named to the committee as representatives of the Board of War. Gates, however, objected to attending, and Congress then exempted all members of the board from the Committee at Camp. The delegates then named Charles Carroll—in late 1777 skeptical of Washington but soon to become a firm supporter—and Gouverneur Morris, a Washington ally, to replace the exempted board members. Ibid., 65–67; *LDC*, 8:619n4. According to a disgusted Thomas Conway, who had considered Carroll a friend, by June 1778 Carroll was convinced that any officers who did not stand behind Washington should get out of the army. Thomas Conway to Horatio Gates, 7 June 1778, Horatio Gates Papers, NHi.

72. Cornelius Harnett to William Wilkinson, 8, 28 Dec. 1777, *LDC*, 8:392, 489.
73. James Lovell to Horatio Gates, 9 June 1778, ibid., 10:58.

Chapter 3

1. Stryker, *Battle of Monmouth*, 22; "Return of the Number of Men, Wagoners, Women & Children victualled at Monmouth the 27 & 28th June 1778 inclusive," Henry Clinton Papers, Vol. 36, No. 5, MiU-C; "State of the Forces under . . . Sir Henry Clinton," 3 July 1778, PRO CO, p. 77. Again, the balance of the combat troops were Hessians and loyalists.
2. The unit sent home was a battalion of the 71st Regiment of Foot (Fraser's Highlanders); the 27th Regiment arrived in March 1778. Katcher, *British, Provincial, and German Army Units*, 67–68; Trimble, *27th Inniskilling Regiment*, 38.
3. Stryker, *Battle of Monmouth*, 22; Curtis, *Organization of the British Army*, 51; Katcher, *British, Provincial, and German Army Units*, 13.
4. On the Brigade of Guards in America, see Burke and Bass, "Brigade of Guards," accessed 31 Dec. 2012; and Katcher, *British, Provincial, and German Army Units*, 24–26.
5. Katcher, *British, Provincial, and German Army Units*,21, 33.
6. The infantry (foot) regiments were numbered in order of their establishment on the army list. Clinton had the following regiments during the Monmouth campaign: 4th (King's Own), 5th, 7th (Royal Fusiliers), 10th, 15th, 17th, 23rd (Royal Welch Fusiliers), 26th (Cameronians), 27th (Enniskillings), 28th, 33rd, 37th, 40th, 42nd (Royal Highlanders, or the Black Watch), 44th, 46th, 49th, 55th, 63rd, and 64th. "Return . . . at Monmouth the 27 & 28th June 1778 inclusive," Clinton Papers, MiU-C; Katcher, *British, Provincial, and German Army Units.*
7. "War of the Revolution," accessed 30 Dec. 2012.
8. Curtis, *Organization of the British Army*, 4. Curtis lists typical English regiments at 477 men and Irish regiments at 474.
9. "Military Annals of the Highland Regiments," accessed 6 Jan. 2013; Katcher, *British, Provincial, and German Army Units*, 67.
10. "Return . . . at Monmouth the 27 & 28th June 1778 inclusive," Clinton Papers, MiU-C.
11. Houlding, *Fit for Service.*
12. Spring, *With Zeal and Bayonets Only*, 139–44.
13. Curtis, *Organization of the British Army*, chap. 1; "Return. . . . at Monmouth the 27 & 28th June 1778 inclusive," Clinton Papers, MiU-C.
14. Curtis, *Organization of the British Army*, 6.
15. Cannon, *Record of the Sixteenth*, 26–31; Cannon, *Record of the Seventeenth Regiment of Light Dragoons*, 15–24. After the Monmouth campaign, the horses and many of the effective men of 16th were merged into the 17th. Ibid., 23–24; "Return. . . . at Monmouth the 27 & 28th June 1778 inclusive," Clinton Papers, MiU-C.

16. Katcher, *British, Provincial, and German Army Units,* 91; "Return. . . . at Monmouth the 27 & 28th June 1778 inclusive," Clinton Papers, MiU-C.
17. For Simcoe's command through the evacuation of Philadelphia, see Simcoe, *Military Journal,* 18–61. For the number of rangers at Monmouth, see "Return. . . . at Monmouth the 27 & 28th June 1778 inclusive," Clinton Papers, MiU-C.
18. "Return. . . . at Monmouth the 27 & 28th June 1778 inclusive," Clinton Papers, MiU-C.
19. Stryker, *Battle of Monmouth,* 22. The strength of loyalists under arms at any given time has been difficult to assess. The closest studies of the subject to date have been Calhoon, *Loyalists in Revolutionary America,* and P. Smith, *Loyalists and Redcoats.* Paul Smith found only "scattered, conflicting provincial returns . . . available before the end of 1777." By this time, army returns showed some 4,400 loyalists in provincial units, a figure inclusive of units in all of the colonies, not just those with Howe in Pennsylvania. Smith cited no returns for mid-1778, by which time concern over French entry into the war stimulated greater British attention to loyalist recruiting. Even so, Howe stated that when he left the city, the three largest of the new tory units totaled only 648 men. Jackson, *With the British Army in Philadelphia,* 100. Philip Katcher estimates that at peak strength these units may have totaled some 2,700 men. But they were never at peak at the same time, and some strength reports may have dated from after the Monmouth campaign. *British, Provincial, and German Army Units,* 83–101. Certainly, some of the figures are inflated. For example, in one report Katcher found a tally of 871 in the Volunteers of Ireland, an outfit raised in Philadelphia in late 1777. Ibid., 101. But this flies in the face of Howe's much lower total for his strongest tory regiments. Had the Volunteers of Ireland been that numerous, Howe (or some other British officer) certainly would have said as much. Katcher also cited 200 men in the Pennsylvania Loyalists, and 425 in the Maryland Loyalists, whereas Howe counted only 132 and 336, respectively. Ibid., 92, 950. The later tabulations are more reliable and roughly match the conclusions of the contemporary British tabulation, which found 168 Pennsylvanians and 370 Marylanders at Monmouth. "Return. . . . at Monmouth the 27 & 28th June 1778 inclusive," Clinton Papers, MiU-C. Whatever the precise numbers, loyalist recruiting efforts drew far fewer men than the British had hoped. Jackson, *With the British Army in Philadelphia,* 99–101. Many of the loyalist muster rolls, which also show a dearth of strength reports for tory units in 1778, are in the National Archives of Canada and are accessible online. See "Loyalist Muster Rolls," updated 1 Feb. 2001.
20. Stryker, *Battle of Monmouth,* 22.
21. On the Hessians, see Eelking, *German Allied Troops,* 258; and Katcher, *British, Provincial, and German Army Units,* 103–27.

22. Selesky, *Encyclopedia of the American Revolution*, 1:594–95.
23. Eelking, *German Allied Troops*, 100–101; "Return. . . . at Monmouth the 27 & 28th June 1778 inclusive," Clinton Papers, MiU-C.
24. D. Michael Ryan, "Brown Bess—Musket Misconception," *Concord Magazine* (Jan./Feb. 2002), http://www.concordma.com/magazine/janfeb02/brownbessmusket.html (subscription required).
25. For technical details on the Brown Bess and its capabilities, see Neumann, "Redcoats' Brown Bess," accessed 2 Jan. 2013.
26. Simcoe, *Military Journal*, 28.
27. Thomas J. McGuire puts the number of patriot dead at fifty-three, but notes that these were only the bodies found on the field the next day; the total could have been higher. *Battle of Paoli*, 132, 146. Edward Lengel thinks the deaths could have numbered "two to three hundred Americans." *General George Washington*, 247. Whatever the numbers, Paoli was a disaster for patriot arms.
28. Frey, *British Soldier in America*, 102–103.
29. Duncan, *Royal Regiment of Artillery*, chap. 10 passim.
30. Ibid., 104, 165, 251, 317–18, 319, 321. Later in the conflict, detachments of the 1st and 3rd Battalions, along with seventy men of the Irish Artillery, deployed to America as well, but they played no role in the Monmouth campaign. Ibid., 169, 220, 264, 307. For mention of the specific artillery pieces with the army, see ibid., 317–18; André, *Journal*, 76–77, 80; and "28th June 1778. Memorandum—Battle of Monmouth," Unidentified British Army Notebook, Sol Feinstone Collection 409, PWacD.
31. "Black Loyalists," The Loyalist Pages, American Revolution.org, http://www.americanrevolution.org/blackloyalists.php; Katcher, *British, Provincial, and German Army Units*, 83; "Return. . . . at Monmouth the 27 & 28th June 1778 inclusive," Clinton Papers, MiU-C.
32. Higginbotham, *War of American Independence*, 124; Robson, "Purchase and Promotion in the British Army," 57–72; Sylvia R. Frey, "British Armed Forces and American Victory," in Ferling, *World Turned Upside Down*, 174–75.
33. Selesky, *Encyclopedia of the American Revolution*, 1:220.
34. Ibid., 2:730.
35. Frey, "British Armed Forces and American Victory," 173. For a full discussion of the subject, see Frey, *British Soldier in America*.
36. Higginbotham, *War of American Independence*, 123–24.
37. Katcher, *British, Provincial, and German Army Units*, 24–25, 29, 52–53 passim.
38. On women in the armies of the period, see DePauw, *Founding Mothers*; Blumenthal, *Women Camp Followers*; and Hargreaves, *Bloodybacks*, 290–91, 304.
39. DePauw, *Fortunes of War*, 25–26 (commissary quoted on 25). Actual commissary returns are in the Daniel Wier–John Robinson Correspondence, pp. 8–10, 55, 81, Ferdinand J. Dreer Collection, Soldiers of the Revolution Series, PHi.

40. On service life, see Hargreaves, *Bloodybacks;* and Frey, *British Soldier in America.*
41. Simcoe, *Military Journal,* 60.
42. Montresor, *Journals,* 498.
43. Feilitzsch and Bartholomai, *Diaries of Two Ansbach Jaegers,* 38–39.
44. Serle, *Journal,* 299–302.
45. Clinton, *American Rebellion,* 85.
46. Elias Boudinot to Hannah Stockton Boudinot, 11 June 1778, Boudinot Collection, Princeton University, Princeton, N.J.
47. *JCC,* 12:866.
48. Baurmeister, *Revolution in America,* 185.
49. General Orders, 7 June 1778, 2BtnBrGrenOrBk.
50. RM [unknown] to Mr. Cooper, 29 June 1778, Haskell Collection, NjFrHi.
51. On the decision to raise a regular Continental Army, see Martin and Lender, *Respectable Army,* 65–97. Unless noted otherwise, the following account is derived from this work.
52. GW to John Hancock, 2 Sept., 16 Dec. 1776, *PGWde,* RWS, 6:199–200, 7:351–52.
53. GW to John Hancock, 25 Sept. 1776, ibid., 6:393–95.
54. Martin and Lender, *Respectable Army,* 76–77.
55. Berg, *Encyclopedia of Continental Army Units,* 141; Katcher, *British, Provincial, and German Army Units,* 141.
56. On Continental troop strength for a given month, see Lesser, *Sinews of Independence.*
57. Papenfuse and Stiverson, "General Smallwood's Recruits," 117–32; Lender, "Social Structure of the New Jersey Brigade," 27–44; Sellers, "Common Soldier in the American Revolution," 151–61; Sellers, "Origins and Careers of the New England Soldier."
58. Quarles, *Negro in the American Revolution,* 33–50, 182–200; Martin and Lender, *Respectable Army,* 91.
59. General Orders, 31 May 1778, *PGWde,* RWS, 15:280; DePauw, *Fortunes of War,* 28–29; Martin and Lender, *Respectable Army,* 92. For the most thorough discussion of women with the Continental forces, see Mayer, *Belonging to the Army.*
60. Martin and Lender, *Respectable Army,* 131–32.
61. For examples of Washington's concern in this regard, see GW to Lord Stirling, 21 Mar. 1778, *PGWde,* RWS, 14:262; GW to Stephen Moylan, 11 Apr. 1778, ibid., 479–80; and GW to John Banister, 21 Apr. 1778, ibid., 573–74.
62. See, for example, Lender, "Social Structure of the New Jersey Brigade," 31, 35–36.
63. John Laurens to Henry Laurens, 28 Feb. 1778, Laurens, *Army Correspondence,* 132–33.
64. For Steuben, I have relied on Palmer, *General von Steuben,* esp. the early chapters and 122–23; and Lockhart, *Drillmaster of Valley Forge.* For examples of Washington's concern in this regard, see GW to Lord

Stirling, 21 Mar. 1778, *PGWde*, RWS, 14:262; GW to Stephen Moylan, 11 Apr. 1778, ibid., 479–80; GW to John Banister, 21 Apr. 1778, ibid., 573–74. See also Lender, "Social Structure of the New Jersey Brigade," 31, 35–36.

65. [Steuben], *Regulations*, 3, 5–6.
66. Spring, *With Zeal and Bayonets Only*, 144–45; [Steuben], *Regulations*, 7.
67. On Steuben's program and its implementation, see William Irvine to Capt. Bostlethwait, 4 June 1778, Society Collection, PHi; "Instructions from Baron Steuben," in Adam Hubley, Military Journal, Vol. 1, ibid.; Wright, "'Nor Is Their Standing Army to Be Despised,'" 70–71; Bodle and Thibaut, "This Fatal Crisis," 342–52.
68. [Steuben], *Regulations*, 13, 14, 31.
69. Washington to William Smallwood, 1 May 1778, *PGWde*, RWS, 15:7–8; Bloomfield, *Citizen Soldier*, 135.
70. Henry Laurens to Baron Steuben, 4 Apr. 1778, *LDC*, 9:368.
71. Ewald, *Diary*, xxiv–xxvii.
72. Ibid., 108.
73. Wright, "'Nor Is Their Standing Army to Be Despised,'" 68–79; Bodle and Thibaut, "This Fatal Crisis," 349–51.
74. General Orders, 4 May 1778, *PGWde*, RWS, 15:27–28.
75. Walker, *Engineers of Independence*; Hawke, *Benjamin Rush*, 210, 212–13, 214–20, 223, 238, 244; Blanco, *Physician of the American Revolution*, 78, 85–87, 96–99.
76. Lesser, *Sinews of Independence*, 60–73.
77. Plans to reduce the number of regiments are mentioned in GW to Lord Stirling, 21 Mar. 1778, *PGWde*, RWS, 14:262; GW to William Heath, 25 Mar. 1778, ibid., 304; and GW to Henry Laurens, 30 Apr. 1778, ibid., 680.
78. General Arrangement, 27 May 1778, *JCC*, 11:538–43.
79. Ibid.
80. Lesser, *Sinews of Independence*, 69.
81. This account of Knox relies on Callahan, *Henry Knox*, 142; Selesky, *Encyclopedia of the American Revolution*, 1:592–94; and Berg, *Encyclopedia of Continental Army Units*, 24.
82. Bodle and Thibaut, "Vortex of Small Fortunes," 362–63, 374, 429. Knox suggested that the mortars remain on the Hudson.
83. For the rejuvenation of Continental logistics, see Mark Edward Lender, "Logistics and the American Victory," in Ferling, *World Turned Upside Down*, 106–107. Greene's complaint is in a letter to Washington, 24 Apr. 1779, *PNG*, 3:427. See also Golway, *Washington's General*, 170–73.
84. Lender, "Logistics and the American Victory," 106–107; Johnson, *Administration of the American Commissariat*, 136–37; Risch, *Supplying Washington's Army*, 46; Bodle and Thibaut, "Vortex of Small Fortunes," 361, 426–29. It is probably impossible to tell what proportion of the men carried a particular shoulder arm. By mid-June, most evidence points to a majority having Charlevilles.

85. These regulations and procedures are traced in Washington's various general orders and communications with Congress and subordinate officers over late 1777 and early 1778. For examples, see General Orders, 2 Nov. 1777 (securing wagons), 9 Dec. 1777 (keeping arms dry), 10 Dec. 1777 (accounting for tools), 18 Dec. 1777 (fabricating substitute building materials), and 25 Dec. 1777 (threshing army grain), 27 Mar. 1778 (officers to campaign only with essential baggage, cutting size and increasing speed of baggage train), 14 Apr. 1778 (cleanliness of latrines), and 22 Apr. 1778 (regiments to grow their own forage), *PGWde*, RWS, 12:91, 581, 585, 627, 700, 13:325–26, 508, 583.
86. Bodle and Thibaut, "Vortex of Small Fortunes," 361.
87. General Orders, 5 May 1778, *PGWde*, RWS, 15:38–39.
88. Bloomfield, *Citizen Soldier*, 134; Washington to the President of Congress, 4 May 1778, *PGWde*, RWS, 15:32; General Orders, 5 May 1778, ibid., 15:38–39.
89. Fleming, *Washington's Secret War*, esp. chap. 8.
90. Lengel, *General George Washington*, 273–74, 279–80; General Orders, 17 Dec. 1777, *PGWde*, RWS, 12:620.
91. Ezra Selden to Samuel Mather, 15 May 1778, in "Letters from Valley Forge," accessed 4 Feb. 2013.
92. Washington's aides are discussed and their roles assessed in detail in Lefkowitz, *Washington's Indispensable Men*. See also Kahler, "Gentlemen of the Family."
93. See, for example, John Laurens to Henry Laurens, 1 Jan. 1778, Laurens, *Army Correspondence*, 100. In this letter John complains that "the promotion of Genl Conway has given almost universal disgust." In another letter, dated 17 February 1778, he warns his father that the troops are close to mutiny for lack of food. Ibid., 126. The senior Laurens learned of these matters directly from Washington as well, though hardly in such graphic terms.
94. *PAH*, 1:428.

Chapter 4

1. GW to Henry Laurens, 18 Apr. 1778, *PGWde*, RWS, 14:546; GW to Henry Laurens, 23 Apr. 1778, ibid., 601. In his letter to Laurens of the twenty-third, Washington added a postscript: "It is confidently reported and I have little doubt of the truth of it, that Sir Wm Howe is recalled, & that Genl Clinton is to succeed him in command."
2. GW to the General Officers, 20 Apr. 1778, ibid., 567; GW to Major General Stirling, 21 Apr. 1778, ibid., 581.
3. Varnum to GW, 23 Apr. 1778, ibid., 607–608.
4. Stirling to GW, 23Apr.1778, ibid., 605–607; Nelson, *Lord Stirling*, 124–25.
5. Anthony Wayne to GW, 21 Apr. 1778, *PGWde*, RWS, 14:581.
6. Poor to GW, 23 Apr. 1778, ibid., 604.
7. Wayne to GW, 21 Apr. 1778, ibid., 581.
8. Hugh F. Rankin, "Anthony Wayne: Military Romanticist," in Billias, *George Washington's Generals*, 260–90.

9. Duportail to GW, c. 20 Apr. 1778, *PGWde*, RWS, 14:559–65.
10. Steuben to GW, 25 Apr.1778, ibid., 636–38; Layfayette to GW, 25 Apr. 1778, ibid., 628–31.
11. "Washington's Thoughts upon a Plan of Operation for Campaign 1778," c. 26–29 Apr. 1778, ibid., 641–45.
12. GW to Laurens, 23 Apr.1778, ibid., 600.
13. All these developments are discussed in William Livingston to GW, 2 May 1778, ibid., 15:17; Israel Shreve to GW, 4 May 1778, ibid., 33; Greene to GW, 3 May 1778, ibid., 19; and GW to Greene, 5 May 1778, ibid., 41.
14. Council of War, 8 May 1778, ibid., 79–81.
15. From a Council of War, 9 May 1778, ibid., 83–87.
16. Jackson, *With the British Army in Philadelphia*, 251.
17. Oliver Wolcott to Laura Wolcott, 5 June 1778, *LDC*, 10:33; Clinton, *American Rebellion*, 88–89.
18. Elizabeth Sandwith Drinker, Diary, 23, 24 May 1778, Drinker Diaries, 1758–1807, Collection 1760, PHi.
19. Serle, *Journal*, 295–99.
20. Jackson, *With the British Army in Philadelphia*, 257.
21. Ewald, *Diary*, 130–31.
22. Supreme Executive Council of Pennsylvania, *Minutes*, 11:483–85. Not all patriots thought this policy wise. Gouverneur Morris considered that the step would only injure "the small Fry" among the tories, while pardoning all but the most notorious would win loyalist troops away from the King. Morris to the New York Assembly, 23 July 1778, *LDC*, 10:342–43.
23. Carlisle quoted in Willcox, *Portrait of a General*, 230.
24. Commissioners for Quieting Disorders to Lord George Germain, 15 June 1778, in Davies, *Documents of the American Revolution*, 15:140–41.
25. *JCC*, 11:614–15; GW to Laurens, 18 June 1778, *PGWde*, RWS, 15:450.
26. Montresor, *Journals*, 486–91. For military engagements, see Munn, *Battles and Skirmishes*, 131–32; and Peckham, *Toll of Independence*, 50–52.
27. Thomas Paine to GW, 5 June 1778, *PGWde*, RWS, 15:327. There is no record of Washington having responded.
28. Joseph Reed to Esther Reed, 9 June 1778, *LDC*, 10:62; James Lovell to Horatio Gates, 9 June 1778, ibid., 56; John Wentworth to John Langdon, 10 June 1778, ibid., 69.
29. William Livingston to GW, 17 May 1778, *PGWde*, RWS, 15:144; Philemon Dickinson to GW, 19, 27 May 1778, ibid., 163, 236; GW to Livingston, 21 May 1778, ibid., 180; William Maxwell to GW, 28 May 1778, ibid., 247–48. On 15 June Dickinson emphatically reiterated his belief that Clinton was determined to march through New Jersey. Dickinson to GW, 15 June 1778, ibid., 399.
30. GW to Henry Laurens, 28 May 1778, ibid., 246.
31. GW to Landon Carter, 30 May 1778, ibid., 269.
32. GW to Charles Lee, 30 May 1778, ibid., 274. As part of this possible movement, on 28 May Washington had prepared detailed plans for the

order and routes of march to the Hudson River for the entire army. See Orders for March from Valley Forge, [17 June 1778], editorial note, ibid., 274. Lee may have received this communication, with a postscript, on 18 June. The three brigades were those of Brig. Gens. Enoch Poor (944 officers and men fit for duty), James Varnum (692), and Jedediah Huntington (829). Lesser, *Sinews of Independence*, 68–69.

33. For a good contemporary account of the preparations for evacuation, see Baurmeister, *Revolution in America*, 173. See also Krafft, *Journal*, 39; and Muenchhausen, *At General Howe's Side*, 54.
34. Stryker, *Battle of Monmouth*, 31; Ewald, *Diary*, 403n36; GW to John Augustine Washington, 4 July 1778, *PGWde*, RWS, 16:25–26.
35. Popp, *Hessian Soldier*, 1–2; Baurmeister, *Revolution in America*, 9.
36. Krafft, *Journal*, 39; Feilitzsch and Bartholomai, *Diaries of Two Ansbach Jaegers*, 39; Baurmeister, *Revolution in America*, 179; Doehla, "Diary," 9 June 1778, copy enclosed with letter, Bruce E. Burgoyne to Garry Stone, 25 Feb. 1995, in author's possession; Popp, *Hessian Soldier*, 9.
37. Jaeger captain Johann Ewald was familiar with the Ansbach-Bayreuth regiments, describing them as "handsome and well-drilled people" and "fit for use," But he explained their departure with the vague observation that they "cannot march," which sheds no light on the matter. *Diary*, 132.
38. Jackson, *With the British Army in Philadelphia*, 261–62; Henry Laurens to John Rutledge, 3 June 1778, *LDC*, 10:18–20; Henry Laurens to John Laurens, 5 June 1778, ibid., 28–29.
39. Nathanael Greene to Moore Furman, 15 June 1778, *PNG*, 2:431–32; Greene to Furman, 18 June 1778, ibid., 441; Greene to Furman, 21 June 1778, ibid., 442.
40. Ibid., 446n1.
41. Jeremiah Wadsworth to GW, 4 June 1778, *PGWde*, RWS, 15:315.
42. John Shreve, "Personal Narrative of the Services of Lieut. John Shreve of the New Jersey Line of the Continental Army," in Allen, *Genealogy and History of the Shreve Family*, 614–15, 624.
43. GW to Israel Shreve, 19 Mar. 1778, *PGWde*, RWS, 14:232.
44. Simcoe, *Military Journal*, 46–54.
45. On general preparations, see GW to Henry Knox, 17 May 1778, *PGWde*, RWS, 15:142. On Maxwell's deployment, see GW to William Maxwell, 25 May 1778, ibid., 220–21. For other orders and communications with the New Jersey detachment, see GW to Israel Shreve, 7May 1778, ibid., 77; and GW to Maxwell, 29 May 1778, ibid., 259.
46. Lesser, *Sinews of Independence*, 68; Woodhull, "Memoir of Brig. Gen. Anthony Walton White," 106–15; Garden, *Anecdotes of the American Revolution*, 76–83.
47. Ward, *General William Maxwell.*
48. For the activities of the New Jersey Brigade in the countryside, see Israel Shreve to Washington, 28 Mar. 1778, *PGWde*, RWS, 14:338; Philemon Dickinson to GW, 6 June 1778, ibid., 15:334; William Maxwell to Philemon Dickinson, 6 June 1778, GWP, 4th ser.; Shreve to GW, 9 Apr. 1778, Israel Shreve Papers, NjRV; John Shreve, "The Days of the

Revolution," *New Jersey Mirror and Burlington County Advertiser*, 29 Dec. 1853; Bloomfield, *Citizen Soldier*, 135.

49. GW to Lafayette, [18 May 1778], *PGWde*, RWS, 15:151.
50. Historian Lynn Montross and others have suggested that Steuben's training played a key role in Lafayette's escape at Barren Hill. Montross argued that until the training regimen of the inspector general, American units generally had moved slowly and in single file, with outfits strung out for hundreds of yards and with straggling the norm. Troops moving in or out of action in such fashion were terribly vulnerable; an enemy could overwhelm either end of the line before unengaged sections could come up to help. Lafayette, however, had marched his soldiers in compact platoon columns, which ensured better speed and control. See *Rag, Tag, and Bobtail*, 280. But independent researcher John U. Rees has convincingly challenged this notion, pointing out that the weight of other evidence (which he discusses at length) is that Continental outfits generally moved in column formations; the units at Barren Hill were no exception. John U. Rees to the author, 8 Dec. 1992, in author's possession.
51. Lengel, *General George Washington*, 288–89; GW to Gouverneur Morris, 29 May 1778, *PGWde*, RWS, 15:261.
52. Landon Carter to GW, 10–20 Mar. 1778, *PGWde*, RWS, 14:125–26; GW to Carter, 30 May 1778, ibid., 15:286.
53. Dennis P. Ryan, "William Livingston," in Stellhorn and Birkner, *Governors of New Jersey*, 77–81.
54. Lender, "Conscripted Line," 23–46.
55. On New Jersey in the early movement for independence, see Gerlach, *Prologue to Independence*.
56. Israel Shreve to GW, 28 Mar. 1778, *PGWde*, RWS, 14:338–40.
57. Munn, *Battles and Skirmishes*, 131–32.
58. Mark Edward Lender, "The 'Cockpit' Reconsidered: Revolutionary New Jersey as a Military Theater," in Mitnick, *New Jersey in the American Revolution*, 50–51.
59. On the Dickinson family and its politics, see Flower, *John Dickinson*. Biographical sketches of Philemon Dickinson (he has no full biography) are in Dickinson, "Philemon Dickinson: Major-General," 420–27; and Johnson and Malone, *Dictionary of American Biography*, 302–303. On Dickinson in patriot politics, see Gerlach, *Prologue to Independence*, 290, 376, 483n19, 484nn26–28.
60. Between 9 May and 18 June, Washington and Dickinson exchanged no fewer than twenty-four letters on the military situation in New Jersey and related subjects. See *PGWde*, RWS, 15:88ff.
61. GW to Maxwell, 29 May 1778, *PGWde*, RWS, 15:259; GW to Dickinson, 24 May 1778, ibid., 208; Dickinson to GW, 9, 15, 17 June 1778, ibid., 362, 399, 419; Dickinson to Shreve, 25 May 1778, Shreve Papers, NjRV; *New-Jersey Gazette*, 27 May 1778.
62. Stryker, *Battle of Monmouth*, 24.
63. New Jersey militia pension applications are on file in NjTSA and in RWPBLW microcopies. Of thirty randomly selected pension applications of Monmouth veterans, all cited prior service; some had served tours of duty since 1776.

64. James Kirby Martin, "The Continental Army and the American Victory," in Ferling, *World Turned Upside Down*, 20, 34.
65. William Maxwell to GW, 14 June 1778, *PGWde*, RWS, 15:395–96.
66. See, for example, William Maxwell to GW, 1 June, 1778, ibid., 292–93; Israel Shreve to Philemon Dickinson, 2 June 1778, GWP; William Maxwell to Dickinson, 1, 14 June 1778, ibid.; Dickinson to GW, 1, 2, 4 June 1778, *PGWde*, RWS, 15:290, 300, 309; GW to Dickinson, 15 June 1778, ibid., 398–99.
67. Ewald, *Diary*, 132.
68. Huber, *Compound Warfare*, vii; Jerry D. Morelock, "Washington as Strategist: Compound Warfare in the American Revolution, 1775–1783," in ibid., 54–56.
69. Morelock, "Washington as Strategist," 54–56, 78–80.
70. Wirth, *British Encampment in Evesham*, 2.
71. Krafft, *Journal*, 40.
72. Dickinson to GW, 15 June 1778, *PGWde*, RWS, 15:399.
73. Muenchhausen, *At General Howe's Side*, 60.
74. Clinton was not happy about this, and in general orders he asked for a count of these women and to know which corps they had joined. He also wanted to know "by whose Permission those women Rejoined the army." General Orders, 23 June 1778, 2BtnBrGrenOrBk.
75. On the final evacuation, see André, *Journal*, 74; Stryker, *Battle of Monmouth*, 22–23, 31–32; Clinton, *American Rebellion*, 90; and Ewald, *Diary*, 132.
76. Elizabeth Sandwich Drinker, Diary, 18 June 1778, Drinker Diaries, 1758–1807, Collection 1760, PHi; Baurmeister, *Revolution in America*, 182.
77. Wister, *Journal*, 183; Journal of Capt. John Peebles, 18 June 1778, Book 6, Cunninghame of Thorntoun Papers, GD 21, Scottish Records Office, Edinburgh. For congressional reaction to the evacuation, see, for example, Samuel Adams to James Warren, 19 June 1778, *LDC*, 10:135; and Committee for Foreign Affairs to Benjamin Franklin, 20 June 1778, ibid., 144.
78. Orders for March from Valley Forge, [17 June 1778], *PGWde*, RWS, 15:424–25; GW to Charles Lee, 30 May 1778, postscript of 18 June 1778, ibid., 274.
79. Council of War, 17 June 1778, ibid., 414–17.
80. Charles Lee to GW, 15 June 1778, ibid., 403–405.
81. The written responses of the general officers to GW, all dated 18 June 1778, are found in *PGWde*, RWS, vol. 15. Those attending were Maj. Gens. Charles Lee, Nathanael Greene, Benedict Arnold, William Alexander (Lord Stirling), the marquis de Lafayette, and Friedrich Steuben, and Brig. Gens. William Smallwood, Henry Knox, Enoch Poor, John Paterson, Anthony Wayne, William Woodford, Peter Muhlenberg, Jedediah Huntington, and Louis Duportail. Not attending but submitting recommendations were Brig. Gen. Charles Scott and Pennsylvania militia major general John Cadwalader. See also GW to Henry Laurens, 18 June 17778, ibid., 449–50.
82. Knox to GW, 18 June 1778, ibid., 446–48.

83. Lee to GW, 18 June 1778, ibid., 457–58; Greene to GW, 18 June 1778, ibid., 441–43.
84. Wayne to GW, 18 June 1778, ibid., 468–69.
85. Jordan, *Encyclopedia of Pennsylvania Biography*, 720–23; Cadwalader, *The Cadwaladers.*
86. Cadwalader to GW, 18 June 1778, *PGWde*, RWS, 15:435–36.
87. GW to George Bryan, 18 June 1778, ibid., 434.
88. GW to Henry Laurens, 18 June 1778, ibid., 449.
89. General Orders, 18 June 1778, ibid., 429–30; GW to Anthony Wayne, 18 June 1778, ibid., 468.
90. GW to Henry Jackson, 18 June 1778, ibid., 445; GW to Benedict Arnold, 19 June 1778, ibid., 472; General Orders, 18 June 1778, ibid., 429–30; Philemon Dickinson to GW, 18 June 1778, ibid., 439; GW to Henry Laurens, three letters of 18 June 1778, ibid., 448–51; GW to Horatio Gates, 18 June 1778, ibid., 440.
91. General Orders, 20 June 1778, ibid., 475; Greenman, *Diary*, 120.

Chapter 5

1. Unless noted otherwise, this sketch of Lee is based on Alden, *General Charles Lee;* John Shy, "Charles Lee: The Soldier as Radical," in Billias, *George Washington's Generals*, 22–53; and Papas, *Renegade Revolutionary.*
2. "Sir Henry Bunbury, 3rd Bt.," accessed 10 Feb. 2013.
3. Katcher, *British, Provincial, and German Army Units*, 53.
4. *Lee Papers*, 1:3–5.
5. Alden, *General Charles Lee*, 14.
6. "103rd Regiment of Foot," accessed 11 Feb. 2013. The history of this regiment is complicated, as it came on and off the army list at least four times between 1760 and 1817; the "1st Raising" was Lee's regiment.
7. Burgoyne to Lord North, [11 July?] 1775, Burgoyne, *Political and Military Episodes*, 174, 176.
8. Snell, "General Charles Lee House. 'Prato Rio.'"
9. Papas, *Renegade Revolutionary*, 4.
10. Shy, "Charles Lee," 23. Shy borrowed from Eric Hoffer in calling Lee a "true believer, the fanatic whose very strength lies in his lack of balance, judgment, and self-restraint."
11. Quoted in Alden, *General Charles Lee*, 30.
12. Papas, *Renegade Revolutionary*, 93–113. For a contrary view—that Lee's radicalism was essentially self-serving opportunism, a means to hoped-for preferment in America—see Mazzagetti, *Charles Lee.* Papas, however, has the best of the argument.
13. Burgoyne to Lord North, [11 July?] 1775, Burgoyne, *Political and Military Episodes*, 174.
14. Joseph Reed to Charles Lee, 21 Nov. 1776, in Reed, *Life and Correspondence of Joseph Reed*, 1:255–56; Reed to Lee, 21 Nov. 1776, *Lee Papers*, 2:293–94; Lee to Horatio Gates, 12–13 Dec. 1776, ibid., 348.
15. GW to Charles Lee, 3 Dec. 1776, *PGWde*, RWS, 7:257. Washington also wrote Lee another letter a few days later, urging him to move. It has

been lost, but its existence is verified through other sources. GW to Lee, 7 Dec. 1776, ibid., 271. The best account of Lee's dilatory march is in Lefkowitz, *Long Retreat*, 107–11.

16. Shy, "Charles Lee," 39; Lee to GW, 4 Dec. 1776, *PGWde*, RWS, 7:259–60.
17. James Flexner, without any evidence other than an allegation that "Lee had a propensity for sleeping in strange places (and with strange women)," has hinted at this. *George Washington in the American Revolution*, 167.
18. A full account of the British operation that led to Lee's capture is in McBurney, *Kidnapping the Enemy*, chap. 2.
19. Parole, 5 Apr. 1778, *Lee Papers*, 2:382.
20. In fact, there was considerable concern in Congress over Lee's treatment and for measures of retaliation. See Samuel Adams to James Warren, 8 Jan. 1777, *LDC*, 6:49; Samuel Adams to John Adams, 9 Jan. 1777, ibid., 64; Thomas Burke's Notes of Debates, 20 Feb. 1777, ibid., 327–28; and Richard Peters to GW, 21 Feb. 1777, *PGWde*, RWS, 8:400–401.
21. Lee to Guiseppi Minghini, 4 Apr. 1777, *Lee Papers*, 2:367–68; Morgan, *Naval Documents of the American Revolution*, 78, 234; Alden, *General Charles Lee*, 184–85.
22. Cox, *Proper Sense of Honor*, 199–200, 224.
23. Otway Bryd to Lee, 1 June 1778, *Lee Papers*, 2:396.
24. Lee's correspondence from December 1776 and April 1778, ibid., 356–82; Thomas Burke's Notes of Debates, 21 Feb. 1777, *LDC*, 6:336. Richard Henry Lee to Charles Lee, [Feb. 1777], *LDC*, 6:337n2; Lee to Guiseppi Minghini, 4 Apr. 1777, *Lee Papers*, 2:367–68.
25. "Scheme for Putting an End to the War, Submitted to the Royal Commissioners, 29th March, 1777," *Lee Papers*, 2:361–66.
26. George H. Moore, "The Treason of Charles Lee, Major General," *Lee Papers*, 4:339–427. This item was also published separately. See Moore, *Treason of Charles Lee.*
27. Alden, *General Charles Lee*, 175–79; Shy, "Charles Lee," 40–41.
28. Charles Thomson to GW, 21 July 1777, *LDC*, 7:358–59; ibid., 377n1; Parole, 5 Apr. 1778, *Lee Papers*, 2:382.
29. U.S. Coast Guard, "Situational Awareness," accessed 9 Feb. 2013.
30. Boudinot, *Journal*, 78.
31. Ibid., 79.
32. Lee probably met with Richard Henry Lee in York on his way back from Virginia before his return to Valley Forge. Richard Henry Lee to John Page, 4 May [1778], *LDC*, 9:599. He also met with delegates John Banister of Virginia and Charles Carroll of Carrollton (whom Lee considered friends). John Banister to St. George Tucker, 15 Apr. 1778, ibid., 416; Charles Carroll of Carrollton to Charles Carroll, Sr., 20 Apr. 1778, ibid., 448. The general probably met with other delegates as well. Gates also wanted to meet with him at York, although Lee's travel may have prevented this. Henry Laurens to GW, 24–25 Apr. 1778, *PGWde*, RWS, 14:613–14.
33. Thomas Burke to Richard Caswell, 9 Apr. 1778, *LDC*, 9:393.

34. Henry Laurens to John Laurens, 6 July 1778, ibid., 10:230, 323n3; Alden, *General Charles Lee*, 191; Lee to Henry Laurens, 17 Apr. 1778, *Lee Papers*, 2:390. In this letter, Lee also suggested that Congress include Burgoyne in the upcoming prisoner exchange, not knowing that Washington already was making final arrangements for exchanging Prescott.
35. Henry Laurens to John Laurens, 17 June 1778, *LDC*, 10:126.
36. Lee to Benjamin Rush, 4 June 1778, *Lee Papers*, 2:397.
37. Charles Lee to Henry Laurens, 13 May 1778, ibid., 392–93.
38. GW to Lee, 15 June 1778, *PGWde*, RWS, 15:406–407.
39. Timothy Pickering to John Pickering, 6 July 1778, Timothy Pickering Papers, MHi.
40. Charles Carroll of Carrollton to Charles Carroll, Sr., 17 May 1778, *LDC*, 9:691.
41. Memorandum, [May 1778], *Lee Papers*, 2:394–95; Lee to GW, 15 June 1778, *PGWde*, RWS, 15:403–406. The memorandum was not addressed to Washington, though he did receive a copy. Elias Boudinot recalled the conversation with Lee but said nothing about agreeing with him on Clinton's intentions. *Journal*, 81.
42. GW to Charles Lee, 15 June 1778, *PGWde*, RWS, 15:406.
43. Charles Pettit to Thomas Bradford, 19 May 1778, *Lee Papers*, 2:393–94.
44. Nathanael Greene to William Greene, 27 May1778, *PNG*, 2:408.
45. Nathanael Greene to Griffin Greene, 25 May 1778, ibid., 406.
46. Papas, *Renegade Revolutionary*, 237. John Alden has posited that Lee's remark at swearing the oath was aimed at Congress, an implied protest against any effort to dictate his opinion as a condition of retaining his commission. *General Charles Lee*, 202. Recently, Thomas Fleming has suggested that Lee intended the remark as a subtle jab at Washington—that perhaps he obliquely referred to the tendency of British opposition politicians to rally to the prince when they disagreed with the King; the implication here is that Lee saw Washington as the King. *Washington's Secret War*, 301. Phillip Papas cautiously agrees that Lee may have intended a dig at Washington. *Renegade Revolutionary*, 237. This interpretation seems strained, but there is little doubt that the commander in chief failed to appreciate Lee's performance on the occasion.
47. Alden, *General Charles Lee*, 200–201.
48. Lockhart, *Drillmaster of Valley Forge*, 132–33; James Varnum to GW, 5 May 1778, *PGWde*, RWS, 15:54–56; Alexander Hamilton to Elias Boudinot, 26 July 1778, *PAH*, 1:528–29.
49. "Plan for the Formation of the American Army in the least Expensive Manner possible . . . ," [13 Apr. 1778], *Lee Papers*, 2:383. Unless noted otherwise, all references to Lee's plan are from this document.
50. Lee to GW, 13 Apr. 1778, ibid.
51. GW to Lee, 22 Apr. 1778; *PGWde*, RWS, 14:585.
52. Lee, "Plan for the Formation of the American Army," *Lee Papers*, 2:384, 388.
53. In his "Plan" Lee expressly mentioned his admiration of Brig. Gen. Kasimir Pulaski's legion, authorized in March 1778. The unit eventually

had horse and foot components and may have had some light artillery. Berg, *Encyclopedia of Continental Army Units*, 101.

54. Warren, *Rise, Progress, and Termination of the American Revolution*, 2:95; Shy, "Charles Lee," 42.
55. Boudinot, *Journal*, 78.
56. Lee to Gates, 4 Apr. 1778, *Lee Papers*, 3:321.

Chapter 6

1. Maxwell to Washington, 14 June 1778, *PGWde*, RWS, 15:395–96; Feilitzsch and Bartholomai, *Diaries of Two Ansbach Jaegers*, 40; Krafft, *Journal*, 41; Ewald, *Diary*, 132; Downman, *Services*, 65; *PGWde*, RWS, 15:473.
2. On the geography and soils of colonial New Jersey, and the Inner and Outer Coastal Plains, see Wacker, *Land and People*, chap. 1.
3. James Pattison to Lord Townsend, 12 June 1778, Pattison, *Papers*, 131. The artillery train consisted of two medium 12-pounder cannons, four light 12-pounders, twenty-six 6-pounders, twelve 3-pounders, and two 5.5-inch howitzers. Pattison to Henry Clinton, 22 May 1778, Pattison Papers, Royal Artillery Institution, Woolwich, London. Brig. Gen. James Pattison was chief of artillery.
4. General Orders, Haddinfild [*sic*], 18 June 1778, 2BtnBrGrenOrBk.
5. For the jaegers' deployment with the 1st Division, see Ewald, *Diary*, 132–34; and Simcoe, *Military Journal*, 63–64. For their listing in the 2nd Division, see "Return of the Number of Men, Wagoners, Women & Children victualled at Monmouth the 27 & 28th June 1778 inclusive," Sir Henry Clinton Papers, vol. 36, no. 5, MiU-C; and "State of the Forces under . . . Sir Henry Clinton," 3 July 1778, Manuscripts Division, PRO CO, p. 77, DLC. The loyalist horse unit was the Philadelphia Light Dragoons, under Capt. Richard Hoveden. See the sources above and [S. P. Adye], "Account of the Evacuation of Philadelphia, the March through the Jerseys, Battle of Freehold or Monmouth Courthouse, and Arrival of the British Army in New York, as Recorded in Brigade Order Book No. 2," in Downman, *Services*, 66; and General Orders, Camp at Mount holey [*sic*], 21 June 1778, 2BtnBrGrenOrBk.
6. Ritchie, "New York Diary of the Revolutionary War," 236. This diary was extracted from the Pattison Papers and probably was the Artillery Brigade orders and a journal kept by Capt.-Lt. Stephen Adye, 17 June 1778–31 December 1779. See also James Pattison to [Henry Clinton], Pattison, *Papers*, 144–47.
7. Simcoe, *Military Journal*, 63; Krafft, *Journal*, 40; Feilitzsch and Bartholomai, *Diaries of Two Ansbach Jaegers*, 40; Robertson, *Archibald Robertson*, 173–74. For Hoveden's loyalist horse, see Stephen Adye, "Brigade Orders," in Ritchie, "New York Diary of the Revolutionary War," 234; and Order Book of the 7th British Foot Regiment, 17, 19, 21, 22, June 1778, [New Jersey] Numbered Miscellaneous Revolutionary War Manuscripts, Department of Defense Record Group, Loyalist Manuscripts, Box 3, NjTSA.

8. Robertson, *Archibald Robertson*, 174; "Journal Kept by Distinguished Hessian Field Jaeger Corps during the Campaigns of the Royal Army of Great Britain in North America," trans. by Bruce E. Burgoyne, 1986, Lidgerwood Collection of Hessian Transcripts of the American Revolution, Letter L, Microfiche 245, NjMoHP; Philemon Dickinson to GW, 19 June 1778, *PGWde*, RWS, 15:472–73, 473n.
9. Ewald, *Diary*, 132.
10. Ibid., 132–33.
11. Clinton quoted in Stryker, *Battle of Monmouth*, 52–53; Bell, MS Diary, 19 June 1778; "Journal Kept by Distinguished Hessian Field Jaeger Corps," Letter L, Microfiche 245, NjMoHP; Wirth, *British Encampment in Evesham*, 9. The Beesley story is actually a bit complicated. In his journal André claimed that the Queen's Rangers had shot the patriot captain, but Simcoe said only that on 19 June the jaegers were in front of Leslie's advance and that there had been a skirmish, with a British deserter captured. Had his men been involved with Beesley, he would have noted as much. André, *Journal*, 75; Simcoe, *Operations of the Queens Rangers*, 63.
12. Wirth, *British Encampment in Evesham*, 9, quoting an account in *NJHC*.
13. Ewald, *Diary*, 132–34; Bell, MS Diary, 20 June 1778.
14. Thomas Sullivan, Journal, 1775–1778, pp. 402–403, Collection 1098, PHi (typescript of original in the American Philosophical Society, Philadelphia).
15. Dann, *Revolution Remembered*, 123.
16. Ewald, *Diary*, 133. The British did inflict some losses on the Americans. The First New Jersey Regiment had two men killed and one captured; John U. Rees, "They Answered Him with Three Cheers . . . ," *New Jersey Brigade Losses in the Monmouth Campaign*, Resource Library, RevWar'75, http://revwar75.com/library/rees/NJlosses.htm.
17. Ewald, *Diary*, 133; Bell, MS Diary, 20 June 1778; Clinton, *American Rebellion*, 90. If Washington had been at Mount Holly, Clinton was prepared to fight. He had a plan to turn Washington's left—a flanking maneuver reminiscent of Long Island in 1776—and cut off his retreat. Ibid., 90. In all likelihood this would have forced Washington to fight a general action. But only Maxwell and militia were at Mount Holly.
18. Leslie's orders quoted in Stryker, *Battle of Monmouth*, 53.
19. Wirth, *British Encampment in Evesham*, 7; Ewald, *Diary*, 133.
20. Ritchie, "New York Diary of the Revolutionary War," 235–36. For the West Jersey Volunteers, see Katcher, *British, Provincial, and German Army Units*, 102. In his account of the march, Knyphausen mentioned encountering no serious opposition until 28 June. Knyphausen to the Landgrave of Hesse-Kassel, 6 July 1778, Lidgerwood Collection of Hessian Transcripts of the American Revolution, 37:361, NjMoHP. Loyalist Andrew Bell mentioned that Knyphausen arrived at Mount Holly with "no kind of interruption." Bell, MS Diary, 21 June 1778.
21. Ewald, *Diary*, 38–39; Munn, *Battles and Skirmishes*, 57. Quite accidentally, this engagement (also called Iron Mill Hill), which took place on

23 December 1776, had the effect of tying down royal troops who might otherwise have helped defend Trenton against Washington's raid on the twenty-sixth. See Fischer, *Washington's Crossing*, 199–200.

22. For the colonial and Revolutionary history of Mount Holly, see the early chapters of Rizzo, *Mount Holly.*
23. John André, *Map of Mount Holly*, bound in a manuscript journal, Henry E. Huntington Library, San Marino, Calif., microfilm, PWasD. A map by John Hills of the Evesham encampment shows a similarly careful defensive arrangement. See back cover of Wirth, *British Encampment in Evesham.*
24. This was in paragraph form in the original; it is shown as a list for clarity with punctuation added as noted in brackets. General Orders, Camp at Mount holey [*sic*], 21 June 1778, 2BtnBrGrenOrBk. The order of march is given slightly differently in Kemble, *Journals*, 596–97.
25. Dickinston to GW, 22 June 1778, Bordentown, *PGWde*, RWS, 15:496.
26. Leslie had the 7th, 26th, and 63rd Regiments, as well as the Philadelphia Light Dragoons and the jaegers. While Clinton's orders had the jaegers with the 1st Division, jaeger records reveal that this was changed. General Orders, Camp at Mount holey [*sic*], 21 June 1778, 2BtnBrGrenOrBk; [Adye], "Account of . . . the March through the Jerseys," 66; Ewald, *Diary*, 134; "Journal Kept by Distinguished Hessian Field Jaeger Corps," Letter L, Microfiche 245, NjMoHP; André, *Journal*, 75.
27. Dickinson to GW, 24 June 1778, 6:30 A.M., *PGWde*, RWS, 15:523.
28. Simcoe, *Operations of the Queen's Rangers*, 63–64.
29. Feilitzsch and Bartholomai, *Diaries of Two Ansbach Jaegers*, 40.
30. General Orders, Camp at Black Horse, 22 June 1778, 2BtnBrGrenOrBk; André, *Journal*, 78.
31. Stryker, *Battle of Monmouth*, 82–83.
32. An Officer [Thomas Anburey], *Travels*, 1:1, 4–5. For a sketch of Anburey's military career, see "Northern Campaign of 1777 Primary Sources," accessed 5 Oct. 2015. On the nature of his British acquaintances, see the subscription list for his book in volume 1, preceding p. 1.
33. Ibid., 2:381–82.
34. Ibid., 2:381.
35. Clarke and Phillips did know and work with one another in captivity at the time of Anburey's writing, which is about all that can be said about the relationship. Jonathan Clarke, Assistant Commissary, "Government in Account with Jonathan Clarke, Esquire," 24 Sept. 1779 ["Approved W Phillips MG"], Bland-Ruffin Papers, image 47, accessed 16 Mar. 2013.
36. Philemon Dickinson to GW, 23 June 1778, 11:30 P.M., *PGWde*, RWS, 15:513; [Adye], "Account of . . . the March through the Jerseys," 66; Ewald, *Diary*, 134.
37. Ewald, *Diary*, 135, 403n50.
38. "Inventory of the Goods, Chattels & Effects of Robert Lewis and Sons, Plundered, Burnt and Destroyed by the Troops of the British army . . . ," Damage Claims, 1776–1782, Reel 1:173–74, No. 333, Burlington County, NJSA.

39. Ewald, *Diary*, 134; "Journal Kept by Distinguished Hessian Field Jaeger Corps," Letter L, Microfiche 245, NjMoHP; Philemon Dickinson to GW, 23 June 1778, 10:00 A.M., *PGWde*, RWS, 15:511–12; Dickinson to GW, 23 June 1778, 1:30 P.M.; and Dickinson to GW, 23 June 1778, 11:30 P.M., ibid., 512–13; Feilitzsch and Bartholomai, *Diaries of Two Ansbach Jaegers*, 40–41.
40. Philemon Dickinson to GW, 24 June 1778, 6:30 A.M., *PGWde*, RWS, 15:523.
41. William Maxwell to GW, 24 June 1778, 8:00 A.M., ibid.,15:531.
42. Dann, *Revolution Remembered*, 123.
43. Also spelled "Stevenson" in some accounts. See, for example, Bell, MS Diary, 23 June 1778. William Stryker, without citing a source, states that the captain survived his wounding (which agrees with British accounts) and remained in action, only to be shot again by a Burlington County militiaman named Caleb Shreve. *Battle of Monmouth*, 86. This is unlikely, and the story may be local lore. Captain Stephenson was one of Simcoe's men, and Simcoe, who left a detailed account of the Queen's Rangers at Crosswicks, would have mentioned such an incident. No other British account mentions it either.
44. Bell, MS Diary, 23 June 1778; Simcoe, *Operations of the Queen's Rangers*, 64–65.
45. Philemon Dickinson to GW, 23 June 1778, *PGWde*, RWS, 15:510–11.
46. Bell, "Journal," 16–17; Simcoe, *Operations of the Queen's Rangers*, 64–65.
47. Stryker, *Battle of Monmouth*, 86.
48. Simcoe, *Operations of the Queen's Rangers*, 64.
49. Ibid., 64–66; Bell, MS Diary, 23 June 1778; André, *Journal*, 76; Bloomfield, *Citizen Soldier*, 136; Robertson, *Archibald Robertson*, 175.
50. Henry Clinton to George Germain, 5 July 1778, in Davies, *Documents of the American Revolution*, 3:160. In neither his letter to Germain nor his postwar narrative of the campaign did Clinton mention exposing himself to enemy fire at Crosswicks. But Simcoe mentioned the incident; and given Clinton's personal conduct in action on other fields (including Monmouth), it has the ring of truth. *Operations of the Queens Rangers*, 65. See also Peckham, *Toll of Independence*, 52; Jacob Morris to GW, 24 June 1778, *PGWde*, RWS, 15:532–33; and Bell, MS Diary, 23 June 1778. Stephenson survived and was exchanged; after the war he settled in New Brunswick, Canada. Munn, *Battles and Skirmishes*, 25; fragment, Elias Dayton to unknown, Oct. 1777, Elias Dayton Papers, MG 94, NjHi.
51. Elizabeth Sandwith Drinker, Diary, 27 June 1778, Drinker Diaries, 1758–1807, Collection 1760, PHi.
52. Simcoe, *Operations of the Queen's Rangers*, 65; John André, "23d June 1778," map from Journal of John André, 1777–78, Henry E. Huntington Library, San Marino, Calif., microfilm copy at PWacD, courtesy John U. Rees; John Hill, "Sketch of the Road from Black Horse to Crosswicks, June 1778," digital maps, DLC, www.memory.loc.gov; anonymous British journal, Clinton Papers, MiU-C, copy courtesy of Joseph Lee Boyle, historian, Valley Forge National Historical Park.

53. Jacob Morris to GW, 24 June 1778, *PGWde*, RWS, 15:532. A three-pound round shot remains embedded in the north wall of the 1773 Friends' meetinghouse.
54. Sullivan, Journal, 403; Simcoe, *Operations of the Queen's Rangers*, 66; Bell, MS Diary, 24 June 1778.
55. Baurmeister, *Revolution in America*, 183; Krafft, *Journal*, 42.
56. Available records indicate that the army convened three courts-martial on the way to Freehold "for the trial of Such prisoners as Shall be Brought before them": 19 June in Evesham, 21 June in Mount Holly, and 26 June in Monmouth Court House. There were only four trials, with two convictions for desertion and plundering, and two acquittals for plundering. See those dates in General Orders, 2BtnBrGrenOrBk.
57. Stryker, *Battle of Monmouth*, 55–56; William Livingston to GW, 22 June 1778, and Livingston to Charles Lee, 22 June 1778, Livingston, *Papers*, 2:372–73.
58. Sullivan, Journal, 403; Ewald, *Diary*, 132, 135.
59. Duncan, *Royal Regiment of Artillery*, 322–23. The regimental history states that this was the first time the artillery troops were allowed to carry only their personal arms and ammunition pouches. Krafft, *Journal*, 44.
60. Rees, "' . . . the Soldier's Necessaries.'" Rees based his conclusions on research in an impressive number of British military records and secondary sources.
61. Clinton, *American Rebellion*, 89; Henry Clinton to George Germain, 5 July 1778, in Davies, *Documents of the American Revolution*, 15:159–61.
62. Dickinson to GW, 23 June 1778, 11:30 P.M., *PGWde*, RWS, 15:513.
63. The West Jersey Volunteers, one of the loyalist outfits raised under General Howe's tenure, had helped garrison Billingsport. Katcher, *British, Provincial, and German Army Units*, 102. Between 2 March and 17 June 1778, there were some thirty-one skirmishes or engagements in the Delaware River counties of New Jersey across from the Philadelphia area. After the Monmouth campaign, there were *no* recorded engagements in these counties for the rest of the year. Munn, *Battles and Skirmishes*, 131–33.
64. Bell, MS Diary, 22 June 1778; André, *Journal*, 76.
65. General Orders, Haddonfield, 18 June 1778, 2BtnBrGrenOrBk; Simcoe, *Military Journal*, 63; André, *Journal*, 77.
66. Krafft, *Journal*, 45; Baurmeister, *Revolution in America*, 185.
67. Peebles, *American War*, 191; Wirth, *Encampment in Evesham*, 8–9; "Inventory of the Goods, Chattels & Effects of John Wilkenson, Plundered, Burnt and Destroyed by the Troops of the British army in June 1778," Damage Claims, 1776–82, Reel 1:175, No. 335, Burlington County, NJSA.
68. John Andrews, "Memorandum, His Surveying Book/Likewise, Painting," [Upper Freehold Township, N.J.], 25 June 1778, Private Collection, courtesy C. Andrew Beagle, South Plainfield, N.J.
69. Krafft, *Journal*, 45.

70. "Inventory of the Goods and Effects of Colonel William Shreve, Plundered, Burnt and Destroyed by the Troops of the British army the 23rd June 1778," Damage Claims, 1776–82, Reel 1:73–76, No. 125, Burlington County, NJSA. A number of sources have confused William Shreve with his brother Israel, assuming that it was Israel's home that went up in flames. For this, see Allen, *Genealogy and History of the Shreve Family*, 262–63, 345; Woodward and Hagemen, *Burlington and Mercer Counties*, 29; and Stryker, *Battle of Monmouth*, 53–54. In fact, there is no evidence indicating that Israel's immediate family suffered any damage during the British march. That Col. William Shreve was in the field when his home was attacked is verified in "Accounts of militia paymasters," Book B, Ledger A, p. 135, Abstracts of Pay-rolls discharged by William Hough, Microfilmed Military Records, Reel 186, NJSA; and Affidavit of Alexander Douglas, 18 June 1833, Jabesh Ashmore Pension Application, RWPBLW, Microcopy 804, Roll 83, Widow 5647.
71. General Orders, Crosswich [Crosswicks], 23 June 1778, 2BtnBrGrenOrBk.
72. Seventh Regiment of Foot, Orderly Book, 1778, p. 77, PHi. For Clarke, see Groves, *Records of the 7th or Royal Regiment of Fusiliers*, 310.
73. Krafft, *Journal*, 43; Baurmeister, *Revolution in America*, 185.
74. For example, see General Orders, Camp at Mount holey [*sic*], 21 June 1778, 2BtnBrGrenOrBk. Of the three defendants tried before this court martial, none were soldiers, all were civilians. Two were acquitted and one, "Penmes Coffee a negro," was sentenced to receive 500 lashes. During the entire march, these were the only courts-martial in the 2nd Battalion of Grenadiers for plundering. Between 5 and 25 September 1778, three loyalist officers were charged with plundering and other offenses on the march through New Jersey. Court-Martial Verdicts, 5–25 Sept. 1778, Flushing Fly, Long Island [N.Y.], Public Records Office, WO 71/87, 173–81. In October two were convicted, one was acquitted. Clayton, "Extracts from the Orderly Book," 100–101.
75. Krafft, *Journal*, 46.
76. Livingston, *Papers*, 2:378.
77. J. P. Martin, *Private Yankee Doodle*, 123–24.
78. Krafft, *Journal*, 42–45; Philemon Dickinson to GW, 24 June 1778, 9:30 P.M., *PGWde*, RWS, 15:523.
79. Sullivan, Journal, 404–409.
80. Knyphausen to the Landgrave of Hesse-Kassel, 6 July 1778, Lidgerwood Collection of Hessian Transcripts of the American Revolution, 37:287, NjMoHP; Baurmeister, *Revolution in America*, 185.
81. On American reaction to British desertion during the Monmouth campaign, see GW to Patrick Henry, 4 July 1778, *PGWde*, RWS, 16:21; and GW to Laurens, 7 July 1778, ibid., 34–35. Mark Boatner notes a total of more than 600 deserters, over two-thirds of them Hessians, returning to Philadelphia by 6 July. *Encyclopedia of the American Revolution*, 725. In a more recent study, however, historian Daniel Krebs has added a note of caution in assessing desertion among the Hessians. While it is impossible to compile a precise count, such losses evidently were not as great as many historians have assumed. Many deserters returned to

their units, and patriots may well have inflated reports of desertions for propaganda purposes; Washington and other senior patriots frankly were disappointed in the relatively low number of Hessian deserters. See Krebs, *Generous and Merciful Enemy*, 249, 396n30. Losses to desertion on the Monmouth campaign among German and British troops, however, clearly were a serious problem for General Clinton.

82. General Court-Martial, 21 June 1778, PRO WO 71/87, pp. 202–208, courtesy Don N. Hagist. The full story of John Fisher is in Riddle and Hagist, "Lessons from the Court," 9.
83. Simcoe, *Operations of the Queen's Rangers*, 63; Bell, MS Diary, 20 June 1778; General Orders, Camp at Mount holey [*sic*], 21 June 1778, 2BtnBrGrenOrBk; Krafft, *Journal*, 42; [Adye], "Account of . . . the March through the Jerseys," 66.
84. Boyle, "Summary of Weather Conditions," 6–7. Drawn from over thirty contemporary journal, diary, newspaper, military, and other accounts of weather conditions, Boyle's manuscript is a remarkable piece of work that deserves publication in its own right.
85. Serle, *Journal*, 314.
86. Chambers, *George Washington in Cranbury*, 3–4.
87. Clinton, *American Rebellion*, 90.
88. Ibid., 91.
89. Clinton to Germain, 5 July 1778, in Davies, *Documents of the American Revolution*, 15:160–61; Thayer, *Making of a Scapegoat*, 28–29.
90. Simcoe, *Operations of the Queen's Rangers*, 66–67; Baurmeister, *Revolution in America*, 184, Bell MS Diary, 25 June 1778.
91. "Shelburne, William Petty, 2nd earl of," in Cannon, *Dictionary of British History.*
92. Charles Grey to Lord Shelburne, 15 June 1778, British Library, London (transcription by Garry Stone, May 2009).
93. General Orders, Allentown, 24 June 1778, 2BtnBrGrenOrBk; "Return of the Number of Men, Wagoners, Women & Children victualled at Monmouth the 27 & 28th June 1778 inclusive," Clinton Papers, MiU-C; Ewald, *Diary*, 135.
94. General Orders, Allentown, 24 June 1778, 2BtnBrGrenOrBk.
95. On forming the army into a single column, see Simcoe, *Operations of the Queen's Rangers*, 67; and [Adye], "Account of . . . the March through the Jerseys," 67.
96. Peebles, *American War*, 190–92; [Adye], "Account of . . . the March through the Jerseys," 67.
97. With the British evacuation of Philadelphia, Jackson had remained to help the city's military governor, Benedict Arnold, restore order. Per Washington's orders, however, Arnold sent Jackson north on 23 June. Arnold to Jackson, 22 June 1778, *Christies Auction Catalogue*, Spring 1999, Lot 157. On Cadwalader's imminent arrival, see Philemon Dickinson to GW, 23 June 1778, 10:00 A.M., *PGWde*, RWS, 15:511–12.
98. Kemble, *Journals*, 599; André, *Journal*, 77; Ritchie, "New York Diary of the Revolutionary War," 239; "Journal Kept by Distinguished Hessian Field Jaeger Corps," Letter L, Microfiche 245, NjMoHP.

99. Craig, "In Search of the Rising Sun Tavern," 65. The tavern, known as the Willow Tree Tavern for most of its existence after the war, was demolished in 1948. Ibid., 61.
100. Simcoe, *Operations of the Queen's Rangers*, 67.
101. Morgan to GW, *PGWde*, RWS, 15:544; Bloomfield, *Citizen Soldier*, 136; Feilitzsch and Bartholomai, *Diaries of Two Ansbach Jaegers*, 41.
102. "Journal Kept by Distinguished Hessian Field Jaeger Corps," Letter L, Microfiche 245, NjMoHP; Feilitzsch and Bartholomai, *Diaries of Two Ansbach Jaegers*, 41; Simcoe, *Operations of the Queen's Rangers*, 68.
103. Simcoe, *Operations of the Queen's Rangers*, 68; Knyphausen to the Landgrave, 6 July 1778, Lidgerwood Collection of Hessian Transcripts of the American Revolution, NjMoHP.
104. Ewald, *Diary*, 135.
105. The best map of the 2nd Division encampments is Reinhart Martin, *Affaire bei Monmouth, 20 August 1778*, Hessian Archives, Marburg, Germany. It locates the artillery park, provision train, and the 4th Foot. The location of the light dragoons is implied by Continental reconnaissance reports from Steuben and Moylan to GW, *PGWde*, RWS, 15:565–66. Col. Silvanus Seeley locates the 2nd Light Infantry picket in his diary. Silvanus Seeley Diaries, 12 May 1768–17 Mar. 1821, NjMoHP. See also Dickinson to GW, *PGWde*, RWS, 15:573.
106. Clinton, *American Rebellion*, 91; Henry Clinton to George Germain, 5 July 1778, in Davies, *Documents of the American Revolution*, 15:160–61.
107. Morgan to GW, 27 June 1778, 2:00 P.M., *PGWde*, RWS, 15:564.

Chapter 7

1. Fisher, "Journal," 22.
2. GW to Livingston, 21 June 1778, *PGWde*, RWS, 15:491–92; GW to Dickinson, 21 June 1778, ibid., 15:489; McHenry, *Journal*, 3.
3. Gordon, *Rise, Progress, and Establishment of the Independence of the United States*, 3:150; J. P. Martin, *Private Yankee Doodle*, 125; Boyle, "Summary of Weather Conditions," 1–7.
4. The modern town of Hopewell is in Mercer County.
5. General Orders, 22 June 1778, *PGWde*, RWS, 15:492–93. Lee's wing had the brigades of Brigadier Generals Woodford, Scott, Poor, Varnum, and Huntington as well as the North Carolina Brigade. Stirling had the First and Second Pennsylvania Brigades and the brigades of Glover, Learned, and Paterson. Strength totals are from Lesser, *Sinews of Independence*, 72–73.
6. Wacker and Clemens, *Land Use in Early New Jersey*, 8–12.
7. General Orders, 22 June 1778, *PGWde*, RWS, 15:492–93.
8. Fisher, "Journal," 275–92.
9. Nathanael Greene to Henry Marchant, 25 July 1778, *PNG*, 2:471. In acknowledging Greene's contributions, Washington also gave appropriate credit to Commissary General Jeremiah Wadsworth. GW to Henry Laurens, 3–4 Aug. 1778, *PGWde*, RWS, 16:238–39. While Greene's

department kept the army adequately supplied, some accounts have waxed too enthusiastic. Thayer thought that Greene had selected nightly campsites along the route of march and that quartermaster personnel arranged for the prior digging of latrines and the delivery of firewood, bedding straw, and other goods. *Making of a Scapegoat*, 27. He cites no sources on this, and it is unlikely that such quartermaster support was the norm. Certainly, the advanced contingents of the army did not enjoy it, as their encampments were not always predictable as they reacted to Clinton's movements. Even some troops in the main body grumbled that they had to sleep in the open on wet bare ground. Chambers, *George Washington in Cranbury*, 11. It is enough to note that Greene's efforts kept the army operational through a critical period, and after Valley Forge that was high praise.

10. Brigham, "Revolutionary Diary," 25; Dearborn, *Revolutionary War Journals*, 124.
11. James Abeel to Nathanael Greene, 25 June 1778, *PNG*, 2:448.
12. Richard Henry Lee to Thomas Jefferson, 23 June 1778, *LDC*, 10:184; Charles Carroll of Carrollton to Charles Carroll, Sr., 23 June 1778, ibid., 178; Henry Laurens to John Houston, 22 June 1778, ibid., 173.
13. Finney, "Old Tennent Church," 264. Finney probably had been wounded at Long Island in 1776. Heitman, *Historical Register of Officers*, 227.
14. Willett, *Military Actions*, 65–66; J. P. Martin, *Private Yankee Doodle*, 123–24; Beatty, "Journal," 112–13.
15. Nicholas Haugessegger, "Orderly Book," 1 June 1778, Haugessegger Orderly Books, PHi. The standard order of march was detailed in General Orders, 1 June 1778, *PGWde*, RWS, 15:287–89. The order of march from Valley Forge, including such matters as road repairs and flanking parties, was dealt with in General Orders, 17, 22 June 1778, ibid., 424–25, 492–93.
16. Ege, *Pioneers of Old Hopewell*, 19–20.
17. Stryker, *Official Register*, 325, 342, 359. There is no record in Stryker's compilation of Houghton having served in the siege of Boston. That does not rule out the possibility of his having been there, as New Jersey volunteers did march to join patriot forces around the city in 1775.
18. This sketch of Hart was drawn from his only full-length biography, Hammond, *John Hart*.
19. Ibid., 69–70, 73.
20. Ege, *Pioneers of Old Hopewell*, 31, 36; Stryker, *Official Register*, 608.
21. Stout had been wounded during September 1777, although the cause of his death is unknown. Stryker, *Official Register*, 413.
22. General Orders, 23 June 1778, "Head-Quarters Hunt's-House," *PGWde*, RWS, 15:509–10.
23. Hammond, *John Hart*, 72; McHenry, *Journal*, 4.
24. GW to William Heath, 24 June 1778, "Hopewell Township, Jersey near the Baptist meeting house," *PGWde*, RWS, 15:527.
25. GW to Henry Laurens, 18 June 1778, ibid., 449.
26. The standard biography of Morgan is Higginbotham, *Daniel Morgan*.

27. Morgan's corps was in the field before the crossing into New Jersey. See Benedict Arnold to GW, 20 June 1778, *PGWde*, RWS, 15:476. The original companies are noted in a payroll for May 1778, MBSP. Regimental histories and strength reports are in Berg, *Encyclopedia of Continental Army Units*, 130; and Lesser, *Sinews of Independence*, 68, 72.
28. Fisher, "Journal," 279; General Orders, 22 June 1778, *PGWde*, RWS, 15:493. The North Carolina Brigade supplied two light-infantry companies instead of the twenty-five picked men. McHenry, *Journal*, 3; GW to Daniel Morgan, 23 June 1778, *PGWde*, RWS, 15:518. Lt. Thomas Blake of the First New Hampshire was clear on the composition of Morgan's command: "Col. Morgan with his regiment of riflemen [a reference to Morgan's corps] and a detachment under his command marched toward the enemy." Thomas Blake, "Lieutenant Thomas Blake's Journal," in Kidder, *First New Hampshire*, 42.
29. Dickinson to GW, 23 June 1778, 1:30 P.M., Trenton, *PGWde*, RWS, 15:513.
30. Affidavit of Alexander Douglas, 18 June 1833, Jabesh Ashmore Pension Application, RWPBLW, Microcopy 804, Roll 83, Widow 5647, DNA; Philemon Dickinson to GW, 24 June 1778, 6:30 A.M., *PGWde*, RWS, 15:523; Dickinson to GW, 24 June 1778, 9:30 P.M., ibid., 523–24; Daniel Morgan to GW, 25 June 1778, 5:00 A.M., "Crosswick bridge," ibid., 543–44; Morgan to GW, 25 June 1778, 11:00 A.M., Allentown, ibid., 544.
31. Morgan to GW, 25 June 1778, 11:00 A.M., Allentown, *PGWde*, RWS, 15:544. On the militia with Morgan, see "Disposition of the Militia Belonging to the State of New Jersey, Made by Major Genl. Dickinson," 25 June 1778, *Lee Papers*, 2:413. The battalions were those of Cols. Samuel Forman and Asher Holmes, both of Monmouth County, and Lt. Col. Joseph Haight of Burlington County. Stryker, *Official Register*, 344–45, 359.
32. GW to Philemon Dickinson, 24 June 1778, *PGWde*, RWS, 15:522.
33. The eleven letters of these dates (23 and 24 June 1778) are in ibid., 510–24.
34. Philemon Dickinson to GW, 23 June 1778, 10:00 A.M., ibid., 511–12. Cadwalader probably brought something over 100 volunteer militia with him. They were recruited in Philadelphia with the help of Benedict Arnold, then military governor of the city. Pennsylvania militia Brig. Gen. John Lacey also raised some volunteers from the militias of Bucks County, Pennsylvania, and Cumberland County, New Jersey. These men also were with Cadwalader. Stryker, *Battle of Monmouth*, 73–74. On Cadwalader's march into New Jersey, William Stryker has this: Cadwalader's "contingent carried to the American Army a new supply of cartridges, which the troops greatly needed. The cartridges had been made by the deft fingers of the patriotic women in Philadelphia during the four days previous, using, for paper wrappers, it is said, some of the sermons on defensive warfare by the famous minister Gilbert Tennent, preached during the French war for the purpose of enlisting men for that struggle. These sermons had been stowed away

in Benjamin Franklin's printing room and were brought forth to wrap the ammunition to be fired on the plains of Monmouth." Ibid., 73. The tale is as delightful as it is improbable and unattributed. In fact, upon arriving in New Jersey, Cadwalader had to ask Dickinson for a supply of ammunition. See Dickinson to GW, 23 June 1778, 10:00 A.M., *PGWde*, RWS, 15:511–12.

35. Philemon Dickinson to GW, 23 June 1778, no time, "Drawbridge" [Bordentown], *PGWde*, RWS, 15:510–11; Dickinson to GW, 23 June 1778, 10:00 A.M., "Drawbridge," ibid., 511–12; Dickinson to GW, 24 June 1778, 6:30 A.M., "Trenton," ibid., 523.

36. Dickinson to GW, 23 June 1778, "Drawbridge [Bordentown], ibid., 510–11; Dickinson to GW, 24 Jun 1778, ibid., 524; Dickinson to GW, 27 June 1778, ibid., 562.

37. Stone, "Militia Service at the Battle of Monmouth," 1–2; "Abstracts of Pay Rolls," Book B, Auditors Accounts, [New Jersey] Numbered Miscellaneous Revolutionary War Manuscripts, NjTSA. Cape May County, the southernmost in New Jersey, and Sussex and Bergen, the northernmost counties, had no organized militia units in the fight (there may have been individual militiamen present). These counties had their own security concerns and in any case were too far away to get men to the line of action. The militia payroll records show no Gloucester County units during the campaign; nor do other primary sources mention Gloucester units. The fighting earlier in the spring clearly took a toll on the Gloucestermen. At least one battalion collapsed as some of its men dispersed while most of the others mutinied, arrested their officers, and went over to the British. These were the men who filled the ranks of the loyalist West Jersey Volunteers. Another Gloucester battalion could muster less than twenty men; patriot morale was evidently at rock bottom throughout the county. See Joseph Ellis to William Livingston, 23 Mar. 1778, GWP, 1741–99, ser. 4, General Correspondence, 1697–1799, DLC, accessed online 2 Apr. 2012, image 164, http://memory.loc.gov/cgi-bin/ampage?collId=mgw4&fileName=gwpage048.db&recNum=163; and Katcher, *British, Provincial, and German Army Units*, 102. There were Gloucester militia in the campaign, but barring any new evidence to the contrary, we must assume that they fought within units from other counties.

38. Dickinson had wanted help from Maxwell at Bordentown, but the New Jersey Brigade was then at Trenton, exhausted from marching in the heat and short of supplies. Ward, *General William Maxwell*, 99.

39. Dann. *Revolution Remembered*, 123. References to these deployments are scattered throughout the sources. See Dickinson to GW, 23 June 1778, "Drawbridge [near Bordentown], *PGWde*, RWS, 15:511–12; Dickinson to GW, 24 June 1778, 6:30 A.M., ibid., 523; and Stone, "Militia Service at the Battle of Monmouth," 1. See also the pension applications of Godfrey Clair, W24829; Abraham Voorhees, S11610; and Tunis Hoagland, S1023, all of Somerset County and in *Index of Revolutionary War Pension Applications in the National Archives*;

the actual applications and supporting documentation are found in RWPBLW, Microfilm M804.

40. Henry Jackson to GW, 24 June 1778, *PGWde*, RWS, 15:527; Lesser, *Sinews of Independence*, 73.
41. See note 37 above.
42. GW to William Winds, 27 June 1778, *PGWde*, RWS, 15:567.
43. William Winds to GW, 27 June 1778, ibid., 568–69; Dickinson to GW, 27 June 1778, 10:00 P.M., ibid., 562, 567–68n1; Stryker, *Official Register*, 350; Tuttle, *Biographical Sketch of General William Winds*, 23. Even Joseph Tuttle's friendly sketch of Winds found the conduct of the militia general seriously wanting. At his death in 1789, feelings were such that there was (unsuccessful) opposition to granting him a military funeral.
44. Dickinson to GW, 23 June 1778, 11:30 P.M., *PGWde*, RWS, 15:513.
45. "Return of the Number of Men, Wagoners, Women & Children victualled at Monmouth the 27 & 28th June 1778 inclusive," Sir Henry Clinton Papers, vol. 36, no. 5, MiU-C.
46. Council of War, 24 June 1778, *PGWde*, RWS, 15:520–21.
47. Lee to GW, ibid., 457–58.
48. Lafayette, *Memoirs*, 50–51; Jared Sparks, "Life of Charles Lee, Major-General in the Army of the Revolution," *Lee Papers*, 4:302; Thayer, *Making of a Scapegoat*, 29.
49. Council of War, 24 June 1778, *PGWde*, RSW, 15:521; Lafayette to GW, ibid., 528–29; Lafayette, *Memoirs*, 52.
50. Alexander Hamilton to Elias Boudinot, 5 July 1778, *PAH*, 1:510.
51. Lengel, *General George Washington*, 293.
52. On Scott's early career, see Ward, *Charles Scott*, chap. 1; GW to Charles Scott, 24 June 1778, *PGWde*, RWS, 15:534.
53. Joseph Plumb Martin makes it clear that he was part of a picked contingent. *Private Yankee Doodle*, 122. Maj. Henry Dearborn, of the Third New Hampshire, also specifically said that the 1,500 men were "pick'd." *Revolutionary War Journals*, 124. William Stryker specifically lists the First New Hampshire, Ninth Pennsylvania, First Virginia, and Fourth Maryland Regiments as being with Scott, although this is unlikely. *Battle of Monmouth*, 78. In June these regiments totaled only some 909 men, so any references Stryker may have found (his book cites none) probably referred to officers from these regiments. Lesser, *Sinews of Independence*, 72–73.
54. J. P. Martin, *Private Yankee Doodle*, 123. Joseph Plumb Martin's rhapsody on Jersey girls predated that of Tom Waits by two centuries. And for those mystified by the reference, Tom Waits released the popular song "Jersey Girl" in 1980 on his *Heartattack and Vine* album; the Bruce Springsteen cover of 1981 made it even more popular. Waits was clearly of the same opinion as Private Martin.
55. In later years Lafayette claimed that after the council meeting he, Greene, and Hamilton called on Washington to argue for the dispatch of a stronger detachment. Lafayette, *Memoirs*, 51. Yet neither Greene

nor Hamilton mention such a meeting in their papers, although if it took place, it was probably after they had sent their letters. Thereafter, a conversation would have been a logical follow-up. Theodore Thayer thinks there was a meeting. *Making of a Scapegoat*, 30. Whatever the exact means or timing of communications with Washington, he clearly understood the thinking of his subordinates.

56. These terms had filled Wayne's advice to Washington the previous April. See Wayne to GW, 21, 23 Apr. 1778, *PGWde*, RWS, 14:582, 610.
57. Anthony Wayne to GW, 24 June 1778, ibid., 15:535.
58. Lafayette to GW, 24 June 1778, ibid., 528–29; Lafayette, *In the Age of the American Revolution*, 10.
59. Nathanael Greene to GW, 24 June 1778, *PNG*, 2:447.
60. GW to Lafayette, 25 June 1778, *PGWde*, RWS, 15:539; Thayer, *Making of a Scapegoat*, 30; Alden, *General Charles Lee*, 209.
61. Dave Richard Palmer, in his interesting strategic study of the Revolution, overstated his case when he concluded that Washington's caution was an indication that Lee had "carried the debate" at the council of war. *Way of the Fox*, 151. In fact, Washington had been cautious from the beginning of the campaign, and his search for a middle ground at Hopewell was consistent with his earlier behavior.
62. Hamilton, "Eulogium on Major-General Greene," 68.
63. Charles Lee to GW, 25 June 1778, *PGWde*, RWS, 15:541.
64. McHenry, *Journal*, 4.
65. GW to Lafayette, 25 June 1778, *PGWde*, RWS, 15:539; GW to Dickinson, 25 June 1778, ibid., 536–37. As issued, the orders still called for Enoch Poor to head the new detachment.
66. Chambers, *George Washington in Cranbury*, 9.
67. Alexander Hamilton to Lafayette, 25 June 1778, *PAH*, 1:503.
68. Lafayette to GW, 25 June 1778, Cranbury, 9:30 P.M., *PGWde*, RWS, 15:539–40.
69. Lafayette to GW, 26 June 1778, 5:00 A.M., ibid., 550; Lafayette to GW, 26 June 1778, 7:15 A.M., ibid., 551.
70. GW to Lafayette, 26 June 1778, 9:45 A.M., ibid., 552–53.
71. Craig, "In Search of Robin's Tavern," 67; Alexander Hamilton to GW, 26 June 1778, 12:00 P.M., Robin's Tavern, *PGWde*, RWS, 15:547.
72. Lafayette to GW, 26 June 1778, 4:30 P.M., *PGWde*, RWS, 15:553.
73. Alexander Hamilton to GW, 26 June 1778, 12:00 [P.M.], *PAH*, 1:505; Hamilton to GW. 26 June 1778, ibid., 506.
74. Chambers, *George Washington in Cranbury*, 11.
75. GW to Lafayette, 26 June 1778, 9:45 A.M., Cranbury, *PGWde*, RWS, 15:552–53; Alexander Hamilton to GW, 26 June 1778, ibid., 547; Hamilton to GW, 26 June 1778, *PAH*, 1:506.
76. GW to Lafayette, 26 June 1778, *PGWde*, RWS, 15:554.
77. Lafayette to GW, 26 June 1778, 10:30 P.M., Robin's Tavern, ibid., 555–56.
78. Dearborn, *Revolutionary War Journals*, 125; "Diary of Bernardus Swartwout, 2d NY Regiment, 10 Nov. 1777–9 June 1783," Bernardus Swartwout Papers, NHi.

79. GW to Lafayette, 26 June 1778, *PGWde*, RWS, 15:552–53; Alexander Hamilton to Elias Boudinot, 5 July 1778, *PAH*, 1:510; "Anonymous Revolutionary War Diary" [probably Jonathan Forman, Fourth New Jersey Regiment], Box 2, Fellows Papers, Department of Rare Books and Special Collections, Rush Rhees Library, University of Rochester, Rochester, N.Y., transcription by Bob McDonald and John U. Rees.
80. Theodore Thayer has a similarly skeptical view of Lafayette's performance. *Making of a Scapegoat*, 31–32. Howard K. Peckham has expressed a contrary view, arguing that it was unfortunate for the Americans that Lafayette was unable to hit Clinton. He said nothing, however, about how Lafayette might have prevailed in the face of Clinton's superior numbers. Peckham, "Marquis de Lafayette: Eager Warrior," in Billias, *George Washington's Generals*, 212–38.
81. H. Lee, *Memoirs of the War*, 1:58.

Chapter 8

1. McHenry, *Journal*, 5; S. Adams, Diary, 27 June 1778, Samuel Adams Papers, 1758–1819, ZL-307, Manuscript Collection 19, Manuscripts and Archives Division, NN; Wild, "Journal," 110.
2. For example, see William Willcocks to Lord Stirling, 26 June 1778, GWP, ser. 4, Microfilm Roll 50; Dickinson to GW, 27 June 1778, *PGWde*, RWS, 15:562–63; and Steuben to GW, ibid., 566.
3. GW to Stirling, 27 June 1778, *PGWde*, RWS, 15:566–67.
4. H. Lee, *Memoirs of the War*, 1:58; Gottschalk, *Lafayette Joins the American Army*, 213–14.
5. Charles Lee to GW, 25 June 1778, *PGWde*, RWS, 15:541–42.
6. Hamilton to Elias Boudinot, 5 July 1778, *PAH*, 1:511.
7. Ibid.; Nelson, *Lord Stirling*.
8. Rossie, *Politics of Command*, 135–53. These disputes extended even to junior officers, with captains arguing over who was senior and in line for the next opening for major. Enoch Poor Orderly Book, 15, 18 Feb. 1778, PHi.
9. Hamilton to Boudinot, 5 July 1778, *PAH*, 1:511.
10. GW to Lee, 26 June 1778, *PGWde*, RWS, 15:556; GW to Lafayette, 26 June 1778, ibid., 555.
11. Lafayette to GW, 26 June 1778, 7:15 P.M., ibid., 552. Many years later Lafayette was not so gracious. In his *Memoirs* he claimed that "everything was going on extremely well" with his command of the forward detachment "when Lee changed his mind, and chose to command the troops himself." As Lafayette told it, he agreed to the change of command only because Lee asked him so nicely. *Memoirs*, 51–52. Not only is this version contrary to Lafayette's letters to Washington on 25 June but also to all other accounts of the transaction.
12. Joseph Cilley to Thomas Bartlett, 22 July 1778, in Ryan, *Salute to Courage*, 132–34. Varnum's four regiments amounted to only two battalions.
13. Stone and Lender, "Lee's Advance Force." Durkee had the First and Second Rhode Island Regiments and the Fourth and Eighth Connecticut;

Grayson had the Fourth, Eighth, and Twelfth Virginia and his own and Patton's Additional regiments.

14. Minutes 1778 [Orderly Book of Larned's Brigade], 21 June 1778, Larned Family Papers, Vol. 4, Collection 1695, PHi.
15. General Orders, 27 June 1778, Penelopen, *PGWde*, RWS, 15:559.
16. Testimony of Scott and Wayne, 4 July 1778, *PLCM*, 5–8.
17. Ibid., 117–19 (Mercer).
18. Lee to GW, 27 June 1778, 7:00 P.M., *Lee Papers*, 2:426; *PLCM*, 7 (Wayne), 202 (Lee).
19. Lee to GW, 27 June 1778, 7:00 P.M., *Lee Papers*, 2:426; *PLCM*, 9 (Fitzgerald).
20. *PLCM*, 11–14 (Hamilton).
21. Ibid., 161 (Edwards), 9 (Mercer, Edwards), 34 (Grayson), 102 (Mercer).
22. Ibid., 11–14 (Hamilton).
23. Ibid., 19–21 (Meade).
24. Hastedt, *Espionage*, 2; Heitman, *Historical Register of Officers*, 157; Clark, "Letters," 1–36.
25. John Clark to Lee, with enclosure, 2 Sept. 1778, *Lee Papers*, 3:230–31.
26. GW to Henry Laurens, 28 June 1778, 11:30 A.M., *PGWde*, RWS, 15:578.
27. GW to Horatio Gates, 28 June 1778, 6:00 A.M., ibid., 578.
28. There are two other known accounts purporting to deal with this question; both are problematic, and one is probably spurious. The first is a journal entry by a Pennsylvania militia captain, Samuel Massey. He apparently was at Monmouth (perhaps with Cadwalader or attached to a Pennsylvania Continental regiment—we do not know). His undated journal entry recorded that Lee had orders to "attack unless (there were) very powerful Reasons to the Contrary," which would support the argument for discretionary orders. But how would a militiaman know this? And why would he use language so similar to some of the court-martial testimony? Other elements of his account also appear drawn from the published statements of witnesses to the battle. Valley Forge National Historical Park historian Lee Boyle has suggested that Massey's account is a postbattle composition, written when the results of the court-martial and details of the battle had become public. This is almost certainly the case. See Samuel Massey, Journal, n.d., PaVfNHP. Another account, this one by a Maj. Thomas Massie of Virginia—no known relation to the militia Massey—claims a direct connection to Washington. In his pension application (no date, but long after the war), Massie related that "on the 28th day June, 1778 (an intense hot day), Gen. Washington ordered Gen. Lee to attack in full force. This, the said Massie, knows to be the fact, the orders having been communicated verbally by Gen. Washington through him (the said Massie), the evening before." It was only Lee's "flagrant disobedience of orders," he claimed, that prevented a major victory over Clinton. However, no other officer recalled such an incident, and there is no evidence that Massey was with the general when he claims to have spoken with him. Why would he have been? In the same narrative, Massie states that he was attached to Colonel Morgan's command during the Monmouth campaign. And even if he

was with Washington, there is no known reason why the commander in chief would have entrusted such vital orders to Massie, an officer with no known connection to the general. Indeed, the only time Massie claimed to have conversed with the general during the entire course of the war was when Washington supposedly issued the verbal orders for Lee. Had Washington sent Massie as a courier on the night of the twenty-seventh, certainly someone at headquarters would have known of it and it would have come out in court-martial testimony. Nothing of the sort occurred. During all of the controversy in the aftermath of Lee's court-martial, no one mentioned Massie, and evidence such as his would have been ammunition for the attacks on Lee. Massie's claim to knowledge of an unequivocal attack order to Lee is the only supposedly contemporary claim to come to light, and it has no basis in fact. Any motives Massie may have had for his invention—perhaps he wanted to bolster his pension application—let alone his decades-long delay in telling his story, are unknown. Massie, "Pension Declaration," 188.

29. *PLCM*, 14 (Lafayette), 40–41 (Grayson).
30. Ibid., 137 (Mercer).

Chapter 9

1. Wellington quoted in Croker, *Papers*, 276.
2. Stone, "Agrarian Landscape of Monmouth Battlefield," 1. This chapter has drawn heavily from this paper. For the tavern and tanyard, see "Newspaper Extracts, New Jersey Colonial Documents," in *NJA*, 31:38.
3. For the lawyer's property, see "Newspaper Extracts, New Jersey in the Revolution," in *NJA* 2, 2:76–77.
4. Garlick, *St. Peter's Church*, 68.
5. Morgan, *Old Tennent Church*, 1; Symmes, *History of the Old Tennent Church*. The Rev. William Tennent was the younger brother of Gilbert Tennent, one the greatest of colonial evangelicals. *NJHC*, 346–47.
6. Quoted in Ellis, *Monmouth County*, 463, 384–85.
7. *NJHC*, 330.
8. Stone, "Agrarian Landscape of Monmouth Battlefield," 1; "History of the Burlington Path," accessed 15 May 2013.
9. When the road was realigned in 1735, part of the road on the Rhea farm followed an "old Indian path." Monmouth County Deeds, H:163, Office of the County Clerk, Freehold, N.J. For deeds referring to the Indian Path from Weamaconk Point to New Manalapan, see East Jersey Deeds, D:189, 345, E:7, 308, F:573, NjTSA; and Monmouth County Deeds, D:199, M:118.
10. McHenry, *Journal*, 5; General Orders, 27 June 1778, Penelopen, *PGWde*, RWS, 15:559.
11. Ellis, *Monmouth County*, 101–102.
12. Freehold Township Ratables, July 1784 (tax list 1130), [New Jersey] Township Ratables, NjTSA; Stone, "Agrarian Landscape of Monmouth Battlefield," 2.
13. "Journal Kept by Distinguished Hessian Field Jaeger Corps during the Campaigns of the Royal Army of Great Britain in North America,"

trans. by Bruce E. Burgoyne, 1986, Lidgerwood Collection of Hessian Transcripts of the American Revolution, Letter L, Microfiche 245, NjMoHP; Peebles, *American War*, 192.

14. "John Bowne sells to Garrett Stoothoff, Garrett Wyckoff, John Wyckoff, Derrick van Sutvant, Peter Couwenhoven, and Jacob Tysen, 'Gawen Lawries 1000 acres,'" 20 June 1699, East Jersey Deeds, G:117–18, NjTSA.
15. Several maps of the area are available online from the Library of Congress. For a 1685 map of the Burlington roads, see John Reid, *A map of the Raritan River, Millstone River, South River . . . Along with the Plantations thereon*, engraved by R. Simson, Digital Collections, DLC, http://www.loc.gov/item/97683564/. See "American Revolution and Its Era: Maps and Charts of North America and the West Indies, 1750–1789," which contains three manuscript versions of a map by British Army cartographer John Hills, *Sketch of part of the road from Freehold to Middle Town shewing the skirmish . . . June 28th. 1778*. Hills's maps roughly locate buildings and orchards. He and other foreign cartographers frequently confused the Baptist meetinghouse with "Monmouth Court House."
16. Freehold Township Ratables, July 1779 (tax list 1124), [New Jersey] Township Ratables, NjTSA; "Rea, Robert Capt.," Freehold Township Ratables for the Poor Tax, 1776, NjHi.
17. Wacker and Clemens, *Land Use in Early New Jersey*, 135, 145, 175–88, 190; Stone, "Agrarian Landscape of Monmouth Battlefield," 6, 8–9.
18. Stone, "Agrarian Landscape of Monmouth Battlefield," 3.
19. Feilitzsch and Bartholomai, *Diaries of Two Ansbach Jaegers*, 41.
20. General Orders, 26 June 1778, 2BtnBrGrenOrBk; Seventh Regiment of Foot, Orderly Book, 1778, 27 June 1778, pp. 83–84, PHi.
21. Krafft, *Journal*, 46.
22. Stephen Moylan to GW, 27 June 1778, 11:00 A.M., *PGWde*, RWS, 15:565; Moylan to GW, 27 June 1778, 12:30 P.M., ibid.; Friedrich Steuben to GW, 27 June 1778, ibid., 566.
23. Ewald, *Diary*, 135; Peebles, *American War*, 193; Baurmeister, *Revolution in America*, 185–86.
24. Moses Estey Pension Application, 2 Oct. 1835, 10304, [New Jersey] Numbered Miscellaneous Revolutionary War Manuscripts, Department of Defense, Adjutant General, NjTSA; Silvanus Seeley, diary, 27 June 1778, Seeley Diaries, 12 May 1768–17 Mar. 1821, NjMoHP.
25. Peebles, *American War*, 193; Rhoda Sutfin Pension Application, 4 Aug. 1836, RWPBLW, Microcopy 804, Widow 6607; Daniel Morgan to GW, 27 June 1778, *PGWde*, RWS, 15:564.
26. Callahan, *Daniel Morgan*, 163.
27. Rhoda Sutfin Pension Application, 4 Aug. 1836, RWPBLW, Microcopy 804, Widow 6607.
28. The turmoil in Revolutionary Monmouth County, with a focus on the Pine Robbers, is explained in David Fowler's meticulous "Egregious Villains, Wood Rangers, and London Traders." As Fowler explains, patriots never did fully suppress the Pine Robbers, who remained a

threat through the end of the war. The role of blacks, free and slave, is detailed in Hodges, *Slavery and Freedom.* See also Ward, *Between the Lines.*

29. Simcoe, *Military Journal*, 66–67.
30. John Leonard Pension Application, 25 Jan. 1786, Halifax, Ref. A.O. 12–15, PRO.
31. Adelberg, *American Revolution in Monmouth County*, 11, 38.
32. Livingston quoted in ibid., 11.
33. Ibid., 33, 102–104.
34. Munn, *Battles and Skirmishes*, 19, 51, 95, 110; *NJA*, 2:327; Peckham, *Toll of Independence*, 51; Adelberg, *Revolution in Monmouth County*, 19–20.
35. Benjamin Van Cleave, "Autobiography of Benjamin Van Cleave," Microfilm MMS50, NHi; "Mrs. Elizabeth Covenhoven, Reluctant Hostess to Sir Henry Clinton; or, Where was Mr. Covenhoven," *Battle Cry* 14, no. 2 (Mar.–Apr. 2004): 4.
36. Krafft, *Journal*, 45–46.
37. Adelberg, *Revolution in Monmouth County*, 26.
38. Letter of Thomas Henderson, *New Jersey Gazette*, 5 Aug. 1778. Henderson got Covenhoven's name wrong, giving it as "Conover." "Mrs. Elizabeth Covenhoven," 4.
39. Adelberg, *Revolution in Monmouth County*, 20.
40. Van Cleave, "Autobiography," NHi.
41. The political affiliations of the property owners in question are identified in Adelberg, *People of Revolutionary Monmouth County.*
42. Steuben to GW, 27 June 1778, *PGWde*, RWS, 15:566.
43. Letter of Thomas Henderson, *New Jersey Gazette*, 5 Aug. 1778.
44. Baurmeister, *Revolution in America*, 185; Krafft, *Journal*, 46.
45. General Orders, 27 June 1778, 2BtnBrGrenOrBk.
46. Seventh Regiment of Foot Orderly Book, 27 June 1778, PHi. "General Court Martial held at Freehold . . . 27th June 1778," PRO WO 71/86, pp. 151–58, transcription courtesy of Don N. Hagist.
47. Seventh Regiment of Foot, Orderly Book, 27 June 1778, p. 84, PHi.

Chapter 10

1. Stryker, *Battle of Monmouth*, 115.
2. Clausewitz, *On War.*
3. Morgan letter of 29 June entered into evidence, 21 July 1778, *PLCM*, 138.
4. S. Smith, *Battle of Monmouth*, 8–9. William Stryker found Morgan's failure to engage an inexcusable blunder, although this harsh judgment takes no account of the confused situation facing Morgan. See *Battle of Monmouth*, 155–56.
5. *PLCM*, 117–18 (Mercer).
6. GW to Daniel Morgan, 28 June 1778, *PGEde*, RWS, 15:580. Fitzpatrick fixed the time of this message at 12:30 in the morning on the twenty-eighth. Don Higginbotham, however, has it as 12:30 in the afternoon.

Daniel Morgan, 91. But Fitzpatrick is almost certainly correct, which means that Morgan sent two riders north on the twenty-eighth. The first man probably left late on the twenty-seventh and reached Washington with Morgan's message shortly before 12:30 A.M. on the twenty-eighth. This was the message to which the commander in chief responded. There was a second rider, who (as noted below) reached the battlefield sometime after 10:00 A.M., when he spoke with Anthony Wayne. Higginbotham's account would have this messenger riding around the battlefield for some two and a half hours after the encounter with Wayne before finding Washington, who then took the time to send a letter to Morgan. This was unlikely. At about 12:30 P.M. on the twenty-eighth, Washington was approaching the battlefield himself, if he had not already arrived and found himself in the middle of his confrontation with Lee; Col. John Laurens, who penned the note to Morgan, also was in action. The last letter Washington wrote on the twenty-eighth was a brief missive to Henry Laurens, president of Congress, at 11:30 A.M.; the next was another note to Laurens on the twenty-ninth. There is no record of any written order or letter composed over his name in the interim.

7. *PLCM*, 11–14 (Hamilton).
8. Ibid., 28 (Wayne).
9. Higginbotham, *Daniel Morgan*, 91.
10. *PLCM*, 10–11 (Meade).
11. Ibid., 32 (Scott), 103 (Maxwell); GW to Henry Laurens, 28 June 1778, *PGWde*, RWS, 15:578–79.
12. *PLCM*, 27 (Scott), 90 (Maxwell), 102–103 (Mercer), 120 (Jackson).
13. Ibid., 162 (Edwards).
14. Ibid., 103 (Mercer).
15. Ibid., 7 (Meade), 90 (Maxwell), 103–104 (Mercer).
16. Ibid., 7 (Meade). The hypothesis that Lee met Walker before talking to the militia officers at the meetinghouse is based upon Meade's description of the general's reaction to Walker's news. If Lee had received similar information from the militia, it is unlikely that he would have initially disbelieved Walker's report.
17. The militia officers were wrong. All of the 1st Division remained at the courthouse.
18. *PLCM*, 18 (Wayne), 104 (Mercer), 144 (Brooks).
19. Ibid., 40–42 (Grayson). Most historians refer to the church as Tennent's Meeting House or Church, as does this book. Other accounts use the more usual contemporary name of the New Meeting House, or simply Presbyterian meetinghouse. As chapter 8 explains, the brook names are a matter of some confusion. Until the nineteenth century, all deed references are to Spotswood North Brook, Spotswood Middle Brook, and Spotswood South Brook. The deeds also show the East Morass as the head of Spotswood Middle Brook. Weamaconk Brook, as then known, was the stream between Wemrock Point (the junction of Spotswood South and Middle Brooks) and Topanemus Brook. There the merged

brooks became the Matchaponix River. For the eighteenth-century deeds locating Weamaconk Brook, see Monmouth County Deeds, F:75–76, 90–92, Office of the County Clerk, Freehold, N.J.

20. *PLCM*, 34–35 (Grayson), 131 (Oswald), 162 (Edwards).

21. Steuben to GW, 27 June 1778, 12:30 P.M., *PGWde*, RWS, 15:566; John Laurens to GW, 28 June 1778, ibid., 579; John Laurens to Henry Laurens, 30 June, 1 July 1778, *PHL*, 13:532–33, 545–46. The account of Simcoe's skirmish with the militia is based on information in *PLCM*, 41 (Grayson); Simcoe, *Military Journal*, 68–71; André, *Journal*, 78–79; and Bell, MS Diary, 28 June 1778. That Simcoe engaged Steuben's party and the militia on the twenty-eighth is further confirmed by a 28 June 1778 entry in an anonymous British journal: "Some General Officers of the Enemy were seen Reconnoitering on the left Flank—some scouting parties of the Militia were dispersed by the Queens Rangers." "Unidentified British Journal," 19 June–1 July 1778, Clinton Papers, MiU-C, copy at PaVfNHP. Another British journal, also anonymous, has Simcoe engaged "with a large body of the enemy" on the twenty-eighth. "28th June 1778, Memorandum—Battle of Monmouth," Unidentified British Army Notebook, Sol Feinstone Collection 409, PWacD.

22. Steuben to GW, 27 June 1778, 12:30 P.M., *PGWde*, RWS, 15:566. That Steuben was out on two mornings was confirmed in this letter to Washington and his testimony at Lee's court-martial. See *PLCM*, 109 (Steuben).

23. Simcoe, *Military Journal*, 68. Cathcart was appointed Clinton's aide-de-camp on 25 May. Baule and Gilbert, *British Army Officers*, 34. For another of Clinton's morning orders written by Cathcart, see Clinton, *American Rebellion*, 93n12.

24. Simcoe places the encounter with the "vedettes" just east of the Rheas' barrack meadow "rivulet." But he marched across two rivulets—Rhea Run to the east and the rivulet in the barrack meadow to the west. Schenck's account suggests that the rangers encountered the vedettes just east of Rhea Run. Steuben appears to have started back unaware of the rangers. If his party had known of the threat, the men would have accompanied him; neither Walker nor Laurens was adverse to danger. For more about Walker, see Lefkowitz, *Washington's Indispensable Men*, 155, 256–57. For Laurens, see ibid., esp. 301–302.

25. "Abstracts of Payrolls," Book B, Auditors Accounts, [New Jersey] Miscellaneous Revolutionary War Manuscripts, 161–64, 183–84, NjTSA; pension applications of Abesh Ashmore, W5647; James Britton, S12293; Robert Carhart, W3941; William Vliet, R10958; Jacob Francis, W459; Moses Estey, S3339; and Lewis Ayres, I799, all in RWPBLW; Silvanus Seeley Diaries, 12 May 1768–17 Mar. 1821, NjMoHp; Dickinson memorandum, *Lee Papers*, 2:413. We are grateful for information from pension records provided by John U. Rees, William Schleicher, and Sue Winters.

26. The stories of Pvt. Ralph Schenck and Lt. Moses Estey are from S. M. Schenck, [Schenck] Family Notes, Bk. 3, 1890s, 66–70, NjFrH; and pension applications of Schenck, W17788, and Estey, S3339, RWPBLW.

27. Edward Taylor Pension Application, S7679, RWPBLW.
28. All references to Schenck and Estey are from S. M. Schenck, [Schenck] Family Notes, Bk. 3, 1890s, 66–70, NjFrHi.
29. With Snook wounded, company command fell to Lt. Jacob Johnson. Garry Wheeler Stone, comp., "Abstracts of Militia Pension Applications," Jacob Johnson, W796, MBSP.
30. There is a postscript to Ellison's story. In 1781 the hussar was with the Queen's Rangers when they took part in the invasion of Virginia led by then–British brigadier general Benedict Arnold. Ellison was wounded and captured in a skirmish but soon exchanged. Simcoe recorded that Ellison "had been ill-treated" during his brief captivity, "but nothing hurt him equally with the being robbed of the silver half moon which he wore on his huzzar cap, with the word 'Monmouth' engraven on it, as a mark of his bravery in that action." Simcoe, *Operations of the Queen's Rangers*, 184–85.
31. The preceding account of Simcoe's skirmish with the militia is based on information in Simcoe, *Military Journal*, 68–71; *PLCM*, 41 (Grayson); and André, *Journal*, 78–79.
32. The Queen's American Rangers initially was a strictly loyalist regiment, but over time it enrolled European troops as well—the only tory unit to do so. In 1778 it was still predominantly loyalist in composition. See James Hannay, "History of the Queen's Rangers," *Royal Society of Canada Transactions*, 3rd ser., 2, no. 2 (1908–1909): 124, 132–33, 155–56.
33. Simcoe, *Military Journal*, 70–71. Virtually all other published histories of the Battle of Monmouth have confused this opening conflict with actions occurring later on that morning. While aware of the skirmish, other authors have placed the wounding of Simcoe in an exchange of light fire between the rangers and a detachment commanded by Col. Richard Butler that took place near Freehold about an hour and a half later, or they further confuse it with yet another incident involving a horse charge against Butler's men. In fact, Simcoe was not present during the shooting around the courthouse, and the rangers did not make the later charge. The confusion may have come from Andrew Bell's mistaken contemporary account of where and when the Queen's Rangers were engaged on the morning of 28 June. See Bell, MS Diary, 28 June 1778.
34. John Graves Simcoe, "Return of Killed, Wounded & Taken Prisoners to October 15th 1780," John Graves Simcoe Papers, 1774–1824, MiU-C, transcription and copy courtesy Todd W. Braisted.
35. Simcoe, *Operations of the Queen's Rangers*, 68–69. For another account has the 17th Dragoons chasing Steuben's party, see Hayes, *Saddlebag Almanac*, 16–17. The weight of available evidence, however, favors the Simcoe version of events. William Stryker has it, without attribution, that the pursuit would have killed Steuben but for orders to the contrary from Knyphausen—a pretty story, but no more. *Battle of Monmouth*, 104.

Chapter 11

1. In this role the Queen's Rangers were replacing the 2nd Light Infantry. Later, as soon as the rangers moved toward the courthouse, Morris County militia colonel Sylvanus Seeley advanced and began skirmishing with the British horse. Seeley Diaries, 28 June 1778, Seeley Diaries, 12 May 1768–17 Mar. 1821, NjMoHP.
2. Clinton, *American Rebellion*, 92–93, 96–97; Ewald, *Diary*, 135–36; Bell, MS Diary, 28 June 1778; André, *Journal*, 78–79.
3. *PLCM*, 18 (Steuben), 41 (Grayson), 59–60 (Lawrence), 109, 111 (Langfrang), 205 (Lee).
4. Ibid., 205 (Lee, quoting Dickinson).
5. Clinton, *American Rebellion*, 91.
6. *PLCM*, 120 (Mercer).
7. Ibid., 22 (Wayne), 120 (Mercer), 161 (Cumpiton), 165 (Brooks), 205 (Lee).
8. This point is explained admirably in Roy K. Flint, "Lifting the Fog of Battle: Charles Lee at the Battle of Monmouth," in Murrin and Waldron, *Conflict at Monmouth Court House*, 53–55.
9. Ibid., 55. A successful movement to contact is no simple matter. Among historians, Lee's critics have overlooked this fact. Dominick Mazzagetti, for example, never mentions the issue in his biography of the major general. If, as Mazzagetti and others have suggested, Lee's heart was not in the fight, why would he have advanced with so much care and with his most aggressive brigadier forward?
10. *PLCM*, 206 (Lee).
11. The formation of Lee's plans to envelop the enemy emerge clearly from the court-martial testimony of Edwards, Forman, Mercer, and Lee himself in ibid., 30 (Edwards), 121 (Forman), 122 (Mercer), 187–88 (Lee). The timing is important, as other historians have placed Lee's decision to march around the enemy *after* the engagements by Wayne and Butler. In fact, Lee ordered Wayne's advance (which led to Butler's clash with the British dragoons) as part of his plan to encircle the enemy, and he had his own column in motion to the left even as Wayne advanced to contact.
12. *PLCM*, 23 (Wayne), 51 (Butler), 120–21 (Mercer), 187–88 (Edwards).
13. Selesky, *Encyclopedia of the American Revolution*, 2:862; Thayer, *Making of a Scapegoat*, 43.
14. *PLMC*, 23–25 (Wayne).
15. Stryker, *Official Register*, 16, 31, 66. Francis Heitman mistakenly has Rhea transferred to the Fourth New Jersey in January 1777; there is no evidence of this. See *Historical Register of Officers*, 464.
16. David Rhea to Israel Shreve, 17 Apr. 1778, Israel Shreve Revolutionary War Letters, 1768–1894, Special Collections, University of Houston Libraries, accessed 4 Oct. 2015, http://digital.lib.uh.edu/collection/p15195coll12/browse.
17. *PLCM*, 58 (Rhea).
18. Ibid., 188 (Edwards).

19. André, *Journal*, 79; *PLCM*, 52 (Jackson), 139–40 (Butler).
20. Abraham Voorhees Pension Application, 30 Jan. 1833, S11610, RWPBLW; *PLCM*, 152 (Oswald).
21. "28th June 1778, Memorandum—Battle of Monmouth," Unidentified British Army Notebook, 32–34, Sol Feinstone Collection 409, PWacD.
22. *NJHC*, 343.
23. *PLCM*, 188–89 (Edwards); "Memorandum—Battle of Monmouth, 28th June 1778," 32, Feinstone Collection 409, PWacD.
24. C. Malcolm B. Gilman thinks this was Maj. Charles William Gilman, M.D., of Woodbridge, N.J., having had access to family papers suggesting this. See a quote on the inside cover of Gilman, *Monmouth Road to Glory.* William Stryker's *Official Register* lists *no* Gilman among New Jersey officers. Francis Heitman identifies Gilman as a lieutenant colonel in the New Hampshire Line. *Historical Register of Officers*, 249.
25. *PLCM*, 17 (Lafayette), 89–90 (McHenry), 148–50 (Gilman).
26. Ibid., 43 (Grayson), 51–52 (Butler), 122–23 (Brooks), 175–76 (Mercer), 188 (Edwards).
27. Ibid., 145–46 (Olney).
28. Ibid., 152–53 (Oswald), 189 (Edwards), 208 (Lee).
29. Ibid., 152–53 (Oswald), 208 (Lee).
30. Ibid., 15 (Lafayette), 208 (Lee).
31. Ibid., 124–25 (Mercer), 189 (Edwards).
32. Ibid., 153–54 (Oswald).
33. Ibid., 146 (Olney); Deposition of Andrew Griswold, John Durkee Pension Application (Anna Young, heir), BLWt 580-500, Reel 857, RWPBLW.
34. *PLCM*, 189 (Edwards).
35. Ibid., 64 (Butler), 140–41 (Jackson, Laurens), 144–45 (Olney).
36. Peebles, *American War*, 193; Baurmeister, *Revolution in America*, 186.
37. Clinton, *American Rebellion*, 92–94.
38. *PLCM*, 43–45 (Grayson), 125–26 (Mercer).
39. Unless noted otherwise, this account of the attempted stand at Freehold and the subsequent retreat to Ker's house, the so-called Duportail Line, is drawn from the testimony of twelve witnesses (Capt. Edwards, Maj. Gen. Lee, Lt. Col. Brooks, Capt. Cumpston, Col. Duportail, Lt. Col. Oswald, Capt. Steth, Lt. Col. Laurens, Brig. Gen. Wayne, Maj. Gen. Lafayette, Col. Grayson, and Capt. Stewart) in *PLCM*, 15, 20, 19–21, 44–45, 47–49, 61–64, 100–102, 153–58, 160, 162, 166–68, 177, 192–94, 209–14.
40. As he got closer to the advancing redcoats, Lafayette may have personally reconnoitered toward the British artillery positions. Tradition has it that one of his escorts was mortally wounded in this foray, and as the marquis stopped to aid the man, Clinton, recognizing him, chivalrously stopped British gunners from shooting him down. It is a pleasant story but unattributed and unlikely. See *NJHC*, 343. There was yet another tale of chivalry connected with this stage of the action. Grenadier lieutenant William Hale recorded it as follows: "Before the action began the Marquis La Fayette, who commanded the first part of the Rebels we

engaged, rode out and very politely saluted Major Gardner with whom he was formerly well acquainted in France." Lafayette himself never mentioned the incident, and Hale's account is probably apocryphal. See William Hale to his father, 4 July 1778, in Wilkin, *Some British Soldiers*, 261.

41. As Captain Mercer recrossed the ravine to report to Lee, he met Captain Edwards and related Scott's disappearance. As they rode back, they saw "a body of troops and artillery" marching down the lane toward the Amboy Road. They surmised that this was Scott's detachment when in actuality it was Maxwell's brigade. *PLCM*, 126–27 (Mercer), 190 (Edwards).
42. *PLCM*, 195 (Steth), 127 (Mercer), 209–210 (Lee).
43. Ibid., 15–16 (Lafayette), 209–210 (Lee).
44. Olney quoted in Williams, *Biography of Revolutionary Heroes*, 247; Heitman, *Historical Register of Officers*, 420.
45. William Ker was the tenant at the Rhea homestead. See Lord Stirling to William Henry Drayton, 15 Aug. 1778, Alexander, "Letters," 174. Stirling spelled it "Kerrs' house." The Kers were longtime residents of the area and founders of the Presbyterian congregation. In most accounts of the battle, historians have spelled (or rather misspelled) "Ker" as "Carr." Contemporary British accounts used "Carr" as well, perhaps indicating how the name was pronounced.
46. *PLCM*, 61 (Meade), 73 (Laurens).
47. "Diary of Bernardus Swartwout, 2d NY Regiment, 10 Nov. 1777–9 June 1783," 28 June 1778, Bernardus Swartwout Papers, NHi.
48. *PLCM*, 168 (Brooks), 211 (Lee).
49. For a summary of the complaints of disorder in Lee's command, see Stryker, *Battle of Monmouth*, 164–65.
50. The regiment breaking ranks at the morass is in the testimony of Captain Edwards on 27 July; the charge of the dragoons is noted in *PLCM*, 47–48 (Stewart), 177 (Brooks), 194 (Edwards). A few historians have reported a volley from the Americans on this occasion, but there is no evidence for this.
51. Bloomfield, *Citizen Soldier*, 135; Greenman, *Diary*, 119.
52. *PLCM*, 62 (Lawrence).
53. Ibid., 29 (Wayne), 49 (Stewart), 73 (Meade), 124, 133 (Mercer).
54. Henry Clinton to the Duke of Newcastle, 11 July 1778, Newcastle Collection, NeC 2645, Nottingham University Library, copy at PaVfNHP.
55. Clinton, *American Rebellion*, 94, 95, 95n16; Spring, *With Zeal and Bayonets Only*, 97.
56. Clinton gave a full account of his deployment in the counterattack, as well as his understanding of the terrain and the rebel force he was facing, in his narrative of the battle. See Clinton, *American Rebellion*, 93–96 (including footnotes on these pages).
57. Journal of Capt. John Peebles, Book 6, 28 June 1778, Cunninghame of Thortoun Papers, GD 21, Scottish Records Office, Edinburgh; Lord

Stirling to William Henry Drayton, 15 Aug. 1778, Alexander, "Letters," 174.

58. Peebles, *American War*, 194; Sivilich, GIS mapping of battlefield archaeology, BRAVO, MBSP, digital files.
59. Simcoe, *Military Journal*, 72.
60. Peebles, *American War*, 193; "28th June 1778, Memorandum—Battle of Monmouth," Unidentified British Army Notebook, 32–33, Sol Feinstone Collection 409, PWacD.
61. Lafayette commanded this reserve. He had crossed to the west side of Perrine's Hill after the final retreat over the West Morass (see chap. 13).
62. See Appendix C for troop strength among the rangers and light infantry. On unit movements and the condition of the troops, see Journal of Capt. John Peebles, Book 6, 28 June 1778, Cunninghame of Thortoun Papers, GD 21; André, *Journal*, 80; and Henry Clinton to George Germain, 5 July 1778, in Davies, *Documents of the American Revolution*, 15:161–62.
63. Lord Stirling to William Henry Drayton, 15 Aug. 1778, Alexander, "Letters," 174; J. P. Martin, *Private Yankee Doodle*, 130.
64. Daniel M. Sivilich, "Ammunition in Colonial America: Musket Balls and Their Uses," 2012, unpublished manuscript, 81–82, 92–93, MBSP.
65. Rawdon became Rawdon Hastings after succeeding to the title of Marques of Hastings (he was also 2nd Earl of Moira). Matthew and Harrison, *Oxford Dictionary of National Biography*, 743–48.
66. Lt. F. Champagne to Lord Rawdon, 29 June 1778, PaVfNHP, original in the Clinton Papers, MiU-C.
67. Kemble, *Journals*, 152.
68. Clinton, *American Rebellion*, 93, 93n12.
69. Lt. William Hale to his father, 4 July 1778, in Wilkin, *Some British Soldiers*, 257.
70. *PLCM*, 213 (Lee), 197–99 (deposition of Peter Wikoff).
71. Ibid., 213–14 (Lee). Captain Edwards did eventually find another horse, and Lee did send him after Wikoff, but by then Washington had come up, rendering Edwards's mission pointless. Ibid., 214.
72. Ibid. 215; enclosure, John Clark to Charles Lee, 3 Sept. 1778, AMs 785/15, PPFR. This enclosure was published in *Lee Papers*, 3:231–32.
73. Berg, *Encyclopedia of Continental Army Units*, 50, 56, 61–62. The regiments of Lee and Henley were merged with Jackson's in 1779, and in 1780 Jackson's was incorporated into the Massachusetts Line as the Sixteenth Massachusetts. On Smith and Tyler, see Heitman, *Historical Register of Officers*, 508, 553.
74. *Jackson Court of Enquiry*, in *Lee Papers*, 3:214 (Trescott), 222–23 (Turner), 226–27 (Jackson).
75. Ibid., 223 (Turner); enclosure, Clark to Lee, 3 Sept. 1778, AMs 785/15, PPFR.
76. *Jackson Court of Enquiry*, in *Lee Papers*, 3:209–10 (Trescott); *PLCM*, 224–27 (Jackson), 83–86 (Smith).
77. There were repercussions from Jackson's withdrawal. On 26 July 1778 sixteen of his officers signed a statement to "openly protest against

Col. Henry Jackson's conduct [at the Battle of Monmouth], and in the strongest terms recommend he should be called to answer for his misdemeanors before a Court appointed by authority." *Jackson Court of Enquiry*, in *Lee Papers*, 3:209–10. In July 1779 a court of enquiry found no case against Jackson sufficient to warrant a court-martial. Ibid., 228.

78. *PLCM*, 142 (Jackson), 97–98 (Smith).
79. Enclosure, Clark to Lee, 3 Sept. 1778, AMs 785/15, PPFR.

Chapter 12

1. Finney, "Old Tennent Church," 265; Beatty, "Journal," 113.
2. Gordon, *Rise, Progress, and Establishment of the Independence of the United States*, 3:150.
3. GW to John Laurens, 28 June 1778, *PGWde*, RWS, 15:578.
4. Washington is placed at Englishtown at this time by Lt. Col. Jeremiah Gilman. *PLCM*, 148–49 (Gilman); GW to Henry Laurens, 28 June 1778, *PGWde*, RWS, 15:578–79. Local tradition, derived from a militia officer also present in the English mansion, has it that about this time Washington expressed his regrets on engaging on the Sabbath but conceded that "he must yield for the good of the country." One doubts this story, but it is a good one. Stryker, *Battle of Monmouth*, 175.
5. There is a persistent legend that New Jersey governor William Livingston had recently sent Washington a gift of a magnificent white stallion, so the commander in chief supposedly rode in style. See Stryker, *Battle of Monmouth*, 81. Unfortunately, there is no contemporary confirmation of the story; significantly, neither the papers of Livingston nor those of Washington mention the alleged gift. Thus in all likelihood the story is just that—a story.
6. Ibid., 120. Stryker cites an army field return of 28 June. The heat-blistered men had left their packs in Englishtown.
7. *PLCM*, 91 (Tilghman); Stryker, *Battle of Monmouth*, 175. William Stryker's assertion is unattributed, but it has the ring of accuracy since the rest of his account accords with contemporary sources.
8. *PLCM*, 106–108 (Maxwell), 197–99 (Wikoff deposition), 214, 218 (Lee). There is no indication that Lee's request to Major Clark that he hasten artillery officers over the bridge to the high ground had any greater effect. Enclosure, John Clark to Charles Lee, 3 Sept. 1778, AMs 785/15, PPFR. See also chap. 10, notes 32 and 33, above.
9. Officers quoted in Stryker, *Battle of Monmouth*, 177.
10. *PLCM*, 218–19 (Lee).
11. Ibid., 169 (Brooks), 215 (Lee).
12. Morton is quoted in Fiske, *Essays Literary and Historical*, 90–91. We need to be careful of this account, however. Morton, who supposedly became a Continental major, is not listed in Francis Heitman's compilation of Revolutionary officers; of the Mortons who are listed, none fits the description of the old soldier cited in Fiske. *Historical Register of Officers*, 404. But the Daughters of the American Revolution accepts Morton as a major—DAR research standards are high—and in 1900 the

organization reprinted the Morton quote as presented in Fiske. But in a footnote, a "Mrs. Lockwood" wrote of the account, "Like the rest of the world I accepted the legend." The authors believe the proper emphasis here should be on "*the legend*" (our italics). See [Morton], "Washington at Monmouth," 1189–92.

13. Quoted in Thayer, *Making of a Scapegoat*, 52–53.
14. Lewis, "Was Washington Profane at Monmouth?" 149–62. In 1919 William Jackson Johnstone published a little-known but able and well-documented (not to mention entertaining) refutation of allegations that Washington had sworn at Lee. A devoutly religious Minnesota author, Johnstone was arguing that Washington was a believing Christian, which in his view required a counter to efforts "made by some, holding infidel views, to bring down Washington to the common level of other men, by conveying the impression that he was in the habit of swearing." *George Washington the Christian*, 115.
15. Over many years, of course, there was plenty of embellishment—so much that there is little point in dealing with all of the secondary accounts. The worst and most inaccurate of them not only had Washington swearing at Lee but also sending him immediately to the rear in disgrace. But perhaps the most vivid image in this regard is not literary at all. This is *Washington Rallying the Troops at Monmouth* (c. 1852), a large—23′ by 13′—oil painting by the celebrated German American artist Emanuel Leutze, now in the collection of the University of California, Berkeley. (In 1857 Leutze painted a one-third-size copy, now in the possession of the Monmouth County Historical Society, Freehold.) Leutze already had completed the iconic *Washington Crossing the Delaware* (1851), and he painted the Monmouth canvass on commission in the same patriotic and romantic genre. Not as famous as the *Crossing*, *Rallying the Troops* still captures what has become the prevailing view of the Washington-Lee confrontation. It shows a plainly dejected and humiliated Lee confronted by a heroic Washington, sword upheld on a dashing horse and surrounded by cheering troops and perfectly uniformed aides. If a picture is worth a thousand words, *Rallying the Troops* is worth several hundred thousand. For a full discussion of the painting, see "*Washington Rallying the Troops at Monmouth*," http://www.americanrevolution.org/leutze.php.
16. Quoted in Thayer, *Making of a Scapegoat*, 54.
17. Selesky, *Encyclopedia of the American Revolution*, 2:961–62, 1113–14. Nathaniel spelled his last name with an "e" and not the second "a."
18. Lesser, *Sinews of Independence*, 68, 73; "Return of the Number of Men, Wagoners, Women & Children victualled at Monmouth the 27 & 28th June 1778 inclusive," Donald W. Holst Private Collection, Washington, D.C.
19. *PLCM*, 129 (Mercer), 179–80 (Knox), 230 (Lee).
20. Ibid., 230 (Lee). Captain Mercer also witnessed the exchange with Hamilton and recalled it almost exactly as Lee did. Ibid., 130–31 (Mercer).

21. Hamilton and Irvine, "Battle of Monmouth," 148.
22. Reed, *Life and Correspondence of Joseph Reed*, 1:368; Reed, *Life of Esther De Berdt*, 294.
23. Dearborn, *Revolutionary War Journals*, 127.
24. Willett, *Military Actions*, 69; Shaw, *Journals*, 48; Lafayette, *In the Age of the American Revolution*, 11.
25. James McHenry to George Lux, 30 June 1778, in McHenry, "Battle of Monmouth," 356.
26. Enclosure, John Clark to Charles Lee, 3 Sept. 1778, AMs 785/15, PPFR; Morrissey, *Monmouth Courthouse*, 70.

Chapter 13

1. Henry Beekman Livingston to Robert R. Livingston, 31 June 1778, New Jersey Letters, Acc. 3097, Special Collections and University Archives, NjRV.
2. Sivilich, GIS mapping of artillery projectiles, BRAVO, MBSP, digital files; William Hale to his father, 4 July 1778, in Wilkin, *Some British Soldiers*, 258.
3. *PLCM*, 158 (Lee & Knox), 166–67 (Edwards).
4. Ibid., 77 (Ogden), 130 (Mercer).
5. Ibid., 113 (Mercer).
6. An unknown British participant stated that the volley was at twenty yards (or 60 feet). "A Guard's Account—Published in the *London Chronicle*, 19–22 Sept. 1778," in "Notes on the Battle of Monmouth," 46. Solomon Parson's remembered firing when the redcoats were eight rods (or 132 feet) away. Parsons quoted in Washburn, *Historical Sketches*, 257–63, courtesy Jason Wickersty.
7. This account is based on *PLCM*, 81 (Fitzgerald), 81 (Lee), 87 (Harrison), 87 (Mercer).
8. Journal of Capt. John Peebles, 28 June 1778, Cunninghame of Thortoun Papers, GD 21, Scottish Records Office, Edinburgh; Peebles, *American War*, 193.
9. O. Williams to P. Thomas, 29 June 1778, in Brackenridge, "Cave of Vanhest," May 1779, 213.
10. "Guard's Account," in "Notes on the Battle of Monmouth," 46; Morrissey, *Monmouth Courthouse*, 69. Trelawny survived his wounds but was left behind in no condition to move when the British pulled out of Monmouth Court House after the battle. The Americans treated him well. Lt. William Hale to his father, 14 July 1778, in Wilkin, *Some British Soldiers*, 264. After a long career (mostly with the Coldstream Guards) and successive promotions, Trelawny became a lieutenant general in 1793. MacKinnon, *Origin and Services of the Coldstream Guards*, 484–85; *London Gazette*, no. 11802, 2 Sept. 1777, p. 1.
11. "Guard's Account," in "Notes on the Battle of Monmouth," 46–47.
12. Extracted from Washburn, *Historical Sketches*, 257–63, courtesy Jason Wickersty.
13. *PLCM*, 130 (Mercer).

14. Lt. William Hale to his father, 4 July 1778, in Wilkin, *Some British Soldiers*, 259.
15. *PLCM*, 130 (Mercer), 147 (Olney), 156 (Oswald), 163 (Cumpston), 180–81 (Knox), 216 (Lee).
16. Ibid., 81 (Fitzgerald).
17. Ibid., 87–88 (Harrison), 180 (Knox), 182 (Shaw).
18. Ibid., 76, 87–88 (Harrison), 136 (Oswald), 157, 180 (Knox), 182 (Shaw).
19. Ibid., 76 (Harrison), 142 (Cumpston), 161 (Seward).
20. Ibid., 163 (Cumpston).
21. Ibid., 184 (Seward).
22. Ibid., 182 (Shaw), 144–45 (Olney).
23. William Hale to his father, 14 July 1778, in Wilkin, *Some British Soldiers*, 263.
24. Ibid.
25. Clinton, *American Rebellion*, 94.
26. Anonymous British officer, 1st Battalion British Grenadiers to Lord Amherst, [23–25 July 1778], Amherst Papers, PRO WO 34/111, p. 71, microfilm copy at PWacD; McHenry, *Journal*, 7.
27. Baurmeister, *Revolution in America*, 187.
28. Lt. William Hale to his father, 4 July 1778, in Wilkin, *Some British Soldiers*, 257–61.
29. Ibid.
30. Baurmeister, *Revolution in America*, 187; McHenry, *Journal*, 7.
31. Henry Beekman Livingston to Robert R. Livingston, 31 June [1 July] 1778, NjRV; John Laurens to Henry Laurens, 30 June 1778, *PHL*, 13:535n17.
32. Ichabod Spencer, 1st Connecticut, Pension Declaration, 29 Sept. 1820, RWPBLW, Microcopy 804, Film 27, Reel 2255, copy at PWacD, reference courtesy of George Quintal, Jr.
33. Stryker, *Battle of Monmouth*, 200; Heitman, *Historical Register of Officers*, 538; *PLCM*, 147 (Olney); William Watson to Joseph Lyman, 4 July 1778, New Jersey Letters, Acc. 3096, Special Collections and University Archives, NjRV.
34. *PLCM*, 150 (Oswald).
35. Ibid., 136 (Oswald), 142–43 (Cumpston), 157–58 (Knox).
36. J. P. Martin, *Private Yankee Doodle*, 128; McHenry, *Journal*, 7.
37. Greenman, *Diary*, 122.
38. We do not know the size of the force that crossed the bridge to the west. Clinton stated that "some battalions" engaged beyond the morass, but that may include Grey and Erskine's men. The best conjecture is that only the 2nd Battalion forced a crossing. Clinton, *American Rebellion*, 94. British captain Archibald Robertson also implies that the British got across the West Morass, noting that the redcoats, including the grenadiers, "drove them from Rail to Rail across Another swamp [the morass] where their 2d line was form'd." Robertson, *Archibald Robertson*, 177. The location of the grenadiers and of Wayne's command is approximately at position 15 of the Capitaine map. Michel

Capitaine du Chesnoy, *Carte de l'affaire de Monmouth: ou le G'al Washington commandon l'armée americaine et le G'l Clinton l'armée angloise le 28 Juin 1778*, G3812.M6453 17778 .C3, Geography and Map Division, DLC.

39. Sivilich and Sivilich, "Surveying, Statistics, and Spatial Mapping," 50–71.
40. Finney, "Old Tennent Church," 265.
41. "Guard's Account," in "Notes on the Battle of Monmouth," 47. Monckton was the lieutenant colonel of the 45th Foot, detached to command the 2nd Grenadier Battalion.
42. These unattributed quotes are from Preston, *Revolution 1776*, 331; and Stryker, *Battle of Monmouth*, 216.
43. Lieutenant Hale implies that Monckton was killed outright. See William Hale to his parents, 14 July 1778, in Wilkin, *Some British Soldiers*, 264. But the chevalier de Pontgibaud very specifically stated that the lieutenant colonel "died of his wounds after suffering for twenty-four hours." *French Volunteer*, 56. The fact that patriot troops brought Monckton back to Tennent's Meeting House, the grounds of which served as a field hospital, suggests that Pontgibaud was correct. For soldiers of both sides noting Monckton's death, see Dudley Coleman to his wife, 3 July 1778, Dudley Coleman Manuscripts, MHi; Peebles, *American War*, 194; "Guard's Account," in "Notes on the Battle of Monmouth," 47–49; and Baurmeister, *Revolution in America*, 187. Controversy and lore grew around Monckton's demise. Some accounts put his death in action later in the day, leading a charge against Wayne's position at the Parsonage. See, for example, Watts, "Memoir," 428. The fact that Pennsylvania troops were in the thick of the fighting at the Parsonage, and that at least one Pennsylvania officer claimed that his platoon had brought the grenadier commander down, probably contributed to this belief. Lt. Alexander Dow ordered his platoon to aim at a mounted officer he thought was Monckton and thought his men had killed him. But in the heat of battle, it was difficult to identify any particular officer, and no British account or casualty list noted a ranking officer killed in the Parsonage action. See Alexander Dow to the Continental Congress, 23 May 1781, Microcopy M-247, Roll 94, Frame 387, PCC. There was also a tale of a struggle between rebels and redcoats over the fallen officer and the grenadier colors that supposedly fell with him. Stryker, *Battle of Monmouth*, 216–18. This legend included a claim that the grenadiers secured the dead colonel and in "relays . . . buried his body, taking turns during the battle and using bayonets for shovels, mingling tears with the earth they cast upon his body." Stedman, *Origin, Progress, and Termination of the American War*, 2:23; also in Stryker, *Battle of Monmouth*, 218. These stories are romantic but apocryphal. No contemporary accounts mention an event as unlikely as a battlefield struggle over a body, the grenadiers carried no colors on the twenty-eighth, and Monckton's grave remains where it has always been—at the Tennent Church. Morrissey, *Monmouth Courthouse*, 76.

In 1888 Samuel Freyer, of Heightstown, New Jersey, erected a stone over Monckton's grave. The inscription reads: "Hic Jacet. Lt. Col. Henry Monckton who on the plain of Monmouth June 28, 1778 Sealed with his life his duty to his King and Country. Courage is considered on all hands as an essential of high character." Freyer's father was British. "Guard's Account," in "Notes on the Battle of Monmouth," 49.

44. Journal of Capt. John Peebles, 28 June 1778, Cunninghame of Thortoun Papers, GD 21, Scottish Records Office, Edinburgh; Unidentified British Journal, 28 June 1778, Clinton Papers, MiU-C, copy at PaVfNHP.
45. *PLCM*, 77 (Ogden); Ramsay, *American Revolution*, 83.
46. McHenry, *Journal*, 7.
47. Anthony Wayne to Polly Wayne, 1 July 1778, Anthony Wayne Papers, Phi.
48. Lee to unknown, 22 Apr. 1780, Gratz Collection, Case 4, Box 13, PHi.
49. *PLCM*, 217–18 (Lee).
50. Clinton, *American Rebellion*, 96; Stedman, *Origin, Progress, and Termination of the American War*, 2:22.
51. Pontgibaud, *French Volunteer*, 56; "Reminiscences of Dr. William Read, Arranged from His Notes and Papers," in Gibbes, *Documentary History*, 257.
52. Thayer, *Making of a Scapegoat*, 58.
53. *PLCM*, 94–95 (Griffith), 232–33 (Lee).
54. In the nineteenth century the Griffith-Lee encounter received considerable embellishment. According to some, Griffith allegedly sought out Washington on the eve of the battle, warning him of treachery on Lee's part. There is not a shred of evidence to support this astonishing charge. Griffith apparently never mentioned the incident, even in correspondence to his wife only days after the fighting. But long after Griffith's death, members of his family continued to believe the story even as they conceded that no one knew how the reverend might have come by such startling intelligence. Had Griffith made such a midnight call on Washington, he had ample opportunity to reveal the matter at the court-martial, where Lee's enemies would have made the most of it. He never did; but the midnight warning appeared as fact in the serious literature of the Revolution well into the twentieth century. David Griffith to Hannah Griffith, 2 July 1778, Griffith Letters, Miscellaneous Manuscripts Collection, NjFrHi. On what the Griffith family thought and on their lack of evidence, see G. W. P. Custis to Benson Lossing, 13 Dec. 1851, Sol Feinstone Collection, PWacD; and Stryker, *Battle of Monmouth*, 111–12.
55. *PLCM*, 110–11 (Steuben), 218 (Lee).
56. This estimate of the strength of the reserve is derived from unit returns in Lesser, *Sinews of Independence*, 72–73.

Chapter 14

1. Wright, *Continental Army*, 104, 150.
2. McKenney, *Organizational History of Field Artillery*, 13.

3. The artillery action under Lee and Oswald has garnered considerably more attention than the cannonade of the afternoon, even in sources from which we might have expected more scrutiny of the artillery duel. See, for example, Trussell, "Artillery and the Battle of Monmouth," 221–23. A U.S. Army Field Artillery School publication notes only that Knox concentrated his guns in groups of eight to ten. *Right of the Line*, [5].
4. The artillery regiments did not receive numerical designations until 1779; until then, they were called after their commanding officers: for example, "Colonel [Charles] Harrison's Artillery Regiment." Washington called Harrison's regiment north from Virginia to make good artillery strength lost through desertions from Col. Thomas Proctor's regiment. With 331 men of all ranks, Harrison's was the only full regiment in the action, the others being represented by various companies. Harrison's appears to have been in the thick of things at Monmouth. See Lesser, *Sinews of Independence*, 73; Carlton, "Captain-Lieutenant William Miller," 3; and Konigsberg, "Edward Carrington," 30–33. Col. John Lamb's regiment (later designated the Second) had four or five companies at Monmouth; Lamb thought it was four, but muster rolls for June 1778 noted five, and it is possible that a company may have joined after the battle when the muster rolls were compiled. Oswald commanded Lamb's companies, along with the two independent companies; Lamb himself was posted with artillery in the Hudson Highlands. See Henry Knox to John Lamb, 2 June 1778, in Leake, *Memoir of the Life and Times of General John Lamb*, 198–99; ibid., 202; and Lesser, *Sinews of Independence*, 73–74. Muster rolls for Col. John Crane's regiment (eventual Third) list nine companies present in New Jersey in June, and there is no reason to presume they were not all at Monmouth, although they may not all have been in action. There were guns with the reserve at Englishtown. See Lesser, *Sinews of Independence*, 73. At least four companies—the Fourth, Sixth, Tenth, and Eleventh—suffered casualties. See Stone, "Artillery Casualties at the Battle of Monmouth."

   Proctor's regiment, while serving under Washington, was technically a Pennsylvania state unit (it would later formally join the Continental roster as the Fourth Continental Artillery Regiment). Proctor's had suffered heavy desertions at Valley Forge, and during the Monmouth campaign most of the outfit remained in Philadelphia on garrison duty. It replaced Col. Henry Jackson's detachment, which had marched to join Washington. See Benedict Arnold to GW, 22 June 1778, *PGWde*, RWS, 15:495. The fullest biography of Colonel Proctor fails to place him at Monmouth. See Nead, "Biographical Sketch of Gen. Thomas Proctor," 454–70. Unfortunately, there are no known surviving muster rolls to provide locations for the various companies of Proctor's regiment in June 1778. One company, under Capt. Francis Proctor, Jr., the colonel's younger brother, apparently was in action on the twenty-eighth. There is no evidence that it marched with Jackson, but Maj. Gen. John

Cadwalader led a contingent of Pennsylvania militia to Monmouth, and Proctor's men may have joined with their fellow Pennsylvanians. During the action at Monmouth, a seemingly reliable eyewitness specifically indicated that Washington identified Proctor on the field. See "Reminiscences of Dr. William Read, Arranged from His Notes and Papers," in Gibbes, *Documentary History*, 256. For the Proctor family, see Bluemilk, "Proctors in Eastern Pennsylvania," accessed 19 June 2013. Captain Proctor's service record, maintained by the Society of the Cincinnati, cannot confirm his presence at Monmouth—there is a gap between 19 June 1778 and July 1779—but most historians accept that his company was in action on 28 June, with a note in *Pennsylvania Archives* specifically stating that elements of Proctor's regiment fought at Monmouth. See Bluemilk, "Continental Line. Fourth Regiment of Artillery," accessed 21 Sept. 2013. See also "Military History of Francis Proctor," accessed 18 June 2013. Other sources all have Proctor's represented at Monmouth: see Morrissey, *Monmouth Courthouse*, 88; Boatner, *Encyclopedia of the American Revolution*, 497; and Rees, "'Very Smart Cannonading,'" 38–39. In his pension application, Sgt. Battas Collins stated specifically that he was wounded at Monmouth while serving in "Col. Proctor's Battalion of Artillery." Battas Collins Pension Application, "Abstracts of Pension Applications on File in the Division of Public Records, Pennsylvania State Library," *PennArch*, 4:558.

5. [Lord Stirling] to William Henry Drayton, 15 Aug.1778, in Alexander, "Letters," 173. Capt. Walter Finney—the Pennsylvania officer with the silver plate in his skull—remembered six guns coming on line, which may have been in addition to the ten mentioned by Stirling. "Old Tennent Church," 265. Dearborn thought the patriots had "about 12 Pieces of Artillery," while a British officer counted fourteen American guns. *Revolutionary War Journals*, 127; William Hale to Admiral Hale, 4 July 1778, in Wilkin, *Some British Soldiers*, 260. Knox may have had a few more guns after he was done collecting them from the various patriot commands. Enos Barnes, a sergeant in the Fifth Connecticut, thought that each brigade had contributed two guns and that the "grand park of artillery"—the army's central reserve—was in action, which would have given Knox a higher number. "Journal of Enos Barnes," 28 June 1778, NjMoHP, transcript. Knox's personnel strength is in Lesser, *Sinews of Independence*, 73.
6. Birkhimer, *Organization, Administration, Materiel, and Tactics of the Artillery*, 12; Ward, *For Virginia and for Independence*, 103.
7. Carrington receives high marks for his role in Dastrup, *King of Battle*, 27.
8. We are not sure of exactly where Pattison was during the battle. One account mentions only company commanders engaged during the cannonade, which hardly precludes Pattison being on the scene. See [S. P. Adye], "Account of the Evacuation of Philadelphia, the March through the Jerseys, Battle of Freehold or Monmouth Courthouse, and Arrival of

the British Army at New York, as Recorded in Brigade Order Book No. 2," in Downman, *Services*, 68. But Pattison's own version of the battle and report of Royal Artillery casualties has the ring of an eyewitness account. See Pattison to Viscount Townsend, 7 July 1778, Pattison, *Papers*, 144–47. As the cannonade increased in tempo, it is difficult to believe that the chief British artillerist would have missed the action—anymore than Knox would have missed it.

9. Roche, "From Commander to Commandant," 10–12, 21.
10. Katcher, *British, Provincial, and German Army Units*, 24; Boatner, *Encyclopedia of the American Revolution*, 724; André, *Journal*, 80; Letter Book, 22 May 1778, Pattison, *Papers*, 125.
11. Dearborn, *Revolutionary War Journals*, 127.
12. Israel Shreve to Polly Shreve, 29 June 1778, Israel Shreve Papers, Buxton Special Collections, LRuL; Israel Shreve to Polly Shreve, 2 July 1778, Ferdinand J. Dreer Collection, Soldiers of the Revolution Series, Box 4, Ser. 52:2, Vol. 4, PHi.
13. Samuel Adams to Sally Adams, 2 July 1778, Stuart Goldman Private Collection, Randolph, Mass.; Joseph Cilley to Thomas Bartlett, 22 July 1778, in Cogswell, *Nottingham, Deerfield, and Northwood*, 182.
14. William Hale to Admiral Hale, 4 July 1778, in Wilkin, *Some British Soldiers*, 260.
15. James Chambers to Kitty Chambers, 30 June 1778, in Garrard, *Chambersburg*, 52.
16. Jason Wickersty, [Account of the Battle of Monmouth], *Dover (N.H.) Gazette & Strafford Advertiser*, 17 July 1827.
17. [William Alexander] to William Henry Drayton, 15 Aug. 1778, Alexander, "Letters," 173; David Griffith to Hannah Griffith, 2 July 1778, Griffith Letters, Miscellaneous Manuscripts Collection, NjFrHi; André, *Journal*, 80.
18. "Return of the killed, wounded and missing of the American Army in the battle of Monmouth on the 28th day of June 1778," 7 July 1778, PCC, Reel 187:374. A modern tally of artillery losses has largely confirmed Washington's report. Including soldiers mortally wounded and succumbing after the battle, the number of dead was eleven, while the number of wounded (minus the mortally wounded included in the death toll) was thirteen. See Stone, "Artillery Casualties at the Battle of Monmouth."
19. James Pattison to Viscount Townsend, 7 July 1778, Pattison, *Papers*, 144–47.
20. Morgan, *Old Tennent Church*, 3.
21. Wild, "Journal," 110.
22. "Abstracts of Pension Applications on File in the Division of Public Records, Pennsylvania State Library," *PennArch*, 4:954.
23. Israel Shreve to Polly Shreve, 2 July 1778, Dreer Collection, Soldiers of the Revolution Series, Box 4, Ser. 52:2, Vol. 4, PHi. There were four Samuel Leonards in an extended Monmouth County family, including some active loyalists. The Samuel killed at Monmouth had gone over

to the British in early 1777 and served as a guide during the Monmouth campaign. Two weeks before his death, the state had initiated forfeiture proceedings against his property. Michael Adelberg to Garry Stone, e-mail, 2 Oct. 2013, copy in MBSP.

24. Dearborn, *Revolutionary War Journals*, 127.
25. Cilley to Bartlett, 22 July 1778, in Cogswell, *Nottingham, Deerfield, and Northwood*, 182; Dearborn, *Revolutionary War Journals*, 127; J. P. Martin, *Private Yankee Doodle*, 132–33.
26. "28th June 1778, Memorandum—Battle of Monmouth," Unidentified British Army Notebook, 34, Sol Feinstone Collection 409, PWacD; William Hale to Admiral Hale, 4 July 1778, in Wilkin, *Some British Soldiers*, 261.
27. Custis, *Recollections and Private Memoirs of Washington*, 224. William Stryker accepted the story as fact. See *Battle of Monmouth*, 202.
28. Custis, *Recollections and Private Memoirs of Washington*, 224. The Custis account of the Battle of Monmouth (chapter 5 in his book) is colorful to say the least and will be revisited in a later chapter. Billy Lee remained Washington's body servant until broken knees prevented his riding and hunting. Upon Washington's death, Lee was offered his freedom and an annuity as a condition of the president's will. Instead, he chose to remain at Mount Vernon as a cobbler, often conversing with former Continental officers who visited. See "Lee, William ("Billy")," in Grizzard, *George Washington*, 187–88. That Washington held Billy Lee in high regard, however, became a useful fact for antebellum Southern apologists for slavery, who argued that their "peculiar institution" was characterized by harmonious relationships between masters and slaves. See Eastman, *Aunt Phillis's Cabin*, 275–76.
29. "Reminiscences of Dr. William Read," in Gibbes, *Documentary History*, 255–56.
30. Custis, *Recollections and Private Memoirs of Washington*, 223.
31. Mayer, *Belonging to the Army.*
32. S. Smith, *Molly Pitcher Chronology*, 10–13. This is the best factual account of Molly Pitcher of Monmouth. His research is quite thorough and convincingly demolishes the oft-repeated story that Molly was Mary Ludwig of Carlisle, who married a John Caspar Hays. Smith's research was massively expanded by David G. Martin in *A Molly Pitcher Sourcebook.* Martin found a 19 March 1779 return for Proctor's artillery listing William Hays as on furlough in Carlisle, Pennsylvania.
33. J. P. Martin, *Private Yankee Doodle*, 132–33.
34. Note that Martin says nothing about a fallen husband, quite the contrary; he probably just saw a woman carrying ammunition. Hearing what she said is almost certainly a fiction.
35. Linda Grant DePauw has emphasized this point in her discussion of the Molly Pitcher legend. See "Women in Combat," 215.

36. John Todd White, "The Truth about Molly Pitcher," 99–105, in Martin and Stubaus, *American Revolution*, 105. White's is probably the most useful examination of the entire Molly Pitcher legend.
37. Stockton, *Stories of New Jersey*, 186–92.
38. Waldo and Clendenin quoted in Martin, *Molly Pitcher Sourcebook*, 2–5; S. Smith, *Battle of Monmouth*, 22.
39. On the stories of other women at Monmouth, see Stryker, *Battle of Monmouth*, 188–91; and S. Smith, *Molly Pitcher Chronology*, 4–5.
40. S. Smith, *Molly Pitcher Chronology*, 5–7; Stryker, *Battle of Monmouth*, 191.
41. Landis, "American Tradition of a Woman Known as Molly Pitcher," 83; Stryker, *Battle of Monmouth*, 191–92. There is an entire literature on "Molly Pitcher," whoever she was, or they were, in reality. Most of it is fanciful, some of it wildly so. See Klaver, "Molly Pitcher." A substantial part of this literature is devoted to Mary Hays McCauley, and the best of it is grounded in careful research. See S. Smith, *Molly Pitcher Chronology.* Samuel Smith puts McCauley at Monmouth but stops short of naming her as the actual Molly Pitcher. For the best single source of documents and other material on Molly Pitcher, see Martin, *Molly Pitcher Sourcebook.*

Chapter 15

1. Clinton, *American Rebellion*, 94.
2. Ibid., 94.
3. Anonymous officer, 1st Bat. Grenadiers to Lord Amherst, 23–25 July 1778, British Record Office, WO 34/111, p. 7, microfilm copy at WPacD.
4. William Dansey to his mother, 28 July 1778, Dansey Papers, DeHi.
5. "Autobiography of Sergeant Steven Jarvis, Queen's American Rangers," typescript, Miscellaneous Microfilms, Roll 17, NHi, courtesy Michael S. Adelberg. Although the lieutenant colonel was not there, the incident was also noted in Simcoe, *Operations of the Queen's Rangers*, 72.
6. David Rhea to GW, 28 June 1778, *PGWde*, RWS, 15:582.
7. Boatner, *Encyclopedia of the American Revolution*, 888; Wright, *Continental Army*, 139–40.
8. Ogden, *Autobiography*, 8.
9. Ibid.
10. After the battle, in a private letter Stirling claimed to have ordered the attack. [William Alexander] to William Henry Drayton, 15 Aug. 1778, Alexander, "Letters," 174. Technically, this was probably true, assuming Washington issued his attack order through the chain of command (that is, through Stirling).
11. Kidder, *First New Hampshire*, 94–95.
12. Joseph Cilley to Thomas Bartlett, 22 July 1778, in Cogswell, *Nottingham, Deerfield, and Northwood*, 182. The brigades and regiments represented were Poor's (1st, 2nd, 3rd New Hampshire, 2nd, 4th New York); Glover's (1st, 4th, 13th, 15th Massachusetts); Learned's (2nd, 8th, 9th Massachusetts); Paterson's (10th, 11th, 12th, 14th Massachusetts);

Varnum's (1st, 2nd Rhode Island, 4th, 8th Connecticut). Stone, Sivilich, and Lender, "Deadly Minuet," 9.

13. Cilley to Bartlett, 22 July 1778, in Cogswell, *Nottingham, Deerfield, and Northwood*, 182.
14. J. P. Martin, *Private Yankee Doodle*, 129.
15. It is surprising that the Highlanders did not withdraw directly east into the better cover of the swale. The most likely explanation is that the extension of the swale to the southeast was a bushy wasteland offering little protection. Field archaeology has convincingly traced the positions of the battalion in and south of the orchard as well as the position of the Americans harassing the British from the Perrine property. A combination of artifacts, careful survey work, and primary sources have defined the site of this brief but important clash of arms in remarkable detail. The British firing line—marked by a handful of dropped 0.69-inch musket balls—was surrounded by impacted 0.65-inch musket balls, buckshot, and rifle balls. Analysis of artillery impact patterns has located the forward position of a Continental cannon. This was new information—nowhere is it recorded that Continental soldiers sniped at the Highlanders. But the archaeological evidence is unarguable. Stone, Sivilich, and Lender, "Deadly Minuet," 2.
16. J. P. Martin, *Private Yankee Doodle*, 129–30; Dearborn, *Revolutionary War Journals*, 127–28; Cilley to Bartlett, 22 July 1778, in Cogswell, *Nottingham, Deerfield, and Northwood*, 182; Peebles, *American War*, 194.
17. The "grasshopper" was a light 3-pounder that could be packed on horses or carried on men's shoulders. Caruana, *Grasshoppers and Butterflies*.
18. Dearborn, *Revolutionary War Journals*, 128.
19. "Diary of Bernardus Swartwout, 2d NY Regiment, 10 Nov. 1777–9 June 1783," Bernardus Swartwout Papers, NHi; Garret Constable Pension Application, 28 Apr. 1818, Continental Soldiers: A–G, 1777–1856, NjFrHi.
20. J. P. Martin, *Private Yankee Doodle*, 129–31.
21. Ibid., 130–31; Cilley to Bartlett, 22 July 1778, in Cogswell, *Nottingham, Deerfield, and Northwood*, 182.
22. Cilley wrote that he "took between twenty and thirty prisoners." Cilley to Bartlett, 22 July 1778, in Cogswell, *Nottingham, Deerfield, and Northwood*, 182. But these prisoners probably included stragglers from several units.
23. Stevens, *Facsimiles*, no. 1114; Stewart, *Charter, Manners, and Present State of the Highlanders*, 1:398; Muster Rolls, PRO WO 12/5479, pp. 11–20. British casualties are explained more fully in Stone, Silivich, and Lender, "Deadly Minuet," 15–16.
24. André, *Journal*, 80; [Anonymous Officer, 1st Battalion British Grenadiers] to General Amherst, [23–25 July 1778], Amherst Papers, PRO WO 34/111, p. 71, microfilm copy at PWacD; Peebles, *American War*, 194.

25. Clinton, *American Rebellion*, 95.
26. Ibid., 95.
27. Stirling to Drayton, 15 Aug. 1778, Alexander, "Letters," 174.
28. Anthony Wayne to [GW?], 14 Oct. 1778, *Lee Papers*, 3:241. Wayne's fury with St. Clair led him to consider resignation from the army. See Stillé, *Major-General Anthony Wayne and the Pennsylvania Line*, 168–69.
29. No list of the exact regiments crossing the bridge with Wayne is extant, although based on personnel known to have fought in this action, the regiments of the Third Brigade were the most likely units. Burr, who lost a horse in the fighting, was with Wayne, and Spencer's presence is confirmed in Alexander Dow to Congress, 23 May 1781, Microcopy M-247, Roll 94:387, PCC. For confirmation of the Third, Ninth, and Twelfth Regiments being with Wayne, see Watts, "Memoir," 427–28; and Barney Hasson Pension Application, "Abstracts of Pension Applications on File in the Division of Public Records, Pennsylvania State Library," *PennArch*, 4:511, courtesy Jason Wickersty. There is no reason to suppose the Sixth Pennsylvania did not advance with the rest of the regiments. Some of the brigade may have advanced only as far as the West Morass bridge and remained there in reserve, but this is conjectural barring the discovery of new documentation (courtesy John U. Rees). Strength estimates for the Third Brigade for May (715 present and fit for duty) and June (619) are noted in Lesser, *Sinews of Independence*, 69, 72. It appears most figures for June were compiled after the battle, accounting for the lower numbers of "present fit for duty & on duty." We have made our estimate of Wayne's command—around 500 men—bearing in mind that these regiments already had provided men for the "picked" battalions.
30. The lieutenant colonel's surname is also spelled "Medows" in sources. See Katcher, *British, Provincial, and German Army Units*, 60; and "Preferments," *Scots Magazine* (Edinburgh) 40 (1778): 55.
31. [Anonymous Officer, 1st Battalion British Grenadiers] to General Amherst, [23–25 July 1778], Amherst Papers, PRO WO 34/111, p. 71, microfilm copy at PWacD; Clinton, *American Rebellion*, 95. For the location of the 1st Grenadiers when Wayne attacked them, see Michel Capitaine du Chesnoy, *Carte de l'affaire de Monmouth: ou le G'al Washington commandon l'armée americaine et le G'l Clinton l'armée angloise le 28 Juin 1778*, position 21, G3812.M6453 17778 .C3, Geography and Map Division, DLC.
32. Lord Barrington to Henry Clinton, 1 Dec. 1778, PRO WO 4, reel 247:150.
33. Katcher, *British, Provincial, and German Army Units*, 47. The 33rd Foot is now (2015) part of the Yorkshire Regiment, with Prince Andrew, the Duke of York, as colonel in chief. See "Yorkshire Regiment History," accessed 12 Nov. 2013; and The Yorkshire Regiment Association, http://www.yorkshireregiment.com/, accessed 4 Jan. 2015.
34. "Return of the Number of Men, Wagoners, Women & Children victualled at Monmouth the 27 & 28th inclusive," Donald W. Holst Private

Collection, Washington, D.C.; Wayne to [GW], 14 Oct. 1778, *Lee Papers*, 3:241.

35. Alexander Dow to the Continental Congress, 23 May 1781, Microcopy M-247, Roll 94:387, PCC; Stryker, *Battle of Monmouth*, 288–90.
36. Stryker, *Battle of Monmouth*, 288–90. A less extravagant version of this is in *NJHC*, 341.
37. Alexander Dow to the Continental Congress, 23 May 1781, Microcopy M-247, Roll 94:387, PCC. Dow was not the only American mistakenly to think Monckton died advancing on Wayne. See James McHenry to "his friend in this City" [John Cox in New Brunswick, N.J.?], 1 July 1778, in McHenry, "Battle of Monmouth," 358.
38. McHenry, "Battle of Monmouth," 358; *NJHC*, 343.
39. [Anonymous Officer, 1st Battalion British Grenadiers] to General Amherst, [23–25 July 1778], Amherst Papers, PRO WO 34/111, p. 71, microfilm copy at PWacD. There is some question as to how close to the Parsonage the British were able to get. The building itself suffered relatively minor damage; a round shot went through the roof, though probably from the cannonade earlier in the day. No doubt musket fire hit the structure as well. But the church (Tennent's Meeting House) congregation saw no reason to undertake major repairs until 1795, suggesting the building was not the direct seat of major fighting and that the grenadiers or the 33rd never reached it. Symmes, *History of the Old Tennent Church*, 55.
40. The relative positions of the grenadiers and Continentals is based on archaeological evidence recovered by BRAVO members. The site of the former orchard contains a mixture of British- and Continental-sized impacted musket balls. The implication is that when Continentals within the orchard fired at the grenadiers, some of their musket balls struck apple trees. Sivilich, GIS mapping of iron and lead shot, BRAVO, MBSP, digital files.
41. Ibid.; Caruana, *British Artillery Ammunition*, 15–16.
42. The story of the single ball disarming a platoon is in "The Royal Grenadiers at Monmouth," in Lossing, *American Historical Record*, 263; *NJHC*, 341; and Henrietta Cooper, ed., "Extracts from the Diary of Captain John Nice, of the Pennsylvania Line," *PMHB* 16 (1892): 406.
43. See, for examples, André, *Journal*, 80; McHenry, *Journal*, 7; and John Laurens to Henry Laurens, 30 June 1778, in Salter, *History of Monmouth and Ocean Counties*, 414. Some accounts have Cornwallis ordering an attack on Combs Hill to silence the American guns; the attacking column supposedly including elements of the grenadiers, the guards, and two regiments of foot. See, for example, Stryker, *Battle of Monmouth*, 211–13; and *PNG*, 2:455n1. This attack was never ordered.
44. Alexander Dow to the Continental Congress, 23 May 1781, Microcopy M-247, Roll 94:387, PCC.
45. [Anonymous Officer, 1st Battalion British Grenadiers] to General Amherst, [23–25 July 1778], Amherst Papers, PRO WO 34/111, p. 71, microfilm copy at PWacD.

46. Lesser, *Sinews of Independence*, 73, 76–77; Morrissey, *Monmouth Courthouse*, 87–88.
47. GW to Henry Laurens, 1 July 1778, *PGWde*, RWS, 16:4–5. The number of guns is unknown, although a brigade normally had two.
48. Ramsay, *American Revolution*, 84; GW to Henry Laurens, 1 July 1778, *PGWde*, RWS, 16:45.
49. "Journal of Enos Barnes," 28 June 1778, NjMoHP.
50. Lafayette, *In the Age of the American Revolution*, 11.
51. [Smith], "Papers of General Samuel Smith," 91. See also Henry B. Livingston to Robert Livingston, 31 June 1778, New Jersey Letters, Acc. 3097, Special Collections and University Archives, NjRV.
52. Sivilich, GIS mapping of howitzer-shell fragments, BRAVO, MBSP, digital files.
53. Bell, MS Diary, 29 June 1778.
54. A point made in Morrissey, *Monmouth Courthouse*, 75.
55. André, *Journal*, 81; Downman, *Services*, 68.
56. John Hills, "Sketch of Part of Road . . . Shewing the Skrimish between the Rear of the British Army . . . and the advanced Corps of the Rebel Army . . . ," Clinton Papers, Map 239, MiU-C.
57. John Neilson to Philemon Dickinson, 29 June 1778, enclosed with Dickinson to GW, 29 June 1778, *PGWde*, RWS, 15:585n1.
58. Pension applications of John B. Field, 6 June 1833, Invalid 643, and Jeremiah B. Field, 14 July 1833, Invalid 872, Abstracts of Revolutionary War Service, NjTSA; Pension Declaration of James T. Dunn, 17 June 1833, RWPBLW, Microcopy 804, Widow 732; Ritchie, "New York Diary of the Revolutionary War," 240. A farm family tried to care for the mortally wounded Michael Field. Unlike most casualties of the battle, his grave was marked and is now the focus of the tiny Colts Neck Memorial Park.
59. Inman, "Battles of Bunker Hill and Monmouth," 92 (28 June 1785); Inman, "Narrative of the Revolution," 243; Letter Book, October 1777–?, p. 145, James Pattison Papers, Royal Artillery Institution, Woolwich, London; Pension Declaration of Samuel Carman, 20 July 1832, Invalid 965, RWPBLW, Microcopy 804, Roll 472.

Chapter 16

1. David Griffith to Hannah Griffith, 2 July 1778, Griffith Letters, Miscellaneous Manuscripts Collection, NjFrHi; William Irvine to John Davis, 30 June 1778, *PMHB* 2 (1878): 148; Persifer Frazer to Polly Frazer, 30 June 1778, in Frazer, *General Persifor Frazer*, 183. Frazer was lieutenant colonel of the Fifth Pennsylvania. Heitman, *Historical Register of Officers*, 236.
2. David Griffith to Hannah Griffith, 2 July 1778, NjFrHi; Israel Shreve to Polly Shreve, 2 July 1778, Ferdinand J. Dreer Collection, Soldiers of the Revolution Series, Box 4, Ser. 52:2, Vol. 4, PHi; Anthony Wayne to Richard Peters, 12 July 1778, Wayne Papers, PHi.
3. General Orders, 29 June 1778, *PGWde*, RWS, 15:583. Woodford's men rejoined the army on 30 June. John Parke to Timothy Matlack, 30 June

1778, *PennArch*, microcopy, Roll 14, Frames 0338–39, reference courtesy Lee Boyle.

4. General Orders, 30 June 1778, *PGWde*, RWS, 15:590.
5. Stephen Moylan to GW, two letters of 29 June 1778, ibid., 588–89; Anthony Walton White to GW, 29 June 1778, ibid., 589.
6. Morrissey, *Monmouth Courthouse*, 76.
7. GW to Philemon Dickinson, 29 June 1778, *PGWde*, RWS, 15:585–86; Dickinson to GW, two letters of 19 June 1778, ibid., 584–85; John Taylor to John Neilson, 29 June 1778, Neilson Papers, Acc. 584, Special Collections and University Archives, NjRV.
8. Daniel Morgan to GW, 2 July 1778, *PGWde*, RWS, 16:12.
9. Israel Shreve to Mary Shreve, 29 June 1778, Israel Shreve Papers, Buxton Special Collections, LRuL; [Smith], "Papers of General Samuel Smith," 92.
10. Pontgibaud, *French Volunteer*, 56; Samuel Adams, "Diary of Dr. Samuel Adams, 1758–1819," 29 June 1778, Samuel Adams Papers, 1758–1819, Manuscript Collection 19, Manuscripts and Archives Division, NN.
11. John Laurens to Henry Laurens, 30 June 1778, *PHL*, 13:536.
12. Unknown American officer, "An Estimate of the Loss of the British Army . . . ," SA 183, NjFrHi; *New Jersey Gazette*, 15 July 1778, in *NJA*, 2:296; [William Livingston], "Account of the Battle of Monmouth," *New Jersey Gazette*, 24 June 1778 [*sic*, 1 July 1778], in *PWL*, 2:378. Some POWs may have ended up in Virginia. William Day, a Virginia Continental and Monmouth veteran, reported escorting British prisoners south from Philadelphia after his discharge following the battle. William Day Pension Application, in Dorman, *Virginia Revolutionary War Pension Applications*, 28:58.
13. For example, after the Battle of Cowpens in 1780, Morgan (by then a brigadier) had to provide security for British POWs as he avoided pursuit by Cornwallis, who very much wanted to get his redcoats back. See Babits, *Devil of a Whipping*, 142–44. After Monmouth Clinton took approximately seventy American prisoners with him to New York. Had his march been longer, securing them could have posed problems. *New York Gazette and Weekly Mercury*, 6 July 1778, in *NJA*, 2:274.
14. Cornelius Van Dyck, "A Report of the No. of Slain buried in the Field of Battle near Monmouth Court Ho. 29th June 1778," GWP, ser. 4, Microfilm Roll 50; James Chamber to Edward Hand, 30 June 1778, in Linn and Egle, *Pennsylvania in the War of the Revolution*, 318; "Journal of Enos Barnes," 28 June 1778, NjMoHP, transcript.
15. Thomas Blake, "Lieutenant Thomas Blake's Journal," in Kidder, *First New Hampshire*, 43.
16. Cox, *Proper Sense of Honor*, 71.
17. General Orders, 29 June 1778, *PGWde*, RWS, 15:583.
18. Henry Beekman Livingston to Robert R. Livingston, 31 [*sic*] June 1778, New Jersey Letters, Acc. 3097, Special Collections and University Archives, NjRV; Finney, "Old Tennent Church," 266; Heitman, *Historical Register of Officers*, 227.

19. William Walton to Joseph Lyman, 4 July 1778, New Jersey Letters, Acc. 3096, NjRV.
20. "Pericles," *Pennsylvania Packet*, 22 Sept. 1778, *NJA* 2, 2:439–40.
21. Otho Williams to Dr. Phil Thomas, 29 June 1778, Gen. Otho H. Williams Papers, Maryland Historical Society, Baltimore.
22. Cowen, *Medicine in Revolutionary New Jersey*, 12. Army regulations called for the establishment of field hospitals at least 3,000 yards to the rear—that is, well out of musket and most artillery range. Eichner, "Military Practice of Medicine during the Revolutionary War," 26, accessed 21 Nov. 2013.
23. Cox, *Proper Sense of Honor*, 148–49.
24. Blanco, *Physician of the American Revolution*, 188–89. On the turmoil within the Medical Department, see Hawke, *Benjamin Rush*, esp. 208–13.
25. "Reminiscences of Dr. William Read, Arranged from His Notes and Papers," in Gibbes, *Documentary History*, 256; S. Adams, Diary, 28 June 1778.
26. J. P. Martin, *Private Yankee Doodle*, 131.
27. General Orders, 29 June 1778, *PGWde*, RWS, 15:583; Saffron, *Surgeon to Washington*, 53, 53n143.
28. "Reminiscences of Dr. William Read," in Gibbes, *Documentary History*, 257; Archilaus Lewis, "Archilaus Lewis Orderly Book," in Ryan, *Salute to Courage*, 131; Henry Vail Pension Application, 8 Aug. 1832, S.6296, RWPBLW, Microfilm 804. Vail had charge of twelve teams collecting the wounded at Monmouth.
29. Stone, "Artillery Casualties at the Battle of Monmouth" (using data from RG 93, DNA, Microfilm M246).
30. Jacob Anderson Pension Application, S.37675, in Dorman, *Virginia Revolutionary War Pension Applications*, 2:26.
31. John Durkee to GW, 14 Nov. 1778, *PGWde*, RWS, 18:147; Heitman, *Historical Register of Officers*, 208.
32. William Walton to Joseph Lyman, 4 July 1778, New Jersey Letters, Acc. 3096, Special Collections and University Archives,, NjRV. "Reminiscences of Dr. William Read," in Gibbes, *Documentary History*, 258–59; Heitman, *Historical Register of Officers*, 582; S. Adams, Diary, 5 July 1778.
33. Heitman, *Historical Register of Officers*, 168; S. Adams, Diary, 4 July–10 Aug. 1778.
34. Brackenridge, "Cave of Vanhest," May 1779, 213, June 1779, 150–51; Heitman, *Historical Register of Officers*, 457.
35. Henry Anderson Pension Application, S.44301, in Dorman, *Virginia Revolutionary War Pension Applications*, 2:23; Baltus Collins Pension Application, "Abstracts of Pension Applications on File in the Division of Public Records, Pennsylvania State Library," *PennArch*, 4:954; Samuel Leonard Pension Application, 11 July 1820, in Pilch, "Morris County [N.J.] Revolutionary War Pension Applications," NjRV; Samuel Leonard Pension Application, S.554, RWPBLW, Microfilm 804. Leonard

is not to be confused with the Monmouth County tory of the same name.

36. "Reminiscences of Dr. William Read," in Gibbes, *Documentary History*, 256–57; Melvin W. Lethbridge, Report Form on Margaret Houck (with genealogical attachments), Montgomery County (N.Y.) Historical Department, 2 Mar. 1936.
37. William Maxwell to GW, 1 July 1778, *PGWde*, RWS, 16:8–9.
38. "Reminiscences of Dr. William Read," in Gibbes, *Documentary History*, 258.
39. William Maxwell to GW, 5 July 1778, *PGWde*, RWS, 16:29–30.
40. General Orders, 29 June 1778, ibid., 15:584. Col. Ephraim Martin, Fourth New Jersey, was tasked with gathering the sick, beginning at Coryell's Ferry.
41. General Orders, 5 July 1778, ibid., 16:27; Stone, "Artillery Casualties at Monmouth"; Troop Return of 18 July 1778, Henry Jackson Papers, 1772–82, Manuscripts Division, Microfilm 17,359-1N-1P, DLC; Saffron, *Surgeon to Washington*, 53n143; William Hampton Pension Application, W.244, in Dorman, *Virginia Revolutionary War Pension Applications*, 51:6.
42. Samuel Adams to Sally Adams, 19–20 July 1778, Sol Feinstone Collection, PWacD.
43. "Reminiscences of Dr. William Read," in Gibbes, *Documentary History*, 259–60. After his recovery, Read had no recollection of having issued the evacuation orders.
44. Cox, *Proper Sense of Honor*, 127.
45. S. Adams, Diary, 30 June, 9 July 1778. We have few names of other doctors serving the army at Monmouth. Adams notes Drs. Upham and Hunt as well as "some other surgeons," although we know little about them.
46. Cox, *Proper Sense of Honor*, 162.
47. For an example, see Babits, *Devil of a Whipping*, 137.
48. Dann, *Revolution Remembered*, 124–25.
49. J. P. Martin, *Private Yankee Doodle*, 131; "Reminiscences Dr. William Read," in Gibbes, *Documentary History*, 258.
50. "Extracts from American Newspapers, Vol. II, 1778," in *NJA* 2 2:284, 292, 309; S. Adams, Diary, 1 July 1778; Samuel Adams to Sally Adams, 2 July 1778, GLC01450.026, Gilder Lehrman Institute, New York; General Orders, 30 June 1778, *PGWde*, RWS, 16:590.
51. Captain Wilson may not have made the claim himself; more likely the story emerged over the years as a family tradition. It was published first in "The Royal Grenadiers at Monmouth," in Lossing, *American Historical Record*, 262–64. The article describes an alleged grenadier standard in the possession of Wilson's descendants. But no British sources indicate that the grenadiers or any other British unit carried colors on the twenty-eighth, and they certainly would have decried the loss of a grenadier standard. Also, it is noteworthy that no other American sources corroborate the Wilson legend.

52. General Orders, 30 June 1778, *PGWde*, RWS, 16:590.
53. Bell, MS Diary, 28 June 1778.
54. Samuel Adams to Sally Adams, 2 July 1778, Stuart Goldman Collection, Randolph, Mass.; Greenman, *Diary*, 122; Dearborn, *Revolutionary War Journals*, 128–19; Anthony Wayne to Richard Peters, 12 July 1778, Anthony Wayne Papers, PHi. See also [William Alexander] to William Henry Drayton, 15 Aug. 1778, Alexander, "Letters," 174.
55. "Return of the killed, wounded and missing of the American Army in the battle of Monmouth on the 28th day of June 1778," PCC, Reel 187:373–74. These figures were published in the *Pennsylvania Evening Post*, Philadelphia, 6 July 1778.
56. "At the Battle of Monmouth June 28th 1778," Jacob Weiss Papers, F-74 (1777–79), PHi; Ramsay, *American Revolution*, 84; Clinton, *American Rebellion*, 95–96. How Clinton came up with these numbers is unclear, though he may have taken them from published copies of Washington's report.
57. This is a conservative estimate. Howard H. Peckham's compilation of Monmouth casualties counted thirty-seven of the Continental missing actually dead from heatstroke or fatigue. See *Toll of Independence*, 52.
58. The number of "sick present" listed with the main army (902 and 1,131 men, respectively) in the June and July returns probably included many of the lightly wounded. Lesser, *Sinews of Independence*, 73, 77.
59. Clinton, *American Rebellion*, 95–96; *New York Gazette and Weekly Mercury*, 6 July 1778. Lt. Col. Stephen Kemble reported virtually identical British losses. *Journals*, 154. No total seems to have included the two women killed in the militia attack on the baggage train.
60. For Van Dyck's report, see note 14 above. It is worth noting, however, that Van Dyck may have fudged his numbers, substantially inflating British losses. A field report dated 29 June from Capt. Ebenezer Frye of the First New Hampshire, in charge of one of the burial details, noted sixteen British buried. But in his official tally, the lieutenant colonel credited Frye with burying twenty-five of the enemy. He accurately record Frye's three American burials. If Van Dyck took similar liberties or made similar transcription errors with other field reports (and we do not know if the discrepancies between the reports were intentional), the accuracy of his official report is questionable indeed. Ebenezer Frye, "Report of Men buried In and Near Monmouth Town June 29th : mo[nday]," microfilm, PaVfNHP. GW to Henry Laurens, 1, 7 July 1778, *PGWde*, RWS, 16:5, 35; GW to John Augustine Washington, 4 July 1778, ibid., 26; "At the Battle of Monmouth June 28th 1778," Weiss Papers, F-74 (1777–79), PHi.
61. Earl of Abington to Earl Harcourt, 1778, Harcourt, *Papers*, 272; Baurmeister, *Revolution in America*, 187; Thayer, "Battle of Monmouth," 50; Bell, MS Diary, 28 June 1778.
62. Shaw, *Journals*, 47–48.
63. Boatner, *Encyclopedia of the American Revolution*, 189, 725. Such a calculation is based on combat-related casualties, not deaths from fatigue.

64. Ewald, *Diary*, 139.
65. For a summary of Monmouth casualty estimates by other historians, see Boatner, *Encyclopedia of the American Revolution*, 725.
66. GW to Horatio Gates, 3 July 1778, *PGWde*, RWS, 16:17; Dearborn, *Revolutionary War Journals*, 129; Blake, "Journal," in Kidder, *First New Hampshire*, 43.
67. General Orders, 2 July 1778, *PGWde*, RWS, 16:10–11.
68. John Laurens to Henry Laurens, 2 July 1778, *PHL*, 13:544.
69. General Orders, 3 July 1778, *PGWde*, RWS, 16:15; General Orders, 4 July 1778, ibid., 19; Dearborn, *Revolutionary War Journals*, 130; Henry Knox to William Knox, 5 July 1778, GLC02437.00715, Gilder Lehrman Institute.
70. John Laurens to Henry Laurens, 2 July 1778, *PHL*, 13:544.
71. Samuel Hodgdon to John Ruddick, 19 July 1778, RG 93, Microfilm M853, Reel 33, 111:96, DNA. At the time of the battle, Hodgdon was deputy commissary general of military stores. Heitman, *Historical Register of Officers*, 293; General Orders, 29 June 1778, *PGWde*, RWS, 15:583.
72. Berg, *Encyclopedia of Continental Army Units*, 82, 98–99, 126–28. The disbanded Pennsylvania regiments were the Sixth, Eleventh, and Thirteenth; the Virginia units were the Fifth, Sixth, and Eighth.
73. John Kinney Pension Application, 2 Oct. 1823, in Pilch, "Morris County [N.J.] Revolutionary War Pension Applications." Kinney went into the iron business after leaving the army, but he was bankrupt when he filed for a pension in 1823.
74. Blake, "Journal," in Kidder, *First New Hampshire*, 43–44; Stryker, *Battle of Monmouth*, 272.
75. Washington to Nelson, 20 Aug. 1778, *PGWde*, RWS, 16:341.

Chapter 17

1. Morrissey, *Monmouth Courthouse*, 75. Morrissey suggested this point, but given Clinton's evidence, there seems no other plausible explanation. Sir Henry stated that even on the Navesink he hoped that Washington would attack him. But the British never realized that only a token American force (Morgan's) had shadowed their retreat. Clinton to Germain, 5 July 1778, in Davies, *Documents of the American Revolution*, 3:162.
2. Downman, *Services in America*, 69.
3. Ewald, *Diary*, 137; Clinton, *American Rebellion*, 98; Clinton to Germain, 5 July 1778, in Davies, *Documents of the American Revolution*, 3:162; Downman, *Services in America*, 67.
4. James Pattison to Lord Townsend, 7 July 1778, Pattison, *Papers*, 144–47.
5. Ewald, *Diary*, 137.
6. Peebles, *American War*, 196.
7. Ibid.
8. Kemble, *Journals*, 154; Downman, *Services in America*, 69; Peebles, *American War*, 199.

9. James Pattison to Lord Townsend, 7 July 1778, Pattison, *Papers*, 144–47; Duncan, *Royal Regiment of Artillery*, 322.
10. Bell, MS Diary, 28 June 1778; Loftus Cliffe to unknown, 5 July 1778, Loftus Cliffe Papers, MiU-C.
11. Hunter, *Journal*, 42.
12. The Erskine comment is related in Henry Laurens to Lachlan McIntosh, 23 Aug. 1778, *LDC*, 10:494.
13. Anonymous Officer, 1st Battalion British Grenadiers, to Lord Amherst, [20 July?] 1778, Amherst Papers, PRO WO 34/111, p. 71, microfilm copy at PWacD; Thomas Davies to Lord Amherst, 5 July 1778, ibid., 63–64.
14. William Dansey to his mother, 21 Aug., 16 Nov. 1778, Dansey Papers, DeHi.
15. Peebles, *American War*, 196; Anonymous Officer, 1st Battalion British Grenadiers, to Lord Amherst, [20 July?] 1778, Amherst Papers, PRO WO 34/111, p. 71, microfilm copy at PWacD.
16. William Hale to his parents, 14 July 1778, in Wilkin, *Some British Soldiers*, 263.
17. Clinton, *American Rebellion*, 98.
18. William Hale to his parents, 14 July 1778, in Wilkin, *Some British Soldiers*, 263–65; Peebles, *American War*, 239.
19. "Account of the Late Action in the Jerseys, between Gen. Clinton's and the American Army," *Public Ledger* (London) 19, no. 5797, 12 Sept. 1778.
20. Post, *Personal Recollections*, 123; Willoughby Bertie, Earl of Abington to Lord Harcourt, [July?] 1778, in Harcourt, *Papers*, 272–73.
21. Clayton, "Extracts from the Orderly Book," *PMHB* 25 (1901): 102–103.
22. O'Shaughnessy, *Men Who Lost America*, 222; William Hale to his parents, 14 July 1778, in Wilkin, *Some British Soldiers*, 268.
23. Kemble, *Journals*, 155.
24. William Hale to his parents, 14 July 1778, in Wilkin, *Some British Soldiers*, 268.
25. Anonymous Officer, 1st Battalion British Grenadiers, to Lord Amherst, [20 July?] 1778, Amherst Papers, PRO WO 34/111, p. 71, microfilm copy at PWacD; Kemble, *Journals*, 155.
26. GW to Henry Laurens, 22 July 1778, *PGWde*, RWS, 16:129–30.
27. Andrew O'Shaughnessy thinks that the Royal Navy was "lucky to escape defeat" at New York. *Men Who Lost America*, 222, 347. Brendan Morrissey thinks d'Estaing would have won an engagement with Howe and thus missed an opportunity "to end the war." See *Monmouth Courthouse*, 78.
28. GW to John Parke Custis, c. 4–8 Aug. 1778, *PGWde*, RWS, 16:242.
29. Morrissey, *Monmouth Courthouse*, 78.

Chapter 18

1. Samuel Adams to John Adams, 25 Oct. 1778, S. Adams, *Writings*, 4:79; John Banister to Theodorick Bland, Jr., 6 July 1778, Bland, *Papers*, 1:96.

See also Titus Hosmer to Thomas Mumford, 10 July 1778, *LDC*, 10:249; and Elias Boudinot to Hannah Boudinot, 7 July 1778, ibid., 232.

2. Warren, *Rise, Progress, and Termination of the American Revolution*, 2:96. Some fine historians have agreed. See, for example, Wallace, *Appeal to Arms*, 190.
3. Henry Laurens to John Laurens, 6 July 1778, *LDC*, 10:229.
4. Nathanael Greene to GW, 24 June 1778, *PGWde*, RWS, 15:526.
5. GW to Henry Laurens, 29 June 1778, ibid., 587.
6. GW to Henry Laurens, 1 July 1778, ibid., 16:2–6.
7. John Hancock to Dorothy Hancock, 1 July 1778, *LDC*, 10:216–17; Titus Hosmer to Richard Law, and Hosmer to Thomas Mumford, 6 July 1778, ibid., 226–27. For similar letters, see Elias Boudinot to Hannah Boudinot, 7 July 1778, ibid., 232; John Mathews to Thomas Bee, 7 July 1778, ibid., 234–35; Thomas McKean to William Atlee, 7 July 1778; ibid., 237; Samuel Adams to John Adams, 25 Oct. 1778, in S. Adams, *Writings*, 4:79; and John Banister to Theodorick Bland, Jr., 6 July 1778, Bland, *Papers*, 1:96.
8. *JCC*, 11:673; General Orders, 11 July 1778, *PGWde*, RWS, 16:51.
9. John Laurens to Henry Laurens, 30 June 1778, in *PHL*, 13:543–35.
10. John Laurens to Henry Laurens, 2 July 1778, ibid., 544.
11. Alexander Hamilton to Elias Boudinot, 5 July 1778, *PAH*, 1:513.
12. William Henry Drayton to William Alexander, 5 July 1778, *LDC*, 10:222; Drayton to GW, 5 July 1778, ibid., 223; Anthony Wayne to Richard Peters, 12 July 1778, Anthony Wayne Papers, PHi.
13. *Pennsylvania Packet*, 6 July 1778. The reference to 1776 was to the successful patriot defense of the fort on Sullivan's Island that guarded Charleston (then "Charlestown"), South Carolina. The climactic battle took place on 28 June 1776, also against Henry Clinton (and a British fleet).
14. Samuel Adams to Samuel P. Savage, and James Lovell to Abigail Adams, 3 July 1778, *LDC*, 13:218–20.
15. Boudinot to Hamilton, 8 July 1778, *LDC*, 10:238.
16. James McHenry to George Lux, 30 June 1778, *MAH*, 3:356.
17. William Irvine to John Davis, 30 June 1778, *PMHB*, 2:148; Samuel Shaw to [?], 3 July 1778, in Shaw, *Journals*, 48; Thomas Clark to James Hogg, 6 Sept. 1778, in Ryan, *Salute to Courage*, 134; Dudley Coleman to his wife, 3 July, Dudley Coleman Manuscripts, MHi.
18. Lewis Nicola to Horatio Gates, 3 July 1778, Nicola, "Unpublished Letters," 277; Timothy Pickering to John Pickering, 6 July 1778, Timothy Pickering Papers, MHi; John Sullivan to John Langdon, 7 July 1778, GLC06521, Gilder Lehrman Institute, New York; Horatio Gates to GW, 6 July 1778, *PGWde*, RWS, 16:32.
19. David Salisbury Franks to GW, 4 July 1778, *PGWde*, RWS, 16:21. Brig. Gen. Samuel Patterson of Delaware thought Conway responded to Cadwalader questioning his (Conway's) conduct at the Battle of Germantown. Samuel Patterson to Caesar Rodney, 6 July 1778, in *Washington-Madison Papers Collected and Preserved by James*

Madison, 238. A quite fanciful account of the duel is in Blanchard, *American Military Biography*, 37.

20. Greene quoted in Stern, *David Franks*, 3.
21. Thomas McKean to William Atlee, 7 July 1778, *LDC*, 13:237.
22. Livingston, *Papers*, 2:375–79. Livingston's article was misdated 24 June; it probably came out on 1 July.
23. *Pennsylvania Evening Post*, 4, 6 July 1778; *Pennsylvania Packet*, [?], 16 July, 8 Aug. 1778; *New Jersey Gazette*, 8, 15 July, 12 Aug. 1778; all in *NJA* 2, 2:272–73, 274–79, 285–92, 296–97, 303–306, 333–41, 343–44.
24. Stiles, *Literary Diary*, 282; Reed, *Life of Esther Reed*, 294.
25. Josiah Bartlett to Mary Bartlett, 6 July 1778, *LDC*, 10:225; Titus Hosmer to Richard Law, 6 July 1778, ibid., 226–27. For congressional reactions similar to Bartlett's, see note 7 above.
26. William Gordon to GW, 23 July 1778, *PGWde*, RWS, 16:140; GW to Elizabeth Watkins, 11 July 1778, ibid., 57. Watkins was living in Paramus, New Jersey, after fleeing British-occupied New York.
27. "Reminiscences of Dr. William Read, Arranged from His Notes and Papers," in Gibbes, *Documentary History*, 255.
28. Bloomfield, *Citizen Soldier*, 136–37.
29. John Laurens to Henry Laurens, 30 June 1778, *PHL*, 13:534–35; Alexander Hamilton to Elias Boudinot, 5 July 1778, *PAH*, 1:513; James McHenry to George Lux, 30 June 1778, in McHenry, "Battle of Monmouth," 355–56.
30. Anthony Wayne and Charles Scott to GW, *Lee Papers*, 2:438–40.
31. Charles Lee to Richard Henry Lee, 28 [29?] June 1778, ibid., 430.
32. Lee and GW exchanged five letters on 30 June, three from Lee, two from GW. See *PGWde*, RWS, 16:594–97. The letters between Lee and Washington were presented as evidence at Lee's trial. See *Lee Papers*, vol. 3; and *PLCM*, 113–16.
33. Ramsay, *American Revolution*, 85. See, for example, Aaron Burr, "Orderly Book as Commander of Malcolm's Continental Regiment, 17 June–28 July 1778," 30 June 1778, in Papers of Aaron Burr, ser. 2, Orderly Books & European Journal, microfilm, Reel 12, Library of Virginia, Richmond.
34. Gordon, *Rise, Progress, and Establishment of the Independence of the United States*, 3:151.
35. GW to Joseph Reed, 12 Dec. 1778, *PGWde*, RWS, 18:397.
36. Neagles, *Summer Soldiers*, 41, 52.
37. See, for example, Anthony Walton White to Phillip Schuyler, 16 Sept. 1776, Emmet Collection, Em 9319, NYPL.
38. Charles Lee to GW, 30 June 1778, *PGWde*, RWS, 15:596.
39. Alexander Hamilton to Elias Boudinot, 5 July 1778, *Lee Papers*, 2:471.
40. Wayne to Peters, 12 July 1778, Anthony Wayne Papers, PHi; Wayne to Irvine, 14 July 1778, ibid.; Wayne to Delany, 20 July 1778, ibid.
41. Henry Beekman Livingston to Robert Livingston, 31 [*sic*] June 1778, New Jersey Letters, Acc. 3097, Special Collections and University Archives, NjRV; Nathanael Greene to Jacob Greene, 2 July 1778, *PNG*, 2:451.

42. Samuel Shaw to John Eliot, 3 July 1778, in Shaw, *Journals*, 48–49.
43. The brigadiers were William Smallwood, Enoch Poor, William Woodford, and Jedediah Huntington. The colonels were William Irvine, William Shepard, Heman Swift, Edward Wigglesworth, Israel Angell, Thomas Clarke, Otho Holland Williams, and Christian Febiger. *PLCM*, 1. For background on these officers, see Selesky, *Encyclopedia of the American Revolution*, 1:23, 216, 354, 534, 559–60, 2:922, 1064, 1135, 1274, 1282; and Heitman, *Historical Register of Officers*, 493, 530, 590–91.
44. *PLCM*, 4.
45. Ibid., 238.
46. Alden, *General Charles Lee*, 279; Papas, *Renegade Revolutionary*, 276.
47. Ramsay, *American Revolution*, 85–86.
48. See, for example, Henry Laurens to Rawlins Lowndes, 18 Aug. 1778, *LDC*, 10:478; Gouverneur Morris to George Washington, 26 Oct. 1778, ibid., 11:127; and Laurens to Lowndes, 7 Dec. 1778, ibid., 297.
49. Lee to Rush, 13 Aug. 1778, *Lee Papers*, 3:229; Lee to Burr, Oct. 1778, ibid., 238.
50. Lee to Robert Morris, 3 July 1778, ibid., 2:458.
51. John Penn to Richard Caswell, 15 July 1778, in *LDC*, 10:287–88; Reed to Nathanael Greene, 5 Nov. 1778, *Lee Papers*, 3:250; Washington to Reed, 12 Dec. 1778, ibid., 274.
52. GW to Joseph Reed, 12 Dec. 1778, *PGWde*, RWS, 18:397–98.
53. James McHenry to "his friend in this City" [John Cox in New Brunswick, N.J.?], 1 July 1778, in McHenry, "Battle of Monmouth," 357–58; McHenry to Elias Boudinot, 2 July 1778, Emmet Collection, Em 9284, NYPL.
54. Hamilton to Elias Boudinot, 5 July 1778, in *PAH*, 1:512; John Laurens to Alexander Hamilton, Dec. 1778, *Lee Papers*, 3:273; John Cadwalader to Nathanael Greene, 5 Dec. 1778, ibid., 270; Reed to Greene, 5 Nov. 1778, ibid., 249–50.
55. Charles Lee to Robert Morris, 3 July 1778, *Lee Papers*, 2:457.
56. Reed to Greene, 5 Nov. 1778, ibid., 3:249.
57. Charles Lee to Isaac Collins, 3 July 1778, *New Jersey Gazette*, 8 July 1778, *Lee Papers*, 2:452.
58. Charles Lee to Benjamin Rush, 29 Sept. 1778, ibid., 3:236. See also Charles Lee, "General Lee's Vindication to the Public," *Pennsylvania Packet*, 3 Dec. 1778, ibid., 255–65.
59. Joseph Reed to Nathanael Greene, 5 Nov. 1778, 250.
60. John Cadwalader to Nathanael Greene, 5 Dec. 1778, ibid., 270.
61. *An Impartial History of the War in America between Great Britain and Her Colonies, from Its Commencement to the End of the Year 1779* (London: Printed for R. Faulder, 1780, 565.
62. "A Short History of the Treatment of Major General Conway, Late in the Service of America," *Lee Papers*, 3:265–69; Lee to Horatio Gates, 18 Dec. 1778, ibid., 278.
63. Stryker, *Battle of Monmouth*, 256; Alexander Hamilton and Evan Edwards, "Narrative of a Duel between General Lee and Colonel

Laurens," 24 Dec. 1778, *Lee Papers,* 3:283–85; Baron Steuben to Charles Lee, 2 Dec. 1778, ibid., 253; Alexander Hamilton to Baron Steuben, 19 Dec. 1778, ibid., 254. Ron Chernow thinks Washington may have known of Laurens's challenge to Lee, believing it unlikely Laurens and Hamilton (Laurens's second) would have flagrantly ignored their chief's known disapproval of dueling unless confident the general was going to wink at their conduct. *Washington,* 346. Not provable—but plausible.

64. Charles Lee to Horatio Gates, 18 Dec. 1778, *Lee Papers,* 3:278.
65. Edward Langworthy, *Memoirs of the Late Charles Lee, Esq.* (London: Printed for J. S. Jordan, 1792), 68.
66. Lafayette, "Memoir of 1779," *In the Age of the American Revolution,* 11.
67. John F. Mercer to "Col. Simms," n.d., in Hunt, *Fragments of Revolutionary History,* 29; Hunt, ibid., iv–v, Heitman, *Historical Register of Officers,* 389.
68. J. S. [John Skey] Eustice to "The Philadelphia Editors," [July 1778], *Lee Papers,* 3:348; Heitman, *Historical Register of Officers,* 218.
69. *JCC,* 13:24. GW agreed to accept Oswald's resignation on 14 Oct. 1778. GW to Eleazer Oswald, 14 Oct. 1778, *PGWde,* RWS, 17:377–78. That Oswald was angry is fully evident in his letter of two weeks later. See Oswald to GW, 28 Oct. 1778, ibid., 620–22. Essentially, he objected to being ranked behind Edward Carrington in seniority. General Orders, 15 Sept. 1778, ibid., 1.
70. [Charles Lee], "Some Queries, Political and Military, Humbly Offered to the Consideration of the Public," 6 July 1778, *Maryland Journal and Baltimore Advertiser,* in *Lee Papers,* 3:341–44. The ensuing uproar produced letters admiring and denouncing Lee's "Queries," and on 7 July 1778, a pro-Washington mob threatened Goddard. Goddard then printed a recantation of the decision to publish the "Queries," but when Maryland authorities upheld his right to publish, he recantation his recantation. *Lee Papers,* 3:345–50; Wheeler, *Maryland Press,* chap. 3.
71. Harold Selesky has Oswald resigning in 1779. *Encyclopedia of the American Revolution,* 2:862. Heitman, however, incorrectly has it on 28 June 1778. *Historical Register of Officers,* 421. Oswald lacks a full biography; the most complete treatment being Wheeler, *Maryland Press,* chap. 3.
72. Evans to Lee, 30 Aug. 1778, *Lee Papers,* 3:229.
73. Charles Henry Hart, "Notes and Queries," *PMHB* 36 (1912): 127–28.
74. Lee, "Vindication," *Lee Papers,* 3:265; Charles Lee to Aaron Burr, Oct. 1778, ibid., 238–39; Lomask, *Aaron Burr,* 58; James Monroe to Charles Lee, 15 June 1780, Monroe, *Writings,* 2; Evan Edwards to Charles Lee, 21 Oct. 1781, ibid., 463–64.
75. GW to Joseph Reed, *PGWde,* RWS, 18:397.
76. For a similar view of Washington's qualities as a diplomat-commander, see Higginbotham, *War of American Independence,* 85–88.

Chapter 19

1. For a decidedly different opinion on the military significance of Monmouth—that the battle "marked a turning point in the American War of Independence"—see Bilby and Jenkins, *Monmouth Court House*, 237.
2. Bell, MS Diary, 28 June 1778.
3. "Monmouth, New Jersey," in Selesky, *Encyclopedia of the American Revolution*, 2:733.
4. The only exceptions were the troops of the New Jersey Brigade (which did not engage) and three battalion-sized units: the composite battalion of Virginians that fought at the Point of Woods, Jackson's detachment, and Varnum's Brigade.
5. Lesser, *Sinews of Independence*, 58, 73.
6. John Laurens to Henry Laurens, 28 Feb. 1778, Laurens, *Army Correspondence*, 132–33.
7. Henry Knox to Lucy Knox, 29 June 1778, Henry Knox Papers, Vol. [Reel] 4, Item 116, MHi; Charles Lee to Isaac Collins, 3 July 1778, in *NJA* 2, 2:278; General Orders, 29 June 1778, *PGWde*, RWS, 15:583–84.
8. Greene to George Weedon, 25 July 1778, *PNG*, 2:472.
9. Elizabeth Grey to Lord Shelburne, 22 Aug. 1778, Papers of William Petty, Lord Shelburne, Additional MS 88906/01/016, Folios 16–18, 20, British Library, London. Elizabeth Grey was the wife of Maj. Gen. Charles Grey; she wrote Shelburne quoting from her husband's letter to her.
10. Kemble, *Journals*, 154.
11. William Hale to his parents, 14 July 1778, in Wilkin, *Some British Soldiers*, 263.
12. Samuell Johnson to Lord Amherst, 13 July 1778, Amherst Manuscripts, U1350 079/22, Kent County (U.K.) Archives, copy at PaVfNHP.
13. Spring, *With Zeal and Bayonets Only*, 74–75.
14. Matthew Spring describes the conduct of senior British commanders similarly. Ibid., 71–72.
15. Bruce Chadwick presents Lee as a bungler who had lost control of his command. *George Washington's War*, 303–304. His account of the battle is generally inaccurate and makes no mention of Washington putting Lee in charge of the holding action at the Hedgerow. Ron Chernow drops Lee from the scene entirely after his confrontation with Washington. *Washington*, 342–43. Joseph Bilby and Katherine Jenkins have described Lee's retreat as "the inevitable result of Lee's haphazard battle preparation and lack of terrain knowledge"; but they advanced no explanation of how Lee might have planned any differently given the circumstances of the run-up to the battle. *Monmouth Court House*, 200. As to the matter of "terrain knowledge," Lee had the advice of local guides (e.g., Forman, Rhea, Wykoff, and others), and he clearly understood that the east–west bias of the terrain favored the oncoming British. Most recently, Dominick Mazzagetti has criticized virtually every aspect of Lee's conduct on 28 June, even questioning whether the difficulty in finding guides for his advance early that day was deliberate

and stating that "Lee found himself in the undesirable position of leading an army against a foe he had just recently embraced." *Charles Lee,* 162–72, 175–76.

16. Spring, *With Zeal and Bayonets Only*, 71–72.
17. Lender, "Lee's Advanced Force." Cols. John Durkee (Connecticut), Joseph Cilley (New Hampshire), Richard Butler (Pennsylvania), and Elias Dayton (New Jersey) had served in the French and Indian War. Selesky, *Encyclopedia of the American Revolution,* 1:139, 301; Johnston, *Record of Connecticut Men*, 182.
18. General Orders, 22 Dec. 1777, *PGWde*, RWS, 12:663.
19. "A Plan for the Formation of the American Army in the least Expensive Manner possible . . . ," *Lee Papers*, 2:384; Spencer Pension Application, 29 Sept. 1820, Microfilm 27, Reel 2255, PWacD.
20. Garson, *Light-Horse Harry*, 61.
21. Wayne to Henry Lee, 20 July 1778, Anthony Wayne Papers, PHi.
22. Wright, "'Nor Is Their Standing Army to Be Despised,'" 64.
23. *Lee Papers*, vol. 3; *PLCM*, 228 (Lee).
24. William Maxwell to the New Jersey Legislature, 9 Nov. 1778, Charles Clark Papers, 1777–1815, Acc. 645, Special Collections and University Archives, NjRV; James Chambers, Orderly Books, 1778–80, 5 Aug. 1778, PHi.
25. Lender, "Logistics and American Victory," 108–10.
26. Garry Wheeler Stone, "Sheriff Joseph Ellis, Colonel-Commandant, South Jersey Militia," 14 Feb. 2014, Indian King Tavern State Historic Site, typescript. Gloucester County then spanned the state; it no longer reaches to the Atlantic.
27. Munn, *Battles and Skirmishes*, 52.
28. Samuel Adams to Sally Adams, 19–20 July 1778, Sol Feinstone Collection, PWacD.
29. Selesky, *Encyclopedia of the American Revolution*, 1:640. The deserters were from Pulaski's command, Hessians who had gone over to the Americans but now wanted to return to the British.
30. Adelberg, *Revolution in Monmouth County*, 20.
31. William Tallman Pension Application, W.1510, DNA; Benjamin Van Cleave Pension Application, W.6354, ibid.
32. On the Black Brigade, Refugeetown, and Tye, see Slater, *History of Monmouth County*, 121–22; Hodges, *Slavery and Freedom*, 96–99; and Adelberg, *American Revolution in Monmouth County*, 75, 84–89.
33. Philemon Dickinson to GW, 29 June 1778, *PGWde*, RWS, 15:584.
34. Mark Edward Lender, "New Jersey, Mobilization," in Selesky, *Encyclopedia of the American Revolution*, 2:802–808.
35. Washington to Dickinson, 25 June 1778, *PGWde*, RWS, 15:536–37.
36. Shy, "American Revolution," 121–56.
37. James Abeel to Nathanael Greene, 25 June 1778, *PNG*, 2:449; André, *Journal*, 76.
38. On the Springfield campaign, see Fleming, *Forgotten Victory.*
39. Ewald, *Diary*, 244–45.

40. Ferling, *Ascent of George Washington.*
41. This last paragraph is adapted from Mark Edward Lender, "The Politics of Battle: Washington, the Army, and the Monmouth Campaign," in Lengel, *Companion to George Washington*, 243–44.

Epilogue

Epigraph. Thomas Ward, "Our Gallant State," in Armstrong, *Patriotic Poems of New Jersey*, 1.

1. J. Stryker, *Oration, Delivered at Woodbridge*, 15–16.
2. Cumming, *Oration, Delivered at Newark*, 15, 17; [Westcott], *Address Delivered to the Inhabitants of the township of Fairfield*, 12.
3. S. M. Schenck, [Schenck] Family Notes, Bk. 3, 1890s, NjFrHi, 66–67, typescript. This account was transcribed verbatim from the *Johnston (N.Y.) Republican*, 1835. According to the family notes, it was reprinted in the *New York Tribune* around 10 January 1844.
4. J. Stryker, *Oration, Delivered at Woodbridge*, 12.
5. Custis, *Recollections and Private Memoirs of Washington*, 222–23.
6. Ibid., 219.
7. Ibid., 218–19. In a footnote Custis actually contradicts himself, noting that Washington allowed Lee to remain forward to fight a holding action. Ibid., 219n.
8. Irving, *Works of Washington Irving. Life of George Washington*, 3:178, 182–83; Bancroft, *History of the United States*, 130–32.
9. Brown, *Battle of Monmouth*, 59–71; Armstrong, *Battles in the Jersies*, 7, 18.
10. Royster, "'Nature of Treason,'" 163–93.
11. This observation is supported only by a *very* unscientific survey: A Google search (28 March 2014) of "Major General Charles Lee Traitor" produced 106,000 hits; in comparison, a search of "Major General Benedict Arnold Traitor" produced only 50,600. But given the literary efforts of Bancroft, Irving, Custis, Benson J. Lossing, and a host of other authors, the Google results are not surprising. The line of poetry is from Will Carleton, "The Longest Battle," in Armstrong, *Patriotic Poems of New Jersey*, 77.
12. Rail service began on 18 July1853. Helme, "Jamesburg & Helmetta Post Offices," 93.
13. "Local Affairs, Notes from the Field of Monmouth," *New Jersey Mirror* (Mount Holly), 5 Nov. 1874; Joseph J. Ely, "The Battle Ground," *Hightstown (N.J.) Gazette*, 24 Jan. 1878, reference courtesy John Orr.
14. Bilby and Jenkins, *Monmouth Court House*, 249.
15. S. S. Forman to the editors, 12 June 1854, *Monmouth Democrat* (Freehold, N.J.), 6 July 1854; "An Interesting Theory," *Trenton State Gazette*, 24 May 1879; "Old Times in Monmouth," *Monmouth Democrat*, 15 Aug.1878, reprinted in Gilman, *Monmouth Road to Glory*, book 3:9.
16. The next known reenactment was an 1844 crossing of the Delaware River in commemoration of Washington's crossing in 1776. Osborne, *Where Washington Once Led*, 74.

17. Revolutionary Officer, "For the True American," *True American* (Trenton, N.J.), 12 July 1828.
18. "Celebration of the Battle of Monmouth," *New York Herald*, 30 June 1854, reprinted in *Monmouth Democrat* (Freehold, N.J.), 6 July 1854; Eliza Smith to Sarah Waln, June 1854, in "Letters from Eliza Smith to Sarah Waln, Jr.," Monmouth County Board of Recreation Commissioners, Lincroft, typescript, 53–54 (also in Battle of Monmouth Collection, NjFrHi).
19. "Celebration of the Battle of Monmouth," *New York Tribune*, 29 June 1854, reprinted in *Monmouth Democrat* (Freehold, N.J.), 6 July 1854.
20. Eliza Smith to Sarah Waln, 6 July 1854, in "Letters from Eliza Smith to Sarah Waln, Jr.," 56.
21. "Celebration of the Battle of Monmouth," *New York Daily Times*, 29 June 1854, reprinted in the *Monmouth Democrat* (Freehold, N.J.), 6 July 1854.
22. "Local Affairs, Notes from the Field of Monmouth," *New Jersey Mirror* (Mount Holly), 5 Nov. 1874. For virtually all sources touching on the Molly Pitcher legend, see Martin, *Molly Pitcher Sourcebook*. Our account has generally followed Martin's sensible conclusions on the identity of "Molly Pitcher." A popular New Jersey version of the legend appeared in 1896 in Stockton, *Stories of New Jersey*, 186–92. Stockton, who drew on earlier nineteenth-century sources, had a vivid imagination when it came to Molly. She "was born with the soul of a soldier," he assured his readers, and when she took her dead husband's place at the cannon, "her eyes flashed with fire." After the battle Stockton had Molly presented to Major General Greene, who in turn took her to Washington, who made her a sergeant and had her formally review the troops. Schoolboy stuff, indeed, but widely popular.
23. Carleton, "Longest Battle," in Armstrong, *Patriotic Poems of New Jersey*, 76. For another example, see New Jersey Farmer, "The Retreat of the British Army," ibid., 66: "On Monmouth's plains where Lee in duty failed." The Armstrong compilation has eight Monmouth poems, most first published in the nineteenth century. For verse of similar character, see Platt, *Ballads of New Jersey in the Revolution*, 60. Monmouth was only typical as a subject for patriotic poets. For similar treatment of the Saratoga campaign, see Stone, *Ballads and Poems Relating to the Burgoyne Campaign*.
24. Martin and Lender explain the rise and persistence of the yeoman farmer myth at the expense of the Continental regulars. See *Respectable Army*, chap. 6.
25. Carleton, "Longest Battle," in Armstrong, *Patriotic Poems of New Jersey*, 66. For similar verse, see ibid., 66–87.
26. Crane, *Oration Delivered in the Presbyterian Church, at Elizabeth-Town*, 10–13.
27. J. Stryker, *Oration, Delivered at Woodbridge*, 15–16; Macwhorter, *Festive Discourse*, 13. For a similar view, see Dow, *Discourse*, 16: "It pleased God, at this period, to awaken generally in the breasts of our

citizens a spirit of pure patriotism, a glowing ardour for liberty." There were exceptions that did mention the Continentals, especially orations before the Society of the Cincinnati, composed, of course, of former Continental officers. See, for example, Boudinot, *Oration, Delivered at Elizabeth-Town.* Boudinot himself had held a Continental commission.

28. "Celebration of the Battle of Monmouth," *New York Herald*, 30 June 1854, reprinted in *Monmouth Democrat* (Freehold, N.J.), 6 July 1854. The article's only reference to the Continentals came in praise of the fighting of Wayne and the usual denunciation of Lee.
29. Bilby and Jenkins, *Monmouth Court House*, 250–52. For full details on the construction and subsequent preservation of the battle monument, see "Gov. Parker's Call Leads to Monument's Creation," WelcomeToFreehold.com, accessed 8 Apr. 2014, http://freeholdnj.homestead.com/monument.html.
30. Bilby and Jenkins, *Monmouth Court House*, 254–56.
31. The struggle to preserve the battlefield and establish a state park is related admirably in ibid., 256–60.
32. To gauge the distance the modern state-park interpretation has come from the old victory narrative, see the elaborate brochure prepared for the celebration of the 225th anniversary of the battle, [MBSP], *June 28, 1778, Battle of Monmouth: 225th Anniversary, Battlefield State Park, June 28–29, 2003* (2003).

Appendix B

1. Gist was commissioned colonel of Gist's Additional Continental Regiment in January 1777, but the regiment's three companies probably never took the field as a battalion. Heitman, *Historical Register of Officers*, 249; Wright, *Continental Army*, 321–22, 325.
2. Tunis Hoagland Pension Application, S1023, *Index of Revolutionary War Pension Applications in the National Archives*.
3. Hunterdon Horse served as "Lifeguards" to Major General Dickinson. Pension file of Elisha Jewell, Invalid 13,533, DNA.
4. On 28 June served as infantry with 1st Burlington. Pension file of Jabesh Ashmore, Widow 5647, DNA.
5. Silvanus Seeley Diaries, 12 May 1768–17 March 1821, NjMoHP.
6. William Stryker has Neilson listed as brigadier general as of 21 February 1777. *Official Register*, 350.
7. At the Manalapan Bridge muster, only three colonels were in the brigade. It is not clear whether Henry Bicker (2nd Pennsylvania) or George Nagel (10th Pennsylvania) was absent.
8. Apparently present at Monmouth, though subsequently unwell. Frazer, *General Persifor Frazer*, 185.
9. Probably absent, as the brigade had only two colonels present at Manalapan Bridge.
10. The Manalapan field return lists no colonels and only three lieutenant colonels present, but Craig and Spencer are known to have taken part in the battle.

11. Brig. Gen. John Glover was commanding at West Point. The colonel commanding the brigade on 28 June is unknown. Billias, *General John Glover*, 161.
12. The initial commander, Col. James Wesson (9th Massachusetts), was wounded at Monmouth Court House. His second, Lt. Col. Nathaniel Ramsey (3rd Maryland), was captured at the Point of Woods.
13. Joseph Lummis Pension Application, S41784, RWPBLW.
14. Jackson's, Henley's, and Lee's regiments were formally reconstituted as one regiment on 22 April 1779.

Appendix C

1. "State of the Forces under . . . Sir Henry Clinton, 3 July 1778," PRO CO, p. 77, DLC; "Return of the Number of Men, Wagoners, Women & Children victualled at Monmouth the 27 & 28th June 1778 inclusive," Sir Henry Clinton Papers, vol. 36, no. 5, MiU-C. Other sources include *A List of All the Officers in the Army* (London: War Office, 30 June 1780); The On-Line Institute for Advanced Loyalist Studies, www.royalprovincial.com; muster rolls, PRO WO 12; and Baule and Gilbert, *British Army Officers.*
2. This was the number of permitted women—the other women of the army were to go on the shipping to New York City. Yet entries in the British orderly books make it clear that many women left the shipping and followed the army on its march. See Kemble, *Journals*, 595–96, 598.
3. Grant commanded the 2nd Brigade, but he may have been acting commander of the 1st Brigade on 28 June. PRO WO 12/6471, p. 120. When Lt. F. Champagne wrote a report on taking an order from Clinton to Knyphausen, he described communicating the "Substance to Major Genl Grant at the Head of the British as I passed along." Lt. F. Champagne to Lord Rawdon, 29 June 1778, PaVfNHP, original in the Clinton Papers, MiU-C.
4. Simcoe, *Operations of the Queen's Rangers*, 72.

Bibliography

The literature on the Battle of Monmouth is vast. This bibliography is by no means a complete record of all the works and sources consulted, only those actually cited in *Fatal Sunday*. Over the course of our research, we visited a large number of manuscript and rare-book repositories, but we also relied on the assistance of library staff members and other scholars who were kind enough to secure copies of documents for us. They have our deepest gratitude, and collections they visited in our behalf are marked with an asterisk [*]. Other sources are contained in various bibliographical compilations we have deposited in the files of the Monmouth Battlefield State Park, Freehold, New Jersey.

Manuscript Collections

Samuel Adams Papers, 1758–1819. Manuscript Collection 19, Manuscripts and Archives Division, New York Public Library, New York.

André, John. *Map of Mount Holly*. Map bound in manuscript journal. Henry E. Huntington Library, San Marino, Calif. Microfilm, David Library of the American Revolution, Washington Crossing, Pa.

Journal of John André, 1777–78. Henry E. Huntington Library, San Marino, Calif.*

Andrews, John. Memorandum, His Surveying Book/Likewise, Painting [Upper Freehold Township, N.J.]. Private collection, courtesy C. Andrew Beagle, South Plainfield, N.J.

"The Journal of Enos Barnes, Sergeant in Capt. Joseph Wright's Company, Fifth Connecticut Regiment." Morristown National Historical Park Library, Morristown, N.J. Transcribed by James L. Kochan, 1991, while on loan from Kim Chysler.

Battle of Monmouth Collection. Monmouth County Historical Association, Freehold, N.J.

Andrew Bell Papers. New Jersey Historical Society, Newark.

Bland-Ruffin Papers. Special Collections, University of Virginia.

Boudinot Collection. Princeton University, Princeton, N.J.

[Bucks County Historical] Society Manuscript Collection. Bucks County Historical Society, Doylestown, Pa.

Papers of Aaron Burr. Microfilm, ser. 2, Orderly Books & Journals. Library of Virginia, Richmond.

Michel Capitaine du Chesnoy. *Carte de l'affaire de Monmouth: ou le G'al Washington commandon l'armée americaine et le G'l Clinton l'armée angloise le 28 Juin 1778*. G3812.M6453 1778 .C3. Geography and Map Division, Library of Congress, Washington, D.C.

Diary of Jonathan Clark, 1777–78. New Jersey Historical Society, Newark.
Loftus Cliffe Papers. William L. Clements Library, University of Michigan, Ann Arbor.*
Henry Clinton Papers. William L. Clements Library, University of Michigan, Ann Arbor.
Dudley Coleman Manuscripts. Massachusetts Historical Society, Boston.
Papers of the Continental Congress, 1774–89. Microfilm edition, National Archives, Washington, D.C.
Cunninghame of Thortoun Papers. Scottish Records Office, Edinburgh.*
Damage Claims, 1776–82. Microfilm, New Jersey State Archives, Trenton.
Dansey Papers. Historical Society of Delaware, Wilmington.
Elias Dayton Papers. New Jersey Historical Society, Newark.
Ferdinand J. Dreer Collection. Soldiers of the Revolution Series. Historical Society of Pennsylvania, Philadelphia.
Elizabeth Sandwith Drinker Diaries, 1758–1807. Collection 1760. Historical Society of Pennsylvania, Philadelphia.
Early American Orderly Books Collection. Microfilm, New-York Historical Society, New York.
Emmet Collection. New York Public Library, New York.
Ely Collection. New Jersey Historical Society, Newark.
Sol Feinstone Collection. David Library of the American Revolution, Washington Crossing, Pa.
Fellows Papers. Department of Rare Books and Special Collections, Rush Rhees Library, University of Rochester, Rochester, N.Y.*
Peter Force Collection. Manuscripts Division, Library of Congress, Washington, D.C.
Horatio Gates Papers. New-York Historical Society, New York.
Gilder Lehrman Collection. Gilder Lehrman Institute, New York.*
Gratz Collection. Historical Society of Pennsylvania, Philadelphia.
Charles Grey to Lord Shelburne, 15 June 1778. British Library, London.*
Griffith Letters. Miscellaneous Manuscripts Collection, Monmouth County Historical Association, Freehold, N.J.
Haskell Collection. Monmouth County Historical Association, Freehold, N.J.
Haugessegger Orderly Books. Historical Society of Pennsylvania, Philadelphia.
William Irvine Papers. Historical Society of Pennsylvania, Philadelphia.
Henry Knox Papers. Massachusetts Historical Society, Boston.*
Larned Family Papers. Collection 1695, Historical Society of Pennsylvania, Philadelphia.
Lee Family Papers. Virginia Historical Society, Richmond.
George Bolling Lee Papers. Virginia Historical Society, Richmond.
Lidgerwood Collection of Hessian Transcripts of the American Revolution. Morristown National Historical Park, Morristown, N.J.
James McHenry Papers. William L. Clements Library, University of Michigan, Ann Arbor.*
Allen McLane Papers. New-York Historical Society, New York.
Monmouth County Deeds. Office of the County Clerk, Freehold, N.J.

Montgomery County Historical Department, Fonda, N.Y.
National Archives of Great Britain (Public Records Office), London: Colonial Office 5, vol. 96; War Office 4, American Letter Books; War Office 4, Out Letters; War Office 34, Amherst Papers.*
Neilson Papers. Special Collections and University Archives, Rutgers University Libraries, New Brunswick, N.J.
Newbold-Irvine Collection. Historical Society of Pennsylvania, Philadelphia.
Newcastle Collection. NeC 2645. Nottingham University Library, Nottingham, U.K.*
New Jersey Letters. Special Collections and University Archives, Rutgers University Libraries, New Brunswick, N.J.
[New Jersey] Manuscripts, 1680s–1970s. New Jersey State Archives, Trenton.
[New Jersey] Numbered Miscellaneous Revolutionary War Manuscripts. Department of Defense, Adjutant General, New Jersey State Archives, Trenton.
[New Jersey] Township Ratables. New Jersey State Archives, Trenton.
New York State Revolutionary War Manuscripts. New York State Library, Albany.*
Park Collection. Morristown National Historical Park, Morristown, N.J.
Papers of William Petty, Lord Shelburne. British Library, London.*
James Pattison Papers. Royal Artillery Institution, Woolwich, London.*
Timothy Pickering Papers. Massachusetts Historical Society, Boston.
Joseph Reed Papers. New-York Historical Society, New York.
Revolutionary War Pension and Bounty-Land-Warrant Application Files. National Archives, Washington, D.C.
Revolutionary War Records, War Department. Record Group 93. National Archives, Washington, D.C.
Rosenbach Museum and Library, Philadelphia.*
[Schenck] Family Notes. Monmouth County Historical Association, Freehold, N.J.
Silvanus Seeley Diaries, 12 May 1768–17 March 1821. E275 A3S4, in 30 parts. Morristown National Historical Park, Morristown, N.J.
Seventh Regiment of Foot, Orderly Book, 1778. Historical Society of Pennsylvania, Philadelphia.
Israel Shreve Papers. Buxton Special Collections, Louisiana Technical University, Ruston.*
Israel Shreve Papers. Special Collections and University Archives, Rutgers University Libraries, New Brunswick, N.J.
Israel Shreve Revolutionary War Letters, 1768–1894. Special Collections, University of Houston, Houston, Tex.*
John Graves Simcoe Papers, 1774–1824. William L. Clements Library, University of Michigan, Ann Arbor*
Society Collection. Historical Society of Pennsylvania, Philadelphia.
Timothy Sullivan Journal, 1775–78. Collection 1098, Historical Society of Pennsylvania, Philadelphia. Typescript of original in American Philosophical Society, Philadelphia.*

Bernardus Swartwout Papers. New-York Historical Society, New York.
Van Cleave, Benjamin. "Autobiography of Benjamin Van Cleave." Microfilm MMS50. New-York Historical Society, New York.
George Washington Papers. Manuscripts Division, Library of Congress, Washington, D.C.
Anthony Wayne Papers. Historical Society of Pennsylvania, Philadelphia.
Jacob Weiss Papers. Historical Society of Pennsylvania, Philadelphia.
Gen. Otho H. Williams Papers. Maryland Historical Society, Baltimore.

Memoirs, Published Papers, and Related Items

Adams, John. *Diary and Autobiography of John Adams*. Edited by L. H. Butterfield et al. 4 vols. New York: Atheneum, 1964.
Adams, Samuel. *The Writings of Samuel Adams*. Edited by Harry Alonzo Cushing. 4 vols. New York: G. P. Putnam's Sons, 1907.
Alexander, William [Lord Stirling]. "Letters of William Alexander, Lord Sterling." *Proceedings of the New Jersey Historical Society* 60, no. 3 (1942): 173–76.
André, John. *Major André's Journal: Operations of the British Army . . . June 1777 to November 1778*. Edited by Henry Cabot Lodge. 1903. Reprint, New York: Arno, 1968.
Archives of the State of New Jersey. *Documents Relating to the Colonial History of the State of New Jersey*. 33 vols. Newark, 1880–1928.
Archives of the State of New Jersey. *Documents Relating to the Revolutionary History of the State of New Jersey*. 2nd ser., 5 vols. Trenton, 1901–1907.
Balderstone, Marion, and David Syrett, eds. *The Lost War: Letters from British Officers during the American Revolution*. New York: Horizon, 1975.
Baurmeister, Carl Leopold. *Revolution in America: Confidential Letters and Journals, 1776–1784, of Adjutant General Major Baurmeister of the Hessian Forces*. Translated and edited by Bernard A. Uhlendorf. New Brunswick, N.J.: Rutgers University Press, 1957.
Beatty, William. "Correspondence of Captain William Beatty, of the Maryland Line, 1776–1781." *Historical Magazine*, 2nd ser., 1, no. 3 (March 1867): 147–49.
———. "Journal of Capt. William Beatty, 1776–1781." *Maryland Historical Magazine* 3, no. 2 (1908): 104–13.
Bell, Andrew. "Copy of a Journal kept during a March through New-Jersey, in June 1778." *Proceedings of the New Jersey Historical Society* 6 (1851–53): 15–19.
Bland, Theodorick. *The Bland Papers: Being a Selection from the Manuscripts of Colonel Theodorick Bland, Jr.; To Which Are Prefixed an Introduction, and a Memoir of Colonel Bland*. Edited by Charles Campbell. Petersburg, Va.: Edmund & Julian C. Ruffin, 1840.
Bloomfield, Joseph. *Citizen Soldier: The Revolutionary War Journal of Joseph Bloomfield*. Edited by Mark E. Lender and James Kirby Martin. Newark: New Jersey Historical Society, 1982.

Boudinot, Elias. *Journal or Historical Recollections of American Events during the Revolutionary War.* Philadelphia: F. Bourquin, 1894.

Brackenridge, H. H., ed. "The Cave of Vanhest." *United States Magazine: A Repository of History, Politics, and Literature* (Philadelphia), (March 1779): 206; (April 1779): 110–11; (May 1779): 213; (June 1779): 150–51.

Brigham, Paul. "A Revolutionary Diary of Captain Paul Brigham." Edited by Edward A. Hoyt. *Vermont History* 34 (1966): 3–30.

Burgoyne, John. *Political and Military Episodes in the latter Half of the Eighteenth Century Derived from the Life and Correspondence of the Right Hon. John Burgoyne, General, Statesman, Dramatist.* Edited by Edward Barrington De Fonblanque. London: Macmillan, 1876.

Clark, John, Jr. "Letters from Major John Clark, Jr., to General Washington during the Occupation of Philadelphia by the British Army." *Bulletin of the Historical Society of Pennsylvania* 1 (1845–47): 1–36.

Clark, Joseph. "Dairy of Joseph Clark." *New Jersey Historical Society Proceedings* 7 (1853–55): 95–110.

Clayton, Robert. "Extracts from the Orderly Book of Major Robert Clayton, of the Seventeenth Regiment of British Foot, 1778." *Pennsylvania Magazine of History and Biography* 25 (1901): 100–103.

Clinton, Henry. *The American Rebellion: Sir Henry Clinton's Narrative of His Campaigns, 1775–1782, with an Appendix of Original Documents.* Edited by William B. Willcox. New Haven, Conn.: Yale University Press, 1954.

Continental Congress. *Journals of the Continental Congress, 1774–1789.* Edited by Worthington C. Ford et al. 34 vols. Washington, D.C.: Government Printing Office, 1904–37.

Croker, Wilson. *The Croker Papers: The Correspondence and Diaries of the Late Right Honourable John Wilson Croker, LL.Dm F.R.S, Secretary of the Admiralty from 1809 to 1830.* Edited by Louis J. Jennings. Vol. 3. New York: C. Scribner's Sons, 1884.

Dann, John C., ed. *The Revolution Remembered: Eyewitness Accounts of the War for Independence.* Chicago: University of Chicago Press, 1980.

Davies, Kenneth Gordon, ed. *Documents of the American Revolution, 1770–1783.* 21 vols. Dublin: Irish University Press, 1972–81.

Dearborn, Henry. *Revolutionary War Journals of Henry Dearborn, 1775–1783.* Edited by Lloyd A. Brown and Howard H. Peckham. Chicago: Caxton Club, 1939.

Dorman, John Frederick, abstr. & comp. *Virginia Revolutionary War Pension Applications.* 51 vols. Washington, D.C.; Falmouth, Va.; Fredericksburg, Va.: n.p., 1958–95.

Downman, Frances. *The Services of Lieut.-Colonel Francis Downman, R.A., in France, North America, and the West Indies, between the Years 1758 and 1784.* Edited by F. A. Whinyates., Woolwich, U.K.: Royal Artillery Institution, 1898.

Ewald, Johann. *Diary of the American War: A Hessian Journal.* Translated and edited by Joseph P. Tustin. New Haven, Conn.: Yale University Press, 1979.

Feilitzsch, Heinrich Carl Philipp von, and Christian Friedrich Bartholomai. *Diaries of Two Ansbach Jaegers: Lieutenant Heinrich Carl Philipp von Feilitzsch and Lieutenant Christian Friedrich Bartholomai.* Translated and edited by Bruce E. Burgoyne. Bowie, Md.: Heritage Books, 1997.

Finney, Walter. "Old Tennent Church, N.J., and the Battle of Monmouth: Captain Finney's Diary." *Journal of the Presbyterian Historical Society* 14 (1930–31): 264–66.

Fisher, Elijah. "Elijah Fisher's Journal While in the War for Independence and Continued Two Years after He Came to Maine, 1775–1784." Edited by William B. Lapham. *Magazine of History, with Notes and Queries* 2, extra no. 6 (1909): 275–92.

Force, Peter, and M. St. Clair, eds. *American Archives: Consisting of a Collection of Authentick Records, State Papers, Debates, and Letters and Other Notices of Publick Affairs, the Whole Forming a Documentary History of the Origin and Progress of the North American Colonies.* 5th ser., 9 vols. Washington, D.C.: M. St. Clair Clarke and Peter Force, 1837–53.

Frazer, Persifor. *General Persifor Frazer: A Memoir Compiled Principally from His Own Papers.* Philadelphia: privately printed, 1907.

Gibbes, R. W., ed. *Documentary History of the American Revolution.* New York: D. Appleton, 1857.

Greene, Nathanael. *The Papers of Nathanael Greene.* Edited by Richard K. Showman, Robert E. McCarthy, and Margaret Cobb. Vol. 2, *1 January–16 October 1778.* Chapel Hill: University of North Carolina Press, 1980.

Greenman, Jeremiah. *Diary of a Common Soldier in the American Revolution, 1775–1783.* Edited by Robert C. Bray and Paul E. Bushnell. Dekalb: Northern Illinois University Press, 1978.

Hamilton, Alexander. "Eulogium on Major-General Greene." In *The Works of Alexander Hamilton,* edited by Henry Cabot Lodge, 8:63–82. Federal ed. New York: G. P. Putnam's Sons, 1904.

———. *The Papers of Alexander Hamilton.* Edited by Harold C. Syrett and Jacob E. Cooke. 27 vols. New York: Columbia University Press, 1961–87.

Hamilton, Alexander, and William Irvine. "The Battle of Monmouth: Letters of Alexander Hamilton and General William Irvine, Describing the Engagement." *Pennsylvania Magazine of History and Biography* 2 (1878): 139–48, 466.

Harcourt, Edward William, ed. *The Harcourt Papers.* Vol. 8. Oxford, U.K.: James Parker, [1880].

Hunt, Gaillard, ed. *Fragments of Revolutionary History.* Brooklyn, N.Y.: Historical Printing Club, 1892.

Hunter, Martin. *The Journal of Gen. Sir Martin Hunter, G.C.M.G., G.C.N., and Some Letters of His Wife, Lady Hunter Put Together by Their Daughter, Miss A. Hunter, and by Their Dear Friend, Miss Bell, and Caused to be Printed by Their Grandson, James Hunter.* Edinburgh, U.K.: Edinburgh Press, 1894.

Huntington, Jedediah. "Battle Letter." Edited by John F. Reed. *Manuscripts* 29 (1977), 201–202.

Inman, George. "Battles of Bunker Hill and Monmouth." *Pennsylvania Magazine of History and Biography* 44 (1920): 92–93.

———. "George Inman's Narrative of the Revolution." *Pennsylvania Magazine of History and Biography* 7 (1883): 237–48.

Kemble, Stephen. *Journals of Lieut. Col. Stephen Kemble, 1773–1789; and British Army Orders: Gen. Sir William Howe, 1775–1778; Gen. Sir Henry Clinton, 1778; and Gen. Daniel Jones, 1778*. Boston: Greg, 1972.

Krafft, John Charles Philip von. *Journal of Lieutenant John Charles Philip von Kraft*. 1883. Reprint, New York: Arno, 1968.

Lafayette, Marie Joseph Paul, marquis de. *Lafayette in the Age of the American Revolution: Selected Letters and Papers, 1776–1790*. Edited by Stanley J. Idzerda, Roger E. Smith, Linda J. Pike, and Mary Ann Quinn. Vol. 2, *April 10, 1778–March 20, 1780*. Ithaca, N.Y.: Cornell University Press, 1979.

———. *Memoirs: Correspondence and Manuscripts of General Lafayette, Published by His Family*. London: Saunders and Otley, 1837.

Laurens, Henry. *The Papers of Henry Laurens*. Edited by David R. Chesnutt and C. James Taylor. 16 vols. Columbia: University of South Carolina Press, 1968–2002.

Laurens, John. *The Army Correspondence of Colonel John Laurens in the Years 1777–8: Now First Printed from Original Letters to His Father, Henry Laurens, President of Congress; with a Memoir by Wm. Gilmore Simms*. Edited by W. M. Gilmore Simms. New York: Bradford Club, 1867.

Lee, Charles. *Anecdotes of the Late Charles Lee, Esq . . . Second in Command in the Service of the United States of America, during the Revolution*. 1792. 2nd ed. Edited by Edward Langworthy. London: printed for S. Jordan, 1797.

———. *The Lee Papers, 1754–1811*. 4 vols. Collections of the New-York Historical Society. New York: New-York Historical Society, 1871–74.

———, defendant. *Proceedings of a General Court Martial, Held at Brunswick, in the State of New Jersey, by Order of His Excellency General Washington . . . for the Trial of Major General Lee, July 4th, 1778. Major General Lord Stirling, President*. Philadelphia: printed by John Dunlap, 1778.

———, defendant. *Proceedings of a General Court Martial, Held at Brunswick, in the State of New Jersey, by Order of his Excellency General Washington . . . for the Rrial of Major General Lee. July 4th, 1778. Major General Lord Stirling, President*. Cooperstown, N.Y.: printed by J. H. Prentiss, 1823.

———, defendant. *Proceedings of a General Court Martial, Held at Brunswick, in the State of New Jersey, by Order of His Excellency Gen. Washington . . . for the Trial of Major-General Lee. July 4th, 1778. Major-General Lord Stirling, President*. New York: privately printed, 1864.

Lee, Henry. *Memoirs of the War in the Southern Department of the United States*. 2 vols. Philadelphia: Bradford and Inskeep, 1812.

Lesser, Charles H., ed. *The Sinews of Independence: Monthly Strength Reports of the Continental Army*. Chicago: University of Chicago Press, 1976.

Livingston, William. *The Papers of William Livingston*. Edited by Carl E. Prince and Dennis P. Ryan. 4 vols. Trenton: New Jersey Historical Commission, 1979–88.

Martin, Joseph Plumb. *Private Yankee Doodle, Being a Narrative of Some of the Adventures, Dangers, and Sufferings of a Revolutionary Soldier*. Edited by George F. Scheer. Boston: Little, Brown, 1962.

[Martin, Joseph Plumb]. *A Narrative of Some of the Adventures, Dangers, and Sufferings of a Revolutionary Soldier, Interspersed with Anecdotes of Incidents that Occurred within His Own Observations, Written by Himself*. Hallowell, Maine: published anonymously; printed by Glazier, Masters, 1830.

Massie, Thomas. "Pension Declaration of Major Thomas Massie." *Virginia Magazine of History and Biography* 21, no. 2 (1913): 188.

McHenry, James. "The Battle of Monmouth." *Magazine of American History* 3 (1879): 355–63.

———. *Journal of a March, a Battle, and Waterfall, Being the Version Elaborated by James McHenry from His Diary of the Year 1778*. [Greenwich, Conn.]: privately printed, 1945.

Monroe, James. *The Writings of James Monroe: Including a Collection of His Public and Private Papers and Correspondence Now for the First Time Printed*. Edited by Stanislaus Murray Hamilton. Vol. 1. New York: G. P. Putnam's Sons, 1898.

Montresor, John. *The Montresor Journals*. Collections of the New-York Historical Society for the Year 1882. Edited by G. D. Scull. New York: New-York Historical Society, 1882.

Morgan, William James, ed. *Naval Documents of the American Revolution*. Vol. 9. Washington, D.C.: Naval Historical Center, Department of the Navy, 1986.

Morris, Robert. "Letters of Chief Justice Morris, 1777–'79." *Proceedings of the New Jersey Historical Society* 38 (1920): 168–78.

[Morton, Jacob]. "Washington at Monmouth—The Testimony of an Eye-Witness." *Daughters of the American Revolution Magazine* 16 (1900): 1189–92.

Muenchhausen, Friedrich Ernst von. *At General Howe's Side, 1776–1778: The Diary of General William Howe's Aide de Camp, Captain Friedrich von Muenchhausen*. Translated by Ernst Kipping. Edited by Samuel Stelle Smith. Monmouth Beach, N.J.: Philip Freneau, 1974.

Nicola, Lewis. "Unpublished Letters of Colonel Nicola, Revolutionary Soldier." Edited by Howard R. Marrano. *Pennsylvania History* 12, no. 4 (1946): 274–78.

"Notes on the Battle of Monmouth." *Pennsylvania Magazine of History and Biography* 14 (1890): 46–49.

An Officer [Thomas Anburey]. *Travels through the Interior Parts of America, in a Series of Letters*. 2 vols. London: William Lane, 1789.

Ogden, Aaron. *Autobiography of Col. Aaron Ogden, of Elizabethtown*. Paterson, N.J.: Press Printing & Publishing, 1893.

Pattison, James. *The James Pattison Papers, 1777–1781*. Edited by I. F. Burton. Woolwich, U.K.: Royal Artillery Institution, 1963.

Peebles, John. *John Peebles' American War: The Diary of a Scottish Grenadier, 1776–1782*. Edited by Ira D. Gruber. Mechanicsburg, Pa.: Stackpole Books, 1998.

Pennsylvania Archives. 5th ser., 5 vols. Harrisburg: Harrisburg Publishing, State Printer, 1906.

Pontgibaud, Charles Albert, chevalier de. *A French Volunteer of the War of Independence*. Translated and edited by Robert A. Douglas. Port Washington, N.Y.: Kennikat, 1968.

Popp, Stephan. *A Hessian Soldier in the American Revolution: The Diary of Stephan Popp*. Translated by Reinhart J. Pope. N.p.: privately printed, 1953.

Post, Lydia Winturn. *Personal Recollections of the American Revolution: A Private Journal*. Edited by Sidney Barclay. 1859. Reprint, Port Washington, N.Y.: Kennikat, 1970.

Reed, William B. *Life and Correspondence of Joseph Reed*. 2 vols. Philadelphia: Lindsay and Blakiston, 1847.

Ritchie, Carson I. A. "A New York Diary of the Revolutionary War." In *Narratives of the Revolution in New York*. New York: New-York Historical Society, 1975.

Robertson, Archibald. *Archibald Robertson: His Diaries and Sketches in America, 1762–1780*. Edited by Harry Miller Lydenberg. New York: New York Public Library, 1930.

Rush, Benjamin. *Letters of Benjamin Rush*. Edited by L. H. Butterfield, Princeton, N.J.: Princeton University Press, 1951.

Ryan, Dennis P., ed. *A Salute to Courage: The American Revolution as Seen through Wartime Writings of Officers of the Continental Army and Navy*. New York: Columbia University Press, 1979.

Serle, Ambrose. *The American Journal of Ambrose Serle, Secretary to Lord Howe*. Edited by Edward H. Tatum, Jr. San Marino, Calif.: Huntington Library, 1940.

Shaw, Samuel. *The Journals of Major Samuel Shaw, the First American Consul at Canton, with a Life of the Author by Josiah Quincy*. Boston: William Crosby and H. P. Nichols, 1847.

Shreve, John. "Personal Narrative of the Services of Lieut. John Shreve." *Magazine of American History* 3 (1879): 564–79.

Simcoe, John Graves. *A Journal of the Operations of the Queen's Rangers, from the End of the Year 1777 to the Conclusion of the Late American War*. Exeter, U.K.: printed for the author, 1787.

Simcoe, J[ohn] G[raves]. *Simcoe's Military Journal: A History of the Operations of a Partisan Corps, Called the Queen's Rangers, Commanded by Lieut. Col. J. G. Simcoe, during the War of the American Revolution*. New York: Bartlett and Welford, 1844.

Smith, Paul H., ed. *Letters of Delegates to Congress, 1774–1789*. 26 vols. Washington, D.C.: Library of Congress, 1976–2000.

[Smith, Samuel]. "The Papers of General Samuel Smith." *Historical Magazine*, 2nd ser., 7 (February 1870): 91–92.

Stedman, Charles. *The History of the Origin, Progress, and Termination of the American War*. 2 vols. London: printed for the author, 1794.

[Steuben, William Augustine, Baron von]. *Regulations for the Order and Discipline of the Troops of the United States*. Philadelphia: Continental Congress, printed by Styner & Cist, 1779.

Stevens, B. F., ed. *B.F. Stevens's Facsimiles of Manuscripts in European Archives Relating to America, 1773–1783; with Descriptions, Editorial Notes, Collations, References and Translations*. London: printed by Malby & Sons, 1889–95.

Stiles, Ezra. *The Literary Diary of Ezra Stiles, D.D., LL.D*. Edited by Franklin Bowditch Dexter. Vol. 2. New York: Charles Scribner's Sons, 1901.

Sullivan, John. *Letters and Papers of Major General John Sullivan, Continental Army*. Vol. 2, *1778–1779*. Edited by Otis G. Hammond. Collections of the New Hampshire Historical Society 14. Concord: New Hampshire Historical Society, 1931.

Supreme Executive Council of Pennsylvania. *Minutes of the Supreme Executive Council of Pennsylvania, from Its Organization to the Revolution*. Vols. 11–16. Harrisburg: Theo. Fenn, 1852–53.

Washington, George. *The Papers of George Washington*. Revolutionary War Series. Edited by Philander D. Chase et al. Charlottesville: University Press of Virginia, 1985–.

———. *The Papers of George Washington Digital Edition*. Edited by Theodore J. Crackel et al. Charlottesville: University Press of Virginia, Rotunda, 2007. Available online at http://rotunda.upress.virginia.edu/founders/GEWN.html.

Washington-Madison Papers Collected and Preserved by James Madison, Estate of J. C. McGuire. Auction Catalogue. Philadelphia: Thomas Birch's Sons, 1892.

Wilkin, W. H., ed. *Some British Soldiers in America*. London: Hugh Rees, 1914.

Wilkinson, James. *Memoirs of My Own Times*. 3 vols. Philadelphia: printed by Abraham Small, 1816.

Willett, Marinus. *A Narrative of the Military Actions of Colonel Marinus Willett, Taken Chiefly from His Own Manuscript. Prepared by His Son, William M. Willet*. New York: G. & C. & H. Carvill, 1831.

Wister, Sally. *Sally Wister's Journal: A True Narrative Being a Quaker Maiden's Account of Her Experiences with Officers of the Continental Army, 1777–1778*. Edited by Albert Cook Myers. Philadelphia: Ferris & Leach, 1902.

Secondary Sources

Abernethy, Thomas Perkins. *Western Lands and the American Revolution*. New York: D. Appleton-Century, 1937.

Adams, Randolph G. *British Headquarters Maps and Sketches*. Ann Arbor, Mich.: William L. Clements Library, 1928.

Adelberg, Michael S. *The American Revolution in Monmouth County: The Theatre of Spoil and Destruction*. Charleston, S.C.: History Press, 2010.

———. *Roster of the People of Revolutionary Monmouth County, New Jersey*. Baltimore, Md.: Genealogical Publishing, 1997.

Albert, Peter J., ed. *Arms and Independence: The Military Character of the American Revolution*. Charlottesville, Va.: U.S. Capitol Historical Society, 1984.

Alden, John Richard. *General Charles Lee, Traitor or Patriot?* Baton Rouge: Louisiana State University Press, 1951.

Allen, L. P. *The Genealogy and History of the Shreve Family from 1641*. Greenfield, Ill.: privately printed, 1901.

Anderson, Fred. *Crucible of War: The Seven Years' War and the Fate of Empire in British North America, 1754–1766*. London: Faber and Faber, 2001

Anderson, Troyer Steele. *The Command of the Howe Brothers during the American Revolution*. 1936. Reprint, New York: Octagon, 1972.

Armstrong, William Clinton. *The Battles in the Jersies and the Significance of Each*. [Newark]: New Jersey Sons of the American Revolution, 1916.

———, ed. *Patriotic Poems of New Jersey*. [Newark]: New Jersey Sons of the American Revolution, n.d.

Azoy, Anastasio C. M. "Monmouth, the Battle That Was Won at Valley Forge." *Infantry Journal* 46, no. 6 (1939): 566–82.

Babits, Lawrence E. *A Devil of a Whipping: The Battle of Cowpens*. Chapel Hill: University of North Carolina Press, 1998.

Bancroft, George. *History of the United States, from the Discovery of the American Continent*. Vol. 10. Boston: Little, Brown, 1879.

Barber, John Warner, and Henry Howe. *Historical Collections of the State of New Jersey: Containing a General Collection of the Most Interesting Facts, Traditions, Biographical Sketches, Anecdotes, Etc. Relating to Its History and Antiquities, with Geographical Descriptions of Every Township in the State*. New York: S. Tuttle, 1844.

Barkalow, Rees H. "The Battle of Monmouth: A Study of the Performance of Staff Functions, including Military Intelligence." *Journal of the Military Intelligence Association* 2, no. 4 (1939): 4–11.

Baule, Steven M., with Stephen Gilbert. *British Army Officers who Served in the American Revolution*. Westminster, Md.: Heritage Books, 2008.

Bemis, Samuel Flagg. *The Diplomacy of the American Revolution*. Bloomington: Indiana University Press, 1957.

Berg, Fred Anderson. *Encyclopedia of Continental Army Units: Battalions, Regiments, and Independent Corps*. Harrisburg, Pa.: Stackpole Books, 1972.

Bilby, Joseph G., and Katherine Bilby Jenkins. *Monmouth Court House: The Battle That Made the American Army*. Yardley, Pa.: Westholme, 2010.

Billias, George Athan. *General John Glover and His Marblehead Mariners*. New York: Henry Holt, 1960.

———, ed. *George Washington's Generals*. New York: William Morrow, 1964.

Birkhimer, William E. *Historical Sketch of the Organization, Administration, Materiel, and Tactics of the Artillery, United States Army*. Washington, D.C.: James J. Chapman, 1884.

Blanchard, Amos. *American Military Biography: Containing the Lives, Characters, and Anecdotes of the Officers of the Revolution, Who Were Most Distinguished in Achieving Our National Independence*. [Cincinnati]: n.p., 1825.

Blanco, Richard L. *Physician of the American Revolution: Jonathan Potts*. New York: Garland STPM, 1979.

Blumenthal, Walter Hart. *Women Camp Followers of the American Revolution*, Philadelphia: G. S. MacManus, 1952.

Boatner, Mark Mayo, III, ed. *Encyclopedia of the American Revolution*. New York: David McKay, 1974.

Boudinot, Elias. *An Oration, Delivered at Elizabeth-Town, New-Jersey, Agreeably to a Resolution of the Sate Society of the Cincinnati, on the Fourth of July, M.DCC.XCIII*. Elizabeth-Town, N.J.: printed by Shepard Kollock, 1793.

Brace, Richard Munthe. "General Dumouriez and the Girondists." *American Historical Review* 56, no. 3 (1951): 493–509.

Brown, Henry Armitt. *The Battle of Monmouth: An Oration Composed to be Delivered at Freehold, New Jersey, June 28,1878, the One Hundredth Anniversary of the Battle*. Philadelphia: Christopher Sower, 1913.

Brown, Weldon A. *Empire or Independence: A Study in the Failure of Reconciliation, 1774–1778*. Baton Rouge: Louisiana State University Press, 1941.

Cadwalader, Sandra L. *The Cadwaladers, 1677–1879: Five Generations of a Philadelphia Family*. Wawa, Pa.: S. L. Cadwalader, 1996.

Calhoon, Robert M. *The Loyalists in Revolutionary America, 1766–1781*. New York: Harcourt, Brace, Jovanovich, 1973.

Callahan, North. *Daniel Morgan: Ranger of the Revolution*. New York: Holt, Rinehart, and Winston, 1961.

———. *Henry Knox: George Washington's General*. New York: Rinehart, 1958.

Cannon, John Ashton, ed. *A Dictionary of British History*. New York: Oxford University Press, 2009.

Cannon, Richard. *Historical Record of the Seventeenth Regiment of Light Dragoons—Lancers: Containing an Account of the Formation of the*

Regiment in 1759, and of Its Subsequent Services to 1841. London: John W. Parker, 1841.

———. *Historical Record of the Sixteenth, or, The Queen's Regiment of Light Dragoons, Lancers: Containing an Account of the Formation of the Regiment in 1759 and of Its Subsequent Services to 1841*. London: John W. Parker, 1842.

Carlton, Emory L. "Captain-Lieutenant William Miller of Revolutionary Service." *Essex County (Va.) Historical Society* 16 (1979): 3.

Carrington, Henry Beebe. *Battles of the American Revolution, 1775–1781: Historical and Military Criticism with Topographical Illustration*. New York: A. S. Barnes, 1876.

Caruana, Adrian B. *British Artillery Ammunition, 1780*. Bloomfield, Ontario: Museum Restoration Services, 1979.

———. *Grasshoppers and Butterflies*. Bloomfield, Ontario: Museum Restoration Services, 1979.

Chadwick, Bruce. *George Washington's War: The Forging of a Revolutionary Leader and the American Presidency*. Naperville, Ill.: Sourcebooks, 2004.

Chambers, John Whiteclay, II. *George Washington in Cranbury: The Road to the Battle of Monmouth*. 2nd ed. Cranbury, N.J.: Cranbury Historical and Preservation Society, 2010.

Chandler, David, ed. *Napoleon's Marshals*. New York: Macmillan, 1987.

Chernow, Ron. *Washington: A Life*. New York: Penguin, 2010.

Clausewitz, Carl von. *On War*. Edited by Anatol Rapoport. Baltimore, Md.: Penguin Books, 1971.

Cogswell, Elliott C. *History of Nottingham, Deerfield, and Northwood, Comprised within the Original Limits of Nottingham, Rockingham County, N.H., with Records of the Centennial Proceedings at Northwood, and Genealogical Sketches*. Manchester, N.H.: J. B. Clarke, 1878.

Cowart, Samuel Craig. *Address on Battle of Monmouth with Poem Patriot Sires of Monmouth*. Freehold, N.J.: Transcript Printing House, 1928.

Cowen, David L. *Medicine in Revolutionary New Jersey*. New Jersey's Revolutionary Experience 12. Trenton: New Jersey Historical Society Commission, 1975.

Cox, Caroline. *A Proper Sense of Honor: Service and Sacrifice in George Washington's Army*. Chapel Hill: University of North Carolina Press, 2004.

Craig, Robert W. "In Search of the Rising Sun Tavern: A Long-Vanished Landmark on the Road to the Battle of Monmouth." *New Jersey History* 119 (2001): 54–71.

Crane, Isaac Watts. *An Oration Delivered in the Presbyterian Church, at Elizabeth-Town, on the Fourth of July, 1794, at the Request of the Militia Officers, It Being the Eighteenth Anniversary of American Independence*. Newark, N.J.: printed by John Woods, 1795.

Cumming, Hooper. *An Oration, Delivered at Newark, N.J., July 4, 1823. By Hooper Cumming . . . Pastor of the Presbyterian Church in Van De Water Street, New-York*. Newark, N.J.: printed by John Tuttle, 1823.

Curtis, Edward E. *The Organization of the British Army in the American Revolution*. 1926. Reprint, St. Clair Shores, Mich.: Scholarly Press, 1972.

Custis, George Washington Parke. *Recollections and Private Memoirs of Washington*. Philadelphia: J. W. Bradley, 1861.

Darling, Anthony D. *Red Coat and Brown Bess*. Bloomfield, Ontario: Museum Restoration Service, 1970.

Dastrup, Boyd L. *King of Battle: A Branch History of the U.S. Army's Field Artillery*. Fort Eustis, Va.: U.S. Army Training and Doctrine Command, 1992.

DePauw, Linda Grant. *Fortunes of War: New Jersey Women and the American Revolution*. New Jersey's Revolutionary Experience 26. Trenton: New Jersey Historical Commission, 1975.

———. *Founding Mothers: Women of America in the Revolutionary Era*. Boston: Houghton Mifflin, 1975.

———. "Women in Combat: The Revolutionary War Experience." *Armed Forces and Society* 7 (1981): 215.

DePeyster, John Watts. "The Battle of Monmouth Court House or Freehold, Sunday, June 28, 1778." *Magazine of American History* 2 (1878): 407–13.

Dickinson, Wharton. "Philemon Dickinson: Major-General: New Jersey Militia—Revolutionary Service." *Magazine of American History* 7 (1881): 420–27.

Dow, John. *A Discourse, Delivered by Request, July 4, 1806, in the Methodist Church at Belleville*. Newark, N.J.: printed by John A. Crane, 1806.

Duffy, Christopher. *The Military Experience in the Age of Reason*. New York: Atheneum, 1988.

Duncan, Francis. *History of the Royal Regiment of Artillery: Compiled from the Original Record*. London: John Murray, 1842.

Eastman, Mary Henderson. *Aunt Phillis's Cabin; or, Southern Life as It Is*. Philadelphia: Lippincott, Grambo, 1852.

Eelking, Max von. *The German Allied Troops in the North American War of Independence*. 1893. Translated by J. G. Rosengarten. Baltimore: Genealogical Publishing, 1969.

Ege, Ralph. *Pioneers of Old Hopewell with Sketches of Her Revolutionary Heroes*. Hopewell, N.J.: Race & Savage, 1908.

Eichner, L. G. "The Military Practice of Medicine during the Revolutionary War." *Tredyffrin Easttown Historical Society History Quarterly* 26, no. 3 (1988): 90–104. Available online at Tredyffrin Easttown Historical Society, *History Quarterly* Digital Archives, http://www.tehistory.org/hqda/html/v26/v26n3p090.html.

Ellis, Franklin. *The History of Monmouth County, New Jersey*. Philadelphia: R. T. Peck, 1885.

Ferling, John E. *Almost a Miracle: The American Victory in the War of Independence*. New York: Oxford University, 2007.

———. *The Ascent of George Washington: The Hidden Political Genius of an American Icon*. New York: Bloomsbury, 2009.

———. *The Loyalist Mind: Joseph Galloway and the American Revolution*. University Park: Pennsylvania State University Press, 1977.

———, ed. *The World Turned Upside Down: The American Victory in the War of Independence*. New York: Greenwood, 1988.

Fischer, David Hackett. *Washington's Crossing*. New York: Oxford University Press, 2004.

Fiske, John. *Essays Literary and Historical*. Vol. 1. New York: Macmillan, 1902.

Fleming, Thomas. *The Forgotten Victory: The Battle for New Jersey, 1780*. New York: Reader's Digest Press, 1973.

———. *Washington's Secret War: The Hidden History of Valley Forge*. New York: HarperCollins, 2005.

Flexner, James Thomas. *George Washington in the American Revolution, 1775–1783*. Boston: Little, Brown, [1968].

———. *Washington: The Indispensable Man*. Boston: Little, Brown, 1969.

Flower, Milton E. *John Dickinson: Conservative Revolutionary*. Charlottesville: University Press of Virginia, 1983.

Frey, Sylvia R. *The British Soldier in America: A Social History of Military Life in the Revolutionary Period*. Austin: University of Texas Press, 1981.

Garden, Alexander. *Anecdotes of the American Revolution: Illustrative of the Talents and Virtues of the Heroes of the Revolution, Who Acted the Most Conspicuous Parts Therein*. 2nd ser. Charleston, S.C.: A. E. Miller, 1828.

Garlick, Barnard McKean. *A History of St. Peter's Church*. Freehold, N.J.: St. Peter's Church, 1967.

Garrard, Lewis H. *Chambersburg in the Colony and the Revolution: A Sketch*. Publications of the Historical Society of Pennsylvania. Philadelphia: J. B. Lippincott, 1856.

Garson, Noel B. *Light-Horse Harry: A Biography of Washington's Great Cavalryman, General Henry Lee*. Garden City, N.Y.: Doubleday, 1966.

Gerlach, Larry R. *Prologue to Independence: New Jersey in the Coming of the American Revolution*. New Brunswick, N.J.: Rutgers University Press, 1976.

Gilman, Charles Malcolm Brookfield. *Monmouth Road to Glory, Including the Court-Martial and Vindication of Major General Charles Lee*. Red Bank, N.J.: Arlington Laboratory for Clinical and Historical Research, 1964.

Golway, Terry. *Washington's General: Nathanael Greene and the Triumph of the American Revolution*. New York: Henry Holt, 2005.

Goodrich, Charles A. *Our Lives, Our Fortunes, and Our Sacred Honour: The Lives of the Signers to the Declaration of Independence*. New York: William Reed, 1829.

Gordon, William. *The History of the Rise, Progress, and Establishment of the Independence of the United States of America; including an Account of the late War; and of the Thirteen Colonies, from their Origin to that Period*. 4 vols. London: printed for the author, 1788.

Gottschalk, Louis Reichenthal. *Lafayette Joins the American Army*. Chicago: University of Chicago Press, 1965.

Grizzard, Frank E. *George Washington: A Biographical Companion*. Santa Barbara, Calif.: ABC-CLIO, 2002.

Groves, [J.] Percy. *Historical Records of the 7th or Royal Regiment of Fusiliers: Now Known as the Royal Fusiliers (The City of London Regiment), 1685–1903*. Guernsey, U.K.: Frederick B. Guerin, 1903.

Gruber, Ira D. *The Howe Brothers and the American Revolution*. New York: Norton, 1972.

Guthorn, Peter J. *American Map Makers of the Revolution*. Monmouth Beach, N.J.: Philip Freneau, 1966.

———. *British Maps of the American Revolution*. Monmouth Beach, N.J.: Philip Freneau, 1972.

Hallahan, William H. *The Day the American Revolution Began: 19 April 1775*. New York: Perennial, 2001.

Hammond, Cleon E. *John Hart: The Biography of a Signer of the Declaration of Independence*. Newfane, Vt.: Pioneer, 1977.

Hargreaves, Reginald. *The Bloodybacks: The British Serviceman in North America and the Caribbean, 1655–1783*. New York: Walker, 1968.

Hastedt, Glenn. *Espionage: A Reference Handbook*. Santa Barbara, Calif.: ABC-CLIO Inc., 2003.

Hawke, David Freeman. *Benjamin Rush: Revolutionary Gadfly*. Indianapolis: Bobbs-Merrill, 1971.

Hayes, John T. *The Saddlebag Almanac of Cavalry in the American Revolution*. Vol. 4. Fort Lauderdale, Fla.: Saddlebag, 1996.

Heitman, Francis B. *Historical Register of Officers of the Continental Army during the War of the Revolution, April 1775, to December 1783*. Washington, D.C.: Rare Book Shop, 1914.

Helme, James B., comp. "History of Jamesburg & Helmetta Post Offices." *Journal of the New Jersey Postal History Society* 21, no. 4 (1993): 93.

Higginbotham, Don. *Daniel Morgan: Revolutionary Rifleman*. Chapel Hill: University of North Carolina Press, 1961.

———. *The War of American Independence: Military Attitudes, Policies, and Practice, 1763–1789*. New York: Macmillan, 1971.

Hodges, Graham. *Slavery and Freedom in the Rural North: African Americans in Monmouth County, New Jersey*. Madison, Wisc.: Madison House, 1996.

Holst, Donald W. "An Unidentified Flag of the American Revolution." *Military Collector & Historian* 19, no. 3 (Fall 1967): 94.

Houlding, J. A. *Fit for Service: The Training of the British Army, 1715–1795*. New York: Oxford University Press, 1981.

Huber, Thomas M., ed. *Compound Warfare: That Fatal Knot*. Fort Leavenworth, Kans.: U.S. Command and General Staff College Press, 2002.

Index of Revolutionary War Pension Applications in the National Archives. Washington, D.C.: Government Printing Office, 1976.

Ireland, Bernard. *The Fall of Toulon: The Last Opportunity to Defeat the French Revolution*. London: Weidenfeld & Nicolson, 2005.

Irving, Washington. *The Works of Washington Irving. Life of George Washington*. Pt. 4. New York: Cooperative Publication Society, 1904.

Jackson, John W. *The Pennsylvania Navy, 1775–1781: The Defense of the Delaware*. New Brunswick, N.J.: Rutgers University Press, 1965.

———. *With the British Army in Philadelphia, 1777–1778*. San Rafael, Calif.: Presidio, 1979.

Johnson, Allen, and Dumas Malone, eds. *Dictionary of American Biography*. Vol. 5. New York: Charles Scribner's Sons, 1946.

Johnson, Victor Leroy. *The Administration of the American Commissariat during the Revolutionary War*. Philadelphia: University of Pennsylvania Press, 1941.

Johnston, Henry P., ed. *The Record of Connecticut Men in the Military and Naval Service during the War of the Revolution*. Hartford, Conn.: Case, Lockwood, & Brainard, printers, 1889.

Johnstone, William Jackson. *George Washington the Christian*. New York: Abington, 1919.

Jordan, John W. *Encyclopedia of Pennsylvania Biography*. Vol. 3. New York: Lewis Historical Publishing, 1914.

Katcher, Philip R. N. *Encyclopedia of British, Provincial, and German Army Units, 1775–1783*. Harrisburg, Pa.: Stackpole Books, 1973.

Ketchum, Richard M. *Saratoga: Turning Point of America's Revolutionary War*. New York: Henry Holt, 1997.

Kidder, Frederic. *History of the First New Hampshire Regiment in the War of the Revolution*. Albany, N.Y.: Joel Munsell, 1868.

King, Charles. "The Battle of Monmouth Court House. Read before the Society, September 13th, 1849, at Their Meeting at Freehold, Monmouth County." *Proceedings of the New Jersey Historical Society* 4 (1849): 125–42.

Krebs, Daniel. *A Generous and Merciful Enemy: Life for German Prisoners of War during the American Revolution*. Norman: University of Oklahoma Press, 2013.

Landis, J. B. "An Investigation into the American Tradition of a Woman Known as Molly Pitcher." *Journal of American History* 5, no. 1 (1911): 83–96.

Lanning, Michael Lee. *African Americans in the Revolutionary War*. New York: Citadel, 2005.

Leake, Isaac Q. *Memoir of the Life and Times of General John Lamb*. Albany, N.Y.: Joel Munsell, 1857.

Lefkowitz, Arthur S. *George Washington's Indispensable Men: The 32 Aides-de-Camp Who Helped Win American Independence*. Mechanicsville, Pa.: Stackpole Books, 2003.

———. *The Long Retreat: The Calamitous American Defense of New Jersey, 1776*. Metuchen, N.J.: Upland, 1998.

Lengel, Edward G. *General George Washington: A Military Life*. New York: Random House, 2005.

———, ed. *A Companion to George Washington*. Oxford, U.K.: Wiley-Blackwell, 2012.

Lender, Mark Edward. "The Conscripted Line: The Draft in Revolutionary New Jersey." *New Jersey History* 103 (1985): 23–46.

———. *The River War: The Fight for the Delaware, 1777*. Trenton: N.J. Historical Commission, 1979.

———. "Small Battles Won: New Jersey and the Patriot Military Revival." *New Jersey Heritage* 1, no. 2 (2002): 30–37.

———. "The Social Structure of the New Jersey Brigade: The Continental Army as an American Standing Army." In *The Military in America: From the Colonial Era to the Present*, edited by Peter Karsten, 27–44. New York: Macmillan, 1980.

Lewis, Theodore R. "Was Washington Profane at Monmouth?" *New Jersey History* 89, no. 3 (Fall 1971): 149–62.

Linn, John Blair, and William H. Egle, eds. *Pennsylvania in the War of the Revolution, Battalions and Line, 1775–1783*. Vol. 1. Harrisburg, Pa.: Lane S. Hart, 1880.

Lockhart, Paul. *The Drillmaster of Valley Forge: The Baron de Steuben and the Making of the American Army*. New York: Smithsonian Books, 2008.

Lomask, Milton. *Aaron Burr: The Years from Princeton to Vice President, 1756–1805*. New York: Farrar, Straus, Giroux, 1979.

Lookwood, Samuel. "British March to Monmouth." *Beecher's Illustrated Magazine* 6 (1872): 17–25.

Lossing, Benson John, ed. *The American Historical Record, and Repository of Notes and Queries*. Philadelphia: John E. Potter, 1874.

———. "The Battle of Monmouth Court House." *Harper's New Monthly Magazine* 57, no. 337 (1878): 29–47.

———. *The Pictorial Field-Book of the American Revolution; or, Illustrations, by Pen and Pencil, of the History, Biography, Scenery, Relics, and Traditions of the War for Independence*. 2 vols. New York: Harper & Brothers, 1852.

Lurie, Maxine N., and Marc Mappen, eds. *Encyclopedia of New Jersey*. New Brunswick, N.J.: Rutgers University Press, 2004.

MacKinnon, Daniel. *Origin and Services of the Coldstream Guards*. Vol. 2. London: Richard Bentley, 1833.

MacWhorter, Alexander. *A Festive Discourse, Occasioned by the Celebration of the Seventeenth Anninersary* [sic] *of American Independence, in the Town of Newark*. Newark, N.J.: printed by John Woods, 1793.

Matthew, H. C. G., and Brian Harrison, eds. *Oxford Dictionary of National Biography*. Oxford, U.K.: Oxford University Press, 2004.

Martin, David G. "The Battle of Monmouth: The Colonies Take the Offensive, June 28, 1778." *Strategy and Tactics* 90 (1982): 4–16.

———. *A Molly Pitcher Sourcebook*. Hightstown, N.J.: Longstreet House, 2003.

Martin, James Kirby, and Mark Edward Lender. *A Respectable Army: The Military Origins of the Republic, 1763–1789*. 2nd ed. Arlington Heights, Ill.: Harlan Davidson, 1982.

Martin, James K., and Karen R. Stubaus. *The American Revolution: Whose Revolution?* Huntington, N.Y.: Robert E. Krieger, 1977.

Mayer, Holly A. *Belonging to the Army: Camp Followers and Community during the American Revolution*. Columbia: University of South Carolina Press, 1996.

Mazzagetti, Dominick. *Charles Lee: Self before Country*. New Brunswick, N.J.: Rutgers University Press, 2013.

McBurney, Christian M. *Kidnapping the Enemy: The Special Operations to Capture Generals Charles Lee and Richard Prescott*. Yardley, Pa.: Westholme, 2014.

McCormick, Richard P. *New Jersey from Colony to State, 1609–1789*. Rev. ed. Newark: New Jersey Historical Society, 1981.

McGaughy, J. Kent. *Richard Henry Lee of Virginia: A Portrait of an American Revolutionary*. Lanham, Md.: Rowman & Littlefield, 2004.

McGuire, Thomas J. *Battle of Paoli*. Mechanicsburg, Pa.: Stackpole Books, 2000.

McKenney, Janice E. *The Organizational History of Field Artillery, 1775–2003*. Washington, D.C.: Center of Military History, United States Army, 2007.

Mitchell, Broadus. *Decisive Battles of the American Revolution with Thirty-One Maps Designed by the Author*. New York: Putnam, 1962.

Mitnick, Barbara J., ed. *New Jersey in the American Revolution*. New Brunswick, N.J.: Rivergate Books, 2005.

[Monmouth Battlefield State Park]. *June 28, 1778 Battle of Monmouth: 225th Anniversary, Battlefield State Park, June 28–29, 2003*. N.p., 2003.

Montross, Lynn. *Rag, Tag, and Bobtail: The Story of the Continental Army, 1775–1783*. New York: Harper, 1952.

Moore, George H. *The Treason of Charles Lee, Major General*. New York: Charles Scribner, 1860.

Morgan, John D. F. *Old Tennent Church and the Battle of Monmouth Court House*. Haddonfield, N.J.: n.p., 1952.

Morrissey, Brendan. *Monmouth Courthouse, 1778: The Last Great Battle in the North*. Oxford, U.K.: Osprey Publishing, 2004.

Munn, David C. *Battles and Skirmishes of the American Revolution in New Jersey*. Trenton, N.J.: Bureau of Geology and Topography, 1976.

Murrin, Mary R., and Richard Waldron, eds. *Conflict at Monmouth Court House*. New Jersey Occasional Papers 2. Trenton: New Jersey Historical Commission, 1978.

Nead, Benjamin M. "A Biographical Sketch of Gen. Thomas Proctor, with Some Account of the First Pennsylvania Artillery in the Revolution." *Pennsylvania Magazine of History and Biography* 4, no. 4 (1880): 454–70.

Neagles, James C. *Summer Soldiers: A Survey & Index of Revolutionary War Courts-Martial*. Salt Lake City: Ancestry, 1986.

Nelson, Paul David. *General Horatio Gates: A Biography*. Baton Rouge: Louisiana State University Press, 1976.

———. *William Alexander, Lord Stirling*. Birmingham: University of Alabama Press, 1987.

Osborne, Peter. *Where Washington Once Led: A History of Washington Crossing State Park*. Yardley, Pa.: Yardley, 2012.

O'Shaughnessy, Andrew Jackson. *The Men Who Lost America: British Leadership, the American Revolution, and the Fate of the Empire*. New Haven, Conn.: Yale University Press, 2013.

Palmer, Dave Richard. *The Way of the Fox: American Strategy in the War for America, 1775–1783*. Westport, Conn.: Greenwood, 1975.

Palmer, John McAuley. *General von Steuben*. New Haven, Conn.: Yale University Press, 1937.

Papas, Phillip. *Renegade Revolutionary: The Life of General Charles Lee*. New York: New York University Press, 2014.

Papenfuse, Edward C., and Gregory A. Stiverson. "General Smallwood's Recruits: The Peacetime Career of the Revolutionary War Private." *William and Mary Quarterly*, 3rd ser., 30 (1973): 117–32.

Peckham, Howard H., ed. *The Toll of Independence: Engagements and Battle Casualties of the American Revolution*. Chicago: University of Chicago Press, 1974.

Peterson, Harold. *The Book of the Continental Soldier: Being a Complete Account of the Uniforms, Weapons, and Equipment with Which He Lived and Fought*. Harrisburg, Pa.: Stackpole Books, 1968.

Peterkin, Ernest W. *The Exercise of Arms in the Continental Army*. Alexandria Bay, N.J.: Museum Restoration Service, 1989.

Platt, Charles Davis. *Ballads of New Jersey in the Revolution*. Morristown, N.J.: Jerseyman Print, 1896.

Preston, John Hyde. *Revolution 1776*. New York: Washington Square, 1962.

Quarles, Benjamin. *The Negro in the American Revolution*. Chapel Hill: University of North Carolina Press, 1961.

Ramsay, David. *The History of the American Revolution*. Philadelphia: printed by R. Aitken & son, 1789.

Rappleye, Charles. *Robert Morris: Financier of the American Revolution*. New York: Simon & Schuster, 2010.

Reed, John F. "Road to Disgrace." *Manuscripts* 26, no. 4 (1974): 288–90.

Reed, William B. *The Life of Esther De Berdt, afterwards Esther Reed, of Pennsylvania*. Philadelphia: C. Sherman, printer, 1853.

Rees, John U. "'. . . the Soldier's Necessaries': A Discussion of the Contents of the Knapsacks of British Troops during the American War." *Royal Gazette* (Newsletter of the 40th Regiment of Foot) 5, no. 1 (February 1994): 13–16.

———. "'A Very Smart Cannonading Ensued from Both Sides': Continental Artillery at Monmouth Courthouse, 28 June 1778." *Military Historian and Collector* 60, no. 1 (2008): 38–39.

Reich, Jerome R. *British Friends of the American Revolution*. Armonk, N.Y.: M. E. Sharpe, 1997.

Riddle, Gilbert V., and Don N. Hagist. "Lessons from the Court: A Case of Mistaken Identity, and a Woman Child of Nine Years of Age." *Brigade Dispatch* 25, no. 2 (1995): 9.

Risch, Erna. *Supplying Washington's Army*. Washington, D.C.: Center of Military History, U.S. Army, 1981.
Rizzo, Dennis. *Mount Holly, New Jersey: A Hometown Reinvented*. Charleston, S.C.: History Press, 2007.
Robson, Eric. "Purchase and Promotion in the British Army in the Eighteenth Century." *History* 36 (1951): 57–72.
Rossie, Jonathan Gregory. *The Politics of Command in the American Revolution*. Syracuse, N.Y.: Syracuse University Press, 1975.
Royster, Charles. "'The Nature of Treason': Revolutionary Virtue and Reactions to Benedict Arnold." *William and Mary Quarterly,* 3rd ser., 36 (1979): 163–93.
Saffron, Morris H. *Surgeon to Washington: Dr. John Cochran, 1730–1807*. New York: Columbia University Press, 1977.
Salter, Edwin. *A History of Monmouth and Ocean Counties*. Bayonne, N.J.: E. Gardner & Son, 1890.
Selesky, Harold E., ed. *Encyclopedia of the American Revolution*. 2nd ed. 2 vols. Detroit: Thomson Gale, 2006.
Sellers, John R. "The Common Soldier in the American Revolution." In *Military History of the American Revolution: Proceedings of the Sixth Military History Symposium, USAF Academy,* edited by S. J. Underdal, 151–61. Washington, D.C., 1976.
Shy, John. "The American Revolution: The Military Conflict Considered as a Revolutionary Conflict." In *Essays on the American Revolution,* edited by Stephen G. Kurtz and James H. Hutson, 121–56. Chapel Hill: University of North Carolina Press, 1973.
Sivilich, Eric D., and Daniel M. Sivilich. "Surveying, Statistics, and Spatial Mapping: KOCOA Landscape Analysis of 18th-Century Artillery Placements at Monmouth Battlefield State Park." *Historical Archaeology* 49, no. 2 (2015): 50–71.
Smith, Paul H. *Loyalists and Redcoats: A Study in British Revolutionary Policy*. Chapel Hill: University of North Caroline Press, 1964.
Smith, Samuel Steele. *The Battle of Monmouth*. Monmouth Beach, N.J.: Philip Freneau, 1964.
———. *The Battle of Monmouth*. Trenton: New Jersey Historical Commission, 1976.
———. *A Molly Pitcher Chronology*. Monmouth Beach, N.J.: Philip Freneau, 1972.
———. *Monmouth Battlefield in Maps & Pictures*. Monmouth Beach, N.J.: Philip Freneau, 1978.
———. "Who Won the Battle of Monmouth?" *Cockpit* 2, no. 1 (1964): 8.
Spring, Matthew H. *With Zeal and Bayonets Only: The British Army on Campaign in North America, 1775–1783*. Norman: University of Oklahoma Press, 2008.
Stauber, Leland G. *The American Revolution: A Grand Mistake*. Amherst, U.K.: Prometheus Books, 2010.
Stellhorn, Paul A., and Michael J. Birkner, eds. *The Governors of New Jersey, 1664–1974: Biographical Essays*. Trenton: New Jersey Historical Commission, 1982.

Stern, Mark Abbott. *David Franks: Colonial Merchant*. University Park: Pennsylvania State University Press, 2010.

Stewart, David. *Sketches of the Charter, Manners, and Present State of the Highlanders of Scotland & the Highland Regiments*. 2nd ed. 2 vols. Edinburg, U.K.: Archibald Constable, 1822.

Stillé, Charles J. *Major-General Anthony Wayne and the Pennsylvania Line in the Continental Army*. Philadelphia: J. B. Lipincott, 1893.

Stockton, Frank R. *Stories of New Jersey*. 1896. Reprint, New Brunswick, N.J.: Rutgers University Press, 1961.

Stone, Garry Wheeler, Daniel M. Sivilich, and Mark Edward Lender. "A Deadly Minuet: The Advance of the New England 'Picked Men' against the Royal Highlanders at the Battle of Monmouth, 28 June 1778." *Brigade Dispatch* 26, no. 2 (1996): 2–18.

Stone, William L., ed. *Ballads and Poems Relating to the Burgoyne Campaign*. 1893. Reprint, Port Washington, N.Y.: Kennikat, 1970.

Stryker, James. *An Oration, Delivered at Woodbridge, New-Jersey, July 4, 1823*. Rahway, N.J.: printed by James A. Bennet, 1823.

Stryker, William Scudder. *The Battle of Monmouth, by the Late William S. Stryker*. Edited by William Starr Myers. Princeton, N.J.: Princeton University Press, 1927.

———. "Lee's Conduct at the Battle of Monmouth." *Proceedings of the New Jersey Historical Society* 25 (1897): 95–99.

———, comp. *Official Register of the Officers and Men of New Jersey in the Revolutionary War*. Trenton, N.J.: Wm. T. Nicholson, 1872.

Symmes, Frank R. *History of the Old Tennent Church*. 2nd ed. Cranbury, N.J.: George W. Burroughs, 1904.

Symonds, Craig L. *A Battlefield Atlas of the American Revolution*. Baltimore: Nautical and Aviation, 1986.

Thayer, Theodore B. "The Battle of Monmouth." In *Development and Interpretive Guide, Monmouth Battlefield State Historic Park*, 35–54. Newark, N.J.: Edwards and Kelcey, 1968.

———. *The Making of a Scapegoat: Washington and Lee at Monmouth*. Port Washington, N.Y.: Kennikat, 1976.

Trimble, W. Copeland. *The Historical Record of the 27th Inniskilling Regiment*. London: W. Clowes and Sons, 1876.

Trussell, J. B. B., Jr. "Artillery and the Battle of Monmouth." *Field Artillery Journal* 39, no. 5 (1949): 221–23.

Trussell, John B. *The Pennsylvania Line: Regimental Organization and Operations, 1776–1783*. Harrisburg: Pennsylvania Historical and Museum Commission, 1977.

Tuttle, Joseph F. *Biographical Sketch of General William Winds, of Morris Co. New Jersey*. Newark, N.J.: Office of the Daily Advertiser, 1853.

U.S. Army Field Artillery School. *Right of the Line: A History of the American Field Artillery*. Fort Sill, Okla.: U.S. Army Field Artillery School, 1984.

Wacker, Peter O. *Land and People: A Cultural Geography of Preindustrial New Jersey: Origins and Settlement Patterns*. New Brunswick, N.J.: Rutgers University Press, 1975.

Wacker, Peter O., and Paul G. E. Clemens. *Land Use in Early New Jersey: A Historical Geography*. Newark: New Jersey Historical Society, 1995.
Walker, Paul K., ed. *Engineers of Independence: A Documentary History of the Army Engineers in the American Revolution, 1775–1783*. Honolulu: University Press of the Pacific, 2002.
Wallace, Willard M. *Appeal to Arms: A Military History of the American Revolution*. Chicago: Quadrangle Books, 1964.
Ward, Christopher. *The War of the Revolution*. 2 vols. New York: Macmillan, 1952.
Ward, Harry M. *Between the Lines: Banditti of the American Revolution*. Westport, Conn.: Praeger, 2002.
———. *Charles Scott and the "Spirit of '76."* Charlottesville: University Press of Virginia, 1988.
———. *For Virginia and for Independence: Twenty-Eight Revolutionary War Soldiers from the Old Dominion*. Jefferson, N.C.: McFarland, 2011.
———. *General William Maxwell and the New Jersey Continentals*. Westport, Conn.: Greenwood, 1997.
Warren, Mercy [Otis]. *History of the Rise, Progress, and Termination of the American Revolution. Interspersed with Biographical, Political and Moral Observations*. 3 vols. Boston: Manning and Loring, 1805.
Washburn, Emory. *Historical Sketches of the Town of Leicester, Massachusetts*. Boston: John Wilson & Son, 1860.
Watts, Henry Miller. "A Memoir of General Henry Miller." *Pennsylvania Magazine of History and Biography* 11 (1887): 341–429.
[Westcott, James D.]. *An Address Delivered to the Inhabitants of the Township of Fairfield, Cumberland County, New Jersey, on the Fourth of July, 1808; in Conformity with Their Previous Appointment, and Published in Compliance with Their Request*. Philadelphia: printed by John Binns, 1808.
Wheeler, Joseph Towne. *The Maryland Press, 1777–1790*. Baltimore: Maryland Historical Society, 1938.
Wild, Ebenezer. "The Journal of Ebenezer Wild." Edited by James M. Bugbee. *Proceedings of the Massachusetts Historical Society*, 2nd ser., 6 (1890): 78–160.
Willcox, William B. "British Strategy in America, 1778." *Journal of Modern History* 19 (1947): 97–102.
———. *Portrait of a General: Sir Henry Clinton in the War for Independence*. New York: Knopf, 1964.
Williams, [Catherine R.]. *Biography of Revolutionary Heroes: Containing the Lives of Brigadier Gen. William Barton and also, of Captain Stephen Olney*. Providence, R.I.: published by the author, 1839.
Wilson, William. "The Royal Grenadiers at Monmouth." *Historical Record* 3 (1874): 262–64.
Wirth, Edna. *The British Encampment in Evesham Township*. [Evesham, N.J.]: published by the author, 1987.
Woodhull, Ann M. W. "Memoir of Brig. Gen. Anthony Walton White of the Continental Army." *Proceedings of the New Jersey Historical Society*, 2nd ser., 7 (1882): 105–15.

Woodward, E. M., and John F. Hagemen. *History of Burlington and Mercer Counties, New Jersey, with Biographical Sketches of Many of Their Pioneers and Prominent Men.* Philadelphia: Everts & Peck, 1883.

Wright, Robert K., Jr. *The Continental Army.* Washington, D.C.: Center of Military History, U.S. Army, 1983.

———. "'Nor Is Their Standing Army to Be Despised': The Emergence of the Continental Army as a Military Institution." In *Arms and Independence: The Military Character of the American Revolution,* edited by Ronald Hoffman and Peter J. Albert. Charlottesville: U.S. Capital Historical Society, 1984.

Wright, Robert K., Jr., and Morris J. MacGregor, Jr. *Soldier-Statesmen of the Constitution.* Washington, D.C.: U.S. Army Center of Military History, 1987.

Newspapers

The Battle Cry (Friends of the Monmouth Battlefield, Freehold, N.J.)
Boston Gazette
Daily State Gazette (Trenton)
Dover (N.H.) Gazette & Strafford Advertiser
Dunlap's Pennsylvania Packet, or, the General Advertiser (Philadelphia)
Hightstown (N.J.) Gazette
London Chronicle
London Gazette
Maryland Journal and Baltimore Advertiser (Baltimore)
Monmouth Democrat (Freehold, N.J.)
New Brunswick (N.J.) Daily Times
New Jersey Gazette (Trenton)
New Jersey Mirror and Burlington County Advertiser (Mount Holly)
New York Times
New York Tribune
New York Gazette and Weekly Mercury
Pennsylvania Evening Post (Philadelphia)
The Public Ledger (London)
Rivington's Royal Gazette (New York)
The Scots Magazine (Edinburgh)
The True American (Trenton, N.J.)

Theses and Unpublished Sources

Bodle, Wayne K., and Jacqueline Thibaut. "The Vortex of Small Fortunes: The Continental Army at Valley Forge, 1777–1778." Part 1 of "Valley Forge Historical Research Report." Report of the Valley Forge Historical Research Project, Valley Forge National Historical Park, 1979.

———. "This Fatal Crisis: Logistics, Supply, and the Continental Army at Valley Forge, 1777–1778." Part 2 of "Valley Forge Historical Research Report." Report of the Valley Forge Historical Research Project, Valley Forge National Historical Park, 1979.

Boyle, Lee. "Summary of Weather Conditions, 18 June–30 June 1778." Unpublished manuscript, Valley Forge National Historical Park, July 1994.

Doehla, Johann Conrad. "Diary of Johann Conrad Doehla." Translated by Bruce E. Burgoyne, unpublished manuscript, Monmouth Battlefield State Park.

Fowler, David. "Egregious Villains, Wood Rangers, and London Traders: The Pine Robber Phenomenon in New Jersey during the Revolutionary War." Ph.D. diss., Rutgers University, 1987.

Jones, Helen F. "James Lovell in the Continental Congress 1777–1782." Ph.D. diss., Columbia University, 1968.

Kahler, Gerald Edward. "Gentlemen of the Family: General George Washington's Aides-de-Camp and Military Secretaries." Master's thesis, University of Richmond, 1997.

Klaver, Carol. "Molly Pitcher: Myth and Reality." History honors thesis, Rutgers University, 1993.

Konigsberg, Charles. "Edward Carrington, 1748–1810: Child of the Revolution, A Study of the Public Man in Young America." Ph.D. diss., Princeton University, 1966.

Lender, Mark Edward, comp. "Lee's Advanced Force, 28 June 1778: Regimental/Battalion Commanders by Date of Commission, First Rank Held, Date of Promotion to Rank at Battle of Monmouth, and Months in Service as of 28 June 1778." Monmouth Battlefield State Park, February 2014, typescript.

Pilch, Henry W., comp. "Morris County [N.J.] Revolutionary War Pension Applications—1829." N.d. Special Collections, Rutgers University, typescript.

Roche, John David. "From Commander to Commandant: The Transformation of British Major General James Pattison during the American War of Independence, 1777–1780." Master's thesis, University of North Carolina at Chapel Hill, 2011.

Sellers, John R. "The Origins and Careers of the New England Soldier: Noncommissioned Officers and Privates in the Massachusetts Continental Line." Paper presented at the American Historical Association Convention, 1972.

Sivilich, Daniel, comp. Battlefield Restoration and Archaeological Volunteer Organization (BRAVO), 1987–. Monmouth Battlefield State Park, digital files.

Snell, Charles W. "General Charles Lee House. 'Prato Rio.'" National Register of Historic Places Inventory, Nomination Form. National Park Service, 27 July 1972.

Stone, Garry Wheeler. "The Agrarian Landscape of Monmouth Battlefield, New Jersey, c. 1775–1790." Annual meeting of the Society for Historical Archaeology, Quebec, Canada, 6 January 2000 (revised, 4 May 2000).

———. "Artillery Casualties at the Battle of Monmouth Courthouse." Unpublished manuscript, 2001, Monmouth Battlefield State Park.

———, comp. "Militia Service at the Battle of Monmouth." 1994. Unpublished manuscript, Monmouth Battlefield State Park.
Stone, Garry Wheeler, and Mark Lender. "Lee's Advance Force." Unpublished manuscript, Monmouth Battlefield State Park, 1993 (revised 2001).

Internet Sources

"Black Loyalists." The Loyalist Pages, American Revolution.org. Retrieved from http://www.americanrevolution.org/blackloyalists.php.
"The American Revolution and Its Era: Maps and Charts of North American and the West Indies, 1750–1789." American Memory, Library of Congress. Retrieved from http://www.loc.gov/teachers/classroommaterials/connections/amrev-maps/file.html.
"The American Revolution's One-Man National Security Agency." *Cryptologic Almanac—NSA/CSS*. Retrieved from http://www.nsa.gov/about/cryptologic_heritage/center_crypt_history/almanac/.
Biographical Directory of the United States Congress. Retrieved from http://bioguide.congress.gov/scripts/biodisplay.pl?index=L000463.
Bland-Ruffin Papers. Revolutionary War Collections, Special Collections, University of Virginia Library. Retrieved from http://ead.lib.virginia.edu/vivaxtf/view?docId=uva-sc/viu01144.xml.
Bluemilk, Donna. "Proctors in Eastern Pennsylvania." USGenWeb Archives Pennsylvania. Retrieved from http://www. usgwarchives.net/pa/1pa/1picts/proctor/pf1.html.
Bluemilk, Donna, transcriber. "Continental Line. Fourth Regiment of Artillery, February 6, 1777–November 3, 1783. Pennsylvania State Regiment of Artillery." From *Pennsylvania Archives*, ser. 5, vol. 3. USGenWeb Archives. Retrieved from http://files.usgwarchives.net/pa/1pa/military/revwar/paarty01.txt.
Burke, William W., and Linnea M. Bass. "Brigade of Guards in the American Service." 4th Coy., Brigade of Guards. Retrieved from http://brigadeofguards.org/history.
"History of the Burlington Path." Freehold History, Township of Freehold. Retrieved from http://twp.freehold.nj.us/history-of-the-burlington-path.
"Letters from Valley Forge." Americanrevolution.org. Retrieved from http://www.americanrevolution.org/vlyfrgeltrs.html.
"Loyalist Muster Rolls." The On-Line Institute for Advanced Loyalist Studies. Retrieved from http://www.royalprovincial.com/military/musters/musters.htm.
"Military Annals of the Highland Regiments, Fraser's Highlanders or Seventy-First Regiment." ElectricScotland.com. Retrieved from http://www.electricscotland.com/history/sketches/highlandsketches68.htm.
"Military History of Francis Proctor, Jr. (c. 1751–c. 1798?)." State Society of the Cincinnati of Pennsylvania. Retrieved from http://pasocietyofthecincinnati.org/Names/FrancisProctorJr.html.

Neumann, George. "The Redcoats' Brown Bess." *American Riflemen* (9 December 2009). Retrieved from http://www.americanrifleman.org/articles/2009/12/9/the-redcoats-brown-bess/.

"Northern Campaign of 1777 Primary Sources," His Majesty's 62d Regiment of Foot, Retrieved from http://www.62ndregiment.org/sources.htm#letters.

"103rd Regiment of Foot." Last modified 28 August 2010. Families in British India Society, Retrieved from http://wiki.fibis.org/index.php?title=1 03rd_Regiment_of_Foot.

Israel Shreve Revolutionary War Letters. Special Collections, University of Houston. Retrieved from http://archon.lib.uh.edu/?p=collections/controlcard&id=359.

"Sir Henry Bunbury, 3rd Bt." Last edited 6 April 2011. Person Page, The Peerage. Retrieved from http://www.thepeerage.com/p18814.htm#i188133.

Smith, Shirley Hunter. "Abraham Clark." 2008, (posted 11 Dec. 2011). Society of the Descendants of Signers of the Declaration of Independence. Retrieved from http://www.dsdi1776.com/signers-by-state/abraham-clark/.

Tredyffrin Easttown Historical Society *History Quarterly*. Retrieved from http://www.tehistory.org/index.html.

U.S. Coast Guard. "Situational Awareness." *Team Coordination Training Student Guide*. August 1998. Retrieved from http://www.uscg.mil/auxiliary/training/tct/chap5.pdf.

"The War of the Revolution, 1775 to 1783: The British Army in the Revolutionary War." Britishbattles.com. Retrieved from http://www.britishbattles.com/american-revolution.htm.

Washington Rallying the Troops at Monmouth. Art Gallery Foyer, AmericanRevolution.org. Retrieved from http://www.americanrevolution.org/leutze.html.

"A Yorkshire Regiment History." British Army. Retrieved from http://www.army.mod.uk/infantry/regiments/26215.aspx.

Index of Military Units

Page numbers in italics indicate illustrations.

British Forces

1st Division, *125–27*, 130–33, *160*; Crosswicks to Monmouth, 136–40, 150, 153–56; at Monmouth, 157, 182, *185*, 217, 222, 257, 262–70, 273–77, 283, 291–93, 299–313, *321*, 331–50

2nd Division, *125*, 127, 130–33, 139–41, 145, 153–54, 156–57, *160*, *185*, 212, 217, 248, 249, 265, 276–77, 331, 332, 349–52

Artillery

Royal Artillery, 4th Battalion, 50, 53–54, 57, 59, 86, 97, 126, 127, 131, 132, 142, 408, 482n30, 493n3; at Crosswicks, 138–139; at Allentown, 140, 151, 154; at battle of Monmouth, 157, 208, 210, 257, 262, 264, 267–68, 270, 272, 274, 276, *301*, *307*, 500n105, 526n8; great cannonade, 318, 320–26, 333–35, 341, 404, 408, 439; retreat, 332, *334*, 335, 338–39, 344, 349, 365, 374, 375

Infantry Brigades

Brigade of Guards, 48, 52, 60, 139, 154, 267, 273, 292–93, 299, *301–308*, 315, *321*, *334*, 375, 386; 1st Battalion Guards, 302, 520n10; 1st, 2nd, and 3rd Regiment Foot Guards, 16, 48, 55, 56, 60, 72

British foot brigades

- 1st Brigade, 98, 375; 4th Regiment, 157; 28th Regiment, 131, 149
- 2nd Brigade, 98, 375; 10th Regiment, 49; 40th Regiment, 350; 55th Regiment, 106, 131
- 3rd Brigade, 98, *231*, 267, 274–76, 284, 318, *321*, 325, 331–40, 344; 15th Regiment, 131, 379; 17th Regiment, 379; 42nd Regiment (Royal Highlanders/Black Watch), 49, 56–57, 131, 144, 206, 210, 274–76, 332, *334*–40, 379, 414, 529n15; 44th Regiment, 106, 275, 379
- 4th Brigade, 98, 132, 139, 267, 274, *301*, *334*, 344; 33rd Regiment, 98, *343*–47, 404, 530n33, 531n39
- 5th Brigade, *125*, 127, 132–33, 135–36, 139, 152, 267, 274, 375; 26th Regiment, 352

Infantry Detachments and Other Units

British flank companies, 49, 376

- grenadiers, 48–49, 52, 56, 60, 98, 128, 138, 139, 148, 154, 182, 210–11, 267, 273, 293, 299–312, *321*, 333–35, 353, 356, 362, 365, 374–76, 386, 390–91, 404, 413
- 1st Battalion Grenadiers, *301*, 304, 307–308, *311*, 329, 340–47, 404, 530n31
- 2nd Battalion Grenadiers, *301*, 304, 307–308, 310–13, 318, 331, 333, 344, 412
- Erskine's detachment (Queen's Rangers, 1st Light Infantry), during battle, 275–276, 297, 310, 332–333, 340, 344, 404, 538n12
- light infantry, 3, 48–50, 59, 98, 138, 139, 140, 154–55, 158, 274, 356, 376, 379, 386, 404
- 1st Light Infantry, 139, 249, 254, 257, 262, 267, 275, 332, *334*, 338–40, 375
- 2nd Light Infantry, 157, 210, 244, 254, 500n105, 514n1

German auxiliaries (Hessians), 47, 49, 50–53, 58, 60, 62, 63, 79, 83, 111, 131, 165, 428; desertion, 59–60, 148, 498n81, 544n29; on march, 124, 126–27, 142, 145–47, 149, 157, 209–210, 214, 216, 274, 375

Ansback-Bayreuth regiments, 87, 487n37
Hessian artillery, 51, 263
Hessian grenadiers, 97, 139, 182, 262, 267, 274
Jaeger Corps, 51–52, 59, 67, 83, 97, 124, 127–28, 130–32, 135–36, 140, 154–56, 158, 205, 249, 369, 373, 404, 424, 493n5, 494n11, 495n26
Loo's Brigade, 97
Stirn's Brigade, 97, 127
Leslie's detachment, *125*, 127–128, 130–133, 139, 153, *160*; at the drawbridge, 135–136, 163, 168
Loyalist forces, 47, 50–53, 58, 60, 83, 89, 93, 96, 127, 146, 201, 211, 213, 215, 258, 324, 375, 420–22, 481n19, 486n22, 497n63, 498n74, 526n23; recruiting, 10–11; garrison Sandy Hook, 151, 211, 373, 421–22
"Black Brigade" (irregulars), 421–22
Bucks County Volunteers, 51
Loyal Americans, 51, 60
Maryland Loyalists, 50–51, 481n19
New Jersey Volunteers, 50–51, 132, 143
Pennsylvania Loyalists, 10–11, 132, 481n19
Queen's American Rangers, 51, 58, 127, 131–32, 137–40, 144, 153–58, 212, *225*, *242*–48, 249, 251, 254–55, *257*, *267*, *275*, 332–*34*, 418, 437, 494n11, 513n30, 515n33, 514
Volunteers of Ireland, 51, 481n19
West Jersey Loyalists, 51, 131, 143, 503n37
71st British Foot (returned to NY 1777), 47, 48, 480n2
vanguard. *See* Leslie's detachment

Horse

British light dragoons, 50, 97, 253, 255, 417; 16th Light Dragoons, 50, 98, 107, 110, 127, 137–38, 249, *257*–60, 262, 267, 270, 272, 274, 279, *301*–302, 304, 306–308, 310, 407, 413, 414; 17th Light Dragoons, 50, 97, 127, 157, 352
Loyalist horse, 127, 132, 466; Philadelphia Light Dragoons, 127, 153, 466, 493n5, 495n26

Support Departments

non-combatants: Black Pioneers, 54, 131; Bridgemaster's Department, 54, 127, 154; Commissary General, 144, 147; Engineer's Department, 54 , 127; Paymaster's guard and suite, 54, 127; pioneers, 139; Quartermaster General's Department, 54, 127; Royal Artillery Conductors and Artificers, 54; surgeons and medical staff, 54, 127, 248, 349–50, 362–63; women and children, 57–58, 86, 98, 126–27, 146, 216, 350, 489n74

Continental Forces

Artillery

Artillery Brigade, 69–70, *229*, 234, *252*, 256–59, 263, 266, 271, 275, 277, 284, *287*, 298–99, *301*–302, 307, *311*–13, 318–30, 333–35, *343*–34, 346, 408, 524n4
Crane's or Third Regiment, 319, 524n4; Frothingham's (Fourth) Co., 524n4; Seward's (Sixth) Co., 277, 299, *301*–302, 305–306, 524n4; Well's (Tenth) Co., 256–57, 259, 262–63, 524n4; Cook's (Eleventh) Co., 277, 299, *301*–302, 305–10, 524n4
Harrison's or First Regiment, 319–20, 361, 408, 524n4
Lamb's or Second Regiment, 319–20, 361, 524n4
Proctor's or Fourth Regiment, *311*, 319, 524n4; Proctor's Co., 319, 326–28, *334*, 527n32

Horse

light dragoons, light horse, 139, 154, 157, 164, 166, 170, 194, 198, 210, 296, 350, 355

Infantry Brigades

Glover's Brigade (First, Fourth, Thirteenth, Fifteenth Massachusetts), 189, 297, 500n5, 528n12
Huntington's Brigade (First, Second, Fifth, Seventh Connecticut), 297, 326, 487n32, 500n5

Learned's Brigade (Second, Eighth, Ninth Massachusetts), 297, 500n5, 528n12
First Maryland Brigade (Delaware; First, Third, Fifth, Seventh Maryland), 458
Second Maryland Brigade (Second, Forth, Sixth Maryland), 161, 317, 348, 359
Maxwell's Brigade, 89–90, 92, 94–96, 100, 104, 129–30, 132, 136–37, 141, 143, 149, 154, 161, 167, 163, 167, 169–70, 172–73, 177–79, 187, 189, 198, 237–39, 256, *257*, 263, 265, *267*, 269, 279–81, 286–*87*, 298, 316, 354–55, 362, 391, 411, 413, 419, 494n16-n17, 503n38, 516n41; First New Jersey Regiment, 89, 155, *287*–88, 299, *301*, *307*, 309, 335, 494n16; Second New Jersey Regiment, 88–90, 93, 145, 258, 286–*87*, 293; Third New Jersey Regiment, 73, 89, 128, 138–39, 155, *287*, 345, 361, 370, 391; Fourth New Jersey Regiment. 90, *287*, 370, 506n79, 535n40
Muhlenberg's Brigade (First, Fifth, Ninth Virginia; First, Second Virginia State; German), 161, 317, 348
North Carolina Brigade (First, Second North Carolina), 386, 500n5, 502n28
Paterson's Brigade (Tenth, Eleventh, Twelfth, Fourteenth Massachusetts), 316, 348, 500n5, 528n12
First Pennsylvania Brigade (First, Second, Seventh, Tenth Pennsylvania), 295, *311*; First Pennsylvania Regiment, 322, 419
Second Pennsylvania Brigade (First New York; Fourth, Fifth, Eleventh Pennsylvania), 297, *311*; Fourth Pennsylvania Regiment, 312; Rifle Co., 168
Third Pennsylvania Brigade, "late Conway's" (Third, Sixth, Ninth, Twelfth Pennsylvania; Malcolm's, Spencer's), 297, *311*, 342–45, 530n29; Third Pennsylvania Regiment, 329, 342, *343*, 345–46, 530n29; Twelfth Pennsylvania Regiment, 530n29; Rifle Co., 168; Malcolm's Additional Regiment, 342, *343*, 345–46, 397, 414, 530n29, 540n33; Spencer's Additional Regiment, 342, *343*, 346, 530n29
Poor's Brigade (First, Second, Third New Hampshire; Second, Fourth New York), 189, 348–49, 413, 487n32, 500n5, 528n12
Scott's Brigade, 189, 194, *242*, 246, 248–50, *252*–53, 256–*57*, 266, 269, 298, 361; Fourth, Eighth, Twelfth Virginia, 189, 241, 246, 248, *252*, 256–*57*, 265, *287*, 292, 299, *301*, 506–507n13; Grayson's and Patton's Additional Regiments, 189, *252*, 256–*57*, 285, *287*, 293
Varnum's Brigade, 189, 194, *252*, 256–*57*, 261, 263, 298, *301*, 306, *307*, *311*, 337, 500n5, 506nn12–13; First, Second Rhode Island, 189, 261, 269, 506n13; Fourth, Eighth Connecticut, 189, 506n13
Weedon's Brigade (Thirteenth Pennsylvania; Second, Sixth, Tenth, Fourteenth Virginia), 317; Sixth Virginia, Rifle Company, 168
Woodford's Brigade (Third, Seventh, Eleventh, Fifteenth Virginia), 284, 333–35; Seventh and Eleventh Virginia, Rifle Companies, 168

Infantry Detachments and Other Units

Jackson's Detachment, 104, 154, 170–71, 178, 187, 190, 237, 253, 255–66, 279–81, *287*, 305–306, 363, 414–15, 499n97, 517n73, 517n77, 524n4; Jackson's Additional Regiment, 279, 517n73; Henley's Additional Regiment, 279, 517n73; Lee's Additional Regiment, 279, 517n73
Morgan's detachment, 129–30, 136, 154–55, 157–58, *160*, 167–70, 173–74, 177–79, 182, *185*, 187, 193–94, 198, 211, 213, *226*, 233–37, 244, 255, 268, 350, 354–55, 362, 372, 411, 413, 418, 422, 502n28, 510n6; Life Guards (part), 168, 211; rifle battalion, 21, 167–69

picked men, 65, 154, 167–69, 177, 189, 192, 255, 258–59, 261, 274–75, 292, 303–304, *307*, 309, *311*, 336–40, 348, 354, 356, 407, 413–14, 502nn27–28, 504n53, 529n15, 530n29

Scott's detachment, 154, *160*, 174–75, 177–79, 182, 187, 189, 198, 237, 239, *252*, 256–*57*, 262–67, 269, 274–76, 297, *311*, 316, 322, 336–40, 348–49, 356, 413–14, 504n53, 516n41, 529n15; Butler's battalion, 189, 227, 253, 255–67, 269–70, 272, 275, 407, 414, 417–18, 437, 513n33, 514n11; Cilley's battalion, 174–75, 189, 275, *311*, 322, 324, *334*–42, 365, 391, 404, 406–407, 409, 414–15, 504n53, 528n12; Gist's battalion, 189; Parker's battalion, 189, 275, *311*, *334*–40, 348–49, 356

vanguard: at Monmouth, 170, 181, 184–90, 192–99, 204, *229*, *232*–40, 250–55, 257, 261, 265, 267, 273, 278, 280, 283–89, 291–95, 297, 314–16, 385, 391, 397, 410–13, 415–16, 418, 431, 532n56; out of Valley Forge, 86, 99, 104–105, 129; party of observation 28 June, 194, 198–99, 233–34, 238–*42*, 244, 246, 248–50, *252*–53

Washington's Life Guards, 159, 162, 168, 211, 453, 459

Wayne's detachment, 177–78, 180, 189, 198, *232*, 236–39, *252*, 256–*57*, 262–63, 268, 292, 299–305, *307*–12, 316, 318, 409, 413, 415; Livingston's battalion, 189, 268, 298–*301*, 306–*307*, 309–*11*, 313, 358, 361, 406, 413–14; Stewart's battalion, 189, 292, 299–305, 315, 418; Wesson's (then Ramsey's) battalion, 189, 292, 299–305, 315, 361, 396, 416, 418, 437, 548n12

Support Departments

Quartermaster's Department, 11, 34–35, 70, 80, 88, 161, 163, 176, 360, 369–70, 501n9; Artificers and Pioneers, 72, 162

Commissary Department, 11, 61, 70–71, 163, 179–81, 314, 370

Medical Department, 30–32, 63, 68, *230*, 316, 320, 329, 356, 359–64, 534n24, 535n45

Militia

New Jersey Militia, 9, 21, 46, 52, 62, 85, 89–90, 92–96, 110, 143, 405, 407, 420, 422–24; and British march, 90, 100, 104, 128–32; Crosswicks to Monmouth, 137–39, 141, 147, 149, 151, 154–55, 159, 162–63, 165–74, 178, 182; at drawbridge, 135–36; at Monmouth, 184, 190, 192, 198, 203, 208, 210–16, *223*, *224*, *225*, *230*, 233–34, 238, 240–52, 254, 257–60, 278–79, 282, 284, *301*, 305, *307*, 309, 314, 322, *334*, 350–52, 354–55, 388, 428–29, 433–36, 502n31, 503n37, 512n24, 514n1

- artillery, 170, 243, 350
- Burlington County, 135, 137, 145, 170, *242*–44, 247, 496n43, 502n31
- Cumberland County, 9, 128–29, 149, 170, 502n34
- Essex County, 170
- Gloucester County, 420, 503n37
- Hunterdon County, 162, 170, 210, *242*–48, 259, 428–29, 512n24, 527n3
- light horse, 90, 139, 170, 190, 257, 259, 277, *301*, 305, *307*, 309, 314, 322
- Middlesex County, 154, 170, 244, 350–52
- Monmouth County, 129, 137, 170, 211, 244, 278–79, 286, 350–52, 293–94, 422, 502n31, 543n15
- Morris County, 170–71, 210, *242*, 244, 514n1
- Salem County, 9, 170
- Somerset County, 170, 210, *242*, 244, 251–52, *334*

Pennsylvania militia, 8, 30–31, 101, 154, 169, 296, 502n34

General Index

Page numbers in italics indicate illustrations.

Abeel, James, 163
Abercrombie, James, 33
Abington, Earl of, 377
Academy and College of Philadelphia (University of Pennsylvania), 78
Adams, Abigail, 23
Adams, Samuel, 32, 320, 356, 360, 363–66, 421
Adams, John, 23, 24, 26, 29, 33; loses faith in Washington, 29–30, 32, 35, 402
Adams, Samuel, 24, 26–27, 29, 30, 32, 35, 41, 42, 356, 384, 386, 402
African Americans, 325–26, 362, 399, 527n28; military enlistment of, 54, 63; in Monmouth County, 211, 373, 421, 437, 509n28. *See also* Lee, Will (Billy)
agriculture, 64, 124, 369; in Hunterdon County, 162, 166; impact of Monmouth campaign and, 140, 144–45, 166; in Monmouth County, 203–206, *207*; produce in trade, 205
Albany, N.Y., 5, 92
Alden, John, 107, 112, 492n46
Alexander, William (Lord Stirling), 16, 37, 78, 161, 172, 174, 186, 322, 335, 336–37, 338, 341, 345, 348, 349, 385, 391, 395, 402, 410, 412, 442, 456, 525n5, 528n10; and Conway Cabal, 37–38; and dispute over command of army vanguard, 187–88; on Perrine's Hill, 275, 276, 297–98, 310, 312, 318, 319, 409, 439
Allentown, N.J., 124, *125*, 126, 135, 137, 139–40, 148, 150, 151, 154, 156–57, *160*, 167, 168, 171, 174, 175, 179, *185*, 202, 209, 217, 258, 443
Allgood, John, 359
Amboy Road, 157, 243, 249, *257*, 274, 275, 445–46, 516n41. *See also* roads
Amherst, Jeffery, 33
ammunition, 23, 70, 71, 126, 136, 142, 162, 255, 263, 282, 328, 365, 370, 497n59, 503n34, 527n34; cut bullets, 276
Amwell (Mount Airy), N.J., 159, *160*, 161, 162
Anburey, Thomas, 133, 134–35, 495n35
Anderson, Henry, 361
Anderson, Jacob, 361
André, John, 131, 143, 274, 340, 494n11
Andrews, John, 144–45
Andromeda (HMS), 3, 82, 379
Annapolis, Md., 111
Antonidas, John, 215
archaeology, 276; artillery impacts, *311*; evidence of troop dispositions, 338, 519n15; of Monmouth Battlefield, 348
Arnold, Benedict, 256, 399, 489n81; in Philadelphia, 104, 499n97, 502n34, 513n30; treason of, 432
Artificers and Pioneers, 72, 162, 467
artillery, 131, 138, 142, 151, 157, 170, 190, 208, 210, 234, 374–75, 406, 408; at Battle of Monmouth, *218*, 224, *229*, *252*, 254, 256, 262–63, 266, *267*, 269, 271, 275–77, 279, 292, 297–99, *301*, 306, 309, *311*, 315, 318–30, 333, 375, 384; effectiveness of, 346–47, 375, 384, 408, 412; "grasshoppers," 332, 338, 365, 529n17; howitzers, 54, 320, 349, 448, 493n3; with Nathanael Greene, 284, 329, 333, 335, *343*, 346–47, 412; sizes of, 54, 320, 338, 349, 493n3
Austria, 107

Bald Hill, 243
Banister, John, 384, 491n32
Baptist Meeting House, N.J., 164–66, 167. *See also* Hopewell, N.J.
Baptists, 205, 509n15

Barber, Francis, 74, 345, 361, 364
Barrack Meadow, 335, 512n24
Barren Hill, Battle of, 91, 183, 186, 277, 413, 488n50
Bartlett, Josiah, 389
Basking Ridge, N.J., 110
battle reenactments: Monmouth, 433–34, 436–37, 439; Trenton, 545n16
Baurmeister, Carl Leopold, 99, 146, 149, 152, 156, 216, 313
bayonets, 53, 59, 164; at Monmouth, 155–56, 261, 302, 309, 386, 522n43; training for use of, 66; wounds by, 416. *See also* weapons
Beesley, Jonathan, 128–29, 149, 494n11
Bell, Andrew, 129, 152, 366, 368, 375, 405, 494n20, 513n33
Bennington, Battle of, 30
Bermuda, 108
Bilby, Joseph, 437, 474n16, 543n15
Billingsport, N.J., 96, 123–24, *125*, 131, 442, 497n63
Black Company of Pioneers, 54. *See also* African Americans
Black Horse (Columbus), N.J., *125*, 132–34, 135–36, 139–40, 170–71, 443
Black Horse Tavern, 132
Black's Creek, 135, 140
Blake, Thomas, 371, 502n28
Bloomfield, Joseph, 73, 90, 155, 391–92, 395
Blue Book (Steuben), 68
Board of War, 36, 40, 41, 368, 394, 478n52, 479n71
Boise, John, 352
Bordentown, N.J., *125*, 132, 135–36, 147, *160*, 163, 168–70, 216, 443, 503n38
Boston, Mass., 28, 49, 69, 90, 109, 148, 165, 167, 389, 501n17
Boudinot, Elias, 116, 187, 384–86, 392, 394, 399; arranges exchange of Lee, 114; as Commissary of Prisoners, 59; denigrates Lee, 121; political support of Washington, 114, 396
bounties, 60–62, 162, 330, 437
Braddock, Edward, 33, 36, 106
Brandywine, Battle of, 6–7, 20, 22, 26, 27, 31, 33, 38, 50–51, 54, 67, 89, 258, 353, 361, 406
British army, 47–60; composition, 47–50; loyalist units, 50–51; Hessians, 51–52; officers of, 54–56; social structure, 56; strength, 47; weapons of, 52–54
Broadhead, Daniel, 27
Brooklyn Heights, 4, 34
Brooks, John, 188–89, 198, 240, 258, 270–71, 279, 289–90, 451
Brown Bess, 51–52, 365. *See also* weapons
Buckingham, Pa., 104
Bucks County, Pa., 148, 502n34
Bunbury, Henry, 105
Bunker Hill, Battle of, 16, 28, 148, 368, 410
Bunner, Rudolph, 345, 360–62
Burgoyne, John, 3, 5, 16–17, 21, 23, 30–31, 46, 48, 55, 70, 236, 384, 492n34; and Charles Lee, 107–109; Convention Army, 134–35, 167; "to Burgoyne" or "Burgoyning," 133, 142–43, 163, 423
Burke, Thomas, 33, 114
Burlington, N.J., 20, *125*, 132, 203
Burlington County, 124, 127, 135, 137, 139, 144–45, 170, 204, 243–44, 247, 420, 496n43
Burlington Path (Great Path), 203, 205, 208, 214
Burr, Aaron, 342, 397, 530n29; friendship with Charles Lee, 402
Burrows' Mill, N.J., 213
Bury St. Edmunds, Suffolk, 106
Butler, Richard, 189, 227, 253, 255–56, 257, 258–60, 270, 272, 275, 407, 414–15, 417–18, 446; in Lee's planned envelopment, 261–63; retreat of Lee's vanguard, 264–66, *267*, 269
Byng, John, 33
Byrd, Otway, 108, 111
Byrd, William, 108

Cadwalader, John, 93, 95, 489n81; duel with Conway, 387–88, 425, 455, 539n19; at Monmouth, 154, 169, 296, 502n34, 507n28; urges aggressive pursuit of British, 101–103
camp followers, 57–58, 126, 146, 166. *See also* women
Campbell, John (Lord Loudon), 33
Canada, 5, 90, 103, 225, 256, 258, 478n52
Cape May County, 89, 503n37

Carleton, Will, 436, 545n11
Carlisle, Pa., 327, 329–30, 527n32
Carlisle Commission, 13, 15, 18, 59, 83–85, 112, 152
Carrington, Edward, 319, 408
Carroll, Charles, 41, 479n71, 491n32
Carter, Dennis Malone, 435
Carter, Landon, 91
casualties, 52, 248, 339, 365–66; American, 136, 264, 270, 360–62, 524n4, 536n57; British, 7, 123, 128, 156, 260, 276, 306, 315, 323, 366–69; treatment of, 138, 360–64
Caswell, Richard, 33, 114
Cathcart, William, 243, 276–77, 512n23
cavalry, 50, 151, 259, 314, 392, 394, 418; American, 61, 72, 186, 356, 417; British, 48–49, 56, 240, 244–45, 254, 272, 278–79, 308, 404, 441; in Lee's retreat, 302, 394, 396, 410, 417
Centurion (HMS), 111
Chambers, James, 322, 357–58, 419, 456
Champagne, Forbes, 277, 548n3
Chappel, Alonzo, 226, 435
Charleston, S.C., 16, 21, 54, 109, 319, 427, 539n13
Charleville musket, 71, 365, 484n84. *See also* weapons
Chelsea Hospital, 363
Chesapeake Bay, 6, 21, 116–17
Chester, Pa., 86
Chester County, Pa., 78
children, 89, 92, 127–28, 213, 350, 465, 468, 470
Cilley, Joseph, 189, 275, 322, 324, *334*, 336–40, 341–42, 365, 391, 404, 406–407, 409, 414–15, 452, 456–57
Clark, Abraham, 27, 32, 38, 43
Clark, John, 195–96, 279–81, *287*, 288–89, 297
Clark, Thomas, 348, 386, 458
Clarke, Alured, 145, 470
Clarke, Jonathan, 134–35
Clarksburg, N.J., 154
Clausewitz, Carl von, 46, 234
Clendenin, John, 329
Clendenin, Rebecca, 329
Clevenger, Job, 137–38
Clinton, George (British colonial governor), 16
Clinton, George (rebel New York governor), 74
Clinton, Henry, 3, 5, 45–47, 88, *185*, 186, 192–95, 423, 442–50; assessment of Monmouth campaign, 314, 367, 375; career of, 16–17, 48, 55; and Carlisle Commission, 83–83; character of, 16; contemplates burning baggage, 133–35; and Cornwallis, 222, 308; counterattacks at Monmouth, *229*, 264–66, *267*, 269–70, 273–77, 284, 291; courage of, 137–38, 306–308, 410; critics of, 314, 376–77, 410; at Crosswicks, 135, 137–39; decision to abandon Philadelphia, 58–59; decision to march to Sandy Hook, 150–53, 380; evacuates Philadelphia, 84–87, 96–98; and Hessians, 51–52, 67, 87; hopes for general engagement, 143, 157, 172–73; and loyalists, 50, 82–83; march to Monmouth Court House, 123–58, *125*, 209; movement to Sandy Hook and New York, 372–75; orders from Germain, 17–18, 76, 83–84; patriot reactions to, 89–90, 98–104, 129–30, *160*, 167, 184; and plundering, 128, 136, 143–48, 214, 216; portrait of, *220*; relieves Howe, 12, 15; and Wayne, Anthony, *334*, 342, *343*, 344–47, 433; withdraws from Monmouth Court House, 237, 249, 251, 331, 332–33, *334*, 335, 340–41, 349–50, *351*, 352
Clunn, Joseph, 243, 454
Cochran, Humphrey, 248
Cochran, John, 360. *See also* medical services
Coercive Acts, 13
Coles, Abram, 434
College of Philadelphia, 78, 93. *See also* Academy and College of Philadelphia (University of Pennsylvania)
Collegium Carolinum, Kassel (Germany), 67
Collins, Battas (Baltis), 323, 361, 525n4
Combs, Thomas, 206, *207*, 208, *242*, *334*
Combs Hill, 208, *242*, 278, 329, 333, *334*, 335, 343, 347–48, 406, 409, 412, 439, 449, 531n43
commissary general of prisoners, 59, 114

commissary general of purchases, 71, 144, 500n9
Committee at Camp, 43, 70, 479n71
compound warfare, 96, 423
Comte d'Estaing, Jean Baptiste Charles Henri Hector, 18, 372, 378–80, 538n27
Concord, Mass., 30, 109, 164, 436
Constantinople, 107
Continental Army: assessment of after Monmouth, 404–20; casualties of, 136, 264, 270, 360–62, 524n4, 536n57; combat effectiveness of, 405–16; councils of war, 76–81, 99–103, 171–77; deficiencies of, 63–64, 68–70, 72, 416–20; desertions from, 63–64; discipline in, 61–62; formation of, 61; French alliance and, 14, 72–73, 372, 378–80; Monmouth vanguard, 189–90, 451–53; order of battle, 451–62; organization of, 61; recruiting of, 62–63; routes of march, 159, *160*, 162–63, 178, 180–81; social structure of, 62–53; Steuben's reforms and, 65–68, 406–407, 415; strength of, 70, 173, 189–90; at Valley Forge, 65–74, 76. *See also* Board of War; Committee at Camp; councils of war; equipment; uniforms; weapons
Continental Congress, 8, 34, 92, 165, *223*, *228*; appoints Washington commander in chief, 26; army reforms and, 61, 65, 68, 70–71, 115; Battle of Monmouth and, 384–86, 389–90; Board of War, 36, 40–41, 386, 394, 478n52; Charles Lee and, 61, 109, 111–12, 114–16, 120–21, 396–97, 400–401; and Committee at Camp, 43, 70, 479n71; congressional critics of Washington, 19–44; dismisses Lee from army, 401; Horatio Gates and, 29, 31, 35–36, 38, 41–42, 43; Philadelphia campaign and, 22–24, 26; sustains Lee court martial verdict, 400; votes thanks for victory at Monmouth, 384; in York, Pa., 4, 31, 36–37, 66, 82, 99, 113–15. *See also* Board of War; Committee at Camp; Conway Cabal; Laurens, Henry
Continental Line. *See* Continental Army
Convention Army, 134–35, 167
Conway Cabal, 33–41, 387, 398, 402, 425
Cooch's Bridge, 6
Cook, David, 299, *301*, 305–306, *307*, 309–10, 361, 364, 452
Coopers Point (Camden), N.J., 80
Corbin, Margaret, 327
Corlies, John, 421
Cornwallis, Charles, 87, 98, 127–28, 133, 136, 154, 276, 349, 402, 410, 531n43; career of, 55; as colonel of 33rd Foot, 345; commands 1st Division, 126, 130, 132, 468; counterattacks at Monmouth, *257*, 262, 265, 273, 439, 446; at Hedgerow, 277, 308; portrait of, *222*
Coryell's Ferry (Lambertville), N.J., *20*, 88, 99, 104, 159, *160*, 161, 363, 442–43, 535n40
councils of war: at Hopewell, 171–77; at Valley Forge, 76–81, 99–103
courts-martial, 58, 104, 141, 146, 209, 497n56, 498n74; Anthony Wayne, 393–94; Arthur St. Clair, 393; Charles Lee, 390–96, 400; Phillip Schuyler, 393
Covenhoven, Albert, *257*, 263
Covenhoven, Benjamin, 215
Covenhoven, Cornelius, 215
Covenhoven, David, 215
Covenhoven, Elizabeth, 214–15, 510n38
Covenhoven, William, *125*, 156, *202*
Covenhoven Road, 238
Cox, Caroline, 357
Craig, John, *185*, 206, *207*, 276
Craig, Thomas, 346, 457
Craig, William, 206
Craig's Mill, 238, 240, 283–84, *334*,
Craik, James, 363, 430
Cranbury, N.J., *125*, 140, 150, *160*, 178–79, 180, 184, 187, *202*, 243, 250–51, 443–44
Crane, Isaac Watts, 436
Crane, John, 319–20, 451–52, 461–62, 524n4
Crosswicks, N.J., *125*, 135–40, 141, 148, *160*, 168, 496n43, 496n50
Crosswicks Creek, skirmish at, 132, 135, 168, 443

Cumberland County, 9, 89, 128, 170, 420, 502n34
Cumpston, John, 306, 310, 452, 461
Currier and Ives, 435
Custis, George Washington Parke, 325–26, 430–31, 545n7

Danbury, Conn., 363
Dansey, William, 332, 376
Davies, Thomas, 376
Dayton, Elias, 138, 453, 462
Dearborn, Henry, 296, 320, 324, 338, 366, 458, 504n53, 525n5
Declaration of Independence, 30, 32, 165
Delany, Sharp, 394
Delaware Bay, 3, 6, 150, 378, 420
Delaware River, 4, 6–7, 15, 20, 22, 30, 86, 89, 94, *125*, 497n63; American crossings of, 25, 66, 102, 103–104, 159, *160*, 161; British crossings of, 9, 84, 96–97, 99, 441; Royal Navy and, 18, 86, 442
Dennis, Rebecca, 214
desertion, 498n81; from British Army, 7, 11, 47, 58, 60, 63, 95, 102, 118, 148–49, 169, 172, 356, 369, 387; from Continental Army, 63–64, 248, 421, 524n4, 544n29; among Hessians, 60, 63, 87, 498n81; among loyalists, 60
Dickinson, Edmund, 358
Dickinson, John, 93
Dickinson, Philemon, 129, 132, 136, 143, 157, 173, 181, 203, 422, 428, 433, 436, 454–55; career of, 92–94; Charles Lee and, 192, 194, 198, 237–39, *252*; and Conway duel, 387; family of, 93; as intelligence source, 85, 94–97, 104, 149, 172, 184, 198, 237, 249–50, 486n29; and John Cadwalader, 93, 95, 503n34; as militia commander, 94–96, 141, 143, 157, 169, 170–71, 178, 241, 243–45, 355; portrait of, *223*; skirmish with Queen's Rangers, 243–47; warns Lee against advance, 250–51, 254, 273, 300, 446; and Washington, 95, 161, 167–69, 178, 355, 422; William Livingston and, 93–94
Director of Hospitals. *See* medical services
discipline, 27, 29, 246, 407, 414, 436; in British army, 58, 126, 145–47, 214–15; in Continental Army, 61–63, 81, 121, 264, 271; among Hessians, 87, 214
Doctors Creek, 138
dogs, 106, 111, 117, 198, *218*
Douglas, Stephen A., 434
Dow, Alexander, 345–46, 415; supposed death of Monckton and, 346, 522n43
dragoons, 50, 97, 110, 137, 139–40, 154–55, 171, 259–62, 265, 302, 308–10, 350, 355, 375, 413, 417–18, 448
Drayton, William Henry, 385–86
Drinker, Elizabeth Sandwich, 82, 89, 139
duels, 67, 107, 121; Cadwalader and Conway, 387–88; Lee and Laurens, 400; Lee and Steuben, 400; Peters and Morgan, 40
Duke of Newcastle, 16
Du Plessis, Thomas Antoine, chevalier de Mauduit, 329, 333, 334, 335, *344*, 347, 408, 459
Duportail, Louis, 79, 172, 176, 186, 269, 271–72, 278, 451, 489n81
Durkee, John, 189, 256, *257*, 264, 361, 364, 452, 506n13

East Morass (East Ravine), 207, 208, 511n19; in morning battle, 250, 255–56, 263, 266–68, 477; Wayne urges defense of, 411–13
Easton, Pa., 99, 103
Eayrestown, N.J., *125*, 129
Edwards, Enoch, 402
Edwards, Evan, 189, 194, 198, 235, 238, 240, 241; defends Lee, 402–403; in morning battle, 28 June, 254, 256, 259–60, 262, 264, 266, 270, 279, 446, 451, 517n71
Ege, Ralph, 164–65
Egg Harbor, N.J., 294, 420–21
Eisenhower, Dwight, 424
Eliot, John, 395
Elizabethtown, N.J., 92, 171, 423, 436
Ellis, Joseph, 420
Ellison, British hussar, 246; captured in Virginia, 513n30

English, James, 282–83, 294, 518n4
Englishtown, N.J., *125*, 157, *160*, 195–96, 250–51, 253, 271, 282–83, 285–86, 293, 297, 326, 355, 369, 418, 446–47; Lafayette withdraws to, 181–82, 183, 186; as Lee's headquarters, 184, *185*, 188, 198, 315–16, 444, 451; post-battle activities in, 355, 360–64, 421, 450; as reserve position, 316, 326, 331, 336, 348–49, 391, 449, 460, 524n4; Washington meets with Lee at, 191–92
equipment, 53–54, 70, 72, 124, 132, 141, 145. *See also* artillery; weapons
Erskine, William, 54, 59, 375, 467–68; commands light troops at Monmouth, 275; maneuvers on American left, 275–76, 297, 310, 332–33, 404, 521n38
Essex County, 423
Estey, Moses, 245–46, 428–29
Eustice, John Skey, 401–402
Evening Post (Philadelphia), 389
Evesham, N.J., *125*, 127–28, 130, 144, 494n11, 495n23
Ewald, Johann, 131, 135–36, 382, 424; assessment of American officers, 67; casualty estimates by, 136, 156, 369; education of, 67; and jaegers, 67; screens British advance to Monmouth, 83, 96, 128–30, 153, 155, 158; withdrawal from Monmouth, 374

Fabian tactics, 22, 26
Fallen Timbers, Battle of, 79
Farmer, Lewis, 302
Feilitzsch, Heinrich von, 59, 136, 155, 209–10
fences, 145, 166, 337; Hedgerow, 241–42, 244–48, *252*, 253, 273, 277, 280–81, *287*, 298–300, *301*, 304–306, *307*, 308–309, 312–14, *321*, 322, 331, 332–33, *334*, 335, 339–41, *343*, 346–47, 349, 358, 361, 394, 406–407, 410, 412–15, 417–18, 431–32, 433, 437, 439; as military positions, *311*, 339, 344, 346; as terrain features, 206, *207*, 252
Ferdinand of Brunswick, Duke, 67
Ferguson, Patrick, 421
Field, Michael, 352
field communications, 68, 270, 411, 416
Finney, Walter, 163, 312, 358, 525n5
Fishbourne, Benjamin, 256
Fisher, John, 149. *See also* courts-martial
Fiske, John, 290, 518–19n12
Fitzgerald, John, 74, 193, 270, 285, 288, 398
Fitz Randolph, Stelle, 352
flank companies, 49, 376
Fleming, Thomas, 42, 73, 478n58, 492n46
Flexner, James, 491n17
foraging: American, 74, 369, 417; British, 7–9, 16, 21, 80, 89, 135, 209–10, 212, 355; by troops, 58, 146, 369
Forman, David, 198, 210, 212–13, 254, 258, 451
Forman's Mill, 157, *185*, *202*, *207*, 210, *242*, 244, 256, *257*, 455
Fort Mercer, 7, *20*, 22, 30–31, 37, 125
Fort Mifflin, 7, *20*, 22, 30–31, 37, 125
Fort Niagara, 106
Fort Ticonderoga, 23, 106, 256, 296, 393, 476n6
Fort Washington, 25
Fostertown, N.J., *125*, 128, 149
Fourth of July, 370, 386, 427–28, 436, 450
France, 14, 65, 83, 108, 376, 378, 381, 387, 402, 516n40; celebration of alliance with, 72–73, 76; Franco-American alliance, 5, 12, 14, 17, 72–73, 76, 80, 81, 102, 173, 316, 371, 378, 419; military assistance from, 371, 378, 419
Franklin, Benjamin, 10, 65, 109, 502–503n34
Frederick the Great, 51, 65
Freehold (Monmouth Court House), N.J., *20*, *125*, 141, 149–50, 154, *160*, *185*, 193, 340, 443–44, 446–47; British occupation, 209–17; described, 201, *202*, 205–206, *207*, 208–209, 417; founded, 201; morning battle, 28 June, 236–38, *242*, 250–51, *252*, 253–56, *257*, 258, 265–66, *268*, 269–72, 290, 314;

post-battle, 349, 352, 354, 356, 360, 362–64, 407, 421; public events and memory, 431–37
Freehold, Borough of, 201
Freehold and Jamesburg Railroad, 432, 434
Freehold Sandy Loam, 204
Freehold Township, N.J., 126, 150, 154, 203–204, 211
Frelinghuysen, Frederick, 244, 251, 454
French and Indian War, 33, 36, 67, 90, 106, 165, 167, 174, 415, 544n17
French Revolution, 402
Frey, Sylvia, 56
Friedrich, Karl (Margrave of Ansbach), 87
Frye, Ebenezer, 536n6
fusee. *See* weapons

Gage, Thomas, 33
Galloway, Joseph, 8, 10, 82–83
Galloway Plan, 8
Gates, Horatio, 6, 24, 80–81, 88, 151, 164, 312; as alternative to Washington, 31, 34–36, 41, 74, 403; and Board of War, 36–37, 41, 43, 478n52; career of, 35; Charles Lee and, 108, 110, 121, 400–401, 496n6, 491n71; and Congress, 23, 29, 36, 42, 469n6, 479n71; Conway Cabal, 37–42, 399, 425, 478n54; criticisms of Washington, 25, 27; and James Lovell 29, 44, 85; and Washington, 92, 104, 146, 369, 387
Gates, Robert, 121
George III (King of Great Britain), 107–108, 117, 131, 344, 377
Germain, George, 3–4, 13, 17–18, 33, 55, 82, 143, 496n50
Germantown, Battle of, 6, 9, *20*, 22, 27, 38, 50, 138, 258, 312, 335, 361, 539n19
Gerry, Elbridge, 21–22, 24, 30, 32, 41
Gibraltar, 48
Gilman, C. Malcolm, 515n24
Gilman, Jeremiah, 261, 518n4
Gist, Nathaniel, 189, 452, 461, 547n1
Gloucester County, 88–89, 93, 143, 149, 171, 420, 503, 544n26
Glover, John, 548n11
Goddard, William, 401, 542n70
Golden, Abraham, 166
Gordon, Cosmo, 303
Gordon, William, 390, 393
Grant, James, 98, 277, 464, 548n3
Grayson, William, 189, 194, 451, 461, 507n13; leads vanguard advanced party, 193, 198–99, 233–34, 236, 238–40, 445–46; and militia skirmish, 241, *242*, 244, 246, 249; in morning battle, 28 June, 250–51, *252*, 253, 256, *257*, 265–66, 269; in morning retreat, 285, 293, 298
Great Awakening, 201
Greene, Nathanael, 78, 80, 100–101, 103, 149, 195, 235–36, 319, 387, 391, 412, 418, 489n81, 522n22; Charles Lee and, 117, 394, 399; commands right wing at Monmouth, 188, 284, 329, 333, *334*, 348, 406, 410, 449, 459; George Washington and, 113, 447, 500n9; Hopewell council of war, 172, 175–77, 383, 504–505n55; as Quartermaster General, 70–71, 88, 161, 163, 369, 408–409, 419; Thomas Mifflin and, 34–35
Greenman, Jeremiah, 366
grenadiers, 56, 97–98, 128, 138–39, 154, 182, *257*, 262, 329, 353, 362, 365, 375–76, 386, 390–91, 449, 468–69; and Anthony Wayne, 340, 342, *343*, 344–47, 404, 449; defined, 48–49; desertions and captures of, 60, 148, 210–11, 357; at Hedgerow, 306, *307*, 308, 312–13, 318, *321*, 333, 335; Hessians, 274, 449; in morning counterattack, 28 June, *267*, 273, 293, 299, *301*; at Point of Woods, 304, *334*, 413; at West Morass, 310, *311*, 312–13, 318, 412, 448
Grey, Charles "No Flint," 332–33, 344, 410, 469–70, 521n38, 543n9; anticipates march to Sandy Hook, 152–53; Battle of Paoli, 53, 59, 152; on evacuation of Philadelphia, 152; flanks American left at Monmouth, *231*, 274, 276, 310, 404; portrait of, *231*
Griffith, David, 316, 353, 523n54
Gruber, Ira, 12

Haddonfield, N.J., *20*, 89–90, 97–98, 123–24, *125*, 126–28, 130, 143, 442

Haines, Hinchman, 128–29
Hale, William, 304, 308, 312–13, 322, 325, 376–77, 410, 434, 515n40, 422n43
Halifax, Nova Scotia, 18, 28
Hamilton, Alexander, 195–98, 235, 271, 298, 305, 414, 431; advance to Monmouth, 283–84, 447; and army politics, 384–85, 389, 392, 394, 398–99, 433; Charles Lee and, 187–88, 194, 293–94, 392, 344, 431, 542n63; at Hedgerow, 306–309; Hopewell council of war and, 174, 176–77, 504n55; and Lafayette's advance, 178–81, 444; Washington's relationship with, 74, 398–99, 431
Hampton, William, 363
Hancock, John, 384
Hancock's Bridge, 9
Hand, Elijah, 9
Harcourt, William, 9, 112, 274, 309, 418, 468
Harnett, Cornelius, 22
Harrison, Benjamin, 40–41
Harrison, Charles, 319, 361, 408, 524n4
Harrison, Robert Hanson, 74, 281, 285, 288, 291, 448
Hart, John, 165–66
Hays, Mary, 327–30, 435, 527n92, 528n41. *See also* McCauley, Mary Hays (also McCalla, McCawly); Molly Pitcher legends; women
Hays, William, 327, 330
Head of Elk, Md., 6, 10, 31, 116
Heard, Nathaniel, 154
Heath, William, 167
Hedgerow, 241–42, 244–48, *252*, 253, 273, 277, 280–81, *287*, 298–300, *301*, 304–306, *307*, 308–309, 321–14, *321*, 322, 331, 332–33, *334*, 335, 339–41, *343*, 346–47, 349, 358, 361, 394, 406–407, 410, 412–15, 417–18, 431–32, 433, 437, 439
Henderson, Rachel, 215
Henderson, Thomas, 215–16, 241; Lee's retreat reported by, 284, 286
Henley, David, 279, 452, 517n73
Henry, Patrick, 42, 479n63
Hesse-Hanau, 51
Hesse-Kassel, 51, 494n20
Hessians, 47, 62, 275; advance to Monmouth, 96, 128–30, 136, 153, 154–55, 158, 209–10; casualties, 136, 156, 369; desertion among, 60, 63, 87, 148, 498n81, 544n29; evacuation of Philadelphia, 83, 87, 148; grenadiers, 274, 449; occupation of Freehold (Monmouth Court House), 216; recruited, 51, 87; strength of, 47, 51, 58; withdrawal from Monmouth, 374–75. *See also* Ewald, Johann; jaegers; Knyphausen, Wilhelm von
Hightstown, N.J., *125*, *160*, 179
Hilford, Richard, 60
Hills, John, 97, 126, 350, 495n23
History of the American Revolution (Ramsay), 396
History of the United States, from the Discovery of the American Continent (Bancroft), 431
Hopewell, N.J., 20, 141, 150, 154, *160*, 161–62, 164, 178, 211; council of war, 171–77, 197, 437, 505n61; encampment at, 164–67, 169, 443; patriot sentiments of, 164–66; picked men detached from, 168, 174–75. *See also* Hart, John
Hopewell Township, N.J., 161, 169
Hosmer, Titus, 384, 390
Houck, Margaret, 362. *See also* African Americans
Houghton, Joab, 164–65, 501n17
House of Burgesses, 40, 425. *See* Washington, George
Houston, Sam, 434
Hoveden, Richard, 127
Howard, Frederick (Fifth Earl of Carlisle), 13, 15, 18, 59, 83–85, 112, 152
Howe, Richard, 86, 378
Howe, William, 3–5, 8, 16–17, 28, 33, 49, 55, 58–59, 82, 86, 111; Barren Hill operation, 91; British views of, 3–4, 15; failure to attack Valley Forge, 11–12, 58, 71, 76; John Burgoyne and, 5–6; and loyalists, 8, 10–11, 50, 82; in New Jersey, 6–7, 9, 20–21, 26, 30, 110; Philadelphia campaign, 6–7, 22, 26, 31, 54; Philadelphia

occupation, 10, 26, 47, 84, 112; political problems of, 4, 19, 55; relieved by Clinton, 4, 15
Huber, Thomas M., 96
Huddy, Joshua, 170, 350, 422, 454, 459
Hudson River, 16, 44, 70, 96, 88, 99–101, 103, 450, 487n32
Hudson River Highlands, 44, 450
Hunt, John, 166
Hunterdon County, N.J., 161–62, 428, 446
Huntington, Jedediah, 297, 326, 457, 487n32, 489n81, 500n5, 541n43
Hussars, 241, 243–45, 247–48. *See also* cavalry

Imlaystown, N.J., *125*, 140, 145, 153, *160*, 443
Independence Day. *See* Fourth of July
Indians (Native Americans), 107, 112, 167, 227
Inman, George, 352
Inman, Mary, 252
Inner Coastal Plain, 124
Inspector General, 39, 65–66, 69, 79, 118, 241, 348, 387, 488n50
Ireland, 51, 102, 106, 148, 402, 466, 481n19
Iron Works Hill, Battle of, 131
Irvine, William, 295, 353, 386, 394, 452
Italy, 107

Jackson, Andrew, 433
Jackson, Henry, 104, 154, 170–71, 178, 187, 190, 306, 363, 415, 499n97, 524n4; court of inquiry, 517n77; in Lee's retreat, 264–66, 279–81, 289, 305; in morning battle, 28 June, 255–56, *257*, *258*, 268, 414; in vanguard's advance, 237, 253
jaegers, 51, 67, 131, 135–36, 382, 424; casualties, 136, 156, 369; definition of, 52; screening British advance to Monmouth, 83, 96, 128–30, 153, 155, 158; withdrawal from Monmouth, 374
Jefferson, Thomas, 108, 163, 296, 401
Jenkins, Katherine Bilby, 347, 479n16, 543n15
Jersey prison ship, 32, 111, 166
Jewstown (Colts Neck), N.J., 350
Jones, Gibbs, 323
Jones, Joseph, 24

Kelly, James Edward, 437
Kelly, John, 361
Ker, William (Carr), 241, *242*, 243, 269–74, 278, 348–49
Ker house, *242*, *267*, 269, 271–72
Keyport, N.J., 213
Kingston, N.J., *160*, 166, 178, 186, 204
Kinney, John, 370–71
Knox, Henry, 284, 335, 348, 370, 395, 405; artillery reorganization and, 69–70; assessment of, 408; at cannonade, 318–20, *321*, 525n5; Charles Lee and, 293, 298; in councils of war, 78, 101, 172, 489n81; at Hedgerow, 293, 298, 301, 305–306, *307*, 309
Knyphausen, Wilhelm von, 212, 248, 265, 276–77, 423–24; advance to Monmouth, 124, *125*, 127, 131, 139–40, 153, 156, *160*, 443; and baggage train, 132–34, 217, 249, 442; career of, 51; evacuation of Philadelphia, 97–98, 442–23; march to Sandy Hook, 331, 349–50, 352, 443, 445–50
Krafft, John von, 147–48

Lafayette, Marquis de, 24, 79, *160*, 186, 191, 243, 383, 402; advance on 26 June, 169, 178–83, 409, 443–44; assessment of, 183, 410, 413; Barren Hill operation, 91, 186, 277; Charles Lee and, 118, 184, 188–89, 401; commands Continental reserve, 161, 320, 448; Conway Cabal and, 39, 41; George Washington and, 74, 113, 296, 349, 398; at Hedgerow, 305–306; Hopewell council of war and, 172–76; morning battle, 28 June, 256, *257*, 261–68, 286, 411; with vanguard at Monmouth, 192, 198, 236, *252*, 253, 447; Washington-Lee confrontation, 290–91. *See also* France
Laing, Harmanus, 352
Lamb, John, 319, 361, 451, 524n4
Lane, Matthias, 215
Langworthy, Edward, 401

Laurens, Henry, 24, 66, 80, 84, *228*, 383, 386; on Battle of Monmouth, 196, 237, 382; on British evacuation of Philadelphia, 85, 87, 103, 163; Charles Lee and, 114, 196; defends Washington, 31, 35, 39, 40–42; and George Washington, 120, 167, 196, 282, 383; portrait of, *228*

Laurens, John, 326, 356, 369; army politics, 385, 389, 393, 398–99, 433; defends Washington, 35, 74; duel with Lee, 400, 402, 542n63; at Hedgerow, 309, 414; intelligence mission, 241; in morning battle, 28 June, 272; and Thomas Conway, 64–65, 408, 485n93

Lee, Charles, 234–35, 336, 348, 366, 375, 407–408, 413, 425; ad hoc attack plan at Battle of Monmouth, 254–56, *257*, 258; assessment of, 406, 410–12; association with Washington's critics, 25–26, 117, 398–401; battlefield confrontation with Washington, *287*, 288–91; command of vanguard at Monmouth, 181, *185*, 186–89, 198, 237; commands delaying action, 293–317; capture and captivity of, 110–12; character of, 107; commissioned major general, 109; conflicting intelligence at Monmouth, 238–40, 249–51, *252*, 281; court martial of, 390–97, 416; criticizes Washington, 25–26, 113–14, 397; death of, 401; defends Conway, 400; defends his conduct at Monmouth, 314, 316, 397, 402; defense of Hedgerow, 305–306, *307*, 308–10; detractors of, 117, 384–85, 391–93, 398–99, 401, 403; discretionary orders, 192, 194–96, 396–97; dismayed at retreat of Scott and Maxwell, 266, 268; dismissed from Continental Army, 401; dogs of, 106, 111, 117; drafts plan to defeat Revolution, 111–12; education of, 106; emigration to America, 108; Enlightenment sympathies, 106, 109; enters British army, 106; estate (Prato Verde) purchase of, 108; European travels, 107–108; exchange of, 101, 113; failure of morning attack, 262–66, *267*; family background, 105–106; first American service of, 106–107; guilty verdict of, 396, 400, 425; Hopewell council of war, 172–76; lack of political and interpersonal skills, 108, 113–14, 118, 121; Lafayette and, 118, 184, 188–89, 401; Laurens, duel with, 400, 402, 542n63; loyalty of, questioned, 365, 398; mental health of, 401; morning advance of, 249–53; movement to contact, 253–54; opposes Steuben's army reforms, 118; orders from Washington before Monmouth, 86, 190–99; patriots' regard for, 109, 114, 401–403; *Plan* for American army, 115–21, 417; portrait of, *221*; radical politics of, 108–109; reasons for retreat at Monmouth, 268–73, 278; refuses vanguard command, 178, 186–87; relations with Congress, 40, 114–15; relations with Washington, 108–109, 110, 113, 117, 197, 393, 398; scholarly and popular views of, 109, 396–97, 431–35, 490n12, 543n15, 492n46; seeks promotion from King, 101, 108; service in Europe, 16, 107–108, 115; strategic views of, 101, 110, 116, 152, 172–76; takes Iroquois consort, 106–107; withdrawal to Englishtown, 313–16, 348

Lee, Francis Lightfoot, 26, 32

Lee, Henry (Light Horse Harry), 12, 155, 183; on Lafayette, 186; misses Battle of Monmouth, 417

Lee, John, 105–106

Lee, Richard Henry, 23, 26, 30, 108, 114, 163, 479n63; Charles Lee and, 392, 399, 491n32; as critic of Washington, 32, 35, 41–42

Lee, Robert E., 12

Lee, Will (Billy), 325–26, 430. *See also* African Americans

Lellorquis, François (Marquis de Malmédy), 189, 279, 451

Lengel, Edward, 73, 482n27

Lenox, David, 256

Leonard, John, 212
Leonard, Sam (tory), 323–24, 353, 437
Leonard, Samuel (Continental), 361
Leonard, Thomas, 201
Leslie, Alexander, *125*, 127, 139, *160*, 470; at Bordentown, 135–36, 163, 168; as 1st Division vanguard, 127–28, 130–35, 153; in reserve on 28 June, 274
Letters from a Farmer in Pennsylvania (Dickinson), 93
Leutze, Emanuel, *218*,
Lewis, William, 135–36, 146–47, 216
Lewis's Mill, N.J., *125*, 135–36, 216
Lexington, Mass., 30, 109, 164–65, 436
Liberty Hall, 92, *224*
Life of George Washington (Irving), 431
Lippincott, John, *125*, 128, 130
Little Egg Harbor, N.J., 421
Livingston, Henry Beekman, 189, 268, 298–300, *301*, 306, *307*, 309–10, *311*, 313, 358, 361, 394, 406, 413–15
Livingston, William, 80, 85, 147, 161, 162, 274; anonymous report of Monmouth by, 147, 274, 388–89; career of, 92–93; Philemon Dickinson and, 93–94; portrait of, *224*; as war governor, 92–94, 213; Washington's relationship with, 92
Lloyd, Thomas, 308
Lloyd, William, 129
logistics, 47, 70–71, 408. *See also* Greene, Nathanael; Wadsworth, Jeremiah
Longbridge (Lawrence's Farm), N.J., 178
Long Island, 152, 201, 205, 373, 375, 389, 450
Long Island, Battle of, 4, 16, 34, 45, 109, 284, 312, 410, 494n17
Long Land Pattern musket. *See* weapons
Longstreet, John, Jr., 201, *202*
Longstreet's Hill, 210
Louisbourg, 106
Louis XVI (King of France), 73
Lovell, James, 22, 24, 436; and Battle of Monmouth, 386; criticizes Washington, 26–32, 35, 41–42, 44; family of, 28; Horatio Gates and, 44, 85; patriotism of, 28, 32
Lovell, John, 28
loyalists (tories), 9–10, 112, 211, *225*, 354, 384, 437; in British army, 47, 50–52, 60, 97, 132, 143, 247–48, 418n19; fates of, 11, 82, 82–83, 86, 143, 212–13, 420–22; Henry Clinton and, 50, 82–83, 86, 390; as intelligence sources, 126, 212; in New Jersey, 89, 93, 126, 143, 212–13, 420–22, 526n23; recruiting of, 10–11, 50, 53; William Howe and, 10–12
Lux, George, 392

MacLeod, John, 138
Manalapan Bridge (Penelopen), *125*, *160*, 184, *185*, 186, 193, 204, 233–34, 444
Manalapan River, 204, 210
Manasquan, N.J., 213
Manasquan River, *125*, *160*, *185*
Mantua Creek, *125*, 131
Marchant, Henry, 23
march security, 356, 362; American army, 88, 117, 164, 181, 253, 407; British army and, 84, 126–27, 131–33, 140, 350, 372–74, 423
Marquis of Rockingham, 152
Martin, James Kirby, 95
Martin, Joseph Plumb, 147, 150, 164, 324, 360, 365, 439, 504n54; with Cilley, 337–39; Molly Pitcher incident, 327–28, 430
Maryland, 6, 8, 10–11, 22, 50–51, 62–63, 101–102, 111, 292, 359, 437
Maryland Journal and Baltimore Advertiser, 401, 542n70
Mason, George, 108
Massie, Thomas, spurious accusation of Lee, 507n28
Mathew, Edward, 48, 469
Mathews, John, 384
matross, 361, 468
Maurice River, 420
Mawhood, Charles, 9–10, 469
Maxwell, William, 78, 100, 161, 163, 178–79, 187, 191–93, 391, 411, 413; career of, 90; cooperation with militia, 149, 169–70, 192; harassing and skirmishing operations in New Jersey, 89–90, 92, 94–96, 104, 129, 141, 154, 167, 169, 442–43; in Lee's vanguard, 189, 191, 237–39; in

Maxwell, William (*continued*)
 morning battle, 28 June, 256, *257*, 269, 279, 280–81, 286, *287*, 298, 447–48; post-battle deployments, 316, 354–55, 362, 419; reports Leslie's feint at Bordentown, 136–37; unable to stop Clinton's march, 130, 132, 143, 172
Mazzagetti, Dominick, 514n9, 543n15
McCauley, John, 329
McCauley, Mary Hays (also McCalla, McCawly), 329–30, 435. *See also* Molly Pitcher legends; women
McDougall, Alexander, 14
McHenry, James, 74, 159, 198, 261, 291–92, 296, 308, 313, 386, 392, 398–99
McKean, Thomas, 384, 387–88
McLane, Allen, 90
McNair, James, 358–59
McWilliams, William, 37
Meade, Richard Kidder, 74, 113, 195–97, 237, 239–40, 270, 511n16
Meadows, William, 344, 468
medical services, 31, 54, 68, 359–64, 367
Mercer, John, 189, 192–93, 198, 235, 298; with Lee in delaying action, 299–300, 304; in morning battle, 28 June, 254, 256, 263–66; in morning retreat, 268, 270, 281, *287*, 288; reacts to Lee court-martial verdict, 401–402; in vanguard's morning advance, 238–39, 251
Meschianza, 4, 82
Middlebrook, N.J., 20
Middle Morass (Middle Ravine), 208, 273–74, 281, 291, 293, 298–99, *303*, 302, 305, 342, 448
Middlesex County, 150, 154, 204, 352
Middletown, N.J., 273–74, 281, 291, 293, 298–99, *301*, 302, 305, 342, 448
Middletown Landing, N.J., 201
Mifflin, Thomas, 41–43, 403; character of, 34; Conway Cabal and, 38–39, 41, 425; critics of Washington and, 34–35, 37, 117, 398; jealousy of Greene, 34–35; leaves Valley Forge, 80; as quartermaster general, 35; relations with Washington, 34, 92; returns to army, 80–81
militia, 8–9, 16, 31, 52, 57, 62, 78, 81, 96, 388, 401; compound warfare and, 96, 423; Hancock's Bridge and Quinton's Bridge, 9; Maryland, 201; morning battle, 28 June, 243–47; New England, 30, 35; New Jersey, 21, 46, 85, 89, 94–96, 110, 120, 128–32, 135–39, 141, 143, 149, 157, 169–71, 178, 192, 241, 243–45, 355, 405, 420, 422–24, 428–29, 433–34; Pennsylvania, 34, 78, 93, 101, 154, 169; problems of, 31, 46, 71, 80, 95, 422; republican ideology and, 28, 30, 31, 41, 403, 436
Minghini, Guiseppi, 111
Minorca, 33
Molly Pitcher legends, 326–30, 432, 435, 437–39
Monckton, Henry, 56, *230*, 312–13, 333, 346, 365, 376, 404, 412, 414, 428, 523n43
Monckton, Robert, 56, 312
Monmouth, Battle of (28 June 1778): American army, effectiveness of, 406–19; artillery actions during, 224, *229*, *252*, 254, 256, 262–63, 266, *267*, 269, 271, 275–77, 279, 292, 297–99, *301*, 306, 308–309, *311*, 315, 318–30, 333, 335, *343*, 346–47, 375, 384, 412; British army, effectiveness of, 375–77; British final retreat after, 348–51; Butler vs. 16th Light Dragoons, 260–62; casualties, American, 264, 270, 360–62, 524n4, 536n57; casualties, British, 260, 276, 306, 315, 323, 366–69; Clinton counterattacks, 262–66, *267*, 268, 273–77; Clinton's leadership during, 273–77, 308–309, 409–10; congressional reactions to, 382, 384–86; Daniel Morgan and, 234–36; effects of heat during, 233, 237, 240, 262–63, 270–71, 276–77, 279–80, 282, 285, 295, 299, 304, 309–10, 313, 315, 328, 336, 339, 245, 360, 366–68, 415; folklore aspects of, 326–30, 432, 435, 437–39; Greene's leadership during, 284, 329, 333, 335, *343*, 346–47, 412; Hedgerow, 299, *301*, 305–306,

307, 308–10, 332–33, *334*, 335, 339–41, *343*, 346–47, 349, 358, 361, 394, 406–407, 410, 412–15, 417–18, 431–32, 433, 437, 439; Lee's leadership during, 253–54, 280–81; Lee's morning advance, 233–41, *252*, 253–56, *257*; Lee's retreat, 268–72, 278–81, 284–85; Lee-Washington confrontation, *287*, 288–91; militia and, 241–48; militia and Queen's American Rangers, 241–48; Monckton's charge, 310, *311*, 312–13; and New Jersey, 420–24; news of reaches Great Britain, 377–78; orders of battle, 451–70; picked men vs. 42nd Foot, 335–40; Point of Woods, 300, *301*, 302–305; popular memory of, 434–38; Washington's leadership during, 283, 292–94, 409–10, 424–25; Wayne's afternoon combat, 340–41, *342*, 343–47; women and, 326–30, 432, 435, 437–39
Monmouth Battlefield State Park, 438–39
Monmouth Battle Monument, 437
Monmouth Battle Monument Association, 437
Monmouth County, 93, 124, 126, 129, 137, 139, 141, 151–52, 156, 163, 204, 211–12, 284, 350, 357, 373, 421–23, 433, 437–38
Monmouth County Historical Association, 218, 438
Monmouth Court House (village), *20*, *125*, 141, 149–50, 154, *160*, *185*, 193, 340, 443–44, 446–47; British occupation, 209–17; described, 201, *202*, 205–206, *207*, 208–209, 417; founded, 201; morning battle, 236–38, *242*, 250–51, *252*, 253–56, *257*, 258, 265–66, *268*, 269–72, 290, 314; post-battle, 349, 352, 354, 356, 360, 362–64, 407, 421; public events and memory, 431–37
Monmouth Democrat (Freehold, N.J.), 434
Monongahela, Battle of, 33, 106
Monroe, James, 402
Montgomery, Robert, *125*, 154
Montreal, 106
Montresor, John, 58, 98
Moore, George H., 111–12
Morgan, Daniel, 21, 129–30, 154, 177–78, 182, 227, 233, 255, 411, 422; attempts to clarify situation at Monmouth, 235; at Bordentown, 136, 168–69; captured grenadiers and, 211; character of, 167–68, 236; confused orders before Monmouth, 193–94, 198, 234–36, 413, 418; detached with picked men, 167–68; fails to engage, 236–37, 268, 350, 418; French and Indian War service of, 167; harasses British advance, 155, 157–58, *160*, 169–70, 173–74, 182, *185*, 244, 433–44; messenger to Wayne, 236, 413; portrait of, *226*; post-battle deployment, 354–55, 450; at Saratoga, 168; Washington's critics and, 40
Morris, Robert, 24, 40–42, 111, 479n63
Morris County, 171, 210, 244, 514n1
Morrissey, Brendan, 380, 537n1, 538n27
Morristown, N.J., 9, *20*, 110, 149, 363, 423, 430
Mount Holly, N.J., *20*, 89, *125*, 128, 130–32, 141, 145, 147, 216, 324, 435, 442–43, 494n17
Mount Laurel, N.J., 128, 130
Mount Vernon, 390, 527n28
Moylan, Stephen, 210, 296, 355, 443
Muhlenberg, Peter, 78, 161, 317, 348
Munro, Edmund, 339
Murphy, Franklin, 438
Murray, British captain, 362
muskets, 51–52, 71, 86, 260, 276, 347, 365, 484n84. *See also* weapons

National Guard, 437
Nauheim, Battle of, 16
Navesink Highlands, *351*, 372–73, 378, 450, 537n1
Navesink River, 350, *351*
Neilson, John, 350, 455
Netherlands, 14, 71, 419
New Brunswick, N.J., 6, 20, 100, 150–51, 171, 363, 369–70, 374, 395–96, 428, 429, 450

Newburgh, N.Y., 86, 99
New Jersey, 26–27, 32, 37–38, 46, 50, 54, 84–86, 88–92; American advance into, 159–83; British military operations in, 123–58; civil conflict in, 93, 211–13, 420–22; Continental Army and, 61–62, 66, 90; foraging in, 9, 21, 58, 80, 89, 135, 146, 209–10, 212, 355, 369; early war effort (1776–1777), 4, 6, 11, 19–23, 25–26, 30; government of, 27, 94, 165; late war effort of, 422–24; loyalists in, 89, 93, 126, 143, 212–13, 420–22, 526n23; militia of, 21, 46, 85, 89, 94–96, 110, 120, 128–32, 135–39, 141, 143, 149, 157, 169–71, 178, 192, 241, 243–45, 355, 405, 420, 422–24, 428–29, 433–34; slavery in, 211, 373, 421–22, 437. *See also* Dickinson, Philemon; Livingston, William; Maxwell, William; Monmouth, Battle of; Monmouth Court House (village); Morristown, N.J.; Sandy Hook; Shreve, Israel
New-Jersey Gazette, 94
New Jersey General Assembly, 165
New Jersey Provincial Congress, 27, 94, 165
New Jersey State Archives, 146
New Manalapan, N.J., 204
Newport, R.I., 16, 111, 379
newspapers, 94, 367, 377, 388–89, 436
New York Bay, 372–73, 389–90
New York City, 18, 20, 21–22, 25, 32, 61, 88, 92, 124, 150, 152, 203, 340, 362, 377, 380, 386, 419, 450; Charles Lee imprisoned in, 109, 111; as garrison, 49, 58, 134, 372; Henry Clinton and, 16, 18, 86, 88, 349, 375; intelligence from, 81; loyalists and, 8, 50, 53, 201, 211, 367, 421–22; possible American attack on, 6, 18, 77–81, 355, 404; Royal Navy and, 151, 373, 375, 379
New York Gazette, 367
New York Herald, 436
New York Historical Society, 111
Nicola, Lewis, 387
North, Frederick, 3–4, 12–13, 15, 59, 83, 103, 108, 152, 377
Nut Swamp, 349–50, 372–73, 445, 449

Ochsenfurth-on-the-Main (Germany), 87
officers, 67–68; British officer corps, 54–56; and Congress, 29–30, 33, 39; expectations of, 33, 47; honors of war and, 128, 358–59; medical treatment of, 364; performance at Monmouth, 409–16; social status of, 54–56, 64; at Valley Forge, 65–66
Ogden, Aaron, 335–36
Ogden, Matthias, 89, *287*, 288, 299–300, 309, 455, 458
Old Burlington Road, 156
Old Tennent Church, 201
Olney, Jeremiah, 189, *257*, 261, 269, 298, 300, 306, 308–10, 313, 366, 406–407, 415, 452
Olney, Stephen, 269
Olney family, 269
orders, Germain to Clinton, 17–18, 76, 83–84; Washington's orders to Lee, 86, 190–99, 396–97
orders of battle, 451–70
Oswald, Eleazer, 256, 319–20, 324, 361, 408; defends Lee, 401–402; French Revolution and, 402; at Hedgerow, 305–306, *307*, 308, 310; on Lee's retreat, 298–99, *301*, 302; in Lee's vanguard, 190, 241; in morning battle, 28 June, 256, 262–64, 266–69, 271, 297–98; portrait of, *229*; radical politics of, 401–402; resigns from army, 401
Ounewaterika, 107
Outer Coastal Plain, 204

Paine, Thomas, 84–85
Palmer, Dave Richard, 505n61
Paoli, Battle of, 53, 59, 78, 152, *231*, 393–94, 482n27
Papas, Phillip, 109, 492n46
Paramus, N.Y., 396, 540n26
Parke, John, 256, *287*
Parker, Joel, 433–34, 437–38
Parker, Richard, 198, 275, *334*, 337, 339–40, 349
parsonage, 206, *207*, *232*, 241, *252*, *287*, 304, *307*, *321*, *334*, 346–48, 376, 406, 414, 433, 449, 522n43, 531n39

Parsons, Solomon, 303–304
partisan warfare, 120, 418
Paterson, John, 78, 172, 316, 348, 460
Pattison, James, 59, 320, 323, 374–75
Patton, John, 256, 293, 451
Paulus Hook (Jersey City), N.J., 422
Peebles, John, 144, 210, 340, 374, 376–77
Peekskill, N.Y., 21, 104, 164, 396
Pennsylvania Council, 83
Pennsylvania Packet, 389, 396
Pericles, 358–59
Perrine, Henry, 206, *207*, 208
Perrine's Hill (Perrine Heights, Perrine Ridge), 208, 218, 275, 279, *287*, 295–96, 298, 305, 309–10, 312, 318–19, 322, 333, 337, 341, 349, 391, 406, 409–10, 412–13, 439
Perth Amboy, N.J., 203
Peters, Richard, 40, 386, 394
Petty, William (Lord Shelburne), 152
Philadelphia, 3, 5–6, 31, 36, 45, 81, 89, 93, 101, 103, 110, 112, 116, 124, *125*, 148–49, 164, 171, 203, 258, 288, 326, 356, 363, 373, 389, 401, 428; American loss of, 4, 21–23, 33; American reoccupation of, 104, 139, 255, 353, 387, 389; British evacuation of, 15, 17–18, 46, 58–59, 84–88, 98–100, 142, 152, 173, 372, 377–78; British occupation of, 7–8, 9–10, 21, 26, 38, 47–50, 58, 60, 195, 378; loyalists and, 9–11, 22, 50–51, 82, 127, 153, 390, 481n19; military operations around (1777–1778), 7, 9, 11, 20, 24, 36–37, 53–54, 90–91, 212; possible American attack on, 30, 76–81; weather in, 282
Phillips, William, 134–35
picked men, 48, 65, 154, 158, 168, 174, 177, 189, 192, *229*, 253, 255, 258–59, 261, 274, 292, 303–304, 309, *311*, 322, 336, 338, 340, 349, 354, 356, 376, 407, 413–14, 448–49
Pickering, Timothy, 116, 387, 478n71
Pine Barrens, 204, 211, 421
Pine Robbers, 211, 421, 509n28
Plan for the Formation of the American Army . . . (Lee), 115–21, 417
plundering, 128, 136, 143–48, 214, 216, 377; American anger at, 164, 210, 214; of casualties, 365; court-martials for, 407n56, 498n74. *See also* Monmouth Court House (village)
Plutarch, 106
Point of Woods, *232*, 281, 292, 298–300, *301*, 302–305, 309–10, 313, 396, 406, 412–13, 415–16, 432, 437, 448, 548n12
Poland, 107
Poniatowski, Stanislaus (King of Poland), 107
Poor, Enoch, 78, 172, 174, 177, 189, 348–49, 409, 413, 449
Portugal, 107–108, 110
Prato Verde (Prato Rio), 108, 111, 113
Presbyterians, 201, 206, *230*, 511n19, 516n45
Prescott, Richard, 132
Price, Rodman, 434
Price, Thomas, 361
Princeton, Battle of, 4, 9, 11, 22, 26, 102, *219*, 296, 389
Princeton, N.J., 20, 27, *160*; hospital at, 363–64; picked men march through, 174–75
prisoners of war, 59, 95, 99, 111, 114, 138, 169, 247, 260, 302, 442; captured on 28 June, 354–56, 362, 366; Charles Lee as, 110–12; commissary general of prisoners, 59, 114; Convention Army, 134–35, 167; as deserters, 149. *See also* Boudinot, Elias
privateers, 420–21
Proctor, Francis, Jr., *311*, 319, 326, *334*, 524n4
Proctor, Thomas, 319, 327, 524n4
Prussia, 46, 51, 65–66, 118, 316
Public Ledger (London), 377
Pulaski, Casimir, 421, 492–93n53, 544n29

Quakers, 34, 82, 88, 127, 131, 137–39
quartermaster general, 34–35, 54, 59, 70, 88, 149, 161, 177, 374. *See also* Erskine, William; Greene, Nathanael; Mifflin, Thomas
Queens, N.Y., 375
Quinton's Bridge, 9

Ramsay, David, 292, 367, 396–97
Ramsey, Nathaniel, 292, 299–300, *301*, 302, 315, 361, 367, 396, 416, 418, 437, 548n12
Rancocas Creek, *125*, 128, 130, 140, 147, 443
Rankin, Hugh F. 79
Raritan Bay, 201, *351*
Raritan River, *20*, 150–51, 369–70; as factor in Clinton's march to Sandy Hook, 151, 380
Rawdon, Francis, 276, 466
Read, William, 326, 360–65. *See also* medical services
Reading, Pa., 37, 163
Recklesstown (Chesterfield), N.J., *125*, 140
recruiting, 10, 27–28, 47, 50–54, 56, 61–63, 65–66, 69, 72, 78, 89–90, 191, 407–408, 420
Red Bank, Battle of, 335
Reed, Esther, 389
Reed, Joseph, 25, 85, 110, 296, 389, 399
Rees, John U., 142, 488n50
Refugeetown, 373, 421. *See also* African Americans; Sandy Hook
Reid, John, 203
republicanism, 19, 28–32, 108, 120, 358, 402, 425, 436
Retaliators, 212
Rhea, David, 258, *287*, 294, 543n15; British dragoon and, 260, 430; family of, 258, 205–206, *207*, 208, 241; guides Tilghman to Perrine's Hill, 292–93
Rhea, Robert, 258
Rhode Island, 70, 201, 269, 298, 387; military operations in, 16, 23, 30, 112, 371, 379, 387
Richmond Mills, 234–35
riflemen, 21, 236, 418, 502n28. *See also* Morgan, Daniel
Rising Sun Tavern (Monmouth County), *125*, 154, *160*, 443
roads, 139, 208, 254; on battlefield, 255–56, *257*, 274, 284; condition of, 47, 54, 124, 142, 161, 209; connecting New York and Philadelphia, 203, 205; in Hunterdon County, *160*, 161; in Monmouth County, 124, 156–57, 201, 350; obstruction of, 90, 141, 162, 164, 172
Robin's Tavern. *See* Rising Sun Tavern (Monmouth County)
Rocky Hill, N.J., *160*, 162, 166, 178, 195, 282
Ross, John, 128–29
Rousseau, Jean-Jacques, 106
routes of march, 46, 88, 90, 99, 103–104; British army, 123, *125*, 127–58, *351*; Continental Army, *160*, 161–83
Royal Military Academy at Woolwich, 53, 55, 320. *See also* artillery
Royal Navy, 3, 7, 9, 14, 18, 97, 111, 150–52, 169, 372–73, 375, 378–79, 424, 442, 450
Rush, Benjamin, 30–33, 35, 42–43, 114, 326, 396–99, 402, 436
Russell, Giles, 189, 461
Russia, 107, 115
Russo-Turkish War, 107

Saint Andrews Church, 131
Salem County, N.J., 9, 89, 170, 420
Samson, Deborah, 326
Samuel, Massey, 507n28
Sandy Hook, 124, 150–53, 157, 167, 177, 181, 204, 209, 211, 213, 217, *351*, 354, 356, 362, 370, 372–74, 378–80, 421–22, 443, 450
Sandy Hook Bay, 373
Saratoga, Battle of, 6, 13, 21, 24, 29–31, 34–36, 38, 48, 57, 134, 168, 236, 348, 386, 423
Schanck family, 437
Schenck, Ralph, 244–46, 248, 259, 428–29, 512n24
Schuyler, Philip, 23, 31, 393, 476n6
Scott, Charles, *160*, 164, 172, 174–75, 177–78, 187, 198, 271, 316, 336, 361, 411; assessment of, 413; career of, 174; complains about Lee, 392; Lafayette and, 178–79, 182; in Lee's vanguard, 189, 194, 237, 239, *252*, 447; in morning battle, 28 June, 256, *257*, 262–65; picked men and, 154, 174, 274, *311*; retreat of, 266, *267*, 268–69, 280–81, 289; Royal Highlanders and, 274–75, 297, 413, 448; Washington-Lee confrontation, 290, 430; Washington's orders to Lee, 191–92, 196
Seely, Silvanus, 244

Selden, Ezra, 73
Seneca Indians, 106–107
Sergeant, Jonathan Dickinson, 27, 32, 42
Serle, Ambrose, 150
Seven Years' War, 3, 14, 16, 33, 36, 67, 90, 106–107, 165, 167, 174, 415, 544n17
Shakespeare, William, 106
Shaw, Samuel, 296, 305–306, 333, 368–69, 386, 395
Sherard's Ferry (Frenchtown), N.J., 99, 103
Shippen, William, Jr., 359
Short Land musket. *See* muskets
Shreve, Israel, 145, 292, 453; career of, 88–89, 258; in battle of 28 June, 286, 320, 323–24, 353, 356; deployed to New Jersey, 88–90, 258; on morning retreat, 286, *287*, 288; New Jersey militia and, 95–96; posted on Perrine's Hill, 293
Shreve, William, 145–47, 216, 243, 324, 454
Shrewsbury, N.J., 154, 157, *185*, 203, 205, 213, 250, *351*, 421, 444
Shrewsbury River, 324, 373
Shrewsbury Road, 153–54, 156
Shy, John, 112, 212, 396
Simcoe, John Graves, 52, 58, 133, 137, 143, 151–52, 273, 275; commands Queen's American Rangers, 50; at Crosswicks, 136–39; Ewald and, 155–56; in militia skirmish, 28 June, *242*, 243–44, 246–48, 259, 418; portrait of, *225*; screens Clinton's march, 154–55, 249
situational awareness, 113
Slabtown (Jacksonville), N.J., *125*, 132
Smallwood, William, 66, 489n81, 541n43
Smith, Eliza, 434
Smith, Paul H., 481n19
Smith, Samuel (historian), 235, 528n41
Smith, Samuel (soldier), 356
Smith, William S., 279–80, *287*
Snook, Phillip (Smock), 245–46
Some Queries, Political and Military, Humbly Offered to the Consideration of the Public (Lee), 401–402, 542n70
Somerset County, N.J., 170, 210, 242, 244, 251, 252
Sons of the American Revolution, 435, 437–38
Sourland Mountains, 165
South Amboy, N.J., 88, 99, 124, 150–52, 163, 166, 181
South Carolina, 16, 21, 36, 54, 109, 384–85, 396, 427
Spain, 14, 107, 419
Spencer, Ichabod, 417
Spencer, Joseph, 23
Spencer, Oliver, 342, *343*, 346, 457
Spotswood, N.J., 171, 369
Spotswood Middle Brook, 206, 208, 241, 250, 278, *301*, *307*, 315, 448–49
Spotswood North Brook, 157, 206, 208, 244, 261, 264, 275–76, 297, 445, 448–49, 511n19
Spotswood South Brook, 208, 511n19
Spring, Matthew, 274, 414
Staten Island, 150, 171, 373, 375, 421, 423, 450
Stauber, Leland G., 475n25
St. Augustine, 17
St. Clair, Arthur, 23, 31, 33, 227, 295; court-martial of, 393–94, 476n6; Wayne and, 341–42, 530n28
Stedman, Charles, 314, 522n43
Stephenson, Charles, 137–38, 496n43, 496n50
Steuben, Friedrich, 68, 113, 187–88, 300, 326, 335, 410, 415; appointed Inspector General, 68; assessment of, 272, 405–408, 412, 430; Benjamin Franklin and, 65; *Blue Book*, 68; Charles Lee and, 118–19, 272, 316, 400; commands reserve, 316–17, 348, 390, 449; in councils of war, 79, 100, 172, 176; opposition to, 118–19; scouting at Monmouth, 210, 216, 239, 241–43, 248–49, 446; training regimen, 65–68, 90, 405–408; Washington's relationship with, 68, 412
Stewart, Walter, 189, 292, 299–300, *301*, 302–303, 315, 418
Stiles, Ezra, 389
Stirn, J. D., 97, 127
Stites, Hezikiah, 179, 181
Stites, Mary, 179, 181
St. Lucia, 17

Stout, Joseph, 166, 501n21
Stryker, James, 427, 429
Stryker, William S., 128, 133–34, 284, 474n16, 502n34, 504n53, 513n35
Sullivan, John, 26, 387
Sullivan, Thomas, 141, 148–49
Susquehanna River, 59, 116–17, 120
Susquehanna Valley, 152
Sutfin, Derick, 207, 211, 240, *242*, *252*, 275–76, 280, 287, 295, 297, *311*, 332, *334*, 335, 338, *343*, 347, 448–49
Sutfin, Joseph, 211
Sutfin, Rhoda, 211
Swartwout, Bernardus, 271

Tallman, Peter, 145–47, 216
Taulman, Peter, 246
taverns, 9, 57, 110, *125*, 132, 154, *160*, 180–81, *185*, 201, *202*, 205, 215, 284, 334, 443
Taylor, Edward, 245
Tea Act, 13
Tennent, Gilbert, 502n34, 508n5
Tennent, William, 201
Tennent Church (Tennent Meetinghouse), *185*, 192, 201, 204, *207*, *230*, 238–40, *242*, 250, 282–83, 315, 323, 433; as field hospital, 312, 360; as militia position, 201–202, 210, 243, 355
Thayer, Theodore, 315, 501n9, 505n55
Thoughts of a Freeman, 31–32, 477n39
Tilghman, Tench, 74, 284, 292–94
Tinton Falls, N.J., 203, 350
Tomson, Thomas, *125*, 156
tories. *See* loyalists (tories)
Townsend Acts, 93
training, 46–47, 61, 64–65, 72, 80, 357, 417, 488n50; in British army, 49, 53, 56–57; Charles Lee and, 113, 118, 120; Friedrich Steuben and, 65–68, 405–408; Henry Knox and, 69–70, 335, 405, 408; in medical staff, 359. *See also* Knox, Henry; Steuben, Friedrich
Travels through the Interior Parts of America (Anburey), 134–35
Treason of Charles Lee (Moore), 112
Treaty of Amity and Commerce. *See* France
Trenton, Battle of, 4, 11, 22, 26, 102, 296, 349, 386, 389–90, 427
Trenton, N.J., 20, 85, 93, 101, *125*, 132, 135–36, *160*, 163, 168, 356, 363, 388
Tye, Colonel (Titus), 421–22
Tyler, John, 279

uniforms, 142, 154, 211, 270, 272, 279–80, 417
Upper Freehold, N.J., 201, 212, 240

Valley Forge, 5, 8, 19, *29*, 31, 39, 76, 85, 87, 105, 113–14, 116–17, 119, 122, 161, 167, 258, 319, 405, 409, 430; army reorganization at, 46, 69–72, 190, 355, 359; and British evacuation of Philadelphia, 103–104; British fail to attack, 8, 12, 58–59; condition of the army at, 43, 71–73; councils of war at, 77–82, 100–103; "military family" formed, 74; portrait of Washington at, *219*; status of Washington and, 73–74, 425; Steuben's training regimen at, 65–68, 272, 295, 406–407
Van Cleave, Benjamin, 213, 215, 422
Vanderveer, Garret, 215
Van Doren's mill, 350, 455
Van Dyck, Cornelius, 357
Varnum, James Mitchell, 77–78, 189, 194, *252*, 256, 261, 263, *301*, 306, *307*, *311*, 337
Vigilant (HMS), 98
Vila Vehla, Battle of, 107
Vindication to the Public (Lee), 399
Virginia capes, 6
Vorhees, Peter, 155

Wadsworth, Jeremiah, 71, 88, 408–409
Waldo, Albigence, 329
Walker, Benjamin, 239–41, 243
Walker, George, 215
Waln's Mill, N.J., *125*, 140, *160*
Walpole, Horace, 5, 13, 36, 109
Ward, Artemus, 109
Warren, Mercy Otis, 121, 382
Washington, George, 3–6, 12, 14, 18, 46, 84–92, 94–96, 123, 151, 159–61, 166, 179–82, 234, 269–70, 280,

354, 358, 360, 365–67, 369–70, 379–80, 387, 421; accounts of at Monmouth, 291–92, 296–97, 326, 385, 388–89; army organization and training and, 19–20, 28, 60–62, 64–69, 405–409, 485n85; assessment of Monmouth campaign by, 370–71, 418–19; biographers and historians of, 42, 73, 121, 390, 396, 425–26, 431–33; Charles Lee and, 25–26, 105, 108–11, 113–22, 181, 184–88, 191–97, 236–37, 281, 284–91, 293, 313–16, 385, 390–403, 492n46, 507n28, 541n63, 542n70, 543n15; Committee at Camp and, 43, 70, 479n71; Conway Cabal and, 33–41, 91–92, 478n58; councils of war and, 76–82, 99–103, 172–77; court martial of Lee and; 392–97; criticisms of, 19, 22–44, 110, 113–15; decides to pursue British in New Jersey, 88–90, 92, 99, 103–104, 167, 174–78, 504n55; fame of, 29, 386, 430–33, 435–36; importance of Monmouth campaign for, 43–44, 382–83, 386–87, 390, 400, 403, 425–26; intelligence operations and, 20, 85, 95, 166, 169–70, 184, 336, 488n60; leadership of; 73–75, 235, 282–83, 291–97, 333, 336, 341–42, 347–48, 409, 424, 511n6; legends and stories about, *218*, 290–91, 325–26, 329, 430–31, 518nn4–5, 519nn14–15, 523n54, 527n28, 546n22; letters and papers of, 390; logistics and supply efforts and, 70–72, 88, 408–409, 419, 500n9; military background of, 9, 45; military family of, 74, 384–85, 393, 398–99; personality of, 38, 73, 121, 398; political acumen of, 38–39, 42–43, 73, 383–84, 387, 397–98, 403, 424–25; popularity of; 73–74; soldiers' views of, 73–75, 291–92, 296–97, 326; strategy and tactics of; 6–8, 11, 20–22, 80–82, 96, 164, 331, 341–42, 347–48, 354, 404, 423, 505n61

Washington, Martha, 113, 121

Washington Rallying the Troops at Monmouth (Leutze), *218*, 435, 519n15

Watchung Mountains, *20*

Watson, William, 309, 359

Wayne, Anthony, 104, 113, 191, 312, 316, 326, *334*, 353, 361, 366, 386, 415, 417; assessment of, 406, 409–10, 413–14, 416; career of, 78; character of, 79; Charles Lee and, 281, 392; councils of war and, 78–79, 81, 101, 103, 172, 174–75; Daniel Morgan and, 236; at Hedgerow and Parsonage, 329, 341–42, *343*, 344–48, 376, 404, 406; with Lafayette, 177–80; on Lee's orders from Washington, 191–92, 196; in Lee's vanguard, 198, 237–40, *242*, *252*, 253; in morning battle, 28 June, 253–56, *257*, 258–64, 268–69; Paoli, 53, 78, 231, 394–98; "picked men" and, 177, 189; at Point of Woods, 292, 297–300, *301*, 302–306, *307*, 308–10, *311*, 313; portrait of, *232*; Washington and, 26, 384

Weamaconk Brook, 208, 511–12n19

weapons, 67, 70–72, 86, 162, 209, 416; bayonets, 53, 59, 66, 156, 164, 261, 302, 309, 386, 416, 522n43; cannon, 54, 320, 338, 349, 493n3; "grasshoppers," 332, 338, 365, 529n17; howitzers, 54, 320, 349, 448, 493n3; muskets, 51–52, 71, 86, 260, 276, 347, 365, 484n84. *See also* artillery; Brown Bess

weather, 6, 150; in advance to Monmouth Court House, 128, 130–31, 140–42, 150, 155–56, 161, 163, 180–81, 184, 209; artillery crews and, 262–63, 309, 324, 328; during battle, 28 June, 233, 237, 240, 262–63, 270–71, 276–77, 279–80, 282, 285, 295, 299, 304, 309–10, 313, 315, 328, 336, 339, 245, 360, 366–68, 415; as factor in casualty counts, 367–68; post-battle, 369–70

Webster, James, 345

Wellington, Duke of, 200

Wells, Thomas, 256, *257*, 259, 262–63, 266

Wesson, James, 189, 361, 364
West Florida, 17
West Morass (West Ravine), 208–209, 218, 230, 241, 250, *252*, 253, *267*, 272–74, 278, 280–81, 283, 285–86, 288, 290–92, 295, 297, 299–300, 304, 310, 312, 314–18, *321*, 333, *334*, 341–42, 348, 362, 365, 391, 393, 409–10, 415
West Virginia, 108
White, Anthony Walton, 90, 139, 170, 259, 309, 354
White Marsh, 7, 22
White Plains, Battle of, 109
White Plains, N.Y., 355, 370–71, 379–80, 387, 396, 419
White's Tavern, 110
Widow Solomon's tavern, 284, *334*
Wikoff, Peter, 278–79, 286, 293–94, *334*
Wild, Ebenezer, 323
Wilkenson, John, 144
Wilkes, John, 108
Wilkins, John, 361
Wilkinson, James, 37–39, 44, 478n54
Willett, Marinus, 164
Williams, Otho, 359
Wilson, William, 365, 535n51
Winds, William, 171, 504n43
women, 57–58, 143, 201, 213; and American army, 63, 282, 326–27, 329, 330, 502n34, 528n41; and British army, 58, 86, 98, 126–27, 146, 216, 375, 489n74, 548n2; Hessians, 58, 127; loyalists, 58, 127, 350
Woodbridge, N.J., 171, 427, 450
Woodford, William, 172, 174, 284, 333, *334*, 348–49, 354, 409, 413, 449
Wrottesly, John, 303

Xenophon, 382

Yale College, 389
York, Pa., 4, 7, 26, 31, 36–37, 66, 80, 82, 99, 113–16, 118–20, 163
Yorktown, Va., *222*, *225*, 319, 418, 421

Printed in the USA
CPSIA information can be obtained
at www.ICGtesting.com
CBHW031322150524
8605CB00002B/37